Lecture Notes in Artificial Intelligence 2308

Subseries of Lecture Notes in Computer Science
Edited by J. G. Carbonell and J. Siekmann

Lecture Notes in Computer Science
Edited by G. Goos, J. Hartmanis, and J. van Leeuwen

Springer-Verlag Berlin Heidelberg GmbH

Ioannis P. Vlahavas
Constantine D. Spyropoulos (Eds.)

Methods and Applications of Artificial Intelligence

Second Hellenic Conference on AI, SETN 2002
Thessaloniki, Greece, April 11-12, 2002
Proceedings

Springer

Series Editors

Jaime G. Carbonell, Carnegie Mellon University, Pittsburgh, PA, USA
Jörg Siekmann, University of Saarland, Saarbrücken, Germany

Volume Editors

Ioannis P. Vlahavas
Aristotle University of Thessaloniki, Dept. of Informatics
54006 Thessaloniki, Greece
vlahavas@csd.auth.gr

Constantine D. Spyropoulos
N.C.S.R. "Demokritos", Inst. of Informatics &Telecommunications
Software and Knowledge Engineering Lab
15310 Aghia Paraskevi, Greece
E-mail: costass@iit.demokritos.gr

Cataloging-in-Publication Data applied for

Die Deutsche Bibliothek - CIP-Einheitsaufnahme

Methods and applications of artificial intelligence : proceedings / Second Hellenic Conference on AI, SETN 2002, Thessaloniki, Greece, April 11 - 12, 2002. Ioannis P. Vlahavas ; Constantine D. Spyropoulos (ed.).

(Lecture notes in computer science ; Vol. 2308 : Lecture notes in artificial intelligence)
ISBN 978-3-540-43472-6

CR Subject Classification (1998): I.2, H.5.2, H.4, I.4

ISSN 0302-9743
ISBN 978-3-540-43472-6 ISBN 978-3-540-46014-5 (eBook)
DOI 10.1007/978-3-540-46014-5

http://www.springer.de

Originally published by Springer-Verlag Berlin Heidelberg New York in 2002

Typesetting: Camera-ready by author, data conversion by PTP-Berlin, Stefan Sossna e.K.
Printed on acid-free paper SPIN: 10846547 06/3142 5 4 3 2 1 0

Preface

In recent times Artificial Intelligence (AI) has proved to be a very fruitful research area whose results have found numerous real-life applications, in the areas of telecommunications, e-commerce, management, medicine, education, etc. The advent and rapid growth of the Internet and the World Wide Web have motivated further the interest and activity in this field, through the increasing demand for intelligent information systems.

This volume includes a collection of papers accepted for oral presentation at the 2nd Hellenic Conference on Artificial Intelligence (SETN 2002), organized by the Hellenic Society for Artificial Intelligence (EETN) and the Department of Informatics at the Aristotle University of Thessaloniki (AUTH), Greece. The conference was held in Thessaloniki, Greece, 11–12 April 2002, and it constituted the first attempt at establishing a regular Hellenic conference on Artificial Intelligence.

EETN was established in 1988 with the aim of organizing and promoting AI research among Greeks in Greece and abroad. Since its foundation, EETN has participated in the organization of various national and international events related to AI and its subfields, including the first Hellenic Symposium on Artificial Intelligence (SETN'96). EETN has also been a member society of the European Coordinating Committee on Artificial Intelligence (ECCAI) since 1996, and organized the advanced school on AI (ACAI'99).

The Department of Informatics of AUTH has been actively engaged in AI research for over 15 years through the Logic Programming & Intelligent Systems group and the Signal Processing group. Both groups have been publishing papers and have been involved in numerous research projects in the areas of Logic Programming, Constraint Solving, Knowledge-Based Systems, Planning, Machine Learning, Image/Video/Speech Processing, Neural Networks, Fuzzy Logic, Biometrics, Distance Learning, etc. Furthermore, the Signal Processing group organized the IEEE-sponsored International Conference on Image Processing (ICIP 2001).

The program of the conference included presentations of research results and applications from distinguished Greek scientists from all over the world. The submission of papers to the conference was overwhelming, both in quantitative and qualitative terms. Each submitted paper was evaluated by two, and in some cases three, independent reviewers on the basis of their relevance to AI, originality, significance, technical soundness, and presentation. The selection was hard, as only 42 papers out of the 121 submitted were accepted for oral presentation and inclusion in this volume, after further discussion with the members of the Advisory Board.

The selected papers cover a broad range of AI topics, such as Knowledge Representation and Reasoning, Natural Language Processing, Human-Computer Interaction, Machine Learning, Machine Vision, Multiagent Systems, etc. In addition, the volume includes two talks given by Christos Papadimitriou (Berkeley University, U.S.A.) and John Mylopoulos (University of Toronto, Canada), the distinguished invited speakers of the conference.

The editors would like to thank all those who contributed to the success of SETN 2002. Especially, they would like to express their gratitude to the sponsors who supported the conference, the Organizing Committee, for implementing the conference schedule in a timely and flawless manner, the Advisory Board, the Program Committee, and the additional reviewers, for the time and effort spent in reviewing the papers, and the two invited speakers for their kind participation. Last but not least, the editors would like to thank all the authors who submitted papers to this conference and would like to invite them to participate in the next Hellenic Conference on Artificial Intelligence, as well.

February 2002

Ioannis P. Vlahavas
Constantine D. Spyropoulos

Conference Chair

Ioannis P. Vlahavas (Aristotle University of Thessaloniki)

Conference Co-chair

Constantine D. Spyropoulos (NCSR "Demokritos")

Organizing Committee

Nick Bassiliades (Aristotle University of Thessaloniki)
Petros Kefalas (City Liberal Studies)
Vangelis Karkaletsis (NCSR "Demokritos")
Constantine Kotropoulos (Aristotle University of Thessaloniki)
Constantine Lazos (Aristotle University of Thessaloniki)
Georgios Paliouras (NCSR "Demokritos")
Ioannis Refanidis (Aristotle University of Thessaloniki)
Ioannis Tsoukalas (Aristotle University of Thessaloniki)

Stavros Stavroulakis (Secretariat)

Advisory Board

Nikolaos Fakotakis (University of Patras)
Constantine Halatsis (National and Kapodistrian University of Athens)
Elias Houstis (University of Patras / University of Thessaly)
Ioannis Kontos (National and Kapodistrian University of Athens)
Vassilis Moustakis (Technical University of Crete / FORTH)
Georgios Papakonstantinou (National Technical University of Athens)
Ioannis Pitas (Aristotle University of Thessaloniki)
Andreas Pomportsis (Aristotle University of Thessaloniki)
Timoleon Sellis (National Technical University of Athens)
Michail-Gerasimos Strintzis (Aristotle University of Thessaloniki / CERTH)
Athanasios Tsakalidis (University of Patras / Computer Technology Institute)
Spyros Tzafestas (National Technical University of Athens)

Program Committee

Ion Androutsopoulos (NCSR “Demokritos”)
Maria Aretoulaki (SemanticEdge, Germany)
Nikolaos Avouris (University of Patras)
Georgios Dimitriou (University of Sheffield, UK)
Ioannis Dimopoulos (University of Cyprus)
Georgios Dounias (Aegean University)
Theodoros Evgeniou (INSEAD, France)
Eleni Galliotou (TEI of Athens)
Petros A. M. Gelepithis (Kingston University, UK)
Emmanouil Gergatsoulis (NCSR “Demokritos” / University of Pireaus)
Nikolaos Hatziargyriou (National Technical University of Athens)
Ioannis Hatzilygeroudis (University of Patras)
Dimitris Kalles (Ahead RM / University of Patras)
Grigoris Karakoulas (Canadian Imperial Bank / Toronto University, Canada)
Stavros Kokkotos (Dynamic Ideas, USA)
Konstantinos Koutroumbas (National Observatory of Athens)
Georgios Magoulas (Brunel University, UK)
Kostas Margaritis (University of Macedonia)
Themistoklis Panayiotopoulos (University of Pireaus)
Christos Papatheodorou (NCSR “Demokritos” / Ionian University)
Stavros Perantonis (NCSR “Demokritos”)
Stelios Piperidis (Institute of Language and Speech Processing)
Dimitris Plexousakis (University of Crete / FORTH)
Georgios Potamias (FORTH)
Demosthenes Stamatis (TEI of Thessaloniki)
Panagiotis Stamatopoulos (National and Kapodistrian University of Athens)
Konstantinos Stathis (City University, UK)
Nikolaos Vassilas (TEI of Athens / NCSR “Demokritos”)
Georgios Vouros (Aegean University)
Emmanouil Yakoumakis (Athens University of Economics and Business)

Additional Referees

Panagiotis Adamidis
Foto Afrati
Lefteris Aggelis
Antonis Argyros
Yannis Avrithis
Panagiotis D. Bamidis
Nick Bassiliades
Constantinos Chandrinos
Eleni Charou
Christofer Child
Stavros Christodoulakis
Vassilis Christofides
Panos Constantopoulos
Dimitrios Dervos
Dimitrios Dranidis
Dimitrios M. Emiris
Attila Fazekas
Cristophe Garcia
Maria Grigoriadou
Nick Ioannidis
Antonis C. Kakas
Achilles D. Kameas
Vangelis Karkaletsis
Dimitrios Karras
Grigoris Karvounarakis
Petros Kefalas
Panayiotis H. Ketikidis
Stefanos Kollias
Constantine Kotropoulos
Manolis Koubarakis
Dimitrios E. Koulouriotis
Yannis Labrou
Isaac E. Lagaris
George K. Lekeas
Aristidis C. Likas
Panagiotis Linardis
Christos Makris
Stratos Malassiotis
Costas Neocleous
Nikolaos Nikolaidis
Christos Nomikos
Penny Noy
George Paliouras
Iraklis Paraskakis
Vasilios Petridis
Ioannis Refanidis
Panagiotis Rondogiannis
George Rovithakis
Dimitrios Sampson
Christos N. Schizas
Kyriakos Sgarbas
Christos Siamitros
Myra Spiliopoulou
Andreas Stafylopatis
Ioannis Stamelos
Yannis Stavrakas
Kostas Stergiou
Chrysostomos Stylios
Francesca Tonny
Athanasios Tsadiras
Ioannis Tsamardinos
Nicolas Tsapatsoulis
Panagiotis Tsarchopoulos
Giorgos Tselentis
George A. Tsihrintzis
Lefteris Tsoukalas
Alexis Tsoukias
Konstantinos Tzafestas
Stavros Varoufakis
Michalis Vazirgiannis
Michael N. Vrahatis
Michael Zervakis

Table of Contents

Invited Talks

Knowledge Representation & Reasoning

Logic Programming & Constraint Satisfaction

Planning & Scheduling

Natural Language Processing

Human-Computer Interaction

Machine Learning

Knowledge Discovery

Neural Networks

Pattern Recognition

Machine Vision

Intelligent Internet & Multiagent Systems

Intelligent Applications

Understanding the Internet

Christos H. Papadimitriou

University of California, Berkeley, USA
http://www.cs.berkeley.edu/~christos

Extended Abstract

The Internet has surpassed the computer as the most complex and intriguing computational artifact of our time, and it is therefore a most natural and worthy subject of study by all fields of Computer Science.

There are several ways in which the Internet is novel, indeed unprecedented, and of special interest to the Artificial Intelligence research community:

- It was not deliberately *designed* in any reasonable sense, and therefore it is the first computational artifact that must be approached as a mysterious phenomenon (or behavior) that we need to understand; this is a little more familiar in Artificial Intelligence than in other fields of Computer Science, because in AI the physiological basis of human intelligence had been of interest for some time.
- The Internet was not designed by a single designer or team for the benefit of a single entity; instead, it is built, operated and used by a dazzling multiplicity of agents, in various and varying degrees of collaboration and competition with each other. As a result, Game Theory and Mathematical Economics are of obvious relevance in this line of research, as is, to a somewhat lesser extent, the Theory of Agents developed by researchers in AI.
- The Internet supports, via the worldwide web but not only, access to information of unprecedented scale, availability, and diversity in content, nature and structure. The problem of accessing all this information, even understanding what is available, especially by vast numbers of inexpert users, promises to affect deeply the research agenda in both Databases and Artificial Intelligence.
- Finally, the Internet is starting to act as “Cambrian Sea” for Artificial Intelligence. Here is what I mean: During the Cambrian period a fantastic diversity of aquatic species evolved, competed, and evolved further; most of today’s animals can be traced to that explosion. The Internet is a perfect medium for all sorts of computational ideas (AI programs in particular) to live and compete, and to be tried, evaluated, combined and improved.

This talk will illustrate this fascinating research area by several recent examples. One of the Internet’s mysterious attributes is the *power law distribution* of various quantities (degrees of the routers and autonomous systems, hops in message routing, even the eigenvalues of the underlying topology) first observed in [3]. We present a simple (and therefore guaranteed to be inaccurate…) model [2] for the growth of the Internet that predicts power law distributions.

In 1998, 52% of web documents were in .com domains. How does one sample uniformly the worldwide web to obtain such statistics? A very interesting method [1]

I.P. Vlahavas and C.D. Spyropoulos (Eds.): SETN 2002, LNAI 2308, pp. 1–2, 2002.

involves random walks in a symmetrized and homogenized version of the web graph (the nodes are all documents, and edges are hyperlinks), and its analysis is based on the spectral properties of this graph.

As the Internet makes possible the interaction of many economic agents –and, as argued above, it is in fact the product of such interaction– it is a natural domain for Mechanism Design, the area of Economics that studies how to provide incentives so that many selfish agents, maximizing their own benefit, end up optimizing the designer's objectives (and in the process reveal truthfully their economic preferences). Recent results [4] indicate that, to be useful in the context of the Internet, this theory must take into account the difficulty in implementing massive distributed algorithms with reasonable communication costs.

Information storage and retrieval in the worldwide web necessitates new languages (such as XML for semi-structured data) but also new techniques for integrating and querying heterogeneous databases –in fact, databases that may have been designed explicitly to resist integration. I shall argue that this new data environment may result in a resurgence of the use of Logic Programming ideas and techniques in Databases.

References

[1] Ziv Bar-Yossef, Alexander Berg, Steve Chien, Jittat Fakcharoenphol, and Dror Weitz, Approximating Aggregate Queries about Web Pages via Random Walks, *Proceedings of the 26th International Conference on Very Large Databases (VLDB)*, 2000, pp. 535-544.

[2] Alex Fabrikant, Elias Koutsoupias, C. H.Papadimitriou "Heuristically Optimized Trade-offs," manuscript 2002, available at http://www.cs.berkeley.edu/~christos/hot.ps

[3] Michalis Faloutsos, Petros Faloutsos and Christos Faloutsos, On Power-Law Relationships of the Internet Topology, *SIGCOMM 1999.*

[4] J. Feigenbaum, C. H. Papadimitriou, S. Shenker Sharing the cost of multicast transactions *STOC 2000*, available at http://www.cs.berkeley.edu/~christos/multicast.ps

Agent-Oriented Software Development

John Mylopoulos[1], Manuel Kolp[2], and Paolo Giorgini[3]

[1] Department of Computer Science - University of Toronto, 6 King's College Road M5S 3H5, Toronto, Canada, tel.: 1-416-978 5180, jm@cs.toronto.edu
[2] IAG - Information Systems Research Unit - University of Louvain, 1 Place des Doyens, B-1348 Louvain-La-Neuve, Belgium, tel.: 32-10 47 83 95, kolp@isys.ucl.ac.be
[3] Department of Mathematics - University of Trento, 4 via Sommarive, I-38100, Trento, Italy, tel.: 39-0461-88 2052, pgiorgini@science.unitn.it

Abstract. The Tropos project is developing concepts, tools and techniques for building agent-oriented software. This paper presents a quick overview of the project and then focuses on a specific problem: the identification of architectural styles for multi-agent systems (MAS). The proposed styles have been adopted from the literature on organization theory and strategic alliances. The styles are represented in *i**, a framework designed to model social and intentional concepts. Each proposed style is evaluated with respect to a set of agent software qualities, such as predictability, adaptability and availability. The use of the styles is illustrated and contrasted with a software architecture for mobile robot reported in the literature.

1 Introduction

The explosive growth of application areas such as electronic commerce, enterprise resource planning and mobile computing has profoundly and irreversibly changed our views on software and Software Engineering. Software must now be based on open architectures that continuously change and evolve to accommodate new components and meet new requirements. Software must also operate on different platforms, without recompilation, and with minimal assumptions about its operating environment and its users. As well, software must be robust and autonomous, capable of serving a naïve user with a minimum of overhead and interference. These new requirements, in turn, call for new concepts, tools and techniques for engineering and managing software.

For these reasons – and more – agent-oriented software development is gaining popularity over traditional software development techniques, including structured and object-oriented ones. After all, agent-based architectures (known as multi-agent systems in the Agent research community) *do* provide for an open, evolving architecture which can change at run-time to exploit the services of new agents, or replace under-performing ones. In addition, software agents can, in principle, cope with unforeseen circumstances because they include in their architecture goals, along with a planning capability for meeting them. Finally, agent technologies have matured to the point where protocols for communication and negotiation have been standardized [7].

I.P. Vlahavas and C.D. Spyropoulos (Eds.): SETN 2002, LNAI 2308, pp. 3–17, 2002.

We are developing a software development methodology for agent-based software systems. The methodology adopts ideas from multi-agent system technologies, mostly to define the implementation phase of our methodology [4]. We are also adopting ideas from Requirements Engineering, where agents and goals have been used heavily for early requirements analysis [5, 26]. In particular, we adopt Eric Yu's *i** model which offers actors (agents, roles, or positions), goals, and actor dependencies as primitive concepts for modelling an application during early requirements analysis. The key assumption which distinguishes our work from others in Requirements Engineering is that actors and goals are used as fundamental concepts for modelling and analysis during *all phases of software development*, not just early requirements[1].

Our methodology, named Tropos, is intended to support five phases of software development:

Early requirements, concerned with the understanding of a problem by studying an existing organizational setting; the output of this phase is an organizational model which includes relevant actors and their respective dependencies;

Late requirements, where the system-to-be is described within its operational environment, along with relevant functions and qualities; this description models the system as a (small) number of actors which have a number of dependencies with actors in their environment; these dependencies define the system's functional and non-functional requirements;

Architectural design, where the system's global architecture is defined in terms of subsystems, interconnected through data and control flows; within our framework, subsystems are represented as actors and data/control interconnections are represented as (system) actor dependencies.

Detailed design, where each architectural component is defined in further detail in terms of inputs, outputs, control, and other relevant information; our framework adopts elements of AUML [19] to complement the features of *i**;

Implementation, where the actual implementation of the system is carried out, consistently with the detailed design; we use a commercial agent programming platform, based on the BDI (Beliefs-Desires-Intentions) agent architecture for this phase.

The motivations behind the Tropos project are presented in [2] and [12], including an early glimpse of how the methodology would work for particular case studies.

In this paper, we focus on a specific problem related to the Tropos methodology: the identification of architectural styles for Tropos models. System architectures describe a software system at a macroscopic level in terms of a manageable number of subsystems/components/modules inter-related through data and control dependencies. The design of software architectures has been the focus of considerable research for the past decade which has resulted in a collection of well-understood architectural styles and a methodology for evaluating their effectiveness with respect to particular software qualities. Examples of styles are pipes-and-filters, event-based, layered and the like [11]. Examples of software qualities include maintainability, modifiability, portability, etc. [1]. Multi-Agent System (MAS) architectures can be considered as organizations (see e.g., [6, 8, 16]) composed of *autonomous* and

---

1 Analogously to the use of concepts such as `object`, `class`, `inheritance` and `method` in object-oriented software development.

proactive agents that interact and cooperate with one another in order to achieve common or private goals. Since the fundamental concepts of multi-agent systems are intentional and social, rather than implementation-oriented, we turn to theories which study social and intentional structures for motivation and insights. But, what kind of social theory should we turn to? There are theories that study group psychology, communities and social networks. Such theories study social and intentional structure as an *emergent property* of a social context. Instead, we are interested in organizational structures that emerge from a *design* process. For this, we turn to organizational theory and strategic alliances for guidance. The purpose of this paper is to present a set of architectural styles for multi-agent systems motivated by these theories. The styles are modeled using the strategic dependency model of *i** [26]. To illustrate these styles, we use a case study comparing organizational with conventional software architectural styles for mobile robot control software.

Section 2 presents our organization-inspired architectural styles described in terms of the strategic dependency model from *i** and specified in Telos. Section 3 introduces a set of desirable software quality attributes for comparing them. Section 4 overviews a mobile robot example while Section 5 discusses related work. Finally, Section 6 summarizes the contributions of the paper and points to further research.

2 Organizational Structures

Organizational theory (such as [14, 18]) and strategic alliances (e.g., [13, 25]) study alternatives for (business) organizations. These alternatives are used to model the coordination of business stakeholders – individuals, physical or social systems -- to achieve common goals. Using them, we view a software system as a social organization of coordinated autonomous components (or agents) that interact in order to achieve specific, possibly common goals. We adopt (some of) the styles defined in organizational theory and strategic alliances to design the architecture of the system, model them with *i**, and specify them in Telos [17].

In *i**, a strategic dependency model is a graph, in which each node represents an actor, and each link between two actors indicates that one actor depends on another for something in order that the former may attain some goal. We call the depending actor the depender and the actor who is depended upon the dependee. The object around which the dependency centers is called the dependum. By depending on another actor for a dependum, an actor is able to achieve goals that it is otherwise unable to achieve, or not as easily or as well. At the same time, the depender becomes vulnerable. If the dependee fails to deliver the dependum, the depender would be adversely affected in its ability to achieve its goals.

The model distinguishes among four types of dependencies – goal-, task-, resource-, and softgoal-dependency – based on the type of freedom that is allowed in the relationship between depender and dependee. Softgoals are distinguished from goals because they do not have a formal definition, and are amenable to a different (more qualitative) kind of analysis [3].

For instance, in the structure-in-5 style (Figure 1), the coordination, middle agency and support actors depend on the apex for strategic management purposes. Since the goal *Strategic Management* is not well-defined, it is represented as a softgoal (cloudy shape). The middle agency actor depends on both the coordination and support actors respectively through goal dependencies *Control* and *Logistics* represented as oval-shaped icons. The operational core actor is related to the coordination and support actors respectively through the *Standardize* task dependency and the *Non-operational service* resource dependency.

In the sequel we briefly discuss ten common organizational styles.

The **structure-in-5** (Figure 1) style consists of the typical strategic and logistic components generally found in many organizations. At the base level one finds the operational core where the basic tasks and operations – the input, processing, output and direct support procedures associated with running the system – are carried out. At the top of the organization lies the apex composed of strategic executive actors.

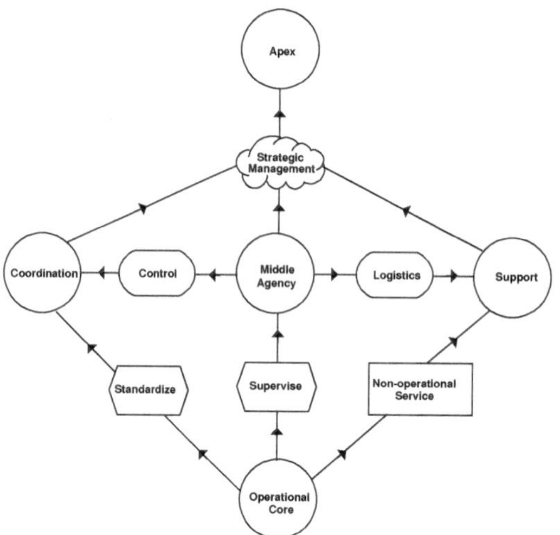

Fig. 1. Structure-in-5

Below it sit the control/standardization, management components and logistics, respectively coordination, middle agency and support. The coordination component carries out the tasks of standardizing the behavior of other components, in addition to applying analytical procedures to help the system adapt to its environment. Actors joining the apex to the operational core make up the middle agency. The support component assists the operational core for non-operational services that are outside the basic flow of operational tasks and procedures.

Figure 2 specifies the structure-in-5 style in Telos. Telos is a language intended for modeling requirements, design, implementation and design decisions for software systems [17]. It provides features to describe metaconcepts that can be used to represent the knowledge relevant to a variety of worlds – subject, usage, system, development worlds – related to a software system. Our styles are formulated as Telos metaclasses, primarily based on the aggregation semantics for Telos presented in [15].

The structure-in-5 style is then a metaclass – *StructureIn5MetaClass* – aggregation of five (*part*) metaclasses: *ApexMetaClass*, *CoordinationMetaClass*, *MiddleAgencyMetaClass*, *SupportMetaClass* and *OperationalCoreMetaClass*, one for each actor composing the structure-in 5 style depicted in Figure 1. Each of these five components exclusively belongs (*exclusivePart*) to the composite (*StructureIn5MetaClass*) and their existence depend (*dependentPart*) on the existence of the composite. A structure-in-5 specific to an application domain will be defined as a Telos class, instance of *StructureIn5MetaClass* (See Section 4). Similarly each structure-in-5 component specific to a particular application domain will be defined as a class, instance of one of the five *StructureIn5Metaclass* components.

```
TELL CLASS StructureIn5MetaClass
  IN Class WITH /*Class is here used as a MetaMetaClass*/
  attribute
           name: String
     part, exclusivePart, dependentPart
           ApexMetaClass: Class
           CoordinationMetaClass: Class
           MiddleAgencyMetaClass: Class
           SupportMetaClass: Class
           OperationalCoreMetaClass: Class
END StructureIn5MetaClass
```

Fig. 2. Structure-in-5 in Telos

Figure 3 formulates in Telos one of these five structure-in-5 components: the coordination actor. Dependencies are described following Telos specifications for *i** models [26].

```
TELL CLASS CoordinationMetaclass
      IN Class WITH /*Class is here used as a MetaMetaClass*/
attribute  name: String
taskDepended
      s:StandardizeTask
              WITH depender OperationalCoreMetaClass: Class
 goalDepended
      c:ControlGoal
              WITH depender  MiddleAgencyMetaClass: Class
 softgoalDepender
      s:StrategicManagementSoftGoal
              WITH dependee ApexMetaClass: Class
END CoordinationMetaclass
```

Fig. 3. Structure-in-5 coordination actor in Telos

The coordination actor is a metaclass, *CoordinationMetaclass.* According to Figure 1, the coordination actor is the dependee of a task dependency *StandardizeTask* and a goal dependency *ControlGoal*, and the depender of a softgoal dependency *StrategicManagementSoftGoal.*

The **flat structure** has no fixed structure and no control of one actor over another is assumed. The main advantage of this architecture is that it supports autonomy, distribution and continuous evolution of an actor architecture. However, the key drawback is that it requires an increased amount of reasoning and communication by each participating actor.

The **pyramid** style is the well-known hierarchical authority structure exercised within organizational boundaries. Actors at the lower levels depend on actors of the higher levels. The crucial mechanism is direct supervision from the apex. Managers and supervisors are then only intermediate actors routing strategic decisions and authority from the apex to the operating level. They can coordinate behaviors or take decisions by their own but only at a local level. This style can be applied when deploying simple distributed systems.

Moreover, this style encourages dynamicity since coordination and decision mechanisms are direct, not complex and immediately identifiable. Evolvability and modifiability can thus be implemented in terms of this style at low costs. However, it is not suitable for huge distributed systems like multi-agent systems requiring many kinds of agents. Even tough, it can be used by these systems to manage and resolve crisis situations. For instance, a complex multi-agent system faced with a non-authorized intrusion from external and non trustable agents could dynamically, for a short or long time, decide to migrate itself into a pyramid organization to be able to resolve the security problem in a more efficient way.

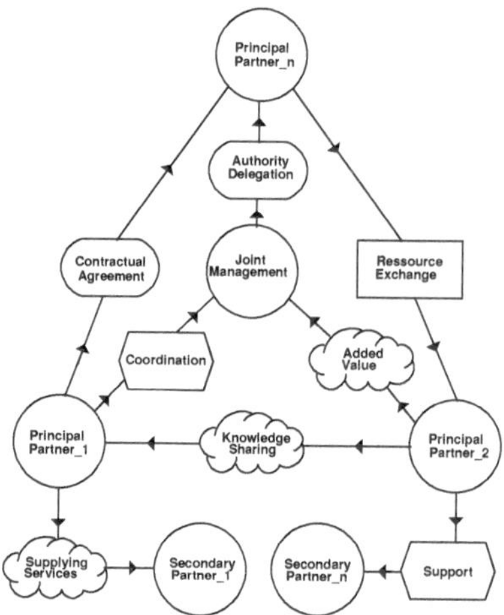

Fig. 4. Joint Venture

The **joint venture** style (Figure 4) involves agreement between two or more principal partners to obtain the benefits of larger scale, partial investment and lower maintenance costs. Through the delegation of authority to a specific joint management actor that coordinates tasks and operations and manages sharing of knowledge and resources they pursue joint objectives and common purpose.

Each principal partner can manage and control itself on a local dimension and interact directly with other principal partners to exchange, provide and receive services, data and knowledge. However, the strategic operation and coordination of such a system and its partner actors on a global dimension are only ensured by the joint management actor. Outside the joint venture, secondary partners supply services or support tasks for the organization core.

The **takeover** style involves the total delegation of authority and management from two or more partners to a single collective *takeover* actor. It is similar in many ways to the joint venture style. The major and crucial difference is that while in a joint venture identities and autonomies of the separate units are preserved, the takeover absorbs these critical units in the sense that no direct relationships, dependencies or communications are tolerated except those involving the takeover.

The **arm's-length** style implies agreements between independent and competitive but partner actors. Partners keep their autonomy and independence but act and put their resources and knowledge together to accomplish precise common goals. No authority is delegated or lost from a collaborator to another.

The **bidding** style (Figure 5) involves competitivity mechanisms and actors behave as if they were taking part in an auction. The auctioneer actor runs the show, advertises the auction issued by the auction issuer, receives bids from bidder actors and ensure communication and feedback with the auction issuer.

The auctioneer might be a system actor that merely organizes and operates the auction and its mechanisms. It can also be one of the bidders (for example selling an item which all other bidders are interested in buying). The auction issuer is responsible for issuing the bidding.

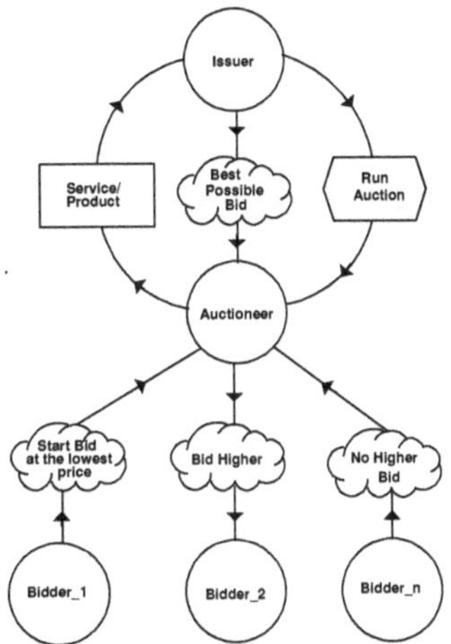

Fig. 5. Bidding

The **hierarchical contracting** style (Figure 6) identifies coordinating mechanisms that combine arm's-length agreement features with aspects associated with pyramidal authority. Coordination mechanisms developed to manage arm's-length (independent) characteristics involve a variety of negotiators, mediators and observers at different levels handling conditional clauses to monitor and manage possible contingencies, negotiate and resolve conflicts and finally deliberate and take decisions. Hierarchical relationships, from the executive apex to the arm's-length contractors (top to bottom) restrict autonomy and underlie a cooperative venture between the contracting parties. Such dual and admittedly complex contracting arrangements can be used to manage conditions of complexity and uncertainty deployed in high-cost-high-gain (high-risk) applications.

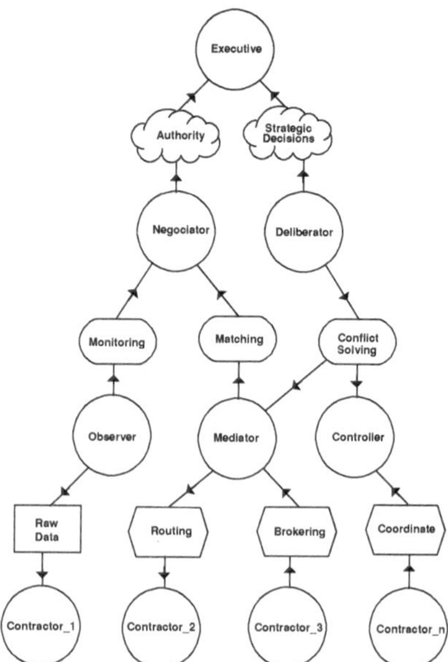

Fig. 6. Hierarchical Contracting

The **co-optation** style (Figure 7) involves the incorporation of representatives of external systems into the decision-making or advisory structure and behavior of an initiating organization.

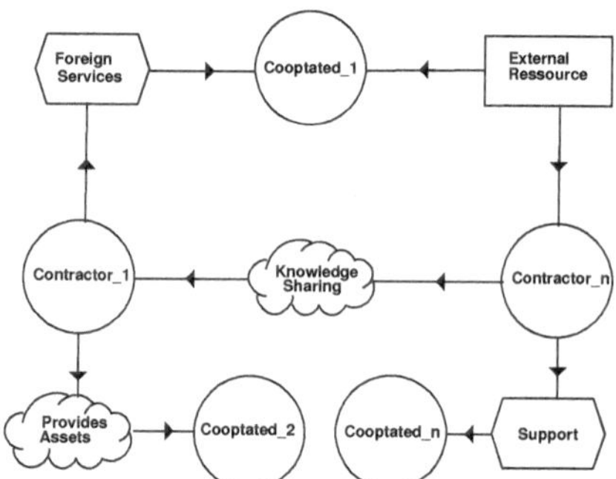

Fig. 7. Cooptation

By co-opting representatives of external systems, organizations are, in effect, trading confidentiality and authority for resource, knowledge assets and support. The initiating system, and its local contractors, has to come to terms with what is doing on its behalf; and each co-optated actor has to reconcile and adjust his own views with the policy of the system he has to communicate.

The **vertical integration** style merges, backward or forward, one or more system actors engaged in related tasks but at different stages of a production process. A merger synchronizes and controls interactions between each of the participants that can be considered intermediate workshops. Vertical integrations take place between exchange partners, actors symbiotically related. Figure 8 presents a vertical integration style for the domain of goods distribution. *Provider* is expected to supply quality products, *Wholesaler* is responsible for ensuring their massive exposure, while *Retailer* takes care of the direct delivery to the *Consumers.*

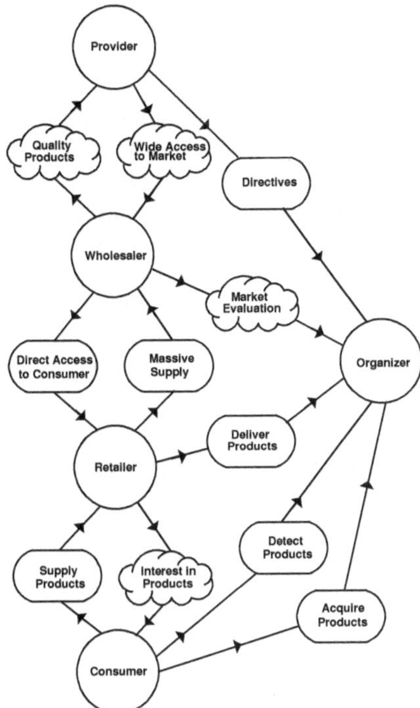

Fig. 8. Vertical Integration

3 Evaluating Architecture

The organizational styles defined in Section 2 can be evaluated and compared using the following software quality attributes identified for multi-agent architectures:

1 – Predictability [24]. Agents have a high degree of autonomy in the way that they undertake action and communication in their domains. It can be then difficult to predict individual characteristics as part of determining the behavior of a distributed and open system at large.

2 – Security. Agents are often able to identify their own data sources and they may undertake additional actions based on these sources [24]. Protocols and strategies for verifying authenticity for these data sources by individual agents are an important concern in the evaluation of overall system quality since, in addition to possibly misleading information acquired by agents, there is the danger of hostile external entities spoofing the system to acquire information accorded to trusted domain agents.

3 – Adaptability. Agents may be required to adapt to modifications in their environment. They may include changes to the component's communication protocol or possibly the dynamic introduction of a new kind of agent previously unknown or the manipulations of existing agents.
Coordinability. Agents are not particularly useful unless they are able to coordinate with other agents. This can be realized in two ways:
4 – Cooperativity. They must be able to coordinate with other entities to achieve a common purpose.
5 – Competitivity. The success of one agent implies the failure of others.
6 – Availability. Components that offer services to other agents must implicitly or explicitly guard against the interruption of offered services. Availability must actually be considered a sub-attribute of security [3]. Nevertheless, we deal with it as a top-level quality attribute due to its increasing importance in multi-agent system design.
7 – Integrity. A failure of one agent does not necessarily imply a failure of the whole system. The system then needs to check the completeness and the accuracy of data, information and knowledge transactions and flows. To prevent system failure, different agents can have similar or replicated capabilities and refer to more than one agent for a specific behavior.

Table 1. Correlation Catalogue

	1	2	3	4	5	6	7	8	9
Flat	--	--	-			+	+	++	-
Struct-5	+	+		+	-	+	++	++	++
Pyramid	++	++	+	++	-	+	--	-	
Joint-Vent	+	+	++	+	-	++		+	++
Bid	--	--	++	-	++	-	--	++	
Takeover	++	++	-	++	--	+		+	+
Arm's-Lgth	-	--	+	-	++	--	++	+	
Hierch Ctr			+	+	+	+		+	+
Vert Integr	+	+	-	+	-	+	--	--	--
Coopt	-	-	++	++	+	--	-	--	

8 – Modularity [23] increases efficiency of task execution, reduces communication overhead and usually enables high flexibility. On the other hand, it implies constraints on inter-module communication.
9 – Aggregability. Some agents are parts of other components. They surrender to the control of the composite entity. This control results in efficient tasks execution and low communication overhead, however prevents the system to benefit from flexibility.

Table 1 summarizes the correlation catalogue for the organizational patterns and top-level quality attributes we have considered. Following notations used by the NFR (non functional requirements) framework [3], +, ++, -, --, respectively model partial/positive, sufficient/positive, partial/negative and sufficient/negative contributions.

4 Example

To motivate our organizational styles, we consider an application domain where distributed and open architectures are increasingly important: mobile robots.

The mobile robot example presented in [22] studies notably the layered architecture (Figure 9) implemented in the Terregator and Neptune office delivery robots [20].

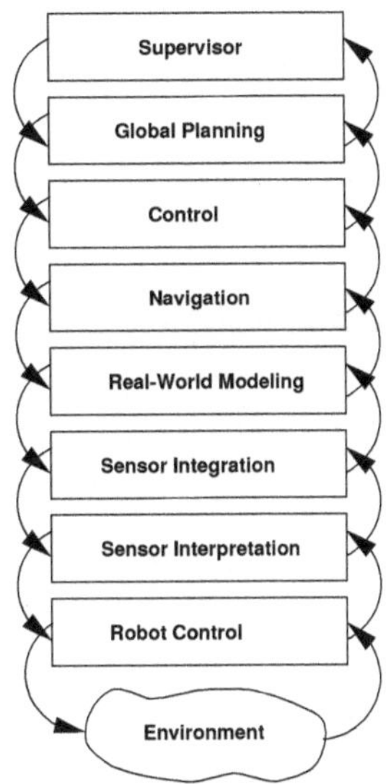

Fig. 9. Classical Mobile Robot Layered Architecture

According to [22] at the lowest level, reside the robot control routines (motors, joints,...). Levels 2 and 3 deal with the input from the real world. They perform sensor interpretation (the analysis of the data from one sensor) and sensor integration (the combined analysis of different sensor inputs). Level 4 is concerned with maintaining the robot's model of the world. Level 5 manages the navigation of the robot. The next two levels, 6 and 7, schedule and plan the robot's actions. Dealing with problems and replanning is also part of the level-7 responsibilities. The top level provides the user interface and overall supervisory functions.

The following software quality attributes are relevant for the robot's architecture [22]: *Cooperativity*, *Predictability*, *Adaptability*, *Integrity*. Let consider, for instance, *Cooperativity* and *Predictability*.

Cooperativity: the robot has to coordinate the actions it undertakes to achieve its designated objective with the reactions forced on it by the environment (e.g., avoid an obstacle). The idealized layered architecture (Figure 9) implemented on some mobile robots does not really fit the actual data and control-flow patterns. The layered architecture style suggests that services and requests are passed between adjacent layers. However, data and information exchange is actually not always straightforward. Commands and transactions may often need to skip intermediate layers to establish direct communication. A structure-in-5 proposes a more distributed architecture allowing more direct interactions between component.

Another recognized problem is that the layers do not separate the data hierarchy (sensor control, interpreted results, world model) from the control hierarchy (motor control, navigation, scheduling, planning and user-level control). Again the structure-in-5 could better differentiate the data hierarchy – implemented by the operational core, and support components – from the control structure – implemented by the operational core, middle agency and strategic apex as will be described in Figure 10.

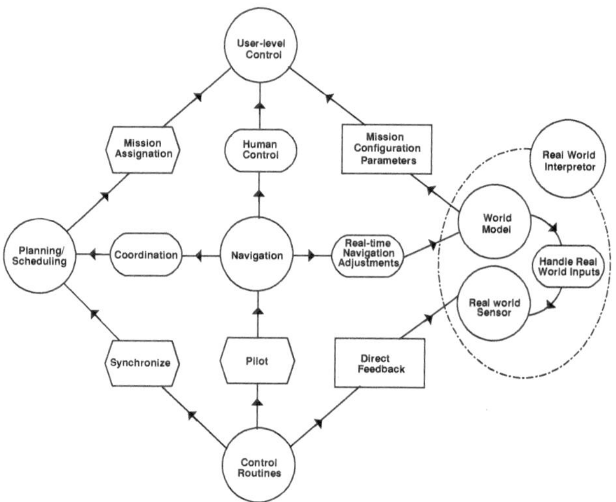

Fig. 10. A Structure-in-5 Mobile Robot Architecture

Adaptability: application development for mobile robots frequently requires customization, experimentation and dynamic reconfiguration. Moreover, changes in tasks may require regular modification. In the layered architecture, the interdependencies between layers prevent the addition of new components or deletion of existing ones. The structure-in-5 style separates independently each typical component of an organizational structure but a joint venture isolating components and allowing autonomous and dynamic manipulation should be a better candidate. Partner components, except the joint manager, can be added or deleted in a more flexible way.

Figure 10 depicts a mobile robot architecture following the structure-in-5 style from Figure 1. The *control routines* component is the *operational core* managing the robot motors, joints, etc. *Planning/Scheduling* is the *coordination* component scheduling and planning the robot's actions. The *real world interpreter* is the *support* component composed of two sub-components: *Real world sensor* accepts the raw input from multiple sensors and integrates it into a coherent interpretation while *World Model* is concerned with maintaining the robot's model of the world and monitoring the environment for landmarks. *Navigation* is the *middle agency* component, the central intermediate module managing the navigation of the robot. Finally, the *user-level control* is the human-oriented *strategic apex* providing the user interface and overall supervisory functions.

Figure 11 formulates the media robot structure-in-5 in Telos. *MobileRobotClass* is a Telos class, instance of the *StructureIn5Metaclass* specified in Figure 2. This aggregation is composed of five exclusive and dependent parts *ControlRoutinesClass, RealWorldInterpreterClass*, *NavigationClass*, *PlanningClass* and *UserLevelControl-Class*, each of them is instance of one metaclass, component of *StructureIn-5MetaClass.*

```
TELL CLASS MobileRobotClass
   IN StructureIn5MetaClass WITH
         attribute
                  name: String
         part, exclusivePart, dependentPart
                  ControlRoutinesClass: OperationalCoreMetaClass
                  RealWorldInterpreter: SupportMetaClass
                  NavigationClass: MiddleAgencyMetaClass
                  PlanningClass: CoordinationMetaClass
                  UserLevelControl: ApexMetaClass
END MobileRobotClass
```

Fig. 11. Mobile Robot Structure-in-5 Architecture in Telos

5 Related Work

Other research work on multi-agent systems offers contributions on using organization concepts such as agent (or agency), group, role, goals, tasks, relationships (or dependencies) to model and design system architectures.

For instance, Aalaadin [6] presents a model based on two level of abstraction. The concrete level includes concepts such as *agent*, *group* and *role* which are used to describe the actual multi-agent system. The methodological level defines all possible roles, valid interactions, and structures of groups and organizations. The model describes an organization in terms of its structure, and independently of the way its agents actually behave. Different types of organizational behavioral requirement patterns have been defined and formalized using concepts such as groups and roles within groups and (inter-group and intra-group) role interactions.

In our work the concepts Aalaadin uses in the concrete level are contained in the concept of actor. An actor can be a single or a composite agent, a position covered by an agent, and a role covered by one or more agents. Unlike ours, Aalaadin's proposal does not include goals in the description of an organization. Moreover, in Aalaadin's work these descriptions include details (e.g., interaction languages and protocols) which we deal with at a later stage of design, typically called *detailed design.*

On a different point of comparison, Aalaadin uses *rules*, *structures* and *patterns* to capture respectively how the organization is expected to work, which kind of structure fits given requirements, and whether reuse of patterns is possible. In our framework, some rules are captured by social dependencies in terms of which one defines the obligations of actors towards other actors. Moreover, other rules can be captured during detailed design instead of earlier phases, i.e., early and late requirements, or architectural design (see [1]).

6 Conclusions

Designers rely on styles, patterns, or idioms, to describe the architectures of their choice. We propose that MAS can be conceived as *organizations* of agents that interact to achieve common goals. This paper proposes a catalogue of architectural styles designing MAS architectures as organizational architectures, i.e, at a macro- and micro-level. The proposed styles adopt concepts from organization theory and strategic alliances literature. The paper also includes an evaluation of software qualities that are relevant to these styles. A standard case study (the mobile robot case control) illustrates and compares them with respect to conventional architecture.

Future research directions include formalizing precisely the organizational structures that have been identified, as well as the sense in which a particular model is an instance of such a style and pattern. We also propose to relate them to social or agent patterns (e.g, the broker, matchmaker, embassy, facilitator, ...) and lower-level architectural components [21] involving (software) components, ports, connectors, interfaces, libraries and configurations [9]. We are still working on contrasting our structures to conventional styles [22] and patterns [10] proposed in the software engineering literature. To this end, as mentioned in the paper, we are defining algorithms to propagate evidences of satisfaction and denial of each conventional or social structure with respect to a set of non-functional requirements.

References

[1] L. Bass, P. Clements, and R. Kazman. *Software Architecture in Practice*, Reading, Addison-Wesley, 1998.

[2] J. Castro, M. Kolp, and J. Mylopoulos. "A Requirements-Driven Development Methodology", In *Proc. of the 13th Int. Conf. on Advanced Information Systems Engineering* (CAiSE'01), Interlaken, Switzerland, June 2001, pp. 108-123.

[3] L. K. Chung, B. A. Nixon, E. Yu and J. Mylopoulos. *Non-Functional Requirements in Software Engineering*, Kluwer Publishing, 2000.

[4] Coburn, M., *Jack Intelligent Agents: User Guide version 2.0*, AOS Pty Ltd, 2000.

[5] A. Dardenne, A. van Lamsweerde, and S. Fickas. "Goal–directed Requirements Acquisition", *Science of Computer Programming, 20*, 1993, pp. 3-50.

[6] J. Ferber and O. Gutknecht."A meta-model for the analysis and design of organizations in multi-agent systems". In *Proc. of the 3rd Int. Conf. on Multi-Agent Systems*, June, 1998.

[7] *The Foundation for Intelligent Physical Agents*, http://www.fipa.org, 2001.

[8] M.S. Fox. "An organizational view of distributed systems". In *IEEE Transactions on Systems, Man, and Cybernetics*, 11(1):70-80, January 1981.

[9] A. Fuxman, P. Giorgini, M. Kolp, and J. Mylopoulos. "Information systems as social structures". In *Proc. of the 2nd Int. Conf. on Formal Ontologies for Information Systems* (FOIS'01), Ogunquit, USA, October 2001.

[10] E. Gamma, R. Helm, R. Johnson and J. Vlissides. *Design Patterns: Elements of Reusable Object-oriented Software*. Addison-Wesley, 1995.

[11] D. Garlan and M. Shaw. "An Introduction to Software Architectures", in *Advances in Software Engineering and Knowledge Engineering*, volume I, World Scientific, 1993.
[12] P. Giorgini, A. Perini, J. Mylopoulos, F. Giunchiglia and P. Bresciani. "Agent-Oriented Software Development: A Case Study". In *Proc. of the 13th Int. Conference on Software Engineering & Knowledge Engineering* (SEKE01), Buenos Aires, Argentina, June 2001.
[13] B. Gomes-Casseres. *The alliance revolution : the new shape of business rivalry*, Cambridge, Mass., Harvard University Press, 1996.
[14] H. Mintzberg. *Structure in fives : designing effective organizations*, Englewood Cliffs, N.J., Prentice-Hall, 1992.
[15] R. Motschnig-Pitrik. "The Semantics of PartsVersus Aggregates in Data/Knowledge Modeling", In *Proc. of the 5th Int. Conference on Advanced Information Systems Engineering* (CAiSE'93), Paris, June 1993, pp 352-372.
[16] T.W. Malone. "Organizing Information Processing Systems: Parallels Between Human Organizations and Computer Systems". In W. Zachry, S. Robertson and J. Black, eds. *Cognition, Cooperation and Computation*, Ablex, 1988.
[17] J. Mylopoulos, A. Borgida, M. Jarke, M. Koubarakis. "Telos: Representing Knowledge About Information Systems" in *ACM Trans. Info. Sys.*, 8 (4), Oct. 1990, pp. 325 – 362.
[18] W. Richard Scott. *Organizations : rational, natural, and open systems*, Prentice Hall, 1998
[19] Odell, J., Van Dyke Parunak, H. and Bauer, B., "Extending UML for Agents", *Proceedings of the Agent-Oriented Information System Workshop at the 17th National Conference on Artificial Intelligence*, pp. 3-17, Austin, USA, July 2000.
[20] R. Simmons, R. Goodwin, K. Haigh, S. Koenig, and J. O'Sullivan. "A modular architecture for office delivery robots". In *Proc. Of the 1st Int. Conf. on Autonomous Agents* (Agents '97), Marina del Rey. CA, Feb 1997, pp.245 - 252.
[21] M. Shaw, R. DeLine, D. Klein, T. Ross, D. Young, and G. Zelesnik. "Abstractions for software architecture and tools to support them." In *IEEE Transactions on Software Engineering*, 21(4), pp. 314 - 335, 1995.
[22] M. Shaw and D. Garlan. *Software Architecture: Perspectives on an Emerging Discipline*, Upper Saddle River, N.J., Prentice Hall, 1996.
[23] O. Shehory. *Architectural Properties of Multi-Agent Systems*, Technical report CMU-RI-TR-98-28, Carnegie Mellon University, 1998.
[24] S. G. Woods and M. Barbacci. *Architectural Evaluation of Collaborative Agent-Based Systems.* Technical Report, CMU/SEI-99-TR-025, Carnegie Mellon University, USA, 1999.
[25] M.Y. Yoshino and U. Srinivasa Rangan. *Strategic alliances: an entrepreneurial approach to globalization*, Boston, Mass., Harvard Business School Press, 1995.
[26] E. Yu. *Modelling Strategic Relationships for Process Reengineering*, Ph.D. thesis, Department of Computer Science, University of Toronto, Canada, 1995.

The Ramification and Qualification Problems in Temporal Databases

Nick Papadakis and Dimitris Plexousakis

Department of Computer Science, University of Crete and
Institute of Computer Science, FORTH
P.O. Box 2208, GR-71409, Heraklion, Crete, Greece
Tel: +30 (81) 393528, Fax: +30 (81) 393501
{npapadak, dp}@csd.uch.gr

Abstract. The ramification and qualification problems are two infamous, hard and ever present problems in databases and, more generally, in systems exhibiting a dynamic behavior. The ramification problem refers to determining the indirect effects of actions, whereas the qualification problem refers to determining the preconditions which must hold prior to the execution of an action. A solution to these problems in database systems permits reasoning about the dynamics of databases and allows proving consistency properties. These two problems become increasingly complex in temporal databases and no satisfactory solution has been proposed as of yet. In this paper, we describe these two problems in the context of temporal databases and we propose a solution of polynomial complexity based on the language of the Situation Calculus. This solution extends previous proposals for the solution of these problems in conventional (non-temporal) databases.

1 Introduction

Reasoning about action and change has been one of the main research themes of the knowledge representation and planning communities of the last two decades. Action theories providing an axiomatic basis for managing change are applicable to a wide area of disciplines including software engineering [1], (cognitive) robotics [20] and data/knowledge base systems [16]. In this paper we consider the case of database systems. Databases are dynamical systems whose contents change as the result of database transactions. An atomic database transaction can be regarded as an action and hence, we can say that the changes in a database occur as the result of actions. Changes to a database may affect its consistency. Appropriate mechanisms must be employed in order to guarantee that a database will never reach an inconsistent state. To enforce this requirement one must be able to prescribe - in a parsimonious fashion - the exact changes (direct or indirect) that are effected by the execution of an action, and consequently determine which actions should be allowed to execute. These interrelated problems have been known as the *ramification* and *qualification* problems and were initially introduced by McCarthy and Hayes in [13].

I.P. Vlahavas and C.D. Spyropoulos (Eds.): SETN 2002, LNAI 2308, pp. 18–29, 2002.

We describe these problems by means of an example. Suppose we are interested in maintaining a database describing the contents of a room as part of a robot's perception of its environment. Suppose that the contents of the database are represented as propositions describing the location of each item in the room, as shown below:

$$on(bookcase, x_1) \quad on(table, x_2) \quad on(book, x_1)$$
$$on(bottle, x_2) \quad on(chair, x_3)\,.$$

Two objects cannot occupy the same room location unless one is stacked on top of the other. As we can observe, the book and the bookcase have the same position. This happens because of the presence of a constraint requiring that books must be on the bookcase (respectively for the bottle and table). The execution of the action $move(chair, x_4)$ has the effect of the *chair* changing position from x_3 to x_4. This action has as its only direct effect the change of the position of the *chair*. However, actions may have indirect effects as well. The action $move(bookcase, x_5)$ has both direct and indirect effects. The direct effect is to change the position of the *bookcase* whereas its indirect effect is to change the position of the *book*, because the *book* is in the *bookcase* and so it moves together with the *bookcase*. Notice that the indirect effect is caused by the presence of the constraint that the book must be on the bookcase.

Whenever an action takes place it is necessary to be able to understand all the direct and indirect effects of this action. Otherwise the contents of database may not satisfy the constraints that describe the consistent states of the database, and thus the database will be inconsistent. In the above example, after the execution of the action $move(bookcase, x_5)$, if the position of the *book* does not change, then the contents of database violate the aforementioned constraint.

Such indirect effects are caused by the presence of constraints. The **ramification problem** [3,4] refers to the concise description of the indirect effects of an action in the presence of constraints.

As far as the actions themselves are concerned, not all actions are allowed to take place in any given situation. For each action there are some preconditions which when true, they permit the action's execution. In the previous example, the action $move(bookcase, x_2)$ is not allowed to execute because a *table* occupies the target position. The action $move(bookcase, x)$ can be executed only if the position x is clear. So the precondition of action $move(p, x)$ is $clear(x)$.

The problem of determining the context in which an action is allowed to execute is the **qualification problem** [22]. As we observe, both problems appear in the context of our example and in the context of any changing world, giving rise to the **qualified ramification problem** [24]. To give a brief description of this problem consider that in above example the table and the chair are somehow connected. When the robot moves the table to a new the location, the chair will be moved too. Now the action $move(table, x_3)$ can be executed because the indirect effect of the action $move(table, x_3)$ is to change location of the *chair*. Hence, the preconditions $clear(x_3)$ holds. Before the execution of the action move $clear(x_3)$ was false. In cases, like this a solution must be able to take into account the fact that the indirect effects of actions may make action preconditions true.

The rest of paper is organized as follows: in section 2 we review the most prevalent solutions which have been proposed for addressing the ramification and the qualification problems in the context of conventional (non-temporal) databases. We also briefly examine the qualified ramification problem. The ramification and qualification problems in temporal databases are examined at section 3, and a solution is presented at section 4. The paper concludes with a summary and directions for further research.

2 Action Theories in Conventional Databases

2.1 The Ramification Problem

For the ramification problem many solutions have been suggested. The majority of them are based on the Situation Calculus [13]. The situation calculus is a second-order language that represents the changes which occur in a domain of interest, as results of actions. One possible evolution of the world is a sequence of actions and is represented by a first-order term, called a situation. The initial situation S_0 is a distinguished term representing the situation in which no action has occurred yet. A binary function, $do(a, s)$ yields the situation resulting from the execution of an action a while in situation s. Predicates, called *fluents*, may change truth value from one situation to another and a situation term is used as one of their arguments. Similarly, one can represent functions whose values are dependent on the situations on which they are evaluated (*functional fluents*). Solutions to the ramification problem aim at providing a parsimonious representation of what changes from one situation to the next, when an action takes place.

Among the simplest solutions proposed are those based on the *minimal change* approach [3,25]. These solutions suggest that, when an action occurs in a situation S, one needs to find the consistent situation S' which has the fewer changes from the situation S. For instance, consider as an example, the modeling of a simple circuit which has two switches and one lamp. When the two switches are up, the lamp must be lit. If one switch is down then the lamp must not be lit. Assume the situation $S = \{up(s_1), \neg up(s_2), \neg light\}$. The action $toggle - switch(s_2)$ change the situation of the circuit to $S^{'} = \{up(s_1), up(s_2), \neg light\}$, which is inconsistent. There are two consistent situations $S_1 = \{up(s_1), up(s_2), light\}$ and $S_2 = \{up(s_1), \neg up(s_2), \neg light\}$. It is sensible to light the lamp, whereas downing the switch s_2 isn't. It is reasonable for the lamp to become lit as indirect effect of "upping" another switch, but it is not reasonable to "down" a switch as indirect effect of "upping" another switch. So we prefer S_1 over S_2. The minimal change approach cannot select one of them, because they are both equally close to the original situation S.

The solutions based on the *categorization of fluents* [9,10,11] solve the above problem. The fluents are categorized in *primary* and *secondary*. A primary fluent can change only as a direct effect of an action, while a secondary one can change only as an indirect effect of an action. After an action takes place, we choose the situation with the fewer changes in primary fluents. In the above example, the separation is $F_p = \{up(s_1), up(s_2)\}$ and $F_s = \{light\}$, where F_p and F_s are the primary and secondary fluents respectively. Now we choose situation S_1 because it does not contain any changes in the primary fluents. The categorization of fluents solves the ramification problem only if all fluents can be categorized. If some fluents are primary for some actions and secondary for some other this solution is not satisfactory. For example, consider the circuit in Figure 1. The integrity constraints specufying the behavior of this system are expressed as the following formulas:

$$light \equiv up(s1) \wedge up(s2)$$
$$relay \equiv \neg up(s1) \wedge up(s3)$$
$$relay \supset \neg up(s2)$$

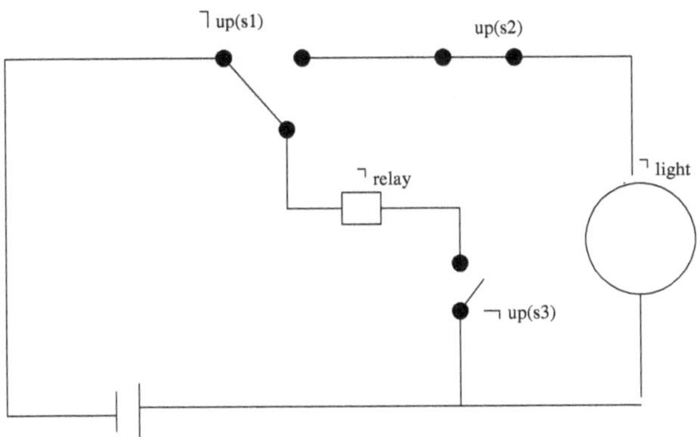

Fig. 1. The complex circuit

Now, the fluents $up(s1)$ and $up(s3)$ are primary, while the fluents *relay* and *light* are secondary. The fluent $up(s2)$ is primary for the action $toggle - switch(s2)$ and secondary for the action $toggle - switch(s1)$. When $up(s1)$ and $up(s3)$ hold after the execution of action $toggle - switch(s1)$, the proposition $\neg up(s1) \wedge up(s3)$ holds. This means that the fluent *relay* become true. When the fluent *relay* is true, it must be the case that $\neg up(s2)$ holds. Thus the action $toggle - switch(s1)$ has as indirect effect $\neg up(s2)$. This means that the fluent $up(s2)$ is secondary for the action $toggle - switch(s1)$. As we can observe, the indirect effect of an action dependends on the context of the database. The context is a conjunctive proposition made up of fluents in the database. and provide the enablity condition for the effects of actions to be realized In the above example, the context which must be in database in order for the action $toggle - switch(s1)$ to have as indirect effect $\neg up(s_2)$ is the fluents $up(s_1) \wedge up(s_3)$.

The above solutions suffer from the drawback that they cannot capture the dependence that exists between the indirect effects of action and the context present in the database.

This dependence is captured by the solution of *causal relationships* [2,12, 5,21,22]. Each causal relationship consists of two parts. The former part, called **context**, consists of one fluent formula which when true, establishes a causal relationship between an action and its effect. The latter part, is the indirect effect of an action (called the cause of this effect). A causal relationship has the form

$$\epsilon \;\; causes \;\; \rho \;\; if \;\; \Phi$$

where ϵ is an action, ρ is the direct/indirect effect and Φ is the context.

One solution based the idea of causal relationships is the language proposed by McCain and Tuner [12]. This language includes static and dynamic laws. A static law is an expression of the form

$$caused \quad F \quad if \quad G\,.$$

The meaning of static law of this form is that when a formula G is true the fluent F must be true. A dynamic law is an expression of the form

$$U \quad causes \quad F \quad if \quad G\,.$$

The meaning of a dynamic law of this form is that an action U has the direct effect F if the proposition G holds. For instance, in the example of the previous section, the following dynamic law is defined

$$move(x,l) \quad causes \quad on(x,l) \quad if \quad free(l)\,.$$

Also, we can define the static law

$$on(x,l) \quad if \quad on(y,l) \wedge on(x,y)\,.$$

This law means that if one object x is on another object y which is at position l (possibly after some move), then x must be at l as well. Note that static laws capture the indirect effects while dynamic laws capture the direct effects of actions.

2.2 The Qualification Problem

We now review briefly solutions proposed for solving the qualification problem. The so-called *default* solution [4] suggests that, for each action a, we must determine a formula F^a which, when true, prohibits action a from executing. The formula F^a is a disjunction of the form

$$F^a \equiv \bigvee F_i\,,$$

where each F_i is a fluent formula. When any of the disjoin F_i is true, the action a can not execute. Returning to our example, the disabling fluent formula of the action $move(x, l)$ has one disjunct:

$$F^{move(x,l)} \equiv on(y, l) \wedge x \neq y \,.$$

We say that when the formula F^a holds then the action a is *disqualified* and thus it cannot execute. This is represented by employing a predicate $disq$ as

$$F^a \supset disq(a)\,.$$

Another solution [24] is an extension of the minimal-change possible-worlds approach that has been suggested for solving the ramification problem. After each action a executes, we try to find a consistent situation which contains all direct and indirect effects of a. If there is at least one such situation, then the action can execute, otherwise it cannot.

3 Temporal Databases

In temporal database systems all action occur at specific points in time. Also objects and relationships among objects exist over time. The value of a fluent is dependent on the time instant at which it is evaluated. Hence, a finer-grained change description mechanism is required here. Recall that, in conventional (non-temporal) databases we only need to determine the value of fluents only after an action occurs.

In this section, we describe the ramification and qualification problems in the context of temporal databases. We describe these problems by means of an example. Assume that the following rule is in effect: if a public employee commits a misdemeanor, then for the next five months he is considered illegal. When a public employee is illegal, then s/he must be suspended for the entire time interval over which s/he is considered illegal. A public employee can receive promotion only if s/he has stayed in the same position for at least five years and is not under suspension. These are expressed in propositional form by the following constraints[1]:

$$occur(misdemeanor(p), t) \supset illegal(p, t_1) \wedge \; t_1 < t + 5m$$
$$illegal(p, t_1) \supset suspended(p, t_1)$$
$$suspended(p, t_1) \vee (sameposition(p, d) \wedge \; d < 5y) \supset \neg receivepromotion(p, t_1)\,,$$

where t and t_1 are temporal variables and the predicate $occur(crime(p), t)$ denotes that the action $crime(p)$ is executed at time t. In a temporal database we need to describe the direct and indirect effects of an action not only in the

[1] Quantifiers are committed in the expression of these propositions. They are considered to be implicitly universally quantified over their temporal and non-temporal arguments.

immediately resulting next situation but possibly for many future situations as well. In the above example, the action *misdemeanor*(p) has the indirect effect that the public worker is in suspension in the next five months. In this five-month period, a number of other actions may execute leading to many different situations. In all these situations, the action *misdemeanor*(p) has the indirect effect *suspended*(p).

The causal relationships cannot solve the ramification problem in temporal databases because they determine the direct and indirect effects only for the next situation. The same weakness characterizes all other solutions of the ramification problem in conventional databases. Furthermore, as we can observe, the execution of the action *misdemeanor*(p) disqualified the action *receivepromotion* for the subsequent five-month period. The solutions proposed for the qualification problem in conventional databases cannot address the qualification problem in temporal databases because they cannot represent the fact that one action can disqualify another for a specific time span.

The above weakness can be alleviated by constructing a correspondence between situations and actions with time. Such a correspondence was suggested in previous works [14,9,7]. We adopt the correspondence which was initially suggested in [14] and which is shown in Figure 2. There are three parallel axes: the first is the situation axis, the second is the time axis and the third is the actions axis. We assume that all actions are instantaneous. When an action takes place, the database changes into a new situation.

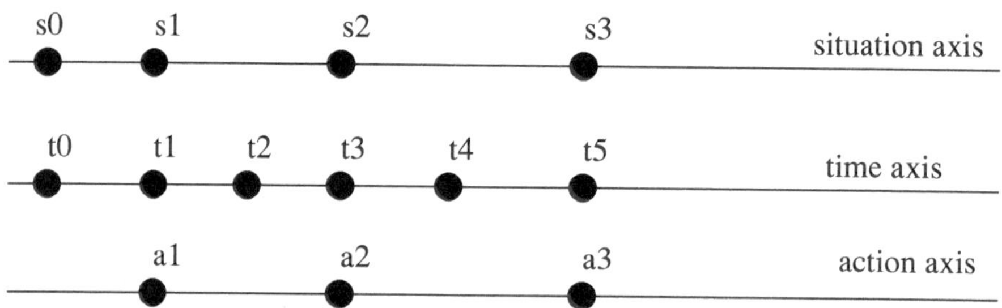

Fig. 2. The correspondence situations and actions with the time

In [14], we have proposed a solution for the ramification problem in temporal databases. More specifically, for each pair (a, f) of an action a and fluent f we define two axioms:

$$a(t) \quad causes \quad f(t') \quad if \quad E^+_{f_a}$$
$$a(t) \quad causes \quad \neg f(t') \quad if \quad E^-_{f_a},$$

where the $E^+_{f_a}$ and $E^-_{f_a}$ are the formulas which must hold, for fluent f to become true or false respectively at time t', after the execution of action a at time t. The above axioms must be specified for any action and the fluents that can be affected by its execution. The maximum number of axioms that need to be defined is $O(2*F*A)$, where F is the number of fluents and A the number of actions. In the next section, we present an improvement to this solution in terms of the number of axioms needed. The improved solution requires the specification of $O(A+2*F)$ such causal laws.

4 An Improved Solution

In this section we present an improvement to our previously proposed solution [14] for the ramification and qualification problems in temporal databases. This solution is an extension of the solution of McCain and Tuner [12] for the ramification problem in conventional databases.

We represent each action A as $A(t)$, meaning that the action A occurs at time t. Each fluent F is represented as $F(t')$, meaning that the fluent F is true for time t' after the current moment. In other words, F is true in time interval $[currentmoment, currentmoment+t']$. When $\neg F_i(t')$ holds, this means that the fluent F is false for time t' after the current moment. As time progresses, the value of t' is decreased by one time unit.

For each action A, we define a law of the form:

$$A \supset \bigwedge L_i(t'),$$

where $L_i(t')$ is $F_i(t')$ or $\neg F_i(t')$. These laws are dynamic and describe the direct effects of an action. Each of these laws are evaluated only when the corresponding action is executed.

Subsequently, for each fluent F, we define two laws

$$G(t) \supset F(1)$$
$$B(t) \supset \neg F(1),$$

where $G(t)$ is a proposition which when true causes the fluent F to become true for the next time-unit. Similarly, $B(t)$ is a proposition which when true causes the fluent F to become false for the next time-unit. These laws are static and describe the indirect effect of the execution of actions. They are evaluated in every state of the database. The formula $G(t)$ and $B(t)$ are more general than the formules $E^+_{f_a}$ and $E^-_{f_a}$ which are described in the previous solution, because $E^+_{f_a}/E^-_{f_a}$ specify what must hold in order for the fluent f to be come true/false after the execution of a specific action a, while the formules $G(t)/B(t)$ specified what must hold in order for the fluent f to be come true/false independently of the specific actions.

Notice that, in reference to the correspondence drawn in Figure 1, the dynamical laws are evaluated only when the corresponding action is executed. The static laws are evaluated at each time unit (on the second axis). The execution of static laws does not necessarily change the situation of the database.

The specification of these causal laws solve the ramification problem in temporal databases, since the dynamic laws capture the direct effects of each action whereas the static ones capture the indirect effects of each action in every state of the database. It is easy to conclude that we need $A + 2 * F$ such laws, where F is the number of fluents and A is the number of actions.

To address the qualification problem we use the predicate *duration* as has been defined in [14]. The interpretation of this predicate is that when $duration(A,$
$t)$ is true, then the action A is disqualified for time t after the current moment. Hence, it represents the duration of the disqualification of the action from executing. At each time unit the value of t is decreased by one time unit. Then, for each action A we define one static law.

$$K_A(t, t') \supset duration(A, t'),$$

where $K_A(t, t')$ is a proposition which when true at time-moment t, disqualifies the action A for a time interval of length t' after the current moment. If some action is disqualified at time instant t, then it is not necessary to examine the above static law. Its examination becomes necessary only when $duration(A, 0)$ holds[2]. Hence, to address the qualification problem we need A laws, where A is the number of actions.

In total, the specification of $O(2*(A+F))$ laws is required for the solution of the ramification and qualification problem in the context of temporal databases. Now let us see how the above solution solves these problems for the example we presented in the previous section[3].

We have one dynamic and one static law, namely:

$$mindemeanor(p, now) \supset illegal(p, 5m) \qquad (1)$$
$$illegal(p, t) \wedge (t > 0) \wedge \ publicemployee(p, t_1) \supset suspended(1) \quad (2),$$

where $misdemeanor(p, now)$ means that p commits a misdemeanor at the present moment. The first law is dynamic and captures the direct effect of the action *misdemeanor*. The second law is static and captures the indirect effects of the action *misdemeanor*.

The action $receive - promotion$ has the following precondition: first the employee must have been in the same position for at least five years, and second, s/he must not have been suspended. These preconditions are represented as:

$$suspended(t) \wedge (t > 0) \wedge \ sameposition(p, t_1) \ \wedge (t_1 < 5y) \ \wedge$$
$$t' = max(t, 5y - t_1) \supset \ duration(receive - promotion, t') \qquad (3).$$

The proposition $K_{receive-promotion}(now, t')$ is specified as

$$K_{receive-promotion}(now, t') \equiv$$
$$suspended(t) \wedge (t > 0) \wedge \ sameposition(p, t_1) \ \wedge (t_1 < 5y) \wedge$$
$$t' = max(t, 5y - t_1).$$

---

[2] This mean that the action A is not disqualified.

[3] We do not deal with the problem of changing time granularities in this paper. We assume that different time units are understood and appropriate conversion functions are available.

Law (3) means that, at any time instant, if a public employee is in suspension or has been in the same position for time less than $5y$, then the action *receive – promotion* becomes disqualified as long as at least one of these two conditions is true. This ensure because the fluent $sameposition(p, 5y)$ is true at time $5y - t_1$ from now and the fluent $\neg suspended$ is true for time t from now. Thus at time $t' = max(t, 5y - t_1)$ from the current monet the two fluents are true.

The above problem becomes even more complex if the actions are not instanteous but have duration. In that case, it is necessary to draw a different correspondece among situations, actions and the time axis than the one of Figure 1. Furthermore, the direct and indirect effects of an action must be determined with regards to the start and/or end of this action. We assume that an action A with duration is equivalent with two instanteous actions one for the start ($start(A, t)$) and one for end ($end(A, t')$). We also assume that the action occurs without interaction through at this interval. The above laws are now defined for each action for two time instants, one for the starting point and one for the end point.

In the previous example, assume that the action $misdemeanor(p, t)$ executes during the interval $[t, t']$. Then the public employee p is considered to be illegal for the interval $[t, t' + 5m]$. Now we must rewrite the dynamic laws as follows

$$start(misdemeanor(p, t)) \supset illegal(p, \infty)$$
$$end(misdemeanor(p, t)) \supset illegal(p, 5m)\,.$$

The symbol ∞ is used to denote that we do not know when the action of committing the misdemeanor ended. The second law changes ∞ to $5m$. We need to specify $O(2 * A)$ such dynamic laws. Notice that the static laws do not need to change. Hence, for the solution of the ramification problem we need $O(2 * A + 2 * F)$ laws and for the solution of the qualification problem we do not need to change the previous specification in the case of actions with duration.

5 Summary and Future Research

The ramification and qualification problems in temporal database are complex and many-faceted problems. We have described a solution to these problems by adherenig to one such facet, namely that the effects of an action (direct and indirect) refer to the current and future situations only. It is very interesting to investigate the case in which actions can change our beliefs about the past. In that case, the effects may be periodically recursive and for the solution of the ramification and qualification problems, it may be necessary to determine what things can change in the past and what things cannot. It is also worth investigating these problems in the presence of concurrent actions (instantaneous or with duration), or in the case of non-deterministic actions. These are topics of current research.

References

1. A. Borgida, J. Mylopoulos and R. Reiter. On the Frame Problem in Procedure Specifications. IEEE Trans. on Software Engineering, 21(10), Oct. 1995, pp.785-798.
2. C. Elkan. Reasoning about action in first order logic. In Proceedings of the Conference of the Canadian Society for Comptutational Studies of Intelligence (CSCSI), pages 221-227, Vancouver, Canada, May 1992.
3. M. Ginsberg and D. Smith. Reasoning about action I: A possible worlds approach. Artificial Intelligence, 35:165-195, 1988.
4. M. Ginsberg and D. Smith. Reasoning about action II: A possible worlds approach. Artificial Intelligence, 35:311-342, 1988.
5. J. Gustafon. Extending Temporal Action Logic for Ramification and Concurency, Thesis No 719 of Linkoping Studies in Science and Technology, 1998.
6. R. Fikes and N. J. Nilsson, STRIPS: A new approach to the application of theorem proving to problem solving. Artificial Intelligence, 2:189-208, 1971.
7. A. Fusaoka. Situation Calculus on a Dense Flow of Time. Proceedings of the AAAI National Conference on Artificial Intelligence, pages 633-638, 1996
8. A. Haas. The Case for Domain-Specific Frame Axioms. In F. Brown, editor. The frame problem in artificial intelligence. Proceedings of the 1987 workshop, pages 343-348, 1987.
9. V. Lifshitz. Towards a metatheory of action. In J.F. Allen, R. Fikes, and E. Sandewall, editors, Proceedings of the International Conference on Principles of Knowledge Representation and Reasoning, pages 376-386, Cambridge, MA, 1991.
10. V. Lifshitz. Frames in the space of situations, Artificial Intelligence, 46:365-376, 1990.
11. V. Lifshitz. Restricted monotonicity. In Proceedings of the AAAI National Conference on Artifical Intelligence, pages 432-437, Washington DC, July 1993.
12. N. McCain and Hudson Turner. A causal theory of ramifications and qualifications. In C. S. Mellish, editor, Proceedings of the International Joint Conference on Artifical Intelligence (IJCAI), pages 1978-1984, Montreal, Canada, August 1995.
13. J. McCarthy and P.J. Hayes. Some philophical problem from the standpoint of artificial intelligence. In B. Meltzer and D. Mitchie, editors, Machine Intelligence 4, pages 463-502. American Elsevier, New York, 1969.
14. Nikos Papadakis and Dimitris Plexousakis. Action Theories in Temporal Databases. 8th Panhellenic Conference on Informatics. Nicosia, Cyprus 8-11 Nov 2001.
15. E. Pednault. ADL: Exploring the Middle Ground between STRIPS and the Situation Calculus. In R.J. Brachman, H. Levesque, and R. Reiter, editors, Proceedings of the 1st International Conference on Principles of Knowledge Representation and Reasoning (KR' 89), pages 324-332. Morgan Kaufmann, 1989.
16. Dimitris Plexousakis, John Mylopoulos: Accomodating Integrity Constraints During Database Design. Proceedings of EDBT 1996, pages 497-513
17. J. Pinto. Temporal Reasoning in the Situation Calculus. Ph.D. Thesis, Dept. of Computer Science, Univ. of Toronto, Jan. 1994.
18. J. Pinto and R. Reiter. Temporal Reasoning in Logic Programming: A Case for the Situation Calculus. Proc. 10th Int. Conf. on Logic Programming, Budapest, Hungary, June 21-24, 1993.
19. R. Reiter A logic for default reasoning. Artificial Intelligence, 13:81-132, 1980.

20. R. Reiter. Khowledge in Action: Logical Foundation for specifying and implementing Dynamical Systems, MIT Press, 2001.
21. M. Thielscher. Ramification and causality. Artifical Intelligence, 89(1-2):317-364, 1997.
22. M. Thielscher. Reasoning about actions: Steady versus stabilizing state constraints. Artifical Intelligence, 104:339-355, 1988.
23. M. Thielscher.Nondeterministic actions in the fluent calculus: Disjunctive state update axioms. In S. Holldobler, editor, Intellectics and Computational Logic. Kluwer, 1999.
24. M. Thielscher. Qualified ramifications. In B. Kuipers and B.Wbber, editors, Proceedings of the AAAI National Conference on Artificial Intelligence, pages 466-471, 1997
25. M. Winslett. Reasoning about action using a possible models approach. In Proceeding of the AAAI National Conference on Artifical Intelligence, pages 89-93, Saint Paul, MN, August 1988.

Multi-inference with Multi-neurules

Ioannis Hatzilygeroudis and Jim Prentzas

University of Patras, School of Engineering
Dept of Computer Engin. & Informatics, 26500 Patras, Hellas (Greece)
&
Computer Technology Institute, P.O. Box 1122, 26110 Patras, Hellas (Greece)
{ihatz, prentzas}@ceid.upatras.gr

Abstract. Neurules are a type of hybrid rules combining a symbolic and a connectionist representation. There are two disadvantages of neurules. The first is that the created neurule bases usually contain multiple representations of the same piece of knowledge. Also, the inference mechanism is rather connectionism oriented than symbolism oriented, thus reducing naturalness. To remedy these deficiencies, we introduce an extension to neurules, called multi-neurules, and an alternative inference process, which is rather symbolism oriented. Experimental results comparing the two inference processes are also presented.

1 Introduction

There have been efforts at combining the expert systems approach and the neural networks (connectionism) one into hybrid systems, in order to exploit their benefits [1]. In some of them, called embedded systems, a neural network is used in the inference engine of an expert system. For example, in NEULA [2] a neural network selects the next rule to fire. Also, LAM [1] uses two neural networks as partial problem solvers. However, the inference process in those systems, although gains efficiency, lacks the naturalness of the symbolic component. This is so, because pre-eminence is given to the connectionist framework.

On the other hand, connectionist expert systems are integrated systems that represent relationships between concepts, considered as nodes in a neural network. Weights are set in a way that makes the network infer correctly. The system in [3] is a popular such system, whose inference engine is called MACIE. Two characteristics of MACIE are: its ability to reason from partial data and its ability to provide explanations in the form of if-then rules. However, its inference process lacks naturalness. Again, this is due to the pure connectionist inference approach.

In a previous work [4], we introduced *neurules*, a hybrid rule-based representation scheme integrating symbolic rules with neurocomputing, which gives pre-eminence to the symbolic component. Thus, neurules give a more natural and efficient way of representing knowledge and making inferences. However, there are two disadvantages of neurules, from the symbolic point of view. Neurules are constructed

I.P. Vlahavas and C.D. Spyropoulos (Eds.): SETN 2002, LNAI 2308, pp. 30–41, 2002.

either from symbolic rules or from learning data in the form of training examples. In case of non-separable sets of training examples, more than one neurule with the same conditions and the same conclusion, but different significance factors exist in a neurule base. This creates neurule bases with multiple representations of the same piece of knowledge [5]. The second disadvantage is that the associated inference mechanism [6] is rather connectionism oriented, thus reducing naturalness.

To remedy the first deficiency, we introduce here an extension to neurules called *multi-neurules.* For the second, we introduce an alternative hybrid inference process, which is rather symbolism oriented. Experimental results comparing the two inference processes are presented.

The structure of the paper is as follows. Section 2 presents neurules and Section 3 mainly the inference process introduced here. In Section 4, an example knowledge base and an example inference are presented. Section 5 presents some experimental results and finally Section 6 concludes.

2 Neurules

2.1 Simple Neurules

Neurules (: *neu*ral *rules*) are a kind of hybrid rules. Each neurule (Fig. 1a) is considered as an adaline unit (Fig.1b). The *inputs* C_i (i=1,...,n) of the unit are the *conditions* of the rule. Each condition C_i is assigned a number sf_i, called a *significance factor*, corresponding to the weight of the corresponding input of the adaline unit. Moreover, each rule itself is assigned a number sf_0, called the *bias factor*, corresponding to the *bias* of the unit.

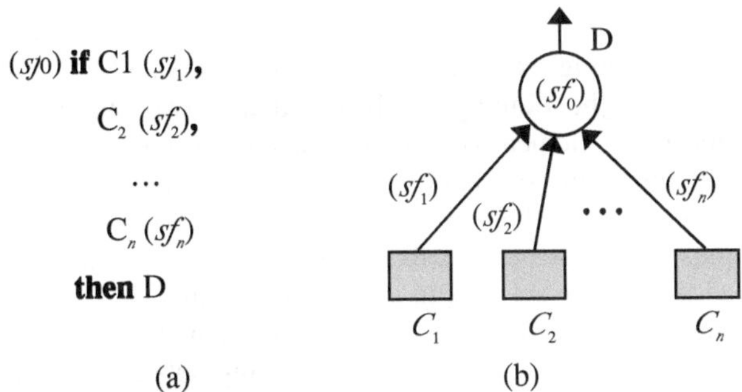

Fig. 1. (a) Form of a neurule (b) corresponding adaline unit

Each input takes a value from the following set of discrete values: [1 (true), -1 (false), 0 (unknown)]. The *output D*, which represents the *conclusion* of the rule, is calculated via the formulas:

$$D = f(\mathbf{a}), \quad \mathbf{a} = sf_0 + \sum_{i=1}^{n} sf_i \; C_i \tag{1}$$

where **a** is the *activation value* and *f(x)* the *activation function*, which is a threshold function:

$$f(a) = \begin{cases} 1 & \text{if a} \geq 0 \\ -1 & \text{otherwise} \end{cases}$$

Hence, the output can take one of two values, '-1' and '1', representing failure and success of the rule respectively.

2.2 Training Neurules

Each neurule is individually trained via a *training set*, which contains *training examples* in the form [v_1 v_2 … v_n d], where v_i, i= 1, …,n are their *component values*, corresponding to the n inputs of the neurule, and d is the *desired output* ('1' for success, '-1' for failure). The learning algorithm employed is the standard least mean square (LMS) algorithm (see e.g. [3]).

However, there are cases where the LMS algorithm fails to specify the right significance factors for a number of neurules. That is, the adaline unit of a rule does not correctly classify some of the training examples. This means that the training examples correspond to a non-separable (boolean) function. To overcome this problem, the initial training set is divided into subsets in a way that each subset contains *success examples* (i.e. with d=1) which are "close" to each other in some degree. The *closeness* between two examples is defined as the number of common component values. For example, the closeness of [1 0 1 1 1] and [1 1 0 1 1] is '2'. Also, we define as *least closeness pair* (LCP), a pair of success examples with the least closeness in a training set. There may be more than one LCP in a training set.

Initially, a LCP in the training set is found and two subsets are created each containing as its initial element one of the success examples of that pair, called its *pivot.* Each of the remaining success examples are distributed between the two subsets based on their closeness to their pivots. More specifically, each subset contains the success examples which are closer to its pivot. Then, the failure examples of the initial set are added to both subsets, to avoid neurule misfiring. After that, two copies of the initial neurule, one for each subset, are trained. If the factors of a copy misclassify some of its examples, the corresponding subset is further split into two other subsets, based on one of its LCPs. This continues, until all examples are classified. This means that from an initial neurule more than one final neurule may be produced, which are called *sibling neurules* (for a more detailed and formal description see [5]).

2.3 Multi-neurules

The existence of sibling neurules creates neurule bases with multiple representations of the same piece of knowledge, which is their main disadvantage. To remedy this deficiency, we introduce multi-neurules.

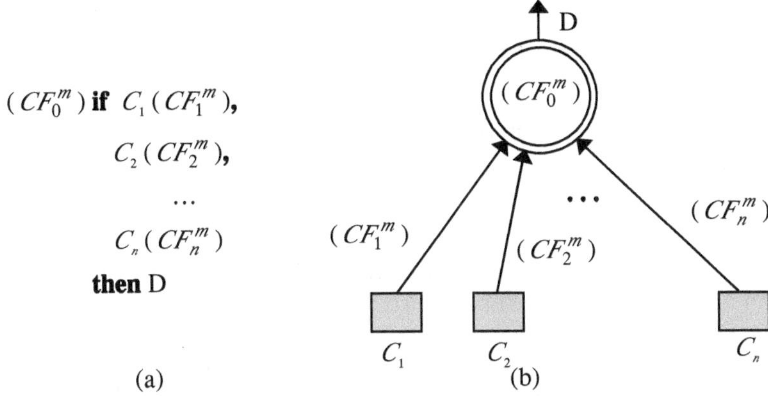

Fig. 2. (a) Form of a multi-neurule (b) corresponding multi-adaline unit

A *multi-neurule* of size *m* has the form presented in Fig. 2a and is considered as a *multi-adaline* unit (Fig. 2b), also introduced here. Each CF_i^m is called a condition *sf-tuple* that consists of *m* significance factors:

$$CF_i^m \equiv < sf_{i1}, sf_{i2}, \ldots, sf_{im} > .$$

A multi-adaline unit of size *m* is a merger of *m* simple adaline units. Correspondingly, a multi-neurule of *size m* is the merger of *m* simple neurules. So, in a multi-unit of size *m* we distinguish *m* different sets of weights, each corresponding to the weights of a constituent unit. Similarly, a multi-neurule of *size m* includes *m* different sets of significance factors, called rule *sf-sets*, each corresponding to the significance factors of a constituent neurule. Thus, the rule sf-set RF_i consists of the *i*th significance factors of the sf-tuples:

$$RF_i = (sf_{1i}, sf_{2i}, \ldots, sf_{ni}), \text{ for } i = 1, m$$

Each RF_i is used to compute the activation $\mathbf{a}_i$ of the corresponding adaline unit.

The output of a multi-unit is determined by the set that produces the maximum activation value. Hence, a multi-unit is activated as soon as any of its constituent units gets activated (i.e. any $\mathbf{a}_i \geq 0$). The output D of a multi-adaline unit is calculated via the formulas:

$$D = f(\mathbf{a})\,, \mathbf{a} = \bigvee_{i=1}^{m} \mathbf{a}_i\,,\ \mathbf{a}_i = sf_{0i} + \sum_{j=1}^{n} sf_{ij} C_j \tag{2}$$

The activation function is the same as in a simple unit.

NR5: (-2.2) **if** Treatment is Placibin (-1.8),
Treatment is Biramibio (1.0)
then Treatment is Posiboost

NR6: (-2.2) **if** Treatment is Biramibio (-2.6),
Treatment is Placibin (1.8)
then Treatment is Posiboost

NR5: (-2.2, -2.2) **if** Treatment is Placibin (-1.8, 1.8)
Treatment is Biramibio (1.0, -2.6)
then Treatment is Posiboost

Fig. 3. Merging sibling neurules into a multi-neurule

In practice, a multi-neurule is produced by simply merging all sibling neurules with the same conclusion. For example, neurule NR5, used in the example knowledge base in Section 4.1, is a multi-neurule produced from merging two sibling neurules of the old knowledge base (NR5, NR6), as shown in Fig.3. Notice that, because the conditions in each simple neurule are are sorted, so that $|sf_1| \geq |sf_2| \geq \ldots \geq |sf_n|$, for efficiency reasons, this information is also attached to multi-neurules. So, NR5 has two sf-sets, $RF_1 = (-1.8, 1.0)$ and $RF_2 = (-2.6, 1.8)$.

2.4 Syntax and Semantics

The general syntax of a neurule, simple or multi, (in a BNF notation, where '{}' denotes zero, one or more occurrences and '<>' denotes non-terminal symbols) is:

<rule>::= (<bias-factors>) **if** <conditions> **then** <conclusions>

<bias-factors>::= <bias-factor> {**,** <bias-factor>}

<conditions>::= <condition> {**,** <condition>}

<conclusions>::= <conclusion> {**,** <conclusion>}

<condition>::= <variable> <predicate> <value> (<significance-factors>)

< significance-factors >::= < significance-factor> {**,** < significance-factor>}

<conclusion>::= <variable> <predicate> <value> .

In the above definition, <variable> denotes a *variable* as in a variable declaration. <predicate> denotes a predicate, which is one of {is, isnot, <, >}. <value> denotes a value. It can be a symbol (e.g. "male", "night-pain") or a number (e.g "5"). <bias-factor> and <significance-factor> are (real) numbers. The significance factor of a condition represents the significance (weight) of the condition in drawing the conclusion. A significance factor with a sign opposite to that of the bias factor of its neurule positively contributes in drawing the conclusion, otherwise negatively.

3 The Hybrid Inference Processes

The inference engine associated with neurules implements the way neurules co-operate to reach conclusions. It supports two alternative hybrid inference processes. The one gives pre-eminence to neurocomputing, and is called *connectionism-oriented* inference process, whereas the other to symbolic reasoning, and is called *symbolism-oriented inference process*. In the symbolism-oriented process, a type of a classical rule-based reasoning is employed, but evaluation of a rule is based on neurocomputing measures. In the connectionism-oriented process, the choice of the next rule to be considered is based on a neurocomputing measure, so the process jumps from rule to rule, but the rest is symbolic. In this section, we mainly present the symbolism oriented process.

3.1 Neurules Evaluation

In the following, WM denotes the working memory and NRB the neurule base.

Generally, the output of a simple neurule is computed according to Eq. (1). However, it is possible to deduce the output of a neurule without knowing the values of all of its conditions. To achieve this, we define for each simple neurule the *known sum* and the *remaining sum* as follows:

$$kn-sum = sf_0 + \sum_{C_i \in E} sf_i C_i \tag{3}$$

$$rem-sum = \sum_{C_i \in U} | sf_i | \tag{4}$$

where E is the set of evaluated conditions, U the set of unevaluated conditions and C_i is the value of condition cond$_i$. A condition is evaluated, if its value ('true' or 'false') is by some way known. So, *known-sum* is the weighted sum of the values of the already known (i.e. evaluated) conditions (inputs) of the corresponding neurule and *rem-sum* represents the largest possible weighted sum of the remaining (i.e. unevaluated) conditions of the neurule. If $|kn\text{-}sum| > rem\text{-}sum$ for a certain neurule, then evaluation of its conditions can stop, because its output can be deduced regardless of the values of the unevaluated conditions. In this case, its output is guaranteed to be '-1' if $kn\text{-}sum < 0$, or '1', if $kn\text{-}sum > 0$.

In the case of a multi-neurule of size m, we define m different *kn-sums* and *rem-sums*, one for each RF_i:

$$kn-sum_i = sf_{0i} + \sum_{C_j \in E} sf_{ji} C_j \,,\ i=1, m \tag{5}$$

$$rem-sum_i = \sum_{C_j \in U} | sf_{ji} | \,,\ i=1, m\,. \tag{6}$$

It is convenient, for the connectionism-oriented process, to define the *firing potential (fp)* of a neurule as follows:

$$fp = \frac{|\,kn-sum\,|}{rem-sum} \; . \tag{7}$$

The firing potential of a neurule is an estimate of its intention that its output will become '±1'. Whenever *fp* > 1, the values of the evaluated conditions can determine the value of its output, regardless of the values of the unevaluated conditions. The rule then evaluates to '1' (true), if *kn-sum* > 0 or to '-1' (false), if *kn-sum* < 0. In the first case, we say that the neurule is *fired*, whereas in the second that it is *blocked*. Notice, that the firing potential has meaning only if *rem-sum* ≠ 0. If *rem-sum* = 0, all the conditions have been evaluated and its output is evaluated based on *kn-sum*. For a multi-neurule, we define as many *fp*s as the size of the multi-neurule.

3.2 Symbolism-Oriented Process

The symbolism-oriented inference process is based on a backward chaining strategy. There are two stacks used, a *goal stack* (*GS*), where the *current goal* (*CG*) (condition) to be evaluated is always on its top, and a *neurule stack (NS)*, where the current neurule under evaluation is always on its top. The conflict resolution strategy, due to backward chaining and the neurules, is based on textual order. A neurule succeeds if it *evaluates* to 'true', that is its output is computed to be '1' after evaluation of its conditions. Inference stops either when a neurule with a goal variable is fired (success) or there is no further action (failure). *WM* denotes the working memory.

More formally, the process is as follows:

1. Put the initial goal(s) on *GS*.
2. While there are goals on *GS* do
   - 2.1 Consider the first goal on *GS* as the current goal (*CG*) and find the neurules having it as their conclusion. If there are no such neurules, stop (failure). Otherwise, put them on *RS*.
   - 2.2 For each neurule NR_i on *NS* (*current rule*: $CR = NR_i$) do
     - 2.2.1 (simple neurule case) While *CR* is not fired or blocked, for each condition C_i of *CR* (*current condition*: $CC = C_i$) do
       - 2.2.1.1 If *CC* is already evaluated, update the *kn-sum* and the *rem-sum* of NR_x. Otherwise, if it contains an input variable, ask the user for its value (user data), evaluate *CC*, put it in WM and update the *kn-sum* and the *rem-sum* of *CR*, otherwise (intermediate or output variable) put *CC* on the top of *GS* and execute step 2.1 recursively until *CC* is evaluated. After its evaluation update the *kn-sum* and the *rem-sum* of *CR*.
       - 2.2.1.2 If (|*kn-sum*| > *rem-sum* and *kn-sum* > 0), mark *CR* as 'fired', mark its conclusion as 'true', put the conclusion in WM and remove the current goal from *GS* (multi-valued variable) or remove from *GS* all goals containing the variable (single-valued variable). If (|*kn-sum*| > *rem-sum* and *kn-sum* < 0), mark *CR* as 'blocked'.

2.2.2 (multi-neurule case) While *CR* is not 'fired' or 'blocked', for each RF_i (*current sf-set*: $CRF = RF_i$) of *CR* do
   2.2.2.1 While *CRF* is not 'fired' or 'blocked', for each for each condition C_i of *CRF* ($CC = C_i$) do
      2.2.2.1.1 The same as 2.2.1.1 (with $kn\text{-}sum_i$ and $rem\text{-}sum_i$ instead of *kn-sum* and *rem-sum*, respectively).
      2.2.2.1.2 If ($|kn\text{-}sum_i| > rem\text{-}sum_i$ and $kn\text{-}sum_i > 0$), mark *CR* as 'fired', mark its conclusion as 'true', put the conclusion in WM and remove the current goal from *GS* (multi-valued variable) or remove from *GS* all goals containing the variable (single-valued variable). If ($|kn\text{-}sum_i| > rem\text{-}sum_i$ and $kn\text{-}sum_i < 0$), mark *CRF* as 'blocked'. If it is the last rule sf-set, mark *CR* as 'blocked'.

2.3 If all neurules on *RS* are blocked, mark their conclusions as 'false', put the conclusions in *WM* and remove the current goal from *GS*.

3. If there are no conclusions in *WM* containing output variables, stop (failure). Otherwise, display the conclusions in *WM* marked as 'TRUE' (output data) and stop (success).

3.3 Connectionism-Oriented Process

Initially, the values of the variables (conditions) may be not known to the system. The *kn-sum* for every simple neurule is then set to its bias factor, whereas its *rem-sum* is set to the sum of the absolute values of all its significance factors. For a multi-neurule, this is done for each RF_i (i=1, m). If the value of a variable becomes known, it influences the values of the conditions containing it and hence the known sums, the remaining sums and the firing potentials of the unevaluated neurules containing them, which are called *affected neurules*. As soon as an intermediate neurule becomes evaluated, the known sums, the remaining sums and the firing potentials of all the affected neurules are also updated. Updating a multi-neurule consists in updating each of its *fps* (*kn-sums* and *rem-sums*). Obviously, a firing potential is updated only if the corresponding remaining sum is not equal to zero.

Unevaluated neurules that are updated, due to a new variable value, constitute the *participating* neurules. The inference mechanism tries then to focus on participating neurules whose firing potential is close to exceeding '1'. More specifically, it selects the one with the maximum firing potential, because it is the most likely, has a greater intention, to fire. In the case of a multi-neurule, its maximum *fp* represents the neurule. The system tries to evaluate the first unevaluated condition, which is the one with the maximum absolute significance factor (recall that the conditions of a neurule are sorted). After evaluation of the condition, *kn-sum, rem-sum* and *fp* of the neurule are computed. If *rem-sum* = 0 or *fp* > 1, it evaluates and its conclusion is put in the WM. If the system reaches a final conclusion, it stops.

A more formal description of this inference algorithm, for a NRB containing only simple neurules, can be found in [6, 11].

4 Examples

4.1 Example Knowledge Base

We use as an example to illustrate the functionalities of our system the one presented in [3]. It contains training data dealing with acute theoretical diseases of the sarcophagus. There are six symptoms (Swollen feet, Red ears, Hair loss, Dizziness, Sensitive aretha, Placibin allergy), two diseases (Supercilliosis, Namastosis) whose diagnoses are based on the symptoms and three possible treatments (Placibin, Biramibio, Posiboost). Also, dependency information is provided. We used the dependency information to construct the initial neurules and the training data provided to train them. The produced knowledge base, which contains five neurules (NR1-NR5), is illustrated in Table 1. An equivalent knowledge base forming a multilevel network is presented in [3]. It is quite clear how more natural is our knowledge base than that in [3].

Table 1.

NR1: (-0.4) **if** SwollenFeet is true (3.6), HairLoss is true (3.6), RedEars is true (-0.8) **then** Disease is Supercilliosis NR2: (1.4) **if** Dizziness is true (4.6), SensitiveAretha is true (1.8), HairLoss is true (1.8) **then** Disease is Namastosis NR3: (-2.2) **if** PlacibinAllergy is true (-5.4), Disease is Supercilliosis (4.6) Disease is Namastosis (1.8), **then** Treatment is Placibin	NR4: (-4.0) **if** HairLoss is true (-3.6), Disease is Namastosis (3.6), Disease is Supercilliosis (2.8) **then** Treatment is Biramibio NR5: (-2.2, -2.2) **if** Treatment is Placibin (-1.8, 1.8), Treatment is Biramibio (1.0, - 2.6) **then** Treatment is Posiboost

4.2 Example Inference

We suppose that the initial data in the WM is: 'HairLoss is true' (TRUE). Since 'Treatment' is the only goal variable, its possible conclusions are initially put on GS. The inference tracing, according to the symbolism oriented process, is briefly presented in Table 2 (follow the left column first in both pages, then the right).

Table 2.

Initial situation and Steps 1, 2-2.1
WM: {'HairLoss is true' (TRUE)}
GS: ['Treatment is Placibin', 'Treatment is Biramibio', 'Treatment is Posi-boost']
CG: 'Treatment is Placibin'
RS: [NR3]
Fired neurules:
Blocked neurules:

Step 2.2-2.2.1
CR: NR3
CC: 'PlacibinAllergy is true' (NR3)

Step 2.2.1.1
User data: 'PlacibinAllergy is true' (FALSE)
WM: {'PlacibinAllergy is true' (FALSE), 'HairLoss is true' (TRUE)}
Updated sums: kn-sum=3.2, rem-sum=6.4 (NR3)

Step 2.2.1.2
|kn-sum| < rem-sum (NR3)

Step 2.2.1
CC: 'Disease is Supercilliosis' (NR3)

Step 2.2.1.1
GS: ['Disease is Supercilliosis', 'Treatment is Placibin', …]
(start of recursion)

Step 2.1-2.2
CG: 'Disease is Supercilliosis'
RS: [NR1, NR3]
CR: NR1

Step 2.2.1
CC: 'SwollenFeet is true' (NR1)

Step 2.2.1.1
User data: 'SwollenFeet is true' (FALSE)
WM: {'SwollenFeet is true' (FALSE), 'PlacibinAllergy is true' (FALSE), 'HairLoss is true' (TRUE)}
Updated sums: kn-sum=-4.0, rem-sum=4.4 (NR1)

Step 2.2.1.2
|kn-sum| < rem-sum (NR1)

Step 2.2.1
CC: 'HairLoss is true' (NR1)

Step 2.2.1.1
User data: 'HairLossis true' (TRUE)
WM: {'HairLoss is true' (TRUE),
GS: ['Treatment is Placibin', 'Treatment is Biramibio', 'Treatment is Posiboost']
(return from recursion)

Step 2.2.1.1
Updated sums: kn-sum=7.8, rem-sum=1.8 (NR3)

Step 2.2.1.2
|kn-sum| > rem-sum and kn-sum > 0 (NR3)
Fired neurules: NR3, NR1
WM: {'Treatment is Placibin' (TRUE), 'Disease is Supercilliosis' (TRUE), 'RedEars is true' (FALSE), …}
GS: ['Treatment is Biramibio', 'Treatment is Posiboost']

Step 2.1-2.2
CG: 'Treatment is Biramibio'
RS: [NR4]
CR: NR4

Step 2.2.1
CC: 'HairLoss is true' (NR4)

Step 2.2.1.1
Updated sums: kn-sum=-7.6, rem-sum=6.4 (NR4)

Step 2.2.1.2
|kn-sum| > rem-sum and kn-sum < 0 (NR4)
Blocked neurules: NR4

Step 2.3
WM: {'Treatment is Biramibio' (FALSE), 'Treatment is Placibin' (TRUE), 'Disease is Supercilliosis' (TRUE), …}
GS: ['Treatment is Posiboost']

Step 2-2.1-2.2
CG: 'Treatment is Posiboost'
RS: [NR5]
CR: NR5

Step 2.2.2-2.2.2.1
CRF: RF_1-NR5
CC: 'Treatment is Placibin' (RF_1-NR5)
Given that both conditions are already evaluated …
Step 2.2.2.1.1-2.2.2.1.2
… finally:
Updated sums: kn-sum_1= -5.0, rem-sum_1= 0
|kn-sum| < 0
Blocked RFs: RF_1-NR5

'SwollenFeet is true' (FALSE), …}
Updated sums: kn-sum=-0.4, rem-sum=0.8 (NR1)

Step 2.2.1.2
|kn-sum| < rem-sum (NR1)

Step 2.2.1
CC: 'RedEars is true' (NR1)

Step 2.2.1.1
User data: 'RedEars is true' (FALSE)
WM:{'RedEars is true' (FALSE), 'HairLossis true' (TRUE), …}
Updated sums: kn-sum=0.4, rem-sum=0 (NR1)

Step 2.2.1.2
|kn-sum| > rem-sum and kn-sum > 0 (NR1)
Fired neurules: NR1
WM: {'Disease is Supercilliosis' (TRUE), 'RedEars is true' (FALSE), 'HairLossis true' (TRUE), …}

Step 2.2.2-2.2.2.1
CRF: RF_2-NR5
CC: 'Treatment is Biramibio'
Given that both conditions are already evaluated …
Step 2.2.2.1.1-2.2.2.1.2
… *finally:*
Updated sums: kn-sum_2= 2.2, rem-sum_2= 0
|kn-sum| > 0
Fired neurules: NR5, NR3, NR1
WM: {'Treatment is Posiboost'(TRUE), 'Treatment is Biramibio' (FALSE), 'Treatment is Placibin' (TRUE), 'Disease is Supercilliosis' (TRUE), …}
GS: [ ]

Step 3
Output data: 'Treatment is Placibin', 'Treatment is Posiboost'

5 Experimental Results

In this section, we present experimental results comparing the two inference processes, the symbolism oriented and the connectionism oriented (see Table 3).

Table 3.

KB	Connectionism oriented process		Symbolism oriented process	
	ASKED	*EVALS*	*ASKED*	*EVALS*
ANIMALS (20 inferences)	162 (8.1),	364 (18.2)	142 (7.1)	251 (12.5)
LENSES (24 inferences)	79 (3.3)	602 (25.1)	85 (3.5)	258 (10.8)
ZOO (101 inferences)	1052 (10.4)	8906 (88.2)	1013 (10)	1963 (19.4)
MEDICAL (134 inferences)	670 (5)	25031 (186.8)	670 (5)	11828 (88.3)

We used four knowledge bases: ANIMALS (from [7]), LENSES and ZOO (from [8]), MEDICAL (from [9]), of different size and content. Numbers in the *ASKED* column (outside the parentheses) represent the number of inputs (variables) whose values were required/asked to reach a conclusion. The numbers within the parentheses represent the mean number of required input values (per inference). The number of inferences attempted for each KB is depicted within the parentheses in the KB column. Furthermore, the numbers in the *EVALS* columns represent the number of conditions/inputs visited for evaluation (the mean value within the parentheses). It is clear, that the symbolism oriented process did equally well or better than the connectionism oriented in all cases, except one (the shaded one). This is clearer for the condition evaluations, especially as the number of inferences increases. Given that the connectionism oriented process is better than the inference processes introduced in [3] and [10], as concluded in [6, 11], the symbolism oriented process is even better.

6 Conclusion

In this paper, we present an extension to neurules, called multi-neurules. Multi-neurules, although they make the inference cycle more complicated, increase the conciseness of the rule base. Simple neurules have the disadvantage that they may produce multiple representations (sibling neurules) of the same piece of knowledge. Multi-neurules merge those representations into one. So, although the overall naturalness seems to increase, interpretation of the significance factors becomes a tedious task, especially in cases that a large number of sibling rules participate.

We also present a new inference process, which gives pre-eminence to the symbolic inference than the connectionist one. Thus, it offers more natural inferences. This new process is proved to be more efficient than the connectionism oriented one.

References

1. Medsker L.R.: Hybrid Neural Networks and Expert Systems. Kluwer Academic Publishers, Boston (1994)
2. Tirri H.: Replacing the Pattern Matcher of an Expert System with a Neural Network. In: , Goonatilake S., Sukdev K. (eds): Intelligent Hybrid Systems. John Wiley & Sons (1995).
3. Gallant, S.I.: Neural Network Learning and Expert Systems. MIT Press (1993)
4. Hatzilygeroudis, I., Prentzas, J.: Neurules: Improving the Performance of Symbolic Rules. International Journal on AI Tools (IJAIT) **9(1)**, (2000) 113-130
5. Hatzilygeroudis, I., Prentzas, J.: Constructing Modular Hybrid Knowledge Bases for Expert Systems. International Journal on AI Tools (IJAIT) **10(1-2)** (2001) 87-105
6. Hatzilygeroudis, I., Prentzas, J.: An Efficient Hybrid Rule Based Inference Engine with Explanation Capability. Proceedings of the 14th International FLAIRS Conference, Key West, FL. AAAI Press (2001) 227-231
7. Fu L.M.: Neural Networks in Computer Intelligence. McGraw-Hill (1994)
8. DataSet. ftp://ftp.ics.uci.edu/pub/machine-learning-databases/
9. Hatzilygeroudis, I., Vassilakos, P. J., Tsakalidis, A.: XBONE: A Hybrid Expert System for Supporting Diagnosis of Bone Diseases. In: Pappas, C., Maglaveras, N., Scherrer J.-R. (eds): Medical Informatics Europe'97 (MIE'97). IOS Press (1997) 295-299.
10. Ghalwash, A.Z.: A Recency Inference Engine for Connectionist Knowledge Bases. Applied Intelligence **9** (1998) 201-215
11. Hatzilygeroudis I., Prentzas, J.: HYMES: A HYbrid Modular Expert System with Efficient Inference and Explanation. Proceedings of the 8th Panhellenic Conference on Informatics, Nicosia, Cyprus, Vol.1 (2001) 422-431

Decision Making Based on Past Problem Cases

Ioannis Stamelos and Ioannis Refanidis

Aristotle University, Dept. of Informatics, Thessaloniki, Greece
{yrefanid, stamelos}@csd.auth.gr

Abstract. This paper deals with the generation of an evaluation model to be used for decision making. The paper proposes the automated selection of past problem cases and the automated synthesis of a new evaluation model, based on the cumulative experience stored in a knowledge base. In order to select the most promising past evaluation cases we propose the use of two metrics: their proximity to the new case and the degree of success. To add flexibility, we allow the user to express his preference on these two factors. After having selected a group of the most promising past evaluation cases, a method for deriving a new evaluation model, i.e. the weights and the scales of the attributes, is presented. The method covers both numerical and nominal attributes. The derived model can be used as a starting point for an interactive evaluation session. The overall process is illustrated through a real world situation, concerning the choice of 1-out-of n candidate ERP products for an enterprise information system.

1 Introduction

Knowledge based evaluation [10] has been recently proposed as a valid approach for decision making in the field of software evaluation. Typical problems in software evaluation [11] are the choice of 1-out-of-n commercial systems, software certification, 'make or buy' an information system, etc. Decision making in software problems is known to be a particularly difficult task, where many factors (such as *cost*, *quality*, *time*), often contradictory have to be taken into account. An important effort for defining a universally accepted evaluation model has been undertaken by the International Standard Organization (ISO), which has published the ISO/IEC 9126-1, 9126-2 and 9126-3 standards [1]. ISO proposes six attributes, which characterize the quality of a software product: *functionality*, *reliability*, *usability*, *efficiency*, *maintainability* and *portability*. These attributes can be further analyzed in lower-level attributes.

One of the most difficult and subjective tasks in software evaluation is the assignment of preferences to the various attributes and the aggregation of the values assigned to the usually heterogeneous basic attributes for each evaluated object, either into an overall value for the object or into an ordering among the several evaluated entities. The fundamental question that has to be answered at each step of the evaluation process is the following: "How can we measure attribute A and what cost are we ready to pay, in terms of any other attribute B, in order to gain one unit on attribute A?"

I.P. Vlahavas and C.D. Spyropoulos (Eds.): SETN 2002, LNAI 2308, pp. 42–53, 2002.

In order to cope with the above problem, the authors developed and presented ESSE, an Expert System for Software Evaluation ([14]). ESSE is a tool that assists an evaluator to develop and maintain an evaluation model, i.e. to define an attribute hierarchy, assign scales and preferences to the various attributes, assign values to the basic attributes for each evaluated object and perform the evaluation using either a multiattribute utility function (e.g. Weighted Average Sum ([9], [13]) or an outranking method (e.g. ELECTRE, [8]).

Moreover, ESSE maintains a knowledge base with past evaluation cases. Each time a new evaluation problem arises, the evaluator can consult this base in order to find a past case, which is close to the new problem. The advantage of using the knowledge base is that the evaluator avoids working with the new problem from scratch. Instead, he/she has a ready-made evaluation model, with pre-assigned preferences and scales to the various attributes and, most importantly, with a known degree of success.

The main disadvantage of ESSE is that only identical past cases are matched. ESSE does not support any automated method for combining similar past cases and for presenting to the evaluator a more complete and general evaluation model, thus exploiting the knowledge base at the maximum possible level.

Motivated by this problem, we present in this paper a case based reasoning generic method for automated generation of hierarchical evaluation models. Each problem case, either past or new, is characterized by a set of descriptors. Distances between cases are computed based on their descriptor values. The past cases, which have been proved more successful and which are closer to the new one, are selected and merged, in order to produce a new evaluation model. The model is proposed to the evaluator, who can use it in order to produce the final evaluation model for the new problem, according to its specific characteristics. Note that the method we propose is general enough and, although we applied it in the area of software evaluation, it can be applied to any other type of case-based evaluation involving the merging of hierarchical case descriptions to produce a solution.

The rest of the paper is organized as it follows: Section 2 presents the basics about software evaluation, providing also the context of the problem we are trying to resolve. Section 3 presents the automatic identification and selection of the most promising past evaluation problems, whereas Section 4 presents the automated merging of the evaluation models of these problems. Section 5 gives an example and Section 6 concludes the paper and poses future directions.

2 The Evaluation Problem

An evaluation problem *P* can be modeled as a 7-ple *MD* = (*A,T,D,M,E,G,R*) where [13]:

- - *A* is the set of alternatives under evaluation.
- - *T* is the type of the evaluation.
- - *D* is the tree of the evaluation attributes.
- - *M* is the set of the associated measures.
- - *E* is the set of scales associated to the attributes.
- - *G* is a set of rules representing the user's preferences.
- - *R* is the preference aggregation procedure.

Usually there is a set A of alternatives to be evaluated and the best must be selected. Type T concerns the desired end result. The possible types are *choice*, *classification*, *sorting* and *description*.

The evaluation attributes D reflect the evaluator's point of view. They are organized in a hierarchy. The leaves of this hierarchy are the *basic* attributes, whereas non-leave nodes are characterized as *compound* attributes. Moreover, a weight w_a is assigned to each attribute a, with the requirement that the sum of the weights of the neighboring attributes is equal to a unit.

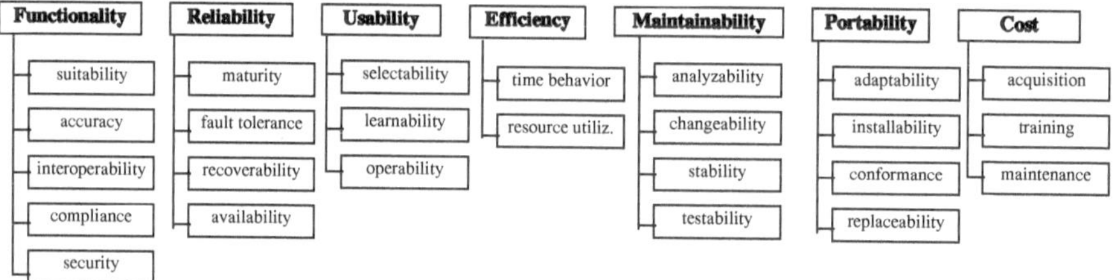

Fig. 1. An attribute hierarchy for software evaluation problems.

There are two different approaches in an evaluation problem. In the first approach, named "fixed models" ([5], [7]), a fixed structure is used, where D has been definitely identified and customized for a particular domain and type of evaluation. In such cases we have just to fill in the measures. This approach is easy to use but lacks flexibility. In the second approach, named "constructive models", a general model must be customized ([1], [3]). In this approach, D is a tree of predefined attributes, depending on the kind of the problem. D may be expanded, modified or reduced. In this case there is more flexibility, but user experience is also required.

For every basic attribute •a method $M_•$ that will be used to assign values to it has to be defined. There are two kinds of values, the *arithmetic values* (ratio, interval or absolute) and the *nominal values*. The first type of values are numbers, while the second type are verbal characterizations, such as "good", "bad", "big", "small", etc. Moreover, a scale e_a must be associated to each basic attribute a. For arithmetic attributes, the scale usually corresponds to the scale of the metric used, while for nominal attributes, e_a must be declared by the evaluator. Scales must be at least ordinal, implying that, within e_a, it must be clear which one of any two values is the most preferred (in some cases there are different values with the same preference).

In case where an outranking aggregation method is going to be used, then for each attribute and for the measures attached to it, a rule has to be defined, with the ability to transform measures to preference structures. This rule compares two distinct alternatives (e.g. two software products), on the basis of a specific attribute. Basic preferences can be combined, using the aggregation method, to produce a global preference structure.

Finally, an aggregation method has to be defined, capable of transforming the set of preference relations into a *prescription* for the evaluator, i.e. an order on A. There are different aggregation methods, which fall into three classes. These are the *multiple attribute utility methods* [2], the *outranking methods* [13] and the *interactive methods* [12]. The selection of an aggregation method depends on several parameters, such as the type of the problem, the type of the set of possible choices (continuous or discrete), the type of the measurement scales, the kind of the importance parameters (weights) associated to the attributes, etc.

The most important component of an evaluation model is the attribute hierarchy. For the software evaluation problem we have selected the ISO 9126 standard [1], being enhanced with the top-level attribute *'cost'*, which could be further analyzed in *'acquisition'*, *'training'* and *'maintenance'* cost. So, the overall hierarchy is the one shown in Fig. 1.

3 Similar Cases Identification

The problem that is treated in this paper is the identification and merging of past evaluation problems that are similar to a new one. This will help the evaluator to have a basis for creating the new evaluation model.

Concerning the identification of similar past cases, we propose to characterize each evaluation case, either past or new, with a set of descriptors, which will be used in order to compute the 'distance' between two problems. Let us consider first a flat set of M descriptors d_1, d_2, ..., d_M, each one of them being accompanied by a weight w_{d_i}. To each descriptor d_i a set of possible values V_i has also to be assigned and for each pair of values v_{i_k}, $v_{i_l} \in V_i$, their distance dist(v_{i_k}, v_{i_l}) has to be defined. For simplicity, we require that all these distances take values in the same interval, e.g. [0, 1], where a zero distance means that the two problems are identical with respect to a specific dimension. In the simplest case, V_i=[0,1] for every descriptor d_i, and the distance between any two values v_{i_k}, $v_{i_l} \in V_i$ is defined as dist(v_{i_k}, v_{i_l})=| v_{i_k} - v_{i_l} |, which obviously ranges in the interval [0,1].

For an evaluation problem P, with $\mathbf{V}(P)$ we denote the N-dimensional vector with the values of P in the descriptors, whereas with $V_i(P)$ we denote the value of its i-th dimension. Let us suppose now that we have two evaluation problems P_1 and P_2. We define the distance between these problems as:

$$Dist(P_1, P_2)=\frac{\sum_{i=1}^{N} w_{d_i} \,|\, V_i(P_1)-V_i(P_2) \,|}{\sum_{i=1}^{N} w_{d_i}} \qquad \textbf{(1)}$$

In Formula 1, a zero distance denotes that the two problems are identical with respect to all of their dimensions. The above definition does not require either that all descriptors are measured in the same scale or that their scales are arithmetic. However, it requires that for each descriptor d_i a mapping will exist from the set V_i x V_i to the interval [0,1]. This mapping may be implemented either by an arithmetic function or by a lookup table.

Other formulas may be also used for distance calculation. The (scaled) Euclidean distance is very often used in case retrieval systems. Other alternatives are the Kaufman-Rousseeuw, the Minkowski, the Canberra, the Czekanowski and the Chebyshev distance, each with different properties [5].

A different expression for distance is the notion of proximity. We denote the proximity between two problems P_1 and P_2 with $prox(P_1, P_2)=1-dist(P_1,P_2)$, ranging over the interval [0,1], with the value 1 denoting two identical problems and the value 0 denoting two completely different problems.

Another metric that is of interest in the selection of the past evaluation cases is their degree of success, i.e. a characterization of how much successful was the application of model MD_i to the past evaluation problem P_i. We denote this value with $succ(MD_i)$ and we suppose that it is an arithmetic value ranging over the interval [0,1], with the value 0 denoting absolute failure and the value 1 denoting absolute success. The degree of success is usually assigned to an evaluation model long after its application and reflects the subjective or objective feeling of the evaluator about the correctness of the decisions taken based on this model.

The two factors, i.e. proximity and success, may not be of equal importance. In order to distinguish the influence of the proximity and the success of the past problems evaluation models to the new one, we assign weights to these two factors. Let w_{prox} and w_{succ} be the weights of proximity and success respectively, with the requirement that $w_{prox}+w_{succ}=1$.

In order to select a subset of the past-evaluation cases knowledge base, which are closer to the new one, we have to take into account both the proximity and the success of the past cases, as well as our relative preference on these two factors. So, the value $Value(P_i)$ of a past evaluation problem P_i with respect to a specific new one P can be expressed by the following formula:

$$Value(P_i)=w_{prox}\cdot prox(P_i,P) + w_{succ}\cdot succ(P_i) \qquad \textbf{(2)}$$

$Value(P_i)$ ranges in the interval [0,1], with the higher values denoting more promising past cases. The selection of the most promising past evaluation cases, based on $Value(P_i)$, can be performed in several ways. Specifically:

- A constant number of the past evaluation problems N, with greater values in *Value*, may be selected.
- All the past problems, whose value *Value* is greater than a threshold $Value_{min}$, may be selected.
- A specific percentage of the problems in the knowledge base, which have the greatest values in *Value*, may be selected.

In the previous paragraphs we considered a flat set of descriptors. However, as in the case of the evaluation attributes, we may have a weighted hierarchy of descriptors. In this case, the distances have to be defined and computed for the basic descriptors only. Then, they are aggregated through the hierarchy to its higher level descriptors using Weighted Average Sum (WAS). The final distance between two models is computed by aggregating the values of the top-level descriptors.

Under this perspective one could consider alternative, non-numeric, methods for aggregating the values of the descriptors. For example, one could consider an outranking method, e.g. ELECTRE [8], for obtaining a ranking of the past evaluation models, from the closest to the farthest, with respect to the new one. However, outranking methods are hard to be applied when the number of the alternatives is large enough, as it is the case with the past evaluation models. So, it seems that a multiattribute value method like WAS is the best choice.

4 Merging of Past Cases

Suppose that for a new problem P, a set of *N* past evaluation cases P_1, P_2, ..., P_N has been retrieved from the knowledge base, based on their values $Value(P_i)$. Each one of these cases is accompanied by two entities:

- An evaluation model MD_i, i.e. an attribute hierarchy with weights for all attributes and scales for the basic ones.
- Its value $Value(P_i)$.

The desired outcome of the past cases merging phase is the derivation of a new evaluation model *MD*, with weights for all attributes and scales for the basic ones. In this process both entities noted above should be taken into account. Without losing the generality of the proposed method, we can assume that all the evaluation models MD_i are identical in their structure, i.e. they have exactly the same attributes in exactly the same places within the attribute hierarchy, and differ only in the weights that have been assigned to the attributes and in the scales of basic ones. In this way we define a universal attribute hierarchy, like the one proposed in Section 3. The case where an attribute or an attribute branch does not appear in an evaluation model MD_i can be considered as if this attribute or the root of the attribute branch has a zero weight. Under this point of view, the attribute hierarchy of Fig. 1 becomes a universal attribute hierarchy (probably being extended with other attributes too), at least for software evaluation problems.

Based on the above assumption, the problem of determining the evaluation model *MD* is transformed to the problem of determining the weights of the attributes and the scales of the basic attributes for *MD*. It is obvious that the model *MD* will be affected more significantly by the models MD_i of the problems P_i that are closer to *P* and had a more successful application.

Formula 3 defines the weight w_a of attribute *a* in model *MD*, based on:

- its weights $w_{a,i}$ in models MD_i, and
- the values $Value(MD_i)$ of the models MD_i.

$$w_a = \frac{\sum_{i=1}^{N} Value(P_i) \cdot w_{a,i}}{\sum_{i=1}^{N} Value(P_i)} \tag{3}$$

It is not difficult to show that the weight w_a ranges over the interval [0,1] and that the sum of the weights in *MD* of the neighboring attributes is equal to 1, provided that these two conditions hold also for the weights of the attributes in the past models MD_i.

After applying Formula 3 to all attributes of the universal attribute structure, weights for all attributes of model *MD* have been derived. However, some attributes may have too small weights, which render them practically of no importance. So, a threshold *t*, $0 \le t < 1$, can be defined, such that all attributes having weights lower than *t* in *MD* will be ignored, i.e. they will be assigned zero weights in *MD*. However, by zeroing the weights of some attributes, the requirement that the sum of the weights of the neighboring attributes is equal to a unit does not hold any more. In order to re-establish this requirement, it is enough to divide the weight of each attribute by the sum of the weights of its neighboring attributes, after having zeroed the weights of the non-important ones.

Concerning the scales of the basic criteria, these can also be based on the scales of the basic criteria in the models MD_i. However, in this case there are two possible scales for a basic attribute a, i.e. either an arithmetic scale or a nominal one. In both cases an approach similar to the one presented for the weights of the attributes can be adopted.

For a basic attribute a that has an arithmetic scale, let us suppose that $[L_{a,i}, R_{a,i}]$ is the interval of this scale in model MD_i and $[L_a, R_a]$ is the respective interval in model MD. We can derive the values L_a and R_a from Formulas 4 and 5 respectively.

$$L_a = \frac{\sum_{i=1}^{N} Value(P_i) \cdot L_{a,i}}{\sum_{i=1}^{N} Value(P_i)} \tag{4}$$

$$R_a = \frac{\sum_{i=1}^{N} Value(P_i) \cdot R_{a,i}}{\sum_{i=1}^{N} Value(P_i)} \tag{5}$$

It can be proved that $L_a<R_a$, provided that $L_{a,i}<R_{a,i}$ holds in every model MD_i.

In case where a basic attribute a has a nominal scale, let us suppose that $N_{a,i}$ is this scale in model MD_i and N_a is this scale in model MD. We require that, within the verbal characterizations in scales $N_{a,i}$ there are no synonyms, i.e. there are no two different verbal characterizations expressing the same concept, as e.g. '*big*' and '*great*'. This requirement can be ensured by defining a universal set of verbal characterizations U_a for each nominal basic attribute a, such that $N_{a,i} \subseteq U_a$ for each model MD_i.

A simple approach for deriving N_a could be to set $N_a = \bigcup_i N_{a,i}$. However, a more sophisticated approach would be to take into account the frequency of the appearance of a value $a_j \in U_a$ within the $N_{a,i}$'s, as well as the values $Value(MD_i)$ of the models MD_i, in a way similar to what has already been presented for the arithmetic scales and for the weights of the attributes in model MD.

For a verbal characterization a_j concerning a nominal basic attribute a (e.g. a_j='*good*'), let us use the notation $a_{j,i}$ to denote whether a_j appears in model MD_i, i.e. $a_j \in N_{a,i}$ or not. Specifically:

$$a_{j,i}=1, \text{ iff } a_j \in N_{a,i}$$

$$a_{j,i}=0, \text{ iff } a_j \notin N_{a,i}$$

Then, the decision of whether a_j will appear in N_a or not can be based on the following value:

$$f(a_j) = \frac{\sum_{i=1}^{N} Value(P_i) \cdot a_{j,i}}{\sum_{i=1}^{N} Value(P_i)} \tag{6}$$

which expresses the frequency of the appearance of value a_j in the models MD_i. It can be proved that $f(a_j)$ ranges always in the interval [0,1]. Note that this process may result in the reduction of the available characterizations, e.g. 'low' and 'very low' may be merged to 'low'. The practical result is that the decision maker has less alternative values to express his opinion. This approach is also frequently used in various procedures in multivariate statistical analysis (e.g. ANOVA combined with multiple range tests to produce characterizations that have significantly different effect on the dependent variable).

Again, a threshold $t_{nominal}$, $0 \le t_{nominal} \le 1$, has to be defined, such that nominal values with frequency smaller than this threshold will be not included in N_a. Eventually, Na can be defined by the following formula:

$$N_a = \{a_j \in U_a : f(a_j) \ge t_{nominal}\} \qquad \textbf{(7)}$$

A more difficult situation arises in cases where for a basic attribute a, in some of the models MD_i an arithmetic scale has been used, whereas in some others a nominal one. In this case Formulas 4 and 5 can be applied to the subset of the models MD_i where an arithmetic scale has been used for attribute a, whereas Formulas 6 and 7 can be applied to the subset of the models MD_i where nominal scales have been used. Consequently, two alternative scales can be defined for attribute a in model MD, an arithmetic and a nominal one. The two scales can be ranked based on the frequency with which we had arithmetic or nominal scales in the models MD_i, as well as on the values of these models. Let us use the notation $number_{a,i}$ to denote whether model MD_i has an arithmetic scale to the basic attribute a. Specifically:

$number_{a,i}=1$, iff a had an arithmetic scale in MD_i
$number_{a,i}=0$, iff a had a non arithmetic scale in MD_i

Similarly we can define $nominal_{a,i}$. In this case, the relative superiority of the arithmetic or the nominal scale for attribute a can be expressed by the following values:

$$number_a = \frac{\sum_{i=1}^{N} Value(P_i) \cdot number_{a,i}}{\sum_{i=1}^{N} Value(P_i)} \qquad \textbf{(8)}$$

$$nominal_a = \frac{\sum_{i=1}^{N} Value(P_i) \cdot nominal_{a,i}}{\sum_{i=1}^{N} Value(P_i)} \qquad \textbf{(9)}$$

Obviously, a greater value either of $number_a$ or of $nominal_a$ denotes preference for an arithmetic or a nominal scale for criterion a in MD respectively. It is not difficult to show that $number_a + nominal_a = 1$. The two values can be presented to the evaluator and he/she can decide whether he/she will use an arithmetic or a nominal scale for a in MD.

In closing this section we have to emphasize the fact that the evaluation model MD produced by the process presented in this section is just a starting point for the new evaluation. In order to get this model, the evaluator has to select appropriate values for several parameters, such as w_{prox} and w_{succ} and the various thresholds. Then, he/she can change the model *MD*, according to the specific needs of the new evaluation problem, which can not always be captured by the case-based similarity analysis of the proposed framework. A friendly graphical user interface would be valuable in this process.

5 Example

In order to demonstrate the application of the approach presented in the previous sections, we consider an evaluation problem concerning the choice of 1-out-of-n commercial ERP systems by an enterprise that wishes to build or modernise its information infrastructure. Such task is typically undertaken by a consulting team that specializes in information systems evaluation and possesses a base of historical past evaluation cases. We assume that a historical base has been built, consisting of couples of problem configurations and evaluation models. In order to select some of them to create the new evaluation model, we have to define some descriptors that characterise the implementation of an ERP system in an enterprise (the problem configuration). We borrow the ones shown in Table 1 from [6] (a study that examined 48 ERP projects). However, the weights have been arbitrarily chosen for the purpose of our example.

Table 1. A set of descriptors for an ERP System implementation.

#	Descriptor	Weight	Scale
1	*System users*	0.20	[7,2000]
2	*Installation sites*	0.05	[0,98]
3	*Plants involved*	0.10	[0,98]
4	*Companies involved*	0.10	[1,35]
5	*User interfaces*	0.10	[0,50]
6	*EDI interfaces*	0.05	[0,10]
7	*No of conversions needed*	0.05	[1,93]
8	*No of modifications needed*	0.10	[0,30]
9	*No of requested reports*	0.05	[0,100]
10	*No of ERP modules acquired*	0.20	[1,8]

Note that in order to compute the distances of the past cases to the new one, the scales in Table 1 have to be transformed to a common one, e.g. [0,1], something that can easily be achieved by linear transformations. The weights denote certain preferences of the user, e.g. he/she wants to put emphasis in the number of system users and number of ERP modules acquired.

For each problem in the knowledge base, a degree of success must have been defined. Let us consider that w_{prox}=0.3 and w_{succ}=0.7, modelling a situation where the user of the method is mostly interested in the success of the past evaluation. So, we can define the value $Value(P_i)$ for each problem in the knowledge base, to select, for example, two of them in order to derive the new evaluation model.

Henceforth we will denote the two selected past evaluation problems with P_1 and P_2 and their models with MD_1 and MD_2. Suppose also that $Value(P_1)$=0.9 and

Value(P_2)=0.7. Table 2 shows the weights for the various criteria in the models MD_1 and MD_2 and the weights derived for the model *MD*, based on Formula 3. The models depend in many aspects on the project case descriptions, e.g. in a situation where many implementation sites are involved, installability would be quite important.

Table 2. The weights of the criteria in models MD_1, MD_2 and *MD*.

#	Attribute	MD_1	MD_2	*MD*	MD'
1	functionality	0.15	0.2	0.17	0.18
1.1	Suitability	0.3	0.2	0.26	0.26
1.2	Accuracy	0.2	0.3	0.24	0.24
1.3	interoperability	0.2	0.1	0.16	0.16
1.4	Compliance	0.2	0.1	0.16	0.16
1.5	Security	0.1	0.3	0.19	0.19
2	Reliability	0.15	0.1	0.13	0.13
2.1	Maturity	0.3	0.25	0.28	0.28
2.2	fault tolerance	0.2	0.25	0.22	0.22
2.3	recoverability	0.2	0.25	0.22	0.22
2.4	Availability	0.3	0.25	0.28	0.28
3	Usability	0.1	0.1	0.10	0.10
3.1	Selectability	0.4	0.4	0.40	0.40
3.2	Learnability	0.2	0.3	0.24	0.24
3.3	Operability	0.4	0.3	0.36	0.36
4	Efficiency	0.2	0.1	0.16	0.16

#	Attribute	MD_1	MD_2	*MD*	*MD'*
4.1	time behavior	0.7	0.5	0.61	0,61
4.2	resource utilization	0.3	0.5	0.39	0,39
5	maintainability	0.1	0.1	0.10	0,10
5.1	analyzability	0.25	0.3	0.27	0,27
5.2	changeability	0.25	0.3	0.27	0,27
5.3	stability	0.25	0.2	0.23	0,23
5.4	testability	0.25	0.2	0.23	0,23
6	portability	0	0.1	0.04	0,00
6.1	adaptability	0	0.25	0.11	0,00
6.2	installability	0	0.2	0.09	0,00
6.3	conformance	0	0.3	0.13	0,00
6.4	replaceability	0	0.2	0.09	0,00
7	cost	0.3	0.3	0.30	0,31
7.1	acquisition	0.5	0.7	0.59	0,59
7.2	training	0.2	0.1	0.16	0,16
7.3	maintainance	0.3	0.2	0.26	0,26

Column *MD* shows the weights of the various criteria, as they have been derived from Formula 3. Column *MD'* considers a threshold in the weights of the criteria, i.e. t=0.1, so criterion portability (and all of its sub-criteria) has been removed from *MD*, whereas the weights of the remaining criteria have been adapted accordingly (note that two decimal points are shown only, so for some criteria the modification in their weight is not shown). Note, that in this specific case, our approach manages to model the low importance that has been given to portability.

Concerning the scales of the basic criteria, let us illustrate the derivation of a scale for criterion '*acquisition cost*'. Suppose that this criterion had the scales $[10^7, 2\cdot10^7]$ and $[1.5\cdot10^7, 3\cdot10^7]$ in the models MD_1 and MD_2 respectively. In this case, the suggested scale in model *MD* would be (according to Formulas 4 and 5) about $[1.22\cdot10^7, 2.44\cdot10^7]$. In a similar way, by applying Formulas 6 to 9, we can treat nominal scales or criteria that appear in one model with an arithmetic scale and in the other model with a nominal scale.

The decision maker may now proceed based on the proposed model. For example, he/she may alter the model parameters to introduce a different preference. He/she may also use the proposed value ranges to prune alternatives (e.g. reject an offer because of inappropriate cost).

6 Conclusions and Future Directions

In this paper we have presented a method for automated synthesis of evaluation models based on a knowledge base with past cases. In order to select the most promising past evaluation cases we proposed the use of two metrics: their proximity to the new case and their successful application. The proximity can be measured based on a set of descriptors and their significance in the new evaluation problem. The success of the application of the past evaluation models is a subjective or objective characterization, given to them long after their application, when the results of the decisions made through these models are clear. The evaluator can express his/her relative preference on these two factors (proximity and success).

After having selected a group of the most promising past evaluation cases, a method for deriving a new evaluation model, i.e. the weights of the attributes and the scales of the lowest level ones, is presented. The method covers both numerical and nominal attributes. The derived model can be used as a good starting point for the new evaluation.

A possible extension to the presented model would involve the capture of the evolution of some quantities over time. For example, one could take into account the evolution of the prices in the market during the last years and adapt the scales of the criteria denoting cost in the past evaluation models to nowadays prices, before applying the proposed method. Another interesting feature would be to enhance the new evaluation model with statistical information such as the standard deviation of the proposed weights and scales.

We are currently implementing the proposed method in the ESSE system and we intend to exploit this functionality in the area of decision making, giving more emphasis in the area of software evaluation. However, it is possible to use the system in other areas of decision making, just by replacing the existing knowledge base with another.

References

[1] ISO/IEC 9126-1, Information Technology – Software quality characteristics and sub-characteristics (1996).

[2] Keeney R.L. and Raiffa H., Decision with multiple objectives, John Wiley, New York (1976).

[3] Kitchenham B., Towards a constructive quality model. Part 1: Software quality modeling, measurement and prediction, Software Engineering Journal (July 1987).

[4] Krzanowski, W.J. 1993. *Principles of Multivariate Analysis: A User's Perspective.* Oxford University Press.

[5] Mosley V., How to assess tools efficiently and quantatively, IEEE-Software (May 1992).

[6] Myrtveit I. and Stensrud S., A controlled experiment to access the benefits of estimating with analogy and regression models, IEEE Transactions on Software Engineering, 25(4):510-525, 1999.

[7] Poston R.M. and Sexton M.P., Evaluating and selecting testing tools, IEEE Software, (May 1992).

[8] Roy B., The outranking approach and the foundation of ELECTRE methods, Theory and Decision, 31 (1991), 49-73

[9] Roy B., Multicriteria Methodology for Decision Aiding, Kluwer Academic, Dordrecht (1996).

[10] Stamelos, I. Vlahavas, I. Refanidis and A. Tsoukias, "*Knowledge Based Evaluation of Software Systems: A Case Study*", Information and Software Technology, Elsevier, vol. 20 (5), 333-345, April 2000

[11] Stamelos, I. and A. Tsoukias, "*Software Evaluation Problem Situations*", European Journal of Operational Research, Special Issue on Decision Support Systems, Elsevier, to appear

[12] Vanderpooten D. and Vincke P., Description and analysis of some representative interactive multicriteria procedures, Mathematical and computer modelling, 12 (1989), 1221-1238.

[13] Vincke P., Multicriteria decision aid, John Wiley, New York (1992).

[14] Vlahavas, I., Stamelos, I., Refanidis I. and Tsoukias A., "*ESSE: An Expert System for Software Evaluation*", Knowledge-Based Systems, Elsevier, vol. 12(4), pp. 183-197, 1999

Relating Defeasible Logic to Extended Logic Programs

George Antoniou

Department of Computer Science, University of Bremen, Germany
ga@tzi.de

Abstract. Defeasible reasoning is a simple but efficient approach to nonmonotonic reasoning that has recently attracted considerable interest and that has found various applications. Defeasible logic and its variants are an important family of defeasible reasoning methods. So far no relationship has been established between defeasible logic and mainstream nonmonotonic reasoning approaches.
In this paper we establish close links to known semantics of extended logic programs. In particular, we give a translation of a defeasible theory D into a program $P(D)$. We show that under a condition of decisiveness, the defeasible consequences of D correspond exactly to the sceptical conclusions of $P(D)$ under the answer set semantics. Without decisiveness, the result holds only in one direction (all defeasible consequences of D are included in all answer sets of $P(D)$). If we wish a complete embedding for the general case, we need to use the Kunen semantics of $P(D)$, instead.

Keywords: logic programming, knowledge representation, nonmonotonic reasoning

1 Introduction

Defeasible reasoning is a nonmonotonic reasoning [18] approach in which the gaps due to incomplete information are closed through the use of defeasible rules that are usually appropriate. Defeasible logics were introduced and developed by Nute over several years [20]. These logics perform defeasible reasoning, where a conclusion supported by a rule might be overturned by the effect of another rule. Roughly, a proposition p can be defeasibly proved ($+\partial p$) only when a rule supports it, and it has been demonstrated that no applicable rule supports $\neg p$; this demonstration makes use of statements $-\partial q$ which mean intuitively that an attempt to prove q defeasibly has failed finitely. These logics also have a monotonic reasoning component, and a priority on rules. One advantage of Nute's design was that it was aimed at supporting efficient reasoning, and in our work we follow that philosophy.

This family of approaches has recently attracted considerable interest. Its use in various application domains has been advocated, including the modelling of regulations and business rules [19,12,1], modelling of contracts [22], legal reasoning [21] and agent negotiations [10]. In fact, defeasible reasoning (in the form of

I.P. Vlahavas and C.D. Spyropoulos (Eds.): SETN 2002, LNAI 2308, pp. 54–64, 2002.

courteous logic programs [11]) provides the foundation for IBM's Business Rules Markup Language and for current developments of RuleML and similar W3C activities. Therefore defeasible reasoning is arguably the most successful subarea in nonmonotonic reasoning as far as applications and integration to mainstram IT is concerned.

Recent theoretical work on defeasible logics has: (i) established some relationships to other logic programming approaches without negation as failure [3]; (ii) analysed the formal properties of these logics [5,16,17], and (iii) has delivered efficient implementations [15].

However the problems remains that defeasible logic is not firmly linked to the mainstream of nonmonotonic reasoning, in particular the semantics of logic programs; the only relevant work concerns the relationship with logic programs without negation as failure [2]. This paper aims at resolving this problem. Our initial approach is to consider stable semantics of logic programs [8] and use a natural, direct translation (defeasible rules translated into "normal defaults"). We discuss why this translation cannot be successful. Then we define a second translation which makes use of control literals, similar to those used in [7]. Under this translation of a defeasible theory D into a logic program $P(D)$ we can show that p is defeasibly provable in D iff p is included in all answer sets of $P(D)$ $(*)$.

However this result can only be shown under the additional condition of *decisiveness*: for every literal q, either $+\partial q$ or $-\partial q$ can be derived. A sufficient condition for decisiveness is the absence of cycles.

If we wish to drop decisiveness, $(*)$ holds only in one direction, from left to right. We show that if we wish the equivalence in the general case, we need to use another semantics for logic programs, namely Kunen semantics [14].

The paper is organised as follows. Sections 2 and 3 present the basics of defeasible logic and logic programming semantics, respectively. Section 4 present our translation and its ideas, while section 5 contains the main results.

2 Defeasible Logic

2.1 A Language for Defeasible Reasoning

A defeasible theory (a knowledge base in defeasible logic) consists of three different kinds of knowledge: strict rules, defeasible rules, and a superiority relation. (Fuller versions of defeasible logic also have facts and defeaters, but [5] shows that they can be simulated by the other ingredients).

Strict rules are rules in the classical sense: whenever the premises are indisputable (e.g. facts) then so is the conclusion. An example of a strict rule is "Emus are birds". Written formally:

$$emu(X) \rightarrow bird(X).$$

Defeasible rules are rules that can be defeated by contrary evidence. An example of such a rule is "Birds typically fly"; written formally:

$$bird(X) \Rightarrow flies(X).$$

The idea is that if we know that something is a bird, then we may conclude that it flies, *unless there is other, not inferior, evidence suggesting that it may not fly.*

The *superiority relation* among rules is used to define priorities among rules, that is, where one rule may override the conclusion of another rule. For example, given the defeasible rules

$$\begin{array}{rl} r: & bird(X) \Rightarrow flies(X) \\ r': & brokenWing(X) \Rightarrow \neg flies(X) \end{array}$$

which contradict one another, no conclusive decision can be made about whether a bird with broken wings can fly. But if we introduce a superiority relation $>$ with $r' > r$, with the intended meaning that r' is strictly stronger than r, then we can indeed conclude that the bird cannot fly.

[5] showed that there is a constructive, conclusion-preserving transformation which takes an arbitrary defeasible theory and translates it into a theory which has only strict rules and defeasible rules. For the sake of simplicity, we will assume in this paper that indeed a defeasible theory consists only of strict rules and defeasible rules.

2.2 Formal Definition

In this paper we restrict attention to essentially propositional defeasible logic. Rules with free variables are interpreted as rule schemas, that is, as the set of all ground instances; in such cases we assume that the Herbrand universe is finite. We assume that the reader is familiar with the notation and basic notions of propositional logic. If q is a literal, $\sim q$ denotes the complementary literal (if q is a positive literal p then $\sim q$ is $\neg p$; and if q is $\neg p$, then $\sim q$ is p).

Rules are defined over a *language* (or *signature*) Σ, the set of propositions (atoms) and labels that may be used in the rule.

A *rule* $r : A(r) \hookrightarrow C(r)$ consists of its unique *label* r, its *antecedent* $A(r)$ ($A(r)$ may be omitted if it is the empty set) which is a finite set of literals, an arrow $\hookrightarrow$ (which is a placeholder for concrete arrows to be introduced in a moment), and its *head* (or *consequent*) $C(r)$ which is a literal. In writing rules often we omit set notation for antecedents and sometimes we omit the label when it is not relevant for the context. There are two kinds of rules, each represented by a different arrow. Strict rules use $\rightarrow$ and defeasible rules use $\Rightarrow$.

Given a set R of rules, we denote the set of all strict rules in R by R_s, and the set of defeasible rules in R by R_d. $R[q]$ denotes the set of rules in R with consequent q.

A *defeasible theory* D is a finite set of rules R.

2.3 Proof Theory

A *conclusion* of a defeasible theory D is a tagged literal. A conclusion has one of the following four forms:

- $+\Delta q$, which is intended to mean that the literal q is definitely provable, using only strict rules.
- $-\Delta q$, which is intended to mean that q is provably not strictly provable (finite failure).
- $+\partial q$, which is intended to mean that q is defeasibly provable in D.
- $-\partial q$ which is intended to mean that we have proved that q is not defeasibly provable in D.

Provability is defined below. It is based on the concept of a *derivation* (or *proof*) in $D = R$. A derivation is a finite sequence $P = P(1), \ldots, P(n)$ of tagged literals satisfying the following conditions. The conditions are essentially inference rules phrased as conditions on proofs. $P(1..i)$ denotes the initial part of the sequence P of length i.

$+\Delta$: If $P(i+1) = +\Delta q$ then
$$\exists r \in R_s[q]\ \forall a \in A(r) : +\Delta a \in P(1..i)$$

That means, to prove $+\Delta q$ we need to establish a proof for q using strict rules only. This is a deduction in the classical sense – no proofs for the negation of q need to be considered (in contrast to defeasible provability below, where opposing chains of reasoning must be taken into account, too).

$-\Delta$: If $P(i+1) = -\Delta q$ then
$$\forall r \in R_s[q]\ \exists a \in A(r) : -\Delta a \in P(1..i)$$

The definition of $-\Delta$ is the so-called *strong negation* of $+\Delta$: normal negation rules like De-Morgan rules are applied to the definition, $+$ is replaced by $-$, and vice versa. Therefore in the following we may omit giving inference conditions of both $+$ and $-$.

$+\partial$: If $P(i+1) = +\partial q$ then either
(1) $+\Delta q \in P(1..i)$ or
(2) (2.1) $\exists r \in R[q]\ \forall a \in A(r) : +\partial a \in P(1..i)$ and
(2.2) $-\Delta \sim q \in P(1..i)$ and
(2.3) $\forall s \in R[\sim q] \exists a \in A(s) : -\partial a \in P(1..i)$

Let us illustrate this definition. To show that q is provable defeasibly we have two choices: (1) We show that q is already definitely provable; or (2) we need to argue using the defeasible part of D as well. In particular, we require that there must be a strict or defeasible rule with head q which can be applied (2.1). But now we need to consider possible "counterattacks", that is, reasoning chains in support of $\sim q$. To be more specific: to prove q defeasibly we must show that $\sim q$ is not definitely provable (2.2). Also (2.3) we must consider the set of all rules which are not known to be inapplicable and which have head $\sim q$. Essentially each such rule s attacks the conclusion q. For q to be provable, each such rule s must have been established as non-applicable.

A defeasible theory D is called *decisive* iff for every literal p, either $D \vdash -\partial p$ or $D \vdash +\partial p$. Not every defeasible theory satisfies this property. For example, in the theory consisting of the single rule

$$p \Rightarrow p$$

neither $-\partial p$ nor $+\partial p$ is provable. However, decisiveness is guaranteed in acyclic defeasible theories [6].

3 Semantics of Logic Programs

We deal with extended logic programs which allow two kinds of negation: classical negation $\neg$ and negation as failure *not*. A literal p preceded by *not* is called a *weakly negated literal*.

A *logic program* P is a finite set of program clauses. A *program clause* r has the form

$$p_0 \leftarrow p_1, \ldots, p_m, not\ p_{m+1}, \ldots, not\ p_n$$

where $n \geq m \geq 0$, and each p_i is a literal. p_0 is the *head* of r, denoted $head(r)$, and $\{p_1, \ldots, p_m, not\ p_{m+1}, \ldots, not\ p_n\}$ the *body* of r, denoted $body(r)$. If $n = m$ then r is a *basic rule* (a rule without weakly negated literals). A program is *basic* iff all its clauses are basic. Finally, we define $body^+(r) = \{p_1, \ldots, p_m\}$ and $body^-(r) = \{p_{m+1}, \ldots, p_n\}$.

3.1 Answer Set Semantics

A set of literals X is *consistent* iff it does not contain a complementary pair, p and $\sim p$, of literals. X is *logically closed* iff it is either consistent, or it equals the set of all literals in the logical language.

Given a basic program P, X *is closed under* P iff for all clauses r in P, $head(r) \in X$ whenever $body(r) \subseteq X$. Given a basic program P, the smallest set of literals which is both logically closed and closed under P is denoted by $Cn(P)$.

The *reduct* P^X of a program P *relative to a set of literals* X is defined by

$$P^X = \{head(r) \leftarrow body^+(r) \mid r \in P \text{ and } body^-(r) \cap X = \emptyset\}.$$

The reduct, often referred to as the *Gelfond-Lifschitz reduction*, constructs a basic program out of a program P, using the set X as the current context.

A set X of literals is an *answer set* of a program P iff $Cn(P^X) = X$. Answer sets were defined in [9] as a generalization of the stable model semantics [8] of programs which do not contain classical negation $\neg$.

3.2 Kunen Semantics

Kunen semantics [14] is a 3-valued semantics for logic programs. A *partial interpretation* is a mapping from ground atoms to one of the three truth values **t**, **f** and **u**, which denote true, false and unknown, respectively. This mapping can be extended to arbitrary formulas using Kleene's 3-valued logic.

Kleene's truth tables can be summarized as follows. If φ is a boolean combination of the atoms **t**, **f** and **u**, its truth value is **t** iff all possible ways of putting t or **f** for the various occurrences of **u** lead to a value **t** being computed in ordinary (2-valued) logic; φ gets the value **f** iff $\neg\varphi$ gets the value **t**; and φ gets the value **u** otherwise. These truth values can be extended in the obvious way to predicate logic, thinking of the quantifiers as infinite conjunctions or disjunctions.

The Kunen semantics of a program P is obtained from a sequence $\{I_n\}$ of partial interpretations, defined as follows:

1. $I_0(\alpha) = \mathbf{u}$ for every atom α.
2. $I_{n+1}(\alpha) = \mathbf{t}$ iff for some clause $\beta \leftarrow \varphi$ in the program, $\alpha = \beta\sigma$ for some ground substitution σ such that $I_n(\varphi\sigma) = \mathbf{t}$.
3. $I_{n+1}(\alpha) = \mathbf{f}$ iff for all clauses $\beta \leftarrow \varphi$ in the program, and all ground substitutions σ, if $\alpha = \beta\sigma$ then $I_n(\varphi\sigma) = \mathbf{f}$.
4. $I_{n+1}(\alpha) = \mathbf{u}$ if neither 2. nor 3. applies.

We shall say that the Kunen semantics of P supports α, written $P \models_K \alpha$, iff there is an interpretation I_n, for some finite n, such that $I_n(\alpha) = \mathbf{t}$.

4 A Translation of Defeasible Theories into Logic Programs

4.1 A Direct Translation That Fails

A natural translation of a defeasible theory into a logic program would look as follows. A strict rule

$$\{q_1, \ldots, q_n\} \rightarrow p$$

is translated into the program clause

$$p \leftarrow q_1, \ldots, q_n.$$

And a defeasible rule

$$\{q_1, \ldots, q_n\} \Rightarrow p$$

is translated into

$$p \leftarrow q_1, \ldots, q_n, not \ \sim p.$$

Unfortunately this translation does not lead to a correspondence between the defeasible conclusions and the sceptical conclusions in answer set semantics, as the following example demonstrates.

Example 1. Consider the defeasible theory

$$\Rightarrow p$$
$$\Rightarrow \neg p$$
$$\Rightarrow q$$
$$p \Rightarrow \neg q$$

Here q is defeasibly provable because the only rule with head $\neg q$ is not applicable, because $-\partial p$. However, the translated logic program

$$p \leftarrow not\ \neg p.$$
$$\neg p \leftarrow not\ p.$$
$$q \leftarrow not\ \neg q.$$
$$\neg q \leftarrow p, not\ q.$$

has three answer sets, $\{p, q\}$, $\{p, \neg q\}$ and $\{\neg p, q\}$. Thus none of $p, \neg p, q, \neg q$ is included in all extensions.

4.2 A Translation Using Control Literals

Above we outlined the reasons why a direct translation of a defeasible theory into a logic program must fail. Here we propose a different translation which uses "control literals" that carry meaning regarding the applicability status of rules.

First we translate strict rules. In defeasible logic, strict rules play a twofold role: on one hand they can be used to derive undisputed conclusions if all their antecedents have been strictly proved. And on the other hand they can be used essentially as defeasible rules, if their antecedents are defeasibly provable. These two roles can be clearly seen in the inference condition $+\partial$ is section 2.

To capture both uses we introduce mutually disjoint copies *strict-p* for all atoms p. For a literal $\neg p$, *strict-*$\neg p$ denotes $\neg$*strict-p*. Given a strict rule

$$r : \{q_1, \ldots, q_n\} \rightarrow p$$

we translate it into the program clause

$$a(r) : strict\text{-}p \leftarrow strict\text{-}q_1, \ldots, strict\text{-}q_n.$$

Additionally, we introduce the clause

$$b(p) : p \leftarrow strict\text{-}p$$

for every literal p. Intuitively, *strict-p* means that p is strictly provable. And the clause $b(p)$ corresponds to the condition (1) in the $+\partial$ inference condition: a literal p is defeasibly provable if it is strictly provable.

Next we turn our attention to defeasible rules and consider

$$r : \{q_1, \ldots, q_n\} \Rightarrow p$$

r is translated into the following set of clauses:

$d_1(r) : p \leftarrow q_1, \ldots, q_n, not \sim strict\text{-}p, ok(r).$
$d_2(r) : ok(r) \leftarrow ok'(r, s_1), \ldots, ok'(r, s_m)$, where $R[\sim p] = \{s_1, \ldots, s_m\}$.
$d_3(r, s) : ok'(r, s) \leftarrow blocked(s)$, for all $s \in R[\sim p]$.
$d_4(r, q_i) : blocked(r) \leftarrow not\ q_i$, for all $i \in \{1, \ldots, n\}$.

In the above, the predicates ok, ok' and *blocked* are new and pairwise disjoint.

- $d_1(r)$ says that to prove p defeasibly by applying r, we must prove all the antecedents of r, the negation of p should not be strictly provable, and it must be ok to apply r.
- The clause $d_2(r)$ says when it is ok to apply a rule r with head p: we must check that it is ok to apply r w.r.t. every rule with head $\sim p$.
- $d_3(r, s)$ says that it is ok to apply r w.r.t. s if s is blocked. Obviously this clause would look more complicated if we had considered priorities, instead of compiling them into the defeasible theory prior to the translation. Indeed, in the present framework we could have used a somewhat simpler translation, but chose to maintain the intuitive nature of the translation in its present form.
- Finally, d_4 specifies the only way a rule r can be blocked: it must be impossible to prove one of its antecedents.

For a defeasible theory D we define $P(D)$ to be the union of all clauses $a(r), b(p), d_1(r), d_2(r), d_3(r, s)$ and $d_4(r, q_i)$.

Example 2. We consider the defeasible theory from Example 4.1:

$r_1 : \Rightarrow p$
$r_2 : \Rightarrow \neg p$
$r_3 : \Rightarrow q$
$r_4 : \ p \Rightarrow \neg q$

Its translation looks as follows:

$d_1(r_1) : \ p \leftarrow not\ \neg strict\text{-}p, ok(r_1).$
$d_2(r_1) : \ ok(r_1) \leftarrow ok'(r_1, r_2).$
$d_3(r_1) : \ ok'(r_1, r_2) \leftarrow blocked(r_2).$
$d_1(r_2) : \ \neg p \leftarrow not\ strict\text{-}p, ok(r_2).$
$d_2(r_2) : \ ok(r_2) \leftarrow ok'(r_2, r_1).$
$d_3(r_2) : \ ok'(r_2, r_1) \leftarrow blocked(r_1).$
$d_1(r_3) : \ q \leftarrow not\ \neg strict\text{-}q, ok(r_3).$
$d_2(r_3) : \ ok(r_3) \leftarrow ok'(r_3, r_4).$
$d_3(r_3) : \ ok'(r_3, r_4) \leftarrow blocked(r_4).$
$d_1(r_4) : \ \neg q \leftarrow p, not\ strict\text{-}q, ok(r_4).$
$d_2(r_4) : \ ok(r_4) \leftarrow ok'(r_4, r_3).$
$d_3(r_4) : \ ok'(r_4, r_3) \leftarrow blocked(r_3).$
$d_4(r_4) : \ blocked(r_4) \leftarrow not\ \neg p.$

5 Properties of the Translation

We begin with an observation on the size of the translation.

Proposition 1. *The size of $P(D)$ is bound by $L + n \times (3 + L) + n^2$, where n is the number of rules in D and L the number of literals occurring in D.*

Next we establish relationships between D and its translation $P(D)$. To do so we must select appropriate logic program semantics to interpret *not*. First we consider answer set semantics.

Theorem 1.

(a) $D \vdash +\Delta p \Leftrightarrow$ *strict-p is included in all answer sets of* $P(D)$.
(b) $D \vdash -\Delta p \Leftrightarrow$ *strict-p is not included in any answer set of* $P(D)$.

Theorem 2.

(a) $D \vdash +\partial p \Rightarrow$ *p is included in all answer sets of* $P(D)$.
(b) $D \vdash -\partial p \Rightarrow$ *p is not included in any answer set of* $P(D)$.
(c) If D is decisive then the implications (a) and (b) are also true in the opposite direction.

That is, if D is decisive, then the answer set semantics of $P(D)$ corresponds to the provability in defeasible logic. However part (c) is not true in the general case, as the following example shows.

Example 3. Consider the defeasible theory

$r_1 : \Rightarrow \neg p$
$r_2 : p \Rightarrow p$

In defeasible logic, $+\partial\neg p$ cannot be proven because we cannot derive $-\partial p$. However, *blocked*(r_2) is included in the only answer set of $P(D)$, so $\neg p$ is a sceptical conclusion of $P(D)$ under answer set semantics.

If we wish to have an equivalence result without the condition of decisiveness, then we must use a different logic programming semantics, namely Kunen semantics.

Theorem 3.

(a) $D \vdash +\Delta p \Leftrightarrow P(D) \vdash_K$ *strict-p*.
(b) $D \vdash -\Delta p \Leftrightarrow P(D) \not\vdash_K$ *strict-p*.
(c) $D \vdash +\partial p \Leftrightarrow P(D) \vdash_K p$.
(b) $D \vdash -\partial p \Leftrightarrow P(D) \not\vdash_K p$.

6 Conclusion

We motivated and presented a translation of defeasible theories into logic programs, such that the defeasible conclusions of the former correspond exactly with the sceptical conclusions of the latter under the answer set semantics, if a condition of decisiveness is satisfied. If decisiveness is not satisfied, we have to use Kunen semantics instead.

This paper closes an important gap in the theory of nonmonotonic reasoning, in that it relates defeasible logic with mainstream semantics of logic programming. This result is particularly important, since defeasible reasoning is one of the most successful nonmonotonic reasoning paradigms in applications.

References

1. G. Antoniou, D. Billington and M.J. Maher. On the analysis of regulations using defeasible rules. In *Proc. 32nd Hawaii International Conference on Systems Science*, 1999.
2. G. Antoniou, D. Billington and M. Maher. Defeasible Logic versus Logic Programming without Negation as Failure. *Journal of Logic Programming* 41,1 (2000): 45-57.
3. G. Antoniou, M.J. Maher and D. Billington. Defeasible Logic versus Logic Programming without Negation as Failure, Journal of Logic Programming, 42 (2000): 47-57.
4. G. Antoniou, D. Billington, G. Governatori and M.J. Maher. A flexible framework for defeasible logics. In *Proc. 17th American National Conference on Artificial Intelligence (AAAI-2000)*, 405-410.
5. G. Antoniou, D. Billington, G. Governatori and M.J. Maher. Representation results for defeasible logic. *ACM Transactions on Computational Logic* 2 (2001): 255–287
6. D. Billington. Defeasible Logic is Stable. *Journal of Logic and Computation* 3 (1993): 370–400.
7. J.P. Delgrande, T Schaub and H. Tompits. Logic Programs with Compiled Preferences. In *Proc. ECAI'2000*, 464–468.
8. M. Gelfond and V. Lifschitz. The stable model semantics for logic programming. In *Proc. International Conference on Logic Programming*, MIT Press 1988, 1070–1080.
9. M. Gelfond and V. Lifschitz. Classical negation in logic programs and deductive databases. *New Generation Computing* 9 (1991): 365–385.
10. G. Governatori, A. ter Hofstede and P. Oaks. Defeasible Logic for Automated Negotiation. In *Proc. Fifth CollECTeR Conference on Electronic Commerce*, Brisbane 2000.
11. B.N. Grosof. Prioritized conflict handling for logic programs. In *Proc. International Logic Programming Symposium*, MIT Press 1997, 197–211.
12. B.N. Grosof, Y. Labrou and H.Y. Chan. A Declarative Approach to Business Rules in Contracts: Courteous Logic Programs in XML. In *Proc. 1st ACM Conference on Electronic Commerce (EC-99)*, ACM Press 1999.
13. H.A. Kautz and B. Selman. Hard problems for simple default theories. *Artificial Intelligence* 28 (1991): 243-279.
14. K. Kunen. Negation in Logic Programming. *Journal of Logic Programming* 4 (1987): 289–308.

15. M.J. Maher, A. Rock, G. Antoniou, D. Billington and T. Miller. Efficient Defeasible Reasoning Systems. In *Proc. 12th IEEE International Conference on Tools with Artificial Intelligence (ICTAI 2000)*, IEEE 2000, 384-392.
16. M.J. Maher. A Denotational Semantics for Defeasible Logic. In *Proc. First International Conference on Computational Logic*, LNAI 1861, Springer, 2000, 209-222.
17. M.J. Maher. Propositional Defeasible Logic has Linear Complexity. *Theory and Practice of Logic Programming*, to appear.
18. V. Marek and M. Truszczynski. *Nonmonotonic Logic.* Springer 1993.
19. L. Morgenstern. Inheritance Comes of Age: Applying Nonmonotonic Techniques to Problems in Industry. *Artificial Intelligence*, 103 (1998): 1–34.
20. D. Nute. Defeasible Logic. In D.M. Gabbay, C.J. Hogger and J.A. Robinson (eds.): *Handbook of Logic in Artificial Intelligence and Logic Programming Vol. 3*, Oxford University Press 1994, 353–395.
21. H. Prakken. *Logical Tools for Modelling Legal Argument: A Study of Defeasible Reasoning in Law.* Kluwer Academic Publishers 1997 .
22. D.M. Reeves, B.N. Grosof, M.P. Wellman, and H.Y. Chan. Towards a Declarative Language for Negotiating Executable Contracts, *Proceedings of the AAAI-99 Workshop on Artificial Intelligence in Electronic Commerce (AIEC-99)*, AAAI Press / MIT Press, 1999.
23. R. Reiter. A Logic for Default Reasoning. *Artificial Intelligence* 13(1980): 81–132.
24. D.D. Touretzky, J.F. Horty and R.H. Thomason. A Clash of Intuitions: The Current State of Nonmonotonic Multiple Inheritance Systems. In *Proc. IJCAI-87*, Morgan Kaufmann 1987, 476–482.

On Algorithms for Decomposable Constraints

Kostas Stergiou

Glasgow University, Glasgow, Scotland. kostas@dcs.strath.ac.uk

Abstract. Non-binary constraints are present in many real-world constraint satisfaction problems. Certain classes of these constraints, like the all-different constraint, are "decomposable". That is, they can be represented by binary constraints on the same set of variables. For example, a non-binary all-different constraint can be decomposed into a clique of binary not-equals constraints. In this paper we make a theoretical analysis of local consistency and search algorithms for decomposable constraints. First, we prove a new lower bound for the worst-case time complexity of arc consistency on binary not-equals constraints. We show that the complexity is $O(e)$, where e is the number of constraints, instead of $O(ed)$, with d being the domain size, as previously known. Then, we compare theoretically local consistency and search algorithms that operate on the non-binary representation of decomposable constraints to their counterparts for the binary decomposition. We also extend previous results on arc consistency algorithms to the case of singleton arc consistency.

1 Introduction

Many problems in the real world can be efficiently modelled as constraint satisfaction problems and solved using constraint programming techniques. Some examples are scheduling, planning, machine vision, temporal reasoning, car sequencing, vehicle routing, belief maintainance, and frequency allocation. Most of these problems can be naturally modelled using n-ary (or non-binary) constraints like the "all-different" and "global cardinality" constraints. Certain classes of these non-binary constraints are *decomposable* [6] as they can be represented by binary constraints on the same set of variables. For example, an all-different constraint can be decomposed into a clique of binary not-equals constraints. As a second example, a monotonicity constraint can be decomposed into a sequence of ordering constraints on pairs of variables. Not all non-binary constraints are decomposable into binary constraints on the same set of variables. For example, the constraint $(x_1 + x_2 < x_3)$ cannot be represented by binary constraints without the introduction of additional variables.

In this paper we make a theoretical analysis of some local consistency and search algorithms for decomposable constraints. In Section 2 we introduce the neccessary definitions from constraint satisfaction. In Section 3 we prove a new lower bound for the worst-case time complexity of arc consistency on binary not-equals constraints. We show that the complexity is $O(e)$, where e is the number of constraints, instead of $O(ed)$, with d being the domain size, as previously

I.P. Vlahavas and C.D. Spyropoulos (Eds.): SETN 2002, LNAI 2308, pp. 65–71, 2002.

known. This new complexity bound is lower than the corresponding complexity bound for the non-binary representation of not-equal constraints (i.e. the all-different constraint). However, as we discuss in Section 4, this does not mean that the binary decomposition is more efficient than the non-binary representation. In Section 4 we compare theoretically local consistency and search algorithms that operate on the non-binary representation of decomposable constraints to their counterparts for the binary decomposition. We show that the non-binary representation is more powerful than the binary one, and this makes up for the worse complexity bound. Finally, we extend previous results on arc consistency algorithms to the case of singleton arc consistency.

2 Formal Background

A *constraint satisfaction problem* (CSP) $\mathcal{P}$ is defined by a triple $(\mathcal{X}, \mathcal{D}, \mathcal{C})$. $\mathcal{X}$ is a set of n variables. Each variable $x_i \in \mathcal{X}$ takes values from a domain $D_i \in \mathcal{D}$. $\mathcal{C}$ is a set of e constraints. Each k-ary constraint is defined over an ordered set of variables $\{x_1, \ldots, x_k\}$ by a subset of the Cartesian product $D_1 \times \ldots \times D_k$ that specifies the set of allowed value combinations (tuples). A constraint can be either defined extensionally by the set of allowed tuples or intensionally by a predicate or arithmetic function.

A value a in the domain D of variable x is *consistent* with a constraint c if x is not included in the variables of the constraint, or if it is included and there exists a valid tuple τ in c where $x = a$. In the latter case we say that τ is a *support* for a in c. Checking whether a tuple is a support for a variable value pair (x, a) is called a *consistency check*. A solution to a CSP is an assignment of values to variables that is consistent with all constraints. Many lesser levels of consistency (usually called local consistencies) have been defined for binary constraint satisfaction problems. A problem is $(i,j)-$*consistent* iff it has non-empty domains and any consistent instantiation of i variables can be extended to a consistent instantiation involving j additional variables. A problem is *arc consistent* (AC) iff it is $(1,1)$-consistent. A problem is *path consistent* (PC) iff it is $(2,1)$-consistent. A problem is *strong path consistent* iff it is $(j,1)$-consistent for $j \leq 2$. A problem is *path inverse consistent* (PIC) iff it is $(1,2)$-consistent. A problem is *neighbourhood inverse consistent* (NIC) iff any value for a variable can be extended to a consistent instantiation for its immediate neighbourhood. A problem is *restricted path consistent* (RPC) iff it is arc consistent and if a value assigned to a variable is consistent with just a single value for an adjoining variable then for any other variable there exists a value compatible with these instantiations. A problem is *singleton arc consistent* (SAC) iff it has non-empty domains and for any instantiation of a variable, the problem can be made arc consistent. Some of the above local consistencies have been extended to the case of non-binary CSPs. The generalizations of AC and SAC to non-binary CSPs are called generalized AC (GAC) and singleton generalized AC (SGAC) respectively. For example, a (non-binary) CSP is generalized arc consistent iff for any variable in a constraint and value that it is assigned, there exist compatible values for all the other variables in the constraint.

Many search algorithms enforce a certain level of consistency at every node in a search tree. For example, the *forward checking* algorithm (FC) maintains a restricted form of AC which ensures that all values of the uninstantiated variables are consistent with the most recent variable instantiation. Various generalizations of FC for non-binary constraints have been proposed. These algorithms, starting from nFC0 up to nFC5 enforce increasingly higher levels of consistency (see [1]). Even higher levels of consistency can be maintained at each node in the search tree. For example, the *maintaining arc consistency* algorithm (MAC) enforces AC at each node in the search tree. For non-binary constraints, the algorithm that *maintains generalized arc consistency* (MGAC) on a (non-binary) constraint satisfaction problem enforces GAC at each node in the search tree.

Following [2], we call a local consistency property A *stronger* than B iff for any problem enforcing A deletes at least the same values as B, and *strictly stronger* iff it is stronger and there is at least one problem where A deletes more values than B. We call A *equivalent* to B iff they delete the same values for all problems. Similarly, we call a search algorithm A stronger than a search algorithm B iff for every problem A visits at most the same search tree nodes as B, and strictly stronger iff it is stronger and there is at least one problem where A visits less nodes than B. A is equivalent to B iff they visit the same nodes for all problems.

3 Arc Consistency on Binary Not-equals Constraints

In this section we correct a result given in [10] regarding the complexity of achieving AC in a network of binary not-equals ($\neq$) constraints. In [10] it is claimed that AC can be optimally achieved with O(ed) worst-case time complexity, where e is the number of constraints and d the domain size of the variables. We will describe an algorithm that achieves AC in networks of binary not-equals constraints with O(e) worst-case complexity. In [10] it is claimed that $O(ed)$ is the optimal worst-case complexity of AC for any subclass of constraints, since, as they say, "it is reasonable to assume that we need to check each value in each domain at least once". We show that this is not the case for not-equals constraints, and as a result, the worst-case complexity is actually $O(e)$.

First, we start from the observation that for a not-equals constraint between variables x_i and x_j AC may remove a value from the domain of variable x_i or x_j only if the other variable has a unary domain. This is also mentioned in [10]. In general, a not-equals constraint between two variables x_i and x_j with domain sizes of more than one is always AC, since every value in the domain of x_i will have a support in the domain of x_j, and vice versa. Whenever a variable x_i is instantiated to a value a, AC will remove a from the domains of the variables adjacent to x_i and will only continue the propagation if some other variable has only one value in its domain. In other words, an optimal implementation of an AC algorithm will never process edges between variables that both have non-unary domains.

We now describe the steps of the AC algorithm with $O(e)$ worst-case complexity.

- For each edge (x_i, x_j), such that x_i has a unary domain mark the edge and put it in a queue.
- Extract the first edge (x_i, x_j) from the queue. Assuming that a is the unique value in the domain of x_i, if a is present in the domain of x_j, remove it.
- If the domain of x_j becomes empty, stop. The network is inconsistent.
- If x_j is left with a unary domain mark all the unmarked edges connected to x_j and put them in the queue. Checking whether a variable has only one value in its domain can be done in constant time through careful implementation. For example, using a flag that is set to 1 when the domain becomes singleton.
- Take the next edge out of the queue and continue in the same way. The algorithm will stop when a domain wipe-out occurs or the queue becomes empty.

Having described the algorithm, we can now prove the following proposition.

Proposition 1. *Arc consistency can be achieved with $O(e)$ worst-case time complexity on a network of e binary not-equals constraints.*

Proof. We need to show that each of the e edges will be processed at most once, and that the processing can be done in constant time. Consider a not-equals constraint between variable x_i with the singleton domain $\{a\}$ and x_j with the domain $\{a, \ldots, z\}$. When this edge is extracted from the queue, AC will remove a from the domain of x_j. If at some point later x_j is left with a singleton domain, the algorithm we described will insert all edges that involve x_j into the queue. However, there is no point in including edge (x_i, x_j), since AC cannot remove a value from either variable. This was done earlier when (x_i, x_j) was first processed. Thus, an edge that has been processed once needs not to be processed again. This means that each of the e edges is made AC at most once. As mentioned, making an edge AC is equivalent to removing a value from a domain (if present) and checking whether the resulting domain has size of 0, 1 or more, both of which can be done in constant time with careful implementation. Therefore, AC can be achieved with $O(e)$ worst-case complexity.

As a result, if we have an all-different constraint on k variables the decomposition of this constraint into binary not-equals constraints can be made arc consistent with $O(k^2)$ worst-case complexity. This is a significant gain over the $O(k^2d^2)$ complexity of a generic optimal AC algorithm like AC-7. Also, the $O(k^2)$ complexity of AC is significantly lower than the $O(k^2d^2)$ complexity of Regin's algorithm for all-different constraints. However, as we discuss in the next section, this does not mean that we should decompose all-different constraints into binary.

4 Local Consistency and Search Algorithms

In this section we review some results from [9,3] where local consistency and search algorithms for non-binary decomposable constraints are compared to the corresponding algorithms for the binary decomposition. [3] first compared the level of consistency achieved by FC on the decomposition to the levels of consistency achieved by the various generalizations of FC on the constraints of the n-ary representation. A lower bound on the performance of FC applied to the binary decomposition was first identified. It was proved that for a decomposable non-binary constraint satisfaction problem, the forward checking algorithm FC on the binary decomposition is strictly stronger than the generalized algorithm nFC0. [3] also gives a simple upper bound on the performance of FC on the binary decomposition. For a decomposable non-binary constraint satisfaction problem the generalized algorithm nFC1 is strictly stronger than FC on the binary decomposition.

[3] also investigated and compared the pruning efficiency of AC on the binary decomposition and GAC on the n-ary representation of decomposable constraints. They first gave a lower bound on the level of consistency achieved by GAC on decomposable constraints with respect to the binary decomposition. It was proved that GAC on decomposable constraints is strictly stronger than AC on the binary decomposition. As a result, an algorithm that maintains GAC on the non-binary representation of a set of decomposable constraints is strictly stronger than an algorithm that maintains AC on the binary decomposition. So, although we showed that AC on the decomposition can be achieved faster that GAC on the non-binary representation, it does not pay off because it is a weaker level of consistency. This is also demonstrated by the empirical results presented in [9,3].

Having established that GAC is stronger than AC, [3] compared GAC to stronger levels of consistency than AC in the binary decomposition. They showed that, in the general case, NIC on the binary decomposition, as well as all the levels of consistency between strong PC and RPC, are incomparable to generalized arc-consistency.

Another result from [3] is that an algorithm that maintains GAC on decomposable constraints strictly is stronger than the strongest generalized forward checking algorithm nFC5. Naturally, this means that it is also stronger than algorithms nFC0-nFC4 and also FC applied to the binary decomposition.

5 Singleton Arc Consistency

We now extend the analysis of [3] to the case of SAC and its generalization SGAC. As shown in [7], these very high levels of consistency can be very effective in certain classes of CSPs. First we prove that SGAC on on the non-binary representation is strictly stronger than SAC on the binary decomposition.

Theorem 1. *Singleton generalized arc consistency on decomposable constraints is strictly stronger than singleton arc consistency on the binary decomposition.*

Proof. SGAC ensures that every variable in the problem can be instantiated to any of the values in its domain and the resulting problem will be GAC. Since GAC on decomposable constraints is strictly stronger than AC on the binary decomposition, for any instantiation of a variable, the binary decomposition of the resulting problem will be AC. Hence, the binary decomposition of the original problem is SAC.

To prove strictness, consider a problem with three all-different constraints on $\{x_1, x_2, x_3\}$, on $\{x_1, x_2, x_4\}$, and on $\{x_1, x_3, x_4\}$, in which all variables have the domain $\{1, 2, 3\}$. The binary decomposition of this problem is SAC, but enforcing SGAC on the original problem shows that it is insoluble. For example, if we assign 1 to x_2 then GAC on the all-different constraint $\{x_1, x_3, x_4\}$ detects inconsistency and, therefore, the resulting problem is not GAC. So 1 is removed from the domain of x_2. With similar arguments, values 2 and 3 are also removed from the domain of x_2 resulting in a domain wipe-out.

A corollary of this theorem is that SGAC is strictly stronger than PIC and RPC on the binary decomposition.

Corollary 1. *Singleton generalized arc consistency on decomposable constraints is strictly stronger than path inverse consistency and restricted path consistency on the binary decomposition.*

Proof. It trivially follows from Theorem 1 and the results of [2] where it is proved that SAC is strictly stronger than PIC and RPC.

The following theorem shows that NIC and strong PC on the binary decomposition are incomparable to SGAC on the n-ary representation of decomposable constraints.

Theorem 2. *Singleton generalized arc consistency on decomposable constraints is incomparable to neighbourhood inverse consistency and to strong path consistency, on the binary decomposition.*

Proof. For an example where NIC is stronger than SGAC, consider a problem with five variables $\{x_1, x_2, x_3, x_4, x_5\}$ and six all-different constraints on $\{x_1, x_2, x_3\}$, on $\{x_1, x_3, x_4\}$, on $\{x_1, x_4, x_5\}$, on $\{x_1, x_2, x_5\}$, on $\{x_2, x_3, x_4\}$, and on $\{x_3, x_4, x_5\}$. All variables have the domain $\{1, 2, 3, 4\}$. This problem is SGAC because any instantiation of every variable results in a problem that is GAC. Enforcing NIC, however, shows that the problem is insoluble. Now, for an example where strong PC is stronger than SGAC, consider a problem with three variables $\{x_1, x_2, x_3\}$ and three not-equals constraints, $x_1 \neq x_2$, $x_1 \neq x_3$, $x_2 \neq x_3$. The domain of x_1 is $\{1, 2\}$ and the domains of x_2 and x_3 is $\{1, 2, 3\}$. This problem is SGAC but enforcing strong PC adds the constraint that either x_2 or x_3 must be 3.

For an example where SGAC is stronger than NIC, consider the following 2-colouring problem. We have 5 variables, x_1 to x_5 which are arranged in a ring. Each variable has the same domain of size 2. Between each pair of neighbouring variables in the binary decomposition, there is a not-equals constraint. In the non-binary representation, we post a single constraint on all 5 variables. This problem is NIC, but enforcing SGAC on the non-binary representation shows that the problem is insoluble. Finally, for an example where SGAC is stronger than strong PC, consider an all-different constraint on 4 variables, each with the same domain of size 3. The binary representation of the problem is strong PC but enforcing SGAC shows that it is insoluble.

6 Conclusions

We made a theoretical analysis of local consistency and search algorithms for decomposable constraints. We proved a new lower bound for the worst-case time complexity of arc consistency on binary not-equals constraints. We showed that the complexity is $O(e)$ instead of $O(ed)$, as previously known. We compared theoretically local consistency and search algorithms that operate on the non-binary representation of decomposable constraints to their counterparts for the binary decomposition. We also extended previous results on AC and GAC algorithms to the case of SAC and SGAC. In general we showed that the representation of problems can have a very large impact on the efficiency of search. Also, a non-binary representation can offer considerable advantages over a binary representation in certain classes of constraints, such as decomposable constraints.

Acknowledgements. The author is a member of the APES research group and would like to thank Ian Gent, Patrick Prosser, and Toby Walsh.

References

1. C. Bessière, P. Meseguer, E. Freuder, and J. Larrosa. On forward checking for non-binary constraint satisfaction. In *Proceedings CP-99*, pages 88–102.
2. R. Debruyne and C. Bessière. Some practicable filtering techniques for the constraint satisfaction problem. In *Proceedings of IJCAI-97*, pages 412–417.
3. I. Gent, K. Stergiou, and T. Walsh. Decomposable Constraints. *Artificial Intelligence*, 123:133–156, 2000.
4. C. P. Gomes and B. Selman. Problem structure in the presence of perturbations. In *Proceedings of AAAI-97*, pages 221–226.
5. C. P. Gomes, B. Selman, and N. Crato. Heavy-tailed probability distributions in combinatorial search. In *Proceedings of CP-97*, pages 121–135.
6. U. Montanari. Networks of Constraints: Fundamental Properties and Applications to Picture Processing. *Information Science*, 7:95–132, 1974.
7. P. Prosser, K. Stergiou, and T. Walsh. Singleton consistencies. In *Proceedings of CP-2000.*
8. J. C. Régin. A filtering algorithm for constraints of difference in csps. In *Proceedings of AAAI-94*, pages 362–367.
9. K. Stergiou, and T. Walsh. The difference all-difference makes. In *Proceedings of IJCAI-99.*
10. P. Van Hentenryck, Y. Deville, and C. Teng. A Generic Arc Consistency Algorithm and its Specializations. *Artificial Intelligence*, 57:291–321, 1992.

CSPCONS: A Communicating Sequential Prolog with Constraints

Ioannis P. Vlahavas[1]*, Ilias Sakellariou[1], Ivan Futo[2], Zoltan Pasztor[2], and Janos Szeredi[2]

[1] Department of Informatics, Aristotle University of Thessaloniki, 54006 Thessaloniki Greece
{vlahavas, iliass}@csd.auth.gr
[2] ML Consulting and Computing Ltd, ML Kft, H-1011 Budapest, Gyorskocsi u. 5-7., Hungary.
{futo, pasztor, szeredi}@ml-cons.hu

Abstract. CSPCONS is a programming language that supports program execution over multiple Prolog processes with constraints. The language is an extended version of CSP-II, a version of Prolog that supports, among other features, channel-based communicating processes and TCP/IP communication and is based on the CSP model introduced by Hoare. CSPCONS inherits all the advanced features of CSP-II and extends it by introducing constraint solving capabilities to the processes. In CSPCONS each Prolog process has one or more solvers attached and each solver is independent from the others, following the original CSP-II model, thus resulting to a communicating sequential constraint logic programming system. Such a model can facilitate greatly the implementation of distributed CLP applications. Currently CSPCONS offers a finite domain constraint solver, but the addition of new solvers is supported as they can be integrated in the system in the form of linkable C libraries. This paper briefly describes the original CSP-II system along with the extensions that resulted to the CSPCONS system.

1 Introduction

In the past decade, constraint programming has proven to be a suitable platform for tackling large combinatorial problems with significant applications in industry, like scheduling, resource allocation, etc. However even with the most advanced techniques, solving such problems is both space and time costly.

The introduction of new sophisticated sequential algorithms for constraint satisfaction is one way to overcome the problem. However the availability of a large number of machines connected by some local network, naturally led to the approach of distributing the problem to multiple processing units, often called agents or workers, that cooperate to solve the problem more efficiently.

* This work was supported by the Bilateral Cooperation Program Greece-Hungary 2000-2002

I.P. Vlahavas and C.D. Spyropoulos (Eds.): SETN 2002, LNAI 2308, pp. 72–84, 2002.

CSPCONS is a logic programming language for building such systems. The language is an extension of the Communicating Sequential Prolog II (CSP-II) a version of Prolog that is based on the notion of communicating sequential processes. CSPCONS supports independent CLP processes each having its own constraint store that communicate through message exchange over channels. Communication is possible both between processes that reside in the same host and on different hosts over TCP/IP networks. Constraint facilities in CSPCONS are implemented as C libraries, thus permitting the incorporation of new constraint just by the addition of the appropriate library. The current version includes a library for constraint satisfaction over finite domains (FD).

The combination of the channel based communication and constraint satisfaction, all under the logic programming framework, offers a powerful platform for the rapid implementation of any distributed CSP application.

This paper is organized as follows. Section 2 briefly presents related work in the field of distributed constraint satisfaction. An overview of the features of the CSP-II language is presented in Section 3, considered necessary since all its features are inherited to the CSPCONS language. The necessary extensions for the support of constraints together with the description of the implementation of the FD solver that form the CSPCONS language is given in Section 4. Section 5 shows an example of a distributed implementation of the N-queens problem along with some experimental results. Finally conclusions and future work are stated in section 6.

2 Distributed Constraint Satisfaction Problems

Informally, a constraint satisfaction problem (CSP) consists of finding an assignment of values from a given domain to a set of variables, such that a set of constraints on the variables is satisfied. Constraints are imposed on a subset of the domain variables and restrict the values which can be simultaneously assigned to them.

A distributed constraint satisfaction problem is a CSP in which the variables/constraints are distributed over some network of agents. Agents are constraint solvers which co-operate to solve the original problem. The need for distributed constraint programming applications derives mainly from two facts: a) more efficient implementations, in terms of execution time, can be achieved by decomposing the original problem into subproblems and b) representing problems that are naturally distributed is significantly facilitated, as for example production planning in a factory in which independent departments must meet their local constraints and at the same time co-operate to achieve global constraints.

A number of approaches have been reported to the literature that address the issue of building distributed constraint programming applications. In the sequel we will restrict our presentation to systems that belong to the logic programming framework and also present some algorithms proposed.

The approach followed for the implementation of the distributed capabilities of the CIAO language[5] is described in [1]. CIAO is a system based in Prolog extended with constraints, parallelism and concurrency. The distributed execution capabilities are based on the Linda library for implementing communication between processing units (referred to as workers), i.e. it adopts a blackboard architecture and the use of attributed variables[6].

A different approach to solving CSP problems in parallel has been proposed by Tong and Leung in [12]. Their model, called Firebird, is based on an extension of the Andorra principle and is an attempt to build a concurrent constraint logic programming system on a massively parallel SIMD computer, that will exploit OR-Parallelism. In Firebird execution interleaves between *indeterministic derivation steps* that consist of guard tests, commitment and spawning in the same manner as committed-choice languages and *non-deterministic derivation steps* which consist of setting up a choice point on a domain variable and attempting all the alternative values in its domain in an OR-parallel manner.

Apart from the above systems a number of algorithms have been proposed that address the issue of distributed constraint satisfaction. A class of such algorithms performs distributed arc consistency, as for example a distributed version of the AC4 algorithm, based on an message passing communication model [9]. In [16] Zhang and Mackworth present parallel and distributed algorithms for computing consistency by formulating a CSP as a *dual network*, in which constraints correspond to nodes and variables to arcs. These algorithms were tested on a transputer based machine.

In [14,15] authors propose an asynchronous backtracking algorithm and its modification, the asynchronous weak-commitment search, that efficiently solves distributed constraint satisfaction problems. In the proposed algorithm a problem variable is assigned to each agent who instantiates it and communicates its value through messages to other agents. Upon the detection of an inconsistency, agents exchange appropriate messages in order to backtrack and achieve a consistent assignment of values.

In the distributed backtracking algorithm (DIBT) introduced in [4], a different approach is followed. Agents compute their position in a total ordering of the network, each having a set of parent and child agents. Upon variable instantiation the agent's children are informed of the chosen value and failure to determine a consistent value in this set initiates backtracking to the parent agents. The algorithm employs message passing communication.

Finally, an algorithm that integrates distributed consistency techniques into asynchronous backtracking is presented in [11]. The proposed algorithm combines a distributed bounds consistency algorithm, called DHC, with a distributed search technique called Asynchronous Aggregation Search [10]. Agents communicate information by message exchange as in the previous algorithm.

To our knowledge no language that combines communicating sequential processes, to the extent that CSPCONS does, with constraints has been proposed in the literature till now.

3 The CSP-II Prolog

The CSP-II distributed Prolog system is being developed since 1995 [2],[3]. The syntax and the built-in procedures of the language follow those of the standard Prolog (ISO/IEC 13211-1); furthermore the language is extended with features like modularity, multitasking, real-time programming and network communication.

The main feature of the CSP-II system is that it supports the communicating sequential process [7] programming methodology in a Prolog environment. Processes run in parallel and communication between them is achieved through message passing over channels. This process-based model allows the implementation of parallel and distributed algorithms.

The channel-based communication has been extended with networking capabilities over the TCP/IP protocol, thus providing the ability to establish connections between different CSP-II applications across the Internet. Furthermore, under this schema CSP-II also provides communication with foreign (non CS-Prolog) applications, an interface to relational data base systems, real-time programming methods like cyclic behavior, reaction to predefined events, timed interrupts, etc.

The system consists of three main components: a compiler, a linker and a runtime system. The Prolog source is compiled into a binary format containing the WAM code, although in some points different. This code is interpreted by a "byte code interpreter" when executing the CS-Prolog runtime system. Among other things the system includes a pre-processor similar to what is found in C compilers and an integrated development environment with a multi-window trace utility.

3.1 CSP-II Processes

CSP-II processes are defined as the execution flow of a Prolog goal and every process has its own Prolog execution environment and dynamic database. Thus the progress of a process is independent of the execution of other processes. This separation of dynamic databases ensures that CSP-II processes may have influence on each other only by the CSP-II provided communication techniques, i.e. channels, events and interrupts, or through external objects like files. On a single processor machine a time-sharing scheduler controls the concurrent processes.

Processes are identified by a unique system-wide symbolic name. Two kinds of processes are provided:

- self-driven or normal processes, which is the most usual kind.
- event-driven or real time processes.

A *self driven* process is characterized by its (Prolog) goal; after its creation, it will begin the execution of this goal. The non-fatal termination of a self-driven process is determined by the termination of its goal. At the moment of its termination the process disappears from the CSP-II system and will never reappear.

A *real time* process is characterized by one goal for the initialization, one goal for the event handling and by the description of the events that trigger its execution. The initialization goal is executed once and provides the means for performing any necessary setup actions. After the successful termination of the initializing goal the process switches to a cyclic behavior. From that moment on it is controlled by the incoming events. For every real time process, the incoming events are gathered in a separate first-in-first-out input queue, from which the process consumes them by initiating its event-handling goal. The number of events that real time processes can be triggered for is unlimited. The successful termination of a process is signaled by the failure of its event-handling goal. Such termination is considered as regular; it does not affect the overall success or failure of the application.

Inter-process communication is achieved by synchronous messages or by event passing. Messages are passed through *communication channels*. A *message* can be any Prolog term except a single unbound variable, however compound terms containing unbound variables are allowed. Communication channels act as system-wide available resources, identified by unique names and may appear and disappear dynamically during the program's lifetime. A channel implements an one way communication between two processes. In such a connection one process has the sending end of the channel and the other the receiving end. The total number of channels in the system and the number of the channels a process can be connected to are unlimited.

As stated *events* serve for triggering real time processes and are also identified by system-wide unique names. They can be generated explicitly by built-in predicates or implicitly by the internal clock of the CSP-II scheduler. The latter allows to invoke execution of the real-time process in specific time intervals. The number of the available events in a program is unlimited. It should be noted that every occurrence of an event may have an optional data argument that can be used to provide some additional information. The event data is an arbitrary Prolog term, except the case of a single unbound variable.

Finally it should be noted that processes can backtrack, however communication is not backtrackable.

3.2 TCP/IP Communication

As a natural extension of the original inter-process channel concept, the external communication conceptually consists of message streams. In order to facilitate speed-up of external communication, asynchronous message passing is introduced as an option. The *send* operation in this case still remains blocking but the condition for continuing execution is the availability of sufficient buffer space instead of the commencement of the matching *receive* operation.

For the Prolog programmer the communication environment appears as a homogeneous address space (community) in which all fellow applications (partners) are accessed via channel messages. A separate mechanism is introduced for connecting channels to other CSP-II applications. Two notions are introduced in this mechanism: the port and the connection.

A *port* represents an incoming message substream. This entity should not be confused with the normal TCP/IP port. A CSP-II port is the entry point of all incoming messages for the local application. It is explicitly created by a corresponding predicate and a local channel is associated with it at the time of its creation. The application receives all messages through that channel. A parameter set during port creation determines the size of the message buffer so that asynchronous communication can take place.

A *connection* is the representation of an outgoing message stream. It is also explicitly created by the programmer and is associated with a partner's port to where it forwards all outgoing messages that it receives from a specific local channel of the sender application. All previous information is defined at the creation of the connection, including a parameter indicating the number of messages stored in the connection buffer.

In order to be able to communicate with a partner, a configuration process has to be performed using a special built-in predicate. Though this, all necessary network information of the partner is defined, i.e. its name, port, IP address or hostname, IP port it listens to, etc. Although this operation requires detailed knowledge of the partner's network information, it provides a more versatile connection schema. We are currently considering the idea to introduce some sort of naming service in a future version, however this will not require modifications of the current communication model, since it will be added in the form of a simple Prolog library.

A CSP-II application can also establish communication with a non-Prolog application through an appropriate mediator, that handles all data and protocol conversions. Currently CSP-II supports an ASCII mediator for plain text communication and one for communication with a specific network management platform (HNMS).

CSP-II has been successfully employed in the development of a distributed expert system for the management of a TCP/IP based WAN [13].

4 Extending the CSP-II Framework for Constraint Programming

CSPCONS is an extension of the CSP-II system that inherits all its advanced features and at the same time provides constraint solving capabilities.

The system consists of two main subsystems: the *solver* and the *core*. The solver is responsible for maintaining the constraint store and performing any constraint related tasks, i.e. is responsible for storing domain variables and the set of constraints as well as for constraint propagation. It should be noted that several solvers are allowed to each program. The core is the extended CSP-II system that keeps track of the active instances of the different solvers, dispatches requests originated by the Prolog program to the appropriate solver instance, and performs other system-related tasks, including all normal Prolog predicate calls.

In general, each CSPCONS process can have active instances of several different solvers, as for example an FD and a Linear solver. However the set of constraints and domain variables maintained by instances of a solver that belong to different processes are independent of each other, resulting to a communicating sequential CLP system.

In order to support the above model, CSPCONS introduced to the original CSP-II system a new set of built-in predicates, an appropriate C interface between the core and the solver and a new variable type, called constraint variable.

The CLP-related predicates that are defined in the new built-in predicate set can be divided into three groups. The first group is concerned with the term type system extension, i.e. their use is the identification of constraint variables. The second group consists of the solver-independent predicates used for obtaining information about the installed solvers and selecting a particular solver. The third group consists of the "normal" interface predicates used for the introduction of new domain variables, constraints and for labeling. The predicates in the third group require cooperation between the core subsystem and the particular solver that is currently selected. This cooperation is achieved through a dedicated for the purpose C language interface.

Solvers are implemented in the form of linkable C libraries. Each solver must expose for the core a table containing pointers to specific functions (entry points). These entry points are mainly implementations of the normal interface predicates, i.e. a CLP related predicate call corresponds to an entry point. For example the `clp_constraint/1` predicate used to introduce new constraints in a program corresponds to the `constraint()` entry point function. However the implementation of the entry points depends on the use of a set of functions provided by the core, called *callback* functions, that provide various services such as constraint variable creation and removal, introduction of new trail points in the backtrack stack, etc.

Finally, constrained variables are introduced as a new term type in the original set of term-types. They are always associated with a corresponding internal variable of the solver. Their creation and removal is the responsibility of the solver, who requests it by appropriate callback function calls from the core. Upon unification of a constraint variable to a term in a Prolog program three cases can occur, depending on the state of the variable:

- If the unification involves a constraint and a normal unbound variable then it simply succeeds and the latter simply refers to the former in the computations that follow.
- If the variable is fixed to a specific value then unification is handled by the core. The solver in this case is called by a special entry point only to inform the solver about the status of the variable and its value if it is fixed.
- If the variable is being unified with another constraint variable or any other term then the unification is the responsibility of the solver who treats it as a newly introduced equality constraint. The solver in this case is called via an appropriate entry point and must either add the new constraint to the store if it is consistent or simply reject it, yielding a unification failure.

4.1 The CSPCONS Execution Model

The solver subsystem is initialized when the first constraint predicate call is issued by the user program in the process. The solver instance starts with an empty system of constraints and during forward execution, new constraints are incrementally added to the model. The solver evaluates the resulting constraint set and if it is consistent, it accepts the additions and the call succeeds, otherwise rejects them, i.e. the call fails. If the predicate, which passes the new constraint succeeds, then all unbound variables occurring in the passed constraints become constrained variables and their behavior during unification is determined through a solver-core cooperation.

If the Prolog program backtracks over a CLP-predicate call or a unification of a constraint variable, the solver must revert to the state that was in effect before that call. Thus the state of the constraint store maintained by a solver instance must be synchronized with the state of the evaluation stack of the Prolog host process. Any change in the constraints store caused by the evaluation of a CLP-predicate or a unification involving constrained variables must be "undone" when the interpretation backtracks over the predicate that originated the change.

In the CSPCONS system there are two trail stacks: the core and the solver trail. The first is used by the Prolog interpreter itself for registering normal variable bindings that should be undone during backtracking. The solver trail is used for registering changes in the constraint store. To achieve synchronization between these two areas the interface offers the ability to introduce identifiers of the solver trail to the core trail. On backtracking a special entry point function (`backtrack()`) is invoked and an identifier is passed back to the solver as argument to this function. The identifier indicates the appropriate stack level that the solver should backtrack to. Any necessary actions for restoring the state of the constraint store are organized based on this information.

The model offers independence of the code concerning the constraint handling and provides the means to easily extend the system to support any constraint domain. Currently CSPCONS supports a finite domain solver while there also exists an experimental linear equations-disequations solver.

4.2 The Finite Domain Solver

Since our main aim was to test the ideas and the extension model, the implementation of the FD solver had to be kept as simple as possible. Thus the solver was based on the AC-3 [8] algorithm. Although the latter is not considered state of the art, it was selected due to its simplicity.

Currently the solver supports constraints of the form: $x \in \{n_1, n_2, .., n_m\}$ and $exp_1\ R\ exp_2$ where $\{n_1, n_2, .., n_m\}$ is a set of natural numbers, $R \in \{=, \neq, <, >, \geq, \leq\}$ and exp_1, exp_2 are linear expressions on constraint variables. All constraints are posted through the `clp_constaint/1` predicate as shown in the following examples:

```
clp_constraint([X in [1..10], Y in [1..10]]),
clp_constraint([3*X < 2*Y +10]),
```

All unary and binary constraints are handled internally by the consistency algorithm. Higher arity constraints are delayed until they become ground and are then handled as unary constraints. The solver also provides a set of predicates for labeling including one that uses the fail-first principle.

As mentioned in a previous paragraph backtracking involves synchronizing the solver and the core trail. The solver trail stack contains entries that belong to four types. Two of them concern variable creation and constraint addition, and the third type concerns value removal, while the last type records constraint variable unification with an integer. Upon value removal only a pointer to the specific value is recorded. This pointer is sufficient for restoring the value since what is required is flipping the `valid` field of the structure that stores the value. Each trail entry has an identifier associated with the core trail entry according to the extension model described above. Multiple solver trail entries can share the same identifier value since they belong to the same choice point and thus the core trail is not overtaxed with entries.

It should be noted that the implementation has been tested on a variety of benchmarks, including the well-known cryptarithmentic and alpha problems and some artificial ones and has performed adequately. However the system performance cannot be compared with systems such as ECLIPSE or SICStus that employ far more sophisticated constraint handling algorithms.

5 Solving the N-Queens Problem

To show the suitability of the proposed system for the implementation of any distributed CSP program, we have implemented a single process and two multi-process versions of the well-known N-Queens problem. The single process version is in fact the standard implementation of the problem but without using the first-fail principle.

The multi-process versions consist of two independent processes each having its own store. Both versions divide the problem of N Queens in half, assigning N/2 Queens to each process. On each subset of these variables local constraints are applied, stating the relations between N/2 Queens in a (N/2)xN chessboard. A priority is set between the two processes having one of them assigning values first and passing them via a channel to the second process. Messages are passed via inter-process channels, since the program is executed in the same host, however the implementation of TCP/IP communication between processes of different hosts is straightforward.

The two versions implement different search algorithms between the two independent processes. The first version employs synchronous backtracking (SB), as that is described in [14], to solve the problem. Under the synchronous backtracking algorithm the first process instantiates its variables to consistent values according to the local constraints and communicates them to the second process. The latter upon reception of this partial solution, introduces to the store new constraints based on the set of values received and searches for a solution. If such a solution is found then the program terminates with success otherwise a backtrack message is passed back to the first process. The above loop continues until a solution is found.

The second version is an enhancement of the synchronous backtracking algorithm (ESB). In this algorithm the sender process communicates the value of a variable as soon as it is instantiated, i.e. at each step of the labeling phase. To achieve early pruning of inconsistent values, the sender process remains blocked after the transmission of the message, until the receiver process responds with an acceptance or rejection of the value. In order to provide such a response the receiver process introduces to the store all constraints that derive from the received value.

When all variables of the first process are instantiated an `end` message is sent to the second process which in turn searches for a solution. If such is found then the program terminates with success, otherwise it sends a `backtrack` message to the sender process and backtracks itself to the last choice point. However

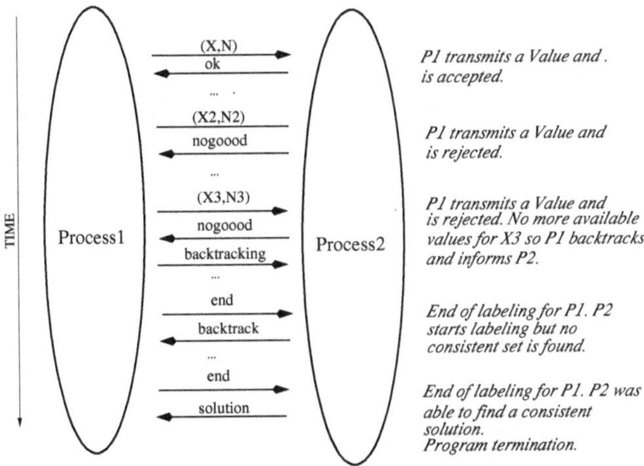

Fig. 1. Message exchange in the Multi-process version.

since the sender process might backtrack not only over the last choice point but also over previous points, the receiver has to be notified so that it can it turn remove any constraints from the store that were introduced because of the previous values transmitted. This extra synchronization is achieved by an appropriate `backtracking` message sent by the first process to the second. If for some reason no solution can be found, the first process sends a failure message to the second indicating that no valid values were possible to be found. The types of messages that are exchanged under in the ESB algorithm are listed in Table 1. Message exchange is shown in Figure 1. We have run several tests for the above versions for various number of queens from N=8 to 28. Speedups for various N compared with the single process version are shown in Figure 2.

Table 1. Types of Messages

Message	Description
`value(X)`	Transmission of a value X, to which a variable was instantiated.
`ok`	Acceptance of a value.
`nogood`	Rejection of a value.
`backtrack`	No labeling found for local variable set. Backtracking of sender process is forced.
`backtracking`	Sender process informs backtracking over a previous choice point.
`end`	The first process has finished with the assignment of values.
`solution`	Reporting that a consistent solution was found.
`failure`	No solution was found. Program termination.

As shown in the figure the multi-process versions are less efficient for a small number of queens justified by the fact that the communication overhead for these cases is comparable to the actual time of computing the solution. However as the number of queens grows the situation is reversed. The speedup obtained is justified by the fact that each process has to solve an easier problem compared to the full N queens problem.

As expected the ESB version performs significantly better that the simple synchronous version, since communicating each value as soon as it is instantiated allows early detection of inconsistencies.

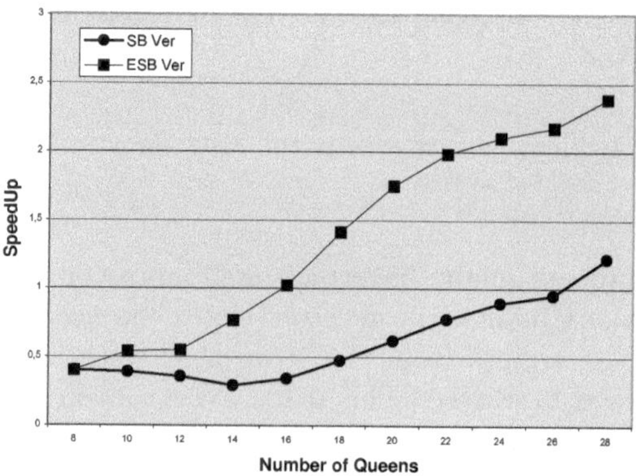

Fig. 2. Speed Up of the Multi-process versions.

6 Conclusions and Future Work

The CSPCONS language, presented in this paper, offers a suitable platform for the development of any DCSP application. Programming through the use of communicating sequential processes and constraints in a logic programming environment can successfully address the issues of easily developing applications that require agent based program distribution and communication. In such an application each agent can be an independent CSPCONS process that exchanges messages with other agents in order to achieve a global consistency.

One of the main points that we are going to concentrate on, is the implementation of a more efficient FD solver. Our plans include the implementation of either the indexical approach to constraint solving or the incorporation of new arc consistency algorithms.

We are currently investigating the implementation of other DCSP algorithms as for example those reported in [15],[4] and in [11]. Such implementation might require both further development of the constraint solver or the introduction of new programming facilities. One of the main issues that has to be addressed is to provide to the programmer the necessary primitives in order to declare which agents share variables under which constraints and propagate messages automatically. Our ambition is to develop a framework that will relieve the programmer of the burden to explicitly encode all the above and just concentrate on the program development.

Possible areas of application include distributed planning and scheduling. Our immediate plans also include the development of a distributed scheduling application for university course scheduling, that will fully test the potential of the current implementation of the language.

References

1. D. Cabeza and M.Hermenegildo. Distributed Concurrent Constraint Execution in the CIAO System. In *Proceedings of the 1995 COMPULOG-NET Workshop on Parallelism and Implementation Technologies, U. Utrecht / T.U. Madrid*, September 1995.
2. Ivan Futo. Prolog with Communicating Processes: From T-Prolog to CSR-Prolog. In D.S. Warren, editor, *Proceedings of the 10th International Conference on Logic Programming*, pages 3–17. The MIT Press, 1993.
3. Ivan Futo. A Distributed Network Prolog System. In *Proceedings of the 20th International Conference on Information Technology Interfaces, ITI 99*, pages 613–618, 1998.
4. Y. Hamadi, C. Bessière, and J. Quinqueton. Backtracking in Distributed Constraint Networks. In Henri Prade, editor, *Proceedings of the 13th European Conference on Artificial Intelligence (ECAI-98)*, pages 219–223, Chichester, August 23–28 1998. John Wiley & Sons.
5. M. Hermenegildo, F. Bueno, D. Cabeza, M. Garcia de la Banda, P. Lopez, and G. Puebla. The CIAO Multi-Dialect Compiler and System: An Experimentation Workbench for Future (C)LP Systems. pages 65–85, April 1999.

6. M. Hermenegildo, D. Cabeza, and M. Carro. Using Attributed Variables in the Implementation of Concurrent and Parallel Logic Programming Systems. In Leon Sterling, editor, *Proceedings of the 12th International Conference on Logic Programming*, pages 631–646, Cambridge, June 13–18 1995. MIT Press.
7. C. A. R. Hoare. Communicating Sequential Processes. *Communications of the ACM*, 21(8):666–677, August 1978.
8. Alan K. Mackworth. Consistency in Networks of Relations. *Artificial Intelligence*, 8(1):99–118, 1977.
9. T. Nguyen and Y. Deville. A distributed arc-consistency algorithm. *Science of Computer Programming*, 30(1–2):227–250, January 1998. Concurrent constraint programming (Venice, 1995).
10. Marius Calin Silaghi, Djamila Sam-Haroud, and Boi Faltings. Asynchronous Search with Aggregations. In *Proceedings of the 7th Conference on Artificial Intelligence (AAAI-00) and of the 12th Conference on Innovative Applications of Artificial Intelligence (IAAI-00)*, pages 917–922, Menlo Park, CA, July 30– 3 2000. AAAI Press.
11. M.C. Silaghi, D. Sam-Haroud, and B.V. Faltings. Maintaining hierachical distributed consistency. In EPFL, editor, *Proceedings of the CP2000 Workshop on Distributed Constraint Satisfaction*, Tech. Report # 00/338, 2000.
12. Bo-Ming Tong and Ho-Fung Leung. Data-parallel concurrent constraint programming. *The Journal of Logic Programming*, 35:103–150, 1998.
13. I. Vlahavas, N. Bassiliades, I. Sakellariou, M. Molina, S. Ossowski, I. Futo, Z. Pasztor, J. Szeredi, I. Velbitskiy, S. Yershov, S. Golub, and I. Netesin. System Architecture of a Distributed Expert System for the Management of a National Data Network. In Fausto Giunchiglia, editor, *Proceedings of the 8th International Conference on Artificial Intelligence: Methodology, Systems, and Applications (AIMSA-98)*, volume 1480 of *LNAI*, pages 438–451, Berlin, September 21–23 1998. Springer.
14. Makoto Yokoo, Edmund H. Durfee, Toru Ishida, and Kazuhiro Kuwabara. The Distributed Constraint Satisfaction Problem: Formalization and Algorithms. *IEEE Trans. on Knowledge and Data Engineering*, 10(5):673–685, 1998.
15. Makoto Yokoo and Katsutoshi Hirayama. Algorithms for Distributed Constraint Satisfaction: A Review. *Autonomous Agents and Multi-Agent Systems*, 3(2):185–207, June 2000.
16. Ying Zhang and Alan K. Mackworth. Parallel and Distributed Finite Constraint Satisfaction: Complexity, Algorithms and Experiments. Technical Report TR-92-30, Department of Computer Science, University of British Columbia, November 1992.

Genetic Evolution of Software Microorganisms

Themistoklis Panayiotopoulos, Harry Kalogirou, Anthony Petropoulos, and Dionisis Dimopoulos

Knowledge engineering Lab, Department of Informatics
University of Piraeus, Piraeus, 185 34, Greece
themisp@unipi.gr, {harkal,anthony,ddemo}@rainbow.cs.unipi.gr

Abstract. Genetic Algorithms have been used in many areas of Artificial Intelligence and Artificial Life. The GA approach comes from the area of Biology and uses the ideas of natural selection and Genetics.
In this paper we present the SoftGene platform consisting of a Virtual Machine as well as a number of evolutionary software microorganisms, which reside in it. Every microorganism is in fact a virtual machine program the code of which corresponds to its DNA. It tries to reproduce itself but there is a possibility of failure in this reproduction. This process, drives to a generation of a mutated copy of the initial microorganism. Certain constraints must be satisfied in order to keep a microorganism alive.

1 Introduction

What we expect from a natural living system is the ability of the organisms living in it to maintain their existence, reproduce and be able to adapt to the conditions of their environment. Using the concept of randomly mutating microinstructions we can simulate the creation and evolution of living organisms. Such systems can be considered as platforms for creating and developing organisms residing and functioning in an Artificial Life environment [1].

Genetic Algorithms have been used in many areas of Artificial Intelligence, especially when global optimization techniques are needed. The GA approach comes from the area of Biology and uses the ideas of natural selection and Genetics. We have been inspired by this approach, but we have developed a different evolutionary technique for the proposed system.

In this paper we present the SoftGene platform consisting of a Virtual Machine as well as a number of evolutionary software microorganisms, which reside in it. Every microorganism is in fact a virtual machine program the code of which corresponds to its DNA. It tries to reproduce itself but there is a possibility of failure in this reproduction. This process, drives to a generation of a mutated copy of the initial microorganism.

Certain constraints must be satisfied in order to keep a microorganism alive. As a result the virtual space is populated by cooperating or competing generations of evolving software microorganisms which try to survive as long as possible. Many interesting types of microorganisms have been created, such as very short parasitic ones, microorganisms depending on each other, etc.

I.P. Vlahavas and C.D. Spyropoulos (Eds.): SETN 2002, LNAI 2308, pp. 85–96, 2002.

The ultimate goal is to mimic a biological environment, in which these microorganisms may compete with each other for survival. In such an environment we could possibly make the microorganisms have a useful objective and using this evolutionary process to produce better solutions. This paper however focuses on the description of the environment created, leaving such applications as future work.

Similar systems to SoftGene, have been created that operate on the same principles, such as those by Ray and Sims, [2]. Ray's Tierra system, [6], is based on a very similar concept. The differences among this systems are discussed later in this paper.

2 Evolving Software Microorganisms

The whole purpose of the SoftGene system is to provide a platform on to which microorganisms constructed in software can reproduce and evolve. In this section we will discuss how a piece of software can reproduce and evolve.

Considering the aim of SoftGene, there are some characteristics that must be present in the system. The microorganisms existing in SoftGene must have a well defined life cycle, including birth, death and perhaps reproduction. The microorganisms must also live in a competitive environment, wherein some resources are limited. An important aspect of the whole system is the ability for the genetic code of those organisms to mutate, either during their life or when they reproduce. Moreover they may have additional functionalities, as well as perhaps being able to interact with one another.

The approach used to implement such an environment in SoftGene if for the microorganisms to consist of instructions that can be executed by a machine, not unlike a computer's CPU. In this context, living can be considered the execution of a microorganism's code by the machine and mutation the alteration of its code. This machine recognizes a very specific instruction set, described below.

2.1 Instructions as Genetic Code

Contrary to biological microorganisms that are identified by their DNA, the software microorganisms are identified by their sequence of instructions. These instructions act as the DNA of the software microorganism, defining and controlling its behavior. These instructions are executed on a machine thus allowing the microorganism to handle its survival operations. The instructions that are implemented in SoftGene are categorized into many categories :

First of all there are the register manipulation instructions. These instructions give to the microorganisms the ability to store and retrieve the contents of the registers. These are the "*mov register,register*" and "*reset register*" instructions.

The next category is the arithmetic instructions. These instructions handle arithmetic operations in registers. The "*neg register*" instruction reverses the sign of the value in the register. The "*inc register*" and "*dec register*" increment and decrement respectively the value of the specified register. "*shl register*" and "*shr register*" binary shifts the value in the specified register left and right by one. The "*add register,register*" adds the value of the second register to the first register.

The next major category of instructions is the execution flow control instructions. These are "*jzf*", "*jzb*", "*jbf*", "*jbb*". These instructions control the flow of execution based on whether the last arithmetic operation resulted in zero or in a positive number. There are also unconditional flow control instructions namely "*jmpf*", "*jmpb*", "*call*" and "*ret*". The jump target in all of the above instructions is not specified by an absolute nor relative address. Instead the target is a specific pattern of "*mark*" instructions in the code.

There are also stack manipulation instructions named "*push register*" and "*pop register*". These instructions push and pop the values in the specified register to and from the microorganisms stack.

Other useful instructions are "*mal*" and "*fork*". There are used from the microorganism to reserve memory space (*mal*) and later spawn a new microorganism using that allocated memory (*fork*).

The copying of genetic code is performed by using the "*puti*" instruction, which copies the contents of a specific address of the memory to another, being owned by the same microorganism.

We can get the absolute numeric address of a location in memory using the "*getadrf*" and "*getadrb*" instructions. These instructions return the address wherein exist a specified pattern of "*mark*" instructions.

2.2 Reproduction

The main operation that every microorganism has to handle is its reproduction. If the microorganism does not reproduce, as it will eventually age and die, its generation will extinct. There are some specific actions that the microorganism has to make in order to reproduce. The reproduction is not done with an instruction that will automatically create a new microorganism that is the child of the original. Instead the microorganism has to "manually" allocate (If it can) the required memory for its child, then copy its genetic material to the allocated memory and finally separate itself from the child. With this separation the child becomes an new self supported microorganism, so the mother loses the write rights on the child's memory. As we can see the reproduction code of a microorganism can be implemented in many different ways, less efficient or more efficient.

2.3 Mutation

The base of the Darwin evolution theory is mutation. Without it we can't have any change, not towards worst nor towards better. Mutation is also the base of evolution of our software microorganisms. Mutation occurs during the reproduction of the microorganisms leading to new kinds of microorganisms. The "quality" of the mutated generations will be evaluated by natural selection. The environment should be equipped with mutation mechanisms, applied on microorganisms, for evolution to take place.

With software organisms we chose to have two different mutation methods. We call the first one *soft mutation*. Soft mutation is applied onto a byte during any access. We call the second one just *mutation*. This one is applied any time a byte is written in memory. The frequency of mutations occurrence is adjusted by per mutation method factors. As said before, soft mutation is applied onto a byte during any access. Soft mutation produces a value varying slightly from the old one. The variance depends on the value of the soft mutation's factor, and produces either increase or decrease. Therefore, soft mutation does not create logical faults on a microorganism, but arithmetic ones. Hard mutation occurs when data are written in memory. Any time a write operation in memory is performed, hard mutation might take place. Since reproduction is a write-based process, hard mutation is frequent during the reproduction procedure. Thus, it is very likely for descendants to be different from their ancestor. Moreover, since hard mutation affects descendant's op-codes, it is possible that logical faults will have been produced.

Each time a microorganism is mutated, a new generation is born. This new generation may have the same microorganism size or not and it is called a descendant generation. Descendants are automatically registered as new microorganisms.

2.4 Microorganism Survival and Extinction

All microorganisms share some resources of the machine, such as memory and execution time. In order for them to be able to reproduce, thus raising the resources requirements there has to be a mechanism to kill an entity. Once an entity is killed, all resources that it held up are freed and its execution stops. Through selective entity extinction, we can implement an effective evolution process, wherein entities that fit certain criteria are developed.

Microorganism' s chance of survival is dependent on how well each entity fares against some criteria and restrictions imposed by the machine, namely instruction execution correctness and age, which will be described below.

Instruction execution of an entity's code may not be flawless. For some instructions, there are conditions in which their execution will fail (like pushing a variable on a stack that is already full). This failure does not result in the entity's termination. Instead, the error will be recorded and the measure of the entity's "correctness" will be adjusted accordingly. Frequent faults include: trying to allocate more memory than available, performing an operation on an uninitialized register, writing in memory blocks that the microorganism do not own etc.

Simulating natural microorganisms, the age of an entity is a major factor that determines its chance of survival. Younger entities have a much greater probability to survive than older ones.

On regular intervals, the entities must be checked to decide whether they should be terminated or not. The probability to terminate an entity at a given time is dependent on the two factors detailed above. Through this process we keep microorganisms that work well, while giving newer ones the chance to develop their potential.

3 The SoftGene System

The SoftGene platform implements all the characteristics described previously using three separate components: The Virtual Machine which is the main component managing the execution of the various entities, the monitoring client, which connects to the Virtual Machine via the network providing most of the human interaction with it, and the Assembler / Disassembler that can convert entities from an executable by the Virtual Machine to human readable code and vice versa.

3.1 The Virtual Machine

The virtual machine consists of the following units, the instruction interpreter, the scheduler, the memory manager and the controller along with the networking subsystem. At Fig. 1 we can see a diagram describing visually the units that make up the virtual machine along with how they cooperate.

The *Scheduler* is responsible for assigning execution time to microorganisms that exist in SoftGene. It chooses the microorganism that will be executed next, and passes it to the Instruction interpreter. Subsequently, the *Instruction Interpreter* executes the microorganism's instructions until the time slice, that the scheduler chooses for this microorganism, is exhausted. Finally, the *Scheduler* decides which will be the next microorganism to profit execution time and makes the context switch.

The main differences of the SoftGene virtual machine against regular virtual machines have their roots to the architecture specialties of the *Instruction Interpreter*. The main difference of this implementation is that all operations have some sort of slackness. In a regular instruction interpreter, all operations are strictly defined and the results are always predictable.

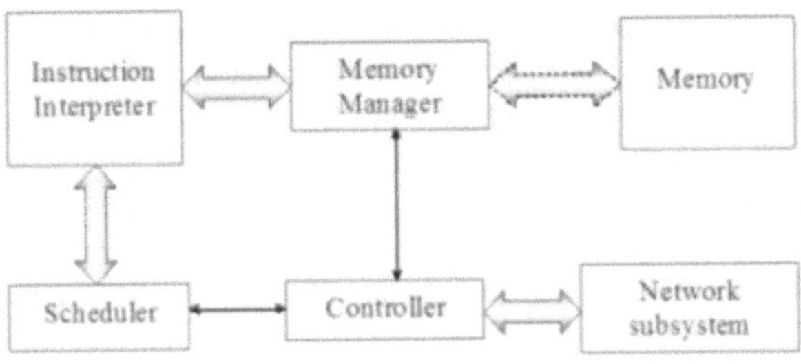

Fig. 1. The VM diagram

In SoftGene, however, this is not the case. Errors can happen during the execution. For example, the transfer of a byte from one memory location to another does not guarantee the correct transfer of the byte. This is the source of mutation in SoftGene.

The interpreter's arithmetic unit architecture is *register based.* This is the architecture mostly used in hardware processors. With this architecture, the instruction interpreter contains a number of registers on which the instructions operate. This is contrary to most virtual machines which are *stack based* like the well known *Java Virtual Machine* [8].

The *Memory manager* is responsible for managing the memory that is available to the entities. It provides facilities to the *Instruction interpreter* to allocate and release memory.

All the units of the virtual machine are communicating with the *Controller*, which is responsible for abstracting the inner workings of the virtual machine and report them to the monitoring client through the network. The commands that the client sends over the network are interpreted to appropriate commands and sent towards the virtual machine units. This way the client can control the simulation, beyond just monitoring it.

The Virtual Machine is a console application written in C. Upon startup, it listens to a network port, waiting for a connection from a monitoring client, whereby it accepts commands and can communicate with the user. Some commands and parameters can be set using the command line of the Virtual Machine, or the monitoring client. The execution of entities will begin when an entity is imported, either using the *add_entity* command from the command line or using the monitoring client.

The Virtual Machine can be asked by the monitoring client to perform some operations, using a custom network protocol. Some of these operations are sending an entity's code or importing a new entity, sending a memory map describing the entities' distribution, pausing and resuming execution as well as changing configuration parameters (like mutation probabilities).

3.2 The Monitoring Client

In order to monitor a SoftGene virtual machine we created the *SoftGene monitor.* This monitor connects to a given SoftGene virtual machine. It gives us the ability to inspect the whole system and control the whole simulation process.

The monitoring client is a graphical application written in Java that communicates with the Virtual Machine via the network. Upon connecting to the Virtual Machine, the monitoring client can retrieve and display information concerning the entities' execution, change the Virtual Machine configuration on the fly, or import new entities for execution.

The monitoring client is a comprehensive tool that can represent various aspects of the execution state of the Virtual Machine. The main visualization tool available is a memory map representing all entities as they are distributed in the Virtual Machine memory, colored according to their generation or size. Moreover, interesting results can be extracted by the histogram representation of the entities' population according to their sizes. Both these views are updated close to real time (according to network speed and client processing power). An instance of the monitoring client in action can be seen in Fig. 2.

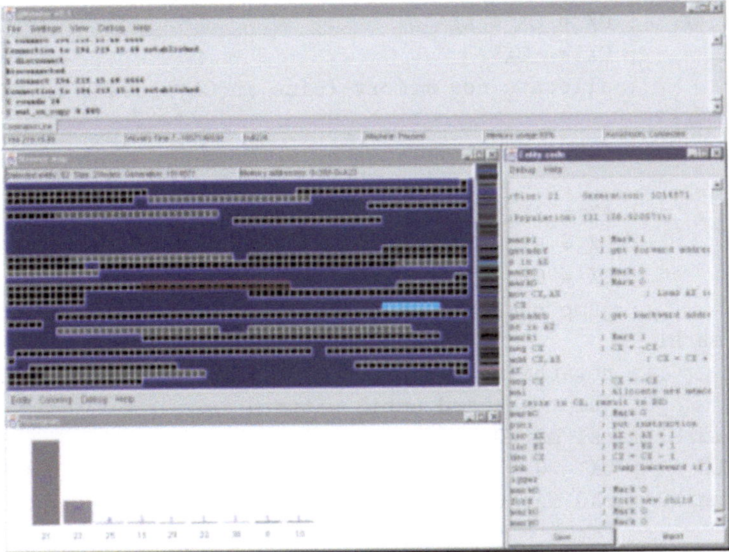

Fig. 2. The monitoring client

3.3 Assembler / Disassembler

Using the SoftGene Assembler, a console application written in C, a user can create his own entities to be run in the Virtual Machine, as well as reviewing binary entities exported by the VM by other means.

4 An Illustrative Example

After bringing up the SoftGene VM, and importing a sample entity (we call it Adam), we are able to watch the evolution procedure through the *gClient* application. Adam's program is illustrated on the frame below.

```
;Code size : 38

mark1 mark1 mark1 mark0
getadrf      ; get forward address in AX
mark0 mark0 mark0
```

```
mov BX,AX    ; Load AX in BX
mov CX,AX    ; Load AX in CX
getadrb      ; get backward address in AX
mark1 mark1 mark1
neg CX       ; CX = -CX
add CX,AX    ; CX = CX + AX
neg CX       ; CX = -CX
mal          ; allocate new memory (size in CX, result in BX)
mark0 mark1
puti         ; put

inc AX       ; AX = AX + 1
inc BX       ; BX = BX + 1
dec CX       ; CX = CX - 1
jbb          ; jump backward if bigger
mark0 mark1
fork         ; new child
jmpb         ; jump backward until pattern
mark1 mark1 mark1 mark0
reset CX     ; CX = 0
mark1 mark0 mark0 mark0
```

Adam's main purpose of existence is to be propagated. Adam is sized 38 bytes in SoftGene machine code. Once the time is running, the evolution procedure takes place. Its descendants may vary in size.

At first, we start the SoftGene virtual machine using the default values. The soft mutation limit is set to 2. Mutation on access and mutation on copy are set to 0.0001 (0.01% probability to mutate on every access) and 0.001 (0.1% probability to mutate on every copy instruction) respectively.

We can import entities to the SoftGene virtual machine from the console, either from the local one or the one that the SoftGene client is equipped with. In order to import Adam, we perform an *add_entity multp.obj* command. After importing Adam, the population chart (snapshot 1) assures us that a new entity is imported. Upon the commencement of execution the SoftGene virtual machine sequentially passes control from one microorganism to another. Observing the very first steps of the virtual machine, we can watch Adam being divided (snapshot 2).

In short time, the population has grown enough, and some different sized descendants have appeared (snapshot 3). The evolution mechanism has provided us with smaller entities, having the same purpose as Adam. Till now, they are faulty enough for not being able to survive. This is the reason why Adam is still the dominating microorganism.

After some time, a new microorganism, sized 30 bytes has dominated (snapshot 4). The latter was better than the other microorganisms, and therefore it overstepped them. Subsequently, a lighter and probably less faulty microorganism, sized 27 bytes, starts to show good potential to overcome it. Its population grows fast while the dominating one goes weak. It is some seconds later that the new microorganism overtakes the other generations in population (snapshot 5).

Later, the situation stabilizes itself after a microorganism, sized 21 bytes in SoftGene machine code, and takes the lead (snapshot 6). The code of the prevalent microorganism is shown below.

```
;Size: 21    Generation: 1014571
;Population: 132 (58.928571%)

mark1         ; Mark 1
getadrf       ; get forward address in AX
mark0 mark0
mov CX,AX     ; Load AX in CX
getadrb       ; get backward address in AX
mark1         ; Mark 1
neg CX        ; CX = -CX
add CX,AX     ; CX = CX + AX
neg CX        ; CX = -CX
mal           ; allocate new memory (size in CX, result in BX)
mark0         ; Mark 0
puti          ; put instruction
inc AX        ; AX = AX + 1
inc BX        ; BX = BX + 1
dec CX        ; CX = CX - 1
jbb           ; jump backward if bigger
mark0         ; Mark 0
fork          ; fork new child
mark0 mark0
```

We can see that this smaller microorganism doesn't include the op-codes referencing BX in the first part of Adam. Moreover, some not necessary mark instructions have been removed by the evolution procedure.

Now that we have run an example, we are able to perform an experiment. It is interesting to have a look on the way microorganisms react, in case of an environmental change. We will try to increase the mutation factor that refers to the copy procedure of microorganisms. Suppose that we have the situation illustrated on snapshot 7, and we set the mutation factor on copy to 0.005, five times the original one. The environment causes a higher rate of mutations. As shown in snapshot 8, the global population decreases. The new born microorganisms suffer from mutation, and thus they are much faulty. This leads to decimation on the global population. Finally, no microorganism survives and the SoftGene virtual machine remains inactive.

Another interesting part is that among microorganisms, there had been some too small in size, which seems not to work properly. Their op-codes do not form the appropriate reproduction algorithm. Instead, they perform an "illegal" jump, according to a pattern, that it is only matched on a neighbor's op-code sequence. Their instruction pointer moves either on another microorganism, either on "lost" bytes (bytes that had been in use by a dead microorganism and are not cleared, just disallocated). These microorganisms, act as parasites, using foreign code to reproduce themselves.

This short example is probably unable to illustrate the full procedure, but it has illustrated some of its principles. The SoftGene virtual machine may continue running until someone interrupts it. Until then, even better microorganisms may have appeared.

Snapshot 1. Adam is imported to the SoftGene virtual machine

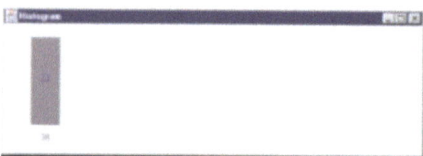

Snapshot 2. The virtual machine has started executing Adam. Adam produces children, and its children, children of their own

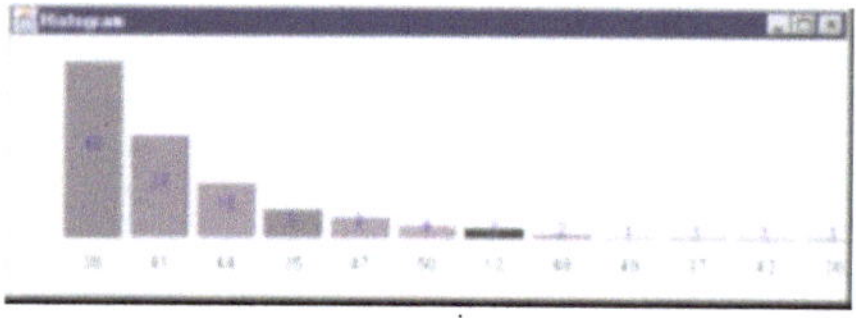

Snapshot 3. Other microorganisms have appeared. They vary in size, population, faultiness but not in purpose.

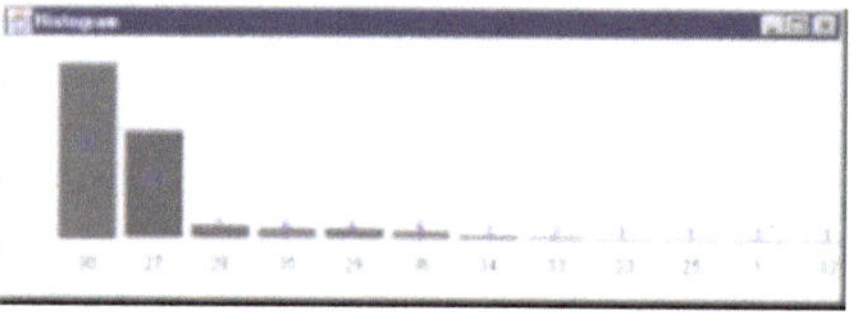

Snapshot 4. The microorganism sized 30 bytes is the dominating one. The one that is sized 27 bytes, tend to reach the dominating one in population.

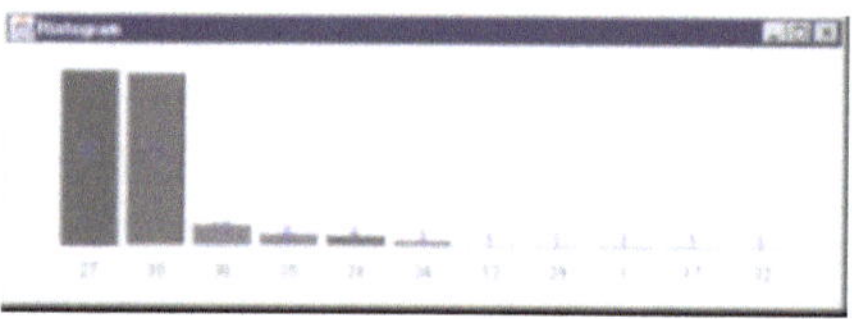

Snapshot 5. Some time later, the forthcoming microorganism, is set to the top.

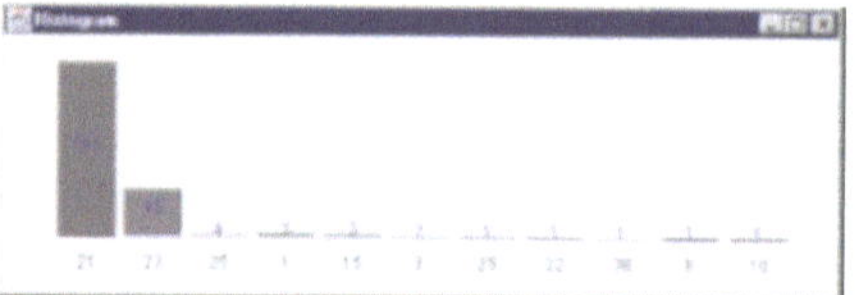

Snapshot 6. The current dominating microorganism is the one that is sized 21 bytes. This one is adequately optimized.

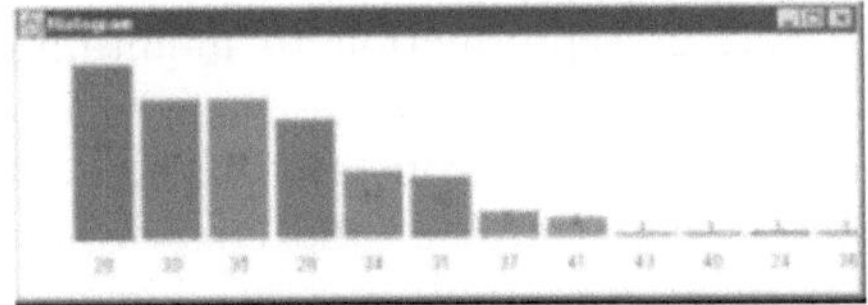

Snapshot 7. Just before tuning the hard mutation factor (on copy).

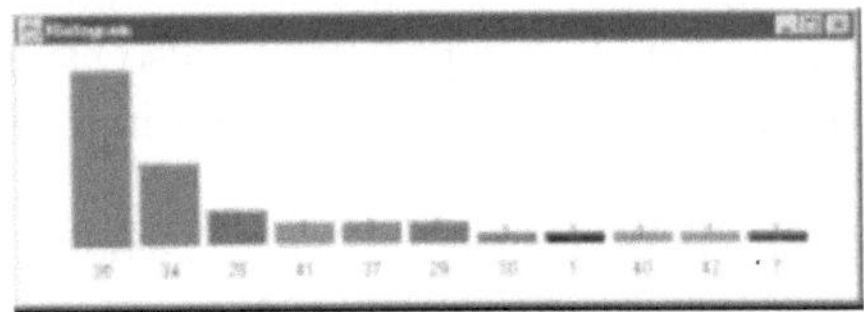

Snapshot 8. Microorganisms are copied with high mutation ratio. Thus, they are faulty enough for not being able to be reproduced. The global population shrinks.

5 Conclusions

SoftGene can be considered as another effort to simulate a biological living environment in a computer simulation. Microorganisms are replaced with snippets of code being executed in a Virtual Machine, sharing the same memory resources. Using natural selection as an evolution technique we are able to create evolving entities that adapt to the requirements and restrictions imposed by the Virtual Machine.

This process produces some interesting results. First of all, since an entity consisting of few instructions is prone to run faster than a bigger one, since it has to copy itself instruction-by-instruction, small entities are favored by the Virtual Machine. This leads ultimately to small entities dominating this virtual environment, most of them consisting of code that looks optimized by a human.

Moreover, as a side effect, very small programs were created that live in the expense of others, usually attaching themselves to them and executing part of their code. On other cases, some entities cooperatively execute its other's code, and being unable to exist without each other.

By changing system parameters during the simulation, we can observe how the microorganisms living in SoftGene adapt to their environment. If we increase the probability of mutation drastically, the system gets unstable, producing newer generations more rapidly and perhaps killing the whole system. Under conditions of high probability of soft mutation, entities that double-check the results of their most crucial parts are favored and therefore survive.

As stated in the introduction similar systems to SoftGene, have been created that operate on the same principles. Some of the differences found between them are the way entities are selected for termination as well as a more dynamic mutation environment.

Tierra [6] implements a queue (called reaper queue) wherein all entities reside and move towards the start or the end according to how correctly they execute. Once a certain memory limit is hit entities at the top of the queue get terminated. SoftGene's method is different, ensuring that each entity has a finite lifespan whether correct or not. We depend on correct reproduction to maintain the population of a generation.

Moreover, mutation in the SoftGene system is not constant through time. The probabilities for mutation changes periodically through time, creating stable and unstable periods. During unstable periods, mutation rates are higher and many varied entities are created, which may prove to be useful or not, while during stable periods entities are given a chance to reproduce more smoothly, thus increasing their numbers. During that period the population is also cleaned from faulty mutated entities. Such a method proves to be more efficient in rapidly deploying interesting entities.

However the Tierra system has some interesting features, such as being effectively distributed in a network environment as well experimenting with multicellular organisms.

The Sims' system [7], though similar in concept, follows a much different approach. Sim uses similar evolutionary methods as SoftGene to create the body of rivalling entities that try to capture an object in 3D space. Selection between them takes place after direct confrontation of two entities at a time and, in that respect, differs from SoftGene's method of selection.

SoftGene is still a long way from successfully simulating a convincing biological environment. Nevertheless it is interesting to note that similar behavior to that of a biological system can be found in a system like SoftGene. Further improvements can be applied to the SoftGene system such as support for multicellular organisms and more complex environments. Also the platform can move towards a more practically interesting direction, rather than the scientific one, by making the microorganisms do something useful, like finding the solution to a practical problem.

References

1. Chr. Adami. *Introduction to Artificial Life.* Springer-Verlag, 1998.
2. R. A. Brooks. Steps torwards living machines. *ER 2001*, LNCS 2217:72–93, 2001.
3. A. D. Channon. Three evolvability requirements for open-ended evolution. In Carlo C. Maley and Eilis Boudreau, editors, *Artificial Life VII Workshop Proceedings*, pages 39–40, 2000.
4. J. R. Koza. *Genetic Programming: On the Programming of Computers by Means of Natural Selection.* MIT Press, 1992.
5. R. Morris. *Artificial Worlds : Computers, Complexity, and the Riddle of Life.* Perseus Press, 1999.
6. Th. S. Ray. An approch to the synthesis of life. *Proceedings of Artificial Life II*, pages 371–408, 1990.
7. K. Sims. Evolving 3d morphology and behavior by competition. *Artificial Life IV : Proceedings of the Fourth International Workshop on the Synthesis and Simulation of Living Systems*, pages 28–99, 1994.
8. Frank Yellin, Tim Lindholm. *The Java Virtual Machine Specification.* Addison-Wesley Publishing Company, 1999.

A Probabilistic Approach to Robust Execution of Temporal Plans with Uncertainty

Ioannis Tsamardinos

Department of Biomedical Informatics, Vanderbilt University,
Eskind Biomedical Library, Room 444,
2209 Galrand Ave, Nashville, TN 37232-8340,
USA
ioannis.tsamardinos@vanderbilt.edu

Abstract. In Temporal Planning a typical assumption is that the agent controls the execution time of all events such as starting and ending actions. In real domains however, this assumption is commonly violated and certain events are beyond the direct control of the plan's executive. Previous work on reasoning with uncontrollable events (Simple Temporal Problem with Uncertainty) assumes that we can bound the occurrence of each uncontrollable within a time interval. In principle however, there is no such bounding interval since there is always a non-zero probability the event will occur outside the bounds. Here we develop a new more general formalism called the Probabilistic Simple Temporal Problem (PSTP) following a probabilistic approach. We present a method for scheduling a PSTP maximizing the probability of correct execution. Subsequently, we use this method to solve the problem of finding an optimal execution strategy, i.e. a dynamic schedule where scheduling decisions can be made on-line.

1 Introduction

Planning is a major area of Artificial Intelligence researching the following problem: given a description of available actions and desired goals, discover a course of action that achieves the goals. This is a notoriously hard problem in general and Classical Planning [1] was developed as a set of assumptions, restrictions, formalisms, and representations to solve it. Classical planning assumes actions are instantaneous and thus there is no need to represent time explicitly. Temporal Planning is the effort of enriching Classical Planning with an explicit representation of time and dealing with durative actions and temporal constraints. Recently, there is a revived interest in temporal planners [2, 3], because of the successes in new, interesting, and real-world situated domains (e.g. Remote Agent [2]). A temporal planning competition in the next Artificial Intelligence Planning and Scheduling conference has also been announced.

Temporal planners are typically based on temporal reasoning formalisms such as the Simple Temporal Problem (STP) [4]. Most often, a planning action A is represented in an STP with two temporal variables *start(A)* and *end(A)* corresponding to the instantaneous events of starting and ending A respectively. Then, constraints on the variables can be defined. The STP and other related formalisms are able to answer

I.P. Vlahavas and C.D. Spyropoulos (Eds.): SETN 2002, LNAI 2308, pp. 97–108, 2002.

the question whether a set of constraints is consistent. *Consistency* is defined as the existence of an assignment to the temporal variables that respects the constraints.

Even though the STP allows the construction of temporal planners that significantly extend Classical Planning's capabilities, it still makes the unrealistic assumption that all events are controllable, i.e. under the direct control of the executing agent, and thus the latter can assign any time it desires to the variables in order to execute the plan in a way that respects all the constraints. In the real world however, certain events are *uncontrollable*; it is Nature[1] that determines their exact timing. For example, the event corresponding to *end(A)*, where *A* is the action of driving a truck from one place to another is uncontrollable. The planning agent can set the time for *start(A)*, i.e. the time the truck will leave its origin, but it is traffic conditions that determine the exact time assigned to *end(A)*, i.e. the time the truck will arrive to its destination.

The first formalism that explicitly models uncontrollable events is the STPU (STP with Uncertainty) [5]. In an STPU, the uncontrollable events are presumed to occur within certain bounds. A new concept in place of consistency is introduced; that of *controllability*. In particular, if there is an assignment to the controllables that respects the constraints no matter what values (within the bounds) Nature selects for the uncontrollables, the STPU is *strongly consistent* (two other related concepts, *dynamic* and *weak controllability* are also defined for STPUs).

The STPU formalism can be used to model the uncertainty of the timing of events in temporal plans; nevertheless, it has certain serious drawbacks. The first is that *in principle there are no such bounds*: there is always a non-zero probability that exogenous factors will cause an event to occur some time outside the bounds. The second problem is that *there is no principled way of selecting the bounds according to some optimality criterion*. The person who encodes the domain is responsible for the difficult task of choosing reasonable approximate bounds for such constraints. If these bounds are loose, Nature will likely respect them, but it will be less probable that the STPU will be strongly consistent. In the latter case, STPU algorithms provide no help as to how to execute the plan. If, on the other hand, the bounds are too tight, it might be easier to find assignments that respect the constraints no matter the values of the uncontrollables, yet less likely for Nature to respect the defined bounds.

In this paper, we take a new and more general, probabilistic approach to the problem of executing temporal plans with uncertainty in which we model the uncontrollable events using random variables following conditional probability distributions. Our approach does not have the above two STPU drawbacks. It also subsumes STPUs since each STPU uncontrollable variable constrained to occur within a lower and upper bound is equivalent in our approach with a random variable following a uniform distribution within these bounds.

To represent such probabilistic information, we develop a new temporal reasoning formalism that we call *Probabilistic Simple Temporal Problem* (PSTP). In STPUs we seek for an assignment to the controllables that respects the constraints in all cases, assuming bounds on the contingent links. The problem in PSTPs is, instead, to find the assignment that *maximizes the probability* that Nature will select values that will respect all constraints. We subsequently show how to solve this optimization problem for the class of PSTPs in which the probability distributions are time-invariant, there are no constraints between two uncontrollable events, and the probability distributions

[1] By Nature we will call all exogenous factors outside the agent's control.

are continuous. The new formalism can be used to robustly execute temporal plans with uncontrollable events. We also present an algorithm for dynamically executing a temporal plan while maximizing our chances of executing it while respecting the constraints.

The structure of the paper is as follows: Section 2 presents the necessary background information; Section 3 defines the PSTP while Section 4 solves the problem of maximizing the probability of successful execution when committing to a specific schedule. Section 5 deals with the problem of executing PSTPs and dynamically deciding the execution time of the controllable events. Sections 6 and 7 provide with a discussion and conclusion to the paper.

2 Background

Definition 1: A *Simple Temporal Problem* (STP) is a tuple $<V, E>$, where V is a set of temporal variables (also called nodes, time-points, and events) and E a set of constraints of the form $l \leq x - y \leq u$, where $x, y \in V$ and $l, u \in \Re$. A *Simple Temporal Problem with Uncertainty* (STPU) is a tuple $<V, E, C>$ where V, E are defined as in the STP case, and C is a set of contingent constraints of the form $l \leq x - y \leq u, x, y \in V$ where x is an uncontrollable variable. The semantics of contingent constraints is that Nature will select a time for x in the interval $[y+l, y+u]$.

Because STPs and STPUs contain only binary constraints (i.e. involving only two variables) we can represent them with graphs where the nodes correspond to the variables and the edges correspond to the constraints. To be able to express unary constraints of the form $l \leq x \leq u$ we define a new variable TR (time reference) that is associated with an arbitrary point in time that is considered the time zero. Then, unary constraints $l \leq x \leq u$ are expressed as binary constraints $l \leq x - TR \leq u$. The graph of an example STP that expresses a simple plan to complete a surgical operation is shown in Fig. 1 (a). The operation will last between 20' to 35' minutes and we would like to exit the operating room at most 5' late for the next operation or at most 10' early. The next operation is set to take place any time between 8:00 and 9:00 in the morning.

The set of time-points V is the set {*TR, Operation-Start, Operation-End, Next-Operation-Start*} with obvious semantics that we will abbreviate as {*TR, OS, OE, NOS*}. The set of constraints E corresponds to the set of edges; each edge from y to x is annotated with an interval $[l, u]$ and expresses the constraint $l \leq x - y \leq u$. E.g. the edge from OS to OE annotated with the interval $[20', 35']$ expresses the constraint $20' \leq OE - OS \leq 35'$ that can be read as "OE follows OS by at least $20'$ minutes and at most $35'$ minutes". Similarly, the edge form OE to NOS annotated with the interval [-5',10'] corresponds to the constraint $-5' \leq NOS - OE \leq 10$, i.e. the fact that we finish the first operation at most 5' late and at most 10' early. An STP is *consistent* if there is an assignment to the variables that respects the constraints. The example of Fig. 1 (a) is consistent since the assignment $\{TR \leftarrow 0, OS \leftarrow 7{:}30, OE \leftarrow 8{:}00, NOS \leftarrow 8{:}00\}$ satisfies all constraints. There are a number of polynomial time algorithms that determines consistency in STPs [6].

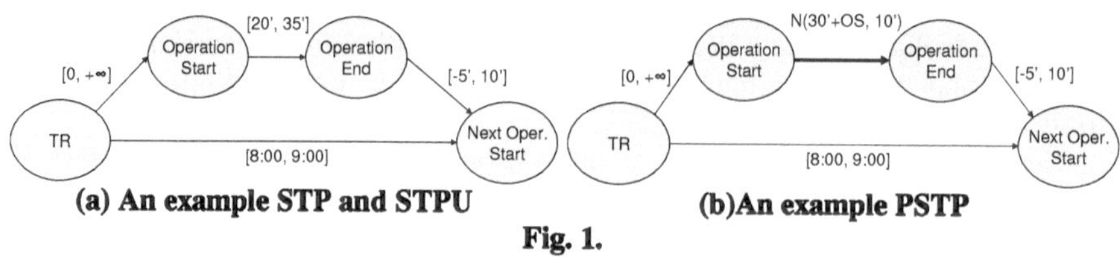

(a) An example STP and STPU **(b)An example PSTP**

Fig. 1.

As already mentioned, STPs do not explicitly distinguish between controllable and uncontrollable variables. In the above example, *OE* is an uncontrollable variable since the doctor cannot predict or determine the exact moment the operation will end. Thus consistency does not guarantee correct execution. The STPU performs this distinction by defining contingent constraints. The graph of Fig. 1 (a) can be thought of as expressing an STPU if we define that $\{20' \leq OE - NOS \leq 35'\}$ to be a contingent constraint.

The question that arises is whether it is possible to execute such an STPU in a way that respects the constraints in which case we will call the STPU *controllable*. We distinguish the following cases: If there is a single assignment that respects the constraints no matter when the uncontrollables occur then the STPU is *strongly controllable*. In this case we can schedule the controllables without any knowledge about the uncontrollables. A different case is when it is possible to schedule the controllables if we are given full knowledge about the times of uncontrollables. Then the STPU is *weakly controllable*. Finally, if it is possible to schedule the controllables dynamically (on-line) by using information of only the uncontrollables observed thus far, then the STPU is *dynamically controllable*. Strong controllability is polynomial, while weak controllability is co-NP-complete [7]. A recent important result is that dynamic controllability can be determined in polynomial time [5].

The STPU of Fig. 1 (a) is strongly consistent because the assignment $\{TR \leftarrow 0, OS \leftarrow 7{:}30, NOS \leftarrow 8{:}00\}$ respects the constraints no matter when *OE* occurs. To see this take the extreme situations for *OE*: if we finish after only *20'*, time will be *7:50,* which is no more than *10'* early. If we finish after *35'*, then we will be done at 8:05, which is no more than 5' late. Notice however, that if the bounds on the contingent link were not *[20', 35']* but looser, e.g. *[10', 40']*, then the STPU would not be strongly controllable. In this case, a controllability-checking algorithm would only return a "no" answer without any further information as to how to execute the STPU. In addition, there is no principled way to select the bounds *[20', 35']* since in general there is always a non-zero probability a value outside these bounds will be selected by Nature. We now define the PSTP that deals with these problems by employing a probabilistic representation.

3 The Probabilistic Simple Temporal Problem

Definition 2: A *Probabilistic Simple Temporal Problem* (PSTP) is a tuple $<V_1, V_2, E, S, Pa>$ where:

V_1 is a set of controllable variables (interchangeably also called events, nodes, and time-points) each with domain the set of reals $\Re$

V_2 is a set of uncontrollable random variables each with domain the set of reals $\Re$

E a set of constraints of the form $x - y \leq b_{yx}$ where $x, y \in V_1 \cup V_2$ and $b_{yx} \in \Re \cup \{-\infty, +\infty\}$

Pa a function $V_2 \rightarrow V_1$ providing for each uncontrollable x, its parent $Pa(x)=y \in V_1$

S a set of conditional probability density functions (pdf) $p(x \,/\, Pa(x) = t)$ for each $x \in V_2$

Notice that the constraints in a PSTP have the form $x - y \leq b_{yx}$ instead of $l \leq x - y \leq u$ as in the STP/STPU case. However, the two definitions are equivalent since we can represent the latter with the former and vice versa: $(l \leq x - y \leq u) \Leftrightarrow (x - y \leq u) \wedge (y - x \leq -l)$. We preferred the definition using a single inequality because it is more convenient for algebraic manipulations. Also notice that each *pdf* p in a PSTP defines a corresponding cumulative probability function (*cdf*) P.

An example PSTP is shown in Fig. 1 (b) where the same plan as in the STP of is depicted. The set of controllable variables V_1 is the set $\{TR, OS, NOS\}$ while the set of uncontrollable variables V_2 is the set $\{OE\}$. The pdf for the only uncontrollable event OE is shown with the bold edge in the figure denoting that the parent of OE is OS ($Pa(OE)=OS$) and that $p(OE \mid OS) = N(OS+30', 10')$, where $N(\mu, \sigma)$ is a Gaussian (normal) density function with mean μ and standard deviation σ. In other words, if we start operating at some time OS, we expect to finish, on average, in 30 minutes. The constraints E correspond to the non-bold edges in the figure. Notice that, even though it is the end of actions that are uncontrollable events in the example, this is not a general restriction of PSTPs and any event can be defined uncontrollable.

The problem now becomes *executing a PSTP so that the probability that all constraints are satisfied is maximized.* Similar to the STPU case the answer to this problem depends on the assumptions we make regarding our knowledge about the uncontrollable variables. We distinguish between two cases:

- The controllables have to be pre-scheduled (off-line) before execution begins, i.e. at scheduling time we have no knowledge about the uncontrollables during execution. This is the case for example, if the scheduling algorithm is not part of the executive of the plan. We will call this problem the *Static Scheduling Optimization Problem* and it corresponds to finding a *strong execution strategy* in STPUs.
- We schedule the controllables dynamically (on-line) using information about the uncontrollables that have already been observed and the information that some have not been observed yet. This is the most typical case in planning and corresponds to finding a *dynamic execution strategy* in STPUs. We will call it *Dynamic Scheduling Optimization Problem.*

The above two cases describe two optimization problems that arise when executing a temporal plan represented as a PSTP. We now turn our focus to the static scheduling optimization problem.

4 Static Scheduling Optimization

Let us denote with *P(Success/T)* the probability that all constraints will be satisfied during execution if the controllables are executed according to schedule *T*. Then, the static optimization problem can be cast as the following mathematical program:

maximize P(Success/T),

subject to:

$$y - z \leq b_{zy},\ y,z \in V_1,\ b_{zy} \in \Re$$

We will see that it is actually easier to maximize the logarithm of the objective function. Later in this section we derive an analytical expression for log*P(Success/T)* under certain assumptions about the PSTP, from which it becomes obvious that log*P(Success/T)* is not linear. Therefore, the optimization problem is a non-linear constrained optimization problem with linear constraints. There are several methods for solving such problems in the literature and can be broadly categorized in terms of the derivative information, i.e. whether it is available or not. If it is not available then only function evaluations can be used for finding an optimum. If the derivative is available then a search can be performed in the direction of the steepest ascent ∇*P(Success/T)* (gradient ascent). Using the gradient is more efficient in general when the derivative is continuous. With constrained optimization one has to pay attention to the constraints so that search remains in the feasible region during gradient ascent.

Later in this section we provide analytical expressions for both the function and the derivative. One can then use standard optimization solvers such as the one included with the software package MATLAB; the latter uses a version of the Sequential Quadratic Programming (SQP) described in [8]. Most of these methods however, do not guarantee finding the global optimum and only discover local optima.

In order to be able to derive analytical expression and use the SQP method we make the following *assumptions*:

1. All pdf *p(x/Pa(x)=t)* are time-invariant, meaning that their shape does not depend on the particular value *t* of *Pa(x)* (the value of *Pa(x)* may only translate them on the *x*-axis). Thus, there is a pdf *p'(x)* for which *p(x/Pa(x)=t)=p'(x+t)*. If *P* and *P'* are the cdf corresponding to the pdf *p* and *p'* respectively, then $P(x \leq b \mid Pa(x)=t) = P'(x \leq b\text{-}t)$. Notice that the pdf *N(30'+LH, '10)* of Fig. 1 (b) satisfies this assumption. The shape of the density function does not depend on the exact value of *OS*: we will finish the operation in half an hour, on average, no matter when we start operating.
2. There are no constraints among two variables in V_2, i.e. there are no constraints $l \leq x - y \leq u$ where $x, y \in V_2$.
3. The pdf are continuous.

Let us first derive *P(Success/T)* for the case when there is a single uncontrollable variable x in V_2. Variables y_i will denote the controllables in V_1.

$$P(Success \mid T) = P(\wedge_{ij} z_i - z_j \leq b_{z_j z_i} \mid T), z_i, z_j \in V_1 \cup V_2 \quad \textbf{(1)}$$

$$= P((\wedge_j y_j - x \leq b_{xy_j})(\wedge_i x - y_i \leq b_{y_i x})(\wedge_{ij} y_i - y_j \leq b_{y_j y_i}) \mid T)$$

The equation above means that the probability of *Success* given a schedule *T* is the probability that all the constraints of the form $x - y \leq b$ are satisfied, all the constraints of the form $y - x \leq b$ are satisfied, *and* all the constraints $y_i - y_j \leq b$ between the controllables are satisfied. Since we perform a search in the space of feasible schedules T, all constraints among the controllables are satisfied and so the above equation becomes:

$$P(Success \mid T) = P((\bigwedge_j y_j - x \leq b_{xy_j})(\bigwedge_i x - y_i \leq b_{y_i x}) \mid T) \tag{2}$$

which can be simplified to:

$$\begin{aligned} P(Success \mid T) &= P((\bigwedge_j y_j - b_{xy_j} \leq x)(\bigwedge_i x \leq y_i + b_{y_i x}) \mid T) \\ &= P(\max_j (y_j - b_{xy_j}) \leq x \wedge x \leq \min_i (y_i + b_{y_i x}) \mid T) \\ &= P(L_T(x) \leq x \leq U_T(x) \mid T) \end{aligned} \tag{3}$$

where $U_T(x) = \min_i (y_i + b_{y_i x})$ and $L_T(x) = \max_j (y_j - b_{xy_j})$ for the given schedule T. When there are more than one uncontrollables x_i then the above equation becomes:

$$P(Success \mid T) = P(\bigwedge_i L_T(x_i) \leq x_i \leq U_T(x_i) \mid T) \tag{4}$$

Note that (i) the random variables x_i are independent of each other (their probability distribution only depends on the value of their parent) and (ii) each conjunction, by assumption (2) contains only one random variable (i.e. it can never be the case that an uncontrollable x_i may appear in $U(x_j)$ or $L(x_j)$). So, the probability of the conjunction of the constraints being satisfied is the product of the probabilities each one of them being satisfied. Using the above facts and maximizing the logarithm of the probability instead we get:

$$\boxed{\log P(Success \mid T) = \log P(\bigwedge_i L(x_i) \leq x_i \leq U(x_i) \mid T) =} \tag{5}$$

$$\boxed{\begin{aligned} &= \log \prod_i P(L_T(x_i) \leq x_i \leq U_T(x_i) \mid T) = \sum_i \log P(L_T(x_i) \leq x_i \leq U_T(x_i) \mid T) = \\ &\sum_i \log \{P(x_i \leq U_T(x_i) \mid T) - P_T(x_i \leq L(x_i) \mid T)\} \end{aligned}}$$

Where:

$$P(x_i \leq U(x_i) \mid T) - P(x_i \leq L(x_i) \mid T) = \int_{L(x_i)}^{U(x_i)} p(x_i) dx_i \tag{6}$$

Notice that the value of the integral is easily computable for most pdf in the literature. For example, most introductory statistics textbooks contain tables of the function $\Phi(t)$

which is the probability $P(x_i \leq t)$ when x_i follows a normal distribution $N(0, 1)$. When x_i follows a normal distribution $N(\mu,\sigma)$ then $P(x_i \leq t)$ is given by the function $\Phi((t-\mu)/\sigma)$.

Equation (5) can be used to calculate $P(Success/T)$ for any given feasible schedule T when the PSTP satisfies assumption (2). Thus, a search procedure in the space of feasible schedules could be used to optimize this quantity. Nevertheless, such an uninformative search procedure is probably highly inefficient. We now develop analytical expressions for the partial derivatives of $\log P(success/T)$ when assumption (1) is also satisfied. From Equation (5) and the chain rule for derivatives we get that:

$$\frac{\partial \log P(Success \mid T)}{\partial y_m} = \frac{\partial}{\partial y_m}\sum_i \log\{P(x_i \leq U_T(x_i) \mid T) - P(x_i \leq L_T(x_i) \mid T)\} = \tag{7}$$

$$\sum_i \frac{\partial}{\partial y_m} \log\{P(x_i \leq U_T(x_i) \mid T) - P(x_i \leq L_T(x_i) \mid T)\} =$$

$$\sum_i \frac{1}{\{P(x_i \leq U_T(x_i) \mid T) - P(x_i \leq L_T(x_i) \mid T)\}} \frac{\partial}{\partial y_m}\{P(x_i \leq U_T(x_i) \mid T) - P(x_i \leq L_T(x_i) \mid T)\}$$

The partial derivatives in the above equation can be calculated as follows: first we notice that by assumption (1)

$$\frac{\partial P(x_i \leq U_T(x_i) \mid T)}{\partial y_m} = \frac{\partial P'(x_i \leq U_T(x_i) - Pa(x) \mid T)}{\partial y_m} \tag{8}$$

which in turn is:

$$\frac{\partial P'(x_i \leq U_T(x_i) - Pa(x) \mid T)}{\partial y_m} = p'(U_T(x_i) - T(Pa(x)))\left\{\frac{\partial U_T(x_i)}{\partial y_m} - \frac{\partial Pa(x_i)}{\partial y_m}\right\} \tag{9}$$

Notice that by definition of $U_T(x)$, $\partial U_T(x_i)/\partial y_m$ is 1 if y_m is the variable maximizing the quantity $(y_i + b_{y_i x})$, otherwise it is 0. Similarly, $\partial Pa(x_i)/\partial y_m$ is 1 if $Pa(x_i)=y_m$ and 0 otherwise. The calculation of $\partial P(x_i \leq L(x_i) \mid T)/\partial y_m$ is similar and so we finally derive:

$$\begin{aligned}\frac{\partial \log P(Success \mid T)}{\partial y_m} = \sum_i & \frac{1}{\{P(x_i \leq U_T(x_i) \mid T) - P(x_i \leq L_T(x_i) \mid T)\}} \\ & \left(p'(U_T(x_i) - T(Pa(x_i)))\left\{\frac{\partial U_T(x_i)}{\partial y_m} - \frac{\partial Pa(x_i)}{\partial y_m}\right\} - \right. \\ & \left. -p'(L_T(x_i) - T(Pa(x_i)))\left\{\frac{\partial L_T(x_i)}{\partial y_m} - \frac{\partial Pa(x_i)}{\partial y_m}\right\}\right)\end{aligned} \tag{10}$$

We will now apply these formulas to the example of Fig. 1 (b) and for the schedule $T_1 = \{TR \leftarrow 0, OS \leftarrow 7{:}30, NOS \leftarrow 8{:}00\}$:

$$P(Success \mid T_1) = P(-5' \leq NOS - OE \leq 10' \mid T_1) = \\ P(7:50 \leq OE \leq 8:05 \mid T_1) \tag{11}$$

Since OE follows the normal distribution $N(30'+OS,\ 10')=N(8{:}00,\ 10')$ the above probability is given by $\Phi((8{:}05-8{:}00)/10') - \Phi((7{:}50-8{:}00)/10') = 0.53$ or 53%.

The partial derivative of $\log P(Success/T_1)$ over NOS is given by substitution to Equation (10):

$$\frac{\partial \log P(Success \mid T_1)}{\partial NOS} = \frac{1}{P(Success \mid T_1)} \\ (p'(8:05-7:30)\left\{\frac{\partial U_T(OE)}{\partial NOS} - \frac{\partial Pa(OE)}{\partial NOS}\right\} - \\ -p'(7:50-7:30)\left\{\frac{\partial L_T(OE)}{\partial NOS} - \frac{\partial Pa(OE)}{\partial NOS}\right\}) = \\ \frac{1}{0.53}(p'(45') - p'(20')) = 1.88(p'(45') - p'(20')) \tag{12}$$

This is because $Pa(OE)=OS$ and so $\frac{\partial Pa(OE)}{\partial NOS}=0$, while $\frac{\partial U_{T1}(OE)}{\partial NOS}=\frac{\partial L_{T1}(OE)}{\partial NOS}=1$, and also because $U_T(OE)=T(NOS)+b_{NOS,OE} = 8{:}00 + 5' = 8{:}05$ and $L_T(OE)=T(NOS)-b_{OE,NOS} = 7{:}50$. In other words, if schedule the next operation an infinitesimal time $dNOS$ later, we will be adding $p'(45')dNOS$ probability to satisfy the upper bound of the constraint $7{:}50+dNOS \leq OE \leq 8{:}05+dNOS$ and subtracting $p'(20')dNOS$ probability to satisfy the lower bound of this constraint. Because $p'(45') > p'(20')$ for p' being $N(30,\ 10')$, by scheduling the next operation for a little later than 8:00 we increase our chances of executing the plan correctly. The reader is encouraged to work out the partial derivative $\frac{\partial \log P(Success \mid T_1)}{\partial OS}$ and notice that it is equal to $-\frac{\partial \log P(Success \mid T_1)}{\partial NOS}$ (the formula is the same, but now $\partial PA(OE)/\partial OS=1$ and also $\partial U_T(OE)/\partial OS=0$). That is, we get the same change in probability of success by starting the operation a little earlier instead of scheduling the next one a little later, as we would expect by symmetry. For this simple example, it is easy to see that an optimal solution is the schedule $\{TR\leftarrow 0,\ OS\leftarrow 7{:}27{:}30,\ NOS\leftarrow 8{:}00\}$. There is actually an infinite number of optimal solutions where the next operation is scheduled for a time $t \in [8{:}00, 9{:}00]$ and OS is set to $t-0{:}32{:}30$, i.e. thirty two and a half minutes earlier.

5 Dynamic Optimization

Unfortunately, deriving analytical expressions for the function and its derivative for the dynamic case is much harder. If we are allowed to use information from observations of the uncontrollables to decide what and when to schedule next, then we are not looking any more for a single optimizing schedule T; instead we are looking for an execution strategy (policy) St that maps the current history of the system, i.e. our decisions about the controllables and our observations about the uncontrollables to the next decision of what and when to execute next.

Nevertheless, a sketch algorithm to the problem would be to find an initial optimal static schedule T and then loop on the steps below:

1. If it is time to execute a controllable according to T, execute it.
2. If an uncontrollable x has occurred at time t, remove it from V_2, remove its pdf from the set of pdf S, insert the constraint $t \leq x - TR \leq t$ to the set of constraints E, and update (recalculate) the optimal T.
3. If an uncontrollable x has not occurred by time t', update its cdf $P(x \leq t' \mid Pa(x))$ with the posterior $P(x \leq t' \mid Pa(x), x > t)$, and update the optimal T.

In step (2) whenever we observe an uncontrollable, then we take into consideration this observation and recalculate the optimal schedule T. Not observing an uncontrollable also provides with useful information since it changes the posterior probability of the occurrence of the uncontrollable and should also be taken into account (Step (3)).

Unfortunately, even though the above algorithm constructs a PSTP schedule dynamically, it does not answer the question what is $P(Success/St)$ where St is a dynamic execution strategy. The latter is important for planning purposes since a planner might decide to keep searching if this probability is below a given threshold or accept a plan if it is above this threshold.

6 Discussion

In order to apply the PSTP framework one needs to obtain the probability distributions of the uncontrollable events. These can reflect the beliefs of the domain encoder about their occurrence or can be estimated with experimentation. In addition, a system can learn and calibrate them by using the previous observations of the events.

Even though we presented a way to solve the static optimization schedule problem, there are still many limitations to our approach. First of all, the method does not necessarily provide the global optimal. We are investigating cases where the global optimal can be found, for example by the use of Lagrange multipliers or similar optimization techniques. Another (minor) limitation is the assumption that the conditional pdf are time-invariant. In the example of Fig. 1 (b) a better model would use a pdf for the event AO that depends on the time we leave home so that, for example, it would take longer on average to reach the office if we leave during rush hour. The use of assumption (1) for time invariance, was used in Equation (8) to derive the partial derivatives of $P(Success/T)$. If we know exactly how $p(x \mid Pa(x)=t)$ changes with t, then it is possible that we could still calculate the partial derivative and then assumption (1) could be dropped.

Solving the problem without assumption (2) holding is harder. Recall that assumption (2) was used in Equation (5) to derive $\log P(Success/T)$ and in order to split the probability of the conjunction of a number of constraints holding to the product of the probability of single constraints being satisfied. For example, $P(x\text{-}y \leq 5 \wedge x\text{-}TR \leq 10)$

when both x and y are random variables, does not necessarily equal $P(x\text{-}y\leq5)P(x\text{-}TR\leq10)$ because the satisfaction of the two constraints are not two independent events. Assumption (2) restricts us from being able to have PSTPs in which the synchronization of two uncontrollable events is required, e.g. two trucks arriving at around the same time. Finally, assumption (3) prohibits the use of pdf with discontinuities in their graph such as the uniform distribution. Nevertheless, such distributions could typically be adequately approximated by continuous ones.

A restriction of the PSTP model is the use of conditional pdf that depend only on the value of a single parent. The model is geared towards representing uncertain durations of actions in planning and scheduling for which a single parent is typically enough. Nevertheless, one can think of situations where this model is inadequate. For example, if the duration of heating up the engines of a spacecraft depends on when we started the action, but also on the amount of power we are willing to spend, then the probability distribution for the end of this action would require two parent variables: the time of the start of the heating action (temporal variable) and the amount of power used (non-temporal variable). It is possible to extend PSTPs to allow for multiple parent variables and optimally schedule events in the same fashion as for the single parent case presented in this paper. We are currently working to overcome these limitations and extend our model.

PSTPs can be derived from temporal planners in various ways. The planner can either use STPs or STPUs to generate a temporal plan that can be directly converted to a PSTP for execution. Alternatively, a planner might directly reason with PSTPs, perform a search in the space of PSTP plans and accept one that is above a threshold of probability of correct execution.

We would like to add that other related formalisms that deal with uncertainty are Markov Decision Processes (MDP) [9] and Influence Diagrams [10]. However, MDPs use discrete time while Influence Diagrams typically do not reason with continuous decision variables.

7 Conclusions

We presented a new constrained-based and probabilistic temporal reasoning formalism called the Probabilistic Simple Temporal Problem (PSTP) for representing plans and schedules with uncontrollable events and uncertain durations. We also provided methods that under certain conditions discover the schedule that maximizes the probability of executing the plan in a way that respects the temporal constraints. PSTP significantly extends previous formalisms that also deal with uncertainty of duration of actions by allowing the representation of and reasoning with probabilistic information. Unlike other models such as the STPU, uncertainty is represented in a principled and intuitive way and does not require guessing of the best approximate bounds. There are still restrictions in our model, such as the assumption that no constraints exist between two uncontrollable variables, and reasoning limitations, such as being incapable of analytically calculating the optimal dynamic execution strategy. We are current researching ways to overcome the limitations.

References

1. Weld, D.S., *An Introduction to Least Commitment Planning.* AI Magazine, 1994. **15**(4): p. 27-61.
2. Jonsson, A., et al. *Planning in interplanetary space: theory and practice.* in *Artificial Intelligence Planning and Scheduling (AIPS-00).* 2000.
3. Ghallab, M. and H.e. Laruelle, *Representation and Control in IxTeT, a Temporal Planner*, in *Proceedings of the Second International Conference on Artificial Intelligence Planning Systems (AIPS-94).* 1994. p. 61-67.
4. Dechter, R., I. Meiri, and J. Pearl, *Temporal constraint networks.* Artificial Intelligence, 1991. **49**: p. 61-95.
5. Vidal, T. and P. Morris. *Dynamic Control of Plans with Temporal Uncertainty.* in *IJCAI-2001 (to appear).* 2001.
6. Chleq, N. *Efficient Algorithms for Networks of Quantitative Temporal Constraints.* in *Constraints'95.* 1995.
7. Vidal, T. and H. Fragier, *Handling consistency in temporal constraint networks: from consistency to controllabilities.* Journal of Experimental and Theoretical Artificial Intelligence, 1999. **11**: p. 23-45.
8. Hock, W. and K. Schittowski, *A comparative performance evaluation of 27 nonlinear programming codes.* Computing, 1983. **30**: p. 335.
9. White, D.J., *Markov Decision Processes.* 1993: John Wiley and Sons.
10. Zhang, N.L. *Probabilistic Inference in Influence Diagrams.* in *Fourteenth Conference on Uncertainty in Artificial Intelligence (UAI-98).* 1998.

Crew Pairing Optimization with Genetic Algorithms

Harry Kornilakis and Panagiotis Stamatopoulos

Department of Informatics and Telecommunications
University of Athens
Panepistimiopolis, 157 84 Athens, Greece
{harryk,takis}@di.uoa.gr

Abstract. We present an algorithm for the crew pairing problem, an optimization problem that is part of the airline crew scheduling procedure. A pairing is a round trip starting and ending at the home base, which is susceptible to constraints that arise due to laws and regulations. The purpose of the crew pairing problem is to generate a set of pairings with minimal cost, covering all flight legs that the company has to carry out during a predefined time period. The proposed solution is a two-phase procedure. For the first phase, the pairing generation, a depth first search approach is employed. The second phase deals with the selection of a subset of the generated pairings with near optimal cost. This problem, which is modelled by a set covering formulation, is solved with a genetic algorithm. The presented method was tested on actual flight data of Olympic Airways.

1 Introduction

Given a timetable containing all the flight legs that an airline company must carry out, the airline *crew scheduling problem* [8] consists of assigning individual crew members to flight legs, so that the assignment is legal and crew costs are minimized. Crew scheduling is separated into two independent subproblems. The *crew pairing problem* (CPP), which will be the focus of this paper, is the process of finding a set of round trips (*pairings*) starting and ending at the home base, covering all flight legs that the company has to carry out with a minimal cost. The *crew assignment problem* is the assignment of individual crew members to pairings and it will not be considered here. What we propose in this paper is to employ a genetic algorithm based approach to deal with the CPP.

The main difficulty of the CPP is the huge size of the search space, which grows exponentially with the number of flight legs. This means that even for average sized problems containing a few hundred flight legs, an intractably large number of legal solutions may exist. Finding the optimal solution among them may not be possible to do efficiently and often methods that produce only a good approximation of the optimal solution have to be used. Another consideration is the nature of the constraints, which are usually based on aviation laws and

I.P. Vlahavas and C.D. Spyropoulos (Eds.): SETN 2002, LNAI 2308, pp. 109–120, 2002.

regulations and, in general, are non-linear. Such constraints tend to be rather difficult to model in an algorithm that automatically solves the CPP.

Crew scheduling is an important problem for airline companies. In fact, crew costs is the second greatest operational expense for airlines, exceeded only by the cost of fuel consumption [2]. As an example, in [1], it is reported that American Airlines spent 1.3 billion dollars on crew costs in 1991. Therefore, a low cost solution to the CPP can save airlines millions of dollars per year. Almost every major airline is using a system that automates crew scheduling. However, computational tests, conducted with actual data, led to the conclusion that many of the solutions provided by these systems needed significant improvement [6].

Much work has been done in the past for tackling the CPP. Traditional approaches are based on Operations Research techniques [19], some of them exploiting parallelism as well [10]. Various methods based on genetic algorithms [7,15,16] or neural networks [14] have been also proposed. Finally, Constraint Programming has been used as a platform for solving the CPP [17], in some cases combined with parallel processing [11].

The paper is organized as follows. In section 2, we deal with the CPP in greater depth and in section 3, we present our proposed method for the CPP, focusing on the optimization procedure and the genetic algorithm that has been implemented for it. Section 4 presents the experimental results on actual flight data of Olympic Airways and finally, our conclusions appear in section 5.

2 The Crew Pairing Problem

The objective of the airline crew pairing problem is to minimize costs associated with assigning crews to flight legs [6]. Every crew has a home base and a pairing is a round trip, consisting of a sequence of flight legs, which starts and ends at the crew's home base. Each pairing is composed of a number of legal workdays, called *duties*, which are separated by rest periods. Airline crew pairing seeks to find a subset of legal pairings such that each flight leg is covered, preferably by only one crew, and so that the total cost of these pairings is minimal.

In order to be legal, the construction of a pairing must take into account a number of constraints. Some of these constraints, like the temporal and spatial constraints, follow directly from the definition of the problem, while others are results of laws and regulations. Specifically, the following types of constraints can be identified:

- Temporal constraints: The departure of a flight leg should obviously take place after the arrival of the previous leg of the pairing. Additionally, a certain amount of time, called transition time, must pass between the arrival of a leg and the departure of the next.
- Spatial constraints: For every two consecutive flight legs in a pairing, the second must depart from the airport that the first arrives at. Also, the first leg of a legal pairing must depart from the home base of the crew and the last leg of each pairing must end at the home base.

– Fleet constraints: Cockpit crew is usually designated to operate only one type of aircraft. Therefore, all flights in a pairing generated for cockpit crew must be performed by the same type of aircraft. On the other hand, cabin crew may be placed in any type of aircraft. Consequently, pairings that are legal for cabin crew may be illegal for cockpit crew, making the cockpit crew problem easier to solve.
– Constraints due to laws and regulations: In order to be legal, pairings must follow government laws and collective agreements. These usually define the maximum duration of a duty, the maximum flight time allowed over a period of time, the minimum length of the rest period between two duties etc. These values may vary depending on the length or the destination of a flight leg and usually are quite different for cockpit and cabin crews.

Another consideration is that it is possible that, besides the crew that is on duty, other crew members are on a plane, travelling as passengers, in order to move to a specific airport and continue a round trip. This process is known as *deadheading* and is an additional cost to the airline, since deadheaded crews get normally paid, even though they are not working, and occupy seats that would otherwise be given to passengers. Obviously, good solutions should avoid deadheaded flights, however it is not always the case that solutions with no deadheading exist. It is also possible that a solution with a few deadheaded flights is better than one with no deadheading. In any case, allowing deadheading results to a larger space of feasible solutions and finding the optimal solution becomes harder.

The cost of a solution is another factor that is critical to the problem. Usually the cost of each pairing is equal to the wages of the crew. This, again, depends on the policy of the airline company, but, in general, it is a function of the flying time, the duty time or the number of duties of a pairing. The total cost of a solution is usually the sum of the costs of all pairings in it, but an additional penalty for deadheaded flights may be introduced.

Looking at the nature of the constraints and the cost function, it becomes obvious that modelling them is not a trivial task. In fact, in most cases, it is impossible to formulate the legal pairings or the cost function as linear equations and therefore use a linear programming framework to solve the entire problem directly. For example, a constraint from the scheduling of Olympic Airways that we used in our test problems was "If a duty starts at a non-domestic airport, it cannot include the home base as an intermediate stop".

3 Solving the Crew Pairing Problem

Due to the large size of the search space, the nature of the constraints and the cost function, which usually are highly non-linear, we follow the approach of decomposing the CPP in two separate phases [18].

1. The pairing generation, where a large number of legal pairings, composed of the flight legs in the timetable, is generated and the cost of each pairing is calculated.

2. The optimization of the solution, where a subset of the generated pairings is selected, so that every flight leg in the schedule is included in at least one pairing and the total cost is minimized.

Furthermore, the pairing generation is itself decomposed in the process of generating a large set of legal duties from the flight legs and in the process of generating the set of pairings by using the duties previously found (Fig. 1).

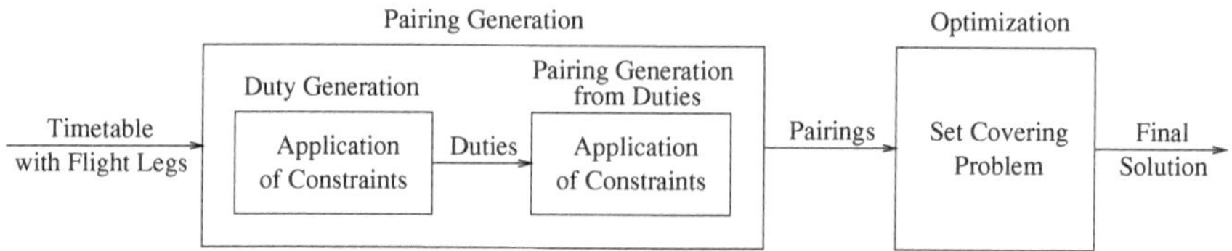

Fig. 1. The parts of the method for solving the CPP

One advantage of this approach is that the constraints and the cost function are taken into account only during the first phase and therefore the optimization is independent of them. In fact, once a large set of legal pairings has been generated, the second phase can be modelled as a *set covering problem*, a widely known combinatorial optimization problem.

3.1 The Pairing Generation

The input to the pairing generation is the set L of all the flight legs that appear in the timetable. The constraints are defined as a function $C : 2^L \rightarrow \{0, 1\}$, where 2^L is the powerset of L, $C(p) = 1$ if p is a legal pairing and $C(p) = 0$, if not. We want to generate the set of pairings $P = \{p \in 2^L \mid C(p) = 1\}$ which contains all pairings that satisfy the constraints. Modelling the constraints as a function like this makes the checking for the satisfaction of the constraints independent of the rest of the search.

Unfortunately, the size of the problems that normally arise in airlines is prohibitive for the complete generation of every valid pairing. For example, in an average sized problem of 1000 legs, we would have to check 2^{1000} pairings for validity, so an exhaustive search of the search space is obviously intractable. Furthermore, the more pairings we generate, the harder the optimization phase, which as we shall see is an NP-complete problem, becomes. Therefore, we wish to keep as few pairings as possible for the optimization, also making certain that these pairing will lead to a solution of high quality after the optimization.

The pairing generation is divided into two parts. During the first part a depth-first search is used, which systematically forms possible duties (sets of flight legs), checks if they satisfy the constraints and stores them if they do. The best of the generated duties are kept and provided as input to the second part, where a similar process is used to initially generate a large number of legal pairings and afterwards keep the best of them. During the entire run of the algorithm, special attention is given so that the number of generated pairings that contain each flight leg is balanced, i.e. each flight leg is part of almost as many pairings as any other. It is also important that each flight is part of a minimum number of pairings, so that not only is the existence of a solution guaranteed, but also there are multiple choices for the pairing that will be chosen to cover each flight leg. The presence of such multiple choices leads to greater diversity in the search space during the optimization phase, making it easier to find a solution of high quality.

Generation of Duties from Legs. We implement the duty generation as a depth-first search in the space of all possible subsets of the set L of all flight legs. Essential to this search is the function we use to model the constraints, which we shall call $validDuty : 2^L \rightarrow \{0,1\} \times \{0,1\}$. This function takes as input a set of flight legs and has two return values. The first return value is equal to 1 if the input legs form a valid duty that satisfies every constraint in the problem, otherwise 0 is returned. The second return value is equal to 1 if it is possible to create a valid duty by adding more legs to the set of input legs. In this case, the search should continue deeper, otherwise the search should stop and the second return value of *validDuty* is 0. A function named `searchForDuties` that can be used to search for valid duties is given next.

```
function searchForDuties(currentDuty, duties)
  [keep, continue] <- validDuty(currentDuty)
  if keep==1 then insert currentDuty into duties.
  if continue==1
    For each leg that departs after the arrival of the last leg of
    currentDuty and from the same airport do
      Insert the leg into currentDuty.
      searchForDuties(currentDuty, duties).
      remove the leg from currentDuty.
```

In the above fragment of pseudocode, `currentDuty` is a set of legs that is used to represent the duty that is checked for validity. The array `duties` holds all the valid duties that have been found. Calling the function `searchForDuties` with `currentDuty` containing only one leg will yield all valid duties that begin with that leg. Therefore, calling `searchForDuties` for each leg in L we obtain every valid duty.

After the completion of the search algorithm, we have generated a very large number of duties. Using so many duties as input to the next phases of the pairing generation and the optimization will cause serious performance problems. Therefore, a subset containing the duties of the highest quality possible should be chosen and kept. To this end, an algorithm that performs the selection of the best duties has been implemented. The criterion for keeping or not a duty is related to how useful this duty will be in the search for an optimal solution to the CPP. This is decided by a heuristic function, which returns the ratio of the flight time of the duty over the total duration of the duty.

This completes the duty generation. The set of duties that is kept will be used as input to the next part of the algorithm, the generation of the pairings.

Generation of Pairings from Duties. The generation of pairings from the duties is performed, using a depth-first search, in practically the same way as the generation of duties. The set of legs that were used as input is replaced by the set of duties and the algorithm instead of generating a set of valid duties generates a set of valid pairings. Since we gave a detailed description of that depth-first algorithm in the previous paragraph, we shall not repeat it here.

3.2 The Optimization

Once we have generated a large set of pairings, we continue to the optimization phase, which is modelled as a set covering problem, defined as follows:

Given a set M with m elements and n subsets $M_j \subseteq M$ with associated costs c_j, $j = 1, 2 \ldots n$, find a subset S of $\{1, 2 \ldots n\}$ such that $\bigcup_{j \in S} M_j = M$ and $\sum_{j \in S} c_j$ is minimized.

In other words, we seek a collection of subsets such that every element of M is contained in a least one selected subset and the total cost of all selected subsets is minimum.

The correspondence to the optimization phase of the CPP is direct, by setting M equal to the set of all flight legs and M_j equal to the generated pairings.

Notice that by modelling the problem as a set covering problem, instead of a set partitioning, we allow solutions which may contain crews travelling as passengers on some flights. As we have mentioned, this is acceptable and in some cases it may even yield better solutions than forcing exactly one crew per flight. Furthermore, it is possible that no feasible solutions exist under the constraint that each leg is covered exactly once. Set covering has been proven to be NP-complete [9] and, therefore, no algorithm is known that can find the optimal solution efficiently, for input data of significant size. In fact, the best reported methods for exact optimization are based on branch-and-bound and deal with problems of sizes around 400 rows (flight legs) and 4000 columns (pairings) [12]. However, the size of problems that commonly arise in airlines is far larger, reaching thousands of rows and millions of columns. Therefore, in order to tackle problems of this size, approximate methods are used, which produce solutions that only approximate the optimal, but can handle large problems efficiently. In [18] and [4], two such methods are presented and success is reported with problems of up to 10000 rows and 1000000 columns.

The method we propose is based on [3], where a genetic algorithm is given that can be used for efficiently solving the set covering problem. We modified this algorithm to better fit the specific characteristics of the set covering problems that arise as part of a CPP.

Overview of Genetic Algorithms. *Genetic algorithms* (GA) are methods for random search based on the evolutionary process of species found in nature. They were introduced in 1975 [13] and since then they have been used successively on a wide range of combinatorial optimization problems.

According to the theory of evolution [5], populations in nature evolve by following the process of natural selection and survival of the fittest. The members of the population that are able to adjust to changes in the environment are more likely to survive and reproduce. On the other hand, individuals who are less fit become extinct. Through this process the genes of the fittest individuals are passed on to future generations and eventually become predominant as generations pass. This mix of characteristics from fit ancestors produces even fitter individuals and in this way species become stronger and better adjusted to the environment.

Genetic algorithms are based on the simulation of the above process, by taking an initial population of solutions and applying a number of genetic operators on it. Each individual of the population is a possible solution to the problem, encoded as a string (usually binary) called *chromosome*. Each character of the chromosome is called a *gene*. The fitness of each individual is represented by an objective function, which is a real valued function defined over the set of all chromosomes. The value of the objective function is representative of the quality of the corresponding solution. The procedure of combining two members of the population to produce offsprings is called *crossover*. Through crossover, individuals containing genes from both parents are produced. By combining high quality solutions we hope that children will inherit the best genes of both parents. In order to avoid getting stuck in local minima during the search, *mutation* is used, i.e. the random change of a few genes of the offspring, after the crossover. Finally, the new individuals replace the weaker members of the existing population and this procedure continues until a satisfactory solution is found.

Genetic Algorithm for Crew Pairing Optimization. The method we use for the set covering problem follows the general framework of GA we presented previously. Certain modifications and additions have been made to accommodate with the specifics of the problem, including a method for correcting solutions that violate constraints, i.e. solutions where there exist flights that are not covered by any selected pairing, turning them into feasible ones.

A binary string coding is used for chromosomes with each chromosome having length equal to the number of pairings. Each gene corresponds to one pairing and when it is 0 it means that the corresponding pairing is not part of the solution. If the gene is equal to 1, then the corresponding pairing is included in the solution. The objective function we use to represent the fitness of each individual is

$$f = \sum_i c_i g_i + deadheadingPenalty \cdot deadheadedFlights$$

where c_i is the cost of the i-th pairing, g_i is the value of the i-th gene of the solution, *deadheadingPenalty* is a constant that is used to penalize flights which are covered more than once in the solution and *deadheadedFlights* is the number of such flights.

By using this cost function, we are able to reach solutions that contain low cost pairings, but also have a low percentage of deadheading, which, as we have mentioned, poses an additional cost to airlines. Furthermore, we have experimentally noticed that a careful assignment of the constant *deadheadingPenalty* may help the genetic algorithm to converge to a high quality solution faster.

The selection of the members of the population that will become parents is based on their order in the population, sorted in descending order based on their fitness function. That means that the fittest individual is the most likely to be selected, the second fittest individual is a little less likely to be chosen, and so on. Note that the probability of selection depends exclusively on the order in the population and not on the absolute value of the fitness function for the individual. In exactly the same way, we choose the member of the population that will be replaced at every generation. The only difference is that in this case the individual that is the least fit has the highest probability of being chosen.

Once two parents have been chosen from the population, the crossover operation is performed on them in order to produce a new solution that inherits characteristics from both parents. We use the *uniform crossover operator*. This means that if a gene has the same value in the chromosomes of both parents, this value is assigned to the same gene of the offspring chromosome. If a gene is equal to 0 for one parent and equal to 1 for the other, the corresponding gene of their offspring may become either 0 or 1, with equal probability. The reason for choosing this variation of the crossover operator was that it provided a better shuffling of the parents' genes in forming the offspring.

After crossover has been used to produce a new individual, the mutation is applied on it. The purpose of mutation is to prevent the search from getting trapped in the local minima, by randomly altering a few genes of the chromosome and therefore directing the search towards new areas in the search space. We propose a method of mutation that depends on the density (the percentage of genes equal to 1) of the fittest individual of the population. Initially, a fixed number of genes are randomly selected from the chromosome. These are the genes that will be mutated. Each of the genes is mutated to 0 with probability equal to the percentage of 0s in the chromosome of the fittest individual, otherwise it is mutated to 1. For example, if in the chromosome of the fittest individual 900 genes are 0 and 100 genes are 1, then each gene is mutated to 0 with probability 90% or to 1 with probability 10%. By mutating in this way, we are able to keep information about the density of fit individuals in the offspring's chromosome. Such information is preserved during crossover, but if mutation to 0 and 1 was made with equal probability, such information, which is quite critical for getting good results, would be lost.

By looking at the way that crossover and mutation are performed, it is obvious that after these operations, the new solution will not necessarily be feasible, i.e. not every flight leg will be present in at least one pairing. In order to avoid having infeasible solutions in the population, after the mutation, we apply a correction algorithm on the new chromosome. This algorithm works by changing the value of some genes to 1 and as a result by adding the corresponding pairings to the solution, until every flight leg is covered and the solution becomes feasible. For each uncovered leg in the solution, we add a pairing that covers that leg. A simple heuristic is used to help us select one pairing among all the pairings which contain that particular leg. That heuristic favours pairings of low cost that when selected cover as many uncovered legs as possible and as few legs that have already been covered as possible. For a more detailed and formal description of the correction method see [3].

One last important thing that should be mentioned about the genetic algorithm is the way that the initial population is created. It is critical to the performance of the search that the initial population is as diverse as possible, so that a large part of the search space will be explored early. Therefore, the best method to initialize the population is one that generates individuals as randomly as possible. Specifically, we randomly insert in the solution new pairings that don't have common legs with the other pairings already selected. Then, once we've reached the point where we can't find such a pairing, we run the correction algorithm on the solution to make it a feasible one. Through this process, we obtain a population whose members are feasible solutions of a reasonably high quality. Furthermore, since a great deal of randomness is present in the generation of individuals, the population created displays the wished diversity.

Having presented the individual parts of the algorithm, we can now give its complete description:

```
Randomly generate an initial population of chromosomes.
Repeat until a satisfactory solution is reached
  Select two of the fittest members of the population for parents.
  Apply crossover on the parents to produce a child chromosome.
  Apply mutation on the child chromosome.
  Correct the child chromosome so that it becomes a feasible solution.
  Select one of the weakest members of the population to be replaced.
  Replace the selected individual with the child.
```

4 Experimental Results

In order to test the efficiency of the proposed algorithm, we ran it using real input data from the flight schedule of Olympic Airways. We used the flight schedule for the 737–200 fleet, for April 1998. The schedule consisted of 2100 flight legs, passing through 29 different airports. The pairings were generated based on the regulations of Olympic Airlines for cockpit crews. Examples of the constraints that were used are the following:

- The minimum transition time between legs in a duty is 45 minutes.
- The flight time of a duty has a maximum value, which is 15 hours for long-range flights, 9 hours for non-domestic flights and 8 hours for domestic flights.
- At most one duty intersects with any calendar day.

As the cost of each pairing we used the value of the function

$$floor(1000 \cdot duration\_of\_pairing/flight\_time\_of\_pairing)$$

where *duration_of_pairing* is the total time that the pairing started from the beginning of its first duty until the end of its last duty, and *flight_time_of_pairing* is the sum of the flight times of all the flight legs in that pairing.

During the pairing generation phase, initially 70358 legal duties were generated, out of which the 22090 best duties were stored for the next phase. The average number of flight legs in each of these duties was 3.88 legs per duty. Afterwards, using these duties as input we generated 66425 legal pairings and kept the 11981 best of them. The average cost of each pairing was 6148.24 and it was composed of 5.3268 flight legs in average. Most of the pairings that were finally kept were composed of either one or two duties. It is easy to see that this is a natural consequence of the cost function we used, which significantly favours smaller pairings.

In the optimization phase, we ran the genetic algorithm to find the best subset of the 11981 pairings, which covered the 2100 flight legs. After some experimentation, it was decided to fix the population of each generation to 10 individuals. Increasing the population size led sometimes to better results, but with a significant decrease in efficiency. In addition, the *deadheadingPenalty* parameter of the fitness function was decided, experimentally, to be fixed to 1000, giving a total penalty of around 1% for deadheaded flights to the fitness of an individual. This contribution, although relatively small, was sufficient to guide the algorithm to solutions with very few deadheaded flights. The cost of the best solution found, plotted against the number of generations that have passed, appears in Fig. 2. The progress of the optimization in greater detail, for various generations, is shown in Table 1. The table gives the total cost, the number of pairings and the number of legs covered by more that one pairing (deadheaded flights) for the best solution of the generation. We can see that as the genetic algorithm runs, the solution constantly gets better. Even though initially many flights are deadheaded and the cost is high, eventually after 20000 generations, we find a solution of zero deadheading and of cost 976004. This requires about 30 minutes of elapsed time on a PC with a 350 MHz Pentium III processor.

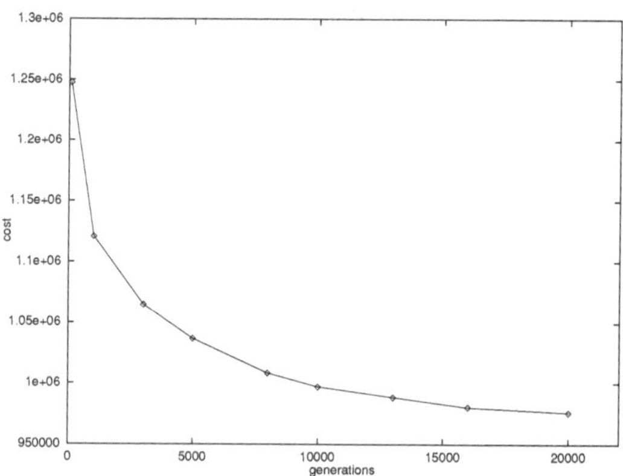

Fig. 2. The progress of the optimization

Table 1. The best solution of various generations

Generation	100	1000	3000	5000	8000	10000	13000	16000	20000
Cost	1247776	1121057	1064647	1036596	1008276	996994	988418	980344	976004
Pairings	635	592	567	551	537	531	529	526	525
Deadheading	71	10	6	6	4	4	2	0	0

Finally, we'll compare the result we found with the result found by the project PARACHUTE [11], a project that combines constraint programming with parallel processing, in order to automatically solve the crew scheduling problem. We ran PARACHUTE on the same data set (April 1998) using the same constraints and the same cost function. The comparative results, showing the total cost of the solution, the number of pairings in the solution and the number of deadheaded flight legs, appear in Table 2. Our proposed method gives a solution of cost lower by 194148 (16.5%) and has no deadheaded flight legs. The running times of both methods were of the same order of magnitude.

Table 2. Comparison of our method and PARACHUTE

	Total Cost	No. of Pairings	Deadheaded Legs
Our Method	976004	525	0
PARACHUTE	1170152	611	25 (1.1%)

Another comparison we carried out was to test our method with the datasets that were used by Beasley and Chu in [3]. It has to be noted, though, that these datasets represented various set covering problems, not necessarily similar in nature to ones coming from crew pairing problems like the one we faced in our work. For example, in these datasets, there exists 30–70% of overcovering in the solutions, while in CPPs the corresponding percentage is 1–5%. In addition, the density of the set covering problems in [3] is 2–20%, while, normally, in CPPs, the density is around 1%. However, the results we obtained by running our method, which is definitely tuned for CPPs, on these set covering problems were of similar, though not better, quality to those achieved by Beasley and Chu.

5 Conclusions

In this paper, we have given a method that can be used to solve the crew pairing problem. We separated the problem into two phases, the pairing generation and the optimization, and we used a depth-first search for the first phase and a genetic algorithm, extending work by Beasley and Chu, for the second. In order to test the performance of the algorithm, we ran it with real data from the schedule of Olympic Airways. The experimental results were very satisfactory, giving a low cost solution and improving on previous results on the same data set. Therefore, through this experiment, we have shown that the method we propose can be a viable solution for the crew pairing process of airlines.

References

1. Anbil R., Gelman E., Patty B., Tanga R. Recent Advances in Crew-Pairing Optimization at American Airlines. *Interfaces*, 21(1):62–74, 1991.
2. Andersson E., Housos E., Kohl N., Wedelin D. Crew Pairing Optimization. in Yu G. (ed.) *Operations Research in the Airline Industry.* Kluwer Academic Publishing, 1997.
3. Beasley J. E., Chu P. C. A Genetic Algorithm for the Set Covering Problem. *European Journal of Operational Research*, 94:392–404, 1996.
4. Carpara A., Fischetti M., Toth P. A Heuristic Algorithm for the Set Covering Problem. *Operations Research*, 47:730–743, 1999.
5. Darwin C. *The Origin of Species.* John Murray, 1859.
6. Desaulniers J., Desrosiers J., Dumas Y., Marc S., Rioux B., Solomon M. M., Soumis F. Crew Pairing at Air France. *European Journal of Operational Research*, 97:245–259, 1997.
7. Eremeev A. A Genetic Algorithm with a Non-Binary Representation for the Set Covering Problem. In *Proceedings of Operations Research '98*, pages 175–181, 1999.
8. Etschmaier M. M., Mathaisel D. F. Airline Scheduling: An Overview. *Transportation Science*, 19:127–138, 1985.
9. Garey M. R, Johnson D. S. *Computers and Intractabitity: A Guide to the Theory of NP-Completeness.* W. H Freeman, 1979.
10. Goumopoulos C., Alefragis P., Housos E. Parallel Algorithms for Airline Crew Planning on Networks of Workstations. In *Proceedings of the International Conference on Parallel Processing*, 1998.
11. Halatsis C., Stamatopoulos P., Karali I., Bitsikas T., Fessakis G., Schizas A., Sfakianakis S., Fouskakis C., Koukoumpetsos T., Papageorgiou D. Crew Scheduling Based on Constraint Programming: The PARACHUTE Experience. In *Proceedings of the 3rd Hellenic-European Conference on Mathematics and Informatics HERMIS '96*, pages 424–431, 1996.
12. Hoffman K. L., Padberg M. Solving Airline Crew Scheduling Problems by Branch and Cut. *Management Science*, 39:657–682, 1993.
13. Holland J. H. *Adaption in Natural and Artificial Systems.* MIT Press, 1975.
14. Lagerholm M., Peterson C., Söderberg B. Airline Crew Scheduling Using Potts Mean Field Techniques. *European Journal of Operational Research*, 120:81–96, 2000.
15. Marchiori E., Steenbeek A. An Evolutionary Algorithm for Large Scale Set Covering Problems with Application to Airline Crew Scheduling. In *Real-World Applications of Evolutionary Computing*, LNCS 1803, pages 367–381, 2000.
16. Ozdemir H. T., Mohan C. Flight Graph Based Genetic Algorithm for Crew Scheduling in Airlines. *Information Sciences*, 133:165–173, 2001.
17. Pavlopoulou C., Gionis A., Stamatopoulos P., Halatsis C. Crew Pairing Optimization Based on CLP. In *Proceedings of the 2nd International Conference on the Practical Applications of Constraint Technology PACT '96*, pages 191–210, 1996.
18. Wedelin D. The Design of a 0-1 Integer Optimizer and its Application in the Carmen System. *European Journal of Operational Research*, 87:722–730, 1995.
19. Yan S., Tung T.-T., Tu Y.-P. Optimal Construction of Airline Individual Crew Pairings. *Computers and Operations Research*, 29:341–363, 2002.

Integration of Topological and Metric Maps for Indoor Mobile Robot Path Planning and Navigation

Panagiotis G. Zavlangas and Spyros G. Tzafestas

Intelligent Robotics and Automation Laboratory
Signals, Control and Robotics Division
Department of Electrical and Computer Engineering
National Technical University of Athens
Zografou 15773, Athens, GREECE
zavlang@central.ntua.gr, Panos.Zavlangas@robotics.ntua.gr,
tzafesta@softlab.ntua.gr

Abstract. Autonomous mobile robots need to use spatial information about the environment in order to effectively plan and execute navigation tasks. The information can be represented at different levels of abstraction, ranging from detailed geometric maps to coarse topological maps. Each level is adequate for some sub-task, but not for others. In this paper, we consider the representation of spatial knowledge at two different levels of abstraction, which are commonly considered in the robotics literature : the geometric level, and the topological level. We propose to represent the environment by local metric maps connected into a topological network. This technique allows us to use maps that are not metrically consistent on the global scale, although they are metrically consistent locally. The structure allows also the combination of abstract global reasoning and precise local geometric computations. Moreover, this structure reflects the typical organization of indoor environments, where rooms and hallways define independent but connected local working spaces. To navigate in the environment, the robot uses the topological information to plan a sequence of sectors to traverse, and uses the metric information in each sector to locally move within the sector and to the next one. The functioning of the proposed system with respect to omnidirectional mobile robots and results of simulated experiments are presented.

1 Introduction

Building a representation of the environment is an important task for a mobile robot that aims at moving autonomously in the surrounding space. In robotics, the common descriptions of the space are metric and topological maps. A metric map represents the environment according to the absolute geometric position of obstacles. A topological map is a more abstract representation that describes relationships among features of the environment, without any absolute reference system. Topological maps are usually represented in graph form [3] [7][11] [19].

Being more abstract, a topological map has the advantage of being more compact and more stable with respect to sensor noise and to small changes in the environment.

I.P. Vlahavas and C.D. Spyropoulos (Eds.): SETN 2002, LNAI 2308, pp. 121–130, 2002.

Unfortunately, the semantics associated to topological maps are still somehow ambiguous. For example, in the maps defined in [11] nodes represent places, characterized by sensor data, and arcs represent paths between places, characterized by control strategies. By contrast, the maps defined in [19] are obtained by partitioning a probabilistic occupancy grid into regions (nodes) separated by narrow passages (arcs) according to some measure of clearance. Perhaps, more puzzling, the topological maps found in the literature seem to be rather detached from descriptions of the environment in terms of the usual notions of mathematical topology [4].

Over the past decades, the problem of building maps and navigating indoor environments has received significant attention in the mobile robotics community. The problem of building maps is the problem of determining the location of certain entities, such as landmarks or obstacles, in a global frame or reference. To build a map of its environment, a robot must know where it is. Since robot motion is inaccurate, constructing maps of large indoor environments requires a robot to solve an inherent concurrent localization problem. There exist two major paradigms for mobile robot maps: metric and topological. Approaches in the metric paradigm generate fine-grained, metric descriptions of a robot's environment [15]. In these representations, the robot's environment is defined by a single global coordinate system, in which all mapping and navigation takes place. Typically, the map is a grid with each cell of the grid representing some amount of space in the real world. These grids became quite sophisticated at representing the spatial structure of the world [14]. These approaches typically work well in bounded environments, with little consistent structure and where the robot has opportunities to realign itself with the global coordinate system using external markers [8].

Approaches in the topological paradigm, on the other hand, generate coarse, graph like descriptions of environments, where nodes correspond to significant, easy-to-distinguish places or landmarks, and arcs correspond to actions or action sequences that connect neighboring places [3]. Topological maps are qualitative descriptions of the robot's workspace, in which the environment is represented as places and connections between places. Indeed, the idea of a map that contains no metric or geometric information, but only the notions of proximity and order, is very attractive because such an approach eliminates the inevitable problems of dealing with movement uncertainty in mobile robots. Movement errors do not accumulate globally in topological maps as they do in maps with global coordinate systems since the robot only navigates locally, between places. Topological maps can also be more compact in their representation of space, in that they represent only interesting places and not the entire environment. Topological maps have become increasingly popular in mobile robotics [1][11].

It has been long recognized, that either paradigm alone, metric or topological, has significant drawbacks [16][11]. In principle, topological maps should scale better than metric maps to large scale indoor environments, because a coarse-grained, graph-structured representation is much more compact than a dense array, and more directly suited to problem solving algorithms [3][11]. However, purely topological maps have difficulty distinguishing adequately among different places, and have not, in practice, been applied successfully to large environments. Recent progress in metric mapping has made it possible to build useful and accurate metric maps of reasonable large-scale environments, but memory and time complexity pose serious problems [13][19]. There have been efforts to combine metric and topological maps so that the strengths of both representations can be used [10].

2 Proposed Strategy

Robot navigation in large scale indoor environments requires an adequate representation of the working space. This representation should be abstract enough to facilitate higher level reasoning tasks like strategic planning or situation assessment, and still be detailed enough to allow the robot to perform lower level tasks like path planning/navigation or self-localization. A common belief in the robotics field is that robots need to represent and reason about information at different levels of abstraction at the same time [9][10].

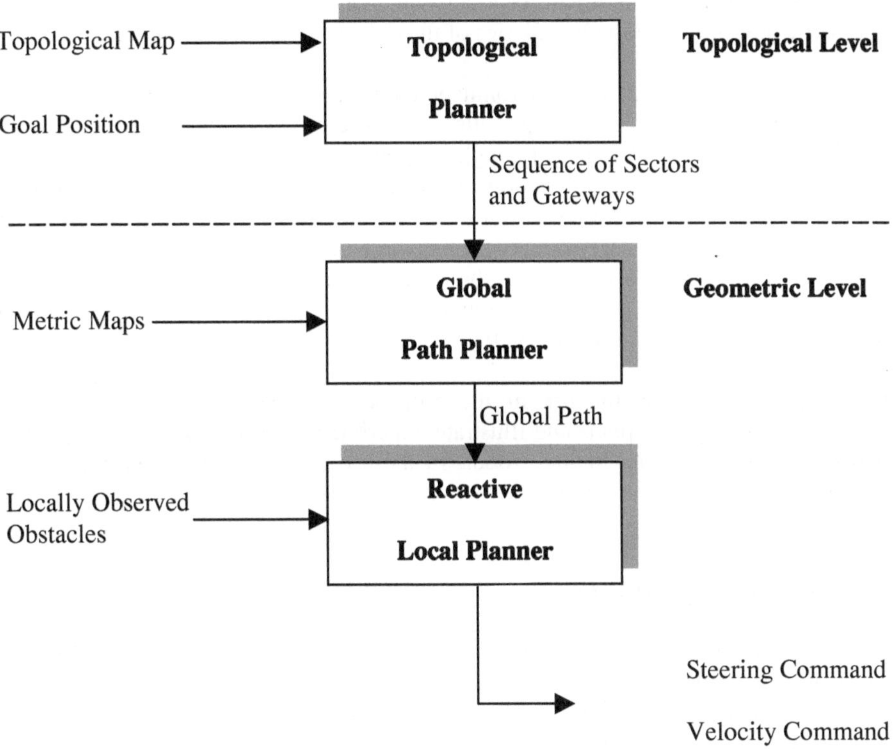

Fig. 1. Control architecture of the proposed system

There are several reasons for that [6]. First is epistemic adequacy: different tasks ask for different types of representation. For example, global path planning strategies are more easily planned using a topological map, where the planner can decide the sequence of rooms and corridors to be traversed. On the other hand, fine motion local navigation needs geometric information to precisely control the motion of the robot among features and obstacles. Second, is computational adequacy : geometric information is difficult to collect and expensive to handle, and we cannot pay the price to maintain a detailed geometric representation of the entire environment where the robot can operate. The final reason is ontological adequacy : fine grained information is difficult to obtain a priori and is likely to change with time; coarse maps are easier to estimate and more prone to remain valid over time.

In this paper, we consider the representation of spatial knowledge at the two different levels of abstraction described above, which are commonly considered in the robotics literature : the geometric level, encoded in a set of local sectors, and the topological level, encoded in a network connecting these sectors. Each sector is a Cartesian representation, with its own reference system, that covers a limited area of the environment, like a room, a hall, or a corridor. Each sector includes an approximate geometric description of the boundaries of the objects in the environment.

We propose to represent the environment by local metric maps connected into a topological network. This technique allows the use of maps that are not metrically consistent on the global scale, although they are metrically consistent locally. The structure allows also the combination of abstract global reasoning and precise local geometric computations. Moreover, this structure reflects the typical organization of indoor environments, where rooms and hallways define independent but connected local working spaces. To navigate in the environment, the robot uses the topological information to plan a sequence of sectors to traverse, and uses the metric information in each sector to locally move within the sector and to the next one.

In this paper we show the use of the proposed strategy for the generation and execution of navigation plans and illustrate experimental results of indoor navigation performed on a simulated mobile robot. In these experiments, both the topological and the local metric maps are given to the robot a priori.

3 Control Architecture

The control architecture, presented in this paper, adopts a two-level model (Fig. 1.). At the higher level of abstraction, we use topological networks to plan a sequence of sectors and gateways to traverse. At the lower level, we perform geometric path planning and navigation within each sector.

The enormous compactness of topological maps, when compared to the underlying grid-based metric map, increases the efficiency of global planning. Paths are planned using the abstract topological map of the robot's environment (Fig. 2). Shortest paths in the topological maps can be easily found using one of the standard graph search algorithms, such as Dijkstra's or Floyd and Warshal's shortest path algorithm, A^*, or dynamic programming. In the proposed strategy the Dijkstra's shortest path algorithm has been used. The task of the topological planner is to find the best/shortest path in the topological map going from the sector that contains the current location of the robot to the one that contains the goal. For example, a plan to get from the "start" position in Fig. 2 to an office desk in room R_2 may be : *first follow corridor C_1 up to junction J_1, then traverse junction J_1, then follow corridor C_2 up to door D_4, get-close-to door D_4, then cross it, then traverse room R_2, and finally get-close-to the desk.*

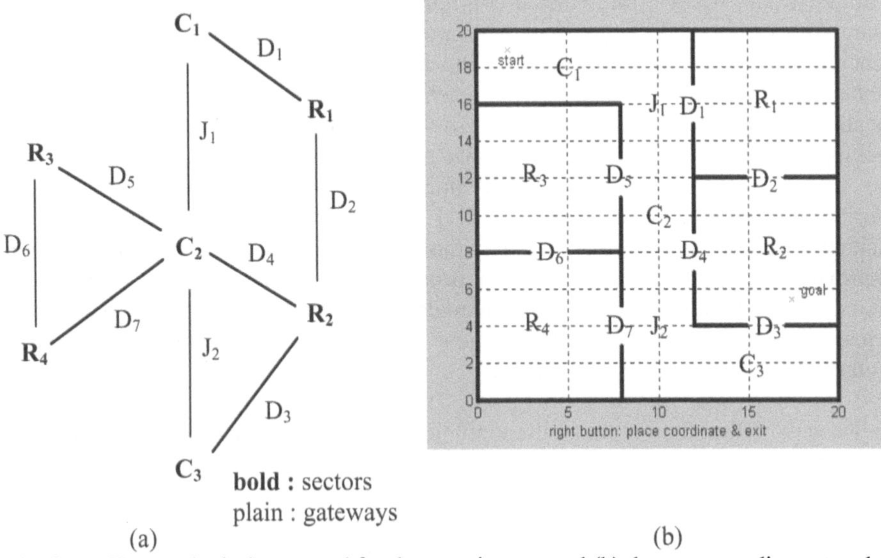

Fig. 2. (a) The topological map used for the experiments, and (b) the corresponding network of the local metric maps.

The path planning and navigation system consists of two modules : a global path planner and a reactive collision avoidance module. Control is generated hierarchically: the global planner, receives from the topological planner a sequence of sectors and gateways, and generates minimum costs paths to the goal, via these sectors and gateways, using the global metric map. As a result, it communicates intermediate subgoals to the collision avoidance routine, which controls the velocity and the exact motion direction of the robot reactively, based on the most recent sensor measurements only. Both approaches – the global path planner and the reactive collision avoidance approach – are characterized by orthogonal strengths and weaknesses. The collision avoidance approach is easily trapped in local minima, such as U-shaped obstacle configurations [12]. However, it reacts in real-time to unforeseen obstacles such as humans and is capable of changing the motion direction while the robot is moving. The global planner, in contrast, does not suffer from the local minimum problem, since it plans globally. It alone, however, is not sufficient to control the robot, since it does not take robot dynamics into account and since learned global maps are incapable of capturing moving obstacles. Thus, the global planning alone would simply not avoid collisions with humans and other rapidly moving obstacle. The task of the collision avoidance technique is to navigate the robot to subgoals generated by the planner while avoiding collisions with obstacles. It adjusts the actual velocity of the robot and chooses the concrete motion direction. For obvious reasons, the collision avoidance module must operate in real-time.

Thus, in the proposed system the control architecture in the geometric level of abstraction relies upon two main complementary modules : a *global path planner*, that receives a sequence of sectors and gateways from the topological level, and computes a nominal path between the current configuration of the robot and its goal position using the local metric maps, and a *reactive local planner*, which purpose is to generate the appropriate commands for the actuators of the robot, so as to follow the global path as close as possible, while reacting in real-time to unexpected events by locally adapting the robots movements, so as to avoid collision with unpredicted or moving obstacles. The global path planner used, is very fast and simple. It connects the various sectors by straight lines, imitating a wall-following behaviour. An artificial potential field based planner [21] has also been employed. However, this planner increases the computational complexity of the system, without any real improvement in performance. This is so, because the topological planner provides the system with a complete sequence of sub goals (sectors and gateways), and there is not a real need for complicated path planning. The global path planner can be easily replaced by a behaviour-based planner.

As we saw earlier, the output of the topological planner is a sequence of sectors and passageways. Each of these sub-tasks can be performed by a specialized behaviour, with concurrent behaviours taking care of real time obstacle avoidance. The actual trajectory followed by the robot depends on how the activated behaviours respond to the environmental contingencies encountered during execution.

The field of behaviour-based robotics has moved beyond the initial emphasis on pure reactivity, and modern behaviour-based architectures typically rely on the use of global models and temporal projection to plan a specific behaviour activation strategy that satisfies the given goals in the given environments [5][16][17][18]. Planning requires the availability of information about the connectivity of the space, given in the form of topological maps. A detailed global metric model is not necessary, since the generation of the actual trajectory is done reactively by the navigation behaviours. However, the planner needs some geometric information in order to correctly instantiate the behaviours: e.g. it should distinguish between a corridor-like space that can be traversed by wall following, and an open space to be crossed by dead reckoning. For this, topological maps can be used annotated with some metric information, as described above. A common limitation, however, is that these maps are given *a priori*.

Though, the application of a behaviour-based planner is under research at this time, and any results will be presented in future publications. The experimental results on Section 4 are obtained using the control architecture described above and is shown on

Fig. 1. The reactive local planner used, consists of two separate fuzzy controllers for global path following and obstacle avoidance. (For more detailed descriptions about the geometric level planners, please refer to [20][21][22]).

4 Experimental Results

The proposed strategy was applied to a simulated model of the Robosoft Robuter III mobile robot using the environment depicted in Fig. 2.

In experiment 1 (Fig. 3. (a)), the mobile robot was in corridor C_1 and was instructed to go to an office desk in room R_2. The output sequence/plan of the topological planner was : *first follow corridor C_1 up to junction J_1, then traverse junction J_1, then follow corridor C_2 up to door D_4, get-close-to door D_4, then cross it, then traverse room R_2, and finally get-close-to the desk.* The robot moved to its goal configuration following the path generated by the path planner. Note, that the final robot path is not equal to the generated global path, due to the local reactive fuzzy navigator.

In experiment 2 (Fig. 3. (b)), the mobile robot was in room R_1 and was instructed to go to a position in corridor C_1. The output sequence/plan of the topological planner was : *first traverse room R_1 up to door D_1, get-close-to door D_1, then cross it, then reverse junction J_1, then follow corridor C_1 and finally get-close-to goal position.* Again, the robot moved to its goal configuration following the local paths generated by the path planner.

During the 3rd experiment (Fig. 3. (c)), the mobile robot was in room R_1 and was instructed to go to an office bookcase in room R_4. The output sequence/plan of the topological planner was : *first traverse room R_1 up to door D_1, get-close-to door D_1, then cross it, then traverse corridor C_2 up to door D_7, then get-close-to door D_7, then cross it, then traverse room R_4, and finally get-close-to the bookcase.* The robot moved to its goal configuration following the local paths generated by the path planner. The same experiment was repeated (Fig. 3. (d)), with the difference that an obstacle (e.g. a chair) was introduced in room R_4. The topological map was not updated, as was the case with the global geometric map of room R_4. The generated global path was the same as in the 3rd experiment (Fig. 3. (c)). However, there was no collision with the obstacle, because the local reactive planner (fuzzy navigator) made all the appropriate adjustments to the robot's motion in order to avoid the collision.

5 Conclusions

In this paper, we proposed a strategy for indoor path planning and navigation for mobile robots. It is based on two distinct levels of abstraction: 1) local geometric information, encoded in a set of local sectors, and 2) global topological information, encoded in a network connecting these sectors. Each sector is a Cartesian representation, with its own reference system, that covers a limited area of the environment, like a room, a hall, or a corridor, and includes an approximate geometric description of the boundaries of the objects in the environment.

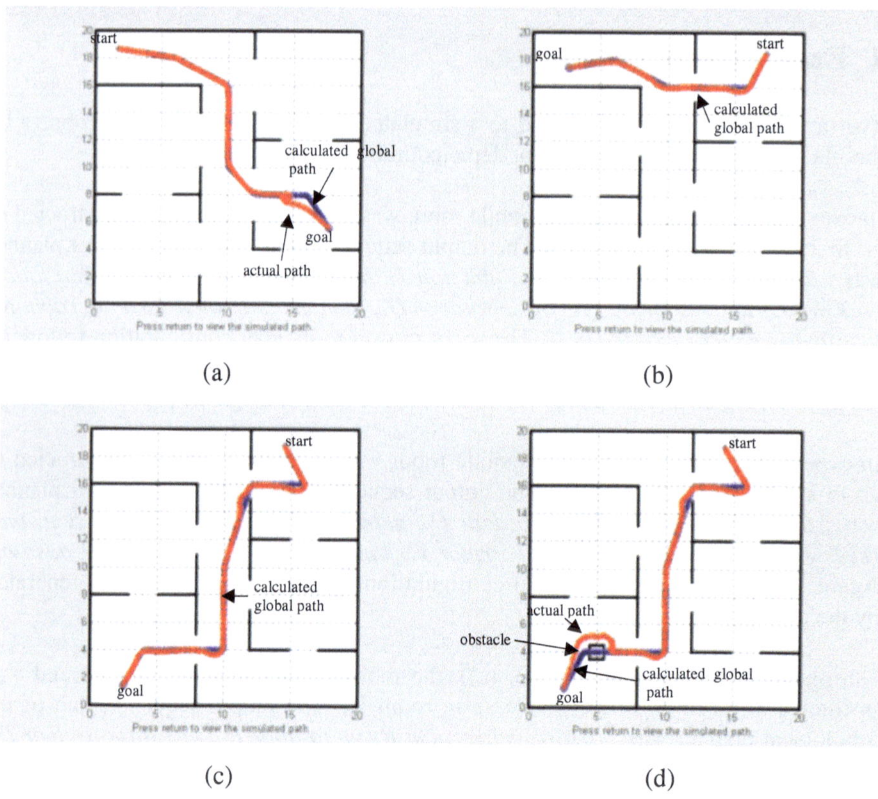

Fig. 3. During the experiments (a), (b), (c) and (d), the robot was instructed to move to different locations in the office. The calculated global path (blue), and the actual robot path (red) are shown.

We propose to represent the environment by local metric maps connected into a topological network. This technique allows the use of maps that are not metrically consistent on the global scale, although they are metrically consistent locally. The structure allows also the combination of abstract global reasoning and precise local geometric computations. Moreover, this structure reflects the typical organization of indoor environments, where rooms and hallways define independent but connected local working spaces. To navigate in the environment, the robot uses, at the higher level of abstraction, the topological information to plan a sequence of sectors and gateways to traverse, and, at the lower level, uses the metric information in each sector to perform geometric path planning and navigation, and to locally move within the sector and to the next one. The use of topological maps offers an enormous compactness to the system compared to grid-based metric maps, and the global path planner is very simple and fast (calculation of the complete path in msecs). Thus, the computational complexity of the system is kept very low, allowing fast calculations. Another, very important advantage, is the incorporation of an intelligent reactive local planner (fuzzy navigator [22]), for global path following and local obstacle avoidance, allowing the use of the system, to partially unknown, time-varying and dynamic environments.

The system has shown a very stable and robust performance, providing each time the mobile robot with a collision free movement. Future research, will aim at the application of a behaviour-based planner, in order to accomplish a complete indoor navigation strategy for mobile robots. Also, an immediate task is the application of the proposed strategy to a real mobile robot to test its functionality under real-world conditions. Finally, issues like map building, localization and dead-reckoning, which have not been mentioned in this paper, will be examined closely.

Acknowledgement. The research carried out by P. G. Zavlangas and S. G. Tzafestas was supported by the European Union and Greek Secretariat for Research and Technology.
(Project HYGIOROBOT – PENED – 99ED623)

References

1. Brooks R. : Visual map making for a mobile robot. *Proc. of the IEEE International Conference on Robotics and Automation*, Los Alamos, CA, USA (1985) 824-829
2. Chatila, R., Laumond, J. P. : Position referencing and consistent world modeling for mobile robots. *Proc. of the IEEE International Conference on Robotics and Automation* (1985)
3. Dudek, D., Jenkin, M., Milios, E., Wilkes, D.: Robotic exploration as graph construction. *IEEE Trans. on Robotics and Automation*, **7(6)** (1991) 859-865
4. Fabrizi, E., Saffiotti, A.: Extracting topology-based maps from gridmaps. *Proc. of the IEEE International Conference on Robotics and Automation*, San Francisco, CA, USA (2000)
5. Fabrizi, E., Saffiotti, A.: Behavioral navigation on topology-based maps. *Proc. of the 8th International Symposium on Robotics and Applications*, Maui, Hawaii, June (2000)
6. Gasos, J., Saffiotti, A.: Integrating fuzzy geometric maps and topological maps for robot navigation. *Proc. of the 3rd International ICSC Symposium on Soft Computing (SOCO'99)*, Genova, Italy (1999) 754-760
7. Kortenkamp, D., Weymouth, T.: Topological mapping for mobile robots using combination of sonar and vision sensing. *Proc. of the AAAI Conf.*, Menlo Park, CA, USA (1994) 979-984
8. Kortenkamp, D., Bonasso, R.P., Murphy, R (editors): Artificial Intelligence and Mobile Robots : Case Studies of Successful Robot Systems. *The AAAI Press/The MIT Press*, Menlo Park, CA, USA (1998)
9. Kuipers, B.: Modeling spatial knowledge. *Cognitive Science*, **2** (1978) 129-153
10. Kuipers, B., Levitt, T.: Navigation and mapping in large scale space. *AI Magazine*, **9** (1988) 25-43

11. Kuipers, B., Byun, Y.T.: A robot exploration and mapping strategy based on a semantic hierarchy of spatial representations. *Journal of Robotics and Automation Systems*, **18(12)** (1996) 1163-1173
12. Latombe, J.C.: Robot Motion Planning. *Kluwer Publishers, Boston* (1991)
13. Lu, F., Milios, E.: Globally consistent range scan alignment for environment mapping. *Autonomous robots*, **4** (1997) 333-349
14. Moravec, H.P., Elfes, A.: High resolution maps from wide angle sonar. *Proc. of the IEEE International Conference on Robotics and Automation*, (1985) pp. 116-121
15. Moravec, H.P.: Sensor fusion in certainty grids for mobile robots. *AI Magazine*, 61-74 (1988)
16. Payton, D.W., Rosebblatt, J.K., Keirsey, D.M.: Plan guided reaction. *IEEE Trans. on Systems, Man, and Cybernetics*, **20(6)** (1990) 1370-1382
17. Ryu, B.S., Yang, H.S.: Integration of reactive behaviors and enhanced topological map for robust mobile robot navigation. *IEEE Trans. on Systems, Man, and Cybernetics*, **29(5)** (1999) 474-485
18. Surmann, H., Peters, L.: The uses of fuzzy control for the autonomous robot Moria. *In D. Driankov and A. Saffioti, eds., Fuzzy Logic in Autonomous Robot.Navigation*, Springer (2000)
19. Thrun, S.: Learning metric-topological maps for indoor mobile robot navigation. *Artificial Intelligence*, **1** (1999) 21-71
20. Zavlangas, P.G., Tzafestas, S.G.: Integrated fuzzy global path following and obstacle avoidance for mobile robots. *Servicerob 2001*, Santorini, Greece (2001)
21. Zavlangas, P.G., Tzafestas, S.G.: Hierarchical Motion Control System for Mobile Robot Path Planning and Navigation. *To appear.*
22. Zavlangas, P.G., Tzafestas, S.G.: Fuzzy Obstacle Avoidance and Navigation for Omnidirectional mobile robots. *ESIT 2000: European Symposium on Intelligent Techniques*, Aachen, Germany (2000)

Symbolic Authoring for Multilingual Natural Language Generation

Ion Androutsopoulos, Dimitris Spiliotopoulos, Konstantinos Stamatakis, Aggeliki Dimitromanolaki, Vangelis Karkaletsis, and Constantine D. Spyropoulos

Software and Knowledge Engineering Laboratory
Institute of Informatics and Telecommunications
National Centre for Scientific Research (NCSR) "Demokritos"
P.O. Box 60228, GR-153 10 Ag. Paraskevi, Athens, Greece
{ionandr, dspiliot, kstam, adimit, vangelis, costass}@iit.demokritos.gr

Abstract. We describe the symbolic authoring facilities of the M-PIRO project. M-PIRO is developing technology that allows personalized multilingual object descriptions, in both textual and spoken form, to be produced from symbolic information in a database and small fragments of text. The technology is being tested in the context of electronic museums, where a prototype that produces dynamically multilingual exhibit descriptions for presentations over the web has already been developed. This paper focuses on M-PIRO's authoring subsystem, which allows domain experts with no language technology expertise to configure the system for new applications. The authoring facilities allow the experts to define or modify the structure of the underlying database, its contents, and the system's domain-dependent linguistic resources. Previews of the generated texts can also be produced during the authoring process to monitor the content and quality of the resulting descriptions.

1 Introduction

This paper presents the symbolic authoring facilities that are being developed within the M-PIRO project.[1] Drawing upon techniques from natural language generation [17], speech synthesis, and user modeling, M-PIRO is developing technology that allows personalized descriptions of objects to be generated dynamically in several languages, in both textual and spoken form, starting from symbolic, language-independent information in a database, and small fragments of text. The resulting technology is expected to have a wide range of applications, from electronic sales catalogues to computer games. During the project, it is being tested in the context of

[1] M-PIRO (Multilingual Personalized Information Objects) is a project of the Information Societies Programme of the European Union, running from February 2000 to January 2003. The project's consortium consists of the University of Edinburgh (UK, co-ordinator), ITC-irst (Italy), NCSR "Demokritos" (Greece), the University of Athens (Greece), the Foundation of the Hellenic World (Greece), and System Simulation Ltd (UK).

I.P. Vlahavas and C.D. Spyropoulos (Eds.): SETN 2002, LNAI 2308, pp. 131–142, 2002.

electronic museums, to enhance web-based interaction with exhibit collections and speech-enabled tours in virtual reality.

Although the project is still in progress, large-scale prototypes have already been implemented, and they will be used in this paper to highlight the functionality of the emerging technology. Figure 1 shows an example from M-PIRO's current web-based prototype. Visitors select exhibits from a catalogue that contains thumbnail images, and the system replies with dynamically generated descriptions of the exhibits. Apart from the sentence that describes the wedding scene, all of the text in Figure 1 has been generated automatically from non-linguistic information in the database. The descriptions can also be generated in Italian and Greek, as demonstrated in Figure 2, from the same underlying database, reducing dramatically translation costs. Furthermore, the descriptions are customized according to what the visitor has already seen, avoiding repeating information that has already been conveyed, and comparing, when possible, the current exhibit to previous ones. The text of Figure 1, for example, points out that the exhibit belongs to the same period as the previous one. The description is also tailored according to the user type. The prototype distinguishes between children, non-expert adults, and experts. Descriptions for children are typically shorter, while expert descriptions contain, for example, additional references to related articles, and avoid explaining common archaeological terms.

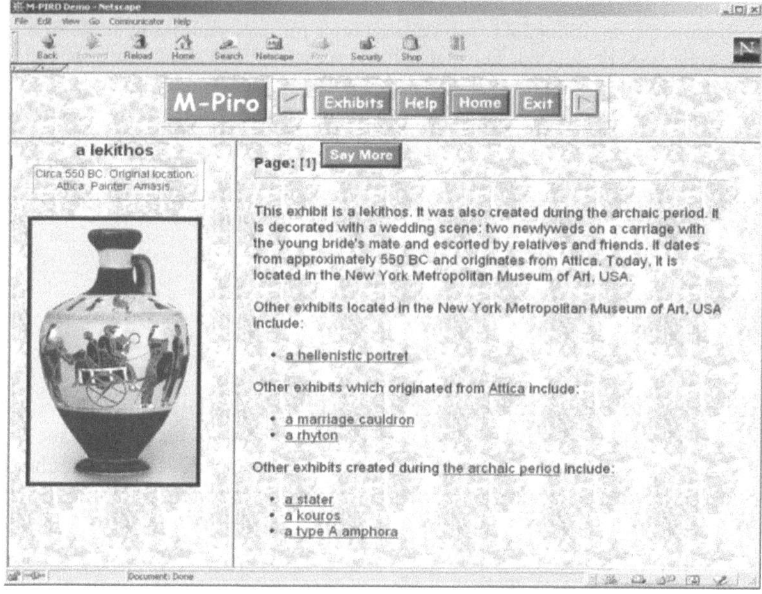

Fig. 1. A dynamically generated exhibit description in English

M-PIRO builds upon the ILEX natural language generation system [12, 13], which was originally used to produce dynamically exhibit descriptions for a web-based electronic gallery of 20th century jewellery. It extends ILEX's technology by incorporating improved multilingual capabilities [5], a more modular core generation engine, and high-quality speech output [3, 19]. The latter is needed in virtual reality tours, where work has just commenced to use M-PIRO's technology as an intelligent guide. One of M-PIRO's most ambitious goals, which also distinguishes it from ILEX and other similar generation systems [4, 10], is that domain experts, such as curators in the context of museums, will be able to configure M-PIRO's technology for new application domains, e.g., new museum collections or collections outside the museum context, without the intervention of language technology experts. This is achieved via M-PIRO's authoring subsystem, which is the focus of this paper; a broader overview of M-PIRO can be found elsewhere [1]. Although familiarity with computers and some training on the use of the authoring subsystem is still required, M-PIRO's authoring facilities constitute a significant advance compared to most natural language generation systems, where porting the system to a new domain requires programming and expertise in natural language generation.

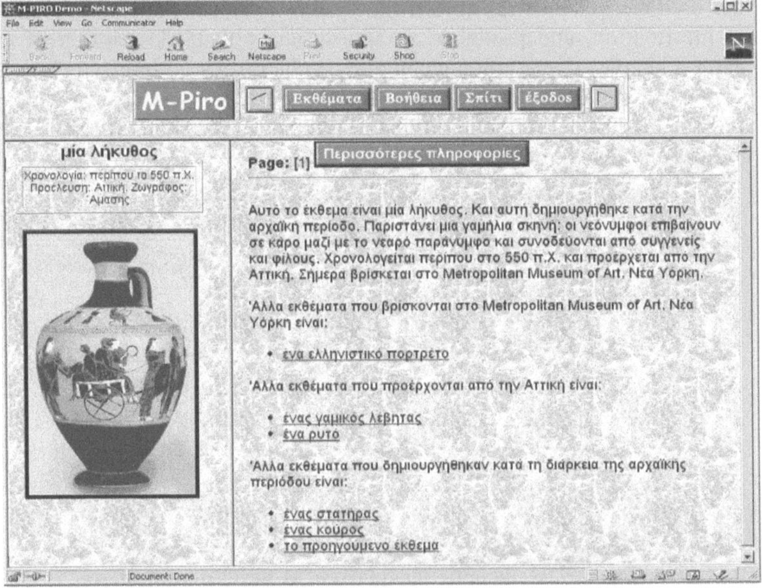

Fig. 2. A dynamically generated exhibit description in Greek

Unlike systems like KPML [2], M-PIRO's authoring subsystem is not intended to assist language technology experts in creating and maintaining domain-independent linguistic resources, such as large-scale grammars. In that sense, M-PIRO's authoring is closer to the symbolic authoring facilities of DRAFTER [14] and GIST [15]. Unlike those systems, however, M-PIRO does not target a specific application domain, and allows the domain experts, hereafter called *authors* to manipulate not only the contents of the database, but also its structure and the domain-dependent linguistic resources that control how the information of the database is rendered in natural language. This allows the authors to control, for example, the vocabulary and form of the generated sentences, as well as, in ongoing work, the rhetorical structure of the resulting descriptions [8].

Section 2 below provides more information about the role of the authoring subsystem in M-PIRO's architecture. Sections 3, 4 and 5 then discuss in more detail some of the facilities that the authoring subsystem provides, namely facilities that allow the authors to manipulate the underlying database, domain-specific aspects of sentence planning, and the domain-dependent lexicon, respectively. Section 6 concludes with targets for future work, which include evaluation plans and ways to re-use information in existing databases.

2 System Architecture and the Role of the Authoring Subsystem

Figure 3 illustrates the role of the authoring subsystem in M-PIRO's architecture. Once the user has selected an object, the system retrieves from the database all the relevant information, and produces an appropriate textual description of the object using natural language generation techniques, to be discussed briefly below. In virtual reality environments, the description is then passed to a speech synthesizer, which produces the audio output, exploiting additional markup made available by the generation components, much as in [18].

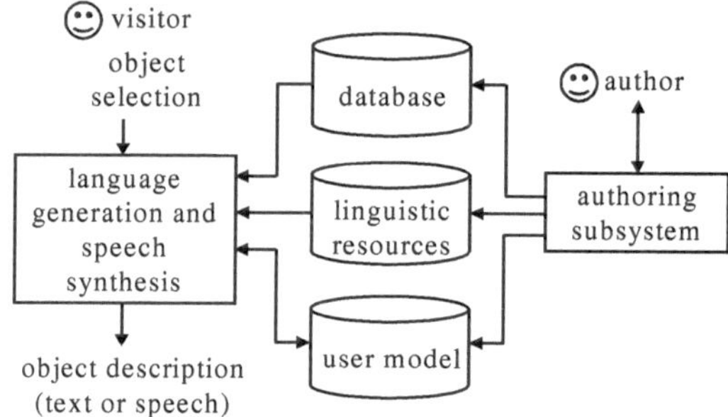

Fig. 3. The authoring subsystem in M-PIRO's architecture

Many of the linguistic resources on which the generation process relies, most notably its systemic grammars [5, 6], are to a large extent domain-independent. Some of these resources, however, are domain-specific, and one of the roles of the authoring subsystem is to allow authors to modify them for new application domains, hiding many of the underlying linguistic complexities. A second role of the subsystem is to allow the authors to manipulate the structure and contents of the database, establishing links between database constructs and linguistic resources where necessary. The third role of the subsystem is to help the authors define the types of visitors and their properties. Among other things, this includes defining stereotypes that indicate the educational value and interest of the various facts in the database for each visitor type. M-PIRO's user modeling mechanisms are based on those of ILEX, which are described in [12] and [13]. We will highlight some of the user modeling tasks that the authoring subsystem is faced with, but since work on these aspects of authoring is still in progress, this paper will focus on facilities that manipulate the database and domain-dependent linguistic resources.

To obtain a clearer view of the authoring tasks, let us now examine briefly the stages of the generation process in M-PIRO, as outlined in Figure 4; we ignore in the rest of this paper issues related to speech synthesis. The input to the generation process is the database, as shaped by the authors using the facilities that allow them to manipulate its structure and contents, and the object to be described. The first stage of the generation process, called *content selection*, is concerned with the selection from the database of the most appropriate facts to be conveyed to the visitor. It exploits user modeling information, such as the stereotypes mentioned above and the interaction history of the visitor, which shows the facts that have already been conveyed. The next stage, *document planning*, outputs an overall document structure, which specifies, for example, the desired sequence of the facts in the generated description, and their rhetorical relations; for example, whether a fact amplifies or contrasts another one [7, 8].

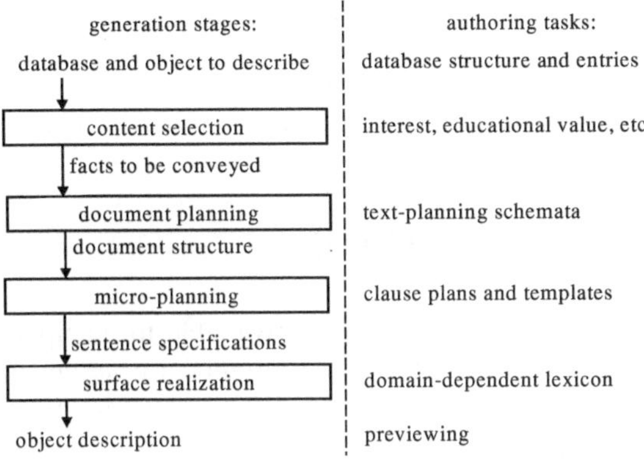

Fig. 4. Generation stages in M-PIRO and the corresponding authoring tasks

M-PIRO has inherited from ILEX a variety of domain-independent document planners, which are being extended to allow the authors to specify domain-dependent schema-like planning rules [9] to capture structural characteristics of object descriptions in particular domains. Descriptions of museum exhibits, for example, typically start with information about the type and creation period of the exhibit. The curator of a collection of coins may wish to specify that descriptions should then proceed with a description of what the two sides of the coin depict, followed by information about the material and style. Work on this aspect of authoring is just starting in M-PIRO, and will not be discussed any further. In contrast, the authoring facilities that are associated with the next two stages of the generation process, *micro-planning* and *surface realization*, are more fully developed.

Micro-planning specifies in abstract terms how a fact can be expressed as a clause in each language; for example, which verb to use, in what tense, and which argument of the fact should be rendered as subject or object. The authoring subsystem allows this information to be specified in two alternative forms, *clause plans* and *templates*, to be discussed in Section 4. Micro-planning also includes the generation of referring expressions, also to be discussed in Section 4, and processing that determines which facts can be aggregated in a single sentence. M-PIRO employs the aggregation rules of ILEX (see [13]), which are domain-independent, and hence require no input from the authors.

The last stage, surface realization, is responsible for producing the final textual form of the descriptions. This includes producing the appropriate word forms (e.g., verb tenses) based on the sentence specifications output by micro-planning, placing the various constituents (e.g., subject, verb, object, adverbials) in the correct order, accounting for number and gender agreement, etc. Surface realization is based on large-scale systemic grammars [6], one for each supported language, that were constructed using ILEX's English grammar as a starting point [5]. While the grammars are domain-independent, a part of the lexicon that they employ, called the *domain-dependent lexicon*, needs to be tuned when the system is ported to a new domain; related authoring facilities will be discussed in Section 5.

Finally, it is important to be able to preview the resulting object descriptions, to monitor the content and quality of the generated texts. The authoring subsystem allows previews to be generated during the authoring process, a point that will be illustrated in following sections. In effect, this introduces a form of interactive symbolic authoring, whereby changes in the symbolic description of the domain and the linguistic resources are immediately reflected on the generated object descriptions.

3 Database Structure and Entries

Let us now examine the facilities that are available to manipulate the structure and content of the database. An entity-relationship model is assumed; i.e., the database is taken to hold information about entities (e.g., statues, artists) and relationships between entities (e.g., the artist of each statue). Entities can be concrete or abstract objects (e.g., historical periods or styles), and they are organized in a hierarchy of entity types, as illustrated in Figure 5. In this example, *exhibit* and *historical-period* are basic entity types; the *exhibit* type is further subdivided into *vessel*, *statue*, and *coin*. Each entity belongs to a particular entity type; for example, *exhibit 2* is a *kouros* and, therefore, also a *statue* and an *exhibit*. To make the authoring subsystem easier to use, we have opted for a single-inheritance hierarchy, although the underlying generation engine can also handle multiple inheritance. There are also mechanisms to link the basic entity types to the Upper Model [2], a built-in domain-independent hierarchy that contains the most common types; this allows making some aspects of the generation process insensitive to the domain-dependent hierarchy.

Relationships are expressed using fields. At each entity type, it is possible to introduce new fields, which then become available to all the entities of the type and its subtypes. For example, the *statue* type in Figure 5 introduces the field *sculpted-by*; consequently, all the entities of this type, including entities of type *kouros* and *portrait*, carry this field. The *creation-period* field is inherited from the *exhibit* type, and is, therefore, also available with non-statue exhibits; inherited fields are shown in different colour. The fillers of each field must be entities of a particular type. In Figure 5, the fillers of *creation-period* must belong to the type *historical-period*; this licenses entities like *archaic-period* and *classical-period* to be used as values of the field. The *Set?* option in Figure 5 allows a field to be filled by multiple fillers of the specified type; in the *made-of* field, this allows entering more than one material.

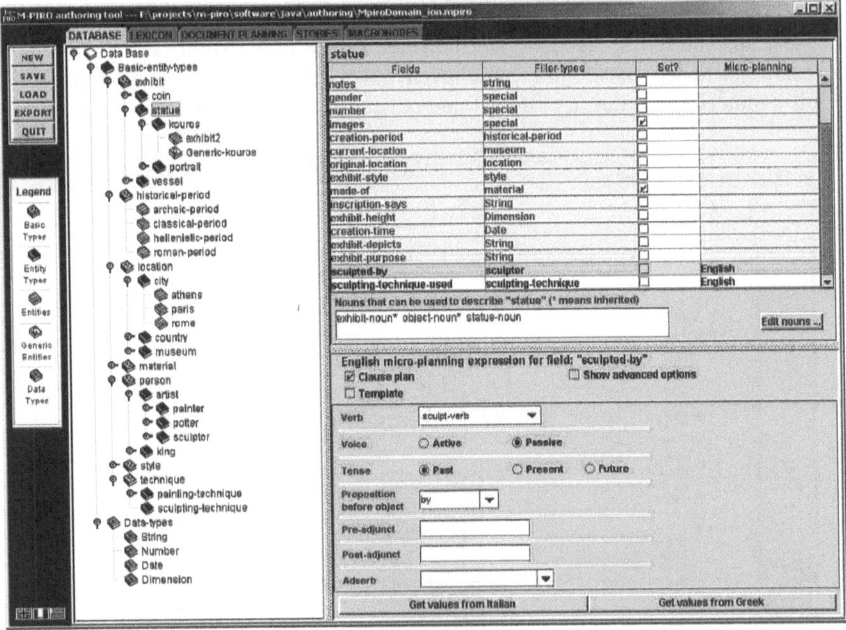

Fig. 5. The structure of the database and a clause-plan

Fields are also used to express attributes of entities, for example, their names or dimensions. Several built-in data-types are available, like *string* and *date*, and they are used to specify the allowed values of attribute-denoting fields. In Figure 5, *exhibit-depicts* and *exhibit-purpose* are string-valued. They are intended to hold canned sentences describing what the exhibits depict and their purposes; the sentence that describes the wedding scene in Figure 1 is the value of an *exhibit-depicts* field. String-valued attributes are used with information that is too difficult to express using full text generation; the drawback is that their values must be entered in all of the supported languages. Notice, however, that some of the benefits of natural language generation are still available with string-valued attributes; for example, they are assigned interest and educational values, like all the other facts in the database, and the text planning schemata can be instructed to place their string values to appropriate positions. Larger, paragraph-long canned texts can be associated with particular entities or entity types via the *stories* tab of Figure 5.

Once the hierarchy and the fields of the entity types have been created, it is possible to insert database entries about particular entities, as illustrated in Figure 6. Pull-down menus and forms guide the authors to select among the allowed values of the fields. Provided that appropriate lexicon entries and micro-plans –to be discussed in following sections– have been entered, previews of the resulting object descriptions can be generated, as shown in Figure 6.[2] The values of language-dependent fields,

---

[2] Work on the integration of the authoring subsystem with the underlying generation engine is currently in progress. Figure 6 illustrates the previewing that will be available once the integration is complete.

such as the string-valued *exhibit-purpose*, which gives rise to the sentence about Kroissos, are entered by clicking on the flags in the upper right part of Figure 6. In this example, content selection has chosen not to convey the information about the exhibit's material, because its interest and educational values are low.

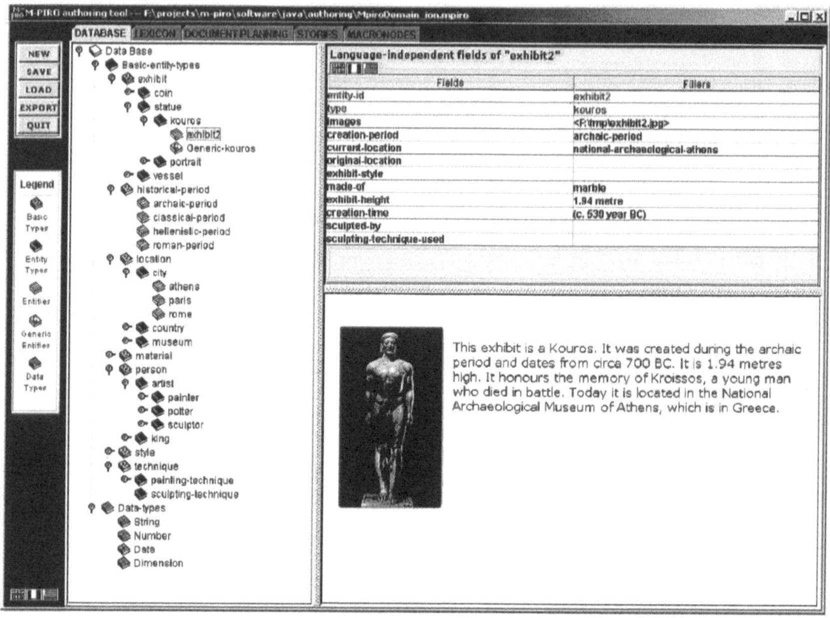

Fig. 6. Entering and previewing information about an object

To capture default information about all the entities of a type, *generic entities* can be introduced. For example, the *creation-period* field of the *Generic-kouros* entity in Figure 6 could be assigned the value *archaic-period.* This would indicate that, unless otherwise mentioned, a kouros belongs to the archaic period.

4 Clause Plans and Templates

During the authoring process, a micro-plan needs to be specified for each database field and language, to specify how the field can be expressed as a clause. Following Ilex, M-PIRO supports two forms of micro-plans: *clause plans* and *templates.*

In clause plans, the author specifies the verb to be used (from those available in the domain-specific lexicon, to be discussed in Section 5), the voice and tense of the resulting clause, the preposition, if any, to be included between the verb and the object, any desired adverb, and strings to be concatenated as adjuncts at the beginning or end of the clause. The micro-plan in Figure 5 leads to clauses like "This statue was sculpted by Polyklitus". Appropriate referring expressions (e.g., "Polyklitus", "a sculptor", "him") are generated automatically by the generation engine. Advanced clause-planning options allow the authors to select manually the case and type of a referring expression, the mood of the clause, and whether or not it can be aggregated. Clause-plans for the supported languages are often very similar, and verbs are kept aligned across the languages, as will be discussed in Section 5. The "get values from" buttons in Figure 5 speed up the authoring process by setting the fields of the clause plan to the same values as their counterparts in the other languages, where possible.

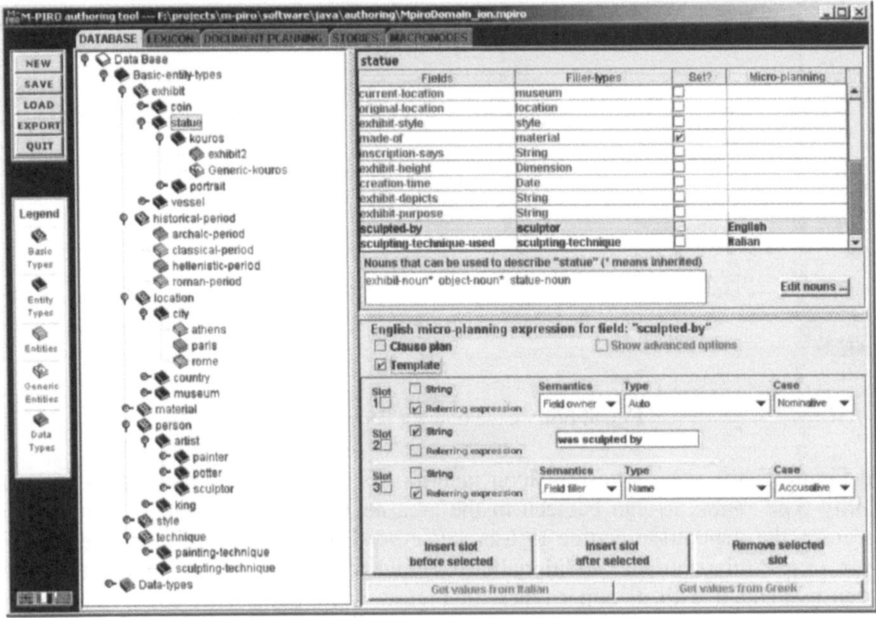

Fig. 7. A micro-plan in the form of a template

Templates provide stricter control over the surface form of the resulting clauses than do clause plans. A template is a sequence of slots, the values of which are simply concatenated to produce a clause. Figure 7 shows an alternative micro-plan for the *sculpted-by* field of Figure 5 in the form of a template. Each slot can be filled by a particular string, an expression referring to the owner of the field (the statue, in the case of *sculpted-by*), or a referring expression for the field's filler (the sculptor). Templates carry less linguistic information than clause-plans, which does not allow the generation engine to exploit its full potential; for example, some forms of aggregation cannot be used with templates. However, templates are the only option when fields need to be rendered in forms other than clauses; e.g., copyright notes.

5 Domain-Dependent Lexicon

The domain-dependent lexicon contains entries for nouns and verbs, as shown in Figure 8. The entries for function words, such as articles and prepositions, are domain-independent and are kept separately. Nouns are associated with entity types;

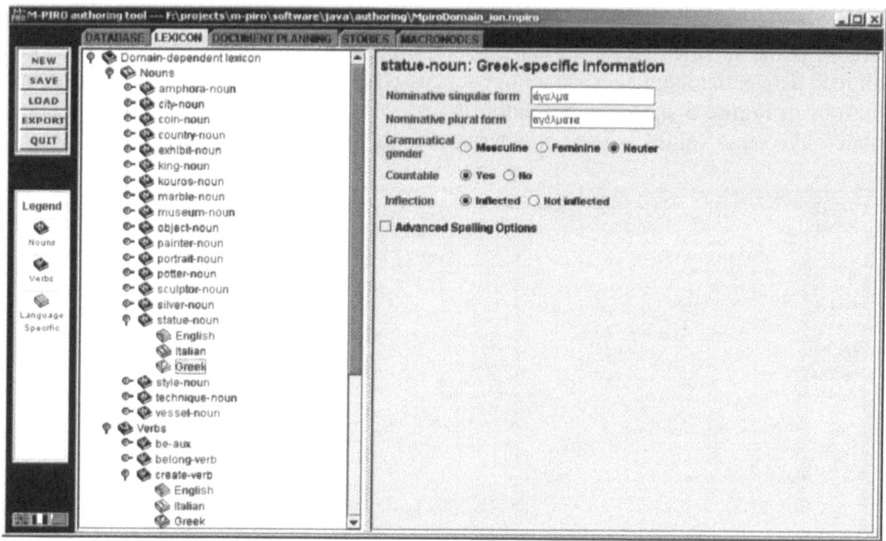

Fig. 8. Editing the domain-dependent lexicon

in Figure 7, the noun whose lexicon identifier is *statue-noun* is associated with the entity type *statue*, as can be seen in the area next to the "edit nouns" button. This licenses the generation engine to use *statue-noun* when referring to entities of this type (e.g., "this statue"). Additionally, each entity type inherits the nouns that have been associated with its super-types. In Figure 7, the entity type *statue* inherits the nouns *exhibit-noun* and *object-noun*, which have been associated with the type *exhibit*; hence, when referring to a statue, those nouns can also be used ("this exhibit" or "this object"). In practice, after defining the hierarchy of entity types, the author associates at least one noun with each entity type by selecting nouns from the domain-dependent lexicon.[3] If the domain-dependent lexicon does not contain the desired nouns, they first have to be inserted into the lexicon as shown in Figure 8. The system encourages the authors to keep the lexicons of the supported languages aligned by treating each entry as a triplet that contains nouns or verbs with equivalent senses in the three languages. For example, the entry of *statue-noun* contains "statue", "statua", and "άγαλμα", for English, Italian, and Greek. This helps maintain the same linguistic coverage across all languages. Entering verbs is similar, except that what leads the author to add a new verb is the need to use it in a clause-plan (Section 4).

Like most natural language generation systems, M-PIRO's domain-dependent lexicon is typically rather small; there are approximately 45 noun and 25 verb entries in the domain of the current web-based prototype, many of which (e.g., "amphora", "kouros") are unlikely to be found in general-purpose dictionaries. Hence, instead of attempting to reuse existing large-scale electronic dictionaries, we have opted for facilities that simplify entering new nouns and verbs. In the case of Greek nouns, for

[3] A few domain-independent noun entries also exist. They are linked to types of the Upper Model, and they are used when an entity type is not associated with any noun of the domain-dependent lexicon.

example, the dictionary of the underlying generation engine contains several features pertaining to the inflection pattern of the noun, the position of the stress in its various forms, etc. The authoring subsystem incorporates facilities that determine and add automatically these features by examining the nominative singular and plural forms of the noun. Morphology rules are also present, which generate automatically the remaining forms of the nouns, and similar facilities are available for verbs. The "advanced spelling options" button in Figure 8 allows those automatically generated forms to be inspected and corrected, if necessary.

6 Conclusions and Future Work

We have presented M-PIRO's authoring facilities, which help domain experts with no language technology expertise configure the system for new application domains. The authoring facilities currently allow the domain experts to manipulate the structure and content of the underlying database, as well as the domain-specific linguistic resources that are used during micro-planning and surface realization. Work is in progress to provide additional facilities for entering user types, stereotypes, and text planning schemata. Additional work is considering how support for *MacroNodes* can be provided; this is a technology deriving from the HIPS project [11] that allows canned texts to be customized according to the user model that has been activated, providing many of the benefits of full-scale generation.

Domain experts are currently using the authoring facilities to extend the domain of the web-based prototype, and the same facilities will be used to port M-PIRO's technology to another collection of exhibits in a virtual reality environment. Both activities will provide feedback on the usability of the authoring subsystem and the portability of the overall technology. A complementary strand of work is considering how existing museum databases can be interconnected with M-PIRO's components.

Finally, it would be interesting to examine how more active forms of previewing can be made available. Additional mark-up could be exploited to allow the authors to inspect database fields, micro-plans, or dictionary entries by selecting the corresponding clauses or words in the generated texts; this would help them repair anomalies in the content or realization of the texts. Mechanisms of this kind could be seen as an attempt to link symbolic authoring to the WYSIWYM approach [16], where authors interact with the system entirely via generated texts that reflect both the content of the database and the options that are available to update it.

References

1. I. Androutsopoulos, V. Kokkinaki, A. Dimitromanolaki, J. Calder, J. Oberlander and E. Not. "Generating Multilingual Personalized Descriptions of Museum Exhibits – The M-PIRO Project". Proc. *29th Conference on Computer Applications and Quantitative Methods in Archaeology*, Gotland, Sweden, 2001.
2. J. A. Bateman. "Enabling Technology for Multilingual Natural Language Generation". *Natural Language Engineering*, 3(1):15–55, 1997.

3. P. Cosi, F. Tesser, R. Gretter and C. Avesani. "Festival Speaks Italian!". Proc. *7th European Conference on Speech Communication and Technology*, Aalborg, Denmark, 2001.
4. R. Dale, S.J. Green, M. Milosavljevic, C. Paris, C. Verspoor and S. Williams. "Dynamic Document Delivery: Generating Natural Language Texts on Demand". Proc. *9th International Conference and Workshop on Expert Systems Applications*, Vienna, Austria, 1998.
5. A. Dimitromanolaki, I. Androutsopoulos and V. Karkaletsis. "A Large-Scale Systemic Functional Grammar of Greek". Presented at the *5th International Conference on Greek Linguistics*, Sorbonne, France, 2001.
6. M. Halliday. *An Introduction to Functional Grammar*. Edward Arnold, London, 1985.
7. E. Hovy. "Automated Discourse Generation Using Discourse Structure Relations". *Artificial Intelligence*, 63(1–2): 341–386, 1993.
8. W. Mann and S. Thompson. "Rhetorical Structure Theory: Towards a Functional Theory of Text Organization". *Text*, 3:243–281, 1988.
9. K.R. McKeown. *Text Generation*. Cambridge University Press, 1995.
10. M. Milosavljevic and J. Oberlander. "Dynamic Hypertext Catalogues: Helping Users to Help Themselves". Proc. *9th ACM Conference on Hypertext and Hypermedia*, Pittsburgh, PA, 1998.
11. E. Not and M. Zancanaro. "The MacroNode Approach: Mediating between Adaptive and Dynamic Hypermedia". Proc. *International Conference on Adaptive Hypermedia and Adaptive Web-based Systems*, Trento, Italy, 2000.
12. J. Oberlander, M. O'Donnell, A. Knott and C. Mellish. "Conversation in the Museum: Experiments in Dynamic Hypermedia with the Intelligent Labelling Explorer". *New Review of Hypermedia and Multimedia*, 4:11–32, 1998.
13. M. O'Donnell, C. Mellish, J. Oberlander and A. Knott. "ILEX: An Architecture for a Dynamic Hypertext Generation System". *Natural Language Engineering*, 7(3):225–250, 2001.
14. C. Paris, K. Vander Linden, M. Fischer, A. Hartley, L. Pemberton, R. Power and D. Scott. "A Support Tool for Writing Multilingual Instructions". Proc. *14th International Joint Conference on Artificial Intelligence*, Montreal, Canada, pp. 1398–1404, 1995.
15. R. Power and N. Cavallotto. "Multilingual Generation of Administrative Forms". Proc. *8th International Workshop on Natural Language Generation*, pp. 17–19, Herstmonceux Castle, U.K., 1996.
16. R. Power and D. Scott. "Multilingual Authoring Using Feedback Texts". Proc. *36th Meeting of the ACL and 17th International Conference on Computational Linguistics*, pp. 1053–1059, Montreal, Canada, 1998.
17. E. Reiter and R. Dale. *Building Applied Natural Language Generation Systems*. Cambridge University Press, 2000.
18. M. Theune, E. Klabbers, J.R. De Pijper, E. Krahmer and J. Odijk. "From Data to Speech: A General Approach". *Natural Language Engineering*, 7(1):47–86, 2001.
19. G. Xydas and G. Kouroupetroglou. "Text-to-Speech Scripting Interface for Appropriate Vocalization of e-Texts". Proc. *7th European Conference on Speech Communication and Technology*, Aalborg, Denmark, 2001.

A User-Sensitive Spoken Dialogue System Incorporating Emotional Responsiveness

Gloria Dabiri, Michael Brown, Maria Aretoulaki, and Matthias Nitzsche

SemanticEdge GmbH, Kaiserin-Augusta-Allee 10-11, 10553 Berlin, Germany
chlor@zedat.fu-berlin.de,
{michael,maria,matthiasn}@semanticedge.com

Abstract. Most commercial dialogue applications are very task-oriented and take little account of indirect user desires or emotional behaviour. As a result, interaction is often inefficient and can lead to user dissatisfaction. The SemanticEdge system described here allows for more responsive dialogue applications, where different users with disparate needs are dynamically classified and their emotions are identified in the course of the dialogue. This reasoning about the specific user (their goals, desires and behaviour), coupled with reasoning about the main interaction task of the dialogue, allows for more appropriate system responses, e.g. in the case of misunderstandings and user anger or in targeted marketing activities.

1 Motivation

A key requirement for a human-computer interface to be user-sensitive is efficiency. By enabling natural language input, as opposed to the limiting pull-down menus of conventional graphical interfaces, efficiency is achieved, because of the economy of language in performing multiple actions simultaneously. In allowing people to interact with a machine via natural language, however, there is the danger that undue intelligence is assumed of the system, which in turn often leads to disappointment and dissatisfaction, when it does not demonstrate all the communication skills of a human operator. One source of frustration can be that the system poses questions and gives answers that the user deems irrelevant. This is caused by the lack of adequate user profiling, i.e. modelling the fact that different types of users have different needs [1], [2]. Users also become impatient, if the system ignores the emotional aspects of their responses; a user that expresses disappointment implicitly expects the system to try and resolve the source of this disappointment rather than continue blasé with the main thread of the dialogue. A practical system for tackling these issues is outlined below.

Recently, an in-house analysis was carried out at SemanticEdge of different natural language dialogue systems available on the Internet, so-called (chat)bots, such as those at http://www.botspot.com/search/s-chat.htm [3]. Available spoken dialogue systems, e.g. those at http://www.ling.gu.se/~sl/dialogue_links.html, were also studied [3]. Both studies showed that the simulation of human-human interaction in the context of an automatic system necessarily entails the accurate assessment of the social situation and the building of a *social relationship* with the user. As in normal social interaction, communication should be taking place on two levels:

I.P. Vlahavas and C.D. Spyropoulos (Eds.): SETN 2002, LNAI 2308, pp. 143–154, 2002.

1. *rational* information is exchanged (e.g. product requirements)
2. *subjective* information is communicated, directly and/or indirectly, namely:

- the *emotional context* restructures the dialogue (e.g. dealing with anger)
- clues as to the interlocutor´s *underlying goals and needs* are exchanged, thereby prioritising the rational content [2]

Typical applications covered by automatic dialogue systems include E-commerce (e.g. on-line bookings) and e-CRM applications (e.g. on-line help-desks). Users may make rational assertions, such as "*I'm_looking for a holiday on a Greek island*". They can also, however, make emotional statements about the content or the system performance ("*Hurry up, I don't have all day!")* or statements about their needs that only indirectly map onto rational information ("*I'd like to go somewhere where I can meet people and have fun*"). Existing dialogue systems only model the interaction with the user according to the more objective level, i.e. rational information exchange. As a result, users often feel hostility towards the service and abandon it quickly, because the underlying system does not react in a context-sensitive way.

2 Main Components of a User-Sensitive Dialogue System

In order to deal with or even prevent user frustration, a dialogue system should model not just the rational content, but also subjective information such as emotional states, user types and needs [2]. Moreover, the system should establish the effects of such knowledge on the dialogue structure itself by dynamically adapting its behaviour (cf. [4]). In this way, the user's illusion of communicating with an "intelligent" system is better preserved. The architecture employed at SemanticEdge to solve these problems is outlined in a simplified form in Fig. 1.

Dialogue management involves the dynamic calling of a number of different knowledge sources. The most elementary are the application-specific lexica and grammars for the recognition of the rational content of the user input. A "rational ontology" is also assumed which models the semantics of what the user says, i.e. the world of the application. Such knowledge is exploited via an inferencing engine and/or query language (See http://www.ontoweb.org/ or http://www.daml.org/ for ongoing research on issues concerning standard ontology languages, querying and inferencing). A mapping mechanism associates ontological concepts with the possible expressions employed by users to refer to them.

The dialogue manager can also access knowledge about different types of user. The related user profiles are defined largely in terms of specific features within the ontology; e.g. mapping the wish to "meet people" to a feature such as " has good nightlife" or "disco nearby". User profiling effects a prioritisation of the standard system goals, focusing on the information that could be most relevant to the known type of user (Section 3.2). Stored profiles can guide the system in dealing with new customers, too, when inferences about their preferences activate a certain profile.

Similarly, specialised lexica and grammars are used to identify emotions in the user input and map them onto emotional states and possible causes of those states. The utterance "*You are too slow!*" reflects dissatisfaction with the system itself,

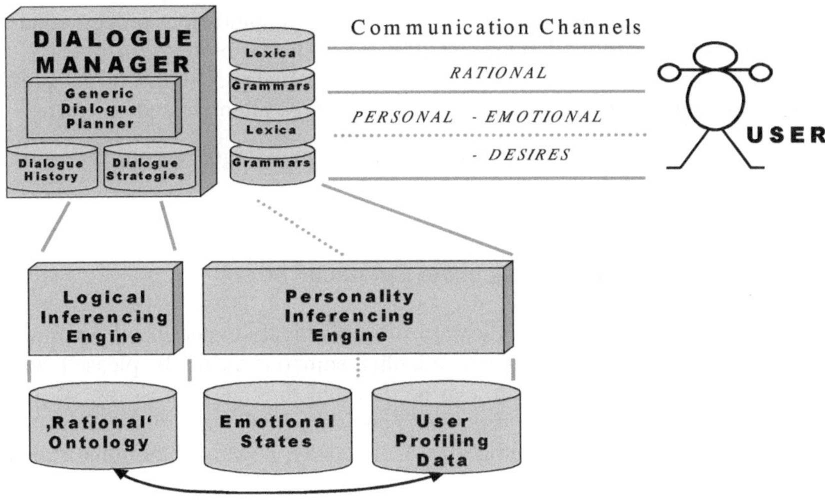

Fig. 1. The system components necessary for user-sensitivity: both rational and subjective information is considered via the *logical* and the *personality inferencing engines*, respectively

whereas "*3 pages per minute is too slow!*" reflects dissatisfaction with a system recommendation of a printer. In addition, dialogue strategies define appropriate system reactions to these emotional states to show the user that the occurrence of such an "extraordinary" event was indeed taken into account (Section 3.1). This responsiveness to emotionality renders the system trustworthy, which increases its "stickiness" [5].

The selective application of different dialogue strategies, e.g. deciding when to repair a misunderstanding, deal with user anger, or activate a user profile, is controlled by a highly-generic planning agent. This agent is supported by a "logical" inferencing engine and a *personality inferencing engine*, which exploits the typically probabilistic nature of the models of emotional state and different user types. The SemanticEdge solution to capturing, expanding, and reasoning about such subjective information is outlined in Section 3.

3 The SemanticEdge Emotion- and User-Sensitive System

What differentiates a user-sensitive from standard human-machine interfaces is the type of input recognised and the type of output produced as a reaction. The system developed at SemanticEdge attempts to identify in the course of the dialogue and interpret different emotional states of the user in order to trigger the appropriate *emotional reaction.* It also tries to probabilistically classify the user and thus infer their needs and preferences in order to select what to say next, as well as how to say it. Appropriate reactions to different emotional and goal-orientated statements serve to modify the user´s present emotional state. More generally, the aim is:

1. to involve the user in such a way in the communication process that their *evaluation* of the information presented by the system is more *positive* [1]
2. to involve the user to such a degree that their mental processing of the presented information has a certain intensity, i.e. they are more attentive and *receptive*

The basis of the user-sensitivity in the SemanticEdge dialogue system is described in Sections 3.1, 3.2 and 3.3.

3.1 Representing and Reasoning about Emotional States

Verbal expressions are useful indicators of subjectively-experienced emotions and their motivational-active component. Whether someone is really pleased with the information offered by the system, can be detected through expressions of joy (e.g. "*Sounds good!*", "*That would be just right*") and used by the system as a confirmation of the current strategies and assumptions. Conversely, negative emotional statements indicate problems:

- either with the performance of the system itself (e.g. "*You are much too slow!*")
- or with the content presented by the system (e.g. "*3 pages per minute! That printer is too slow.*")

This is why an important component of the SemanticEdge system is the *Emotional Lexicon*, which contains words and discourse variants (such as the ones in the examples) which can be used to deduce emotional state characteristics. Knowing the emotional state of a user is not enough, however; some evidence for the cause of the emotion must also be found. Thus, the Emotional Lexicon also contains mappings from surface text to a number of types of emotion cause. The basic emotions defined by Izard have been adopted for the classification of the verbal indicators [6]. A useful definition of emotions is that they are temporary, irregular states of perception which manifest themselves across three dimensions:

1. *Intensity* (the internal excitation level)
2. *Direction* (attraction, avoidance)
3. *Quality* (the subjective experience: interest, joy, fear, anger, etc.)

In addition, every emotion can be associated with a certain action readiness [7], [8]. A complication is that the terms and concepts contained in such a lexicon rarely convey a single emotion, but rather express in most cases a combination of two or more basic emotions that occur concurrently. To capture those emotional patterns, the terms are assigned a weight for each emotion they imply, which represents an estimated value for the intensity of that emotion [9]. For example, the expression "*No, that's no good*" could be assigned the following weights:

- 0 on the JOY scale
- 0,1 on the INTEREST scale
- 0,4 on the ANGER scale

Given the difficulty to accurately and objectively measure, not so much the intensity, as the quality of different emotions, the different weights are assigned by at least two independent coders who are using the same coding scheme, based on established psychological theories of emotion, such as [6], [7], [8] and [9].

The reasoning associated with emotional states can be best thought of in terms of an *emotional barometer.* The emotional barometer represents the combined summation of verbal indicators in the course of a dialogue, with respect to each basic emotion. It calculates actual emotional states in relation to time elapsed. Reasoning about a momentary emotional state can only be reliable, when the full emotional history of a dialogue is taken into account. In Fig. 2, *emotional history* is shown as a series of emotional barometers, representing an initially sceptical user (t1), who is unimpressed by the initial interaction with the system (t2), but is then surprised by positive system behaviour (t3), e.g. through its ability to give a user-sensitive response to negative statements, and ends the dialogue session with a positive, if disconcerted, impression of the system's ability (t4). In general, the dialogue history should also record the frequency of verbal indicators for each different emotion over the course of a dialogue.

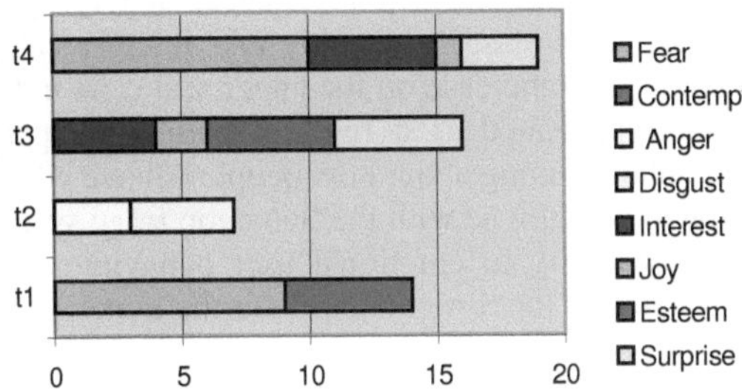

Fig. 2. The Emotional Barometer represents the history of emotions in the course of a dialogue. At t1, the specific user showed *Fear* and *Contempt* towards the system; at t2 *Anger* + *Disgust*; at t3 *Interest* + *Joy* + *Esteem* + *Surprise*; and finally at t4 *Fear* + *Interest* + *Joy* + *Surprise*

The current values of the emotional barometer, in combination with activated causes of emotional states, influence the action plan of the system, i.e. its strategies (Fig. 3). At each dialogue step, the emotional barometer and possible causes of the exhibited emotions are inferred via the emotional lexicon. The inferencing from emotional states is based on a set of positively and negatively weighted associations between each emotional state and the dialogue strategies considered. At all times, some of the currently active plans will be blocked by the emotional states (*red stars*), whereas others will be prioritised (*blue ticks*) (See selections (I) in Fig. 3).

A final decision as to the most appropriate plan to apply requires further inference, however. A second influence are the actual causes of an emotional state. In addition, the dialogue history that brought the emotional response about has to be taken into account (e.g. a sudden switch from negative to positive emotions can be interpreted as user satisfaction with the last exchange). A decay mechanism could be integrated later, once sufficient information has been collected on the specific structure and duration of individual emotions and the way one emotion is followed by another. The corresponding tests require each subject to keep protocols for every emotion they experience at each dialogue step (anger, boredom, satisfaction, etc.). More generally, the system should reason with the proposals made from the personality inferencing engine linked to the emotional states model in order to (see selections (II) in Fig. 3):

1. either take advantage of the user's absorption readiness for *product recommendations* or information gathering
2. or *prevent* user *reactance* to the system [1]

Imagine, for example, a company using the SemanticEdge system for market research purposes: if the system misunderstands the user at two consecutive steps (as represented in the dialogue history), the built-in planning logic will infer a high probability of a system-initiated communication failure. A market research question at this point of the interaction would probably cause "reactance" in the user and would amplify the already negative emotional state [1]. Thus, using the emotional barometer in conjunction with the dialogue logic imposes the need to initiate a repair strategy.

However useful verbal indicators may be, the problem remains of expression variability among different users. In addition, not all users express their current emotional status verbally. This makes the fall-back use of *interaction-analytical assumptions* necessary. It is assumed, for instance, that the purchase of a product leads automatically to an increase on the joy and interest value scales, whereas a misunderstanding leads to an increase on the anger scale. As indicated in Fig. 3, such assumptions are best represented as a rule set within the personality inferencing engine, a kind of default reasoning about how people behave when they interact.

Here is an example of a dialogue with the Semantic Edge system demonstrating the above principles of sensitivity to emotional user behaviour and dealing with user reactance (where *S* stands for the System and *U* for the user):

- S: Welcome to SemanticEdge Holidays. What can I do for you?
- U: *We want to go somewhere in the South with our 2-year old.*
- S: Is it just two adults?
- U: *Yes.*
- S: Are you looking for a hotel with a baby-sitting service?
- U: *Yes, that would be just right.*
- S: Okay, let´s see what there is then. One moment please...
- U: *You´re much too slow! I´m falling asleep here!* (ANGER)
- S: Very interesting! I have found the following child-friendly packages for you:...
- U: *Spain sounds good. But is it warm there yet?* (INTEREST)
- S: If you want to know what the weather is like there, look up www.weather.com
- U: *Smartypants!* (ANGER)
- S: This looks like a good opportunity for me to learn some useful expressions!
- U: *Now you are taking the mickey!* (ANGER + JOY)
- S: That´s nice to hear
- U: *Alright then, can I book it straight away?* (INTEREST)
- S: You can book it straight away with your VISA or Mastercard. ...

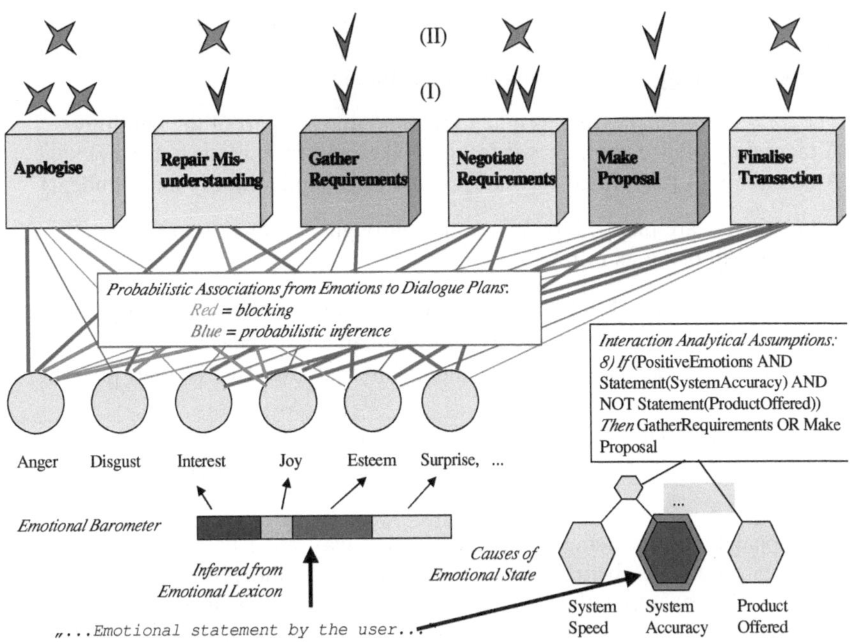

Fig. 3. Dialogue plan selection (e.g. *Gather Requirements* and *Make Proposal*) on the basis of (I) the emotional state of the user (*Interest, Joy, Esteem, Surprise*) and possible causes of this state (*System Accuracy*), and (II) default reasoning rules (*Interaction Analytical Assumptions*)

This dialogue shows that most instances of anger on the part of the user cause an acknowledgement by the system that there is a problem by means of likewise emotional statements (e.g. "*Very interesting*"). In addition, a sarcastic user statement such as "*Smartypants!*" is exploited by the system to demonstrate some humour, i.e. that this is a good opportunity for it to learn some new words. This has the desired effect on the user who now seems to be entertained. The next step in this strategy is to ignore the negative emotion (Anger) and focus on the positive user emotion (Joy). The system thereby manages to bring the conversation from the emotional back to a more factual-rational level. The user now concentrates on the product recommendations by showing renewed interest. Naturally, a considerable part of the system strategy relates to the specific wording of the system prompts at various steps in the course of the dialogue. For the time being, emotional prompts are pre-wired in the system, as reactions to specific user input. However, dynamic and concatenative generation of such prompts is planned for the medium term.

3.2 Representing and Reasoning about User Profiles

The modelling of emotional states and their effect on dialogue strategies is one aspect of user-sensitivity. A second requirement is access to knowledge about different user types in such a way that the system, can predict in the course of interacting with an unknown user the probable type of that user and thus focus the dialogue to address the assumed needs and goals. This is achieved by a mapping between user profiles and the rational ontology. The mapping itself has three levels:

1. The *factual statements* (e.g. product features) that are part of the ontology
2. A taxonomy of *generic user needs* (e.g. make-new-friends, save money)
3. A taxonomy of predefined *user stereotypes* (e.g. single, family man, student)

The three levels are mapped to one another through weighted associations. Typically, inferencing will occur as follows:

- From surface level text, infer Factual Statements, User Needs, User Stereotypes
- From all known Factual Statements, infer probable User Needs
- From all known Factual Statements and/or inferred User Needs, infer probable User Stereotypes
- From all inferred User Stereotypes infer further User Needs
- From all inferred User Needs or User Stereotypes, infer additional Factual Statements

Additional factual statements inferred in this way must be treated by the overall inferencing process as being weak suggestions as to the probable interests of the current user. For example, the statement "*We want to go somewhere in the South with our 2-year-old*" in the dialogue of Section 3.1 might be used to strongly infer a <FamilyPerson> stereotype and to weakly infer the User Needs <relax> and <have-romance>. In turn, this could imply additional needs such as <use-baby-sitting-services> which could lead to the prioritisation of children facilities in the ontological description of a holiday. This may ultimately lead to a system question such as "*Are you looking for a hotel with a baby-sitting service?*" at the next step (See dialogue in Section 3.1).

As already pointed out, weighted associations form the basis for the inferential infrastructure in the SemanticEdge system, for both emotional states and user stereotypes. This helps to gracefully deal with incorrect assumptions about the user, as well as with conflicting profiling information identified in the course of the dialogue, by preserving alternative hypotheses. In practice, a prohibitive factor is that often there is insufficient data to derive such associations with statistical significance. In such cases, SemanticEdge has a fallback position of utilizing *Case-Based Reasoning* as the primary inference engine for carrying out the required weak inferencing. A User Profile Capturing GUI is employed in order to generate specific instances of the required associations from any number of available transcribed dialogues, however small. An overview of the architecture is given in Fig. 4. The following process is followed:

- Representative cases are identified, at least one for each user type (ideally from real dialogues; if necessary on the basis of market reports)
- Each case is analysed so that relevant ontological concepts can be identified

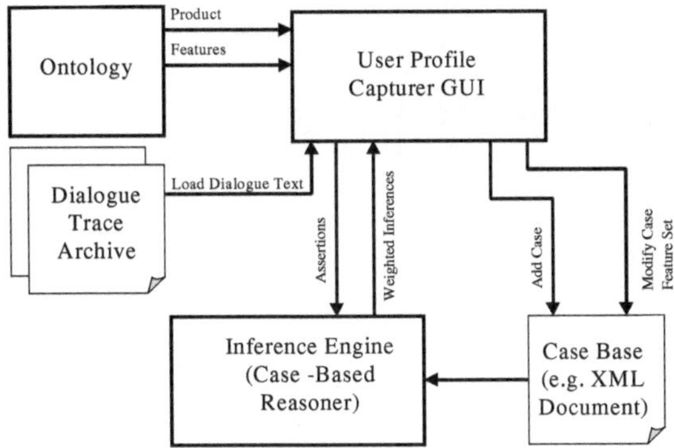

Fig. 4. Case-Based Reasoning in the SemanticEdge system: *Dialogue archives* are annotated with concepts from the *Ontology* and with emotional information using the *User Profile Capturer GUI* in order to collect a series of representative examples (*Case Base*). The *Case-Based Reasoner* identifies new cases on the basis of their similarity to old ones

- User cases are contrasted; a core network of distinctive features (specific goals and preferences) is singled out for each user type
- New cases are employed to augment and refine the existing user profiles

In Section 3.3, the corresponding profiling tool is briefly described.

3.3 The SemanticEdge User Profile Capturer

Fig. 5 shows a mock-up of the prototype environment employed at SemanticEdge in order to allow linguists and psychologists to analyse transcribed dialogues and to model inferences about factual information, user needs, stereotypes and even emotions in a comfortable way.

The user of the GUI starts by selecting a product description or other 'rational' description from the central ontology. This is represented as a flat list of features in a form view. Similarly, the user can load in additional ontologies of user stereotypes. The user can then load one or more dialogue transcripts and highlight various key phrases which correspond to assertions in one or more of the listed features. In this way, *Destination=Caribbean* and *UserNeed->HasNightlife* could be initially asserted in Fig. 5. The user then carries out each step of the inferencing process detailed in Section 3.2 via manual entry of inference weights on additional features; e.g. *UserType->IsSingle* might be strongly inferred from *UserNeed->HasNightlife* and other evidence. At the end of this process, the user can generate a case for the Case Base by selecting the export option; the full collection of associations for this case are

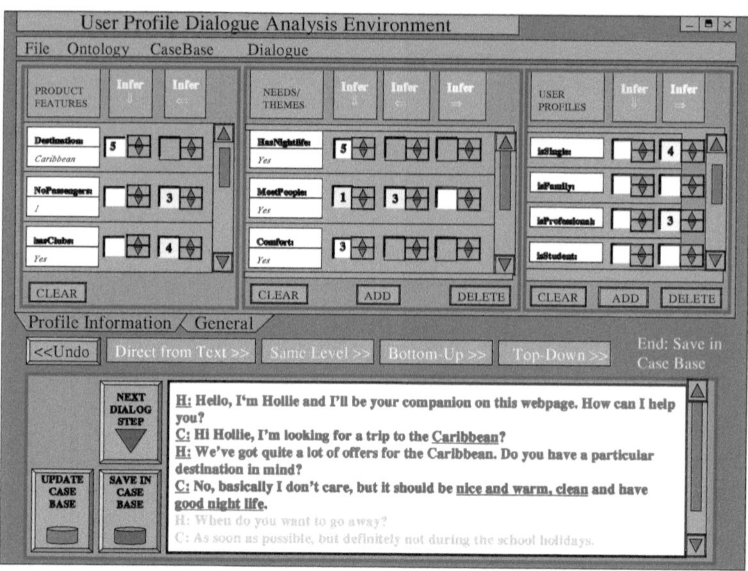

Fig. 5. The User Profile Capturer GUI developed at SemanticEdge: ontological concepts specific to the application (e.g. *Caribbean*) are associated with emotional indicators (e.g. *nice*) and preferences of the specific user (e.g. *good night life*)

exported there (currently represented in XML). Once several cases have been added this way, the actual performance of the CBR system can also be viewed via this GUI.

4 Conclusion and Future Work

The SemanticEdge dialogue system presented here reacts in a user-sensitive way, accounting for (i) *rational assertions*, (ii) indicators of the *user type* and (iii) indications concerning the *current emotional state of the user*. This is largely achieved by specialised grammars and vocabulary, but also interaction-analytical assumptions about the usual triggers of various emotions, in the case where no explicit cues were identified. This additional information about the user guides the system in selecting the most appropriate action to take next, thereby dynamically structuring the dialogue: the questions to pose, the type of information to present, the level of detail, and the communication style to use in the generated prompts. It should even be possible to predict within a dialogue the optimal time to pose a market research question, allowing for a seamless integration of such business research without causing customer offence. This contrasts to standard dialogue systems which predefine a dialogue path and force the user to comply to it. The deployment of such a user-sensitive system ensures effective and efficient communication. Moreover, interaction on the emotional level establishes trust, which can positively influence the end user's attitudes and future behaviour.

Reasoning about emotions and user stereotypes is inherently probabilistic. However, it is often problematic to gather the large volumes of data required to create a reliable statistical model of the various associations outlined here. Hence, SemanticEdge implemented a fall-back strategy: a) providing an environment for the manual capture of examples of emotional behaviour and/or user types and b) using applied case-based reasoning (CBR) as a fuzzy inferencing engine capable of reasoning from small data sets. Future work will investigate how additional examples can be gathered semi-automatically, once a dialogue system has been deployed and will look towards providing a seamless transition from CBR-based inferencing to more probabilistic reasoning, e.g. based on Bayesian Networks.

General emotional states have been addressed here. A further step is to construct user-specific emotional models for repeat customers. Such models will capture the average emotional disposition of a given user and will allow for more accurate predictions of the emotional behaviour of any one individual using the system.

The current version of the SemanticEdge system can identify and react to different user profiles (single and family person), as well as show sensitivity to explicit user anger and joy. Initial evaluation has shown increased user acceptance of repeated system misunderstandings and word recognition errors, when the system – rather than repeating the same question for the third time –visibly changes its strategy in the course of the dialogue by temporarily postponing its current goal and suggesting a related but different topic of discussion (e.g. "*Okay, Let's discuss this later. When do you want to fly out?*"). Annoying repetitions only serve to show that the system does not understand the user either on the rational or on the emotional level. This causes anger and frustration, which in the case of male subjects leads to them hanging up or abandoning the service a lot earlier than female users. A more detailed evaluation of the ability of the system to identify emotional and user-profile-related cues is currently underway in order to validate the suggested mappings between surface form and significance. Problems posed by user irony, negation, and prosody need to be considered in this respect. A more extensive evaluation of the activated dialogue strategies also needs to be done to measure general user satisfaction and acceptance, interface "stickiness", prompt suitability and effectiveness, as well as the more traditional qualitative and quantitative evaluation measures used for spoken dialogue systems (e.g. [10], [11]). Nevertheless, the architecture and tools presented here consist the important first step in building an integrated environment for the establishment and dynamic refinement of emotional and user profiles and for the design and application of appropriate system behaviour to deal with this information.

References

1. Behrens, G.: Konsumentenverhalten, 2nd edn., Heidelberg (1991)
2. Flycht-Eriksson, A.: A Survey of Knowledge Sources in Dialogue Systems. In: Alexandersson, J. (ed.): Proceedings of the IJCAI-99 Workshop on Knowledge and Reasoning in Practical Dialogue Systems. Stockholm, Sweden (1999) 41-48
3. Androutsopoulos, I., Aretoulaki, M.: Natural Language Interaction: Natural Language Interfaces and Spoken Dialogue Systems. In: Mitkov, R. (ed.): Handbook of Computational Linguistics. Oxford University Press (to appear)
4. Aretoulaki, M., Ludwig, B.: Automaton-Descriptions and Theorem-Proving: a Marriage made in Heaven?. Linköping Electronic Articles in Computer and Information Science 4 (1999) Article No. 022. ISSN 1401-9841. URL: http://www.ep.liu.se/ea/cis/1999/022/.
5. Bowlby, J.: Attachment and loss, Vol. 1. Attachment. Basic Books, New York (1969)

6. Izard, C.E.: Die Emotionen des Menschen. Eine Einführung in die Grundlagen der Emotionspsychologie. Beltz, Weinheim (1994)
7. Frijda, N.H.: The Emotions. Cambridge University Press, Cambridge (1986)
8. Frijda, N.H.: Gesetze der Emotionen. Zeitschrift für Psychosomatische Medizin und Psychoanalyse 42 (1996) 205—221
9. Gottschalk, L.A., Gleser, G.C.: The Measurement of Psychological States through the Content Analysis of Verbal Behaviour. University of California Press, Los Angeles (1969)
10. Danieli, M., Gerbino, E.: Metrics for Evaluating Dialogue Strategies in a Spoken Language System. In: Proceedings of the AAAI Symposium on Empirical Methods in Discourse Interpretation and Generation. (1995) 34-39
11. Walker, M.A., Litman, D.J., Kamm, C.A., Abella, A.: PARADISE: a Framework for Evaluating Spoken Dialogue Agents. In: Proceedings of the 35th ACL Annual Meeting and the 8th EACL Conference. Madrid, Spain (1997) 271-280

Transforming Spontaneous Telegraphic Language to Well-Formed Greek Sentences for Alternative and Augmentative Communication

Georgios Karberis and Georgios Kouroupetroglou

University of Athens,
Department of Informatics and Telecommunications,
Panepistimiopolis, Ilisia, Athens, Greece
{grad0350, koupe}@di.uoa.gr

Abstract. The domain of Augmentative and Alternative Communication (AAC) studies appropriate techniques and systems that enhance or accomplish the retaining or non-existing abilities for interpersonal communication. Some AAC users apply telegraphic language, as they attempt to speed up the interactive communication or because they are language impaired. In many AAC aids, a "sentence" is formulated by combining symbols of an icon-based communication system. To be accepted by the communication partner, the output should be a correct oral sentence of a natural language. In this paper we present our effort to develop a novel technique for expanding spontaneous telegraphic input to well-formed Greek sentences, by adopting a feature-based surface realization for Natural Language generation. We first describe the general architecture of the system that accepts compressed, incomplete, grammatically and syntactically ill-formed text and produces a correct full sentence. The NLP techniques of the two main modules, named preprocessor and translator/ generator, are then analyzed. A prototype system has been developed using Component Based Technology (CBT) which is under field evaluation by a number of speech-disabled users. Currently it supports fully the BLISS and MAKATON icon based communication systems. Some limitations of the module are also discussed along with possibilities for future expansions.

1 Introduction

Computer Mediated Interpersonal Communication (CMIC) (or its equivalent term e-communication) launches an important societal role for all citizens. In CMIC either voice or text is commonly used to achieve synchronous (i.e. in real time) or asynchronous (e.g. messaging, mailing) communication between two or more individuals. In some cases an alternative symbolic communication system (such as BLISS, PIC, PCS, MAKATON, SIGSYM, LEXIGRAMS, OACKLAND and REBUS) can be also utilized [1]. Traditionally, interpersonal communication is referred in the context of the assistive technology and the communication aids. However recently, general solutions have been proposed allowing communication between able-bodied and the disabled [2], [3], [4]. The domain of Augmentative and Alternative Communication (AAC) studies the appropriate techniques and the

I.P. Vlahavas and C.D. Spyropoulos (Eds.): SETN 2002, LNAI 2308, pp. 155–166, 2002.

systems that enhance or accomplish the retaining or non-existing abilities for interpersonal communication.

AAC constitutes a highly multilingual communication environment as almost an infinite number of vocabulary sets from various orthographic languages or symbol systems can be created or adapted. In the majority of the AAC aids the two partners in a communication session apply different meaning representations chosen among text and symbols. Some AAC users apply telegraphic language, because either they are language impaired or they attempt to speed up the interactive communication. Telegraphic language is very brief and concise and many words are omitted. Substitutionally, in many AAC aids, one combines elements of an icon-based system to formulate a "sentence". Nevertheless, to be accepted by the communication partner, the output should be a correct oral sentence of a natural language. In this case, as an intermediate step, the icon–based "sentence" is lexical translated to telegraphic language. Research work concerning lexical knowledge in the AAC field has focused primarily on knowledge-based rate enhancement techniques for natural languages, such as COMPANSION [5], [6] and co-generation [7]. The formal description, processing and translation of symbol systems (e.g. BLISSYMBOLICS) have also been investigated: The COMPANSION system [5] uses a statistical model for syntax analysis in English and it accepts input from the keyboard. The PVI system [9] uses Tree Adjoining Grammars (TAG) to generate French sentences. KOMBE produces also French sentences [8] from input in SODI-GRACH, which is not a widely accepted symbolic system compared to BLISSYMBOLICS. Whereas morphological treatment in some languages, like the English, seems to be relatively simple, it can become a central issue for highly inflectional languages, such as Hungarian [17], Basque [18] and Greek. In the literature there are also proposals concerning the exploitation of already existing large-scale lexical resources in AAC [10]. The role of multilingual lexical linguistic information and lexical translation relations for orthographic languages and symbolic systems has been discussed in depth in [11], [12].

This paper presents a new approach for expanding spontaneous telegraphic input in AAC to well-formed sentences for the Greek language. The adopted method consists of a feature-based surface realization for Natural Language generation. We first describe the general architecture of the system that accepts compressed, incomplete, grammatical and syntactically ill-formed text and produces a correct full sentence. The NLP techniques of two main modules, named preprocessor and translator/generator, are then analyzed. Furthermore, a prototype of such a system developed using Component Based Technology (CBT) is given. Some limitations of the module are also discussed along with possibilities for future expansions.

2 General Architecture

The general architecture of a typical AAC system is given in Fig. 1. A language impaired user, through an appropriate to his/her abilities input device (such as switch {either mechanical or infrared or acoustic}, touch screen, trackball, mouse, head-stick, touch tablet) selects a number of symbols from the selection set in order to form a message [13]. This icon-based "sentence" is then lexically translated to telegraphic form [11]. Non-language impaired users can formulate telegraphic sentences directly.

The Telegraphic-to-Full Sentence (TtFS) module produces a well-formed complete sentence to drive either a Text-to-Speech system or to reach the communicator partner through alternative output forms (e.g. chat, e-mail, print).

We concentrate our work on developing the TtFS module, which will work as a language text translator/generator. The input is a compressed, incomplete, grammatical and syntactically ill-formed Greek text. The output of the module is a full Greek sentence, grammatical and syntactically correct. The module uses a database with morphological, syntactic and semantic knowledge.

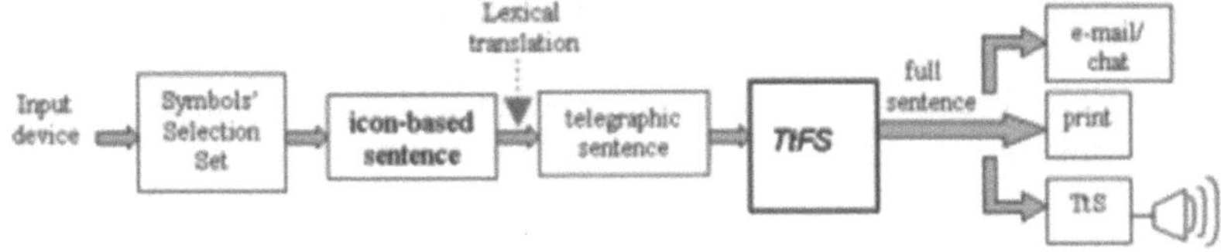

Fig. 1. General architecture of an AAC system

Two modules can accomplish the whole processing of the TtFS:

1. The *preprocessor* module, which splits the sentence into words and identifies the part of speech for each of them. The preprocessor also adds any missed words, such as articles. The output of the module is a full sentence, but grammatical incorrect.
2. The *translator/generator* module, which applies syntactic and grammatical rules as well as semantic information to the output of the preprocessor and generates a well-formed complete Greek sentence.

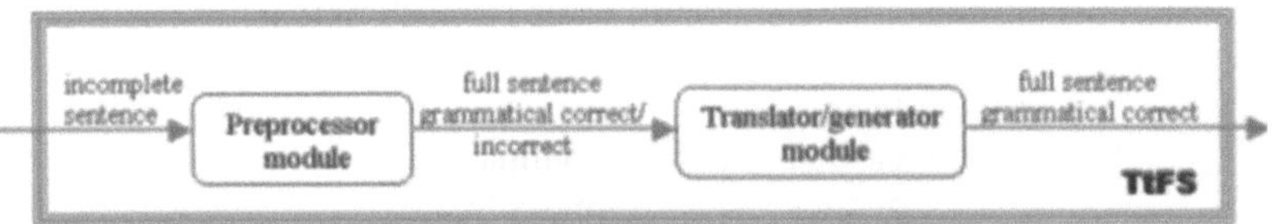

Fig. 2. The architecture of the TtFS

3 The Preprocessor

The preprocessor module has a linear, step-by-step architecture (Figure 3). Initially, the preprocessor module splits the input sentence into words. For every word a small chunk is created. One part of the chunk is the word class of the given word. The above information is retrieved from a computational morphological and syntactic lexicon of Modern Greek. Currently the module includes 3000 lemmas, in order to support the full icon based communication system BLISSYMBOLICS [14], [15],

[16], as well as MAKATON. Then, the preprocessor checks each word and applies the following syntactic rules:

1. If there is not any conjunction in the sentence, it assumes that there is only one main sentence. If there is at least one conjunction, it creates two or more different sentences. The first sentence is the main and the others are subordinate clauses. The remaining processing is taking place for each of them.
2. If the user omits to add an article before a noun, or before an adjective, then a new chunk, which contains the article, is added. The order of this chunk in the list is just before the chunk of the noun or the adjective, correspondingly. This processing is taking place only for nouns and adjectives before the verb of the sentence.
3. It is examined if for each verb a noun follows. If this is the case, the semantics of the noun are checked and the omitted words are added in a chunk between them.

The following cases are checked for the semantics of a noun: place, person, food, drink, object, vehicle. The semantic information for the verbs and the nouns is encoded in the database of the system. In this database there is also stored the lexicon and morphological information for every lemma.

Then, the preprocessor module merges all the words into a sentence. This sentence is a full one, as there are not missed words, but it is grammatical incorrect.

4 The Translator/Generator

The translator/generator module inputs a full sentence from the preprocessor and applies syntactic and grammatical rules to generate a well-formed sentence. Figure 4 presents the architecture of this module.

Initially, it splits the sentence and creates a list of chunks. Every chunk corresponds to a specific word of the sentence. Each chunk has five fields: number, gender, tense, person and case. The default value for each field is:

tense	:	present
case	:	nominative
gender	:	masculine
number	:	singular
person	:	first

After the creation of the chunks list, the word class for each word is retrieved from the lexicon. Then, depending on the word class of each word, the fields' values on its corresponding chunk changes properly. For example, if one word recognized to have a plural number, then the field "number" changes to *plural*, or if a pronoun is "εσύ" ("you") then the "person" changes to *second* and if there is a pronoun like " αυτός" ("he") it changes to *third*. Next, the sentence is checked for conjunctions. Then it is separated in one main and subordinate clauses, if there are any.

After these initializing steps, the module acts out the syntactic analysis. It uses syntactic rules to determine the subject and the object complement for each sentence.

First, it examines each sentence to identify the subject. The identification is accomplished with the use of syntactic patterns. The patterns of subjects that are used in the Greek language are stored in a table of the database (see Table 1). The sentence is checked from the start to its verb, if there is any. The check is performed sequentially using all the patterns of the database. The order of storing them in the database is from the larger to the smaller. If there is no subject in the sentence, the module assumes that the subject is the pronoun "εγώ" ("I"). For the special case a subordinate clause has no subject, the subject of the main sentence is assumed.

The examination for object complements is follwing. The technique used is the same as described above. The rest of the sentence (without the subject) is checked with the patterns for object complements stored in the database. In the case the verb is a transitive one, the object complement is labeled as a predicate.

Table 1. The patterns used to identify the subject and the object complement. Abbreviations: PRE=Ppreposition, ART=article, PAR=particle, NN=noun, PRO=pronoun, ADJ=adjective, CON=conjuction and NUM=number

Subject	Object Complement
PRE+ART+PAR	PRE+ART+NN+CON+ART+NN
ART+NN+CON+ART+ADJ+NN	PRE+ART+ADJ+NN
ART+ADJ+NN+CON+ART+NN	ART+NN+CON+ART+NN
ART+NN+CON+ART+NN	PRE+ART+NN
ART+PAR+NN	PRE+ART+PAR+NN
ART+ADJ+NN	PRE+ART+NN+ART+ADJ
PRO+CON+ART+ADJ+NN	ART+ADJ+NN
ART+ADJ+NN+CON+PRO	ART+ADJ
ART+NN+PRO+CON+PRO	PRE+ART+ADJ
ART+NN+CON+PRO	ART+PAR+NN
PRO+CON+ART+NN+PRO	ART+NN
ART+NN+CON+PRO	PRE+ART+PAR
PRO+CON+ART+NN+PRO	PRE+ART+NUM
PRO+CON+ART+NN	ART+NUM
ART+ADJ	ART+PAR
PRO+CON+PRO	ART+ADJ
ART+NN+PRO	PRE+PRO
ART+NUM	PRE+NN
ART+PRO	PRO
ART+NN	ADJ
ART+PAR	PRE+ADJ
PAR	NN
NN	#
ADJ	#

After the assessment for subjects, object complements and predicates, the module applies some grammatical rules of the Greek language, to the chunks list. During the application of the rules, the field values of the chunks list are changed. The goal of this process is label each chunk with the appropriate number, gender, tense and case, according to the grammatical rules of the Greek language, (described in 4.1).

The final step of the module is to inflect every word to its correct tense, gender and number, according to the values of the labels of its corresponding chunk. The inflection is accomplished with the use of morphological knowledge. The inflection technique is described in section 4.2.

After the generation of the inflected words, the module merges them to produce a well-formed sentence, which represents the output of the whole module.

4.1 Syntactic and Grammatical Rules

The translator/generator module applies the following grammatical and syntactic rules of the Greek language (all the rules are being applied before the inflection of each word):

Agreement between the subject and the verb of a sentence.
The object complement in accusative.
The predicate in nominative.

Agreement between the subject and the verb of a sentence
The verb of a sentence must have the same number and the same person with the subject of the sentence where it belongs. If a subordinate clause doesn't have a subject, then the module assumes that the subject is the same with that of the main sentence. For example:

Input sentence: {αυτός}+{έχω} ({he}+{have})
Output sentence: "Αυτός έχει" ("He has")

At the starting point the default values of the labels for the verb "έχω" ("have") are *singular* for the number and *first* for the person. The label person of the word "αυτός" ("he") is *third*. Before the inflection of each word, the corresponding labels of the verb "έχω" ("have"), changes to become the same as the subject "αυτός". Thus, the inflected word for the verb "'έχω" ("I have") is "έχει" ("he has") and the output sentence is well formed.

The object complement in accusative
The object complement of a sentence must always be in accusative. Thus, for all the words that consist the object complement, the label for case changes to *accusative*. For example, consider the following sentence to be handled by the TtFS system:

Input: {μητέρα}+{κάθομαι}+{καρέκλα}
{mother}+ {sit} +{chair}
Output: "Η μητέρα κάθεται στην καρέκλα"
"The mother is sitting on the chair"

The preprocessor module adds: a) an article before the noun "μητέρα" ("mother") and b) the prepositional article "στο" ("on+the") before the noun "καρέκλα" ("chair"). The word "στο" ("on+the") suits for the verb "κάθομαι" ("sit") if a noun follows with the meaning of an item, like "καρέκλα" . The input sentence for the second module is:

{άρθρο}+{μητέρα}+{κάθομαι}+{στο}+{καρέκλα}. In the second module, every word, by default, has its case label in *nominative*. The object complement of the sentence is: {στο}+{καρέκλα}, thus, the label for the case changes to *accusative* and, after the inflection, the output sentence is well formed.

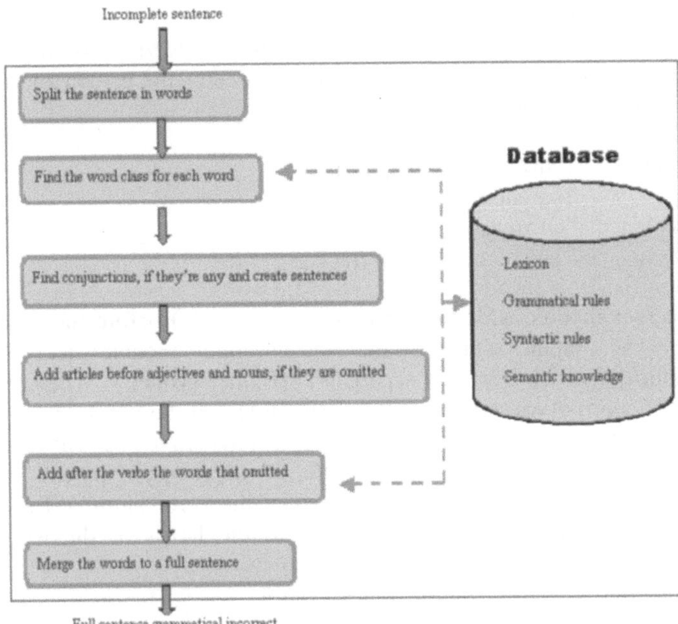

Fig. 3. The architecture of the *Translator/Generator* module

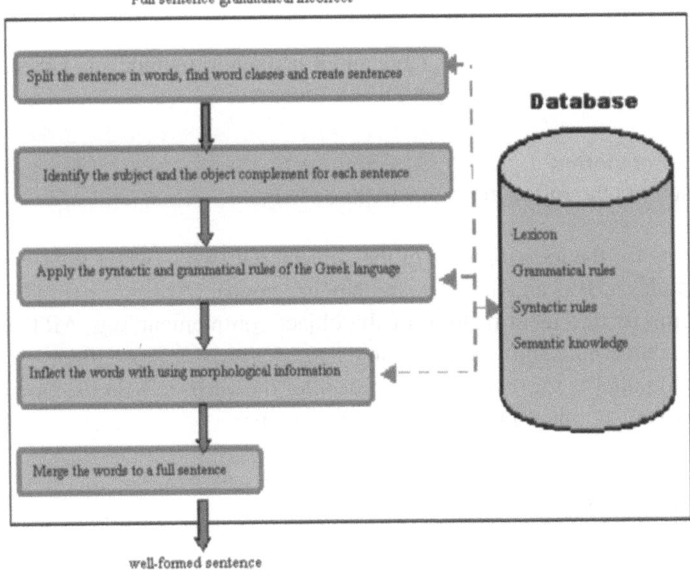

Fig. 4. The architecture of the *Preprocessor* module

The predicate in nominative

The predicate of a sentence must always be in *nominative.* We notice that the predicate gives an attribute to the subject. Hence, it takes the person and the number of the subject. For example:

Input sentence :	{γονείς} + {είμαι}+{νέος}
	{parents}+ {I am} +{young}
Output sentence:	"Οι γονείς είναι νέοι"
	"The parents are young"

The preprocessor module adds the word "άρθρο" (article) before the noun "γονείς" ("parents"). The input sentence for the second module is: {άρθρο} + {γονείς}+{είμαι}+{νέος} ({article}+{parents}+{I am}+{young}). The subject of the sentence is: {άρθρο}+{γονείς} ({article}+{parents}) and the word "νέος" ("young") is a predicate, because the verb "είμαι" ("I am") is a transitive one. The number of the subject is found to be *plural* because after the word "γονείς" ("parents") the article doesn't give any information. Hence, the labels of the verb "είμαι" ("I am") and the predicate "νέος" ("young") change according to the labels of the word "γονείς" ("parents").

4.2 Knowledge Needed

The module uses a specially designed database, which stores the lexicon with appropriate syntactic and morphological knowledge.

Lexicon

The lexicon consists of a database table and it is open to include any Greek word. The module is independent from the symbol selection set.

Syntactic information

The module uses the following syntactic knowledge:

- Patterns for the identification of the subject, e.g. ART+ADJ+NN (where ART is an article, ADJ is an adjective, and NN is a noun).
- Patterns for the identification of the object complement, e.g. ART+NN (where ART is an article and NN is a noun).
- Special patterns for the omitted words after the verbs, e.g. in the case of the verb "πηγαίνω" ("going") the stored information is:

Word	πηγαίνω	going
Item	στο	to+*article*
Person	μαζί+ με+*άρθρο*	with+*article*
Food	για	for+*article*
Drink	για	for+*article*

Place	στο	to+*article*
Game	για	for+*article*
Time	*άρθρο*	at+*article*
Vehicle	με+*άρθρο*	with+*article*
Verb	να	to

For example, if the noun is "σχολείο" ("school") which is a place, then the omitted Greek word is the prepositional article "στο" ("to"+ *article*). If the noun is a vehicle, like "λεωφορείο" ("bus"), then the words are "με"+*άρθρο* ("with"+ *article*)", and if it is a person, like "μητέρα" ("mother") then the words are "μαζί με"+άρθρο ("with"+ *article*)".

Morphological information/ word inflection

At the final step of the process, every word is inflected using the label values from its corresponding chunk. The morphological information for the inflection of each word is stored in the database. In reality, the word class and an inflection code along with its stem are specified for the members of the lexicon. This code corresponds to a pattern of specific endings. We have encoded the complete ending patterns for all the Greek words. For example, all the nouns in the Greek language have one out of 56 different endings. These 56 endings are stored only once. For each noun, adjective, article or verb we stored only the inflection code that corresponds to the correct pattern ending and the stem of the word. The module generates all the inflectional morphemes using the inflection code and the stem of the word. Thus, by combining the stem with the corresponding ending, it can inflect a word in every number, any tense, any gender and any case, according to the label values and the corresponding word class. Thus, the following values are retrieved for each word class:

- Verb tense, person, number
- Noun number, case
- Adjective number, gender, case
- Participle number, gender, case
- Pronoun number case
- Article number, gender, case
- Number number, case
- Adverb null
- Preposition null
- Conjunction null

5 Implementation

The module TtFS described above has been developed using Component Based Technology (CBT) for effective integration, as an independent component, in thorough CMIC applications. As a first test, it has been incorporated under the ULYSSES framework [4], which facilitates the integration of multi-vendor components into interpersonal communication applications. The module has not any user interface in a real AAC aid. Although, a special user interface has been developed to accomplished laboratory alpha tests. The output of the module possesses an appropriate format [19], [20] to drive even advanced modern Text-to-Speech systems [21]. Currently, the system supports fully the icon based languages, BLISS and MAKATON. The software implementation has been accomplished with Visual Basic of the MS-Visual Studio, version 6.0. The module was built as an ActiveX DLL (Dynamic Library Link) and it can be easily installed and used as an independent intermediate component in AAC aids.

6 Discussion

The TtFS prototype is under field evaluation by a number of speech-disabled users at different regions of Greece. Preliminary results are very positive regarding its usability in real time everyday spontaneous interpersonal communication sessions.

The following limitations has to be taken into account for the current version of TtFS:

Unlimited lexicon. TtFS requires a rather large amount of information to be associated with each word. This knowledge must be hand coded on the database of the module. An effort is under way to handle the problem of unrestricted vocabulary using automatic methods for deriving the necessary information from either on-line lexical resources or from corpus-based processing.

User Input Assumptions. The module assumes that the input would reflect the basic word order of the desired output. Additionally, the subject should be first in the sentence and the object complement second. Furthermore, function words may be left out, but content words must be included.

Future expansions of the TtFS may include:

- Extension of the module's functionality to support other major icon-based symbolic communication systems used in AAC.
- Text input from the keyboard.
- Support of random telegraphic input.
- Support the opposite function of TtFS: transforming well-formed Greek sentences to a corresponding symbol sequence "sentence" for a specific icon-based system.

7 Conclusion

In this paper we have presented a novel technique for expanding spontaneous telegraphic input to well-formed sentences for the Greek language by adopting a feature-based surface realization for Natural Language generation. The general architecture of the system that accepts compressed, incomplete, grammatical and syntactically ill-formed text and can produce a correct full sentence has been described along with the NLP techniques of two main modules, named preprocessor and translator/generator. A prototype of such a system has been developed using Component Based Technology (CBT) as a part of a number of AAC aids designed for different user groups. The system supports currently the full icon based AAC systems BLISS and MAKATON. The system is under field evaluation by a number of speech-disabled users at different regions of Greece.

Acknowledgments. Part of the work reported in this paper was carried out within the framework of the AENEAS project (contract 98AMEA19), funded by the EPET II Programme of the Greek General Secretariat for Research and Technology.

References

1. von Tetzchner, S.: Use of Graphic Communication Systems in Telecommunication. In: von Tetzchner, S. (ed.): Issues in Telecommunication and Disability. CEC, DG XIII, Luxembourg (1992) 280-288
2. Kouroupetroglou, G., Viglas, C., Stamatis C., Pentaris, F.: Towards the Next Generation of Computer-based Interpersonal Communication Aids. In: Anogianakis, G., Buhler, C. and Soede, M. (eds.): Advancement of Assistive Technology. Assistive Technology Research Series, Vol. 3. IOS Press, Amsterdam Berlin Oxford Tokyo Washington (1997) 110-114
3. Viglas, C., Stamatis, C., Kouroupetroglou, G.: Remote Assistive Interpersonal Communication Exploiting Component Based Development. In: Edwards, A., Arato, A., Zagler, W. (eds.): Computers and Assistive Technology, Proceedings of the XV IFIP World Computer Congress, 31 August - 4 Sept. 1998, Vienna – Budapest, Congress, ICCHP'98, (1998) 487-496
4. Kouroupetroglou, G., Pino, A.: ULYSSES: A Framework for Incorporating Multi-Vendor Components in Interpersonal Communication Applications. In: Marincek C., Buhler, C., Knops, H., Andrich, R. (eds.): Assistive Technology – Added Value to the Quality of Life. Assistive Technology Research Series, Vol. 10. IOS Press, Amsterdam Berlin Oxford Tokyo Washington (2001) 55-59
5. McCoy, K. F., Pennington, C. A., Badman, A. L.: Compansion: From Research Prototype to Practical Integration. Natural Language Engineering **4** (1): Cambridge University Press, (1998) 73-95
6. McCoy, K., Demasco, P.: Some Applications of Natural Language Processing to the Field of Augmentative and Alternative Communication. Proceedings of the IJCAI '95 Workshop on Developing AI Applications for Disabled People, Montreal, (1995) 97-112
7. Copestake A.: Augmented and Alternative NLP Techniques for Augmented and Alternative Communication. In: Copestake. A., Langer, S., Palazuelos-Cagigas, S. E. (eds.): Proceedings of the 35th Annual Meeting of the Association for Computational Linguistics (ACL) and the 8th Conference of the European Chapter of the ACL.. Morgan Kaufmann, San Francisco (1997) 37-42

8. Guenthner F., Kruger-Thielmann, K., Pasero, R., & Sabatier, P.: Communication Aids for Handicapped Persons. In: Proceedings of the 2nd European Conference on Advances in Rehabilitation Technology (ECART2), May 26-28, 1993, Stockholm (1993) 1-4
9. Vaillant P.,: A semantics-based communication system for dysphasic subjects. Proc. Of the 6th Conf. On Artificial Intelligence in Medicine Europe, AIME '97, Grenoble, France (1997)
10. Zickus, M. W., McCoy, K. F., Demasco, P. W., Pennington, C. A.: A lexical Database for Intelligent AAC Systems. In: Langton, A. (ed.): Proceedings of the 18th Annual Conference of the Rehabilitation Engineering Society of North America (RESNA), Washington, DC: RESNA Press, (1995) 124-126
11. Antona M., Stephanidis C., Kouroupetroglou G.: Access to Lexical Knowledge in Modular interpersonal Communication Aids. Augmentative and Alternative Communication, **15**, (1999) 269-279
12. Antona M., Stephanidis C., Kouroupetroglou G.: Vocabulary Management in Modular Interpersonal Communication Aids. In: Anogianakis, G., Buhler, C. and Soede, M. (eds.): Advancement of Assistive Technology. Assistive Technology Research Series, Vol. 3. IOS Press, Amsterdam Berlin Oxford Tokyo Washington (1997) 200-205.
13. Kouroupetroglou G., Pino, A., Viglas, C.: Managing Accessible User Interfaces of Multi-Vendor Components under the ULYSSES Framework for Interpersonal Communication Applications. In: C. Stephanidis (ed) Universal Access in HCI. Lawrence Erlbaum Ass, (2001) 185-189
14. Bliss C. K.: Semantography-Blissymbolics, 3rd edition. Semantography-Blissymbolics Publications (1978)
15. McDonald, E. T.: Teaching and using Blissymbolics. Blissymbolics Communication Institute, Canada (1985)
16. McNaughton, S.: Communicating with Blissymbolics. Blissymbolics Communication Institute, Canada (1985)
17. Garay-Vitoria, N., Abascal, J. G.: PROFET. Word Prediction for Inflected Languages. Application to Basque Language. Proc. Of the Workshop on Natural Language Processing for Communication Aids. Madrid, Spain (1997) 29-36
18. Olaszi, P., Koutny, I., Kalman, S.: From BLISS Symbols to Grammatically Correct Voice Output: A Communication Tool for People with Disabilities. Int. Journal of Speech Technology, **5** (1) (2002) 49-56
19. Xydas, G., Kouroupetroglou, G.: Text-to-Speech Scripting Interface for Appropriate Vocalisation of e-Texts. Proc. of EUROSPEECH 2001, Aalborg, Denmark (2001) 2247-2250
20. Xydas, G., Kouroupetroglou, G.: Augmented Auditory Representation of e-Texts for Text-to-Speech Systems. In V. Matousek (eds.): Text, Speech and Dialogue. Lecture Notes in Artificial Intelligence Vol. 2166. Springer-Verlag, (2001) 134-141
21. Xydas, G., Kouroupetroglou, G.: The DEMOSTHeNES Speech Composer. Proc. of the 4th ISCA Tutorial and Research Workshop on Speech Synthesis, Perthshire, Scotland (2001)

Role Identification from Free Text Using Hidden Markov Models

Georgios Sigletos, Georgios Paliouras, and Vangelis Karkaletsis

Software and Knowledge Engineering Laboratory
Institute of Informatics and Telecommunications,
N.C.S.R. "Demokritos",
Tel: +301-6503197, Fax: +301-6532175
{sigletos, paliourg, vangelis}@iit.demokritos.gr

Abstract. In this paper we explore the use of hidden Markov models on the task of role identification from free text. Role identification is an important stage of the information extraction process, assigning roles to particular types of entities with respect to a particular event. Hidden Markov models (HMMs) have been shown to achieve good performance when applied to information extraction tasks in both semistructured and free text. The main contribution of this work is the analysis of whether and how linguistic processing of textual data can improve the extraction performance of HMMs. The emphasis is on the minimal use of computationally expensive linguistic analysis. The overall conclusion is that the performance of HMMs is still worse than an equivalent manually constructed system. However, clear paths for improvement of the method are shown, aiming at a method, which is easily adaptable to new domains.

1 Introduction

Role identification is the subtask of *information extraction,* dealing with the assignment of event-specific roles to the various entities mentioned in a piece of text that describes an event. In the information extraction process, as defined in the Message Understanding Conferences [8], role identification is part of the *scenario template-filling* task, which is the ultimate goal of the information extraction process. Thus, role identification is a hard task, often requiring significant use of computationally expensive linguistic processing methods.

In this paper we investigate the problem of role identification using hidden Markov models (HMMs). Hidden Markov modeling is a powerful statistical learning technique with widespread application, mostly in the area of speech recognition [11]. HMMs have also been applied successfully to other language related tasks, including part-of-speech tagging [2], named entity recognition [1] and text segmentation [15]. The main advantage of HMMs in language modeling is the fact that they are well suited for the modeling of sequential data, such as spoken or written language. Another serious motivation behind the use of HMMs for text-based tasks is their strong statistical foundations, which provide a sound theoretical basis for the constructed models. On the other hand, an important concern with the use of HMMs

I.P. Vlahavas and C.D. Spyropoulos (Eds.): SETN 2002, LNAI 2308, pp. 167–178, 2002.

is the large amount of training data required to acquire good estimates of the model parameters.

Recent research has suggested the use of HMMs for the task of role identification from either semistructured or free text. Leek in [7] designed HMMs to extract gene locations from biomedical texts. Freitag & McCallum in [3] and [4], used HMMs for information extraction both from newsgroups and a collection of Reuter's articles. The focus of that work was on techniques that either improve the estimation of model parameters [3] or learn the model structure from training data [4]. However, the use of HMMs for role identification from free text is largely unexplored territory and there are many important issues to be examined.

In this paper we examine for the first time the use HMMs for role identification from Greek texts. For this purpose, we have used a collection of Greek financial articles describing company acquisitions, which was used in the MITOS R&D project [5]. Unlike previous work on HMMs for role identification, we pay particular attention to whether and how linguistic processing of textual data can improve the extraction performance of HMMs. This is a difficult issue, because the initial intuition that linguistic analysis is likely to help in extracting information from natural language, has to face the reality of high computationally costs for using linguistic analysis tools. Therefore, it is important to identify the minimum necessary linguistic processing for improving the performance of information extraction, while maintaining the computational efficiency of the process. Along this line of thought, we performed various types of linguistic preprocessing to our dataset, and considered different data representations, where linguistic information was represented as part of the text in a *sequential* form. The motivation for the sequential representation is the suitability of HMMs for modeling sequential data.

The rest of this paper is structured as follows. In section 2 we review the basic theory of HMMs and discuss how HMMs can be used for role identification. In section 3, we present experimental results on our dataset varying the use of linguistic processing. Finally, we conclude in section 5, discussing potential improvements of the method.

2 HMMs for Role Identification

2.1 Basic Theory

A hidden Markov model is an extension of a Markov process where the observation is a probabilistic function of a state. The elements that characterize an HMM are:

- A set of N individual states $S = \{s_1, s_2, \ldots, s_N\}$, often interconnected in a way that any state can be reached from any other state (*ergodic* model).
- A discrete vocabulary of M observation symbols $V = \{v_1, v_2, \ldots, v_M\}$.
- An NxN state transition probability matrix $A = \{a_{ij}\}$, indicating the probability of transitioning from state i to state j. Here we deal with *first-order* HMMs, which

means that transitioning to the next state j at time $t+1$ depends only on the current state i at time t, i.e., $P[s_j(t+1) \mid s_i(t)\, s_k(t-1)\ldots] = P[s_j(t+1) \mid s_i(t)] = a_{ij}$.

- An NxM observation symbol probability matrix $B = \{b_j(k)\}$ indicating the probability of observing symbol v_k at state s_j.
- An Nx1 initial state matrix $\pi = \{\pi_i\} = \{P[s_i(1)]\}$, indicating the probability of being at state s_i at time $t=1$.

An HMM is a probabilistic generative model, whereby a sequence of symbols, denoted as $O = \{o_1 o_2 \ldots o_T\}$, is produced by starting from an initial state i (with probability π_i), emitting an output symbol $v_k = o_1$ (with probability $b_i(k)$), transitioning to a new state j (with probability a_{ij}) emitting a new symbol and so on until reaching the final state at time T and emitting the output symbol o_T. Here we also deal with *discrete output* HMMs, meaning that O is a sequence of discrete symbols, chosen from the vocabulary V.

The three classic issues with HMMs are the following [12]:

1. Given the parameters $\lambda = (A, B, \pi)$ of an HMM and a sequence of symbols, how can we efficiently compute the probability $P(O \mid \lambda)$, that the observation sequence was produced by the HMM? This is an *evaluation* problem, which allows us to choose the model which best matches the sequence.
2. Given the parameters $\lambda = (A, B, \pi)$ of an HMM and a sequence of symbols, how can we efficiently compute the most likely state sequence $Q=\{q_1 q_2 \ldots q_T\}$ associated with the symbol sequence? The state sequence Q is *hidden* and can be *observed* only through the sequence O. This issue relates to the "uncovering" of the hidden state sequence.
3. How can we efficiently estimate the parameters $\lambda = (A, B, \pi)$ to maximize $P(O \mid \lambda)$? This is the most difficult of the three problems, dealing with the *training* of an HMM given a set of observation sequences.

The above three problems can be solved using the *Forward-Backward*, *Viterbi* and *Baum-Welch* algorithms respectively, as described in [12].

A key insight into the use of HMMs for language related tasks is that state transitions are modeled by a *bigram* model emitting label types from a N-length discrete vocabulary (just as with traditional Markov models), while each state is a label-specific *unigram* language model, emitting tokens from a M-length discrete vocabulary.

2.2 Using HMMs for Role Identification

In order to train HMMs for the role identification task, we make the following assumptions, inspired by related work in [3] and [4].

- An HMM models the entire document, thus not requiring any segmentation of the document into sentences or other pieces of text. Each training document is modeled as a sequence *O*, of lexical units (tokens). The discrete tokens of all the training sequences constitute the discrete alphabet *V* of the HMM.
- A separate HMM is constructed for each role of the event. In this paper we deal with a collection of Greek articles describing company acquisitions. For this event, we are interested in four roles: the *buyer* company, the company that is *acquired*, the acquisition *rate* and the acquisition *amount*. Thus, we construct four different HMMs, one for each role.
- The structure of each HMM is set by hand, and follows the same basic form for each of the four different roles. Each state of an HMM is associated with a specific *label type*. The set of label types that is used, involve a *start* (S) label type that models the first token of the document, an *end* (E) type that models the last token, which is always the EOF (end of file) symbol, two *target* types (T_1 and T_2), which model the tokens that were hand tagged as one of the four target roles, two *prefix* (P_1 and P_2) and two *suffix* (S_1 and S_2) label types which model two tokens around the target tokens, and finally a *background* (B) type that models all the other tokens of the document which are of no particular interest. This set of label types is used to attribute a particular meaning to each state of the HMM, and it should not be confused with the token vocabulary *V* of the model. A typical HMM structure, using these label types is shown in Figure 1. The HMM of Figure 1 is not fully connected. This constraint on the allowable transitions encodes prior knowledge about the task, aiming to improve the extraction performance. For example, the self-transition in state "T2" indicates that a role instance, e.g. a *buyer* company, may consist of more than two tokens. Similarly, the transition from state T1 to state S1, indicates that a role instance may also consist of a single token.

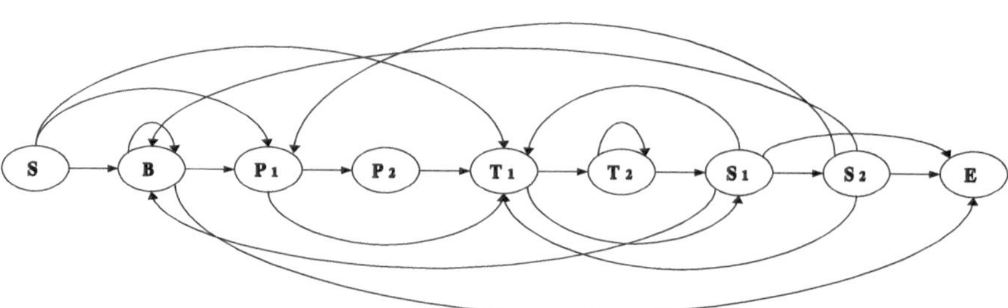

Fig. 1. An example of an HMM structure. Label types are associated to the states of the model (S: *start*, E: *end*, B: *background*, P1 *prefix1*, P2: *prefix2*, T1: *target1*, T2: *target2* S1: *suffix1*, S2: *suffix2*).

- A sequence of labels $L=\{l_1 l_2 \dots l_T\}$ is associated with each training sequence $O=\{o_1 o_2 \dots o_T\}$. *L* encodes the hand tagged information about the roles in a document, and l_i elements take values from the vocabulary of label types, as depicted in Figure 1. An example of a label sequence might be *L*={S B B…P1 P2 T1 T2 T2 S1 S2 B B…E}. When training an HMM for a specific role (e.g. *buyer company*), all tokens that are hand tagged with this role are associated with target tokens.

Since there is a one-to-one mapping between states and labels, the state sequence is no longer *hidden* and thus the Baum-Welch algorithm is not needed to train the HMMs. State transition and token emission probabilities can be acquired directly from the training data and their associated label sequences, by simply calculating ratios of counts (maximum likelihood estimation) as follows:

$$a_{ij} = \frac{c(i \to j)}{\sum_{s \in S} c(i \to s)} \quad \text{and} \quad b_j(k) = \frac{c(j \uparrow k)}{\sum_{v \in V} c(j \uparrow v)}. \tag{1}$$

Where $c(i \to j)$ counts the transitions from state i to state j, and $c(j \uparrow k)$ counts the occurrence frequency of token k in state j. Token emission probabilities often need to be *smoothed*, in order to avoid zero probabilities for vocabulary tokens not observed in the training data for a particular state. For that purpose we chose a widely used smoothing technique, described in [16]. State transition probabilities do not require smoothing, due to the small size and low connectivity of the model.

After the training phase, our four HMMs are evaluated using articles that have not been "seen" during the training process. Given a set of test sequences, each denoted as O, the objective is to find the most likely state sequence, i.e., the most likely label sequence L, and then extract the target tokens. The uncovering of the hidden label sequence corresponds to the second issue concerning HMMs, as described in subsection 2.1 and is achieved by the *Viterbi* algorithm. One issue that arises when following this modeling approach is how to deal with unknown tokens in the test collection, i.e., tokens that do not exist in the training vocabulary V. To deal with that problem we added a special token "unknown" to the vocabulary of the HMMs, during the training phase.

3 Experiments

3.1 Data Preprocessing

For the purposes of our experiments we used a collection of 110 Greek financial articles describing company acquisition events. In these texts, the roles *buyer*, *acquired*, *rate* and *amount* were hand tagged. As mentioned above, *buyer* indicates the company that acts as a buyer, *acquired* indicates the company that is bought, the acquisition *rate* is the percentage of the company that is bought and finally the *amount* is the amount spent by the buyer. Each text describes a single company acquisition event. The text corpus was preprocessed using the *Ellogon* text engineering platform [10] and the following linguistic tools: *tokenizer*, *part-of-speech-tagger* and *stemmer*.

The tokenizer identifies text tokens (i.e., words, symbols, etc.) and characterizes them according to a token-type tag set which encodes graphological information (e.g. the token comprises upper case greek characters). Part of this tag set is shown in Table 1(a). The part-of-speech (POS) tagger identifies the POS of each word token, according to a POS tag set. In addition to the part of speech, the tag set includes also morphological features, such as number, gender and case. Part of this tag set is shown in Table 1(b). The POS tagger that we used is a rule-based one, constructed with the use the transformation-based learning method [2]. The performance of the tagger on Greek financial texts is approximately 95% [9]. Finally, the stemmer converts word tokens to lowercase and unstressed, and removes the inflectional suffixes of Greek nouns and adjectives.

Table 1. (a) Part of the token-type subset used by the tokenizer. (b) Part of the part-of-speech tag set used by the POS tagger

GLW	Greek lowercase word
GUW	Greek uppercase word
GFW	Greek word first capital
EUW	English uppercase word
EFW	English word first capital
PERIOD	.
INT	Integer

(a)

NNF	Noun, feminine, singular number
DDT	Definite article
VBD	Verb past tense
WP	Relative pronoun
FW	Foreign word

(b)

The result of each linguistic processing step is a new collection of articles, where the linguistic information is represented as part of the text in various ways. Due to the sequential modeling nature of traditional HMMs, we represented the linguistic features of each token in sequence with the document text. For example, the result of the tokenizer is a new collection where an extra token is added just before each token, indicating the type of that token according to the tag set. Table 2 shows a sample sentence in the various data representations that we examined.

Table 2. Different representations for a sample sentence, incorporating linguistic information.

Collection A (Baseline)	Στην εξαγορά της εταιρείας ITC προχώρησε η Computer Logic.
Collection B (Type Token)	*GFW* Στην *GLW* εξαγορά *GLW* της *GLW* εταιρείας *EUW* ITC *GLW* προχώρησε *GLW* η *EUW* Computer *EUW* Logic *PERIOD* .
Collection C (POS Token)	*DDT* Στην *NNF* εξαγορά *DDT* της *NNF* εταιρείας *FW* ITC *VBD* προχώρησε *DDT* η *FW* Computer *FW* Logic.
Collection D (Type POS Token)	*GFW DDT* Στην *GLW NNF* εξαγορά *GLW DDT* της *NNF GLW* εταιρείας *EUW FW* ITC *GLW VBD* προχώρησε *GLW DDT* η *EUW* Computer *FW EUW FW* Logic *PERIOD* .
Collection E (Token_Type)	Στην_*GFW* εξαγορά_*GLW* της_*GLW* εταιρείας_*GLW* ITC_*EUW* προχώρησε_*GLW* η_*GLW* Computer_*EUW* Logic_*EUW* PERIOD .

Collection F (Token_POS)	Στην_*DDT* εξαγορά_*NNF* της_*DDT* εταιρείας_*NNF* ITC_*FW* προχώρησε_*VBD* η_*DDT* Computer_*FW* Logic_*FW* .
Collection G (Token_Type_POS)	Στην_*GFW_DDT* εξαγορά_*GLW_NNF* της_*GLW_DDT* εταιρείας_*GLW_NNF* ITC_*EUW_FW* προχώρησε_*GLW_VBD* η_*GLW_DDT* Computer_*EUW_FW* Logic_*EUW_FW* PERIOD .
Collection H (Type_POS)	*GFW_DDT GLW_NNF GLW_DDT GLW_NNF EUW_FW GLW_VBD GLW_DDT EUW_FW EUW_FW* PERIOD
Collection I (Stems)	στην εξαγορ της εταιρι itc προχωρησε η computer logic

3.2 Results

We conducted five groups of experiments. Each group uses collections from Table 2, which represent linguistic information in a similar manner. The first group contains experiments on the baseline collection A of Table 2 without any linguistic information. The second group contains experiments on the collections B, C and D, where the linguistic information (token type or POS or both) is represented as extra tokens added just before each token of the text. The third group contains experiments on the collections E, F and G, where the linguistic information is represented as tokens attached to each token of the text using the underscore character ("_"), as depicted in Table 2. The fourth group comprises the collection H where each token of the text is substituted by the corresponding type and POS, connected with each other using the underscore character (*Type_POS*). Finally, the fifth group contains the collection I, where each token from the baseline collection is substituted by the corresponding stem.

Each experiment on a collection, involves the training of four HMMs, one for each role of the domain. We experimented with various structures for the HMMs on each collection. The model structure, which achieved the best results for the majority of the collections, is shown in Figure 1. We conducted experiments using more than two prefix, suffix and target states, expecting that more complex HMM structures would capture the content of some collections where new tokens have been introduced, e.g. B, C and D, and thus achieve better results. However the results did not justify the additional complexity.

The evaluation of the HMMs was done using the 10-fold cross validation method. According to this evaluation method, the collection is split into ten equally sized subsets and the learning algorithm is run ten times. Each time, nine of the ten pieces are used for training and the tenth is kept as unseen data for the evaluation of the algorithm. Each of the ten pieces acts as the evaluation set in one of the ten runs and the final result is the average over ten runs. The extraction performance of the HMMs was evaluated using three measures per HMM (i.e., per role): *recall*, *precision* and *accuracy*. Recall measures the number of items of a certain role (e.g. buyer) correctly identified, divided by the total number of items of this specific role in the data. Precision measures the number of items of a certain role correctly identified, divided by the total number of items that were assigned to that role by the HMM. Accuracy measures the number of *tokens* of a certain role correctly identified, divided by the total number of *tokens* assigned to that role [13]. In total 12 measures are used for the experiments: recall, precision and accuracy for each of the four roles (*buyer, acquired, rate, amount*) of the company acquisition domain.

The best results for each group of experiments together with the collections that achieved those results are presented in Tables 3 (a-e).

Table 3. Best performance of HMMs for each of the five groups of experiments

	Buyer	*Acquired*	*Rate*	*Amount*
Recall	0,294	0,238	0,856	0,517
Precision	0,567	0,531	0,791	0,397
Accuracy	0,721	0,617	0,806	0,607

(a) Performance on collection A (baseline collection)

	Buyer	*Acquired*	*Rate*	*Amount*
Best Collection	B	B	B	B
Recall	**0,637**	**0,571**	**0,967**	**0,592**
Precision	0,389	0,332	0,687	0,347
Accuracy	0,529	0,413	0,715	0,545

(b) Best performance on collections B, C, D

	Buyer	*Acquired*	*Rate*	*Amount*
Best Collection	G	G	G	G
Recall	**0,310**	**0,250**	0,838	**0,567**
Precision	**0,619**	**0,555**	**0,791**	**0,430**
Accuracy	**0,782**	**0,646**	**0,806**	**0,615**

(c) Best performance on collections E, F, G

	Buyer	*Acquired*	*Rate*	*Amount*
Recall	**0,697**	**0,683**	**0,915**	**0,842**
Precision	0,341	0,351	0,721	0,403
Accuracy	0,410	0,370	0,728	0,482

(d) Performance on collection H

	Buyer	*Acquired*	*Rate*	*Amount*
Recall	**0,309**	**0,286**	**0,856**	**0,567**
Precision	0,501	0,485	**0,796**	0,385
Accuracy	0,685	0,554	**0,814**	**0,631**

(e) Performance on collection I

Comparing the results in Table 3(b) to the baseline results in Table 3(a) we note a significant increase in recall, accompanied by a smaller decrease in both precision and accuracy. This can be justified as follows: Capitalization of the first character of a token usually provides evidence of a name. By using the *Type Token* representation of collection B, our HMMs can learn rules of the form "when emitting one of *GUW, GFW,* etc., then with high probability the next token is a target token". Thus the number of items assigned to the *buyer* and *acquired* roles increases, causing the equivalent increase in recall, followed by a smaller decrease in the other two measures. On the other hand, the *rate* and *amount* roles mostly involve numerical entities. Thus the number of items assigned to those two roles also increases by the presence of a numeric token *Type*, e.g. *INT*, added just before a number. The learned rules in this case can be of the form "when emitting an integer or decimal number then with high probability the next token is a target token".

Comparing the results of Table 3(c) to the results of Table 3(a), we note an overall improvement for the *buyer*, *acquired* and *amount* roles, while the performance for the *rate* role remains almost unaffected. This means that the additional part-of-speech information included in this representation *(Token_Type_POS)* improves the performance of HMMs. The same is not true for collection D (*Type POS Token*), where the encoding of linguistic information as extra tokens causes a significant deterioration in precision and therefore the additional part-of-speech information is not beneficial.

When removing information about the token itself in collection H, the result is a significant increase in recall (comparing tables 3(d) and 3(c)), with a significant decrease in the other two measures. This is an indication of overgeneralization, which is expected due to the generality and simplicity of the linguistic information that is used, i.e., part-of-speech and token type.

The results in Table 3(e) show that stemming improves recall overall, while it hurts precision for the *buyer*, *acquired*, and *amount* roles. This means that the reduction of the vocabulary, with the use of stemming, causes a higher level of generalization, which increases recall and reduces precision. The performance for the *rate* role improves slightly in all three measures, which is justified by the emergence of clearer contextual patterns for this role, with the use of stemmed words.

Another clear conclusion from the experiments is that the performance for the *buyer* and *acquired* roles is worse than that for the *rate* role for all of the experiments. To a lesser extend the same is true for the *amount* role. There are two reasonable explanations for this. First, the *rate* and *amount* roles involve numerical entities, which are easier to detect in the text than detecting named entities, such as companies. This justifies the high recall for these roles. Second, it is more difficult to discriminate between roles for entities of the same type (e.g. *companies*). As a result many *buyer* companies in the collection were also detected by the HMMs as *acquired* and vice versa. On the other hand, *rate* and *amount* are very different from the other roles, and there aren't any other similar roles in the domain such as "*rate*_B" or "*amount*_B". This justifies the low precision for the *buyer* and *acquired* roles. To verify the second explanation we conducted another set of experiments where both *buyer* and *acquired* were tagged as one concept, i.e., "*buyer* OR *acquired*". The experiments were conducted using the collections with the best results in the previous experiments (Table 3). The new results are depicted in Table 4.

Table 4. Performance of the HMMs for the role "*buyer* OR *acquired*" on the collections with the best results from the five groups of experiments.

	Collection A (baseline)	Collection B (type token)	Collection G (token_type_pos)	Collection H (type_pos)	Collection I (stems)
Recall	0,432	0,738	0,426	0,842	0,416
Precision	0,611	0,400	0,620	0,560	0.560
Accuracy	0,758	0,579	0,767	0,648	0,741

As expected, in Table 4 a consistent improvement in all three measures (recall, precision and accuracy) is obtained over the results for the *buyer* and the *acquired* roles in Table 3. That improvement, however, is not as substantial as one would expect. This happens because there are also other company names in the collections that do not have a particular role in the acquisition event and the HMMs erroneously detect those entities as either *buyer* or *acquired*.

The ultimate question that remains unanswered is which representation leads to the best performance for HMMs? From the results of Table 3, we conclude that the best representation for the *buyer* and *acquired* roles is the one used in collection G (*Token_Type_POS*), which leads to a significant increase in all measures, in comparison to the baseline collection A. The representation of collection H (Type_POS) seems to achieve the best performance for the amount role. Finally, for the *rate* role the best representation seems to be the one used in collection I (*stems*). Note however that the *rate* is the role with the least deviation to the performance measures in all the experiments. This happens because the *rate* role involves exclusively numerical entities and the percent (%) symbol which are very little affected by the different representations used in the experiments. On the other hand, the amount role may further involve alphabetic characters (e.g. 40 εκ. δρχ.). Thus the performance for the amount role can be easier influenced by the various representations of Table 2.

4 Discussion and Future Work

In this paper we examined the effect of linguistic pre-processing of the training data to the performance of hidden Markov models in role identification. For the evaluation we used three measures (recall, precision and accuracy) and the 10-fold cross-validation method, in order to gain an unbiased estimate of the performance. The data that we used consisted of 110 Greek articles, announcing company acquisition events. These data were processed by simple and efficient linguistic analysis tools and were translated into training data for the HMMs using various representations, in which the linguistic information was represented as part of the text in a sequential form. The size of the HMMs that we used was small and their structure was simple, with the model parameters easily estimated from the training data, in a straightforward manner.

The experiments showed that using certain representations, simple linguistic analysis improves the extraction performance of HMMs on role identification. The overall performance was high for the two simpler roles (*rate* and *amount*), but it was much lower for the other two roles (*buyer* and *acquired*). The improvement in performance gained by the use of linguistic information was clearer for the harder roles. The difficulty in identifying instances of the *buyer* and *acquired* roles stems mainly from the fact that they both correspond to the same type of entity (organization) and there is insufficient linguistic information for distinguishing between the two roles. Richer linguistic processing, involving syntactic analysis, could improve those results. This conclusion is also supported by the higher performance of an equivalent handcrafted system [5]. Indicative results of this system are shown in Table 5. The manual system performs badly for the *rate* and *amount* roles, due to the weak performance on the detection of numerical entities in text.

However, it does much better in the other two roles, using much more extensive, albeit computationally expensive, linguistic analysis. Finally, our results are comparable to those reported in [3].

Table 5. Performance of a handcrafted system for the company acquisition domain

	Buyer	Acquired	Rate	Amount
Recall	75%	70%	49%	43%
Precision	72%	85%	72%	60%

The extraction performance of HMMs could be improved in several ways. Freitag & McCallum in [3], implemented a statistical technique called *shrinkage* that improves the token emission probabilities of an HMM in the presence of sparse training data. Furthermore, the learning of a probabilistic model such as an HMM, also involves the learning of the structure of the model. In this paper we assumed a fixed model structure, carefully designed for the particular dataset and domain that we used. However, certain structures may capture better the content of some documents straightforwardly affecting extraction performance. Machine learning techniques have been used for learning the structure of HMMs ([4], [13], [14]) from training examples.

Acknowledgments. This work was performed in the context of the CROSSMARC project, funded by the EC (contract IST-2000-25366), and has used data collected for the MITOS project, funded by the Greek Secretariat for Research and Technology (contract NEO EKBAN 2 1.3/102).

References

1. Bikel D.M., Miller S., Schwartz R., Weischedel R. (1997). *Nymble: a high performance learning name finder.* In Proceedings of ANLP-97, 194-201.
2. Brill E. (1995). *Transformation-Based Error Driven Learning and Natural Language Processing: A Case study in Part of Speech Tagging*, Computational Linguistics, vol. 21, n. 24.
3. Freitag D., McCallum A.K. (1999). *Information extraction using HMMs and shrinkage.* AAAI-99 Workshop on Machine Learning for Information Extraction, pp. 31-36. AAAI Technical Report WS-99-11.
4. Freitag D., McCallum A.K. (2000). *Information extraction with HMM structures Learned by Stochastic Optimization,* AAAI-2000, pp. 584-589.
5. Karkaletsis V., Farmakiotou D., Androutsopoulos I. Koutsias J., Paliouras G., Spyropoulos C.D. (2000). *Information Extraction from Greek Texts in the MITOS Information Management System.* Internal Technical Report, Institute of Informatics and Telecommunications, NCSR "Demokritos".
6. Kupiec, J. (1992). *Robust part-of-speech tagging using a hidden Markov model.* Computer Speech and Language, 6, 225-242.
7. Leek T.R. (1997). *Information extraction using hidden Markov models*, Master's thesis, UC San Diego.

8. MUC-6 (1995). *Proceedings of the Sixth Message Understanding Conference*, Morgan Kaufman, for Defense Advanced Research Projects Agency.
9. Petasis G., Paliouras G., Karkaletsis V., Spyropoulos C.D. and Androutsopoulos I. (1999). *Using Machine Learning Techniques for Part-of-Speech Tagging in the Greek Language*, Proceedings of the 7th Hellenic Conference on Informatics, Ioannina, Greece.
10. Petasis G., Karkaletsis V., Paliouras G., Androutsopoulos I., (2001). *Ellogon: A Text Engineering Platform.* Internal Technical Report, Institute of Informatics and Telecommunications, NCSR "Demokritos".
11. Rabiner, L., Juang B. (1986). *An introduction to hidden Markov models.* IEEE Acoustics, Speech & Signal Processing Magazine, 3 ,4-16.
12. Rabiner, L. (1989). *A tutorial on hidden Markov models and selected application in speech recognition.* Proceedings of the IEEE 1977 (2).
13. Seymore K., McCallum A., Rosenfeld R. (1999). *Learning hidden Markov model structure for information extraction.* AAAI-99 Workshop on Machine Learning for Information Extraction., pp. 37-42.
14. Stolcke A., Omohundro S. (1992). *Hidden Markov model induction by Bayesian model merging.* In Advances in Neural Information Processing Systems, volume 5. Morgan Kaufmann.
15. Yamron J., Carp I., Gillick L., Lowe S., Mulbregt P. (1998). *A hidden Markov model approach to text segmentation and event tracking.* In Proceedings of the IEEE ICASSP.
16. Witten, I. H., Bell T.C. (1991). The zero-frequency problem: Estimating the probabilities of novel events in adaptive text compression. IEEE Transactions on Information Theory 37 (4).

Improving SMS Usability Using Bayesian Networks

Manolis Maragoudakis[1], Nikolaos K. Tselios[2], Nikolaos Fakotakis[1], and Nikolaos M. Avouris[2]

[1]Wire Communications Laboratory
{mmarag,fakotaki}@wcl.ee.upatras.gr

[2]Human-Computer Interaction Group
Dept. of Electrical & Computer Engineering
University of Patras, 26500 Patras, Greece
{nitse,n.avouris}@ee.upatras.gr

Abstract. During the last years, the significant increase of mobile communications has resulted in the wide acceptance of a plethora of new services, like communication via written short messages (SMS). The limitations of the dimensions and the number of keys of the mobile phone keypad are probably the main obstacles of this service. Numerous intelligent techniques have been developed aiming at supporting users of SMS services. Special emphasis has been provided to the efficient and effective editing of words. In the presented research, we introduce a predictive algorithm that forecasts Greek letters occurrence during the process of compiling an SMS. The algorithm is based on Bayesian networks that have been trained with sufficient Greek corpus. The extracted network infers the probability of a specific letter in a word given one, two or three previous letter that have been keyed by the user with precision that reaches 95%. An important advantage, compared to other predictive algorithms is that the use of a vocabulary is not required, so the limited memory resources of mobile phones can easily accommodate the presented algorithm. The proposed method[1] achieves improvement in the word editing time compared to the traditional editing method by a factor of 34.72%, as this has been proven by using Keystroke Level Modeling technique described in the paper.

1 Introduction

Throughout the past decade, mobile telephony has boosted wireless communication to a high, most respectable level of public acceptance. Although we usually consider mobile phones as speech input and output devices, novel technologies such as SMS messaging, mobile chat and WAP, have been presented in an obvious attempt to transform the mobile phone into a hyper-node of incoming and outgoing information. As an example, Sonera, Finland's largest teleoperator reports a six-fold increase in text message [13]. Moreover, GSM association revealed that more than 10 billion of messages per month were sent by the end of 2000. However, the basic problem in

[1] This corresponding method is protected under copyright law.

I.P. Vlahavas and C.D. Spyropoulos (Eds.): SETN 2002, LNAI 2308, pp. 179–190, 2002.

mobile phones and pervasive devices in general is input, where the physical dimensions of the devices obstruct the user. User input is a crucial issue concerning mobile devices since there are numerous applications that take it for granted. SMS communication is now one of the most popular features of cellular phones. Myriads of messages are exchanged throughout the world in a growth rate that approximately doubles every year[2]. Apart from messages, input is also of great importance in mobile chat services, a new technology that aims to create mobile chat rooms as well as in WAP pages where the user forms a query for search, fill out forms.

Buchanan et al., [1] report a study concerning mobile phone users complaining about the difficulty of accessing the phone's functions using the key pad. Buchanan et al. [1] carried out extensive analysis to detect reasons for poor subjective users' satisfaction and found that the number of key presses to access all the menu options was 110, while the average number of key presses to access a function was 8.2. These excess numbers, provide a clear idea that mobile input design is of great importance, not only for quick accessing of the phone's menus but for editing text messages as well. Clearly, the problem exists because first, mobile handsets were anticipated as devices to make and receive calls, but actually transformed to complex information appliances delivering a variety of services to the user [7]. Moreover, physical limitations of devices such as tiny keypads and small screens with low resolution further intensifies the problem reducing the possibility for the users to build solid conceptual models of interaction with them.

For the present work, we focus on this issue of mobile input usability, study the existing methodologies and propose a novel, Bayesian approach that appears to improve typing speed without having to incorporate any linguistic information or dictionary at all. In order to determine the efficiency of the new interaction dialogue proposed, we have evaluated its efficiency using Keystroke Level Model as well as by building a software prototype for simulating preliminary real world experiments.

This paper is organized as follows: First, we briefly present current status in mobile usability research area. Subsequently, we present Bayesian networks upon which our proposed alternative text input method is based, followed by predicting text sequence algorithm description. Subsequently, keystroke level model of interaction is presented and alternative text input dialogues are compared. Finally a software prototype emulator is presented used to preliminary evaluate efficiency of the proposed method.

2 Text Entry Usability in Mobile Phones

As mentioned previously, usability in mobile devices still remains a subject under extensive debate [12]. Due to the fact that our work concerns mobile phones input, we shall discuss usability under this perspective. In a mobile phone, the letters of an alphabet have to be mapped onto a nine-key pad. As a consequence, this means that three or more letters have to be grouped in one single key. Due to that reason, usually

---

[2] Source: GSM World Association (www.gsmworld.com)

more than one keystroke required in order for a user to access and enter a letter. Nowadays, two alternative dialogues have been established in order to assist the user in editing a message.

The simpler, yet widely acceptable, which from now will be referred as STEM (Standard Text Entry Method), approach requires tapping the corresponding key as many times as needed to appear on screen for a letter to be entered. The basic disadvantage of multiple keystrokes is the lack of speed. However, as previously described, this lack of speed influences positively the need for user confirmation. So, the user does not have to pay any attention to the mobile phone screen. Another problem appears when typing two letters that lie in the same key. The most common solution is the introduction of a time delay between two taps of the same key, in order to verify that the user wants to type two letters from the same group or one letter by multiple taps. This obviously further deteriorates the message editing speed. Additionally to poor task execution time provided by this method, extensive effort in terms of keystrokes is required from the user to complete typing a message.

Another, similar approach is the two-key input method, in which a user specifies a character by pressing two keys. The first key represents the group of letters (e.g key 2 for A, B or C) and the second disambiguates the letter by selecting its place in the group (e.g key 1 would select A). Studies by Silfverberg et al., [13] have depicted that although two-key is very simple, it is not efficient for Roman characters, since there is great loss of speed by moving between the two keys. That is probably the main reason why this method is not popular among users. Note however that it is very common for typing Katakana characters.

Among the lexicon-based methods, the most popular is called T9©, developed by Tegic©, and uses a dictionary in order to deal with letter disambiguation. More specifically, the user presses the key in which the desired letter lies, only once. By the time a word is completed, which means that a space was entered, the system is trying to output the most probable word that corresponds to the key sequence that the user provided. If the guessed word is incorrect, then using a special key the system outputs a pool of other words that also correspond to the specific key sequence. This method significantly reduces editing speed but requires user attention and since it is based on a lexicon, it cannot efficiently handle unknown or shortened words, slang, names etc., heavily used in mobile text messaging [8]. Another important drawback of T9 is the poor feedback during the process of typing a word. There are times that letter disambiguation occurs at the latter characters of a word, so until then, the user may see a totally different set of characters, a phenomenon that obviously results in user confusion due to reduced sense of progress towards user's text entry goal.

In the following section, we shall provide some fundamental background concerning Bayesian networks theory, which we used in order to obtain knowledge about the probabilistic relations of letter sequences. This information contributes to the effective disambiguation of grouped letters according to the approach presenting in the following.

3 Bayesian Belief Networks

A Bayesian Belief Network (BBN) is a significant knowledge representation and reasoning tool, under conditions of uncertainty [9]. Given a set of variables D = <X_1, X_2...X_N>, where each variable X_i could take values from a set $Val(X_i)$, a BBN describes the probability distribution over this set of variables. We use capital letters as *X,Y* to denote variables and lower case letters as *x,y* to denote values taken by these variables. Formally, a BBN is an annotated directed acyclic graph (DAG) that encodes a joint probability distribution. We denote a network *B* as a pair B=<G,Θ>, [11] where *G* is a DAG whose nodes symbolize the variables of *D*, and *Θ* refers to the set of parameters that quantifies the network. *G* embeds the following conditional independence assumption:

Each variable X_i is independent of its non-descendants given its parents.

Θ includes information about the probability distribution of a value x_i of a variable X_i, given the values of its immediate predecessors. The unique joint probability distribution over <X_1, X_2...X_N> that a network *B* describes can be computed using:

$$P_B(X_1 ... X_N) = \prod_{i=1}^{N} P(x_i \mid parents(X_i)) \tag{1}$$

3.1 Learning BBN from Data

In the process of efficiently detecting the impact that the neighbouring characters apply to the target character, prior knowledge is not always straighforward. Thus, a BBN should be learned from the training data provided. Learning a BBN unifies two processes: learning the graphical structure and learning the parameters Θ for that structure. In order to seek out the optimal parameters for a given corpus of complete data, we directly use the empirical conditional frequencies extracted from the data [3]. The selection of the variables that will constitute the data set is of great significance, since the number of possible networks that could describe these variables equals to:

$$2^{\frac{N(N-1)}{2}} \tag{2}$$

where N is the number of variables [6]. We use the following equation along with Bayes theorem to determine the relation r (or Bayes factor) of two candidate networks B1 and B2 respectively:

$$r = \frac{P(B_1 \mid D)}{P(B_2 \mid D)} \tag{3}$$

$$P(B \mid D) = \frac{P(D \mid B) P(B)}{P(D)} \tag{4}$$

where:

P(B/D) is the probability of a network *B* given data *D*.
P(D/B) is the probability the network gives to data D.
P(D) is the 'general' probability of data.
P(B) is the probability of the network before seen the data.

Applying equation (3) to (4), we get:

$$r = \frac{P(D \mid B_1)P(B_1)}{P(D \mid B_2)P(B_2)} \qquad \textbf{(5)}$$

Having not seen the data, no prior knowledge is obtainable and thus no straightforward method of computing P(B1) and P(B2) is feasible. A common way to deal with this is, is to follow the standard BBN approach and assume that every network has the same probability with all the others, so equation (5) becomes:

$$r = \frac{P(D \mid B_1)}{P(D \mid B_2)} \qquad \textbf{(6)}$$

The probability the model gives to the data can be extracted using the following formula of Glymour and Cooper, [4]:

$$P(D \mid B) = \prod_{i=1}^{n} \prod_{j=1}^{qi} \frac{\Gamma(\frac{\Xi}{q_i})}{\Gamma(\frac{\Xi}{q_i} + N_{ij})} \prod_{k=1}^{ri} \frac{\Gamma(\frac{\Xi}{r_i q_i} + N_{ijk})}{\Gamma(\frac{\Xi}{r_i q_i})} \qquad \textbf{(7)}$$

where:

- Γ is the gamma function.
- n equals to the number of variables.
- ri denotes the number of values in i:th variable.
- qi denotes the number of possible different data value combinations the parent variables can take.
- Nij depicts the number of rows in data that have j:th data value combinations for parents of i:th variable.
- Nijk corresponds to the number of rows that have k:th value for the i:th variable and which also have j:th data value combinations for parents of i:th variable.
- Ξ is the equivalent sample size, a parameter that determines how readily we change our beliefs about the quantitative nature of dependencies when we see the data. In our study, we follow a simple choice inspired by Jeffreys' [5] prior. Ξ equals to the average number of values variables have, divided by 2.

We have applied the above equation to tabular data, meaning that the training file contained columns that correspond to the distinct variables of the network and the rows that correspond to each data entry.

Given the great number of possible networks produced by the learning process, a search algorithm has to be applied. We follow greedy search, which is based on the assumption that all possible network combinations produce a candidate best one, with one modification: instead of comparing all candidate networks, we consider investigating the set that resembles the current best model most, meaning that we consider examining other networks from the group of those that have almost same set of dependency statements. In general, a BBN is capable of computing the probability distribution for any partial subset of variables, given the values or distributions of any subset of the remaining variables. Note that the values have to be discretised, and different discretisation size affects the network. As we shall discuss in the result section, BBN are a significant tool for knowledge representation, visualising the relationships between features and subsets of them. This fact has a significant result on identifying which features are actually affect the class variable, thus reducing training data size without any significant impact in the performance.

4 Predicting Text Sequence

Having discussed the advantages and disadvantages of STEM and T9, our initial goal was simply to incorporate the positive aspects of these into one single approach. Furthermore, resource reduction was a high motivation for our research. As previously mentioned, the most significant problem is ambiguity of letters belonging to the same group. The goal is simply to type the desired character using as less keystrokes as possible. In STEM, the average number of keystrokes for a SMS message reaches 2.072 as measured in a sample of 386870 letters concerning words from a of the DELOS[3] Greek corpus. The ideal number would have to approximate 1. Our approach, which will be referred to as BAPTI (Bayesian Predictive Text Input) from now on, uses Bayesian knowledge to infer about the probability of a letter given the key that was pressed and its immediate predecessors (e.g. sequence of letters entered). We have been experimenting with the Greek language, because it is more ambiguous than English, due to the large number of vowels. We are of the belief that the new proposed methodology, combines speed enhancement with robustness when dealing with words not listed in a dictionary. Moreover, we have managed to incorporate minimal resources, a significant advantage compared with the large dictionary entries of T9 (about five thousand words considered the most popular across an analysis of English texts).

The Bayesian prior probabilities for every letter have been calculated by training Bayesian Belief Networks from large corpora. In our case, we used the DELOS Greek corpus, which is consisted of approximately 70Mb of raw text. BAPTI uses this prior probability to infer about the most probable letter in the group of letters that lie in the key that the user pressed. The level of network complexity is increasing in proportion to the length of the word that the user wishes to enter. However, due to the memory limitations of a mobile phone, we do not consider prefixes consisting of more than three letters. In case the system incorrectly predicts a letter, a special purpose function key (#) can alter the output to the second most probable letter and so on.

---

[3] DELOS Project Nr: EPET II, 98 LE-12

Figure 1 illustrates an example of a BBN taking the three predecessors of a letter as well as the key that was pressed into account. Nodes three letters before, two letters before and one letter before represent the corresponding prefixes. Node KEY symbolizes the key that was pressed, and takes values from two to nine (nominal). Finally, STATE has three distinct values, namely one, two and three that represent the position of a Greek letter in a key group. The network encodes a conditional probability table that can predict which STATE value is most probable, provided the values of all or a subset of the other nodes. As an example, consider that a user wants to write the Greek word "HΛIKIA". Suppose also that the system has correctly guessed the subset "HΛIK". In order to enter letter "I", the user presses key 4 where letters H, Θ and I lie. The network can calculate probability for each of them given the prefix "ΛIK" and key 4. The most probable letter would be returned. In case that it is not the correct one, the system would output the second most probable or the third. Throughout the experimental phase, using prefixes of three, prediction accuracy never dropped below 95.5%.

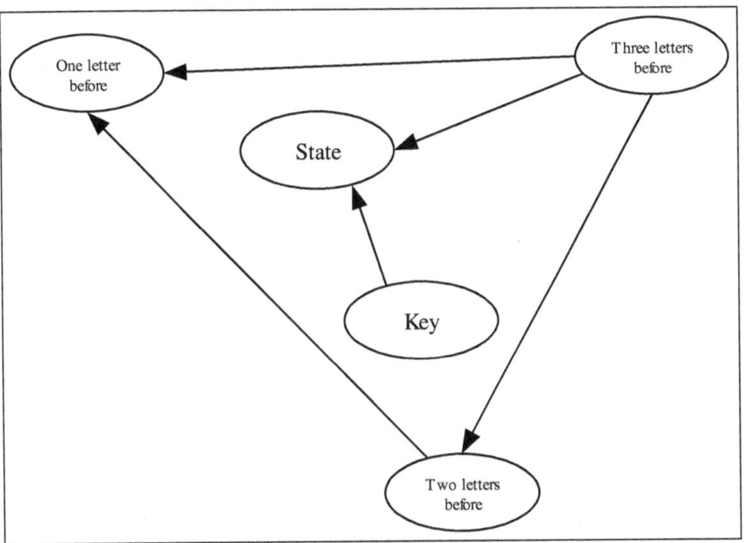

Fig. 1. Diagrammatic representation of Bayesian network obtained

As expected, the more complex a Bayesian network is, the less probable it is for the system to predict the incorrect letter. This of course directly imposes an impact to memory requirements. However, even in the worst case, the number of states that the system should hold in memory is approximately 330.000, a number that seems rational and operative to store.

5 Keystroke Level Model to Evaluate Proposed Method

Keystroke Level Model (KLM) is an analytic predictive method inspired by the Human Motor Processor Model [2]. This model focuses on unit tasks within a user machine interaction environment which consists of a small number of sequenced operations. The model assumes two phases in task execution. During the first phase decisions are made on how to accomplish the task using the primitives of the system. During the second phase the execution of the task takes place without high level mental activity. The model assumes expertise from user. This method has been empirically validated against a range of systems and a wide selection of tasks, and the predictions made were found to be remarkably accurate (prediction errors less than 20%, as stated by Olson and Olson, [10]).

Assuming negligible times for system (mobile device) response and mental operators (the user is assumed to have decided what to write and knows exactly the positioning of letters on the keypad) , we can develop a model to predict times for an expert user to enter a word. According to this model the time to complete entry of a word using STEM is:

$$T_{STEM} = \text{time to enter X letters + time to move to another key} = X[nT_P + T_{PER} + (1-P_{CK})T_{WAIT}] + (X-1)P_{CK}T_{CK} \quad \textbf{(8)}$$

And time to complete entry of a word using the proposed method is:

$$T_{BAPTI} = \text{time to enter X letters (no } T_{WAIT} \text{ required)+ time to move to another key + time to press \# } = X[T_P + T_{PER}] + (X-1)P_{CK}T_{CK} + X(P_{ERROR1} + P_{ERROR2})(T_{CK} + T_P) \quad \textbf{(9)}$$

where:

- X denotes the number of letters for a specific word.
- n denotes the average number of keystrokes to select a specific letter using STEM (calculated 2.0229 from a sample of 386870 letters).
- T_P denotes average key press time. (165 milliseconds (Silfverberg et. al 2000))
- T_{PER} denotes time required from user to perceive correct entry.(500 milliseconds).
- P_{CK} probability of requiring a letter contained in a different key than the previously pressed. (calculated 0.89 from a sample of 386870 letters).
- T_{WAIT} time waiting for cursor to proceed, when successive letter contained in the same key.(depends on phone, for Nokia models is 1500 milliseconds [13]).
- T_{CK} required for a user to move to another key. (approximately calculated by using Fitt's Law: 215 milliseconds [13]).
- P_{ERROR1}, P_{ERROR2} are probability for a proposed letter not be the required one, and probability for the second proposed letter not be the required one, respectively. (calculated as 0.045 and 0.002 respectively).

Applying equations (8) and (9), we obtain T_{STEM} = 5695,8 msec and T_{BAPTI}= 3590,5 msec for an average Greek word length (X=6). Increase in task efficiency is 34,72% in terms of time required and average number of keystrokes required is 12,13 and 6,39 respectively, a difference of 47,35%. Modeling of T9 method does not give accurate results because of the inconsistent behaviour of the algorithm. More specifically, the keystrokes per letter required is reduced to one, except from the cases where the first proposed word is not the one that user wants to enter forcing him to choose across a list of proposed words. Secondly, if the word required is not in T9's dictionary, the user has to alter the text entry method to STEM thus further reducing efficiency of the task. Unfortunately no published study exists concerning the proportion of desired words present in the dictionary –especially for Greek language, and on how often a word other than the desired one appears. Therefore, no accurate dialogue modelling can take place. Direct comparison of BAPTI against T9 should take place using actual prototypes to have an indication of performance. However, lack of such a hardware prototype limits our research in this point.

6 Prototype Implementation and Performance Evaluation

In the present section, we discuss usability issues in the context of STEM and BAPTI. Having already theoretically modeled each technique's dialogue performance concerning the time to complete word entry, we intended to verify BAPTI's performance in the real world. For that reason, we have implemented a mobile phone keypad emulator where users were supposed to edit messages using BAPTI. Figure 2 depicts a snapshot of the described tool. The left part of the tool consists of a single line mobile screen simulator, where the user verifies the system's output and the standard keypad that mobile phones use. The arrangement of the Greek letters in every key was identical to that of Nokia 6110 and 5110 models. For our experiments, we considered only capital letters, since they are most commonly used by the Greek users. Moreover, in the lower part, the system outputs the probability for each state of the last pressed key. Emulator traces the number of keystrokes using BAPTI and compares to those that would be needed by STEM for the same message. The right part of the simulator contains the graphical representation of the number of keystrokes needed by during the editing procedure. This graph is dynamically updated across the editing progress, thus providing a better sense of each method's behavior.

The dashed line represents the number of keystrokes using STEM while the continuous line represents the number of keystrokes using our approach. As we could observe from an example text messaging task, BAPTI is better than STEM throughout the whole editing process with an average keystroke number that approximates 1.06. On the other hand, STEM converges to a value of about 1.94 which agrees to our initial expectations (Figure 2). Performance measurements in terms of time required to complete text entry task could not be compared directly to the KLM model at the moment, because of the non negligible response time required by the system to find the appropriate probabilities due to early prototyping issues.

To evaluate real world performance of the proposed method, we have conducted preliminary experiments using ten SMS prototype phrases of varying length containing high informal word rate. Table 1 tabulates analytic results concerning the number of keystrokes needed from BAPTI and STEM and error rates of single errors and double errors (e.g. second and third keystroke required to access desired letter respectively).

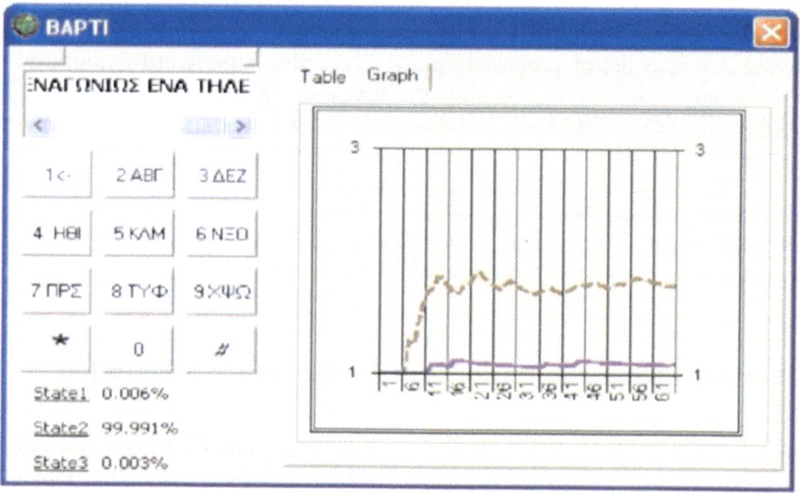

Fig. 2. BAPTI SMS emulator.

Table 1. Comparative results regarding the needed number of keystrokes for STEM and BAPTI methods, obtained from real world preliminary experiment.

Phrase	#of words	Characters	BAPTI	STEM	% Improvem.	S.Errors	D. Errors
1	28	143	158	256	38.3%	9.1%	0.7%
2	29	160	169	268	36.9%	5.6%	0.0%
3	29	158	179	279	35.8%	8.2%	2.5%
4	14	87	102	142	28.2%	8.0%	4.6%
5	25	150	165	265	37.7%	8.7%	0.7%
6	20	122	134	218	38.5%	6.6%	1.6%
7	28	154	169	276	38.8%	7.1%	1.3%
8	16	86	92	150	38.7%	4.7%	1.2%
9	19	117	129	213	39.4%	8.5%	0.9%
10	10	58	63	107	41.1%	8.6%	0.0%
Total	218	1235	1360	2174	37.4%	7.5%	1.3%

Having analyzed the results we could clearly distinguish an improvement of 37.4% concerning the effort required to edit a message in terms of keystroke number. The percentage of correctly predicting a letter by BAPTI is 91.2%. Note that the average keystroke numbers excluding spaces within words for BAPTI and STEM are 1.118 and 1.907 respectively, depicting an improvement of 41.3%. The difference between the methods is considered statistically significant ($p<0.0001$ and the 95% confidence interval of the difference is [-0.86,-0.71]). A notable remark is that the extracted results have a close convergence to our initial predictions derived by KLM modeling.

7 Conclusions

We have presented a novel technique, named BAPTI for improving text entry usability in mobile keypads. BAPTI is based on Bayesian knowledge, obtained by training with raw text corpora, about the probability of a letter that was pressed by the user to be the desired one, among the other candidate letters that belong to the same key, given its predecessors. We have argued that BAPTI performs better than the standard mobile input method in context of keystroke count. A significant advantage of our approach is that it is not restricted to orthographic linguistic knowledge, as with dictionary-based methods, which would decrease its performance in case of unknown words. We have also emphasized on the multilingual character of BAPTI, which allows for easy adaptation to any other language. Concerning the evaluation, we have modeled both BAPTI and STEM using Keystroke Level Modeling and formed a prototype emulator for actual experimentation. Theoretical analysis depicted satisfactory results, with BAPTI to behave better than STEM by a factor of 34.72% concerning time efficiency and approximately 47,35% concerning the number of key presses. Preliminary experiments were carried out using the implemented emulator and have verified the accuracy of KLM predictions. A request for patent concerning the BAPTI technique is in process.

As for future work, our intention is to improve disambiguation accuracy by incorporating more domain specific corpora with the existing, as well as developing an algorithm that would allow quick typing but without reducing the sense of word progress towards the user's entry goal. Prototype should be improved also in terms of system response time thus enabling extensive user testing and comparison of proposed text entry methods in various aspects.

References

1. Buchanan G., Jones M., Thimbleby H., Farrant S., Pazzani M. Improving mobile internet usability. Proceedings of the Web 2001 Conference, Hong Kong, ACM Press (2001)
2. Card, S. K., Moran, T. P., & Newell, A. The keystroke-level model for user performance time with interactive systems. Communications of the ACM, 23 (7), (1980) 396-410.
3. Cooper J., Herskovits E. A Bayesian method for the induction of probabilistic networks from data. Machine Learning, 9 (1992) 309-347.
4. Glymour C., Cooper G. (eds.). Computation, Causation & Discovery. AAAI Press/The MIT Press, Menlo Park (1999)
5. Jeffreys H. Theory of Probability. Clarendon Press, Oxford. (1939)
6. Jensen F.. An Introduction to Bayesian Networks. New York: Springer-Verlag (1996)
7. Ketola P., Roykkee M. Three Facets of Usability in Mobile Handsets, In CHI 2001, Workshop, Mobile Communications: Understanding Users, Adoption & Design Sunday and Monday, April 1 -2, 2001 Seattle, Washington. ACM (2001)
8. Longmate E., Baber C., Trabak A.. A study of text messaging within a digital community, In Human Computer Interaction 2001.Panhellenic conference with international participation, December 7-9 2001, Patras, Greece (2001) 257-262.
9. Mitchell T. Machine Learning. Mc Graw-Hill (1997)

10. Olson J., Olson G. The Growth of Cognitive Modeling in Human-Computer Interaction Since GOMS, Human Computer Interaction ,Vol.5, Lawrence Erlbaum Associates, (1990) 221-265.
11. Pearl J. Probabilistic Reasoning in Intelligent Systems: Networks of Plausible Inference. San Mateo, CA: Morgan Kaufmann (1988)
12. Rodden, T., Cheverst K, Davies N. and Dix A. Exploiting Context in HCI design for Mobile Systems. In Workshop on Human Computer Interaction with Mobile Devices. Glasgow (1998)
13. Silfverberg, M., MacKenzie, I. S., & Korhonen, P. Predicting text entry speeds on mobile phones. Proceedings of the ACM Conference on Human Factors in Computing Systems - CHI 2000, New York: ACM (2000) 9-16.

Fuzzy Inference for Student Diagnosis in Adaptive Educational Hypermedia

Maria Grigoriadou[1], Harry Kornilakis[1], Kyparisia A. Papanikolaou[1], and George D. Magoulas[2]

[1]Department of Informatics & Telecommunications, University of Athens, Panepistimiopolis, GR-15784 Athens, Greece
{gregor, harryk, spap}@di.uoa.gr
[2]Department of Information Systems and Computing, Brunel University, UB8 3PH, U.K.
George.Magoulas@brunel.ac.uk

Abstract. In this paper we propose a method that implements student diagnosis in the context of the Adaptive Hypermedia Educational System INSPIRE – INtelligent System for Personalized Instruction in a Remote Environment. The method explores ideas from the fields of fuzzy logic and multicriteria decision-making in order to deal with uncertainty and incorporate in the system a more complete and accurate description of the expert's knowledge as well as flexibility in student's assessment. To be more precise, an inference system, using fuzzy logic and the Analytic Hierarchy Process to represent the knowledge of the teacher-expert on student's diagnosis, analyzes student's answers to questions of varying difficulty and importance, and estimates the student's knowledge level. Preliminary experiments with real students indicate that the method is characterized by effectiveness in handling the uncertainty of student diagnosis, and is found to be closer to the assessment performed by a human teacher, when compared to a more traditional method of assessment.

Keywords: Student Diagnosis, Fuzzy Logic, Analytic Hierarchy Process, Adaptive Educational Hypermedia Systems.

1 Introduction

Adaptive Educational Hypermedia Systems (AEHSs) (Brusilovsky, 1996; 1999) constitute a new generation of Educational Hypermedia (EH) systems, which possess the ability to make intelligent decisions about the interactions that take place during learning aiming to support students without being directive. Such systems build a model of the goals, preferences and knowledge of each individual student and use this model throughout the interaction with him/her for adapting the content and/or the navigation to the needs of the particular student. Thus, the quality of personalized instruction offered by an AEHS is largely determined by the coverage and accuracy of the information constructing the student model and by the ability of the system to dynamically update it. As the student model is used as a source of system's adaptation,

I.P. Vlahavas and C.D. Spyropoulos (Eds.): SETN 2002, LNAI 2308, pp. 191–202, 2002.

in most cases it includes information regarding student's behavior and knowledge, which have repercussions for his/her performance and learning. However, the construction of such a model is a research challenge from both the Instructional Design and Artificial Intelligence (AI) perspectives, involved in the design of student interaction with the system.

However an educational system, due to the restricted communication channel, is only able to directly obtain raw measurements, by monitoring the interaction with the student. The process of inferring students' internal characteristics from their observable behavior is called *student diagnosis* (VanLehn, 1988). Important issues outlining student diagnosis refer to: (*i*) the observable student's behavior that should be recorded in terms of specific measurements, (*ii*) the internal characteristics that can be inferred based on the recorded information and that are important to learning, and (*iii*) the method adopted for extracting this information through student monitoring and tracking. Thus, with regards to the AI perspective, the main demand is the development of a reliable method that will be able to analyze effectively, in a way a teacher would follow, measurements regarding student's behavior and make estimations on student's internal characteristics updating the student model accordingly. This model will be further used to guide system's adaptive behavior. The main obstacle in the diagnosis process is uncertainty coming partly from the communication among the teacher, the developer and the system and partly from inaccuracies in the measurements conducted.

In this paper we present the method for *student diagnosis* that is being used for supporting the adaptive capabilities of INSPIRE – INtelligent System for Personalized Instruction in a Remote Environment, which is a Web-based AEHS for distance learning, recently developed at the laboratory of "Educational & Language Technology" of the department of Informatics and Telecommunications, University of Athens. In Section 2 an overview of INSPIRE is presented. Section 3 examines the individualities of the student diagnosis problem and proposes several technologies in order to deal with them. In Section 4 the method used for student diagnosis combining the analytic hierarchy process and fuzzy logic is presented. Furthermore, the way this process exploits teacher's expertise in the assessment procedure and simulates his/her individual way of assessing students' knowledge level, is presented. In Section 5 an example of the diagnostic process is shown and the experimental results are discussed. The paper ends with concluded remarks on the advantages and disadvantages of the proposed method and further research.

2 An Overview of INSPIRE

INSPIRE, (Papanikolaou et al, 2001), is an AEHS that aims to assist distance students during their study by constructing and presenting lessons that correspond to specific learning outcomes, accommodating student's knowledge level and learning style. This process of content personalization requires, apart from the information of student's learning style, a thorough knowledge of the student's knowledge level. To this end a number of assessment tests have been developed for INSPIRE, each of them assessing the student's knowledge on the main topics of the domain that s/he studies. Based on the performance of the student on these assessment tests, INSPIRE makes estimations on the knowledge level of the student on the various topics using the student diagnosis process that will be described below in Section 4.2. These estimations are then used to personalize the content that will be delivered to the student. In the following by student diagnosis we refer to the above process of deducing the students' knowledge level on each topic (internal characteristics) from their answers to assessment tests (observable behavior).

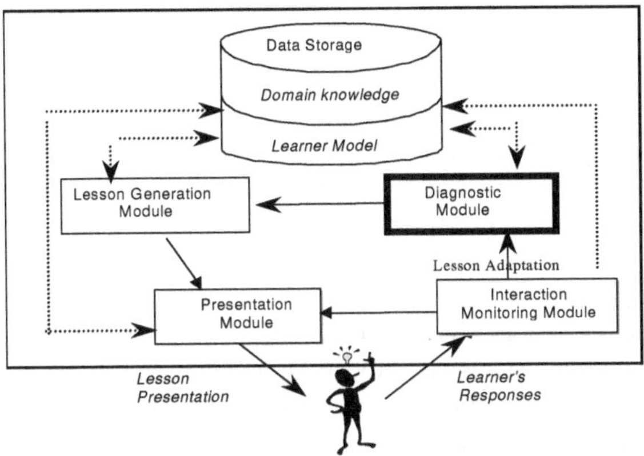

Fig. 1. Schematic of INSPIRE's architecture

INSPIRE is comprised of four modules and the data storage (Fig.1). The modules of the system are: *(i)* the *Interaction Monitoring Module (IMM)* that monitors and handles student's responses, including answers to tests, during his/her interaction with the system, *(ii)* the *Student's Diagnostic Module* that processes data recorded about the student and decides on how to classify the student's knowledge and learning style, *(iii)* the *Lesson Generation Module (LGM)* that generates personalized lessons following students' knowledge level and *(iv)* the *Presentation Module (PM)* whose function is to present the lessons created by the LGM to the student following his/her learning style. The data storage contains the domain knowledge, and the student model, which is the data structure that holds all the information that the system has gathered about the student, and upon which the Diagnostic Module acts. This information includes the number and type of questions the student tried to answer, the attempts s/he made to answer each question, the time s/he has spent on each page, the percentage of the study time that s/he has devoted to each type of material (presentations, examples, simulations etc.) and similar other measurable quantities.

In this paper, we will focus on the operation of the Diagnostic Module, which appears highlighted in Fig.1. The Diagnostic Module receives its input from the IMM, which gathers numeric information about the interaction of the student with the system. Especially, we shall concentrate on the output of the Diagnostic Module that provides an estimation of student's knowledge level in the domain of interest. The

LGM uses this information further, in order to generate the personalized content that will be delivered to the student.

3 The Problem of Student Diagnosis

The presence of uncertainty is an important factor that often leads to errors in student diagnosis. This uncertainty appears partly due to errors and approximations involved when gathering data from measurements, and partly due to the abstract nature of human cognition and the loss of information resulting from its quantification. Uncertainty in measurements stems from several factors such as careless errors and lucky guesses in the student's responses. In an educational system where there is no direct interaction between the tutor and the student the collected data tend to be more haphazard, than those obtained through traditional face-to-face interaction. Furthermore, it is harder for these systems to rely upon background information and relevant experience, as human tutors can (Jameson, 1996). Especially in a web-based learning environment inaccurate measurements caused by technical difficulties, such as network congestion, cannot be ignored. On the other hand, when trying to explicitly represent the mental and emotional states and processes, an additional layer of approximation is introduced. The student's knowledge is constantly changing during the dynamic process of learning and it is therefore quite difficult to be certain about his/her current mental state. Considering the above attributes of the problem, it is obvious that the development of a reliable method for student diagnosis is based on successful handling of uncertainty.

However, the diagnostic process relates to the way a human-expert assesses students' knowledge level on a certain topic focussing on how the assessment tests are marked by him/her. To this end, different approaches are applied, such as the *norm-referenced assessment* that is traditionally used in end examinations and the *criterion-referenced assessment* that is associated with continuous (or intermittent) assessment so that many more of the lesson objectives and competences are assessed (Reece & Walker, 1997). In the first approach tests are marked so that the normal distribution is achieved while in the second one the assessment process is based on specific criteria that are defined in terms of objectives and competences which state what the students must achieve. Thus, the way that the teacher's expertise in assessment is incorporated in the system in order to guide the diagnostic process is an important issue influencing the efficiency of the provided estimations. Furthermore, the system should allow teachers that use the system to convey this knowledge in a simple and comprehensible manner without being forced to make complicated quantifications of abstract knowledge.

In our case, the diagnostic process is based on the criterion-referenced assessment, which is considered as a part of the developmental process of learning aiming to assess the students' quality of learning. This way the educational system is continuously provided with information on students' performance in order to be able to adapt its output accordingly. As a method of dealing with uncertainty and incorporating teacher's expertise and flexibility in student's assessment, we use a combination of fuzzy logic with a multicriteria decision-making approach.

Zadeh (1965) was the first to introduce fuzzy logic and fuzzy systems as a method to handle numerical uncertainty and express imprecision and subjectivity in human thinking. Use of fuzzy logic in numerous applications has shown that it offers high expressive powers, an enhanced ability to model real-world problems, and a methodology for building systems tolerant to imprecision and uncertainty (Lin & Lee, 1996). In multicriteria decision-making, Saaty's Analytical Hierarchy Process (AHP) is widely used to define the relative importance of a number of criteria (Saaty, 1980), which in our case emulate the criteria used by the expert-teacher in order to assess student's knowledge level.

The approach proposed in this paper builds on previous results reported in (Panagiotou & Grigoriadou, 1995; Magoulas et al., 2001) and enhances INSPIRE with the ability to consider multiple criteria simultaneously. Usually the process of assessing student's knowledge level is influenced by several conditions to which the expert adapts the assessment, such as the current knowledge level of the student, the topic being considered, etc. Thus, defining the relative importance of the criteria used according to several preconditions provides the system with knowledge coming from teacher's expertise in the assessment procedure and makes the system flexible enough to accommodate the personal way of assessment of each individual teacher.

4 Student Diagnosis in INSPIRE

Lessons in INSPIRE are generated so as to lead the student to the accomplishment of a specific learning goal, which corresponds to a topic of the domain knowledge. Each learning goal is associated with a subset of outcome topics, in which one must become proficient in order to accomplish the learning goal.

In order to measure the student's knowledge at each of the outcome topics, assessment tests have been developed. Each assessment test covers the material of one topic and it is available to the student while s/he is studying that topic. Questions of an assessment test are grouped in several categories that correspond to specific abilities that the student must exhibit and which are in accordance with the three levels of performance proposed by Merril (1983): (*i*) *Remember Level:* questions that test the ability of students to recall the provided information, (*ii*) *Use Level:* questions that test the ability of students to apply the provided information to specific case(s), (*iii*) *Find Level:* questions that test the ability of students to propose and solve original problems.

When the student selects to take the assessment test, the questions appear one after the other with increasing difficulty, i.e. the easier questions of the Remember Level appear first, then the questions of the Use Level and finally the questions of the Find Level. At any point the student has the option to stop taking the test. Based on the answers given to the questions of a specific topic, we want to make an estimation of the knowledge level of the student on that topic. That estimation should be as close as possible to the way an experienced teacher evaluates a student. We use a qualitative model, which classifies knowledge on a topic to one of the four levels of proficiency {Insufficient, Rather Insufficient, Rather Sufficient, Sufficient}.

Ultimately, the goal of the diagnosis is to obtain information about the knowledge of the student in each topic, in terms of the four characterizations and in a way an expert teacher would. In order to achieve this we need to model the knowledge and experience of the expert and also to model the inference process used by the expert.

4.1 Modeling the Expert's Knowledge

As valuable resources in modeling teacher's expertise in assessing students' knowledge as well as in modeling teacher's personal way of assessing, are considered:

- the criteria that the teacher defines in order to assess student's knowledge level
- teacher's estimations of the importance of different types of assessment questions that correspond to the above criteria, with respect to the student's knowledge level at the time s/he asks to be assessed and the type of the topic under consideration, i.e. a theoretical concept or a procedure etc., and
- teacher's estimations of the relationship between student's correct answers and his/her proficiency of the topic.

Definition of Criteria. Criterion-referenced assessment is associated with the concept of mastery learning, which is important in cases where students need to master a topic prior to moving onto another one (Reece & Walker, 1997). The process of assessing students' knowledge on a certain topic is facilitated by the introduction of specific criteria given in terms of objectives and competences which state what the student must achieve on this topic. These criteria guide also the marking process, e.g. students can achieve full marks if they attain the required standard suggested, or, their marks differentiate according to the objectives of a topic that they achieved.

In our approach, the diagnostic process for assessing students' knowledge level uses three qualitative criteria. These criteria correspond to the three levels of performance *Remember*, *Use*, *Find* (see Section 4), aiming to assess the relative students' abilities.

Importance of Different Types of Questions. As we have mentioned assessment tests in INSPIRE consist of questions of three different categories (see Section 4). The importance of the questions of each category may vary depending on the topic that the questions assess and on the proficiency of the student at the time s/he takes the assessment test. For example, for the topic "The role of cache memory" knowledge of the theory (Remember Level) is more important, while for the topic "Mapping techniques" it is more important that the student is able to solve problems on that topic (Use Level). The importance of the questions of the different categories is one aspect of the knowledge of the teacher that should be modeled when performing student diagnosis. In order to assist the teacher to convey this knowledge to the system we use the AHP for assigning weights to the different criteria expressing their relative importance. These criteria correspond to the three different categories of questions and consequently their weights are also considered as weights of the corresponding questions.

The weights of the various criteria on which the system is based in order to evaluate the knowledge level of the student, change depending on:

- *The knowledge level of the student at the time s/he asks to be assessed.* For example, when the student is a novice on a topic, the weights are specified so that the questions that assess the understanding of the theory (1st criterion) have a greater weight compared to those that assess application of the theory (2nd criterion). In other words, we assume that the student should initially study the theory – Remember Level – and then continue with the application of the theory. As the student progresses, his/her knowledge level changes from {Insufficient} to {Rather Insufficient} (s/he has covered the theory and should move on to the application), the weights of the criteria change, and the weight of the questions of the Use Level increases. After this change, in order to reach a {Rather Sufficient} knowledge level the student should answer the questions about the application and so on.
- *The type of the topic that is being examined.* For example, if a topic is a procedure, then students should learn mainly how to apply it in different cases, and thus the application (2nd criterion) should have greater weight compared to the theory (1st criterion). Accordingly, for a more theoretical topic, understanding the theory is more important compared to its application.

In more detail, the AHP offers a framework that lets someone specify the importance of a number of different criteria, by giving linguistic comparisons expressing the relative importance between pairs of criteria. Suppose that we have n criteria c_1 through c_n and wish to specify the importance of these criteria. According to AHP we only need to give as input their relative importance. For each pair of criteria c_i and c_j, a value α_{ij}, between 1 and 9, is specified, declaring the relative importance of criterion c_i over c_j. For example $\alpha_{ij}=1$, means 'c_i is as important as c_j', $\alpha_{ij}=2$, means 'c_i is slightly more important than c_j', up to $\alpha_{ij}=9$, which means 'c_i is extremely more important than c_j'. Based on these values we generate the pairwise comparison matrix A as follows:

$$A=\begin{bmatrix} 1 & a_{12} & \cdots & a_{1n} \\ 1/a_{12} & 1 & \cdots & a_{2n} \\ \vdots & \vdots & \ddots & \vdots \\ 1/a_{1n} & 1/a_{2n} & \cdots & 1 \end{bmatrix}, \quad a_{ij} \in \{1,2,...9\}, \text{ and } a_{ji} = 1/a_{ij} \tag{1}$$

Then the weight w_i of each criterion c_i is calculated as:

$$w_i = \frac{\left(\prod_{j=1}^{n} a_{ij}\right)^{1/n}}{\sum_{i=1}^{n}\left(\prod_{j=1}^{n} a_{ij}\right)^{1/n}} \tag{2}$$

By letting the teacher specify different weights to the criteria assessing student's knowledge for each topic, it is possible to take into account specific characteristics of the topic, such as if a topic is theory oriented or application oriented, etc. Furthermore, by using different weights for the novice and for the more advanced student it is possible to adapt the diagnosis to his/her current knowledge level. Therefore, knowledge of the theory will be more important when the student is a novice, while as s/he becomes more familiar with a topic, being able to apply the theory and solve problems becomes more important.

In our case we have three categories of questions (see Section 4), which correspond to three different criteria for assessing student's knowledge level (these are in accordance with the three levels of performance Remember, Use, Find). For each topic, the teacher specifies the relative importance of each criterion to the other for the case that the student is a novice, for the case that s/he is more advanced and so on. Therefore, for each topic, multiple 3×3 pairwise comparison matrices are specified, each one corresponding to the state of the learner before taking the test.

Relationship between Correct Answers and Proficiency. The marking of criterion-referenced assessment, as already mentioned, relates to the criteria (objectives/competences) defined by the teacher (Reece & Walker, 1997). The teacher designs questions that assess student's competences in terms of certain objectives and then s/he relates the percentage of questions that a student has answered correctly to the knowledge of the student on the specific topic. In INSPIRE we try to model this marking process through the use of fuzzy sets aiming to combine quantitative measurements (number of right answers in different types of questions) in order to get qualitative characterizations for the student's knowledge.

By the term fuzzy set we mean a function f: $U \rightarrow [0,1]$, where U is the universe of discourse of the function. The value $f(x)$ of the function for an input x, represents the degree of membership of x in the fuzzy set. For example let's suppose we have the fuzzy set "Insufficient knowledge of the Remember Level". The function f is equal to $f(x)=\{1, 0.6, 0.3, 0.1, 0, 0, 0, 0, 0, 0\}$, where $x=\{0, 10, 20, 30, 40, 50, 60, 70, 80, 90\}$ is the percentage of the questions of the Remember level that the student has answered correctly. Then, for input equal to 10 the value of the function f is $f(10)=$ 0.6. The interpretation of this is that the knowledge on the Remember level of a student who has answered 10% of the questions correctly, can be considered {Insufficient} to the degree of 0.6. The degrees of membership can be extracted from the teacher by asking questions such as, "How much do you consider that someone's knowledge on theory is Insufficient, if s/he has answered 10% of the questions on theory correctly?". Note that the universe of discourse is discretized, which results in working with fuzzy sets that have 10 elements. The actual percentage of correct answers is obviously a continuous value, but for practical purposes we make it discrete by rounding it to a multiple of ten.

In total, we need the teacher to provide us with twelve such fuzzy sets. One fuzzy set is required for each of the three different criteria {Remember, Use, Find} and for each of the four levels of proficiency {Insufficient, Rather Insufficient, Rather Sufficient, Sufficient}. So, for example, we will have fuzzy sets describing "Insufficient knowledge of the Remember Level", "Rather Insufficient knowledge of the Remember Level", "Sufficient knowledge of the Use Level" etc. We shall call these fuzzy sets f_L^P, where $L \in \{R, U, F\}$ and $P \in \{I, RI, RS, S\}$. The fuzzy set f_L^P will represent a proficiency level equal to P on the L level of performance.

4.2 The Diagnostic Process

After the student has answered a question of an assessment test, the diagnostic process begins. The diagnosis aims to estimate the knowledge level of the student on a specific topic, i.e. on the topic that the answered question refers to.

We *first* need to divide the number of correctly answered questions of each category by the total number of questions for that category, in order to calculate the percentage of correctly answered questions on each different category. Afterwards that value is rounded to the closest multiple of ten percent as the discrete fuzzy sets have 10 elements with values {0, 10, 20, ...,90} (see previous section). Thus, we get three percentages of correct answers, one for each category of questions. Let us call these percentages x_R, x_U, x_F for the Remember, Use and Find level respectively.

Then, using these three values and the twelve fuzzy sets that the teacher specified (see previous section), we form the matrix D, containing the degrees of membership of the knowledge level of the student to each of the twelve fuzzy sets.

$$D = \begin{bmatrix} f_R^I(x_R) & f_R^{RI}(x_R) & f_R^{RS}(x_R) & f_R^S(x_R) \\ f_U^I(x_U) & f_U^{RI}(x_U) & f_U^{RS}(x_U) & f_U^S(x_U) \\ f_F^I(x_F) & f_F^{RI}(x_F) & f_F^{RS}(x_F) & f_F^S(x_F) \end{bmatrix} \quad \textbf{(3)}$$

At this *point* we need to consider the effect that each of the three criteria will have on the final diagnosis. As we mentioned in our discussion about the importance of the different types of questions, the teacher has specified their importance for each topic and for different levels of students' proficiency before taking the test in the weights w_i. So, based on the current topic and on the knowledge level of the student at the time s/he asks to be assessed, the appropriate vector $W=[w_R, w_U, w_F]$ is selected, where w_R is the weight for the questions assessing the Remember Level (1st criterion), w_U, for the questions assessing the Use Level (2nd) and w_F for the questions assessing the Find Level (3rd). By multiplying the vector W by the matrix D, we calculate the vector $P=W{\cdot}D$, which is the degree of membership of the student's knowledge in each of the four proficiency levels, with respect to all three criteria. Thus, we get the vector $P=[p_1\ p_2\ p_3\ p_4]$, where p_1 is the degree to which the student's knowledge is {Insufficient}, p_2 is the degree to which it is {Rather Insufficient}, etc.

Finally, as we have calculated the vector P it is possible for us to give a final estimation on the knowledge level of the student on the topic. The vector P contains the estimation on the knowledge level with respect to each of the four possible levels {Insufficient, Rather Insufficient, Rather Sufficient and Sufficient}. In order to reach a final result we need to combine the four elements of the vector P, so as to select one of the four alternative levels. This is performed using the Center of Gravity method, according to which we calculate the number v as follows (Lin & Lee, 1996):

$$v = \frac{\sum_{i=1}^{4} p_i i}{\sum_{i=1}^{4} p_i} \quad \mathbf{(4)}$$

and then round v to the nearest integer. Depending on the result, we make the final estimation on the student's knowledge level. So, if *round(v)* = 1, we characterize the knowledge of the student on the topic as {Insufficient}, if *round(v)* = 2 as {Rather Insufficient} and so on.

5 Experimental Results

The data presented in this section come from an experiment, which performed as a part of the formative evaluation of the system, aiming to evaluate the adaptive dimension of INSPIRE. Specifically, the answers that the students gave to an assessment test, were used in order to check the validity of the performance of the diagnostic module of INSPIRE. To this end, the output of the diagnostic module concerning students' knowledge level was compared with the diagnosis of an expert-teacher and with the simple diagnostic process of calculating the percentage of right answers, a method adopted in many AEHSs. In the experiment participated 20 postgraduate students of the Department of Informatics and Telecommunications of the University of Athens, and the professor of the course who had the role of the expert-teacher. The students had already studied the handouts of the module "Computer Architecture" and they had been examined on the module. They worked independently, one on each computer. The students accessed INSPIRE through a common browser and they studied the learning goal "What is the role of cache memory and which are its basic operations" for a period of one hour.

All the tasks that the students had to perform were listed in following a usage scenario (Carroll & Rosson, 1990). Through the scenario and after the students had studied the educational material of the topic "Mapping Techniques", they were asked to submit the corresponding assessment test. The assessment test consisted of fifteen questions organized as follows: *(i)* seven of them tested the Remember Level, *(ii)* five of them tested the Use Level and *(iii)* three questions tested the Find Level.

As each question of the test was being submitted by the student, the diagnostic process of INSPIRE estimated his/her knowledge level on the topic and his/her model was then updated accordingly. The vector of weights of the three criteria, used for assessing student's knowledge (three types of questions) for the topic "Mapping Techniques", had been calculated using the AHP (see Relations (1)-(2)) based on the relative importance of the criteria as provided by the professor before the experiment and was equal to: *(i)* W = [0.1775, 0.5190, 0.3035] for novice students, i.e. those whose knowledge level before answering the question was {Insufficient or Rather Insufficient}, and *(ii)* W = [0.1047, 0.2583, 0.6370] for more experienced students, i.e. those with knowledge level {Rather Sufficient or Sufficient}. The final estimation of the student's knowledge level was the one made after the student had submitted every question of the test (see in Fig. 2 the row labeled "INSPIRE").

After the experiment was completed, the professor examined students' answers to the test and estimated their knowledge level on the topic, based on the number, the type and difficulty of the correctly answered questions and the general impression given by the test (see in Fig. 2 the row labeled "Expert"). Furthermore, we estimated the students' knowledge level based on the percentage of correct answers they had given, based on the heuristic rules that *if* the percentage of correct answers is (see Fig. 2 - in the row labeled "Percentage"): (*i*) between 0% and 25% *then* the knowledge level is considered as {Insufficient}, (*ii*) between 26% and 50% *then* the knowledge level is considered as {Rather Insufficient}, (*iii*) between 51% and 75% *then* the knowledge level is considered as {Rather Sufficient} and (*iv*) over 75% *then* the knowledge level is considered as {Sufficient}.

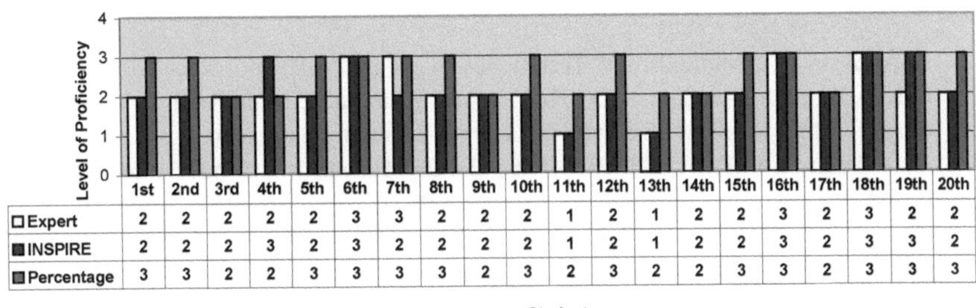

	1st	2nd	3rd	4th	5th	6th	7th	8th	9th	10th	11th	12th	13th	14th	15th	16th	17th	18th	19th	20th
Expert	2	2	2	2	2	3	3	2	2	2	1	2	1	2	2	3	2	3	2	2
INSPIRE	2	2	2	3	2	3	2	2	2	2	1	2	1	2	2	3	2	3	3	2
Percentage	3	3	2	2	3	3	3	3	2	3	2	3	2	2	3	3	2	3	3	3

Fig. 2. The estimations of the knowledge level of 20 students on the topic "Mapping techniques" using different methods of assessment: an Expert-teacher, INSPIRE and the Percentage of students' correct answers. The vertical axis shows the level of proficiency, {Insufficient, Rather Insufficient, Rather Sufficient, Sufficient} which corresponds to {1,2,3,4}. These values are also summarized in the data table below the chart.

From the results of Fig. 2 one can observe that the estimations made by INSPIRE's diagnostic module and the teacher coincide in 17 out of the 20 student cases. On the other hand, only in the case of 9 out of the 20 students the teacher's estimations are the same as estimations based on the percentage of correct answers. Even though the sample is rather small to reach a safe conclusion, the results indicate that INSPIRE can indeed perform diagnosis in a way that gives results similar to the way that a teacher evaluated students.

6 Conclusions

In this paper, the problem of student diagnosis was investigated, as it appears in the context of the adaptive educational hypermedia system INSPIRE, and several difficulties that arise when trying to perform student diagnosis, were pointed out.

A method making use of ideas from the fields of fuzzy logic and multicriteria decision-making has been proposed in order to deal with uncertainty and to incorporate in the system a more complete and accurate description of the expert's knowledge and flexibility in student's assessment. This way the assessment procedure takes into account the individual teacher's personal style of assessing as well as the current knowledge level of the student and accordingly adapts the relative importance of the selected criteria for assessing student's knowledge.

Experimental results have been encouraging, even performed on a limited test group and show that the student diagnosis performed by the proposed method is close to the teacher-expert estimations. Further investigation of the effect of the different parameters and structural features of the proposed diagnostic process, through a sensitivity analysis (VanLehn & Niu, 2001), is necessary in order to determine their influence in the accuracy of the assessment and adjust them accordingly.

References

1. Brusilovsky, P.: Methods and Techniques of Adaptive Hypermedia. User Modeling and User-Adapted Interaction, Vol.6. Kluwer Academic Publ., Netherlands (1996) 87-129
2. Carroll, J.M., Rosson, M.B. (1990). Human-computer interaction scenarios as a design representation. In Proc. of IEEE HICSS-23, 23rd Hawaii Intl. Conf. System Sciences Vol. II, 555-561.
3. Papanikolaou, K., Grigoriadou, M., Kornilakis, H., Magoulas, G.: INSPIRE: An INtelligent System for Personalized Instruction in a Remote Environment. In: Reich, S., Tzagarakis, M.M., De Bra, P. M.E. (eds.): "Hypermedia: Openness, Structural Awareness and Adaptivity". Lecture Notes in Computer Science Vol. 2266. Springer-Verlag, Berlin (2001)
4. Jameson, A.: Numerical Uncertainty Management in User and Student Modeling: An Overview of Systems and Issues. User Modeling and User-Adapted Interaction **5**:3/4 (1996) 193-251
5. Lin, C.T., Lee, C.S.G.: Neural Fuzzy Systems: A Neuro-Fuzzy Synergism to Intelligent Systems. Prentice Hall P T R Upper Saddle River, New Jersey (1996)
6. Magoulas, G.D., Papanikolaou, K.A., Grigoriadou, M.: Neuro-fuzzy Synergism for Planning the Content in a Web-based Course. Informatica **25**:1 (2001) 39-48
7. Merril, M.D.: Component Display Theory. In: C.M.Reigeluth (ed.), Instructional design theories and models: An overview of their current status. Lawrence Elrbaum Associates Hillsdale NJ (1983)
8. Panagiotou M., Grigoriadou M.: An Application of Fuzzy Logic to Student Modeling. In: Proceedings of the IFIP World conference on Computer in Education. (WCCE95), Birmigham (1995)
9. Reece, I., Walker, S.: Teaching, Training and Learning. A Practical Guide. Third Edition. Business Education Publishers Limited, Sunderland (1997)
10. Saaty T.: The Analytic Hierarchy Process, McGraw-Hill, New York (1980)
11. VanLehn, K.: Student Modeling. In: Polson, M. C., Richardson, J.J. (eds.): Foundations of Intelligent Tutoring Systems. Lawrence Erlbaum Associates Hillsdale, New Jersey (1988) 55-78
12. VanLehn, K., Niu, Z.: Bayesian student modeling, user interfaces and feedback: A sensitivity analysis. International Journal of Artificial Intelligence in Education **12** (2001)
13. Zadeh, L. A.: Fuzzy Sets. Information and Control **8**:3 (1965) 338-353

MultiCAD-GA: A System for the Design of 3D Forms Based on Genetic Algorithms and Human Evaluation*

Nikolaos Vassilas[1], George Miaoulis[1], Dionysios Chronopoulos[1], Elias Konstantinidis[1], Ioanna Ravani[1,2], Dimitrios Makris[1,2], and Dimitri Plemenos[2]

[1] Technological Educational Institution of Athens, Department of Computer Science, Ag. Spyridonos St., 122 10 Egaleo, Greece
{nvas, gmiaoul, jrav,demak}@teiath.gr, amico2000@panafonet.gr, coma@onf.com

[2] Université de Limoges, Laboratoire Méthodes et Structures Informatiques, 83 rue d'Isle, 87000 Limoges, France
plemenos@unilim.fr

Abstract. The solution engine of MultiCAD-GA, presented in this work, is a part of a new software environment for efficient search for solutions in heavily demanding applications involving the design of three-dimensional forms, such as those of architectural and interior decoration design. MultiCAD-GA starts by using constraint programming techniques in order to find a set (population) of solutions (forms) that satisfy the spatial constraints imposed by the user and create an initial generation. In the sequel, it applies genetic operators to generate new solutions and interacts with the user in order to evaluate the solutions and increase the speed of convergence to those forms that satisfy his/her aesthetics. The forms are coded into chromosomes using the usual binary strings. Visualization of the results is performed through the VRML graphics language.

1 Introduction

MultiCAD is a software architecture framework for the development of multimedia and intelligent information systems in order to support declarative design processes [1]. The declarative design of forms [2,3] is an approach of the design act based on the following cycle: *description*, *generation of alternative solutions* and *evaluation.* The description of the form is a non-geometrical model on a high level of abstraction which is supplied to a search engine in order to generate alternative solutions. The current solutions engine of prototype "MultiCAD-II" is that of the MultiFormes project [2] based on constraint-programming techniques. Present research develops the principles of a solutions engine based on genetic algorithms.

MultiCAD-II uses constraint programming techniques to generate solutions, i.e., 3D forms satisfying the user's constraints. The main disadvantages of such a *generate and test* search strategy are: a) its exhaustive sequential search nature leading to

* This work was supported by grant 19/6-7-99 EE-TEI-A of T.E.I. of Athens.

I.P. Vlahavas and C.D. Spyropoulos (Eds.): SETN 2002, LNAI 2308, pp. 203–214, 2002.

unacceptably long times in relatively large problem spaces, and b) its inability to interact with the user and derive solutions that satisfy his/her aesthetics.

Both of the above mentioned problems are dealt with in this work by introducing MultiCAD-GA, a genetic algorithm-based search engine that allows global rather than sequential search guided by the user's aesthetic criteria. The search for solutions is performed in more promising parts of the global search space through interaction with the user who is asked to evaluate each time the solutions of the evolving generations.

In problems of architectural design, *solutions* are not what they are in other scientific domains; they are not the classic mathematical solutions, conditionally categorical, and thus capable of being superseded or nullified by modification in the aggregate of supporting conditions. Here, they are solutions insofar as they allow us to think that which cannot be reduced to a definite aggregate of conditions. The function of the design goals is to motivate and inspire activity that in turn will generate new goals [4].

That happens because the nature of these so-called problems involves evolving co-operative behaviour and/or a changing *landscape* and of course, we cannot apply just a function optimizer, no matter how powerful is its performance. It is accepted [5], that the process of architectural design is based on ill-defined problems and it is not a routine process at all. In fact, its inexactitude drives the progress in architectural thinking. Because of this, such processes are not well understood, and therefore cannot be simulated by any simple algorithmic approach. The generation of concepts whose representation is of unknown size and shape is a very difficult task. An example of such a concept is the creation of spatial forms. Composing the three-dimensional spatial structure of a building–space is one of the most important open tasks in architecture. The way architects work imply the formulation of many items of information of varying importance to their designs. They recognize their applicability, while working at the details of the solution. During the design process, it is not possible to start out by making lists of criteria that are supposed to get satisfied with the newly created layout. The whole process for a good solution is also a search for proper information with which to evaluate it [6].

Genetic algorithms [7-10] embody a range of dynamics that permit task-specific knowledge to *emerge* while solving a given problem and they are better suited for global search and global optimization in large and complex search spaces than the traditional exhaustive search algorithms such as breadth-first search or depth-first search [11]. Considering that each generated solution is evaluated according to the user's aesthetic criteria, one can view the problem of finding the optimal solution as a global optimization problem that searches for the maximum of the evaluation function. Typically, these are NP-complete problems and one is satisfied by a "good" solution rather than the optimal one. A wide variety of architectural and spatial evolutionary systems have been proposed by several researchers during the last decade [12-16].

Following a short presentation of MultiCAD-II in Sec. 2, the internal description model is presented in Sec. 3 to elaborate the user interface, the format of the generated script files and the result of scanning and parsing those script files. In Sec. 4 the genetic algorithm approach in the design of the search engine of MultiCAD-GA is presented. Finally, Secs. 5 and 6 present the simulations and conclusions of this work respectively.

2 MultiCAD-II

MultiCAD-II was the first attempt to create a complete conceptual modeling environment that would help users implement three-dimensional (3D) models through an abstract modeling language. Users do not have to deal with dimensional details. The computer generates all possible solutions of a given model and the users' task is to evaluate each according to their personal criteria.

MultiCAD is able to read Internal Model Description (IMD) script files (shown on the right side of Fig.1) and analyzes them in order to create graphic solutions. Each solution is displayed one by one on screen (middle part of Fig. 1) and the user has to either accept it or move on to the next solution.

In MultiCAD-II, the solutions are calculated using constraint programming techniques. Constraint programming is a full search algorithm, which scans the entire search tree exhaustively. It uses a repetitive generate-and-test method to access each valid tree node sequentially. Each node is checked if it meets the model's restrictions. This algorithm is easy to implement using a programming language. The mathematical foundation is relatively simple, because it uses plain comparison operators for calculating bounding boxes for the scenes.

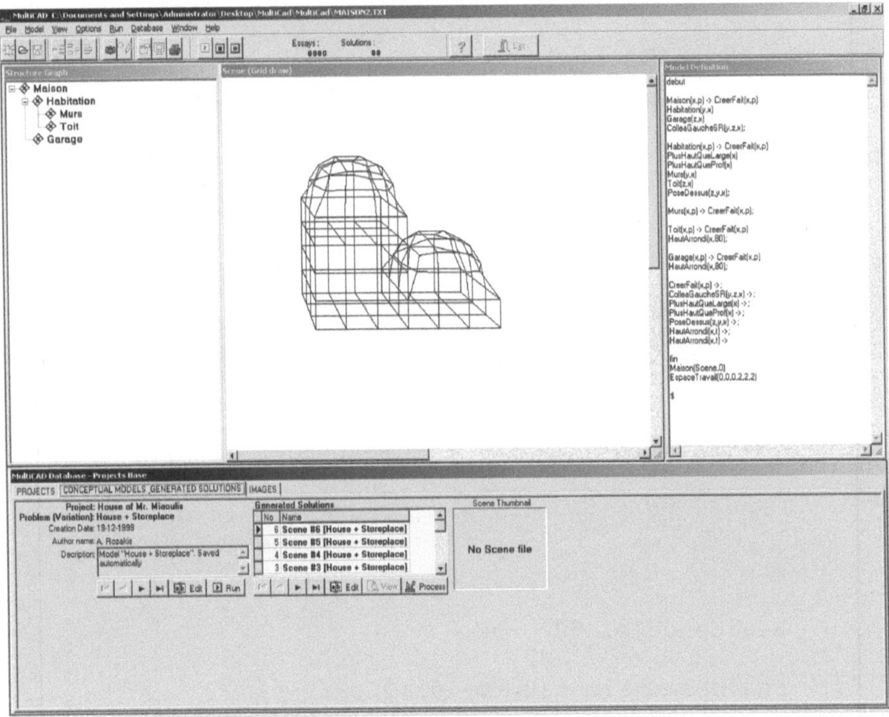

Fig. 1. Example of a MultiCAD-II user interface.

Due to the fact that constraint programming is a sequential method, such a technique is slow and inefficient for large search trees. In addition, the user has to evaluate each solution before he/she moves on to the next one.

3 The MultiCAD Internal Model

MultiCAD-II as well as MultiCAD-GA use a scanner and a parser to analyze internal model script files. A script file fully describes a scene using a Prolog-like language. A scene may have many subscenes in a tree hierarchy. Each scene defines a root (global) bounding box, which should bound all subscenes contained in it. Sibling subscenes should not have overlapped bounding boxes. The global bounding box is defined by the *space dimension property*.

```
# demo script
begin

 Residence (x,p)   ->    CreateFact (x,p)
                         House (y,x)
                         Garage (z,x)
                         PastedLeft (y,z,x);

 House (x,p)       ->    CreateFact (x,p)
                         HigherThanLarge (x)
                         HigherThanDeep (x)
                         Walls (y,x)
                         Roof (z,x)
                         pastedunder (z,y,x);

 Garage (x,p)      ->    CreateFact (x,p)
                         TopRounded (x,80);

 Walls (x,p)       ->    CreateFact (x,p);

 Roof(x,p)          ->   CreateFact (x,p)
                         TopRounded (x,70)
end

Residence(p, 50)

SpaceDimensions(0, 0, 0, 3, 3, 3)
```

Fig. 2. A scene definition using a Prolog-like script file.

Fig. 2 shows an example of such a script defining a scene with name *residence* that contains two subscenes, namely, a *house* and a *garage*, as well as a constraint (spatial relation) requiring the house to be on the left of the garage. Similar descriptions follow for each subscene. The origin of the global coordinate system as well as the dimensions of the global bounding box are defined at the end of the script file. More details regarding the internal description model can be found in [1-3].

Following scanning and parsing, the program converts the internal model script file into a hierarchical tree structure as shown in Fig. 3, for the previous example.

```
Scanning...
Parsing...
Setting up model...
+-Residence
| +-House
| | +-Walls
| | +-Roof
| +-Garage
```

Fig. 3. The tree model of the *residence* scene.

Actual objects are only the *terminal nodes* of that tree. Intermediate nodes are used only for bounding box and relational properties calculations between scenes.

4 Three-Dimensional Form Generation Using Genetic Algorithms

The MultiCAD-GA genetic algorithm-based search engine is described in this section. Specifically, we present, how the terminal subscene bounding boxes of the internal tree model are encoded into chromosomes, which genetic operators are used and in what way and, finally, how are new generations of solutions reproduced and evaluated by the user.

4.1 Chromosome Encoding

Each of the 3D scenes recursively consists of 3D subscenes. As explained above, the scene nodes of the global scene description tree can be considered to be contained within bounding boxes that satisfy a set of constraints imposed on their positions and relative dimensions. Consider the bounding box of such a subscene shown in Fig. 4. The bounding box can be described by the *bottom-front-left* corner (x, y, z) relative to the global (X, Y, Z) coordinate system and by the three dimensions Δx, Δy and Δz for its *width*, *depth* and *height* respectively. The origin of the global coordinate system is assumed to coincide with the *bottom-front-left* corner of the bounding box that corresponds to the root node of the scene description tree (*the global bounding box*).

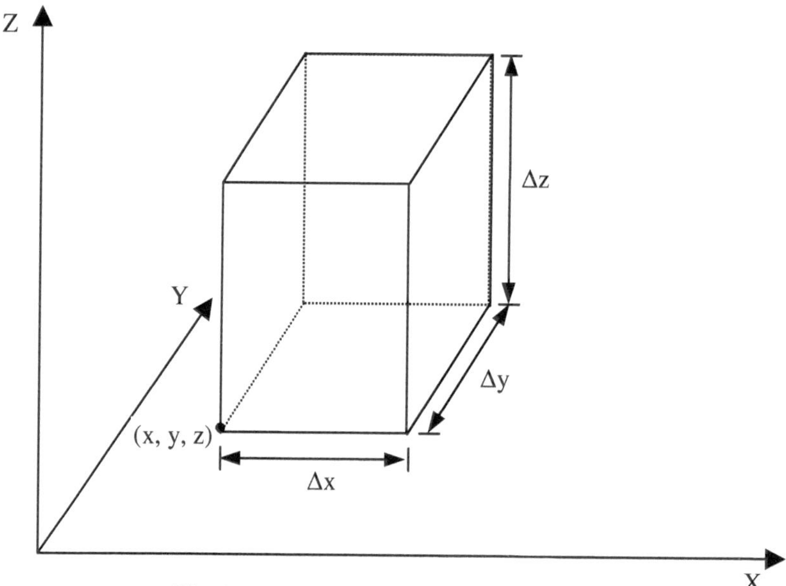

Fig. 4. Specification of a subscene bounding box.

A logical assumption followed in this paper is that the global bounding box is quantized using a three-dimensional homogeneous grid. The elementary grid cell, i.e. the *voxel* (or *volume element*), will thus be the structuring element of any scene. Hence, according to this assumption, all six positive quantities, i.e., x, y, z, Δx, Δy, Δz, will be at integer multiples of the voxel dimensions Vx, Vy and Vz respectively. In the following, in order to simplify matters, we will consider that both the location and dimensions of any bounding box will be integers. The true position and size can easily be found afterwards by multiplying with the corresponding voxel dimensions. More details on 3D space quantization and representation can be found in [17-20].

A natural representation of the six integer quantities, and the one followed in this paper, is using binary string encodings. The length of these binary strings will depend on the required accuracy as well as on practical issues such as, the induced time complexity on the solution generation engine.

Although the length of the binary encoding is treated as parameter L, for clarity reasons, in the following description we frequently assume $L = 3$, i.e., encodings using three bits. In the latter case, each spatial quantity is quantized into 8 equally spaced levels which in decimal notation range from 0 to 7.

A chromosome representation of a scene must contain all spatial information regarding the terminal nodes (subscenes) of the scene description tree. Assuming that a scene contains n such nodes, a chromosome will be represented using nL bits. Fig. 5

shows the encoding for a scene of two subscenes using $L = 3$. The dotted line signifies the end of the first subscene representation and the beginning of the other.

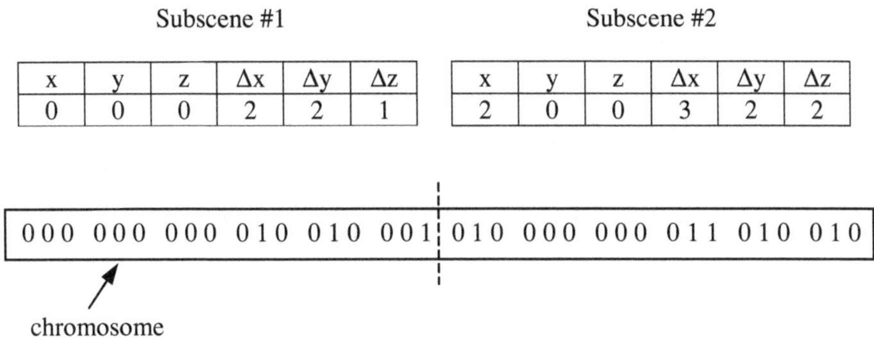

Fig. 5. Chromosome representation of a scene with two subscenes.

4.2 Genetic Operators

The genetic operators used for reproduction of the current generation of solutions are: a) *cloning*, b) *crossover*, and c) *mutation*. The three operators are applied following a user evaluation of all chromosomes and are described in the sequel.

Cloning. In this work, the chromosomes reproduced through cloning are those parents that were successful in generating offspring that corresponded to solutions of the problem. Specifically, since the parents are selected through the *roulette-wheel parent selection* technique (see Sec. 4.2.2), it is expected that cloning will favor those chromosomes with higher fitness (evaluation) scores which at the same time have been proven able to produce solutions.

Crossover. Crossover requires two parents. The parents are selected using the so called *roulette-wheel parent selection* technique. According to this technique, each chromosome is given a probability to be selected equal to the ratio of its fitness score to the sum of the fitness scores of all chromosomes. Following parent selection, one crossover point is selected for each spatial quantity (i.e., for each group of L successive bits) according to the crossover probability that specifies *if* and *where* crossover will take place. The "genes" (i.e., the bits) to the right of the crossover point in each group between the two parents are interchanged. Fig. 6 shows an example for crossover when the chromosomes represent a single subscene ($L = 3$). In this case, the crossover point within a group can be placed in the 0, 1 or 2 positions whereby 3, 2 or 1 genes are mutually changed respectively.

The crossover operator is applied independently on each group of L bits, following the group crossover probability P_{gc}. Given that crossover is going to take place, the crossover point is chosen randomly, i.e. with probability $1/L$. The particular group crossover operator has been found more appropriate than the typical crossover applied to the whole chromosome due to the fact that interchanging bits across several groups certainly has a much higher probability to violate the spatial constraints. A more frequent constraint violation would necessarily lead to the generation and testing of a larger number of chromosomes until the required number of solutions is generated, thus slowing down the whole process.

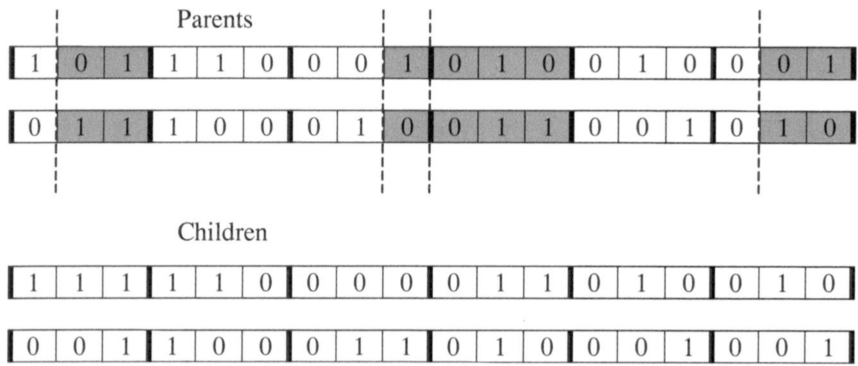

Fig. 6. Example illustrating the crossover operator. The thick vertical lines signify the borders of the groups and the dashed lines show the crossover points. The shaded bits are those to be interchanged.

In practice, there is a very small probability that crossover will not be applied to any group of bits, thus resulting in cloning. If the number of groups encoded in a chrosome is G, the probability that no crossover will take place in any group will be $(P_{gc})^G$. By always copying the successful parents to the next generation of solutions, as the cloning operator suggests, we explicitly set the above probability to one for the successful and to zero for the unsuccessful parents.

Mutation. The mutation operator changes each bit of the children chromosomes according to a low probability of mutation. This operator allows for controlled randomness during the search for problem solutions (i.e. it permits random jumps in the search tree of solutions) and is applied to the bits of every member of the next generation with the mutation probability P_m.

4.3 Reproducing New Generations of Solutions

The genetic algorithm used in this work starts from an initial population of solutions produced through constraint programming (as in MultiCAD-II), then interacts with the user, through a user friendly interface that allows for 3D form visualization, in order to evaluate each chromosome (i.e. to assign a fitness score) and, finally, it applies the genetic operators in order to produce the next generation of solutions. If the user's aesthetics are satisfied by the solutions of a generation, the whole process is stopped. Otherwise, the genetic operators are repeatedly applied until the next generation of solutions is derived according to the diagram shown in Fig. 7.

1. Create an initial population of solutions using constraint programming.
   Define the population size *PS*.
2. Have the user evaluate each chromosome according to his/her aesthetics.
   Assist the user through appropriate visualization aids.
3. Stop, if the user is satisfied by the solutions.
   Else, continue with step 4.
4. Select two parents using the roulette-wheel technique and apply the crossover operator to create two children.
5. Apply the mutation operator to each child.
6. Examine if at least one of the children satisfies the spatial constraints of the scene description. If none is a solution to the problem, go to step 4.
   Else, continue with the next step.
7. Place the children that satisfy the spatial constraints to the new generation. Clone the parents by copying them in the new generation. Do not allow for duplicated chromosomes.
8. If the size of the new generation is smaller than *PS* go to step 4. Else, go to step 2 to evaluate the new generation.

Fig. 7. Generation of 3D forms using the genetic algorithm approach.

5 Simulations

Several simulations have been performed using the MultiCAD-GA solution search engine for different scene descriptions. The population size of each generation was set to 20. Each solution was then visualized through a VRML file which allowed the user to project it onto any viewer supporting VRML, such as Internet Explorer.

All simulations have been performed on a typical 128MB PC Pentium III at 450MHz with no problems being reported even though sometimes the program was left running for several hours. The time required for a complete production of the next generation of 20 chromosome solutions varies from a few seconds to a few minutes depending on the severity of the problem constraints and on the choice of the crossover and mutation probabilities.

Moreover, another advantage of the genetic search engine over the traditional exhaustive linear search strategy is that the user not only directs the search on more promising parts of the search tree but also examines and evaluates the scenes in groups of 20 rather than one by one as in MultiCAD-II. The latter allows for a relative comparison and is found to generally improve the subjective quality of the final solutions.

Fig. 8 shows an instance of the auxiliary file with the encoded chromosomes where the question marks must be replaced by a fitness score (an integer in the [0, 10] interval) by the user and where the existing scores correspond to earlier evaluated chromosomes such as those that have been cloned. The first row of the file shows the generation number.

```
1
0000000000100010100010000100010010010100000000001001010=3
0000000000100010100010000100010010010100000000001001011=4
0000000000100010100000000100010010010100000000001001011=?
00100000000010100100000000010010010001010001000001001001=8
000000000010001010001000010001010001010001010001001001=4
000000000010001010000000001000101000101000101000 1001001=?
00000000000101001000000000100100100010100000001001010001=4
00100000000101001000000000100100100010100000001001010001=?
00000100001001000100000010010010010100100000001001011001=6
00000100001000101000100101000100100101000000000001011001=6
00000100001001001000100101000100100101000000000001011011=?
0000100000010010100000010100010100010010000001010011001=9
0000100000010010100000010100010100010010000000001011001=?
000001000001010010000001010010010001010001000001001001=?
000000000001010010000000010001001001001000001010011001=3
0000000000100100100010010100010010010100000001001011001=?
000000000001010001000000001001010010001000010001001001=4
0000100000010010100000010100010100010010000000010011001=?
0000000000010100100000000010010010001010000000001010001=3
00000000000100101000000000100100100010100000001001010001=?
```

Fig. 8. File shown to the user for evaluating the first generation.

Finally, Fig. 9 shows two solutions for the residence scene described in the script file of Fig. 2, generated with MultiCAD-GA. These solutions were derived within the first ten generations. The crossover and mutation probabilities for this problem were chosen as $P_{gc} = 0.3$ and $P_m = 0.003$ respectively.

6 Conclusions

A new version of the MultiCAD architectural design system enriched with a genetic algorithm-based search engine has been presented in this work. The need for such a search strategy has been raised by the global search qualities of genetic algorithms, which can have an impact even in applications traditionally dealt with declarative methods. The evolutionary character of such an approach offers advantages to the designers since they not only have the possibility to obtain alternative solutions based on a prototype but also to allow for their selective improvement. It also allows, through evaluation of alternative solutions, to inflict the designer's subjective parameters, like his/her aesthetic preferences, without being obliged to translate themes into formal constraints.

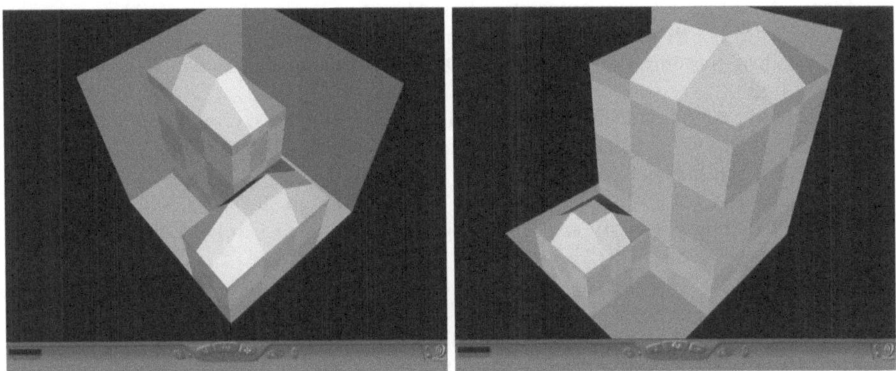

Fig. 9. Two 3D forms produced by MultiCAD-GA for the residence scene.

Although the algorithm does not proceed by exhaustively searching the solution space, it can quickly improve an initial solution. We are persuaded that the proven feasibility of such an approach is the major contribution of this research. MultiCAD-GA is a quite promising solution to the above requirements and allows for user interaction through scene evaluation by relative comparisons in each generation. The latter is made possible through VRML files and appropriate visualization programs (e.g. Internet Explorer).

Following the specification of the scene objects and their spatial constraints, a script file is first generated then scanned and parsed in order to derive the internal description tree model. Bounding box representations of the terminal subscenes using binary strings representing the chromosomes allowed for a genetic formulation of the search engine. Then, repeated application of genetic operators on an initial population of acceptable solutions, derived using constraint programming techniques, reproduce the next generations of solutions taking into account user evaluation of the scenes. The results obtained through simulations on a typical PC are quite encouraging and show that MultiCAD-GA can be a usefull tool in applications involving 3D form design.

Finally, in our future research, we will investigate improved initialization algorithms for the first genetic population so as to guarantee sufficient diversity of the initial solutions as well as the possibility of integrating a neural network into the system for user modeling and scene evaluation.

References

1. Miaoulis, G., Plemenos, D.: Propositions pour un Systeme d'Information Multimedia Intelligent Dedie a la CAO: Le Projet MultiCAD. Rapport de recherche MSI 96-03, Laboratoire Methodes et Structures Informatiques, Universite de Limoges (1996) 1-27
2. Plemenos, D.: Declarative Modeling by Hierarchical Decomposition. The Actual State of the MultiFormes Project. Int. Conf. GraphiCon'95, St. Petersbourg, Russia, July, (1995)
3. Bonnefoi, P.-F., Plemenos, D.: Proposals for Declarative Modeling Parallelization. Int. Conf. SCCG'98, Bratislava, Slovakia, April 23-25, (1998)
4. Simon, H.A.: Sciences of the Artificial. MIT Press, Cambridge, Mass. (1981)
5. Tzonis, A., White, I. (eds.): Automation Based Creative Design. Elsevier (1994)
6. Rychener, M.D.: Research in expert systems for engineering design. In: Rychener, M.D. (ed.): Expert Systems For Engineering Design. Academic Press, San Diego California (1988) 1-33
7. Mitchell, M.: An introduction to Genetic Algorithms. MIT Press, Cambridge, Mass. (1998)
8. Whitley, L.D., Vose, M.D. (eds): Foundations of Genetic Algorithms. Vol. 3. Morgan Kaufmann, San Mateo, CA (1995)
9. Woodbury, R.F.: A Genetic Approach to Creative Design. In: Gero, J.S., Maher, M.L. (eds.): Modelling Creativity and Knowledge-Based Creative Design. Lawrence Erlbaum, Hillsdale, NJ (1993) 211-232
10. Goldberg, D.E.: Genetic Algorithms in Search, Optimization and Machine Learning. Addison-Wesley, Reading, Massachusetts (1989)
11. Rich, E.: Artificial Intelligence. McGraw-Hill, New York (1983)
12. Frazer, J.: Evolutionary Architecture. Architectural Assoc., London, UK (1995)
13. Bentley, P. (ed.): Evolutionary Design by Computer. Morgan Kaufmann, San Francisco (1999)
14. Gero, J.S., Kazakov, V.: Evolving Design Genes in Space Layout Planning Problems. Artificial Design in Engineering **12:3** (1998) 163-176
15. Coates, P., Makris, D.: Genetic Programming and Spatial Morphogenesis. In: Proc. AISB'99: Symp. on Creative Evolutionary Systems. Univ. of Edinburgh, Edinburgh, UK (1999) 105-114
16. Makris, D.: Evolutionary Design ENvironments (EDEN). MSc thesis. School of Architecture, Univ. of East London, London, UK (1999)
17. Mortenson, M.E.: Geometric Modelling. Wiley, New York, (1995)
18. Khemlan, L., Timerman, A., Benne, B., Kalay, Y.: Intelligent Representation for Computer-Aided-Building-Design. Automation in Construction **8:1** (1998) 49-71
19. B. Björk, C.: A Conceptual Model of Spaces, Space Boundaries, and Enclosing Structures. Automation in Construction **3:1** (1994) 193-214
20. Orenstein, G.S.: The 3D approach to design. Fifth Int. Conf. on Computing in Civil and Building Engineering. Anaheim, CA (1993) 51-60

Intelligent Semantic Access to Audiovisual Content

Yannis Avrithis[1], Giorgos Stamou[1], Anastasios Delopoulos[2], and Stefanos Kollias[1]

[1] Image, Video and Multimedia Systems Laboratory
Department of Electrical and Computer Engineering
National Technical University of Athens
9, Iroon Polytechniou Str., 15773 Zographou, Athens, Greece
{iavr,gstam}@image.ntua.gr, stefanos@cs.ntua.gr

[2] Division of Electronics & Computer Engineering
Department of Electrical and Computer Engineering
Faculty of Engineering, Aristotle University of Thessaloniki
Thessaloniki 54006, Greece
adelo@eng.auth.gr

Abstract. In this paper, an integrated information system is presented that offers enhanced search and retrieval capabilities to users of heterogeneous digital audiovisual (a/v) archives. This novel system exploits the advances in handling a/v content and related metadata, as introduced by MPEG-4 and worked out by MPEG-7, to offer advanced access services characterized by the tri-fold "semantic phrasing of the request (query)", "unified handling" and "personalized response". The proposed system is targeting the intelligent extraction of semantic information from a/v and text related data taking into account the nature of useful queries that users may issue, and the context determined by user profiles. From a technical point of view, it will play the role of an intermediate access server residing between the end users and multiple heterogeneous audiovisual archives organized according to new MPEG standards.

1 Introduction

Digital archiving of multimedia content including video, audio, still images and various types of documents has been recognized by content holding organizations as a mature choice for the preservation, preview and partial distribution of their assets. The advances in computer and data networks along with the success of standardization efforts of MPEG and JPEG boosted the movement of the archives towards the conversion of their fragile and manually indexed material to digital, computer accessible data. By the end of last century the question was not on whether digital archives are technically and economically viable, but rather on how digital archives would be *efficient* and *informative*. In this framework, different scientific fields such as, on the one hand, development of database management systems, and on the other hand, processing and analysis of multimedia data, as well as artificial and computational intelligence methods, have observed a close cooperation with each other during the last few years. The attempt has been to develop intelligent and efficient human computer inter-

I.P. Vlahavas and C.D. Spyropoulos (Eds.): SETN 2002, LNAI 2308, pp. 215–224, 2002.

action systems, enabling the user to access vast amounts of heterogeneous information, stored in different sites and archives.

Database management systems (DBMS) have been designed that are able to handle such types of access to the stored information. Attaching information bits, called metadata, to the original data is the means for achieving this goal. The focus of technological attempts has been on the analysis of digital video, due to its large amounts of spatio-temporal interrelations, which turns it into the most demanding and complex data structure. Current and evolving international standardization activities, such as of the EBU, MPEG-4 [3,4,9], MPEG-7 [5-8], or JPEG-2000 [10] for still images, deal with aspects related to data structures and metadata. In particular, the new MPEG standards are object-oriented, i.e., adopt video objects as the information units, which is different from the information units used in the current form of video and film, i.e. scenes or shots. Of major importance is the contribution of MPEG-7 and JPEG-2000 to using metadata related to the visual and acoustic content of archived objects.

In more detail, MPEG-7 will define a standard for describing multimedia content. The objective is to quickly and efficiently search and retrieve audiovisual material. To allow interoperability, the standard adopts some normative elements, such as Descriptors (D's), Description Schemes (DS's), the Description Definition Language (DDL) as well as Coding and System Tools. The Descriptors define the syntax and the semantics of the representation of features, while the Description Schemes specify the structure and semantics of the relationships between Descriptors or other Descriptions. Many descriptors have been submitted for MPEG-7, some of which either accepted and included in the eXperimental Model (XM), which is a platform and tool set to evaluate and improve the tools of MPEG-7, or are in the experimentation (Core Experiments, CE) phase. Two parallel levels of descriptors are defined: the syntactic one, which describes the perceptual properties of the content, such as color and motion of spatio-temporal segments and the semantic one, which describes the meaning of content, in terms of semantic objects and events. Syntactic description seems to be well in hand in MPEG-7, but fleshing out the semantic description has not yet received the required attention.

It becomes clear among the research community dealing with content-based audiovisual data retrieval and new emerging related standards such as MPEG-7, that the results to be obtained will be ineffective, unless major focus is given to the semantic information level, defining what most users desire to retrieve. Mapping, however, low level, subsymbolic descriptors of a/v archives to high level symbolic ones is in general difficult, even impossible with the current state of technology. It can, however, be tackled when dealing with specific application domains. It seems that the extraction of semantic information from a/v and text related data is tractable taking into account [1]:

- *The nature of useful queries that users may issue.* This is only a portion of the general set of questions related to "content understanding". Using all types of multimedia information of the archives makes the task more tractable.
- *The context determined by user profiles.*

In this paper a novel platform is proposed that intends to exploit the aforementioned ideas in order to offer user friendly, highly informative access to distributed audiovisual archives.

2 Architecture of the Proposed System

The general architecture is provided in Figure 1, where all modules and subsystems are depicted, but the flow of information between modules is not shown for clarity. More detailed system diagrams and descriptions of subsystems are provided in the following sections for the two main modes of system operation, i.e. *update mode* and *query mode*. The system has the following features:

- Adopts the general features and descriptions for content-based access to visual information proposed by MPEG-7 and other standards such as JPEG-2000; also adopts existing basic system architectures implementing the MPEG-4 and MPEG-7 standardisation activities.
- Performs dynamic extraction of high level semantic description of a/v content units (movies, scenes, shots, etc.) on the basis of syntactic and lower level semantic information contained in the a/v archives.
- Enables the issuing of queries at a high semantic level. This feature is essential for unifying user access to multiple heterogeneous a/v archives with different structure and description detail.
- Generates, updates and manages users' profile metadata that specify their preferences against the a/v content.
- Employs the above users' metadata structures for filtering the information returned as response to their queries so that it better fits to user preferences and priorities. To this end static, adaptive or dynamic classification of the available a/v content is performed by the a/v classification module, and next "compared" to individual users' profiles.
- Gives users the ability to define and redefine their initial profile.
- Is capable to communicate with existing a/v archives, structured on the basis of scenes/shots and key frames, or with already developed systems with proprietary user interfaces. In the former case, it will permit translation of the basic information units to more complex object-based ones; in the latter, it will accept and adapt a/v data, objects and stored metadata.
- User interfaces employ platform independent tools targeting both the Internet and WWW and broadcast type of access routes.

Additionally, it is important that the system has the following features related to user query processing:

Response time: Internal intelligent modules may use semantic information available in the DBMS (calculated by *Dynamic Thematic Categorization*-DTC and *Detection of Events and Composite Objects*-DECO) to locate and rank multimedia documents very fast, and some times without querying individual a/v archives. In most cases where a/v unit descriptions are required, query processing may be slower due to the large volume of information. In all cases it is important that the overall response time of the system is not too long as perceived by the end user.

Filtering: When a user specifies a composite query, it is desirable that a semantic query interpretation is constructed and multimedia documents are filtered as much as possible according to the semantic interpretation and the user profile, in order to avoid the overwhelming responses of most search engines.

Exact matching: In the special cases where the user query is simple, e.g. a single keyword, the system must return all documents whose description contains the keyword; no information is lost this way.

Ranking: In all cases retrieved documents must be ranked according to the user's preferences and their semantic relevance to the query, so that most important documents are presented first.

Up-to-date information: Since the system is designed for handling a large number of individual a/v archives whose content may change frequently, DBMS must be updated (either in batch updates or updates on demand) to reflect the most recent archive content.

Relevance feedback: It will be useful and probably necessary to provide a relevance feedback mechanism to permit refinement of user queries. Used in modern information retrieval systems, this mechanism allows the user to select those documents among the first retrieval results that are most "relevant" to the original query; the latter is then automatically refined to retrieve similar documents.

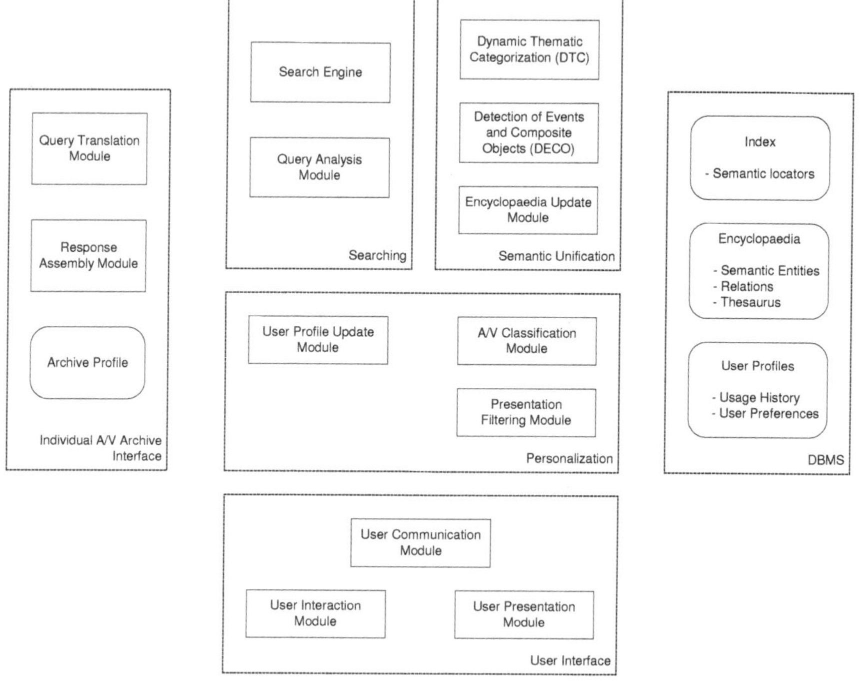

Fig. 1. General architecture of the system

The description of subsystems functionality follows the distinction in two main modes of operation. In *query mode*, the system is online and used to process user requests by translating/dispatching queries to the archives and assembling/presenting the respective responses. The main internal modules participating in this mode are *query analysis*, *search engine*, *a/v classification* and *presentation filtering*.

An additional *update mode* of operation will also be necessary for updating the content description data. In particular, a batch update procedure can be employed at regular intervals to perform DTC and DECO on available a/v units and update the database. Alternatively, an *update on demand* procedure can be employed whenever new a/v units are added to individual a/v archives to keep the system synchronised at all times. The decision will depend on speed, storage and network traffic performance considerations. The main internal modules participating in the update mode are *DTC*, *DECO*, *encyclopaedia update* and *user profile update*.

An overview of the functionality of the subsystems and modules is described below in two separate sections for the query mode and the update mode, where additional diagrams depict detailed flow of information between modules.

3 Query Mode of Operation

In query mode, the system is online accepting user requests, translating / dispatching queries to the archives and assembling / presenting the respective responses. The main internal modules participating in this mode are *query analysis*, *search engine*, *a/v classification* and *presentation filtering*. The overall diagram of this mode of operation is depicted in Figure 2.

The user query is first submitted at the *user interaction* module of the *user interface*. It mainly consists of two parts:

- *Semantic specification*: either keywords with logical operators, free text or composite, structured statements/scenaria designed by special forms and input controls. It may also contain audiovisual content features specified either through text or special input controls.
- *Metadata specifications*: keywords, numbers, dates etc. representing metadata specifications such as creation, media, usage, classification, navigation and access information as defined in MPEG-7.

The metadata part of a query will be finally dispatched to individual a/v archives (after translation at the archive interfaces); the semantic part however is first processed within the internal intelligent modules of Feathon to accommodate for semantic unification. The query is first transformed in a suitable structure (*user query*) by the communication module of the user interface and then transferred at the *query analysis* module of the *searching* subsystem. This module performs three main operations:

- *Query interpretation*: receives the semantic part of queries in the form of vectors or graphs of keywords and replaces the keywords by *semantic entities* (objects, events, concepts, agents etc.) found in the *encyclopaedia*.
- *Query expansion*: takes advantage of the semantic entity relations in the encyclopaedia and the *thesaurus* (an automatically updated association table between semantic entities) to expand queries using entities that do not appear in the original query. E.g. a goal event in football can be expanded in a suitable combination of objects such as a player, a ball and a goal post [2].

- *Profiling*: adds relevant information from the *user preferences* of the user profile (e.g. interest for European or American football) and adjusts the query accordingly to perform *pre-filtering*. The user preferences, apart from the normative elements described in MPEG-7, may contain thematic categories and interests in the form of composite semantic entities.

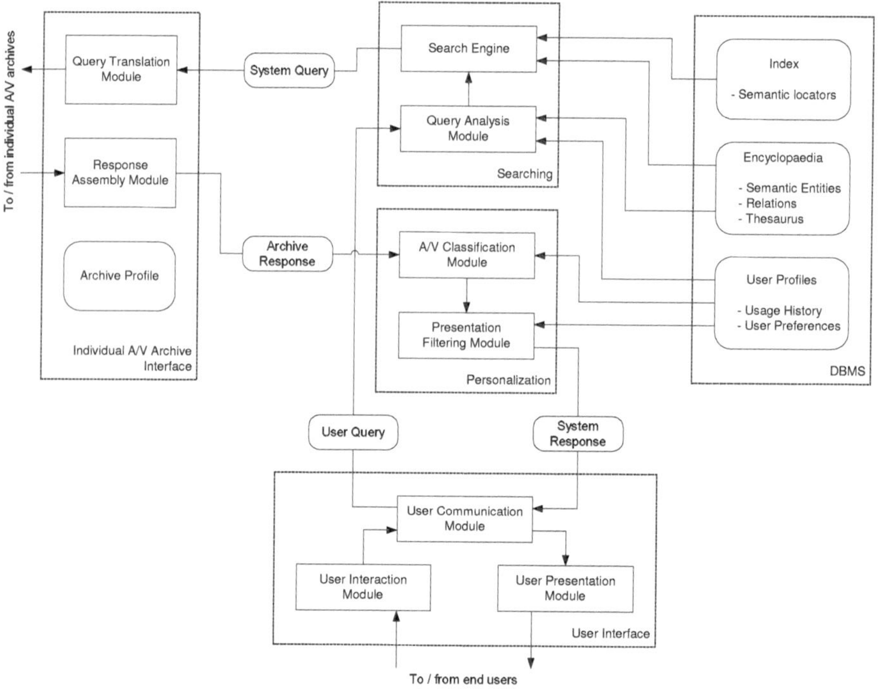

Fig. 2. The system at query mode of operation

The final result of query analysis, the *internal query*, is a structure (vector or graph) of semantic entities along with confidence values. This is transferred to the *search engine* where this structure is tested against the *index*. The index contains sets of document locators for each thematic category and semantic entity of the encyclopaedia (and also for a large set of composite entities), resulting from DTC and DECO procedures. The result is a list of document locators corresponding to documents at different a/v archives. This list is combined by the search engine with the metadata part of the user query to construct the *system query*, which is a unified query dispatched to all individual a/v archive interfaces.

At each *a/v archive interface*, the *query translation* module uses the *archive profile* to associate normative DS's of the system query to the proprietary structures employed in each archive. This translation takes place only for the metadata part of the query; the semantic part has already produced a known list of media locators. Then, depending on the archive interfacing type, the interface either dispatches the query to an existing *archive search engine* (through the query translation module) or communicates directly with the multimedia document descriptions (or even the multimedia documents themselves) included in the archive. The result is a filtered (but not ranked) list of document locators (or links) and possibly their descriptions. The *response assembly* module of the interface constructs the *archive response* as a unified structure of retrieved documents, which is returned to the a/v classification module of the *personalisation* subsystem.

The *a/v classification module* performs ranking (but not filtering) to the retrieved documents of the archive response based on *user interests* contained within the preferences of the user profiles. The user interests consist of (unified) thematic categories and simple or composite semantic entities of the encyclopaedia. Dynamic categorisation and detection of composite entities is performed on the retrieved documents using their entire descriptions and relevance values are assigned after matching with the user interests. The result is the *internal response*, which is a ranked list of a/v documents with their descriptions.

The internal response is transferred to the *presentation filtering* module where further ranking and filtering is performed according to the remaining parts of the user preferences such as creation, media, classification, usage, access, and navigation preferences (e.g. favourite actors / directors or preference for short summaries). The *system response* produced by the presentation filtering module, which is also a ranked list of a/v documents with their descriptions, is transferred to the *communications module* of the user interface and finally to the *user presentation* module. The entire record of user actions during the search procedure (user query, retrieved documents, documents selected as relevant) is stored in the *usage history* of the specific user; this information is then used for tracking and updating the user preferences. Furthermore, *relevance feedback* is supported by the system. This would require modifications in the user interaction and presentation modules of the user interface, and a feedback module in the personalisation subsystem.

4 Update Mode of Operation

The general scope of the information update mode of operation is to adapt and enrich the DBMS used for the unified searching and filtering of a/v content. Its operation is based on the *semantic unification* and the *personalisation* subsystems depicted in Figure 3. The semantic unification subsystem is responsible for the construction and update of the *index* and the *encyclopaedia*, while the personalisation subsystem updates the *user profiles*.

As already mentioned, the index stored in the DBMS consists of a set of semantic document locators, i.e. a set of encyclopaedia terms with links to the a/v unit descriptions (stored in the a/v archives) that semantically "contain" them. The information units of the index are semantic entities (objects, events, concepts, thematic categories, etc.) stored in the encyclopaedia, and composite semantic structures (relations, composite objects or scenarios, probably not contained in the encyclopaedia) representing the abstract semantic meaning of complex concepts and events. It is mentioned that although thematic categories are actually a special case of concepts, they are stored and processed as separate units due to their important role during the searching process.

The modules that update the terms of the index and its links to the a/v units are DTC and DECO. The former takes the thematic categories stored in the encyclopaedia as input, unifies them with the thematic categories of the a/v archives and scans the a/v units in order to find and store (as links) the a/v units that belong to each thematic category, together with a weight representing the degree in which the system believes that the a/v unit is characterised of this thematic category. The latter performs a similar task for the objects, events and concepts of the encyclopaedia. Furthermore, it scans the a/v units and searches for composite semantic structures and links them with the corresponding a/v units.

All update procedures may be performed globally for the entire content of the a/v archives at regular intervals (*batch update*) or whenever the a/v content of an archive is updates (*update on demand*). In the latter case, which is preferable due to low computational cost, the update process is *incremental*, i.e. only the newly inserted a/v unit descriptions are necessary.

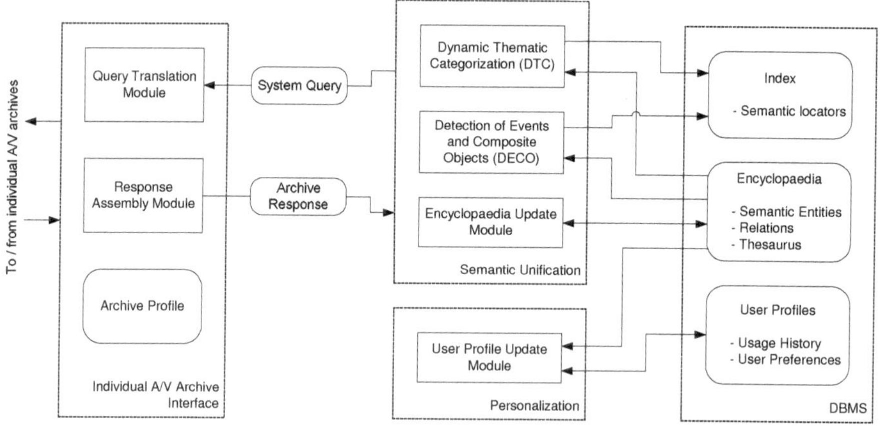

Fig. 3. The system at update mode of operation

The content of the encyclopaedia is updated with the aid of the *encyclopaedia update* module. The main goal of this module is to update the thesaurus that associates semantic entities through semantic relations. Moreover, the semantic entities of the encyclopaedia should be updated, especially when the content of the a/v archives is dramatically changed. Finally, new terms may be inserted in the encyclopaedia (especially composite semantic structures) after the mining process of the DECO and their insertion in the index.

One of the most important tasks of the update mode of operation is the update of the user profiles. This is carried out with the aid of the *user profile update* module of the *personalisation* subsystem. The structures of the DBMS that should be updated within this process are the usage history and the user preferences. The *usage history* is be updated after the end of a user query by storing all transactions of the user during the query process. The above transactions characterise the user and express his personal view of the a/v content. The user profile update module takes these transactions as input and with the aid of the Encyclopaedia and the multimedia descriptions of the a/v units referred to in the usage history, extracts the *user preferences* and stores them in the corresponding user profile. The user preferences are actually a set of semantic entities (objects, events, concepts, thematic categories) taken from the encyclopaedia, with the corresponding weights. Furthermore, they contain a set of more abstract semantic concepts (not as general as the thematic categories), the *interests*. The interests are extracted from the multimedia descriptions of the a/v units selected by the user, through a data mining process.

5 Conclusions

The core technological target of the system is to blend the achievements in characterizing a/v content - especially visual and acoustical content - with state of the art hybrid intelligence technologies in order to

(i) offer unified semantic views to existing a/v archives, if possible, beyond the individual classification schemes and subject indexes of each archive

(ii) personalize those views according to the retained profile of individual users or specific user groups; the latter clearly appreciating that semantic interpretation heavily relies on the context which in turn depends on the specific profile.

The system provides novel tools and methods for extracting high-level semantic information. Finally, using statistical and relevance feedback techniques are used to assist personalization.

Acknowledgements. This work has been partially funded by the project FAETHON of the Information Society Technologies (IST) programme of the European Community.

References

1. Delopoulos, A., Kollias, S., Avrithis, Y., Haas, W., Majcen, K.: Unified Intelligent Access to Heterogeneous Audiovisual Content. In Proc. of Int. Workshop on Content-Based Multimedia Indexing (CBMI), Brescia, Italy, Sept. 2001
2. Akrivas, G., Stamou, G., Kollias, S.: Fuzzy Semantic Association of Audiovisual Document Descriptions. In Proc. of Int. Workshop on Very Low Bitrate Video Coding (VLBV), Athens, Greece, Oct. 2001
3. Battista, S., Casalino, F., Lande C.: MPEG-4: A Multimedia Standard for the Third Millenium, Part 1. IEEE Multimedia **6** (4) (1999) 74-83

4. Battista, S., Casalino, F., Lande, C.: MPEG-4: A Multimedia Standard for the Third Millenium, Part 2. IEEE Multimedia **7** (1) (2000) 76-84
5. Nack, F., Lindsay, A.: Everything You Wanted to Know About MPEG-7: Part 1. IEEE Multimedia **6** (3) (1999) 65-77
6. Nack, F., Lindsay, A.: Everything You Wanted to Know About MPEG-7: Part 2. IEEE Multimedia **6** (4) (1999) 64-73
7. Special Issue on MPEG-7. IEEE Trans. On Circuits and Systems for Video Technology **11** (6) (2001) 685-772
8. ISO/IEC JTC1/SC29/WG11 N4032: Introduction to MPEG-7. Singapure (2001)
9. ISO/IEC JTC1/SC29/WG11 N3747: MPEG-4 Overview (V.16 – La Baule Version). La Baule, France (2000)
10. ISO/IEC JTC1/SC29/WG1 N1646R: JPEG 2000 Part I Final Committee Draft Version 1.0 (2000)

A Multi-clustering Fusion Algorithm

Dimitrios Frossyniotis[1], Minas Pertselakis[1], and Andreas Stafylopatis[2]

National Technical University of Athens
Department of Electrical and Computer Engineering
Zographou 157 73, Athens, Greece
[1]{dfros, mper}@cslab.ntua.gr
[2]andreas@cs.ntua.gr

Abstract. A multi-clustering fusion method is presented based on combining several runs of a clustering algorithm resulting in a common partition. More specifically, the results of several independent runs of the same clustering algorithm are appropriately combined to obtain a partition of the data which is not affected by initialization and overcomes the instabilities of clustering methods. Finally, the fusion procedure starts with the clusters produced by the combining part and finds the optimal number of clusters in the data set according to some predefined criteria. The unsupervised multi-clustering method implemented in this work is quite general. There is ample room for the implementation and testing with any existing clustering algorithm that has unstable results. Experiments using both simulated and real data sets indicate that the multi-clustering fusion algorithm is able to partition a set of data points to the optimal number of clusters not constrained to be hyper-spherically shaped.

1 Introduction

Unsupervised classification, also known as data clustering, is a generic label for a variety of procedures designed to find natural groupings or clusters in multidimensional data, based on measured similarities among the patterns [1]. Clustering is a very difficult problem because data can reveal clusters with different shapes and sizes. Additionally, the number of clusters in the data often depends on the resolution with which the data are viewed. As a consequence, different clustering algorithms have been proposed in the literature and new clustering algorithms continue to appear.

Moreover, the majority of these algorithms are based on the following four most popular clustering methods: iterative square-error partitional clustering, hierarchical clustering, grid-based clustering and density-based clustering [2,3].

Partitional methods can be further classified into two groups. In the first group, each sample is assigned to one and only one cluster, contrary to the second group of methods where each sample can be associated (in some sense) with several clusters. The most commonly used partitional clustering algorithm

I.P. Vlahavas and C.D. Spyropoulos (Eds.): SETN 2002, LNAI 2308, pp. 225–236, 2002.

is K-means, which is based on the square-error criterion. This algorithm is computationally efficient and yields good results if the clusters are compact, hyper-spherical in shape and well separated in the feature space. Numerous attempts have been made to improve the performance of the simple K-means by using the Mahalanobis distance to detect hyper-ellipsoidal shaped clusters [4] or by incorporating a fuzzy criterion function resulting in a fuzzy C-means algorithm [5]. A different partitional clustering approach is based on probability density function (pdf) estimation using Gaussian mixtures. The specification of the parameters of the mixture is based on the expectation-minimization algorithm (EM) [6]. A recently proposed greedy-EM algorithm [7] is an incremental scheme that has been found to provide better results than the conventional EM algorithm.

Hierarchical clustering methods organize data in a nested sequence of groups which can be displayed in the form of a dendrogram or a tree [8]. These methods can be either agglomerative or divisive. An agglomerative hierarchical method places each sample in its own cluster and gradually merges these clusters into larger clusters until all samples are ultimately in a single cluster (the root node). A divisive hierarchical method starts with a single cluster containing all the data and recursively splits parent clusters into daughters.

Grid-based clustering algorithms are mainly proposed for spatial data mining. Their main characteristic is that they quantise the space into a finite number of cells and then they do all operations on the quantised space. On the other hand, density-based clustering algorithms adopt the key idea to group neighbouring objects of a data set into clusters based on density conditions.

However, many of the above clustering methods require additional user-specified parameters, such as the optimal number and shapes of clusters, similarity thresholds and stopping criteria. Moreover, different clustering algorithms and even multiple replications of the same algorithm result in different solutions due to random initializations, so there is no clear indication for the best partition result. Consequently, two main of the challenges in cluster analysis are first to select an appropriate measure of similarity to define clusters, which in general is cluster shape dependent, and second to specify the optimal number of clusters in the data set. In this direction, clustering strategies have been developed which prove to perform very satisfactorily in clustering and finding the number of clusters [9,10,11,12,13]. The present work, following an analogous approach, proposes a clustering algorithm which tackles these two important problems and is able to partition a data set in a shape independent manner and to find the optimal number of clusters existing in the data set.

The paper is organized as follows: Section 2 describes the multi-clustering fusion method, while experimental results for the evaluation of the proposed method are presented in Section 3 and, finally, conclusions are presented in Section 4.

2 Description of the Algorithm

The multi-clustering fusion algorithm consists of two procedures that take place sequentially. The Partitioning procedure, which is used to partition data points of a set in clusters and the Fusion procedure, which determines the true structure of the data.

In the primary stage, the initial number of clusters and the number of iterations are defined for the Partioning procedure, wherein a clustering algorithm and a voting scheme are implemented, in order to produce a distinct partition of the data set. During the Fusion procedure, this partition is processed and neighbour clusters are merged, resulting in an optimal number of clusters for the given data set, according to some specified criteria.

2.1 Partitioning Procedure

The partioning procedure applies the same basic clustering algorithm for a number of iterations, *Iter*, so as to accomplish a distinct partitioning of N data points to a predefined number C of clusters. The experimental study of our work is based on two implementations of the proposed multi-clustering fusion method using different basic clustering algorithms: the K-means and the greedy-EM algorithm.

More specifically, the K-means clustering aims to optimise an objective function that is described by the equation

$$J = \sum_{i=1}^{C} \sum_{\vec{x} \in \mu_i} d(\vec{x}, \vec{v}_i) \tag{1}$$

where $\vec{v}_i$ is the center of cluster μ_i and $d(\vec{x}, \vec{v}_i)$ is the Euclidean distance between a point $\vec{x}$ and $\vec{v}_i$. Thus, the criterion function J attempts to minimize the distance of every point from the center of the cluster to which the point belongs. Starting from arbitrary initial positions for cluster centers and by iteratively updating cluster centers, the algorithm moves the cluster centers to sensible locations within the data set.

As far as the greedy-EM algorithm [7] is concerned, the data are assumed to be generated by several parameterized Gaussian distributions, so the data points are assigned to different clusters based on their posterior probabilities of having been generated by a specific Gaussian distribution. A multivariate Gaussian mixture is defined as the weighted sum:

$$p(\vec{x}) = \sum_{j=1}^{C} \pi_j f(\vec{x}; \vec{\phi}_j) \tag{2}$$

where π_j are the mixing weights satisfying $\sum_j \pi_j = 1,\ \pi_j \geqslant 0$, and $f(\vec{x}; \vec{\phi}_j)$ is the l-dimensional Gaussian density

$$f(\vec{x}; \phi_j) = (2\pi)^{-l/2} \mid S_j \mid^{-1/2} exp[-0.5(\vec{x} - \vec{m}_j)^{\top} S_j^{-1} (\vec{x} - \vec{m}_j)] \tag{3}$$

parameterized on the mean $\vec{m}_j$ and the covariance matrix S_j, collectively denoted by the parameter vector $\vec{\phi}_j$. Usually, for a given number C of kernels, the specification of the parameters of the mixture is based on the *expectation-minimization* algorithm (EM) [6] for maximization of the data log-likelihood:

$$\mathcal{L} = \frac{1}{N} \sum_{i=1}^{N} \log p(\vec{x}^i) \tag{4}$$

The algorithm starts with one kernel and adds kernels dynamically one at a time so as to estimate the true number of components of the mixture (therefore the true number of clusters, if we consider that each kernel corresponds to a group of patterns) as follows. The algorithm is run for a large value of C, and, for the solution obtained for each intermediate value of C, a model selection criterion is applied, e.g., cross-validation using a set of test points, a coding scheme based on minimum description length etc. Finally, the optimal value of C is selected that corresponds to the optimal value of the model selection criterion. In this work, we have used as a criterion for the specification of C, the log-likelihood value on a validation set of points that have not been used for training.

The above procedure is carried out when applying the greedy-EM algorithm as a stand-alone clustering method. When using the greedy-EM as a basic clustering algorithm within the multi-clustering fusion approach we consider only the predefined value of C and no intermediate values, so as to obtain a partitioning to C clusters at each iteration step.

In what concerns the Partioning procedure, the basic clustering algorithm partitions the data set in a different way for each iteration, creating a problem of deciding which cluster of one run corresponds to which in another run. This algorithm tackles this problem using the similarity between the clusters produced during successive runs. By determining the percentage of points of a cluster in the t-th run belonging to clusters of the $t-1$-th run, each cluster of the new run is assigned to one of the previous run, resulting in a cluster renumbering process.

After renumbering, if pattern i is assigned to cluster q, then a positive vote is given to cluster q and a negative one to all other clusters. This process defines a voting scheme, during which a voting table VT (of dimension $N \times C$) is updated, so that $VT(i,j)$ denotes the membership degree of pattern i to cluster j, where $i = 1, \ldots, N$, and $j = 1, \ldots, C$.

At the end of the runs, each pattern i is considered to belong to the cluster C^i_{max}, where

$$C^i_{max} = argmax(VT(i,j)), \;\; j = 1, \ldots, C \tag{5}$$

The procedure thus results in a distinct partitioning of the data set, assigning each data point to one cluster.

Using the VT table and the relation between the data points of one cluster with all the remaining clusters, a table NRT (of dimension $C \times C$) can be produced, so that $NRT(i,j)$ represents the neighbourhood relation between clusters i and j:

$$NRT(i,j) = \sum_{p=1}^{N}(VT(p,j)I(C^p_{max} = i)), \;\; i = 1,\ldots,C, \; j = 1,\ldots,C, j \neq i \quad (6)$$

where $I(z)$ is an indicator function, i.e. $I(z) = 1$ if z =true, otherwise $I(z) = 0$.

2.2 Fusion Procedure

Given the neighbourhood relation among clusters, a Fusion procedure is developed. This procedure starts with the predefined number C of clusters and (after removing the clusters with zero data points) merges the ones which are closest to each other.

More specifically, the procedure searches the neighbourhood relation table ($C \times C$ table) for the two clusters (with indexes $C1$ and $C2$) that fulfill the following conditions: first, both clusters are the closest to each other and, second, these two clusters are the closest of all clusters. The next step is to merge these clusters into one and to reconfigure the voting table accordingly, by adding the votes of the second cluster to the first one as follows:

$$VT(i, C1') = VT(i, C1') + VT(I, C2'), \;\; i = 1, \ldots, N \quad (7)$$

where $C1' = min(C1, C2)$ and $C2' = max(C1, C2)$. The new neighbourhood relation table is created with one cluster less, by removing cluster $C2'$, and the procedure starts again until some stopping criterion is met.

The criterion that derives directly from this procedure is that merging will stop when all clusters end up to have an average 'sureness' of 100%. (The average 'sureness' is defined as the sum of the membership degrees of points assigned to a cluster divided by their total number). That means that in the voting table all data points will be assigned to only one cluster by 100%. Since in practice this condition is not always possible to be realized, due to overlapping clusters for example, it was decided to use methods suitable for quantitative evaluation of the clustering results, which determine the number of clusters better fitting a data set.

The cluster validity methods used in our study are the Root-mean-square standard deviation (RMSSTD) and the R-squared (RS) described in [3]. More specifically, RMSSTD and RS have to be taken into account simultaneously in order to find the correct number of clusters. The optimal values of the number of clusters are those for which significant local change in values of RS and RMSSTD occurs. It should be noted, however, that since these methods give an indication of the quality of the resulting partitioning they should only be considered as a tool at the disposal of the experts in order to evaluate the clustering results.

2.3 Pseudo-Algorithm

- Define number of clusters, C
- Define number of iterations, $Iter$

Procedure 1: Partitioning

- $i = 1$;
  Run the basic clustering algorithm to partition the data set into C clusters
- If sample p ($p = 1, \ldots, N$) belongs to cluster q then
  $VT(p, q) = 1$
  $VT(p, j) = 0, \quad j = 1, \ldots, C, \; j \neq q$
- For $i = 2$ to *Iter*
  - Run the basic clustering algorithm to partition the data set into C clusters
  - Renumber clusters
  - Voting scheme:
    If sample p ($p = 1, \ldots, N$) belongs to cluster q then
    $VT(p, q) = \frac{(i-1)}{i} VT(p, q) + \frac{1}{i}$
    $VT(p, j) = \frac{(i-1)}{i} VT(p, j), \quad j = 1, \ldots, C, \; j \neq q$
- Create neighbourhood relation table NRT ($C \times C$)

Procedure 2: Fusion

- Remove clusters with zero data points
- Repeat until stopping criterion is met
  - From neighbourhood relation table find the two closest clusters
  - Merge pairs, sum the votes
  - Recompute NRT with $C = C - 1$ clusters

The proposed algorithm consists of two procedures that take place sequentially, thus the total complexity is the sum of the respective complexities. The Partioning procedure has the complexity of the basic clustering algorithm, i.e., if the basic clustering algorithm is the K-means then the time complexity is $O(n)$ where n is the number of points in the dataset. The time complexity of the Fusion procedure is $O(C^3)$ where C is the number of clusters produced from the Partition procedure.

3 Experimental Results

In this section we present a comparative experimental evaluation of the proposed methodology using different basic clustering algorithms, namely the K-means and the greedy-EM algorithm. The resulting multi-clustering fusion method with K-means as the basic clustering algorithm will be hereafter referred to as *multi-fusion-k-means*. Similarly, using the greedy-EM as the basic clustering algorithm will be referred to as *multi-fusion-greedy-EM*.

The proposed multi-clustering fusion method has been tested on several data sets. The basic idea for choosing the initial number of clusters is by setting C to a large value, say $\sqrt{N}$, N being the number of patterns in the data set. We used this formula, because partitioning a small data set into a large number of clusters (compared to the actual number of clusters) usually produces clusters of few points or empty clusters. The experiments presented here consist of $Iter = 100$ runs of the basic clustering algorithm in the Partitioning procedure with a number C of clusters. The voting table VT and the neighbourhood relation table NRT are computed between successive runs and the Fusion procedure follows according to the final results of the partition. The optimal values of the number of clusters are those for which a significant local change in values of RS and RMSSTD occurs.

Finally, for comparison purposes, we also present clustering results from running the greedy-EM algorithm as a stand-alone clustering method. In this case, we have applied the procedure described in the previous section for selecting the optimal value of clusters using a validation set of points that have not been used for training.

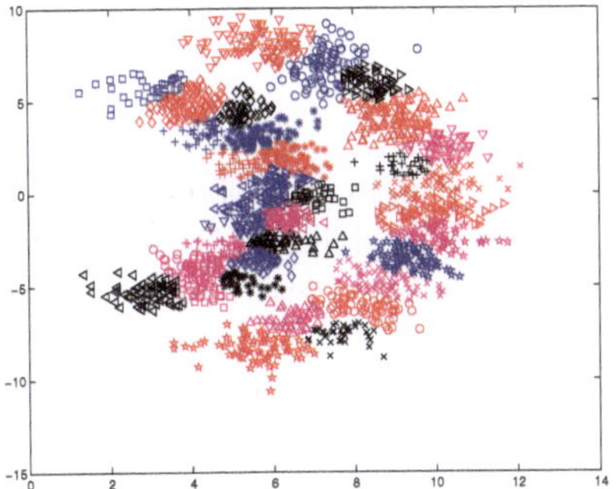

Fig. 1. Lith data set after the Partitioning procedure (multi-fusion-k-means).

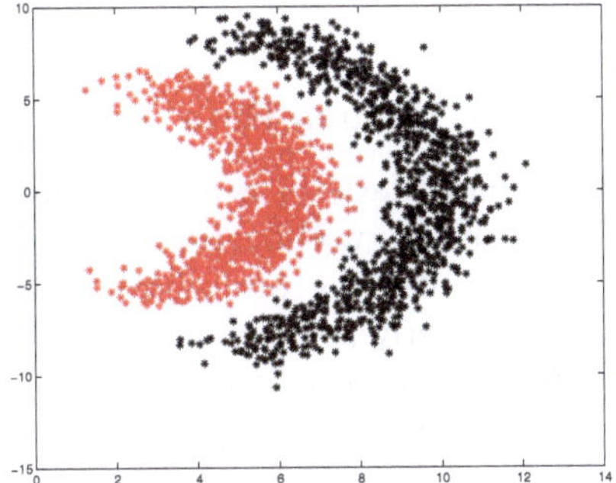

Fig. 2. Lith data set after the Fusion procedure (multi-fusion-k-means).

3.1 The Lith Data

This is a 2-dimensional data set consisting of 2000 data points. The data is uniformly distributed along two sausages and is superimposed by a normal distribution with standard deviation 1 in all directions. We have considered $C = 45$ clusters in the Partitioning procedure. The multi-fusion-k-means partitioned the data points correctly into two clusters (Fig. 1 and 2). The validity indices (RMSSTD and RS) select the clustering scheme of two clusters while we reached an average 'sureness' of the clusters greater than 99%. Similarly, the multi-fusion-greedy-EM method partitioned the data points into two well separated clusters reaching an average 'sureness' of the clusters greater than 99%. For the stand-alone greedy-EM algorithm, we used 1000 data points for training and 1000 for validation. We ran the algorithm for $C = 45$ clusters and the optimal solution obtained was 6 clusters (Fig. 7) with average 'sureness' of the clusters 91.8%.

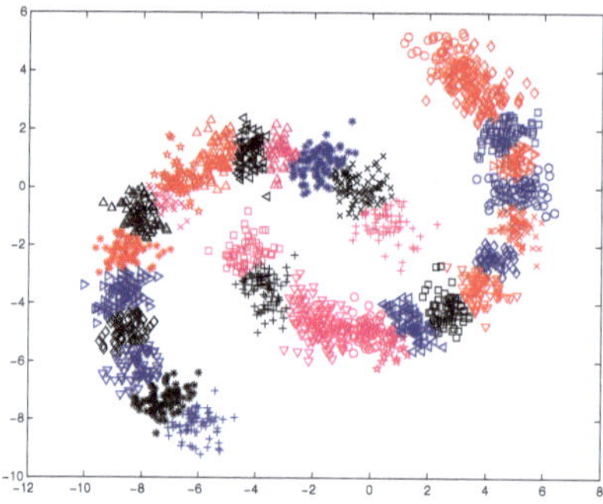

Fig. 3. Banana data set after the Partitioning procedure (multi-fusion-k-means).

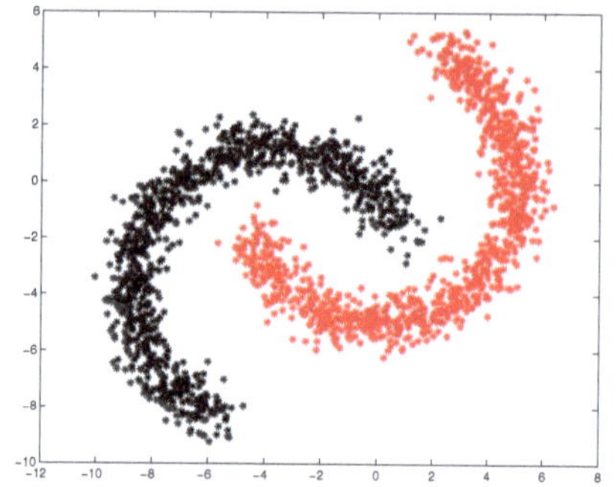

Fig. 4. Banana data set after the Fusion procedure (multi-fusion-k-means).

3.2 The Banana Data

The Banana data set is also a 2-dimensional one consisting of 2000 data points that belong to two banana shaped clusters. We have considered $C = 45$ clusters in the Partitioning procedure. The multi-fusion-k-means partitioned the data points correctly into two clusters (Fig. 3 and 4). The validity indices (RMSSTD and RS) select the clustering scheme of two clusters while we reached an average 'sureness' of the clusters greater than 99%. Similarly, the multi-fusion-greedy-EM method partitioned the data points into two well separated clusters reaching an average 'sureness' of the clusters greater than 99%. For the stand-alone greedy-EM, we used 1000 data points for training and 1000 for validation. We ran the algorithm for $C = 45$ clusters and the optimal solution obtained was 10 clusters (Fig. 8) with average 'sureness' of the clusters 86.8%.

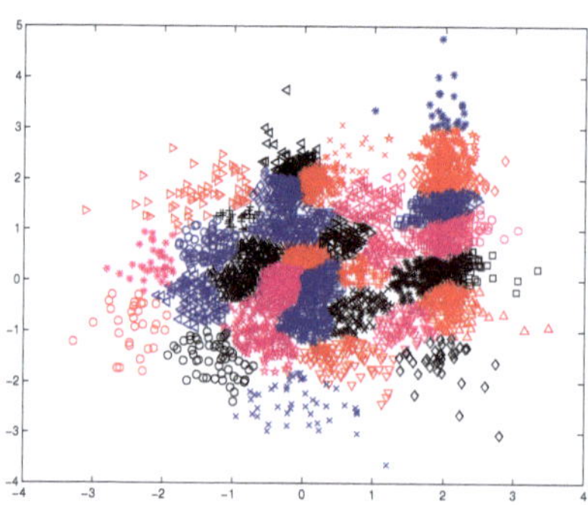

Fig. 5. Clouds data set after the Partitioning procedure (multi-fusion-k-means).

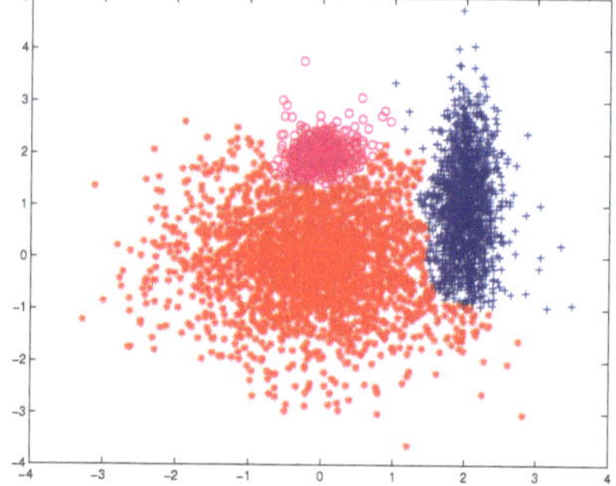

Fig. 6. Clouds data set after the Fusion procedure (multi-fusion-k-means).

3.3 The Clouds Data

The Clouds artificial data from the ELENA project [14] are two-dimensional produced by three different Gaussian distributions. There are 5000 samples in the data set belonging to three clusters which are relatively highly overlapped. We have considered $C = 70$ clusters in the Partitioning procedure. The multi-fusion-k-means correctly identified the true number of clusters (three) (Fig. 5 and 6). The validity indices (RMSSTD and RS) select the clustering scheme of three clusters while we reached an average 'sureness' of the clusters greater than 98.5%. Similarly, the multi-fusion-greedy-EM method partitioned the data points into three clusters reaching an average 'sureness' of the clusters greater than 95.5%. For the stand-alone greedy-EM algorithm, we used 3000 data points for training and 2000 for validation. We ran the algorithm for $C = 70$ clusters and the optimal solution obtained was 4 clusters (Fig. 9) with average 'sureness' of the clusters 94.1%. The average 'sureness' of the clusters is less than that of the previous examples for the proposed method. Indeed, the Lith and Banana data sets have a simple and clear structure, but, unfortunately, in the case of overlapping clusters (especially in real-world data sets) it is very difficult to find a 'very sure' partitioning.

3.4 The Pima Indians Data

The Diabetes set from the UCI data set repository [15] contains 8-dimensional data. It is based on personal data from 768 Pima Indians obtained by the National Institute of Diabetes and Digestive and Kidney Diseases. We have considered $C = 28$ clusters in the Partitioning procedure. The multi-fusion-k-means yielded four clusters. The validity indices (RMSSTD and RS) select the clustering scheme of four clusters, while we reached an average 'sureness' of the clusters greater than 99%. Similarly, the multi-fusion-greedy-EM method partitioned the data points into four clusters reaching an average 'sureness' of the clusters greater than 96.5%. For the stand-alone greedy-EM algorithm, we used 500 data points for training and 268 for validation. We ran the algorithm for $C = 28$ clusters and the optimal solution obtained was 5 clusters with average 'sureness' of the clusters 95%.

3.5 Discussion

An important conclusion that can be drawn from the experimental evaluation is that the proposed multi-clustering fusion method results in a partitioning scheme that fits optimally the specific data set according to some criteria, such as 'sureness', RMSSTD and RS. We used two different basic clustering algorithms and came up with similar clustering results. It can be claimed that the multi-clustering fusion methodology, independently of the basic clustering algorithm used, finds the 'optimal' number and shape of clusters that fit the data, thus

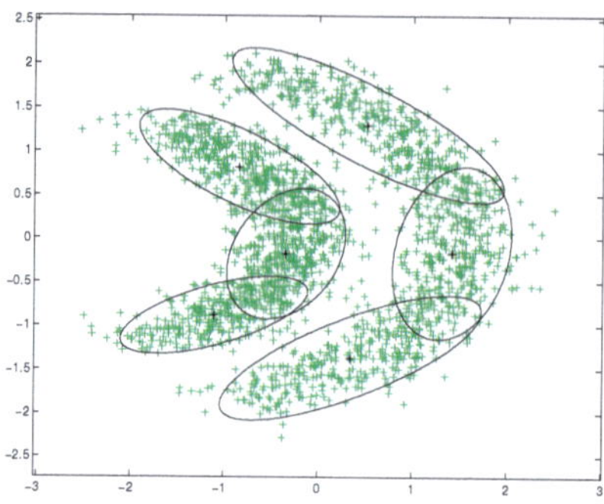

Fig. 7. Means and variances of the kernels using the stand-alone Greedy-EM for the Lith data set.

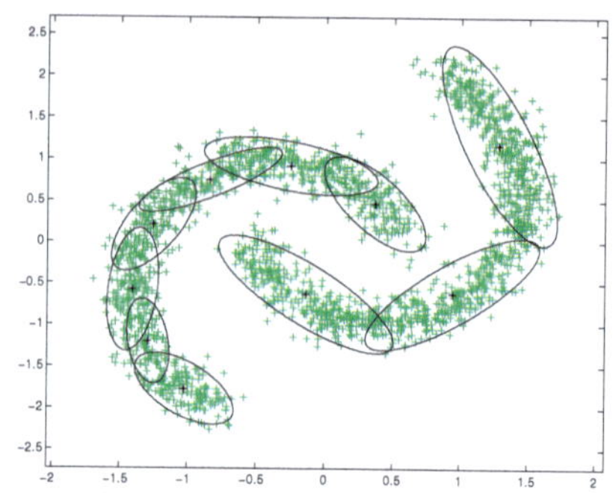

Fig. 8. Means and variances of the kernels using the stand-alone Greedy-EM for the Banana data set.

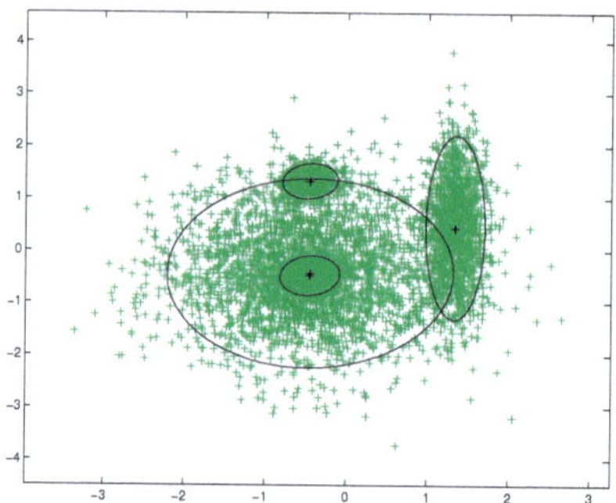

Fig. 9. Means and variances of the kernels using the stand-alone Greedy-EM for the Clouds data set.

dealing with the problem of initialization dependency and selection of the number and shape of clusters.

Another interesting observation is that the proposed multi-clustering fusion method almost always exhibits better clustering performance than the greedy-EM algorithm, according to the adopted cluster validity methods and the term of 'sureness'. However, this comparison should be considered as rather indicative.

4 Conclusions

This paper proposed a general unsupervised learning scheme for combining clustering results produced by several iterations of a basic clustering algorithm. A fusion procedure takes the resulting partition and finds the optimal number of clusters in the data set according to some cluster validity methods. Although the general scheme has been explored here within the framework of K-means and greedy-EM clustering, the data points are typically not uniquely assigned by the fusion procedure to one cluster, so we can also consider 'fuzzy' partitioning.

We have shown that the clustering algorithm implemented in this work can handle the problem of initialization dependency and selection of the number of clusters. Moreover, as illustrated by the experimental results, the algorithm can partition a data set into clusters which are shape independent.

Concluding, the proposed multi-clustering fusion algorithm does not require additional user-specified parameters, since the only parameter needed to be defined is the initial number of clusters. It must be noted, however, that a good value for this parameter was found experimentally depending on the size of the problem. Ongoing work includes the adoption of other basic clustering algorithms and experimentation with different fusion techniques, as well as comparison of the proposed method with other AI clustering methods for selecting the optimal number of clusters. Finally, this multi-clustering methodology can be used for improving the performance of a multi-net classification system, which is based on supervised and unsupervised learning [16].

References

1. A.K. Jain and R.C. Dubes. *Algorithms for Clustering Data.* Englewood Cliffs, N. J.: Prentice Hall, 1988.
2. A.K. Jain, R.P.W. Duin, and J. Mao. Statistical pattern recognition: A review. *IEEE Transactions on Pattern Analysis and Machine Intelligence*, 22(1), 2000.
3. M. Halkidi, Y. Batistakis, and M. Vazirgiannis. Clustering algorithms and validity measures. In *Proceedings of the SSDBM conference*, Virginia,USA, July 2001.
4. J.C. Bezdek and S.K. Pal. *Fuzzy Models for Pattern Recognition: Methods that Search for Structures in Data.* IEEE CS Press, 1992.
5. J.C. Bezdek. *Pattern Recognition with Fuzzy Objective Function Algorithms.* Plenum Press, New York, 1981.
6. A.P. Dempster, N.M. Laird, and D.B. Rubin. Maximum likelihood from incomplete data via the em algorithm. *Roy. Statist. Soc. B*, 39:1–38, 1977.
7. Vlassis N. and Likas A. A greedy-EM algorithm for Gaussian mixture learning. Technical report, Computer Science Institute, University of Amsterdam, The Netherlands, May 2000.
8. E. Boundaillier and G. Hebrail. Interactive interpretation of hierarchical clustering. *Intell. Data Anal.*, 2(3), 1998.
9. A. Fred. Finding Consistent Clusters in Data Partitions. In *Proceedings of the Second International Workshop on Multiple Classifier Systems (MCS 2001)*, LNCS 2096, pages 309–318, Cambridge, UK, July 2-4 2001. Springer.
10. E. Dimitriadou, A. Weingessel, and K. Hornik. A voting-merging clustering algorithm. Working Paper 31, SFB 'Adaptive Information Systems and Modeling in Economics and Management Science', April 1999.
11. P. Smyth. Clustering Using Monte Carlo Cross-Validation. In *Proceedings Knowledge Discovery and Data Mining*, pages 126–133, 1996.
12. P. Cheeseman and J. Stutz. Bayesian Classification (AutoClass): Theory and Results. In Usama M. Fayyad, Gregory Piatetsky-Shapiro, Padhraic Smyth, and Ramasamy Uthurusamy, editors, *Advances in Knowledge Discovery and Data Mining.* AAAI Press/MIT Press, 1996.

13. D.H. Fisher. Knowledge acquisition via incremental conceptual clustering. *Machine Learning*, 2:139–172, 1987.
14. ESPRIT Basic Research Project ELENA (no. 6891). [ftp://ftp.dice.ucl.ac.be/pub/neural-nets/ELENA/databases], 1995.
15. UCI Machine Learning Databases Repository, University of California-Irvine, Department of Information and Computer Science. [ftp://ftp.ics.edu/pub/machine-learning-databases].
16. D.S. Frossyniotis and A. Stafylopatis. A Multi-SVM Classification System. In *Proceedings of the Second International Workshop on Multiple Classifier Systems (MCS 2001)*, LNCS 2096, pages 198–207, Cambridge, UK, July 2-4 2001. Springer.

Distance and Feature-Based Clustering of Time Series: An Application on Neurophysiology

George Potamias[1,2]

[1] Institute of Computer Science, Foundation for Research and Technology – Hellas (FORTH), Vassilika Vouton, P.O. Box 1385, GR-71110, Heraklion, Crete, Greece.
potamias@ics.forth.gr
and
[2] Department of Computer Science, University of Crete, GR-71409, Heraklion, Crete, Greece

Abstract. We present an integrated methodology for the discovery of hidden relations and underlying indicative patterns in time-series collections. The methodology is realized by the smooch integration of: (i) dynamic and qualitative discretization of time-series data, (ii) matching time-series by respective similarity assessment operations, and (iii) a novel hierarchical clustering process, grounded on a graph-theoretic technique, which combines information about the distances between objects and their respective feature-based descriptions. We apply our methodology on in-vivo neuropsychological data targeting the challenging task of patterning brain-developmental events.

1 Introduction

Most data contain time information in an explicit or implicit way. *Time series* organization of data implies time stamping of individual observations. Observations may represent various sequential activities, such as those occurred during brain developmental events, and the respective time-series data acquired via in-vitro or in-vivo neurophysiological experiments [10].

Time series data modelling has been an active area of research in statistics, and a variety of models exist, which manifest interest and provide the interested analyst with analysis tools [4]. Expanding interest in data mining and knowledge discovery has contributed to an increase of research awareness in mining time-series data. Mining tasks referring to *linear precedence* phenomena, i.e., ordering of elements (events) in a sequence as a relation over the time axis, include prediction, characterization, and *clustering* [14].

Clustering of time-series data contributes to the problem of inducing and forming categories (classes) of events. For example the problem of finding trends, seasons and cycles in a sole time-series may be approached by finding *similar* parts (or, segments) of the series itself. Moreover, the identification of time-series coherences could be also approached by the identification of similar ordered sub-sequences between the time-series. During the last years a great-deal of work is devoted on such research aspects [1, 8, 11, 12, 19].

I.P. Vlahavas and C.D. Spyropoulos (Eds.): SETN 2002, LNAI 2308, pp. 237–248, 2002.

In this paper we introduce a data-mining methodology for clustering and identifying coherences between time-series. Coherence refers to data-mining issues related to the assessment of time-series similarity and the discovery of time-series regularities and relations (e.g., causality). The whole endeavour demands and encompasses special operations such as: *transformation*, *matching*, and *clustering* of time-series.

The application domain, the case study and the performed experiments focus on the discovery of indicative and descriptive *patterns* in data from the domain of experimental neurophysiology. The data refer to *protein-synthesis activity* in *developing brain* areas that underlies long-term events, such as changes in *morphology* and *remodelling* [2, 10]. Our study aims to 'uncover' hidden relations and yield insight on the chronological and topographical order of avian brain maturation, providing rules guiding the development of avian brain.

Next section presents the settings of the introduced time-series transformation and matching operations. The time-series mining methodology is integrated with a specially devised graph-theoretic clustering process, presented in section 3. In section 4 we present the specifics of the application domain and the results from the performed experiments. Finally, in the last section we conclude and point to future research and development directions.

2 Transforming and Matching Time Series

Measuring the *similarity* between objects is a crucial issue in many data retrieval and data mining applications. The typical task is to define a function *sim(a,b)*, between two sequences *a* and *b*, which represents how '*similar*' they are to each other. For time-series, the elaboration of such a function is not a trivial task. As it is noted in [1], reliable time-series matching and clustering operations should take in consideration the following operations: (i) ignore small or *not-significant* parts of the series, (ii) translate the *offset* of the series in order to align them vertically, and (iii) *scale* the *amplitude* of the series so that each of the respective segments lie within an envelope of fixed width.

2.1 Qualitative Dynamic Discretization of Time Series

The problems about identifying significant parts in time-series; offset translation and amplitude scaling could be addressed by the intorduction of a *nomilization*-based transformation of time-series. That is, each value of a time-series is transformed into a representative *nominal* value.

In this paper we follow and adjust the *qualitative discrete transformation*- QDT method presented in [13]. The basic idea behind this method is the use of statistical information about the preceding values observed from the series in order to select the discrete value which corresponds to a new continuous value from the series. A new continuous value will be assigned to the same discrete value as its preceding values if the continuous value belongs to the same population (to be decided with the appropriate call on a Student's *t*-statistic computation). Otherwise a static discrete transformation method (see below the *discr* function) will assign a new discrete value to this new continous value. In Figure 1 the QDT method is formally described.

```
Input:
    continuous TS{X};
    significance level t_a;
    number of intervals for discretization s
Discretization:
    v_1 ← discr(X_1)
    init = 1
        for i = 2, ..., n do
        if ((i-ini)) > 1 then
```

$$\hat{X} \leftarrow (\sum_{i=ini}^{i=1} Xj)/(i - ini)$$

$$\hat{\sigma} \leftarrow \sqrt{\frac{\sum_{j=ini}^{i-1} (Xj - \hat{X})^2}{(i - ini) - 1}}$$

$$t_{obs} \leftarrow |Xi - \hat{X}|/\hat{\sigma}^2$$

$$v_i = \begin{Bmatrix} \textbf{discr}\ (Xi) & t_{obs} > t_{a/2} \\ vi - 1 & othrewise \end{Bmatrix}$$

```
        else
            v_i ← discr(X_i)
              if v_{i-1} ≠ v_i then
                  ini = i
Output:
    Discrete TS: {V} = {v_1, ..., v_n}
```

Fig. 1. Time series nominalization: The Qualitative Discrete Transformation - QDT process.

Discrete transformation. The continuous values of a time-series are transformed into s discrete values through s intervals of same length. So, given a time-series X_t over time $t \in \{1, \ldots, n\}$, the discrete value v_i corresponding to a continuous value X_i is an integer from 1 to s computed by:

$$v_i = \textbf{discr}(X_i) = \begin{Bmatrix} s & \textit{if } Xi = max\{ Xt \} \\ [X_i - min\{X_t\})/\mathbf{w}_x] + 1 & otherwise \end{Bmatrix}$$

where,

$$\mathbf{w}_x = \frac{max\ \{X_t\} - min\ \{X_t\}}{s},$$

and *max*, *min* the minimum and maximum values of the series, respectively.

The time-series matching metric. The distance between time-series X_a and X_b, is computed by the distance between their corresponding nominal transforms, V_a and V_b.

$$\boldsymbol{dist}(X_a,X_b) = \boldsymbol{dist}(V_a,V_b) = \frac{\sum_{i=1}^{n} \boldsymbol{distance}\ (v_{a,i},v_{b,i})}{n}$$

where,

$$\boldsymbol{distance}(v_a,v_b) = \begin{cases} 1 & \text{if } v_a \neq v_b \\ 0 & \text{otherwise} \end{cases}$$

3 Graph Theoretic Clustering (GTC)

Having on our disposal two different sources of information, (a) a set of nominalised time-series, and (b) a matrix comprising the distances between the series, the question is how to utilize both of them in order to form a reliable clustering of the series. The problem could be generalised to different kind of objects (other than time-series) and its statement have as follows:

Given:

1. A fully-connected weighted graph, G(V,E), with each node in V representing an object, and each weighted link in E, representing the distance between the linked objects (in our case the nodes are the time-series, and the weight assigned to each of the edges corresponds to the respective time-series distance).
2. A feature-based description of the objects (in our case the description refers to the nominalised time-series transforms).

Find: A clustering of the objects that utilizes both (i) and (ii).

In other words we are confronted with the problem of inventing and forming categories of objects with information coming from different *modalities*, i.e., from distances and from feature-based descriptions of the objects. Towards this end, we elaborate on an innovative *graph-theoretic clustering* – GTC approach which is realised within the following steps.

Step 1. Minimum Spanning Tree (MST)

Given a set *E* of *n* objects, the *minimum spanning tree*- MST of the *fully-connected weighted* graph of the objects is constructed, *mst(E)*; it contain *(n-1)* edges (links).

- A basic characteristic of the MST is that it keeps the shortest distances between the objects. This guarantees that objects lying in 'close areas' in the tree exhibit low distances. So, finding the 'right' cuts of the tree could result in a reliable grouping of the objects. This is a method firstly introduced by Zahn, [18].
- *The Zahn's method and its drawback.* Zahn's MST-based clustering approach takes no advantage of the information provided by the feature-based description of the objects (in our case, the nominalization-based description of the series), a *crucial* source of information for deciding where to cut the formed MST, and

accordingly split the data. The method follows a 'one-shot' partition of the formed MST, i.e., appropriate 'weak' links are identified and cut; the nodes in the separated parts of the MST compose the formed clusters. Because of its 'one-shot' clustering approach the method could not identify special and 'hidden' structures that potentially underlie the data, as for example the potential of a *hierarchical* organization. With this in mind, we devised an *iterative* MST-partitioning process concluding into a *hierarchical clustering* structure. The process is realised within the following steps.

Step 2. Initialize

Set `Clusters = {E}`
`MST`$_{CLUSTERS}$ `= {mst(E)}`

Step 3. CUT[Clusters]

- Compute the *Category Utility*- CU of *Clusters*, `CU(Clusters)`; see below for the specifics of the category utility formula.
- For each `cluster` in `Clusters`, and for all the edges present in the respective `mst(`$G_{cluster}$`)` in `MST`$_{CLUSTERS}$, cut one edge at a time. Cutting an edge results into a *binary split* of each cluster, i.e., its partition into two disjoint sets of nodes (i.e., objects), $G_{cluster,1}$ and , $G_{cluster,2}$; where, $G_{cluster,1} \cup G_{cluster,2} = G_{cluster}$, and $G_{cluster,1} \cap G_{cluster,2} = \emptyset$. For each cluster, a total of `|cluster|-1` binary `splits` could be formed, denoted with: `Splits(cluster)` (`|cluster|` = number of nodes present in the `cluster`).

Step 4. BEST[Splits]

For each cluster in `Clusters`, and for each `split` in `Splits(cluster)`, resulted from step 2, compute :

```
CU(Clusters-split,split)=CU(Clusters-split,Gcluster,1, Gcluster,2)

If    CU(Clusters) <  CU(Clusters-split, split)
then
 Set
 Clusters = {Clusters-split, split}
 MSTClusters = {mst(Clusters-split), mst(Gcluster,1), mst(Gcluster,2)}
 goto  Step 2
else Stop
```

- At each iteration, the GTC procedure search for the best binary split for each of the so-far-formed sub-clusters (note that no MST re-computation is performed for each of the formed sub-clusters). The result is a candidate binary split of the current sub-cluster into two disjoint sets; the best split replaces each of the current sub-clusters.
- The category utility of all so-far-formed clusters- excluding the replaced current cluster, plus the two disjoints sets (i.e., the binary split) of the current cluster, is compared with the category utility of all so-far-formed clusters.

- In the case that the newly formed set of clusters exhibits a higher category utility than the so far formed set of clusters then, it is sub-clustered to its best binary split. Otherwise, it is left unchanged. The whole operation follows a *breath-first* tree growing process, concluding into a *hierarchical clustering* organization of the data.

Category Utility. For the computation and estimation of the utility that each set of clusters exhibits, we rely on the Category Utility formula used in the COBWEB clustering system [9].

$$CU(G1, G2,\ldots, Gg) = \frac{\sum_{k=1}^{g} p(Gk)\left[\left(\sum_i \sum_j p(Ai = Vij/Gk)^2\right) - \left(\sum_i \sum_j p(Ai = Vij)^2\right)\right]}{g}$$

where,

$$p(G_k) = \frac{\#\, examples\_in\_group\_Gk}{Total\_number\_of\_examples},$$

$$p(A_i{=}V_{ij}/G_k) = \frac{\#\, examples\_in\_group\_Gk\_with\_value\_Vij\_for\_feature\_Ai}{\#\, examples\_in\_group\_Gk}$$

$$p(A_i{=}V_{ij}) = \frac{\#\, examples\_with\_value\_Vij\_for\_feature\_Ai}{Total\_number\_of\_Examples}$$

Note 1. The distances between objects, in our case the time-series, may be computed following different methods. For example, a *dynamic time warping* method [2] could be utilized or, other methods like the ones that rely on a *linear piecewise segmentation* and *transformation* of the series (see for example [15]). It could be also the case that the distances are provided by a human itself (i.e., an expert in the application domain).

Note 2. The CU computation is based on the *feature-based description* of the available objects, and deals with the problem of finding the 'best' *distribution* of feature-values in the various formed clusters. On the other hand, the distances between objects could be interpreted as a '*metric-based*' description of the objects, i.e., an information-outsource. In other word the presented clustering method aims to find the '*best fit*' between the two sources of information.

Complexity assessment (preliminary). The overall complexity of the presented iterative clustering approach clustering depends: (i) on the complexity of the category-utility computation, and (ii) on the *depth* of the resulted clustering tree. Denote with F, the number of features; V, the mean number of values per feature, and B the depth of the final clustering tree.

- The category-utility computation needs a time linear to the total number of the feature-values used to represent the data. So, its complexity is ~ $O(F{\times}V)$.
- At the worst case where, the lowest level includes one node for each of the n presented objects we have: $2^B = n$. In order to reach the lowest level, a series of best binary-splits are taking place: 1, 2, 4, …, B-1. Each of the best binary-splits is

found after examining a variable number of potential splits. At the initial node (all n objects belong into the same cluster) a total of $(n-1) = 2^0(n-1)$ cuts of the minimum spanning tree should be evaluated. Assume that each best binary split results into an equal number of objects in the two formed sub-clusters. Then, at the second level we need a total of $2x(2((n-1)/2)) = 2^1x(2^1((n-1)/2^1)) = 2^1(n-1)$ comparisons; at the third level $2^2x(2^2((n-1)/2^2)) = 2^2(n-1)$, and so on. Finally, at level $B-1$ (in order to reach the final level B), a total of $2^{B-1}(n-1)$ splits are examined. So, a total of $(n-1)(1+2^1+2^2+2^3+ \ldots + 2^{B-1}) = (n-1)(2^B-1) = (n-1)^2$ category-utility computations should be performed.

So, in the worst case the GTC-based clustering operation exhibits a complexity of $\sim O(n^2 \times F \times V)$.

4 Application Domain and Experiments

The adult brain is composed of a complex network of fibers interconnecting functional structures, the brain nuclei, lamina of neurons and their connections, which are formed progressively during ontogeny. Brain development is characterized by a series of events that include cell proliferation and migration, growth of axons and dendrites, formation of functional connections and synapses, cell death, myelination of axons and refinement of neuronal specificity [10]. Knowledge of the underlying mechanisms that govern these complex processes and the study of histogenesis and neural plasticity during brain development are critical for the understanding of the function of normal or injured brain.

Biosynthetic activity, such as *protein synthesis*, underlies these long-term effects in the developing brain that involve changes in morphology and remodeling [16] Therefore, the history of in vivo protein synthesis activity of specific brain areas could yield insight on their pattern of maturation and reveal relationships between distantly located structures. Furthermore, the spatial and temporal developmental brain protein synthesis profile would yield information on neuronal interrelations and therefore suggest different roles of the topographically organized brain structures in the maturation processes.

Data. The late embryonic development of avian brain was selected for this study, since chick embryo is the ideal organism for developmental studies. We used the time course of protein synthesis activity of individual brain areas as a model to correlate critical periods during development. The aim is to extract critical-relationships that possibly govern the normal ontogenic processes.

For the determination of the biosynthetic activity, the *in vivo* auto-radiographic method of carboxyl labeled L-Leucine was used [6, 17], as an essential amino acid present in most proteins. The experimental data for the present study concern 30 experimental animals (chick embryos) at different developmental stages.

The late embryonic development between day 11 (E11) and day 19 (E19) as well as the post-hatching day 1 (P1) was studied. The specific stages were selected because it is known that during that time proliferation of neurons has ceased [5] and cell growth, differentiation, migration and death, axon elongation, refinement of connections, and establishment of functional neuronal networks occurs.

A total of 49 *brain-areas* were identified and accordingly measured using an image analysis system (see Figure 3, for the distribution of these areas in the brain). For each area, the means over all chicks were recorded. The final outcome is a set of 49 time-series in a time-span of 6 points (i.e., the 5 embryonic days and one post-hatching day).

4.1 Experimental Results

We applied the presented time-series matching, and GTC clustering algorithm on the brain-development (protein-synthesis) time-series data, aiming to extract the critical relationships that possibly govern the normal ontogenetic processes. A total of three-(3) clusters were identified.

The clusters and the brain-areas included in each of them are shown in Table 1. The biosynthetic activities of each cluster's brain-areas- over the stamped developmental ages, exhibit no statistical-significant deviation from the respective mean of the cluster. So, the mean of each cluster offers an *indicative* and *representative* model for the developmental-pattern underlying the clustered areas. The plots of the discovered clusters' means as well as the respective minimum spanning tree are shown in Figure 2 at the next page.

Table 1. The induced brain-areas clusters.

Cluster	# Objects	Brain Arears
c1 ○	13	CA, CP, E, FPLa, LC, LPO, Mld ,PL, PT, SP, Spi, TPc, VeM
c2 ▲	20	Ac, CDL, DL, FPLp, GLv, IO, MM, N, NI, OcM, Ov, Rt, SM, Slu, Tov, nBOR, Loc, PA, PM, RPO
c3 ■	16	AM, Ad, Bas, Cpi, DM, GCt, HV, Hip, Co, POM, SL, Tn, Lli, PP, Imc, SCA

A straightforward interpretation of these plots could be summarised into the following observations:

- Cluster-1 (c1): *'E11-E17_decreasing'* and *'E17_P1_increasing'* patterns; these areas mature at the late stages, i.e., near the post-hatching day; while potential *neuronal-death* and/or *migration* of the cells take place at the early stages.
- Cluster-2 (c2): *'continuous-decreasing'* – protein-synthetic activity in these areas is steadily decreasing, indicating their early formation and therefore their important role in brain development.
- Cluster-3 (c3): *'continuous-increasing'* pattern; these areas are steadily increasing their activity during the whole brain developmental period suggesting that they are involved in *late* ontogenetic events.

Biomedical Discussion and Interpretation. Determination of the local values of leucine incorporation indicates the protein-synthesis activity that underlies long-term events in the developing brain regions [6]. Some of the open issues in ontogenetic events such us, changes in the cytoarchitecture (growth of axons and dendrites, myelination of axons) and remodeling (formation and refinement of functional connections and synapses, cell death) of the brain [10], could be addressed by the examination of the recorded protein-synthesis time-stamped events. Indeed, chronological mapping of the local cerebral protein-synthesis provides a reliable model for them.

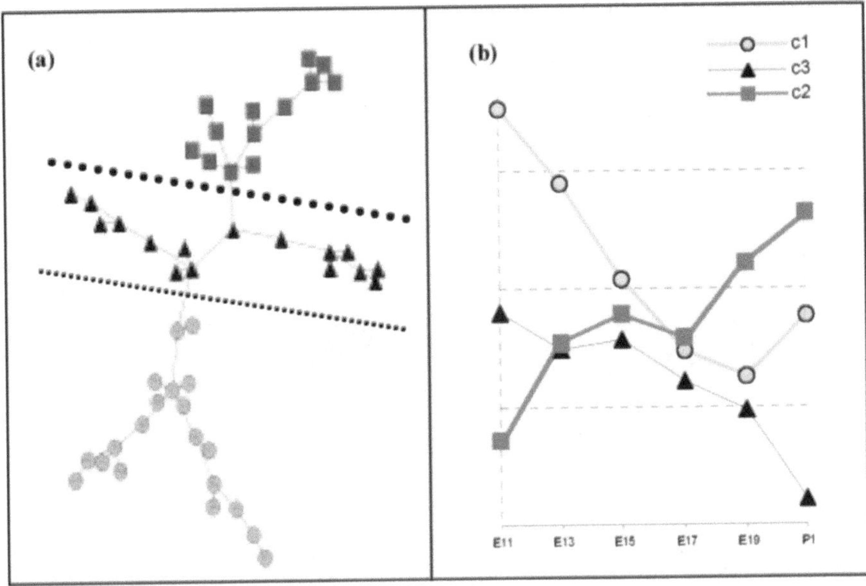

Fig. 2. (a) The minimum spanning tree resulted from the computed time-series distances; the different shapes of the nodes denote the formed sub-clusters, (b) The plots of the clustered brain-areas means (i.e., the means of the original time-series on each of the stamped developmental ages).

Our results indicate that at the stages studied, the revealed developmental patterns follow an <u>*area specific*</u> model rather than a general spatial (caudal to rostral or medial to lateral) model. Previous theories of brain development suggested that its histological maturation followed a caudal to rostral sequence [10]. Our data suggest that the *observed ontogenetic patterns depend on the neuronal specificity of the brain region.*

- Specifically, *somatosensory* and *motor* related brain areas and white matter regions are grouped together in Cluster 3, showing a more-or-less constant increase in protein synthesis (see Figure 2 above). This result possibly reflects the *myelination* process and the motor activity observed in late developmental stages.

- Moreover, most second order *sensory* and *limbic* areas (see [7]) are grouped in Clusters 1, and 2 (see Figure 2), respectively. These clusters exhibit a decline in protein synthesis rates, suggesting that *cell death* or *cell displacement* due to *migration* represent a common phenomenon in many brain regions under development.

Hierarchical structure. Although, sensory and limbic areas follow a common pattern of biosynthetic activity, their activities differ significantly at post-hatching life. The resulted clustering was able to identify this difference. See Figure 3 below where, clusters c1 and c2 are sub-clusters of the same upper-level cluster. This results, demonstrates the utility of the followed *iterative clustering* operation, and reveals the *hierarchical* structure 'hidden' in the data. In particular, it is known that leucine incorporation is further decreased in most of the limbic areas (grouped in Cluster 2) in post-hatching life. The *second order sensory* areas were grouped in Cluster 1, and increase their activity after birth when it is known that they receive sensory inputs.

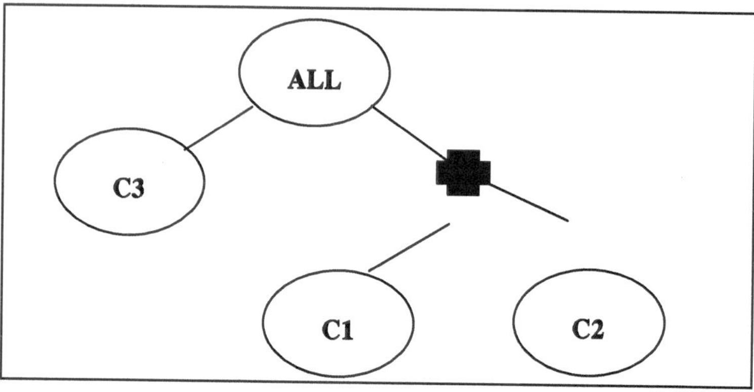

Fig. 3. The induced hierarchical clustering-tree for the specified brain-areas; the tree is indicative of a hierarchical organization of the brain-areas with respect to their developmental activities, i.e., areas in clusters 1 and 2 exhibit 'similar' developmental patterns.

The introduced time-series mining methodology, and the respective analysis on the history of in vivo protein synthesis activity of specific brain areas, yields insight on their maturation patterns and reveal relationships between distantly located structures. Moreover, our study contribute to the identification of common origin of brain structures and provide possible homologies in the mammalian brain, since the concept of homology also implies the existence of identifiable population during embryogenesis.

5 Conclusions and Future Work

We have presented a data-mining methodology for discovering critical-patterns and relations between time-series. The methodology is realized by the smooch integration of: (i) dynamic and qualitative discretization of time-series data, (ii) matching time-series and similarity assessment, and (iii) a novel hierarchical clustering process, grounded on a graph-theoretic technique (GTC). The novelty of the clustering approach relies on the fact that it utilizes and combines information from two different sources: 'metric-based' distance measures between the objects to cluster, and feature-based (mostly 'nominal') descriptions of them.

The aim of the neurophysiology study was to explore quantitative and automatic procedures for the comparison and discussion of functional neurophysiological data and in this way to pave the road for objective meta-analyses. The long-term goal is a tool, which can assist the neuroscientist in quantifying and reporting the information content of a study with respect to the accumulated body of neuroscience.

The presented time-series mining methodology provides easily interpretable and reliable results that uncover hidden and crucial patterns in the course of the brain developmental activities. With the followed iterative-clustering approach we were able to uncover and reveal the hierarchical organization of the events that take place in the developing brain.

Our immediate research plans are moving towards two directions: (a) inclusion in the overall methodology of additional formulas and procedures for computing the distance between time-series, and (b) experimentation on other application domains in order to validate the approach and examine its scalability to huge collections of time-series- initial experiments on economic time-series are already in progress with encouraging preliminary results.

Acknowledgement. Special thanks to Dr. Cathrin Dermon, head of the Neurobiology laboratory, Dept. of Biology, University of Crete, for the provision of the biomedical background material and the respective neurophysiology data, as well as for the interpretation and discussion on the results.

References

1. Agrawal, R., Lin, K., Sawhney, H.S., and Shim, K., Fast Similarity Search in the Presence of Noise, Scaling, and Translation in Time-Series Databases. *Proc. 21st VLDB Conf.* Zurich, Switzerland, 490-501 (1995).
2. Berndt, D. J., and Clifford, J. Using dynamic time warping to find patterns in time series. *In Working Notes of the Knowledge Discovery in Databases* Workshop, 359-370, (1994).
3. Bodeutsch, N., Siebert, H., Dermon, C.R., and Thanos S., Unilateral injury to the adult rat optic nerve causes multiple cellular responses in the contra lateral site. *J. Neurobiol.*, 38, 116-128 (1998).
4. Box, G.E.P., and Jenkins, G.M. *Time Series Analysis, Forecasting and Control.* Prentice Hall (1976).
5. Cowan W.M., Adamson L. and Powell T.P.S., An experimental study of the avian visual system. *J. Anatomy* 95: 545-563 (1981).
6. Dermon, C.R., Deibler, G.E., Jehle, J., L. Sokoloff, and Smith, C.B., Local cerebral protein synthesis in the regenerating hypoglossal nucleus in euthyroid and hyperthyroid rats. *Society for Neuroscience, 23th Annual Meeting.* Washington, USA, abstr. 543.3, 1314 (1993).
7. Dermon C.R., Stamatakis A., Tlemcani O., and Balthazart, J., Performance of appetitive or consummatory components of male sexual behavior is mediated by different brain areas: A 2-deoxyglucose autoradiographic study. *Neuroscience*, 94, 1261-1277 (1999).

8. Faloutsos, C., Ranganathan, M., and Manolopoulos, Y., Fast Sequence Matching in Time-Series Databases. Proc. *SIGMOD'94* (1994).
9. Fisher, D. Knowledge Acquisition Via Incremental Conceptual Clustering. *Machine Learning*, 2, 139-172. (1987).
10. Jacobson, S. *Histogenesis and morphogenesis of cortical structures in the developmental neurobiology.* Plenum Press., 401-451 (1991).
11. Jagadish, H., Mendelzon, A., and Milo, T., Similarity-Based Queries. *Proc. 14th Symp. on Principles of Database Systems* (*PODS'95*). 36-45 (1995).
12. Laird, P., Identifying and using patterns in sequential data. In: Jantke, K., Kobayashi, S., Tomita, E., and Yokomori, T. (Eds), *Algorithmic Learning Theory, 4th International Workshop*, Berlin: Springer Verlag, 1-18, (1993).
13. Lopez, L.M., Ruiz I.F., Bueno, R.M., and Ruiz, F.T. Dynamic Discretization of Continuous Values from Time Series. In Ramon Lopez de Mantaras and Enric Plaza (eds) Proceedings of the *11th European Conference on Machine Learning (ECML 2000)*, Catalonia, Spain, 280-291, May/June 2000.
14. Morik K., The Representation Race – Pre-processing for Handling Time Phenomena. *Proc. European Conference on Machine Learning (ECML).* Springer Verlag (2000).
15. Potamias, G, and Dermon, C. Patterning Brain Developmental Events via the Discovery of Time-Series Coherences. In G. Papadourakis (Ed.), Proceedings of *4th International Conference on Neural Networks and Expert Systems in Medicine and Healthcare*, 281-287, June 20-22, 2001, Milos, Greece, (2001).
16. Sokoloff L. and Smith B.B., Basic principles underlying radioisotopic methods for assay of biomedical processes in vivo, in Tracer Kinetics and Physiologic Modeling Eds. Lambrecht r.M. and Reseigno A., Springer-Verlag pp. 202-234 (1983).
17. Stamatakis A., Balthazart, J., and Dermon, C.R. Sex differences in local cerebral protein synthesis activity in quail as revealed by the in vivo autoradiographic ^{14}C-leucine method. *It. J. Anat. Embryol*, 101, 207-210 (1996).
18. Zahn, C.T. Graph-Theoretical Methods for Detecting and Describing Gestalt Clusters. IEEE Transactions on Computers, 20, 68-86, (1971).
19. Wang, J., Chrin, G.-W., Marr, T., Shapiro, B, Shasha, D., and Zhang, K. Combinatorial patterns discovery for scientific data: Some preliminary results. In: Snodgrass, R., and Winslett, M. (Eds), *Proc. ACM SIGMOD Conference on Management of Data* (*SIGMOD'94*), MI, USA, 115-125 (1994).

Least-Squares Methods in Reinforcement Learning for Control

Michail G. Lagoudakis[1], Ronald Parr[1], and Michael L. Littman[2]

[1] Department of Computer Science, Duke University, Durham, NC 27708, U.S.A.
{mgl,parr}@cs.duke.edu
[2] Shannon Laboratory, AT&T Labs – Research, Florham Park, NJ 07932, U.S.A.
mlittman@research.att.com

Abstract. Least-squares methods have been successfully used for prediction problems in the context of reinforcement learning, but little has been done in extending these methods to control problems. This paper presents an overview of our research efforts in using least-squares techniques for control. In our early attempts, we considered a direct extension of the Least-Squares Temporal Difference (LSTD) algorithm in the spirit of Q-learning. Later, an effort to remedy some limitations of this algorithm (approximation bias, poor sample utilization) led to the Least-Squares Policy Iteration (LSPI) algorithm, which is a form of model-free approximate policy iteration and makes efficient use of training samples collected in any arbitrary manner. The algorithms are demonstrated on a variety of learning domains, including algorithm selection, inverted pendulum balancing, bicycle balancing and riding, multiagent learning in factored domains, and, recently, on two-player zero-sum Markov games and the game of Tetris.

1 Introduction

Linear least-squares methods have been successfully used for prediction problems in the context of reinforcement learning. Although these methods lack the generalization ability of "black box" methods such as neural networks, they are much easier to implement and debug. It is also easier to understand why a linear method succeeds or fails, to quantify the importance of each basis feature, and to engineer these features for better performance. For example, the *Least Squares Temporal Difference* learning algorithm (LSTD) [2] makes efficient use of data and converges faster than conventional temporal difference learning methods.

Unfortunately, little has been done in extending these methods to control problems. Using LSTD directly as part of a policy iteration algorithm can be problematic, as was shown by Koller and Parr [6]. This failure is partly due to the fact that LSTD approximations are biased by the stationary distribution of the underlying Markov chain. However, even if this problem is solved, the state value function that LSTD learns is of no use for policy improvement since a model of the process is not available, in general, for learning control problems.

I.P. Vlahavas and C.D. Spyropoulos (Eds.): SETN 2002, LNAI 2308, pp. 249–260, 2002.

This paper is an overview of our research efforts in using least-squares techniques for learning control problems. First, we consider *Least-Squares Q-learning* (LSQL), an extension of LSTD that learns a state-action value function (instead of a state value function) in the spirit of Q-learning. Then, we present the *Least-Squares Policy Iteration* (LSPI) algorithm which is a form of model-free approximate policy iteration and resolves some limitations of LSQL (approximation bias, poor sample utilization). The algorithms were tested and produced excellent results on a variety of learning domains, including algorithm selection, inverted pendulum balancing, bicycle balancing and riding, and multiagent learning in factored domains. Currently, LSPI is being tested on the game of Tetris and on two-player zero-sum Markov games.

2 MDPs and Reinforcement Learning

We assume that the underlying control problem is a *Markov Decision Process* (MDP). An MDP is defined as a 4-tuple $(\mathcal{S}, \mathcal{A}, P, R)$, where: $\mathcal{S} = \{s_1, s_2, ..., s_n\}$ is a finite set of states; $\mathcal{A} = \{a_1, a_2, ..., a_m\}$ is a finite set of actions; P is a Markovian state transition model — $P(s, a, s')$ is the probability of making a transition to state s' when taking action a in state s ($s \xrightarrow{a} s'$); and, R is a reward (or cost) function — $R(s, a, s')$ is the reward for the transition $s \xrightarrow{a} s'$.

We assume that the MDP has an infinite horizon and that future rewards are discounted exponentially with a discount factor $\gamma \in [0, 1)$. Assuming that all policies are proper, i.e. that all episodes eventually terminate, our results generalize to the undiscounted case as well.

A *deterministic policy* π for an MDP is a mapping $\pi : \mathcal{S} \mapsto \mathcal{A}$, where $\pi(s)$ is the action the agent takes at state s. The *state-action value function* $Q^\pi(s, a)$, defined over all possible combinations of states and actions, indicates the expected, discounted, total reward when taking action a in state s and following policy π thereafter. The exact Q-values for all state-action pairs can be found by solving the linear system of the Bellman equations :

$$Q^\pi(s, a) = \mathcal{R}(s, a) + \gamma \sum_{s'} P(s, a, s') Q^\pi(s', \pi(s')) \qquad \text{or} \qquad Q^\pi = \mathcal{R} + \gamma \mathbf{P}^\pi Q^\pi ,$$

where Q^π and $\mathcal{R}$ are vectors of size $|\mathcal{S}||\mathcal{A}|$ and $\mathbf{P}^\pi$ is a stochastic matrix of size $(|\mathcal{S}||\mathcal{A}| \times |\mathcal{S}||\mathcal{A}|)$. $\mathcal{R}$ is the expected reward for state-action pairs, $\mathcal{R}(s, a) = \sum_{s'} P(s, a, s') R(s, a, s')$, and $\mathbf{P}^\pi$ describes the probability of transitions from pairs (s, a) to pairs $(s', \pi(s'))$.

For every MDP, there exists a deterministic *optimal policy*, π^*, not necessarily unique, which maximizes the expected, discounted return of every state. The state-action value function Q^{π^*} of an optimal policy is the fixed point of the non-linear Bellman optimality equations:

$$Q^{\pi^*}(s, a) = \mathcal{R}(s, a) + \gamma \max_{a'} \sum_{s'} P(s, a, s') Q^{\pi^*}(s', a') .$$

Value Iteration is a method of approximating the Q^{π^*} values arbitrarily closely by iterating the equations above (similar to the Gauss iteration for linear systems). If Q^{π^*} is known, the optimal policy can be constructed simply by finding the maximizing action in each state, $\pi^*(s) = \max_a Q^{\pi^*}(s,a)$. *Policy Iteration* is another method of discovering an optimal policy by iterating through a sequence of monotonically improving policies. Each iteration consists of two phases: *Value Determination* computes the value function for a policy $\pi^{(t)}$ by solving the linear Bellman equations, and *Policy Improvement* defines the next policy as $\pi^{(t+1)}(s) = \arg\max_a Q^{\pi^{(t)}}(s,a)$. These steps are repeated until convergence to an optimal policy, often in a surprisingly small number of steps.

In the absence of a model of the MDP, that is, when P and $\mathcal{R}$ are unknown, the decision maker has to learn the optimal policy through interaction with the environment. Knowledge comes in the form of samples (s,a,r,s'), where s is a state of the process, a is the action taken in s, r is the reward received, and s' is the resulting state. Samples can be collected from actual (sequential) episodes or from queries to a generative model of the MDP. In the extreme case, they can be experiences of other agents on the same MDP. The class of problems that fall under this framework is known as *Reinforcement Learning* (RL) [5,15,1].

Q-learning [17] is a popular algorithm that stochastically approximates Q^{π^*}. It starts with any arbitrary initial guess $\widehat{Q}^{(0)}$ for for the values of Q^{π^*}. For each sample (s,a,r,s') considered, Q-learning makes the update

$$\widehat{Q}^{(t+1)}(s,a) = (1-\alpha)\widehat{Q}^{(t)}(s,a) + \alpha\left[r + \max_{a'}\left\{\widehat{Q}^{(t)}(s',a')\right\}\right] ,$$

where $\alpha \in (0,1]$ is the learning rate. Under certain conditions (e.g., infinitely many samples for each state-action pair, appropriately decreasing learning rate), $\widehat{Q}$ is guaranteed to converge to Q^{π^*}.

3 Least-Squares Methods in Reinforcement Learning

3.1 Least-Squares Approximation of Q Functions

Q functions can be stored in tables of size $|\mathcal{S}||\mathcal{A}|$ for small MDPs. This is, however, impractical for large state and action spaces. In such cases, it is common to approximate Q^π with a parametric function approximator by setting the parameters to a set of values that maximizes the accuracy of the approximator. A common class of approximators, known as *linear architectures*, approximate a value function as a linear combination of k basis functions (features):

$$\widehat{Q}^\pi(s,a,w) = \sum_{i=1}^{k} \phi_i(s,a)w_i = \phi(s,a)^\intercal w ,$$

where w is a set of weights (parameters), and, in general, $k << |\mathcal{S}||\mathcal{A}|$. Let $\boldsymbol{\Phi}$ be the $(|\mathcal{S}||\mathcal{A}| \times k)$ matrix, where row i is the vector $\phi_i(s,a)^\intercal$. We are interested in finding a set of weights w^π that yields a fixed point in value function space, that is, a value function $\widehat{Q}^\pi = \boldsymbol{\Phi} w^\pi$ that is invariant under one step of value determination followed by orthogonal projection to the space spanned by the basis functions. In particular, under the assumption that the columns of $\boldsymbol{\Phi}$ are independent, we require that

$$\boldsymbol{\Phi}(\boldsymbol{\Phi}^\intercal\boldsymbol{\Phi})^{-1}\boldsymbol{\Phi}^\intercal(\mathcal{R} + \gamma\mathbf{P}^\pi\boldsymbol{\Phi}w^\pi) = \boldsymbol{\Phi}w^\pi \implies \boldsymbol{\Phi}^\intercal(\boldsymbol{\Phi} - \gamma\mathbf{P}^\pi\boldsymbol{\Phi})w^\pi = \boldsymbol{\Phi}^\intercal\mathcal{R} \implies \mathbf{A}w^\pi = b ,$$

where $\mathbf{A} = \boldsymbol{\Phi}^\intercal(\boldsymbol{\Phi} - \gamma \mathbf{P}^\pi \boldsymbol{\Phi})$ is a square matrix of size $k \times k$, and $b = \boldsymbol{\Phi}^\intercal \mathcal{R}$. The solution of the system, $w^\pi = \mathbf{A}^{-1} b$, yields the desired set of weights. We note that this is also the standard fixed point approximation method used in the LSTD algorithm with the exception that the problem here is formulated in terms of Q values instead of state values. For any $\mathbf{P}^\pi$, a unique solution is guaranteed to exist for all but finitely many values of γ [6].

3.2 LSQ: Learning the State-Action Value Function

When the model $(\mathcal{R}, \mathbf{P}^\pi)$ of the underlying MDP is not available, $\mathbf{A}$ and b cannot be determined *a priori*, but they can be approximated using samples. Recall that $\boldsymbol{\Phi}$, $\mathbf{P}^\pi \boldsymbol{\Phi}$, and $\mathcal{R}$ are of the form

$$\boldsymbol{\Phi} = \begin{pmatrix} \phi(s_1, a_1)^\intercal \\ \cdots \\ \phi(s, a)^\intercal \\ \cdots \\ \phi(s_{|\mathcal{S}|}, a_{|\mathcal{A}|})^\intercal \end{pmatrix} \quad \mathbf{P}^\pi \boldsymbol{\Phi} = \begin{pmatrix} \sum_{s'} P(s_1, a_1, s') \phi(s', \pi(s'))^\intercal \\ \cdots \\ \sum_{s'} P(s, a, s') \phi(s', \pi(s'))^\intercal \\ \cdots \\ \sum_{s'} P(s_{|\mathcal{S}|}, a_{|\mathcal{A}|}, s') \phi(s', \pi(s'))^\intercal \end{pmatrix} \quad \mathcal{R} = \begin{pmatrix} \sum_{s'} P(s_1, a_1, s') R(s_1, a_1, s') \\ \cdots \\ \sum_{s'} P(s, a, s') R(s, a, s') \\ \cdots \\ \sum_{s'} P(s_{|\mathcal{S}|}, a_{|\mathcal{A}|}, s') R(s_{|\mathcal{S}|}, a_{|\mathcal{A}|}, s') \end{pmatrix}$$

Given a set of samples, $D = \{(s_{d_i}, a_{d_i}, r_{d_i}, s'_{d_i}) \mid i = 1, 2, \ldots, L\}$, we can construct approximate versions of $\boldsymbol{\Phi}$, $\mathbf{P}^\pi \boldsymbol{\Phi}$, and $\mathcal{R}$ as follows :

$$\widehat{\boldsymbol{\Phi}} = \begin{pmatrix} \phi(s_{d_1}, a_{d_1})^\intercal \\ \cdots \\ \phi(s_{d_i}, a_{d_i})^\intercal \\ \cdots \\ \phi(s_{d_L}, a_{d_L})^\intercal \end{pmatrix} \qquad \widehat{\mathbf{P}^\pi \boldsymbol{\Phi}} = \begin{pmatrix} \phi(s'_{d_1}, \pi(s'_{d_1}))^\intercal \\ \cdots \\ \phi(s'_{d_i}, \pi(s'_{d_i}))^\intercal \\ \cdots \\ \phi(s'_{d_L}, \pi(s'_{d_L}))^\intercal \end{pmatrix} \qquad \widehat{\mathcal{R}} = \begin{pmatrix} r_{d_1} \\ \cdots \\ r_{d_i} \\ \cdots \\ r_{d_L} \end{pmatrix}$$

These approximations can be thought of as first sampling rows from $\boldsymbol{\Phi}$ and then, conditioned on these samples, as sampling terms from the summations in the corresponding rows of $\mathbf{P}^\pi \boldsymbol{\Phi}$ and $\mathcal{R}$. The sampling distribution from the summations is governed by the underlying dynamics $(P(s, a, s'))$ of the process as the samples in D are taken directly from the MDP. Therefore, $\mathbf{A}$ and b can be approximated as

$$\widehat{\mathbf{A}} = \widehat{\boldsymbol{\Phi}}^\intercal (\widehat{\boldsymbol{\Phi}} - \gamma \widehat{\mathbf{P}^\pi \boldsymbol{\Phi}}) \qquad \text{and} \qquad \widehat{b} = \widehat{\boldsymbol{\Phi}}^\intercal \widehat{\mathcal{R}} .$$

These equations lead to an incremental update rule for $\widehat{\mathbf{A}}$ and $\widehat{b}$. Assume that initially $\widehat{\mathbf{A}} = 0$ and $\widehat{b} = 0$. For a fixed policy π, a sample (s, a, r, s') contributes to the approximation according to the following update equation :

$$\widehat{\mathbf{A}} \leftarrow \widehat{\mathbf{A}} + \phi(s, a)\Big(\phi(s, a) - \gamma \phi(s', \pi(s'))\Big)^\intercal \qquad \text{and} \qquad \widehat{b} \leftarrow \widehat{b} + \phi(s, a) r .$$

With uniformly distributed samples over pairs of states and actions (s, a), the approximations $\widehat{\mathbf{A}}$ and $\widehat{b}$ are consistent approximations of the true $\mathbf{A}$ and b (scaled by a constant) and the solution $\widehat{w}^\pi$ will converge to the true solution w^π.

We call this algorithm LSQ [7] due to its similarity to LSTD. LSQ learns the state-action value function of a fixed policy. However, unlike LSTD, it computes Q functions and does not expect the data to come from any particular Markov chain. LSQ can use the same set of samples to compute Q values for any policy. The policy merely determines which $\phi(s', \pi(s'))$ is added to $\widehat{\mathbf{A}}$ for each sample.

3.3 LSQL: Least-Squares Q-Learning

In our early work [8,9] we proposed a direct extension of LSQ to control problems in the spirit of Q-learning. Recall that Q-learning uses the current approximation to derive an estimate of the (maximum) value of the resulting state. Applying the same idea to modify LSQ, we arrived at the following update equations for any sample (s, a, r, s'):

$$\widehat{\mathbf{A}}^{(t+1)} \leftarrow \mu\widehat{\mathbf{A}}^{(t)} + \phi(s,a)\phi(s,a)^{\mathsf{T}} \;, \quad \widehat{b}^{(t+1)} \leftarrow \mu\widehat{b}^{(t)} + \phi(s,a)\Big(r + \gamma \max_{a'} \phi(s',a')^{\mathsf{T}} w^{(t)}\Big) \;.$$

The weight vector $w^{(t)}$ at each step t is the solution of the system $\widehat{\mathbf{A}}^{(t)} w^{(t)} = \widehat{b}^{(t)}$. Essentially, the nonlinear term introduced by the maximization operator is explicitly computed using the current estimates and becomes part of the right hand side of the system. Unlike Q-learning, the effect of a sample does not fade out because of the absence of a learning rate. The parameter $\mu \in (0, 1]$ is an exponential windowing factor and is used to discount the oldest, and thus most inaccurate, entries in $\widehat{\mathbf{A}}$ and $\widehat{b}$.

Although LSQL is a reasonable and intuitive extension, it has some limitations. The use of the current estimates introduces significant bias in the approximation, especially in the early steps when the estimates are inaccurate. Also, samples are not used so efficiently since they are discarded after one use. Even if they were stored and reused, numerous passes are required before the inaccurate information entered early in the matrices is replaced by more accurate estimates.

3.4 LSPI: Least-Squares Policy Iteration

LSQ does not suffer from the problems of LSQL because its equations are strictly linear, however it can learn value functions for fixed policies only. Thus, LSQ can be integrated into an approximate policy iteration procedure (performing the value determination step) for solving learning control problems . This is the key insight behind the Least-Squares Policy Iteration (LSPI) algorithm [7]. Note that this is not the same as using LSTD in a policy iteration algorithm. LSQ approximations are not biased by the stationary distribution, since samples can be collected arbitrarily and their distribution can be potentially controlled. More importantly, the policy improvement step of the policy iteration can be realized automatically without ever explicitly representing the policy and without any sort of model. Since LSQ computes Q functions, the improved policy $\pi^{(t+1)}$ is simply the greedy policy over the Q function learned in the previous iteration:

$$\pi^{(t+1)}(s) = \arg\max_a \widehat{Q}^{\pi^{(t)}}(s,a) = \arg\max_a \phi(s,a)^{\mathsf{T}} w^{\pi^{(t)}} \;.$$

In this sense the improved (greedy) policy is represented implicitly by a finite set of parameters ($w^{\pi^{(t)}}$) and can be determined on demand for any given state as shown above. To close the loop, we require that LSQ performs this maximization to find $\pi^{(t)}(s')$ for each s' in the data set when constructing the $\widehat{\mathbf{A}}$ matrix for a policy $\pi^{(t)}$. The LSPI algorithm is summarized in Figure 1.

```
LSPI (k, φ, γ, ε, π0, D0)

    // k  : Number of basis functions
    // φ  : Basis functions
    // γ  : Discount factor
    // ε  : Stopping criterion
    // π0 : Initial policy, given as w0 (default: w0 = 0)
    // D0 : Initial set of training samples, possibly empty

    D = D0
    π' = π0          // In essence, w' = w0

    repeat
        Update D (optional)          // Add/remove samples, or leave unchanged
        π = π'                       // w = w'
        π' = LSQ (D, k, φ, γ, π)     // w' = LSQ (D, k, φ, γ, w)
    until (π ≈ π')                   // that is, (||w − w'|| < ε)

    return π                         // return w
```

Fig. 1. The LSPI algorithm.

4 Experimental Results

4.1 Algorithm Selection

Algorithm selection [13] is the following decision problem: given a set of algorithms for a problem, dynamically choose the best algorithm for any instance of the problem, i.e. the algorithm that minimizes the expected total execution time on a target machine. The problem becomes more challenging with recursive algorithms in the set. A sub-instance generated during a recursive call gives rise to a new algorithm selection problem; any algorithm in the set can be chosen to solve it. We call this sequential decision problem *recursive algorithm selection* [8], since the entire sequence (or tree) of decisions has to be optimized. Uncertainty in algorithm selection stems from the input distribution, the inner workings of the algorithms (e.g. randomized algorithms), and the hardware characteristics.

We can formulate the problem as a kind of MDP. The state of the process consists of a set of instance features, such as problem size. The actions are the different algorithms we can choose from. Non-recursive algorithms are terminal in that they solve the instance completely (terminal state). Recursive algorithms create subinstances and therefore cause (non-deterministic) transitions to other states. The immediate cost of a decision is the real time taken for executing the selected algorithm on the current instance, excluding time taken in recursive calls. Thus, the total (undiscounted) cost during an episode is the total time taken to solve that particular instance. The goal is to find a policy that minimizes the expected total cost/time. This process differs from a standard MDP in that it allows one-to-many state transitions (multiple recursive calls at one level).

We used LSQL to learn good policies for the following problems: order-statistic selection [8], sorting [8], and branching in satisfiability [9]. For sorting, we combined InsertionSort and QuickSort using the array size n as the only state feature. The linear approximator included a block of three terms (n, $n \log_2 n$, and

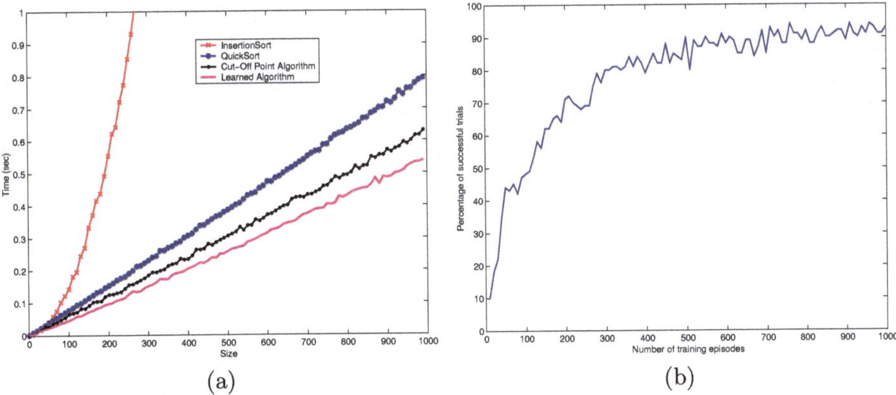

(a) (b)

Fig. 2. Results on: (a) algorithm selection for sorting; (b) the inverted pendulum.

n^2) repeated for each action, thus a total of six basis functions. In effect, each action had its own separate set of weights over the same set of basis functions. After training, the learned policy was tested against the individual algorithms and against an empirical cut-off point algorithm. Averaged results are shown in Figure 2 (a). For sorting, in particular, it is easy to derive the transition model and use a model-based approach to obtain even better selection policies [10].

For satisfiability, we considered the problem of selecting among seven heuristic branching rules at each branching point of a DPLL procedure for the SAT or #SAT problem [9]. The state was the number of free variables n at the current node and the immediate cost was the number of nodes expanded between the current and the next branching nodes. With this definition, the total undiscounted cost of a complete episode is the total number of nodes expanded during the DPLL run. Since the Q function was expected to be exponential in n, we used a polynomial in n of degree 7 (with no constant term) to approximate the logarithm of the Q function separately for each action (49 basis functions total). We used LSQL to learn selection policies on different classes of #SAT problems. The learned policies performed as well as the best of the individual heuristics, and in one class of problems significantly better. In all cases, the learned policies were significantly better than the purely randomized policy.

4.2 Inverted Pendulum

The *inverted pendulum* problem is to balance a pendulum of unknown length and mass at the upright position. The state space is continuous and consists of the vertical angle and the angular velocity of the pendulum. The (nonlinear) dynamics of the system are described in [16]. There are three force actions, $\mathcal{A} = \{-50, 0, +50\}$, but the actual input u to the system is noisy; $u = a + 10n$, where $a \in \mathcal{A}$ and n is a Gaussian noise term. The simulation step is 0.1 seconds. The agent receives zero reward as long as the angle of the pendulum does not exceed $\pi/2$ in absolute value. An angle greater than $\pi/2$ signals the end of the episode and a penalty of -1. The discount factor of the process is 0.9.

We used a set of 30 basis functions (10 for each action) to approximate the value function. These 10 basis functions include a constant term and 9 radial basis functions (Gaussians with $\sigma^2 = 1$) arranged in a 3×3 grid ($\{-\pi/4,\ 0,\ +\pi/4\} \times \{-1,\ 0,\ +1\}$) over the 2-dimensional state space. Training samples were collected from "random episodes", i.e., starting in a random state close to the upright position and following a purely random policy. Figure 2 (b) shows the performance of controllers learned by LSPI. Each (successful) episode was allowed to run for a maximum of 3000 steps (5 minutes) of continuous balancing. LSPI returned very good policies given only a few hundred training episodes.

4.3 Bicycle Balancing and Riding

The goal in the bicycle problem [12] is to learn to balance and ride a bicycle to a target position located 1 km away from the starting location. Initially, the bicycle's orientation is at an angle of 90° to the goal. The state description is a six-dimensional real-valued vector $(\theta, \dot{\theta}, \omega, \dot{\omega}, \ddot{\omega}, \psi)$, where θ is the angle of the handlebar, ω is the vertical angle of the bicycle, and ψ is the angle of the bicycle to the goal. The actions are the torque τ applied to the handlebar (discretized to $\{-2, 0, +2\}$) and the displacement of the rider υ (discretized to $\{-0.02, 0, +0.02\}$). In our experiments, actions are restricted to be either τ or υ (or nothing) giving a total of 5 actions. A shaping reward signal was used to learn both tasks at once. The agent receives a reward equal to the net change in the square of the vertical angle and a reward equal to 1% of the net change (in meters) in the distance to the goal. These two rewards are combined additively at each time step. The discount factor is 0.8. The noise in the system is a uniformly distributed term in $[-0.02, +0.02]$ added to the displacement component of the action. The dynamics of the bicycle are based on the model described in [12] and the time step of the simulation is set to 0.01 seconds.

The state-action value function $Q(s, a)$ for a fixed action a is approximated by a linear combination of 20 basis functions:

$$(1,\ \omega,\ \dot{\omega},\ \omega^2,\ \dot{\omega}^2, \omega\dot{\omega},\ \theta,\ \dot{\theta},\ \theta^2,\ \dot{\theta}^2,\ \theta\dot{\theta},\ \omega\theta,\ \omega\theta^2,\ \omega^2\theta,\ \psi,\ \psi^2,\ \psi\theta,\ \bar{\psi},\ \bar{\psi}^2,\ \bar{\psi}\theta\ ),$$

where $\bar{\psi} = \pi - \psi$ for $\psi > 0$ and $\bar{\psi} = -\pi - \psi$ for $\psi < 0$. Note that the state variable $\ddot{\omega}$ is completely ignored. This block of basis functions is repeated for each of the 5 actions, giving a total of 100 basis functions and weights. Training data were collected by initializing the bicycle to a random state around the equilibrium position and running small episodes of 20 steps each using a purely random policy. LSPI was applied on training sets of different sizes and the average performance is shown in Figure 3 (a). Successful policies usually reached the goal in approximately 1 km total, near optimal performance.

4.4 Multiagent Learning: The SysAdmin Problem

In multiagent domains, multiple agents must coordinate their actions so as to maximize their joint utility. Such systems can be viewed as MDPs where the

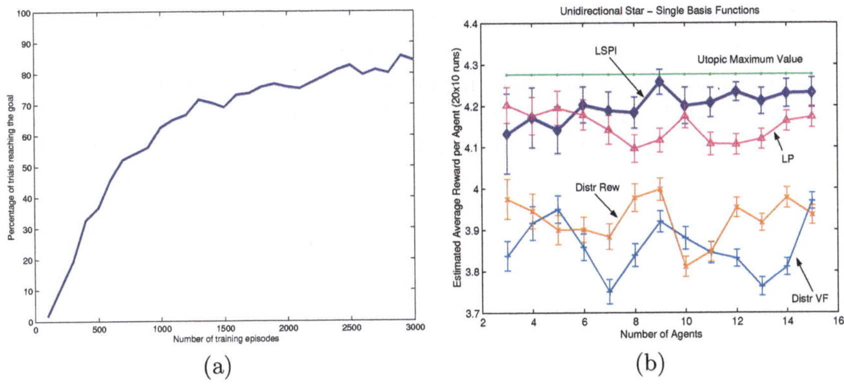

Fig. 3. Results on: (a) bicycle balancing and riding; (b) the SysAdmin problem.

"action" is the joint action and the reward is the total reward for all of the agents. Although, the action space can be quite large, *Collaborative action selection* [3] is a method that allows multiple agents to efficiently determine the jointly optimal action with respect to an (approximate) factored value function using a simple message passing scheme. This joint value function is a linear combination of local value functions, each of which relates only to some parts of the system controlled by a small number of agents. Extending LSPI to multiagent learning in such domains is straightforward. LSPI can learn the coefficients for the factored value function and the improved policy will be defined implicitly by the learned Q-function. However, instead of enumerating the exponentially many actions to find the maximizing action, the collaborative action selection mechanism is used to determine efficiently the policy at any given state.

The *SysAdmin* problem [3] consists of a network of n machines connected in a chain, ring, star, ring-of-rings, or star-and-ring topology. The state of each machine is described by its status (good, faulty, dead) and its load (idle, loaded, process successful). Jobs can be executed on good or faulty machines (job arrivals and terminations are stochastic), but a faulty machine will take longer to terminate. A dead machine is not able to execute jobs and remains dead until it is rebooted. Each machine receives a reward of +1 for each job completed successfully. Machines fail stochastically and they are also influenced by their neighbors. Each machine is also associated with a rebooting agent. Rebooting a machine makes its status good independently of the current status, but any running job is lost. These agents have to coordinate their actions to maximize the total reward for the system. The discount factor is 0.95. The SysAdmin problem has been studied in [3], where the model of the process is assumed to be available as a factored MDP. The state value function is approximated as a linear combination of indicator basis functions, and the coefficients are computed using a Linear Programming (LP) approach. The derived policies are close to the theoretical optimal and significantly better compared to policies learned by the Distributed Reward (DR) and Distributed Value Function (DVF) algorithms [14].

In our work, we assume that no model is available and we applied LSPI to learn rebooting policies [4]. To make a fair comparison, we used comparable sets of basis functions. For n machines in the network, we experimentally found that about $600n$ samples are sufficient for LSPI to learn a good policy. The samples were collected by a purely random policy. Figure 3 (b) shows the results obtained by LSPI on the star topology compared to the results of LP, DR, and DVF as reported in [3]. In both cases, LSPI learns very good policies comparable to the LP approach, but without any use of the model. It is worth noting that the number of samples used in each case grows linearly in the number of agents, whereas the joint state-action space grows exponentially.

4.5 Two-Player Zero-Sum Markov Games

A two-player zero-sum Markov game is defined by a set of states $\mathcal{S}$ and two sets of actions, $\mathcal{A}$ and $\mathcal{O}$, one for each player. In each state, the two players take actions simultaneously, they receive a reward that depends on the current state and their actions, and the game makes a stochastic transition to a new state. The two players have diametrically opposed goals; one is trying to maximize the total cumulative reward, whereas the other is trying to minimize it. Optimality can be defined independently of the opponent in the minimax sense: maximize your total reward in the worst case. Unlike MDPs, the minimax-optimal policy for a Markov game need not be deterministic. Littman [11] has studied Markov games as a framework for multiagent RL by extending tabular Q-learning to a variant called minimax-Q.

We tried to apply LSPI to the same kind of problems. Given an approximate value function $\widehat{Q}(s, a, o)$, the implied policy at any given state s is a probability distribution π_s over actions defined as

$$\pi_s = \arg \max_{\pi_s \in \text{PD}(\mathcal{A})} \min_{o \in \mathcal{O}} \sum_{a \in \mathcal{A}} \pi_s(a) \widehat{Q}(s, a, o) ,$$

where a is the action of our agent and o is the opponent's action. π_s can be found by solving a linear program [11]. Given that the policy is stochastic, the update equations of LSQ within LSPI have to be modified so that the distribution over possible next actions is taken into account:

$$\widehat{\mathbf{A}} \leftarrow \widehat{\mathbf{A}} + \phi(s, a, o) \Big(\phi(s, a, o) - \gamma \sum_{a' \in \mathcal{A}} \pi_{s'}(a') \phi(s', a', o') \Big)^{\intercal} , \quad \widehat{b} \leftarrow \widehat{b} + \phi(s, a, o) r ,$$

for any sample (s, a, o, r, s'). The action o' is the minimizing opponent's action in computing $\pi_{s'}$. In our preliminary experiments on the simplified one-on-one soccer game [11], LSPI was able to learn very good policies using only about $10,000$ samples. This is a fraction of the $1,000,000$ samples required by tabular minimax-Q. Further, with the use of basis functions that capture important features of the game (e.g., scaled distances to the goals and the opponent) for approximating the value function, we have been able to scale to grid sizes much bigger than the original (5×4) grid. We are currently investigating team-based Markov games and the use of coordinated action selection in conjunction with LSPI for efficient multiagent learning in team-based competitive domains.

4.6 Tetris

Tetris is a popular tiling video game. Although the model of the game is rather simplistic and known in advance, the state-action space is so big ($\approx 10^{61}$ states and ≈ 40 actions) that one has to rely on approximation and learning techniques to find good policies. We used 10 basis functions over (s, a) pairs to capture features of state s and the one-step effects of playing action a in s: the maximum height in the current board, the total number of "holes", the sum of absolute height differences between adjacent columns, the mean height, and the change of these quantities in the next step, plus the change in score and a constant term. That results in a single set of 10 weights for all actions.

In our preliminary results, policies learned by LSPI using about $10,000$ samples achieve average score between $1,000$ and $3,000$ points per game. The training samples were collected using a hand-crafted policy that scores about 600 points per game (the random policy rarely scores any point). Knowledge about the model was incorporated in LSPI to improve the approximation: for each sample, instead of considering just the sampled next state in the update equation, we considered a sum over all possible next states appropriatelly weighted according to the transition model.

Our results compare favorably with the results of $\lambda-$policy iteration on Tetris [1], but there are significant differences in the two approaches. $\lambda-$policy iteration collects new samples in each iteration and learns the state value function; it uses the model for greedy action selection over the learved function, and the iteration does not finally converge. On the contrary, LSPI collects samples only once at the very beginning and learns the state-action value function; it uses the model only to improve the approximation, and converges in about 10 iterations. In both cases, the learned players exhibit big variance in performance.

5 Discussion and Conclusion

We presented an overview of our research efforts towards using least-squares methods in reinforcement learning control problems. The key advantages of least-squares methods is the efficient use of samples and the simplicity of the implementation. In all the domains we tested, our algorithms were able to learn very good policies using only a small number of samples compared to conventional learning approaches, such as Q-learning. Moreover, the algorithms required little or no modification in each case. There are also many exciting avenues to explore further: How are the basis functions chosen? What is the effect of the distribution of the training samples? Can we use projection reweighting methods to make LSPI amenable to even "bad" data sets? These are some of the many open questions on our research agenda. In any case, we believe that algorithms like LSPI can easily be good first-choice candidates for many reinforcement learning control problems.

We would like to thank C. Guestrin, D. Koller, and U. Lerner for helpful discussions. The first author would also like to thank the Lilian-Boudouri Foundation in Greece for partial financial support.

References

1. D. Bertsekas and J. Tsitsiklis. *Neuro-Dynamic Programming.* Athena Scientific, Belmont, Massachusetts, 1996.
2. Steven J. Bradtke and Andrew G. Barto. Linear least-squares algorithms for temporal difference learning. *Machine Learning*, 22(1/2/3):33–57, 1996.
3. Carlos Guestrin, Daphne Koller, and Ronald Parr. Multiagent planning with factored MDPs. In *Proceeding of the 14th Neural Information Processing Systems (NIPS-14)*, Vancouver, Canada, December 2001.
4. Carlos Guestrin, Michail G. Lagoudakis, and Ronald Parr. Coordinated reinforcement learning. In *Proceedings of the 2002 AAAI Spring Symposium Series: Collaborative Learning Agents*, Stanford, CA, March 2002.
5. Leslie P. Kaelbling, Michael L. Littman, and Andrew W. Moore. Reinforcement learning: A survey. *Journal of Artificial Intelligence Research*, 4:237–285, 1996.
6. Daphne Koller and Ronald Parr. Policy iteration for factored MDPs. In Craig Boutilier and Moisés Goldszmidt, editors, *Proceedings of the 16th Conference on Uncertainty in Artificial Intelligence (UAI-00)*, pages 326–334, San Francisco, CA, 2000. Morgan Kaufmann Publishers.
7. Michail Lagoudakis and Ronald Parr. Model free least squares policy iteration. In *Proceedings of the 14th Neural Information Processing Systems (NIPS-14)*, Vancouver, Canada, December 2001.
8. Michail G. Lagoudakis and Michael L. Littman. Algorithm selection using reinforcement learning. In Pat Langley, editor, *Proceedings of the Seventeenth International Conference on Machine Learning*, pages 511–518. Morgan Kaufmann, San Francisco, CA, 2000.
9. Michail G. Lagoudakis and Michael L. Littman. Learning to select branching rules in the dpll procedure for satisfiability. In Henry Kautz and Bart Selman, editors, *Electronic Notes in Discrete Mathematics (ENDM), Vol. 9, LICS 2001 Workshop on Theory and Applications of Satisfiability Testing.* Elsevier Science, 2001.
10. Michail G. Lagoudakis, Michael L. Littman, and Ronald Parr. Selecting the right algorithm. In Carla Gomes and Toby Walsh, editors, *Proceedings of the 2001 AAAI Fall Symposium Series: Using Uncertainty within Computation*, Cape Cod, MA, November 2001.
11. Michael L. Littman. Markov games as a framework for multi-agent reinforcement learning. In *Proceedings of the Eleventh International Conference on Machine Learning*, pages 157–163, San Francisco, CA, 1994. Morgan Kaufmann.
12. J. Randløv and P. Alstrøm. Learning to drive a bicycle using reinforcement learning and shaping. In *Proceedings of The Fifteenth International Conference on Machine Learning*, Madison, Wisconsin, July 1998. Morgan Kaufmann.
13. John R. Rice. The algorithm selection problem. *Advances in Computers*, 15:65–118, 1976.
14. J. Schneider, W. Wong, A. Moore, and M. Riedmiller. Distributed value functions. In *Proceedings of The Sixteenth International Conference on Machine Learning*, Bled, Slovenia, July 1999. Morgan Kaufmann.
15. R. Sutton and A. Barto. *Reinforcement Learning: An Introduction.* MIT Press, Cambridge, MA, 1998.
16. K. Wang, H. Tanaka and M. Griffin. An approach to fuzzy control of nonlinear systems: Stability and design issues. *IEEE Transactions on Fuzzy Systems*, 4(1):14–23, 1996.
17. Christopher J. C. H. Watkins. *Learning from Delayed Rewards.* PhD thesis, King's College, Cambridge, UK, 1989.

Association Rules & Evolution in Time

George Koundourakis and Babis Theodoulidis

Information Management Group
Department of Computation, UMIST,
Manchester, United Kingdom
{koundour,babis}@co.umist.ac.uk
http://www.crim.org.uk/

Abstract. In this paper, an algorithm for mining association rules is proposed that is based on the generation of multiple decision trees and extraction of rules from them. This method is quite effective especially in data sets that contain numeric attributes. In this paper, also, it is studied the capturing of the evolution of association rules during time. Since most of the interesting observations involve time, the evolution of association rules during time is quite important. In order to capture and study this evolution, the notion of temporal rules is proposed and a method for mining them is described. Finally, methods for visualisation of temporal rules are proposed in order to offer to the users the opportunity to perform comparisons of support and confidence of consecutive temporal periods easily.

1 Definition and Properties of Association Rules

An association rule is a rule, which implies certain association relationships among a set of objects in a database. Let $I=\{i_1, i_2, \ldots, i_m\}$ be a set of *items*. Let DB be a database of transactions, where each transaction T consists of a set of items such that $T \subseteq I$. Given an *itemset* $X \subseteq I$, a transaction T *contains* X if and only if $X \subseteq T$. An association rule is an implication of the form $X \Rightarrow Y$, where $X \subseteq I$, $Y \subseteq I$ and $X \cap Y = \emptyset$. The association rule $X \Rightarrow Y$ holds in DB with *confidence c* if $c\%$ of transactions in DB that contain X also contain Y. The association rule $X \Rightarrow Y$ has *support s* in DB if $s\%$ of transactions in DB contain $X \cup Y$. A pattern A is *large* in set S if the support of A is no less than its corresponding minimum support threshold σ'. The confidence of a rule $A \Rightarrow B$ in S is *high* if its confidence is no less than its corresponding minimum threshold φ'. A rule $A \Rightarrow B$ in S is *strong* if A and B are large and the confidence of $A \Rightarrow B$ in S is high. The task of mining association rules is to find all the association rules whose support is larger than a *minimum support threshold* σ' and whose confidence is larger than a *minimum confidence threshold* φ'.

Most of the proposed algorithms for the discovery of association rules are variations of the well-known Apriori method. These methods are based on the discovery of large itemsets and the construction and evaluation of bigger itemsets. The generation of the

I.P. Vlahavas and C.D. Spyropoulos (Eds.): SETN 2002, LNAI 2308, pp. 261–272, 2002.

candidate itemsets for evaluation is based on the theorem that no large itemset contains sub-itemsets that are not large. Therefore, at each step k of the algorithm, only the large k-itemsets are used to construct candidate (k+1)-itemsets. The process starts with the discovery of the large itemsets that consist of one item. It continues with the generation and evaluation of bigger candidate itemsets until there are not any candidate itemsets. Most of the algorithms, which are based on Apriori, vary on the method of generating the candidate itemsets. In Apriori algorithm [1] the values of the numeric attributes are replaced by ranges. If the number of ranges is large, the support for any single range is low. On the other hand, if the number of ranges is low, it can lead into rules with low confidence. To determine the number of ranges the algorithm uses k-partial completeness, which is based only on the ordinal properties of the data. This method [1] aims to construct ranges that have support between a minimum and a maximum threshold. Therefore, the partitions of values are useful since they have sufficient support and they are not over-generalised since there is a maximum threshold for their desired support. Although this method generates ranges of sufficient support, the generation of these ranges does not take into account how these ranges are related with values of other attributes. In addition, this method of handling numeric attributes suffers from information loss. This happens because the values of the numeric attributes are separated into fixed ranges before the actual execution of the mining algorithm. This removes from the mining algorithm the flexibility to determine at run-time the most appropriate sub-ranges of values of numeric attributes that should be combined with values of other attributes in order to construct more precise association rules.

2 Mining Association Rules from Decision Trees

In this paper, a new method for mining association rules is proposed. In comparison with the Apriori-based methods, its main advantage is the dynamic handling of numeric attributes as it determines at run time which are the most appropriate conditions for any numeric attribute that should be added to a rule in order to increase its confidence. Because of this difference, the proposed method behaves better than Apriori on data sets containing numeric attributes as it mines not only more rules but also more precise rules.

A decision tree is a collection of *IF-THEN* rules that are expressed by its individual paths. This is a semantic characteristic of decision trees and our proposed method for finding association rules is based on it. Since our method is based on decision trees, it presumes the selection and distinction of a set of attributes that must appear in the "*THEN*" part of the rules. This can be regarded as the main difference between our proposed method and Apriori. In Apriori no attribute is distinguished and moreover any attribute can occur either in the "*IF*" part or in the "*THEN*" part of a rule. Our proposed method consists of two simple steps, which are described in detail in the later paragraphs. These steps are the following:

1. Data Preparation
2. Generation of multiple decision-trees and extraction of strong rules from each decision tree

2.1 Data Preparation

In this stage, the data set is collected and prepared for the mining process. Having completed the data collection and preparation, the *target attribute* is selected and discriminated from the others. The *target attribute* is the one for which there is interest on finding association rules and moreover must appear in the "*THEN*" part of the rules. In the case that there is interest on finding rules with more than one attribute in the consequent of the rules, then the *target attribute* is constructed from the join of the selected and discriminated attributes. Generalisation is performed on the *target attribute* by using relative concept hierarchies, as it has been described in [2] . If any of the selected target attributes is numeric or temporal that has not been generalised by the use of generalisation rules, then it is generalised into a categorical attribute by using ranges or temporal periods as it is mentioned in [2] . By this method, the initial numeric or temporal attribute is converted into a categorical one with only a few values (ranges) that express higher-level concepts. Moreover, the discovered rules X⇒Y have higher confidence since Y has also higher support. Generalisation may also be applied to the remaining attributes of the data set. It is especially recommended for attributes that have a large number of distinct values. In such cases, it reduces data complexity as it substitutes many values with little support with less values of higher support. Such data abstractions are more useful for finding association rules with significant support. Moreover, association rules are more meaningful to the users when they refer to a data set containing a relatively small number of distinct values with significant support.

2.2 Generation of Multiple Decision Trees

After the stage of data preparation, the final *target attribute* can be considered as the classifying attribute of the whole data set. Hence, a set of decision trees can be constructed, based on that classifying attribute. For each of these trees, each path from the root to a node represents one or more rules of the form:

IF (sequence of intermediate conditions) THEN (target attribute value)

For each generated rule from such a path, the confidence is r_j/r and the support is r_j/n, where r_j is the number of records of class j in the final node, r is the number of records of the final node and n is the total number of records of the training set of the decision tree.

Decision-tree building algorithm uses a subset of the available attributes in the test conditions of the internal nodes Therefore, the rules that are extracted from a built decision tree concern only a subset of the available attributes. Although the chosen attributes are the ones that provide the best split conditions, it may exist useful and informative rules with significant support and confidence that concern the remaining attributes. Such rules can not be extracted from a single tree. Thus, several decision trees have to be constructed in order to extract more association rules from the data set. Each of these decision trees has to be trained on a subset of the available attributes in order to be forced to find rules concerning them. At first, a set of combinations of the available attributes is generated. Usually the number of attributes in a data set is significant and therefore the number of the attributes combinations is big. The construction of a decision tree for each of these combinations is computationally expensive. Moreover, many lengthy combinations of attributes do not contribute in the whole process, as it is difficult for human users to interpret rules that concern too many attributes. To avoid the construction of too many decision trees, only a subset of all possible attributes combinations is generated and examined. User defines the maximum size k allowed for a combination of attributes. As candidate fields for constructing those subsets are considered the n attributes that are most relevant to the target attribute, where n is defined by the user as well. To determine the relevance to the target attribute, relevance analysis is initially performed to the set of all available attributes as it is described in [2] . Thus, the generated combinations of attributes are:

$$\sum_{i=1}^{k} \binom{n}{i}.$$

For each of the generated combinations of attributes, a decision tree is constructed. From each of these trees, new rules can be extracted. A rule is considered as new if it refers to all the attributes of the examined combination of attributes. If a rule refers to less attributes, then it is not considered as new as it should be discovered from a smaller combination of attributes. By this way, it is ensured that a rule is not added multiple times in the set of the discovered rules. Having completed the examination of all generated combinations of attributes, a decision tree is trained on all the available attributes. Rules are extracted from this tree and if their conditions refer to more than k attributes, they are considered as new rules and are added to the set of the discovered association rules. If all the strong rules are extracted from these trees, a substantial number of similar rules is created. Most of these rules represent generalisations or specialisations of other rules. This happens because each path from the root of a tree to a node l gives rules that are related with those generated from paths ending to nodes that are ancestors or successors of node l. Moreover, nodes of lower levels generate more specialised rules than the nodes of higher levels. On the other hand, rules generated from nodes of higher levels are more general as they have fewer conditions and they refer to larger number of records. In cases that the mined data set contains numeric attributes, it is possible to extract a series of strong rules that have only small differences on conditions for the range values of numeric attributes. In order to avoid this phenomenon, a restriction has been imposed in the extraction of rules from a decision tree. If any strong rules are extracted from a path ending to a node l, then it is not permitted to extract rules from any of the sub-paths that end to ancestor nodes of l. By this restriction, the set of the extracted rules is more concise and therefore more meaningful and understandable to users.

For all the training sets that are used in the generation of the multiple decision trees, several data structures and operations are common. Therefore, they are computed once and afterwards they are used in the construction of each decision tree. This sharing lowers the computational cost, decreases the running time and increases the efficiency of the overall method. At first, the arrays for the mapping of categorical and class values into integers are built before the reading of the data set [2] . After their construction, the array for the mapping of the class labels into integers is used in every decision tree building process. Moreover, the corresponding mapping arrays are used in the decision tree building for the combinations that contain categorical attributes. Furthermore, when building decision trees for the n training sets that consist of only one of the n most relevant attributes, it is found the best split condition that each of these n attributes provides for the root of a decision tree. Therefore, when examining bigger combinations, the attribute for the splitting of the root node is chosen based on its best split condition that has been calculated from the examination of the training set that contained only the corresponding attribute. Thus, for the building of decision trees based on training sets of more than one attribute, the splitting of the root does not require any evaluation of possible split conditions. Hence, in these cases the splitting of the root is immediate and computationally inexpensive.

3 Association Rules and Their Evolution in Time

Some of the more interesting observations involve time. In reality, only a few rules remain with the same "strength" independently from time. For example, let us consider the following rule that was found in a medical database:

IF a *smoker* has a *stroke then* he *survives*, with *support* =28%, *confidence*=84%

A question that can be asked is: "Does this rule stand with the same strength independently from the Date of Birth of the patients?". The answer is obviously not. Similar questions can be based on other temporal dimensions, like the date of stroke or the date of last medical examination of the corresponding patients or even the date that the mining operation is performed. This is an example of the well-known fact that only a few things remain unchanged in time. Association rules consist another domain that this general principle applies. Most databases contain data that changes over time. Moreover, in most databases there is not just a single temporal dimension that is represented by a single temporal attribute. Usually several temporal attributes are kept in a database in order to record certain events and data evolutions. Each of these attributes represents a different temporal dimension of the data. For example, in a medical database they are recorded the date of birth of a patient, the dates of medical examinations, the dates of important medical incidents and several other dates concerning different facts of the evolution of the health of a patient like subscriptions or special medical treatments. For a specific temporal dimension, the mining of a data set at different temporal periods results into a series of sets of association rules. Each set of association rules is the result of the mining process in one of the examined temporal intervals. The strong association rules of one temporal interval apply to the other temporal intervals with the same, lower or higher support and confidence. Apparently, the rule evolution in a temporal dimension is depicted by the fluctuations of its support and confidence in a series of temporal intervals. For this reason, it is named as temporal rule an association rule accompanied by the fluctuations of support and confidence in a series of temporal periods.

Temporal rules reveal the evolution pattern of the strength of association rules over time. This pattern is quite useful as it identifies the temporal periods that the rule can be trusted more than other temporal periods. In addition, the evolution pattern of the strength of an association rules can be used for discovering possible periodicities in the temporal intervals that an association rule is strong [5]. Moreover, this pattern can be considered as the basis for making any temporal reasoning about the evolution of an association rule in time. Mining of all available data for association rules and considering of all temporal attributes as common ones can not provide this evolution pattern. For this reason, the notion of temporal rules has been proposed in §4 and a method for mining them is provided in §5.

4 Definition of Temporal Rules

Each temporal rule contains the list of the rule conditions (IF part), where each condition refers to the values of an attribute. In addition, each temporal rule contains a string for the result ("*THEN*" part) of the rule. Moreover, every temporal rule contains an array of Date_Period items. The dimension of the *periods_array* is defined by the integer *periods_num*. Each Date_Period object contains information about the statistics of a rule on a temporal period. Therefore, a Date_Period object contains the starting and ending points of a temporal period. Additionally, it holds information about the support and confidence of an association rule for the temporal period that is specified by the starting and ending points. Furthermore, a Date_Period object contains information about the number of records that exist between the starting and ending point of the temporal period.

5 Mining of Temporal Rules

The discovery of temporal rules implies the mining of association rules and capturing the fluctuations of their support and confidence in successive periods of a specific temporal dimension. This procedure is divided in the following subtasks.

1 Data preparation.
2 Selection of a temporal dimension-attribute and creation of a series of temporal intervals of equal length.
3 Mining of strong association rules for each temporal interval.
4 Verification of the support and confidence of each discovered association rule in each of the defined temporal intervals.

The whole process of finding and visualising temporal rules is displayed in Fig. 1.

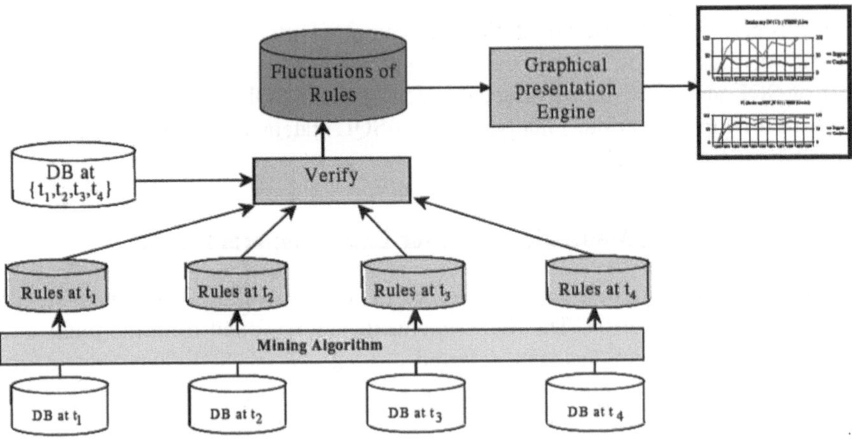

Fig. 1. Mining and Visualisation of Temporal Rules

5.1 Data Preparation

This step is quite similar to the one described in §2.1. For the mining of temporal rules, it is necessary the collection and preparation of the corresponding data set. Moreover, it is required the selection of the *target attributes* and the definition of the thresholds for the minimum support and confidence. In addition, it is defined if it is going to be performed generalisation to the *target attributes* or any of the remaining attributes of the data set. In the case of using generalisation method, the tables containing the relative generalisation rules are identified. The user defines all the necessary data preparation actions once, before the actual mining of the temporal rules. All these selections are collected and recorded in a list of actions. This list of data preparation actions is performed in the data set of each temporal period. Thus, the mining of the data sets of the temporal periods is performed with the same preparations and parameters.

5.2 Specification of Temporal Parameters

In order to discover temporal rules, a specific temporal interval is separated into continuous temporal periods of equal length. These temporal periods are the key in order to find the fluctuations of rules' support and confidence.

At first, the temporal attribute that is considered as the temporal dimension of the data set is specified. In addition, the length of the temporal periods that are going to be examined must be specified. There is the option to choose minute, hour, day, month, or year as period length. Moreover at this stage, they are defined the starting and ending points of the temporal interval that is going to be mined for temporal rules. The starting and ending points are expressed in the same temporal unit that has been defined as period length. Having defined the temporal attribute, the length of the temporal sub-periods and the starting and ending points of the examined temporal interval, a list of SQL statements is constructed. Each of these SQL statements selects the records of a temporal period. Finally, an extra SQL statement selects the data set of the whole temporal interval.

5.3 Mining Strong Association Rules for Each Temporal Period

For each temporal period, the execution of the corresponding SQL statement collects the records of that period. The SQL statements can be found from the relative list of SQL-statements, which has been referred in §5.2. All the SQL-statements of the list are executed for the mining of strong all rules, except the last one that refers to the whole temporal interval. The last SQL-statement of the list is used in the verification stage that is described in §5.4. Having selected the data set of a temporal period, the list of data preparations actions, referred in §5.1, is applied to it. After the execution of the defined data preparations, the selected data set is mined for strong association rules. The discovered strong association rules of each period are the base for creating a list of temporal rules.

For each strong association rule found in a temporal period, a check is performed to the list of the already existing temporal rules. If no temporal rule exists in the list with the same conditions and conclusions as those of the discovered association rule, then a new temporal rule object is created and added to the list. The entry of the *periods_array* that corresponds to the temporal period in which the rule was discovered is updated with the support and confidence of the discovered rule. On the other hand, if a temporal rule exists in the list, with the same conditions and conclusions as those of the discovered association rule, then an update is performed in the corresponding entry of the *periods_array*. More specifically, for the existing temporal rule, the entry of the *periods_array* that corresponds to the period of the discovered rule is updated with the support and confidence of the discovered rule.

5.4 Verification of Support and Confidence for Each Temporal Period

After the examination of all temporal periods, the list of temporal rules has been created. The temporal rules that were discovered as strong association rules in all the examined temporal periods have information about their support and confidence for all the temporal periods. In addition, for each of these temporal rules, the total support and confidence in the whole temporal interval can be computed from the support, confidence and records number of each examined temporal period. For each of these temporal rules, this information is available in the first (*periods_num* – 1) entries of its *periods_array*. The total support, confidence and records number of the whole temporal interval are stored in the last entry of the *periods_array*. For these rules, there is no need for further verification of their support and confidence for any temporal period. Therefore, they are separated from the remaining temporal rules for which the support and confidence are unknown for some temporal periods. For all the remaining temporal rules, the support and confidence of all the entries of the *periods_array* are set to zero. It must be mentioned that the remaining temporal rules refer to association rules that are strong at least in one of the examined temporal periods.

At next, the data set of the whole temporal interval is read by executing the last SQL statement of the relative list that is referred in §5.2. For each of the read records, all the remaining temporal rules are examined in order to find the ones that the record satisfies. The entries of *periods_array* are used for storing temporary statistics that are necessary for the final calculation of the support and confidence for all temporal periods. For the rules whose conditions (*IF*- part) are satisfied by a record, there is an increased by one of the support of the *periods_array* entry that specifies the value of the record for the chosen temporal dimension-attribute. Moreover, for the rules that a record satisfies their conditions (*IF*- part) and their consequences (*THEN* - part), there is an increase by one of the confidence of the *periods_array* entry that specifies the value of the record for the chosen temporal dimension-attribute. When an increase occurs to the support or confidence for a specific temporal period, the support or confidence for the whole time slice increases accordingly.

After the processing of all the records, the temporary statistics stored in the entries of *periods_arrays* are used for calculating the support and confidence of any rule for all the temporal periods. For any period of a *periods_array*, executing the operations displayed below can perform the calculation of its support and confidence.

```
FLOAT temp_num
temp_num  = period.support
period.support = period.confidence / period.records_number
period.confidence = period.confidence / temp_num
```

After the calculation of the support and confidence of all rules for all temporal periods, the list of temporal rules is ready for storing in a table for future visualisation and examination.

6 Visualisation of Temporal Rules

A set of stored temporal rules has to be visualised in such a way that it allows the users to notice and understand the fluctuations of support and confidence as clearly as possible. The methods developed for the visualisation of temporal rules have as main goal to achieve the fast and complete understanding of the rules and their fluctuations. Moreover, these methods try to offer to the users the opportunity to perform comparisons of support and confidence of adjustment temporal periods easily.

Since the body (*IF-THEN*) of a temporal rule is the same for all the temporal periods, one way for visualising temporal rules is by displaying them in a hierarchical form. In Fig. 2(a), one can observe an example of visualisation of a set of temporal rules in hierarchical view. In this view, there is the option to add two extra columns for the support and confidence of a rule for the whole temporal interval.

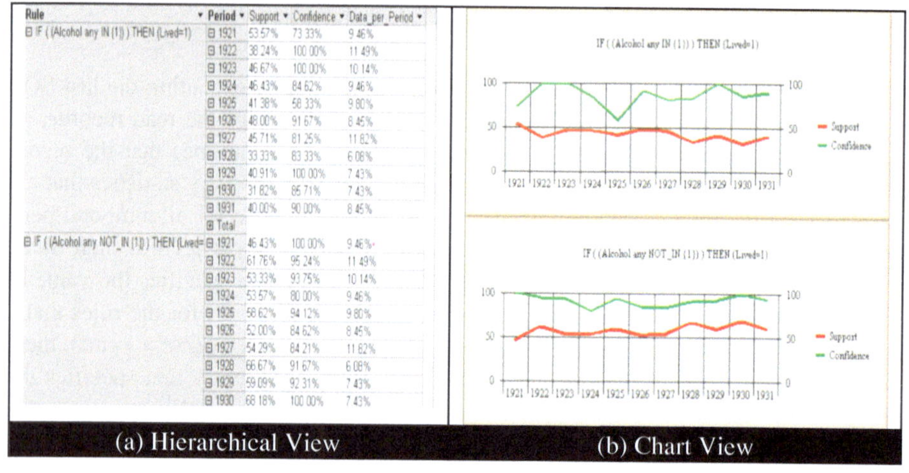

Rule	Period	Support	Confidence	Data_per_Period
IF ((Alcohol any IN {1})) THEN (Lived=1)	1921	53.57%	73.33%	9.46%
	1922	38.24%	100.00%	11.49%
	1923	46.67%	100.00%	10.14%
	1924	46.43%	84.62%	9.46%
	1925	41.38%	58.33%	9.80%
	1926	48.00%	91.67%	8.45%
	1927	45.71%	81.25%	11.82%
	1928	33.33%	83.33%	6.08%
	1929	40.91%	100.00%	7.43%
	1930	31.82%	85.71%	7.43%
	1931	40.00%	90.00%	8.45%
	Total			
IF ((Alcohol any NOT_IN {1})) THEN (Lived=	1921	46.43%	100.00%	9.46%
	1922	61.76%	95.24%	11.49%
	1923	53.33%	93.75%	10.14%
	1924	53.57%	80.00%	9.46%
	1925	58.62%	94.12%	9.80%
	1926	52.00%	84.62%	8.45%
	1927	54.29%	84.21%	11.82%
	1928	66.67%	91.67%	6.08%
	1929	59.09%	92.31%	7.43%
	1930	68.18%	100.00%	7.43%

Fig. 2. Visualisation of Temporal Rules

Although the hierarchical view of Fig. 2(a) is quite informative and effective, it is characterised by the extensive use of text that the user has to read. This view is appropriate for learning the exact values of support and confidence of association rules in a series of temporal periods. In most cases, users are interested on noticing the fluctuations of support and confidence during the time. More specifically, they are interested to identify the temporal periods that there is increase or decrease in the support or confidence of a rule. A popular method for visualisation of fluctuations of numerical functions is the use of charts. Charts are visual and users are able to understand them without having to learn the exact values referred in them. It is easy to identify in a chart increases and decreases and their slope. For this reason, a visualisation method for temporal rules has been implemented based on the use of charts. For each temporal rule, a chart is created in which are depicted the fluctuations of the rule's support and confidence for all the examined temporal periods. An example of this visualisation method is shown in Fig. 2(b). In Fig. 2(b), the same temporal rules are visualised as in Fig. 2(a). The difference is obvious as the visualisation of Fig. 2(b) is graphical and qualitative whereas the visualisation of Fig. 2(a) is textual and quantitative. The choice of the most appropriate method depends each time on the needs of the user at the given moment.

7 Conclusions

The most established algorithms for discovery of association rules have problems when the examining data set contains numerical attributes. The methods that are based on the attribute-oriented induction have to generalise the numerical attributes and convert them into categorical ones. During this human-driven generalisation there is a lost of information because the user-defined generalisation is not always the most adequate and optimum to the request data mining task. In Apriori algorithm, the values of the numerical attributes are replaced by intervals. If the number of intervals is large, the support for any single interval is low. On the other hand, if the number of intervals is low, it can lead into rules with low confidence. To determine the number of intervals the algorithm uses k-partial completeness, which is based only on the ordinal properties of the data.

The method proposed in this paper for mining association rules does not have such problems since numerical attributes values are split into groups according to how well those groups are related to the values of the target attribute. Therefore, it handles them according to the needs of every requested data mining task. Furthermore, the described method is based on the generation of multiple decision trees instead of one decision tree. As a consequence, a better coverage of the area that association rules may exist is achieved as decision-tree building algorithm is biased on choosing and examining only a subset of the available attributes that provide strong split conditions. This methodology gives a good solution to the relative problem stated in [3] that a decision tree uses only a subset of the strong rules in its structure. Although the described method discovers stronger rules by building several decision trees, it is true that it may not discover some strong rules. However, no method is able to discover all the existing strong rules in a data set. As it has been mentioned, the variations of the Apriori algorithm miss a substantial number of strong rules when numeric or temporal attributes exist in the examined data set. Therefore, the proposed method must not be regarded as a method that mines all strong rules from a data set. Instead, it must be regarded as a method that mines more effectively strong rules than other existing methods, especially in the cases of data sets that contain numeric attributes.

The method for mining association rules, takes advantage of a powerful decision-tree building engine and exploits its capabilities, which are stated in [2] . This decision tree building engine uses a new generalisation method that replaces attribute values with more meaningful abstractions. Also, this engine contains a relevance analysis module, which discriminates the attributes that are strongly related with the target attribute. This relevance analysis module is an extension of the method proposed in [4] in order to handle numeric attributes. By this way, it is possible the reduction of the search area for mining interesting and strong association rules by not examining the attributes that are too weakly related with the target attribute(s). In addition, this engine makes effective use of the physical memory as it maps string values into integers of the appropriate size and reduces the size of physical memory that is required to handle the mined data set. Moreover, the single construction of the arrays for mapping string values into integers and the repeatedly usage of them in every tree building contributes in the computationally inexpensive building of multiple decision trees.

Moreover, in the building decision trees for the n training sets that consist of only one of the n most relevant attributes, it is computed the best split condition that each of these n attributes provides for the root of a decision tree. Consequently, the best split condition of the chosen attribute is known from the examination of the training set that contained only the corresponding attribute. Thus, in the process of building decision trees based on training sets of more than one attribute, the splitting of the root does not require any evaluation of possible split conditions. The most appropriate attribute is known from the ranking resulted from relevance analysis and the best split condition of the chosen attribute is known from the examination of the training set that contained only the corresponding attribute. This reduces the amount of operations required for the splitting of the roots of the decision trees. This speeds up the whole process and contributes in its efficiency.

Finally, in this paper has been proposed a method for capturing the evolution of association rules during time. In order to capture and study this evolution, it has been proposed in §4 the notion of temporal rules. The method for mining temporal rules uses the described algorithm for mining association rules and takes advantage of its capabilities and efficiency. The study and understanding of mined temporal rules is possible by the use of the simple but powerful visualisation methods presented in §6. Concluding, this method allows the capturing of the evolution of association rules in time and enables users to identify and understand the fluctuations of the strength of rules in time.

References

[1] Mohammed J. Zaki, Srinivasan Parthasarathy, Mitsunori Ogihara and Wei Li. *New Algorithms for Fast Discovery of Association Rules.* Technical Report 651, University of Rochester, Computer Science Department, New York, July 1997.

[2] George Koundourakis. *EnVisioner: A Data Mining Framework Based On Decision Trees.* A Thesis submitted to the University of Manchester Institute of Science and Technology for the degree of Doctor of Philosophy in December, 2001.

[3] Parsaye, K., *Rules Are Much More Than Decision Trees.* The Journal of Data Warehousing, December 1996.

[4] Micheline Kamber, Lara Winstone, Wan Gong, Shan Cheng, and Jiawei Han. *Generalisation and Decision Tree Induction: Efficient Classification in Data Mining.* In *Proc. of 1997 Int'l Workshop on Research Issues on Data Engineering (RIDE'97)* , pages. 111-120, Birmingham, England, April 1997.

[5] Mohamad Hosssein Saraee. *TempoMiner: Towards Mining Time-Oriented Data.* Ph.D. Thesis submitted to the University of Manchester Institute of Science and Technology, 2000.

Managing Uncertainty and Quality in the Classification Process

Maria Halkidi and Michalis Vazirgiannis

Dept of Informatics, Athens University of Economics & Business
76 Patission Str, 10434
{mhalk, mvazirg}@aueb.gr

Abstract. An important open issue in KDD research is the reveal and the handling of uncertainty. The popular classification approaches do not take into account this feature while they do not exploit properly the significant amount of information included in the results of classification process (i.e., classification scheme), though it will be useful in decision-making. In this paper we present a framework that maintains uncertainty throughout the classification process by maintaining the classification belief and moreover enables assignment of an item to multiple classes with a different belief. Decision support tools are provided for decisions related to: i. relative importance of classes in a data set (i.e., "young vs. old customers"), ii. relative importance of classes across data sets iii. the information content of different data sets. Finally we provide a mechanism for evaluating classification schemes and select the scheme that best fits the data under consideration.

1 Introduction and Motivation

Classification is one of the main tasks in the data mining procedure for assigning a data item to a predefined set of classes. According to [4], *classification* can be described as a function that maps (classifies) a data item into *one* of the several predefined classes.

A well-defined set of classes and a training set of pre-classified examples characterize the classification. On the contrary, the clustering process does not rely on predefined classes or examples[1]. The goal in classification process is to induce a model that can be used to classify future data items whose classification is unknown [1, 12]. For this purpose, many classification approaches have been developed and are available in literature. However, in the vast majority of traditional approaches the data values are classified to one of the classes. Also, the issue of evaluation of classification outcome (i.e., classification scheme) is under-addressed in most of classification approaches. Hereafter we address issues that arise from classification approaches:

i. *The clusters are not overlapping.* The limits of clusters are crisp and each database value may be classified into at most one cluster. This is unlikely to everyday life experience where a value may be classified into more than one classes (clusters)*. For instance a male person 182cm high in Central Europe is considered as of "medium" height as well as "tall" to some degree.

* In this paper we use the terms "classes" and "clusters" interchangeably.

I.P. Vlahavas and C.D. Spyropoulos (Eds.): SETN 2002, LNAI 2308, pp. 273–287, 2002.

ii. *The data values are treated equally in the classification process.* In traditional data mining systems database values are classified in the available classes in a crisp manner i.e., a value either belongs to a category or not. Also, they assume that all values belong to a class, assigned to it with the same degree of belief. The person 182cm high is considered tall and also another person 199cm high is also considered tall. It is profound that the second person satisfies to a higher degree, than the first, the criterion of being "tall". This piece of knowledge (the difference of belief that A is tall and also B is tall) cannot be acquired using the well-established classification schemes.

iii. Classification results may hide "useful" knowledge for our data set. Most of the classification methods define a model that is used to classify new instances to predefined classes. This assignment of data values to classes conveys significant knowledge and when aggregated for many values provides collective indication on a class importance. We can exploit this aggregated knowledge for decision-making as well as for the selection of the classification model that best fits a data set.

Motivation. Our effort is not yet another classification algorithm for learning (discovering) classes. We address a somewhat different issue. Given a data set S consisting of a set of tuples {t} each of which consists of a set of values $\{t.v_i\}$ where v_i corresponds to the value of an attribute A_i, we want to be able to:

- decide to which class(es) a value set v_i can be assigned and what the respective beliefs for each assignment is,
- compare the i. relative importance of classes in a data set (e.g. "young vs. old customers"), ii.relative importance of classes across data sets, iii. the information content of different data sets,
- assess the quality of a classification model i.e., how well it fits a data set. This requirement arises as data sets continuously change due to insertions/ deletions/updates.

In recent literature some efforts based on probabilistic concepts [17] deal with uncertainty. They measure the probability for a data set value to belong to a category, while we measure the degree of belief with which it is classified in a category. Our approach is an alternative for supporting partial classification. It supports the uncertainty using degrees of belief and not probabilities.

In the decision tree family of algorithms successive splits of a data set S into non-overlapping sets $\{S_i\}$ take place. The split is based on the different values of an attribute A_i (selected so that a metric is minimized). Then each successive step splits the subsets in other subsets so that each tuple of the data set is assigned to one class. In each of the splits a crisp decision is made and according to the above discussion potential knowledge is lost. A related approach dealing with uncertainty is fuzzy decision trees [15]. According to it, a data value can be classified to several tree nodes with an attached degree of satisfaction. More specifically, to classify a new value, we should find leaves (i.e., classes) whose restrictions are satisfied by this value. Then we combine the restrictions along the path from root to the specific leaves and their satisfaction degrees into a single crisp response. It is obvious that the classification result of fuzzy decision trees is crisp though they use fuzzy concepts during classification process. Moreover, the classification of a new data value is based on successive tests to internal nodes i.e., it is classified according to one attribute each time with an attached degree of satisfaction. However, as we proved in [19] classification based on multi-dimensional classes (i.e., classes defined taking into account many attributes simultaneously) results in better classification inferences. Even in the fuzzy decision trees approach the eventual assignment is crisp since each item is assigned to the most probable class where as in our approach an item may be classified into different classes. Moreover, the classification belief for each assignment is maintained.

Our contribution. The contributions of this paper are summarized as follows:

- *Maintenance of classification belief* all the way through the classification process. Moreover a value set can be assigned to more than one classes with a different belief.
- *Decision support tools* for decision related to: i. relative importance of classes in a data set (e.g., "young vs. old customers"), ii. relative importance of classes across data sets, and iii. the information content of different data sets.
- *Quality assessment* of a classification model. This procedure will be very useful for evaluating models and select the one that best fits the data under consideration.

It is important to stress that our contribution is independent of any classification algorithm. Indeed, we take as input the classes resulting from the application of any algorithm on a training set and we classify all the data set to these classes introducing uncertainty features. Moreover we take into account aggregate beliefs that will assist for decision support in the data set and across data sets.

The remainder of the paper is organized as follows. Section 2 surveys related work. Section 3 elaborates on the proposed classification approach while in Section 4 we present the fundamental concepts of the proposed classification framework. In Section 5 we define classification information measures so as to exploit the classification belief. Section 6 presents a quality assessment procedure for a classification scheme while in Section 7 we discuss the results of an experimental study we carried out using synthetic and real datasets. We conclude in Section 8 by summarizing and providing further research directions.

2 Related Work

The classification problem has been studied extensively in statistics, pattern recognition and machine learning community as a possible solution to the knowledge acquisition or knowledge extraction problem [12]. A number of classification techniques have been developed and are available in literature. Among these, the most popular are: *Bayesian classification*, *Neural Networks* and *Decision Trees.*

Bayesian classification is based on bayesian statistical classification theory. The aim is to classify a sample x to one of the given classes $c_1, c_2, \ldots, c_N$ using a probability model defined according to Bayes theory[3]. Also, complete knowledge of probability laws is necessary in order to perform the classification [7].

Decision trees are one of the widely used techniques for classification and prediction. A number of popular classifiers construct decision trees to generate classification models. A decision tree is constructed based on a training set of pre-classified data. Each internal node of the decision tree specifies a test of an attribute

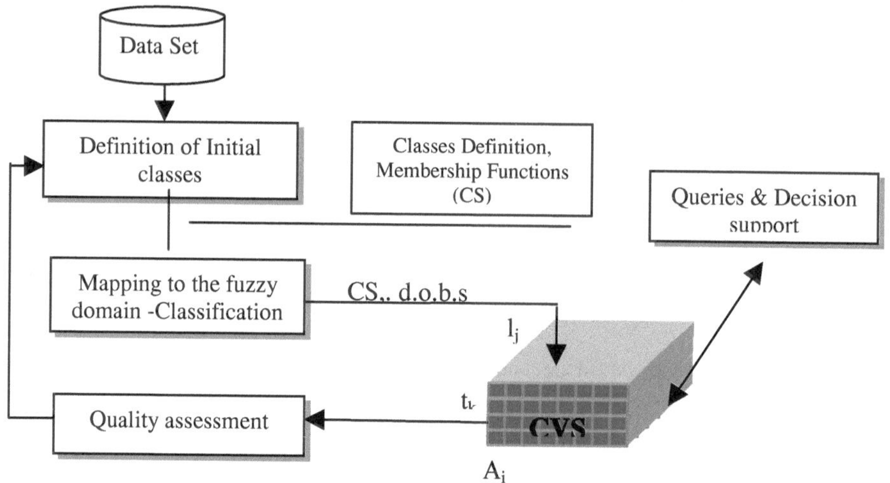

Fig. 1. Steps of the classification approach.

of the instance and each branch descending of that node corresponds to one of the possible values for this attribute. Also, each leaf corresponds to one of the defined classes. Some of the most widely known algorithms that are available in literature for constructing decision trees are: ID3[10], C4.5[11], SPRINT[13], SLIQ[9], CART etc.

Another classification approach used in many data mining applications for prediction and classification is based on neural networks [1].

The above reference to some of the most widely known classical classification methods denotes the relatively few efforts that have been devoted to data analysis techniques (i.e., classification) in order to handle uncertainty. These approaches produce a crisp classification decision, that is an object either belongs to a class or not and all objects are considered to belong in a class equally. It is obvious that there is no notion of uncertainty representation in the proposed methods, though usage and reveal of uncertainty is recognized as an important issue in research area of data mining[14]. For this purpose, the interest of research community has been concentrated on this context and new classification approaches have recently been proposed in literature so as to handle uncertainty. In this point we should mention that the issue of uncertainty handling is not restricted to the classification but there is also an important set of clustering approaches that aims at uncertainty handling [17, 18]. However, in this paper we concentrated on the case of classification process.

An approach for pattern classification based on fuzzy logic is represented in [2]. The main idea is the extraction of fuzzy rules for identifying each class of data. The rule extraction methods are based on estimating clusters in the data and each cluster obtained corresponds to a fuzzy rule that relates a region in the input space to an output class. Thus, for each class c_i the cluster center is defined that provides the rule: *If {input is near x_i} then class is c_i*. Then for a given input vector x, the system defines the degree of fulfillment of each rule and the consequent of the rule with highest degree of fulfillment is selected to be the output of the fuzzy system. As a consequence, the approach uses fuzzy logic to define the best class in which a data value can be classified but the final result is the classification of each data to one of the classes.

In [15], an approach based on fuzzy decision trees is presented and aims at uncertainty handing. It combines symbolic decision trees with fuzzy logic concepts so as to enhance decision trees with additional flexibility offered by fuzzy representation. More specifically, they propose a procedure to build a fuzzy decision tree based on classical decision tree algorithm (ID3) and adapting norms used in fuzzy logic to represent uncertainty [15]. As a consequence, the tree-building procedure is the same as that of ID3. The difference is that a training example can be partially classified to several tree nodes. Thus, each instance of data can belong to one or more nodes with different membership that is calculated based on the restriction along the path from root to the specific node. However, according to the decision tree methodology the classification inferences are crisp. More specifically, to define the classification assigned to a sample, we should find leaves whose restrictions are satisfied by sample and combine their decisions into a single crisp response. Furthermore, there is no evaluation of proposed inference procedures as regards the quality of new sample classification. Also, there is a significant amount of information included in decision tree that is not exploited and thus there is useful knowledge that is not extracted.

In general, there are some approaches proposed in literature, which aim at dealing with uncertainty representation (e.g. fuzzy decision trees). According to these approaches each data value can be assigned to one or more classes with an attached degree of belief. However, they don't propose ways to handle classification information and exploit it for evaluation of classification scheme and decision-making. Another related issue is how well a classification model fits an evolving data set. As new data values are inserted to the data set, it is possible the statistical features of the classes to be affected and then the classification model should be updated. It is obvious that there is a need to define an evaluation procedure for classification schemes, which helps us to understand how successful the classification for a specific data set is. However, the evaluation of classification models is under-addressed by most classification approaches where as we address and tackle the issue.

3 System Architecture

As it is well known, the classification procedure is based on a predefined set of classes. We assume a set of classes as a result of a preceding clustering process, which aims at the definition of the "optimal" clustering scheme that fits a specific data set [6]. More specifically, we apply a clustering algorithm that results in a clustering scheme corresponding to the initial classes on which the classification process is based. However, the majority of clustering algorithms result in crisp clusters (i.e., they assume that each data item belongs to only one cluster), but as we have mentioned in previous sections each value that belongs to a cluster should not be treated equally. Thus, in order to handle uncertainty, we define mapping functions for the clusters, based on fuzzy logic. These functions map the clusters to the fuzzy domain and enable the production of classification uncertainty during the classification process. Then, we use the clusters' definition (e.g. representatives of

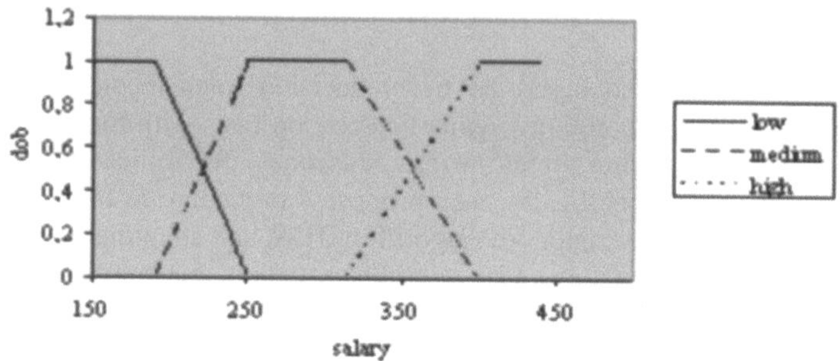

Fig. 2. The transformation function (HMF) for one-dimensional data set.

clusters) and membership functions, in order to define the classification approach introduced in this paper.

The basic modules of the system follow (Figure 1):

- *Definition of initial classes:* A clustering or classification algorithm discovers classes (or clusters) that correspond to the distribution of the data. The result of the module is for each non-categorical attribute (A_i) of a data set a set of classes $L=\{l_i\}$ (where l_i a category) and a set of mapping functions appropriately chosen.
- *Mapping to the fuzzy domain:* The result of this procedure is a set of degrees of belief (d.o.bs)$\{M = \{\mu_{li}(t_k.A_i)\}$. Each member of this set represents the confidence that the specific value $t_k.A_i$ (where t_k is the tuple identifier) belongs to the set denoted by the category l_i. The resulting d.o.bs are stored in a structure called Classification Value Space (CVS).
- *Quality Assessment:* In this module the quality of the classification scheme is assessed in terms of information measures extracted from the CVS. The goal is to assess how well the current classification model is applied to the data set. As the database grows and new instances are classified the system is able to check if it is necessary to redefine the initial clustering scheme.
- *Queries and Decision support.* The CVS includes significant knowledge for our data set. We can exploit this knowledge for decision making, based on the energy metric [5] measure. Then, we exploit the results of these measures in order to make decisions with reference to the knowledge conveyed by CVS.

4 Mapping to the Fuzzy Domain

In this section, we briefly present the procedures for uncertainty representation after the definition of the initial categories on which the classification process is based. The interested reader may consult [19] for more details.

4.1 Classification Space (CS)

Assuming a data set S, we define the initial groups into which our data can be partitioned. A clustering algorithm can be used in order to identify these initial groups of data (clusters), which then used in the classification process. As mentioned before, there is inherent uncertainty in the classification of a value in a set of classes. The set of clusters can be represented by the clusters' representatives and the extent of the partitions. Then, we attach to each class a mapping function that maps each real value to the fuzzy domains and represents the belief that the value belongs to the class. We introduce the term *Classification Space* (CS) that implies the specifications of the classes along with the attached mapping functions. Assuming the appropriate set of value domains for these classes, for each attribute (or set of attributes) A_i we define the corresponding *classification set* $L_{Ai} = \{ct \mid ct$ is a *classification tuple*$\}$. The classification tuples are of the form: $(l_i, [v_1,v_2], f_i)$ where l_i is a user defined lexical category that corresponds to cluster i, $[v_1, v_2]$ is the respective value interval and f_i the assigned mapping function. The value domains may be overlapping, increasing thus the expressive power of the classification mechanism since some values may be classified to one or more classes with different d.o.bs.

The selection of mapping functions is an important issue that can affect the results of the classification process. However, in this paper we do not deal with the evaluation of membership functions or their influence to the classification results. We have currently adopted the *hypertrapezoidal membership functions (HMFs)* [8] (see Figure 2), though we can use any other type of membership functions [5]. The main reason of HMFs selection is that they are proposed as a convenient mechanism for representing and dealing with multidimensional fuzzy sets. The definition of these functions is based on the representatives of clusters and a factor, which determines the ambiguity (overlapping) between the clusters [8]. Thus, we can use them as the appropriate functions for representing the uncertainty in multidimensional datasets.

4.2 Classification Value Space (CVS)

The result of mapping the data set values to the fuzzy domain using the CS can be represented by a 3D structure, further called Classification Value Space (CVS) (see Figure 3). The front face of this structure stores the original data set while each of the other cells $C[A_i, l_j, t_k]$, where j, k >1, stores the d.o.b. $\mu_{li}(S.t_k.Ai)$. In the sequel, we refer to a cell in the CVS as $CVS(t_k.A_i.l_j)$. The higher the d.o.b. is, the higher is our confidence that the specific value belongs to the specific set.

The algorithm for computing the d.o.bs for the data set values with reference to the CS follows:

```
for each attribute Ai in CS
 for each category lj of Ai
  for each value tk.Ai in the data set
    compute μli(S.tk.Ai)
 end
 end
end
```

The time complexity of the above algorithm is $O(d{\cdot}c{\cdot}n{\cdot}f(c,d))$ where d is the number of attributes(data set dimension), c is the number of classes (clusters), n is the number of d.o.b. values for a category l_j (number of tuples in the data set) and $f(c,d)$ is the complexity of degrees of belief computation. Usually $c, d << n$. Thus, the time complexity for computing the d.o.bs for a data set will be $O(n)$.

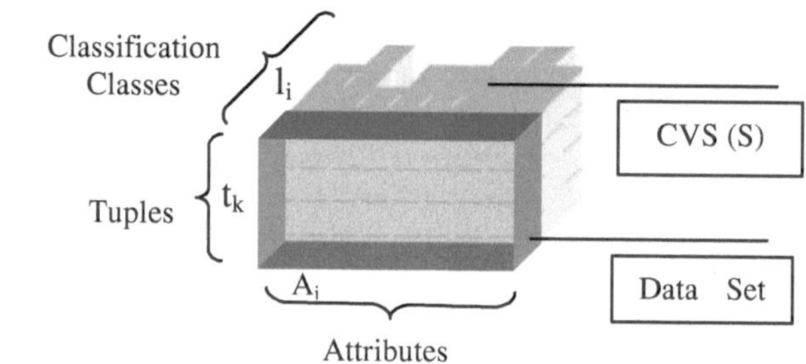

Fig. 3. The CVS holding the "degrees of belief" (d.o.b.s) for the classification of the attributes' values

4.3 CVS Storage

As the expected size of the CVS is very big we designed a scheme that minimizes the storage requirements. The CVS is stored in two database tables, further called *cube dictionary* and *CVS table* respectively. The *cube dictionary* includes information about the CS of the data sets. It stores the name of cube, the name of the data set (i.e., database table) that a specific cube refers to, the name of the data set attributes, the names of the data set classes and the membership function assigned to each of them. The *CVS table* corresponds to CVS cube. It stores the distinct values of our data set and the degree of belief with which a specific value is classified into pre-specified classes of our data set. Each category (cluster) of a data set corresponds to a specific column of the table while there is also a specific column for each attribute of the data set. Each distinct value of the data set and the corresponding d.o.b. is stored only once. Thus, there are no duplicate values and the storage requirements of the proposed structure (i.e., CVS) are minimized to the storage cost for the data set distinct values. Assume a data set S with N tuples and let Dist(N) the number of distinct values of S. Then the cost of storage for cube related to S will be Dist(N)/N of the cost for the whole data set. For instance, in case of a corporate data set consisting of 1000 tuples, there are 74 different values for the attribute "age". Thus, the storage cost of the cube related to "age" classification will be 0.07 of the cost for the whole data set.

5 Information Measures for Decision Support

The CVS conveys significant knowledge included in cumulative information measures. Various information measures have been proposed in literature such as entropy and energy [5]. We adopt the energy metric, which is essentially a measure of the overall information content of a fuzzy set (in our case CVS). We exploit it in order to evaluate classification schemes or support decision making related to a data set. The aim here is to be able to compare

i. relative importance of classes in a data set (e.g., "young vs. old customers")
ii. relative importance of classes across data sets
iii. the information content of different data sets

In the sequel, we assume both the case of one- and multi-dimensional classification. This means that we can define classes for our data set and the corresponding membership functions of its initial classes, taking in account one or more attributes (e.g. "salary", "age", "salary and age").

5.1 Class Energy Metric

This is a measure of the information (significance) of a class l_i in the data set S. Let A_i be a set of attributes (A_{i1}, A_{i2}, ..., A_{im}) and l_i a related category. Then the overall information that S contains, regarding the classification of its data in the category l_i is given by the information measure:

$$E_{li}(S.A_i) = \left(\sum_k [\mu_{l_i}(S.t_k.A_i)]^q \right) \quad (1)$$

where q is a positive integer. The typical value of q is 2. Higher values suppress lower d.o.b. making the contribution of the tuples with high (close to 1) d.o.bs more significant.

For instance assume an attribute "salary" and its category *high*. Applying Equation 1 the overall information included in the data set for the category *high* salaries is given by the formula 1a. In Figure 4 the corresponding slice and column of CVS are selected in order to acquire the information measure E_{high}.

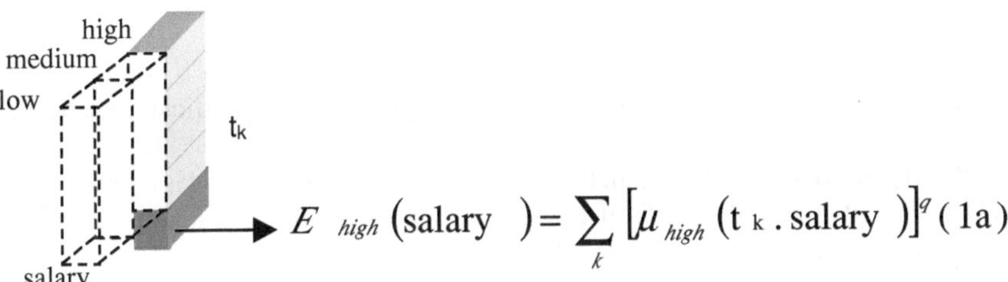

Fig. 4. Representing the *category energy metric* in cube.

5.2 Attribute Energy Metric

The *overall energy* of a set of attributes A_i = (A_{i1}, A_{i2}, ..., A_{im}), is the sum of the energy metric values for all the attribute classes. This measure represents the information content of the attribute. Hence:

$$E_{A_i}(S) = \sum_{li} E_{li} \quad (2)$$

More specifically, $E_{Ai}(S)$ represents the information included in the slice of the CVS cube (Figure 5) corresponding to a specific attribute. For instance, the slice of cube in

Figure 5 represents the overall information for attribute "salary" when we classify the data in the classes *low*, *medium* and *high.*

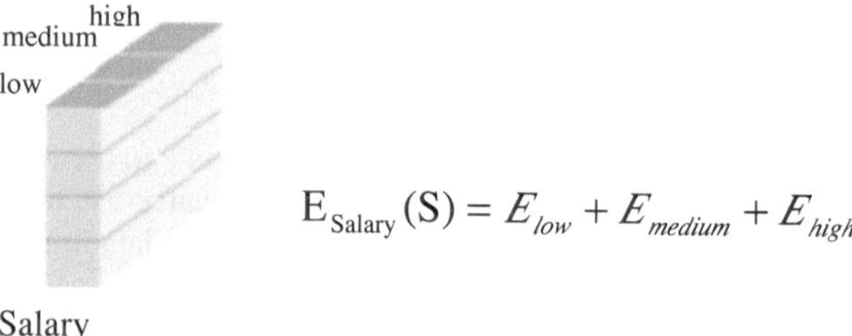

Fig. 5. Attribute energy metric in the CVS

6 Classification Scheme Quality Assessment

One of the most important requirements is the assessment of the classification scheme's quality. This implies how successful a classification scheme is, considering a specific data set and how well the defined classes of an attribute fit the data.
A successful classification scheme should contain a significant amount of information i.e., the value of class/attribute *energy* have to be as high as possible. Another requirement is the minimization of the entropy in the defined classes, i.e., to minimize the cases that the data values are equally assigned to all classes. We introduce a new quality assessment index for classification based on these criteria and concepts of the information theory.

Let C={c_1,..., c_{nc}} to be a classification scheme for a data set S into n_c clusters. The following measures are defined to assess the quality of a classification scheme.

Uncertainty of a class. It evaluates the uncertainty within a class based on the memberships (degrees of belief) of the data into the specific class. This term is also known in the information theory as *surprise*[20].:

$$Unc\_Cl_{c_j} = -\sum_{i=1}^{N} \log_2(\mu_{ij}) \Big/ N \tag{3}$$

where N is the number of tuples in the dataset under consideration. In case that the membership values of the data to the classes are equal i.e., $\mu_{ij}=1/n_c$, Unc_Cl_{cj} obtains its higher value, i.e., $log_2(n_c)$, Moreover, this is an indication that the class c_j does not fit the data under consideration.

Overall belief of a class. The *overall belief* that a data set supports a class is given by the equation:

$$DoB_{c_j} = \sum_{i=1}^{N} \mu_{ij}^{q} \Big/ N \quad (4)$$

where N is the number of tuples in the data set S.

Information coefficient of a class. It is an index of the quality of the class under consideration defined as

$$InfoCl_i = DoB_{cj} \cdot \left(\log_2(n_c) - Unc\_Cl_i\right) \quad (5)$$

where n_c is the number of classes under consideration.

The definition of *Info_Coef* indicates that both criteria of a "good" classification scheme (i.e., amount of information and uncertainty) are properly combined, enabling reliable evaluation of results. The first term, DoB_{cj}, indicates the significance of a class in the data set, i.e., the amount of information included in the specific class. A high value of this term is an indication of a class that is significantly supported by the data. The second term is an indication of the class uncertainty. More specifically, it evaluates the deviation of the class uncertainty from the case that all membership values to a set of classes are equal (i.e., the case of no clustering tendency or improper definition of classes). The highest is the value of this term the highest is our belief that the data are classified to the proper class and thus the defined scheme fits to the data set under consideration. Then the *Information coefficient of the classification scheme C* is given by the equation:

$$Info\_Coef(C) = \frac{1}{n_c} \sum_{i=1}^{n_c} InfoCl_i \quad (6)$$

where n_c is the number of classes under consideration.

Thus, the *Info_Coef* can be used as a measure for finding the best partitioning that fits a data set taking in account the uncertainty included in its values. We consider a variety of classification schemes for our data set, as defining by considering the results of different clustering algorithms. Then, we evaluate them based on the *Info_Coef* measure in order to select the scheme that best fit our data set. In general terms, the best classification scheme corresponds to a local maximum of *Info_Coef* in its graph versus n_c (number of clusters/classes). It is the point (here the number of classes) at which the *Info_Coef* is maximized.

7 Experimental Study

Based on the framework we described in previous sections, we implemented a classification system for handling uncertainty in the data mining process. It is a system implemented in Java using the JDBC application interface to connect to a data set. Using this system, we experimented with synthetic data sets of known structure. The experimental results focus on handling the classification belief and exploiting it for decision-making. Also, we evaluate the use of information measures for assessing the quality of classification schemes.

Table 1. (a) Category and Energy metrics for "salary", (b) Category and Energy metrics for "age"

Salary	
E_{low}	304.2736
E_{medium}	343.2594
E_{high}	348.0000
E_{salary}	995.5320

(a)

Age	
E_{young}	398.75
E_{old}	540.96
E_{age}	939.71

(b)

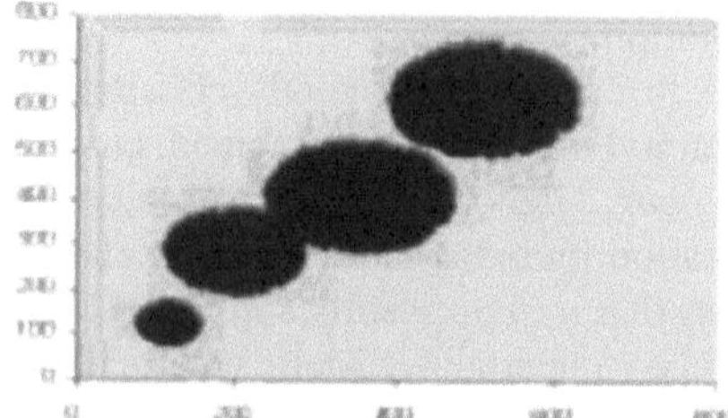

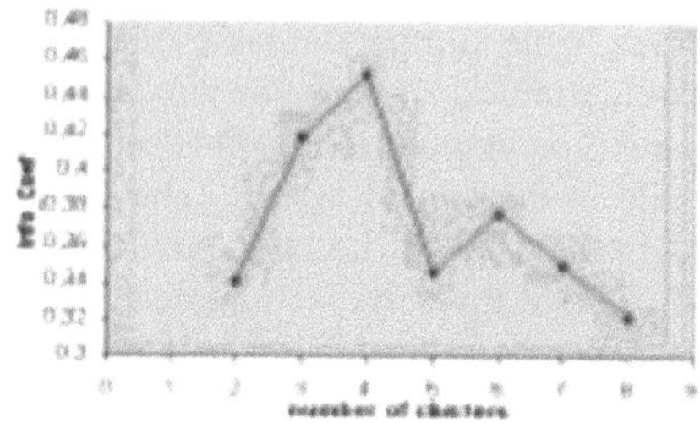

Fig. 6. a. A data set classified in four clusters, **b.** The graph of QoC_{Ai} versus the number of clusters considering a synthetic two-dimensional data set

We assume a synthetic data set maintaining information related to the employees. The schema of this data set is R = {salary, age}. Our system uses the CS (centers, name of categories, value domain and mapping functions) for the data set and transforms it into a CVS. This implies classification of the data set values into classes using HMFs as the mapping functions. Table 1a and Table 1b present the class energy metric values for the attributes "salary", "age" respectively. Some "useful" knowledge about data set can be extracted from these tables. For instance, the class energies in Table1a indicate that our data set supports with more confidence *high* salaries than *low* salaries ($E_{high} > E_{low}$). Also, Table1b indicates that in this data set we are more confident to have *old* employees than *young* ones($E_{old} > E_{young}$).

Selecting the optimal classification scheme. This part of our experiments refers to quality assessment of classification schemes. We experiment with real and synthetic data sets and the goal is to evaluate the different classification schemes, resulting from different learning procedures, so as to select the scheme that best fits our data set.

The evaluation of schemes is based on the quality classification measure *Info_Coef* defined in Section 6. More specifically, we considered different partionings of a data set corresponding to the different sets of initial classes on which the classification process will be based. Then exploiting the appropriate membership functions (in our case HMFs) we map the values to the fuzzy domains. Thus, the data set is transformed into CVSs, one for each classification scheme (partitioning). Using the $Info\_Coef_{Ai}$ measure we evaluate the defined classification schemes so as to select the

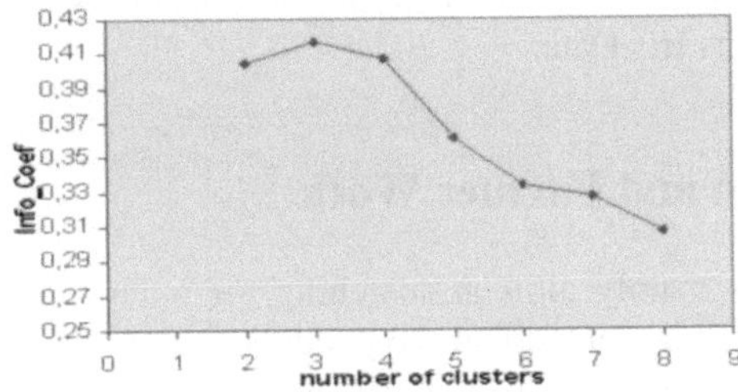

Fig. 7. The graph of QoC_{Ai} versus the number of clusters considering Iris Data Set

scheme that best fits the data under consideration. In the sequel, due to lack of space, we present only some representative examples of our experimental study.

We consider a synthetic two-dimensional data set, following the normal distribution. It is clear from Figure 6a that the data set consists of four overlapping clusters. This is also verified by our approach based on the *Info_Coef* measure. Figure 6b depicts the behavior of *Info_Coef* versus the number of classes. We observe there, that the classification scheme of four classes corresponds to a maximum value of *Info_Coef*. This is an indication that the best classification for the data under consideration is the scheme of four classes.

Also, we use a sample data set (see Fig. 8a) that contains the values of "salary and age". We apply two-dimensional clustering so as to define the initial classes of the data set considering the attributes "salary and age". Fig. 8b shows the graph of the *Info_Coef* measure as a function of the number of clusters. We observe there, that

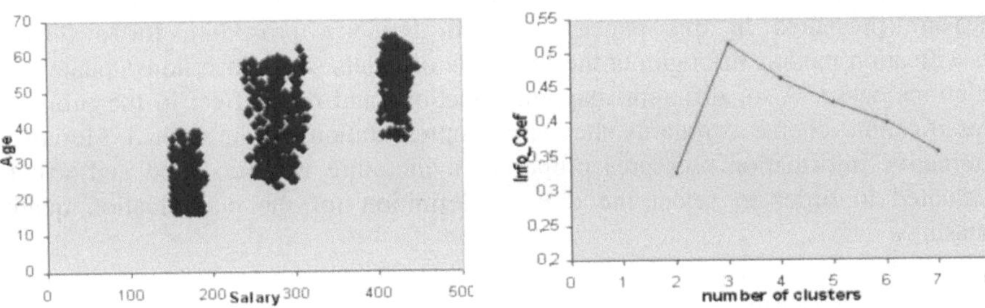

Fig. 8. a. A data set classified in three classes, **b.** The graph of QoC versus the number of clusters considering a two-dimensional data set "salary and age".

the classification scheme with three classes corresponds to a maximum value of *Info_Coef*. This is an indication that the best classification for "salary and age" a scheme of three classes, which is also verified by the distribution of the data set values in Fig. 8a.

We carried out a similar experiment using Iris Data Set. It consists of 150 measurements (length and width of sepal and petal) belonging to three flower varieties. This is also verified by our approach. We consider eight different classifications of Iris Data and we evaluate them based on the *Info_Coef* measure. As Fig. 7 depicts *Info_Coef* takes its maximum value when we consider a scheme of three classes. This is an indication that the classification scheme of three classes is the scheme that best fits Iris Data.

8 Conclusion and Further Work

The KDD process mainly aims at searching for interesting instances of patterns in data sets. It is widely accepted that the patterns must be *comprehensible*. This will be achieved by classifying the data into classes that fit the data set properties to a satisfactory degree. The contributions of this paper are summarized as follows:

- *Maintenance of classification belief* all the way through the classification process. A data set value can be assigned to more than one classes with a different belief.
- *Information measures* enabling decisions related to: i. relative importance of classes in a data set (i.e., "young vs. old customers"), ii. relative importance of classes across data sets, iii. the information content of different data sets
- *Quality assessment of classification models*, so as to find how well a model fits the underlying data set.

It is important to stress that our contribution is independent of the technique used for the definition of initial clusters. Indeed, we take as input the classes resulting from the application of any algorithm on a training set and we classify all the data set to these classes introducing uncertainty features. Moreover we take into account aggregate beliefs that will assist for decision support in the data set and across data sets.

Further work in the incremental production of optimal classification and association rules extraction models. We aim at exploiting the classification quality measure presented in this paper so as to define a procedure for evaluating classification models through out the life cycle of a data set as insertions/updates and deletions occur. Also, different mapping functions and their effect to the proposed classification scheme as regards uncertainty representation will be studied. Moreover, alternative information measures proposed in literature will be tested and will be evaluated in order to select the optimal definition for the classification quality measures.

References

1. M. Berry, G. Linoff. Data Mining Techniques For marketing, Sales and Customer Support. John Willey & Sons, Inc, 1996.
2. S. Chiu. "Extracting Fuzzy Rules from Data for Function Approximation and Pattern Classification". *Fuzzy Information Engineering- A Guided Tour of Applications*.(Eds.: D. Dubois, H. Prade, R Yager), 1997.
3. P. Cheeseman, J. Stutz. "Bayesian Classification (AutoClass): Theory and Results". *Advances in Knowledge Discovery and Data Mining*. (Eds:U. Fayyad,et al), AAAI Press,1996.
4. U. Fayyad, G. Piatesky-Shapiro, P. Smuth & R. Uthurusamy(editors). "From DataMining to Knowledge Discovery: An Overview". *Advances in Knowledge Discovery and Data Mining*. AAAI Press, 1996.

5. M. Gupta, and T. Yamakawa, (eds*).* "Fuzzy Logic and Knowledge Based Systems", *Decision and Control* (North Holland). 1988.
6. M. Halkidi, M. Vazirgiannis. Clustering: Quality measures and uncertainty handling. *Technical report*, Athens Univ. of Economic & Business, 1999
7. T. Horiuchi. "Decision Rule for Pattern Classification by Integrating Interval Feature Values". *IEEE Transactions on Pattern Analysis and Machine Intelligence*, Vol.20, No.4, April 1998, pp.440-448.
8. W. Kelly, J. Painter. "Hypertrazoidal Membership Functions". *5th IEEE International Conference on Fuzzy Systems*, New Orleans, September 8, 1996.
9. M. Melta, R. Agrawal, J. Rissanen. "SLIQ: A fast scalable classifier for data mining". *In EDBT'96, Avigon France,* March 1996.
10. T. Mitchell. *Machine Learning*. McGraw-Hill, 1997
11. J.R Quinlan. *C4.5: Programs for Machine Learning*. Morgan Kaufman, 1993.
12. R. Rastori, K. Shim. "PUBLIC: A Decision Tree Classifier that Integrates Building and Pruning". *Proceeding of the 24th VLDB Conference,* New York, USA, 1998.
13. J.Shafer, R. Agrawal, M. Mehta. "SPRINT: A scalable parallel classifier for data mining". *In Proc. of the VLDB Conference*, Bombay, India, September 1996
14. Glymour C., MadiganD., Pregibon D, Smyth P, "Statistical Inference and Data Mining", in CACM v39 (11), 1996, pp. 35-42
15. Cezary Z. Janikow, "Fuzzy Decision Trees: Issues and Methods", *IEEE Transactions on Systems, Man, and Cybernetics*, Vol. 28, Issue 1, pp 1-14, 1998.
16. M. Vazirgiannis, "A classification and relationship extraction scheme for relational databases based on fuzzy logic", in the proceedings of the Pacific -Asian Knowledge Discovery & Data Mining '98 Conference, Melbourne, Australia, 1999.
17. S. Theodoridis, K. Koutroubas. *Pattern recognition,* Academic Press, 1999
18. Bezdeck J.C, Ehrlich R., Full W., "FCM:Fuzzy C-Means Algorithm", Computers and Geoscience 1984
19. M. Vazirgiannis, M. Halkidi. "Uncertainty handling in the datamining process with fuzzy logic", to appear in the proceedings of the IEEE-FUZZ conference, San Antonio, May, 2000.
20. T. Shneider. "Information Theory Primer", Chapter II, PhD thesis: "The information Content of Binding Sites on Nucleotide Sequences". http://www.lecb.ncifcrf.gov/~toms/paper/primer/

The Role of Domain Knowledge in a Large Scale Data Mining Project

Ioannis Kopanas, Nikolaos M. Avouris, and Sophia Daskalaki

University of Patras, 26500 Rio Patras, Greece
{ikop, N.Avouris}@ee.upatras.gr, sdask@upatras.gr

Abstract. Data Mining techniques have been applied in many application areas. A Data Mining project has been often described as a process of automatic discovery of new knowledge from large amounts of data. However the role of the domain knowledge in this process and the forms that this can take, is an issue that has been given little attention so far. Based on our experience with a large scale Data Mining industrial project we present in this paper an outline of the role of domain knowledge in the various phases of the process. This project has led to the development of a decision support expert system for a major Telecommunications Operator. The data mining process is described in the paper as a continuous interaction between explicit domain knowledge, and knowledge that is discovered through the use of data mining algorithms. The role of the domain experts and data mining experts in this process is discussed. Examples from our case study are also provided.

1 Introduction

Knowledge discovery in large amounts of data (KDD), often referred as data min-ing, has been an area of active research and great advances during the last years. While many researchers consider KDD as a new field, many others identify in this field an evolution and transformation of the applied AI sector of expert systems or knowledge-based systems. Many ideas and techniques that have emerged from the realm of knowledge-based systems in the past are applicable in knowledge discovery projects. There are however considerable differences between the traditional knowledge-based systems and knowledge discovery approaches. The fact that today large amounts of data exist in most domains and that knowledge can be induced from these data using appropriate algorithms, brings in prominence the KDD techniques and facilitates the building of knowledge-based systems. According to Langley and Simon [1] data mining can provide increasing levels of automation in the knowledge engineering process, replacing much time-consuming human activity with automatic techniques that improve accuracy or efficiency by discovering and exploiting regularities in stored data. However the claim that data mining approaches eventually will automate the process

I.P. Vlahavas and C.D. Spyropoulos (Eds.): SETN 2002, LNAI 2308, pp. 288–299, 2002.

and lead to discovery of knowledge from data with little intervention or support of domain experts and domain knowledge is not always true.

The role of the domain experts in KDD projects has been given little attention so far. In contrary to old knowledge-based systems approaches where the key roles were those of the domain expert and the knowledge engineer, today there have been more disciplines involved that seem to play key roles (e.g. data base experts, data analysts, data warehouse developers etc.) with the consequence the domain experts to receive less prominence. Yet, as admitted in Brachman &Anand [2], the domain knowledge should lead the KDD process. Various researchers have made suggestions on the role of domain knowledge in KDD. Domingos [3] suggests use of domain knowledge as the most promising approach for constraining knowledge discovery and for avoiding the well-known problem of data overfitting by the discovered models. Yoon et al. [4], referring to the domain knowledge to be used in this context, propose the following classification: inter-field knowledge, which describes relationship among attributes, category domain knowledge that represents useful categories for the domains of the attributes and correlation domain knowledge that suggests correlations among attributes. In a similar manner Anand et al. [5] identify the following forms of domain knowledge: attribute relationship rules, hierarchical generalization trees and constraints. An example of the latter is the specification of degrees of confidence in the different sources of evidence. These approaches can be considered special cases of the ongoing research activity in knowledge modeling, ontologies and model-based knowledge acquisition, see for instance [6], [7], with special emphasis in cases of data-mining driven knowledge acquisition.

However these studies concentrate in the use of domain knowledge in the main phase of data mining, as discussed in the next section, while the role of domain knowledge in other phases of the knowledge discovery process is not covered. In this paper we attempt to explore our experience with a large-scale data-mining project, to identify the role of the domain knowledge in the various phases of the process. Through this presentation we try to demonstrate that a typical KDD project is mostly a multi-stage knowledge modelling experiment in which domain experts play a role as crucial as in any knowledge-based system building exercise.

2 Identification of Key Roles and Key Phases of a KDD Project

According to Langley and Simon [1] the following five stages are observed in the development of a knowledge-based system using inductive techniques: (a) problem formulation, (b) determination of the representation for both training data and knowledge to be learned, (c) collection of training data and knowledge induction, (d) evaluation of learned knowledge, (e) fielding of the knowledge base. In Fayyad et al. [8] the process of KDD is described through the following nine steps: (a) Defining the goal of the problem, (b) Creating a target dataset, (c) Data cleaning and pre-processing, (d) Data transformation, e.g. reduction and projection in order to obtain secondary features, (e) matching the goals of the project to appropriate data mining method (e.g. clustering, classification etc.), (f) Choosing the data mining algorithm to be used, (g) Data Mining, (h) Interpretation of identified patterns, (i) Using discovered knowledge. By comparing the two processes one should notice the emphasis of the first frame on knowledge and the second on data analysis and processing. However in reality, while the stages proposed by Fayyad et al. do occur in most cases, the role of domain knowledge in them is also important, as discussed in this paper, while the final stage of building the knowledge base and fielding the system is also knowledge-intensive, often involving multiple knowledge representations and demanding many knowledge evaluation and knowledge visualization techniques.

The subject of our case study was the development of a knowledge-based decision support system for customer insolvency prediction in a large telecommunication industry. During the initial problem definition phase the observation of existence of large amounts of data in the industry concerned, led to the decision of extensive use of KDD techniques during this project. However this extensive dataset did not cover all aspects of the problem. While high degree of automation in modern telephone switching centres means that telephone usage by the customers of the company was well monitored, information on the customers financial situation and credit levels, which are particularly important for this problem, were missing. This is a problem that often occurs in real problems; that is different levels of automation in different aspects of the problem domain leads to non-uniform data sets. Also techniques to infer knowledge, based on assumptions, observations and existing data need to be used extensively during the problem definition and modeling phase. So, for instance, if information on the credit levels of a customer is missing, this can be inferred from information on regularity of payment of the telephone bills, based on the assumption that irregular payments are due to financial difficulties of the customers involved. This is a typical example of use of domain knowledge in the so called 'data transformation phase'. From early stages it was deduced that a number of domain experts and sources of data had to be involved in the process. Domain experts, e.g. executives involved in tackling the problem of customer insolvency and salesmen who deal with the problem in day-by-day basis were interviewed during the problem formulation phase and their views on the problem and its main attributes were recorded. An investigation of the available data was also performed and this involved executives of the information systems and the corporate databases who could provide an early indication on sources and quality of data. Other key actors were data analysts, who were also involved together with knowledge engineers and data mining experts.

3 Business Knowledge and KDD

In many KDD projects, like the case study discussed here, the domain knowledge takes the form of business knowledge, as this represents the culture and rules of practice of the particular company that has requested the knowledge-based system. Business knowledge has been a subject of interest for management consultant firms and business administration researchers [9]. Business process re-engineering (BPR) is a keyword that has been extensively used during the last years, while special attention has been put in building the so-called "institutional memory", "lessons learned data bases" and "best practice repositories". While there are but few examples of successful full-scale repositories of business knowledge in large companies today, the widespread application of these techniques makes worth investigating their existence. The relevance of these approaches to KDD projects and the importance of them as sources of domain knowledge to data mining efforts is evident and for this reason they should be taken in consideration. It should also be noticed that a side effect of a major data-mining project could be the adaptation of a business knowledge base with many rules and practices, which resulted from the KDD process. This is also the case with tacit knowledge and implicit knowledge, which is the not documented business knowledge, often discovered during such a project.

The distinction between domain knowledge and business knowledge is that the former relates to a general domain while the latter to a specific business, thus both are required in the case of a specific knowledge based system that is to be commissioned to a specific company. A special case of business knowledge that affects the KDD process relates to the business objectives as they become explicit and relate to problem definition. These can influence the parameters of the problem and measures of performance, as discussed by Gur Ali and Wallace [10]. In the following an example of such mapping of business objectives to measures of system performance is described for our case study.

4 Use of Domain Knowledge in an Insolvency Prediction Case Study

In this section, some typical examples of applying domain and business knowledge in the case study of the customer insolvency problem are provided. The examples are presented according to their order of appearance in the different phases of the KDD process. In the following section a classification of the domain and business knowledge used is attempted. The discussion included in this section does not provide a full account of the knowledge acquisition and modeling case study. It attempts rather through examples to identify the role of domain knowledge in the various phases of the project. A more detailed account would have included details on the modelling process, which involved many iterations and revisions of discovered knowledge.

A detailed description of the problem of customer insolvency of the telecommunications industry is beyond the scope of this paper. For more information on the problem, the approach used and the performance of the developed system, see Daskalaki et al. [11].

4.1 Problem Definition

In this phase the problem faced by a telecommunications organization was defined and requirements relating to its solution were set. The role of domain experts and the importance of domain and business knowledge in this phase is evident. For instance the billing process of the company, the rules concerning overdue payments and currently applied measures against insolvent customers need to be explicitly described by domain experts.

4.2 Creating Target Data Set

Formulation of the problem as a classification problem was performed at this stage. Available data were identified. As often occurs in KDD projects available data were not located in the same database, while discrepancies were observed among the entities of these databases. This phase was not focused on the specific features to be used as parameters for training data, but rather on broad data sets that were considered relevant, to be analyzed in subsequent steps. So the sources of data were: (a) telephone usage data, (b) financial transactions of customers with the company (billing, payments etc.), (c) customer details derived from contracts and phone directory entries (customer occupation, address etc.). As discussed earlier more details of customer credit conditions were not available in the corporate databases and could not become available from outside sources. The role of domain and business knowledge in this stage concerned the structure of the available information and the semantic value of it, so this knowledge was offered mostly by the data processing department, in particular employees involved in data entry for the information systems involved. Serious limitations of the available data were identified during this process. For instance it was discovered that the information systems of the organization did not make reference to the customer as an individual in recorded transactions, but rather as a phone number owner. This made identification of an individual as an owner of multiple telephone connections particularly difficult.

4.3 Data Prepossessing and Transformation

This phase is the most important preparation phase for the data mining experiments; The domain knowledge during this stage has been used in many ways:

(i) elimination of irrelevant attributes
(ii) inferring more abstract attributes from multiple primary values
(iii) determination of missing values
(iv) definition of the time scale of the observation periods,
(v) supporting data reduction by sampling and transaction elimination

In all the above cases the domain knowledge contributes to reduction of the search space and creation of a data set in which data mining of relevant patterns could be subsequently performed. Examples of usage of domain knowledge are:

Example of case i: The attribute "billed amount" was considered as irrelevant since it is known that not only insolvent customers relate to high bills, but also very good solvent customers.

Examples of case ii: Large fluctuation of the amounts in consecutive bills is considered important indication of insolvency, so these fluctuations should be esti-mated and taken in consideration.

Overdue payments have been inferred by comparison of due and payment dates of bills.

Considerable reduction of data was achieved by aggregating transactional data in the time dimension according to certain aggregation functions (sum, count, avg, stddev) and deduced attributes. Domain-related hypotheses of relevance of these deduced attrib-utes have driven this process. An example was the *DiffCount* attribute that represents the number of different telephone numbers called in a given period of time and the deviation of this attribute from a moving average in consecutive time periods. Defini-tion of this attribute is based on the assumption that if the diversity of called numbers fluctuates this is an entity related to possible insolvency.

Example of case iii: In many cases the missing values were deduced through interrelated attributes, e.g. Directory entries were correlated with customer records in order to determine the occupation of a customer, payments were related to billing periods, by checking the amount of the bill etc.

Examples of case iv: The transaction period under observation was set to 6 months prior to the unpaid bill, while the aggregation periods of phone call data was set to that of a fortnight.

Example of case v: Transactions related to inexpensive calls (charging less than 0.3 euros) were considered not interesting and were eliminated, resulting in reduction of about 50% of transaction data.

Sampling of data with reference to representative cases of customers in terms of area, activity and class (insolvent or solvent) was performed. This resulted in a data set concerning the 2% of transactions and customers of the company.

4.4 Feature and Algorithm Selection for Data Mining

At this phase the data mining algorithms to be used are defined (in our case decision trees, neural networks and discriminant analysis) and the transformed dataset of the previous phase is further reduced by selecting the most useful features in adequate form for the selected algorithm. This feature selection is based mostly on automatic techniques, however domain knowledge is used for interpretation of the selected feature set. Also this process is used for verification of the previous phase assumptions, so if certain features do not prove to be discriminating factors then new attributes should be deduced and tested. It should also be mentioned that this feature selection process is often interleaved with the data mining process, since many algorithms select the most relevant features during the training process. In our case a stepwise discriminant analysis was used for feature selection.

4.5 Data Mining

Training a classifier using the cases of the collected data is considered the most important phase of the process. Depending on the mining algorithm selected, the de-rived knowledge can be interpreted by domain experts. For instance the rules defined by a decision tree can be inspected by domain experts. Also the weights related to the input

variables of a neural network reflect their relevant importance in a specific net-work. This is related to the performance of the model.
Extensive experiments often take place using a trial and error approach, in which the contribution of the classes in the training dataset and the input features, as well as the parameters of the data mining algorithm used, can vary. The performance of the deduced models indicate which of the models are most suitable for the knowledge-based system.

In an extensive experimentation that took place in the frame of our case study, 62 features were included in the original data set. Subsequently, 5 different datasets where created that where characterised by different distribution of the classes (S)olvent/ (I)nsolvent customer. These distributions were the following: (I/S: 1:1, 1:10, 1:25, 1:50, 1:100)

A ten-fold validation of each data mining experiment was performed, by redistributing the training/testing cases in the corresponding data sets. This way 50 classifying decision trees were obtained. By inspecting the features that have been used in these experiments, we selected the 20 most prominent, shown in Table 1.

Table 1. Most popular features used in the 50 classifiers

Feature	***Feature description***	***n.***
NewCust	Identification of a new connection	50
Latency	Count of late payments	50
Count_X_charges	Count of bills with extra charges	50
CountResiduals	Count of times the bill was not paid in full	50
StdDif	Std Dev. of different numbers called	50
TrendDif11	Discrepancy from the mov. avg. of four previous periods of the count of different numbers called, measured on the 11th period.	50
TrendDif10	Idem for the 10th period	50
TrendDif7	Idem for the 7th period	50
TrendDif6	Idem for the 6th period	50
TrendDif3	Idem for the 3rd period	50
TrendUnitsMax	Maximum discrepancy from the moving average in units charged over the fifteen 2-week periods.	45
TrendDif5	Idem for the 5th period	43
TrendDif8	Idem for the 8th period	40
Average_Dif	Average # of different numbers called over the fifteen 2-weeks period.	39
Type	Type of account, e.g. business, domestic etc.	33
MaxSec	Maximum duration of the calls in any 2-week period during the study period.	31
TrendUnits5	Discrepancy from the moving average of the units charged, measured on the 5th period.	28
AverageUnits	Average # of units charged over the fifteen 2-weeks periods.	23
TrendCount5	Discrepancy from the moving average of the total # of calls, over the fifteen 2-week periods.	21
CountInstallments	Count of times the customer requested payment by instalments.	18

In Table 1, one may observe that the time-dependent feature most frequently used was the one related with the dispersion of the telephone numbers called (*TrendDif*, *StdDif* etc., 9 occurrences). This is a derived feature, proposed by the domain experts as discussed above, that could not possibly be defined without the domain experts

Case distribution 1:1

If (StdDif<0.382952541) And (MaxSec<1086)
Then
INSOLVENT (confidence 1.4%)

If (StdDif<0.382952541) And (MaxSec>1086) And (ExtraDebt>=1.5)
Then
INSOLVENT (confidence 100%)

If (StdDif>=0.382952541) And (TrendCountMax>=4.625)
Then
INSOLVENT (confidence 5.36%)

Case distribution 1:10

If (CountXCharges<1.5) And (NewCust<0.5) And (TrendDif11<-0.625) And (TrendSec3<-1863.75)
Then
INSOLVENT (confidence 0%)

If (CountXCharges<1.5) And (NewCust>=0.5) And (CountResiduals>=0.5) And (TrendDif7<-0.625)
Then
INSOLVENT (confidence 12.5%)

If (CountXCharges<1.5) And (NewCust>=0.5) And (CountResiduals>=0.5) And (TrendDif7>=-0.625) And (StdDif<0.487950027) Then
INSOLVENT (confidence 10.93%)

If (CountXCharges>=1.5) And (StdDif>=0.305032313) And (TrendUnitsMax>=121.25) And (TrendUnits6<-2.375) And (TrendDif10<-0.125)
Then
INSOLVENT (confidence 12.26%)

If (CountXCharges>=1.5) And (StdDif>=0.305032313) And (TrendUnitsMax>=121.25) And (TrendUnits6>=-2.375) then
INSOLVENT (confidence 7.6%)

Case distribution 1:25

if (CountXCharges<2.5) AND (NewCust>=0.5) AND (CountResiduals>=0.5) AND (TrendCount5>=-1.25) AND (TrendDif6<-0.375)
then
INSOLVENT (confidence 25.8%)

if (CountXCharges<2.5) AND (NewCust>=0.5) AND (CountResiduals>=0.5) AND (TrendCount5>=-1.25) AND (TrendDif6>=-0.375) AND (TrendCount5<1.375) AND (Type<55.5)
Then
INSOLVENT (confidence 55.03%)

if (CountXCharges>=2.5) AND (TrendDif3<-0.125) AND (TrendUnitsMax>=222.625) Then
INSOLVENT (confidence 9.49%)

Fig. 1. Knowledge in form of rules, determining *Customer Insolvency*

contribution. This table demonstrates the important role of the domain experts in suggesting meaningful features during this phase.

4.6 Evaluation and Interpretation of Learned Knowledge

Evaluation of the learned knowledge usually involves measuring the performance using a test data set. However this also involves knowledge interpretation, as discussed in the previous section, which involves domain experts. Knowledge interpretation can be based on the performance on test cases and on inspection of the derived knowledge if adequate knowledge representation formalism has been used. The evaluation criteria for the learned knowledge performance may be related to business objectives as defined by domain experts. An example of evaluation criteria is described in this section.

In figure 1 the knowledge in the form of rules, classifying the minority class cases (INSOLVENT customers) are exposed. It may be noticed that there is a considerable deviation in the parameters contributing to each of the rules, while the measure of performance of the rules vary considerably as indicated by the confidence measure expressing the rule performance in the test data set.

The criteria used for quantitative evaluation of learned knowledge in our case, as suggested by the domain experts, were different than the usual overall success rate and the specific class success rate indices usually applied in this kind of experiments. The domain experts suggested the following two criteria in our case study:

- The precision of the classifier, which is defined as the percentage of the actually insolvent customers in those, predicted as insolvent by the classifier.
- The accuracy of the classifier, which is defined as the percentage of the correctly predicted insolvent out of the total cases of insolvent customers in the data set.

These measures in problems of imbalanced class distributions, like in our case, in which the incidents of insolvent customers are very rare compared to those of solvent ones, seem more appropriate for measuring the effectiveness of the induced knowledge. By introducing these criteria, we discovered that the learned knowledge, despite of the fact that had very high success rates both overall and in specific classes, it did not meet the business objectives as these were defined by the Telecommunication Company (i.e. the requested measure of success was precision > 80% and accuracy > 50%).

An example of such a classifier is presented in the following table 2. In this table the performance of the classifier is shown in the testing data set. From this table one can see that the performance of this particular classifier is over 90 % in the majority class and over 83% in the minority class. However the precision is 113/2844= 3.9% and the accuracy is 113/136= 83%, thus making the performance in terms of the business objective set, not acceptable.

Table 2. Performance of classifier C1-3 for the insolvency prediction problem

		Predicted cases	
	Category	**Insolvent (0)**	**Solvent (1)**
Actual cases	**Insolvent (0)**	113 (83.1 %)	23 (16.9%)
	Solvent (1)	2731 (9.8 %)	25081 (90.2 %)

4.7 Fielding the Knowledge Base

This stage is essential in knowledge-based system development project, while this is often omitted in data mining projects as considered outside the scope of the data mining experiment. During this phase the learned knowledge is combined with other domain knowledge in order to become part of an operational decision support system, used by the company that commissioned the KDD project. The domain knowledge plays an important role during this stage. Usually the learned knowledge is just a part of this knowledge-based system, while heuristics or other forms of knowledge are often used as pre- or post-processors of the learned knowledge. In our case, the domain experts have suggested that the customers classified as insolvent, should be examined in more detail in terms of the amount due, the percentage of this amount that is due to third telecommunication operators, previous history of the customer etc, attributes that did not participate in the classification algorithm's decision, yet important for taking measures against the suspected insolvency.

In the fielded knowledge based system important aspects are also the available means for convincing the decision-maker for the provided advice. This can be achieved by providing explanation on the proposed suggestion or visualizing the data and the knowledge used, as suggested by many researchers, see Ankerst et al [12], Brachman & Anand [2], etc.

5 Conclusion

This paper has focused on the role of domain knowledge in a data-mining project. Eight distinct phases have been identified in the process and the role of the domain experts in each one of them has been discussed. In summary this role is shown in Table 3.

From this table and the discussion of the previous section it can be seen that while it is true that the domain knowledge plays a crucial role mostly in the initial and final stages of the process, it has contributed to some degree in all the phases of the project. If one takes also in consideration that the data mining phase (e), that necessitates comparatively little use of domain knowledge, accounts usually for not more than the 5% of the effort of such project, according to Williams and Huang [13], it is the most demanding stages of the process in which the domain experts and the domain knowledge participate mostly.

A conclusion of this study is that the data mining projects cannot possibly lead to successful knowledge-based systems, if attention is not paid to all the stages of the process. Since the domain knowledge plays such a crucial role in most of these stages, one should consider a data-mining project as a knowledge-driven process.

More support and adequate tools are therefore needed to be devised, which model the domain knowledge and track the contribution of domain experts that influence the assumptions made and the decision taken during the process.

Table 3. Overview of use of domain knowledge in a data mining project

stage	*Use of Domain Knowledge (DK)*	*Type of DK*	*Tools used*
(a) Problem definition	HIGH	Business and domain knowledge, requirements Implicit, tacit knowledge	
(b) Creating target data set	MEDIUM	Attribute relations, semantics of corporate DB	Data warehouse
(c) Data prepossessing and transformation	HIGH	Tacit and implicit knowledge for inferences	Database tools, statistical analysis
(d) Feature and algorithm selection	MEDIUM	Interpretation of the selected features	Statistical analysis
(e) Data Mining	LOW	Inspection of discovered knowledge	Data mining tools
(f) Evaluation of learned knowledge	MEDIUM	Definition of criteria related to business objectives	Data mining tools
(g) Fielding the knowledge base	HIGH	Supplementary domain knowledge necessary for implementing the system	Knowledge-based system shells and development tools

A concluding remark is that in terms of the actors involved in the process, next to the experts related to data analysis, data mining, data warehousing and data processing in a prominent position there should be put the domain experts that should participate actively and guide the process.

Acknowledgements. The research reported here has been funded under project YPER97-109 of the Greek Secretariat of Research and Technology. Special thanks are also due to the group of scientists of OTE S.A. that supplied us with data and continuous support. Special thanks to IBM for providing licenses of the DB2© and Intelligent Miner© products under their academic support programme. Also special thanks are due to the constructive comments of the anonymous reviewers on earlier draft of this paper.

References

1. Langley P., Simon H.A., Applications of Machine Learning and Rule Induction, Com. of the ACM, 38 (11), (1995), 55-64.
2. Brachman R. Anand T., "The Process of Knowledge Discovery in Databases: A Human-Centered Approach", Advances in Knowledge Discovery & Data Mining, AAAI Press & The MIT Press: California, 996, (1996), 37-57.
3. Domingos P., "The Role of Occam's Razor in Knowledge Discovery", Data Mining and Knowledge Discovery, an International Journal, Kluwer Academic Publishers, Vol.3, (1999), 409-425.

4. Yoon S.-C., Henschen L. J., Park E. K., Makki S., Using Domain Knowledge in Knowledge Discovery, Proc. ACM Conf. CIKM '99 1 1/99 Kansas City, MO, USA, pp. 243-250.
5. Anand S. S., Bell D. A., Hughes J. G., The Role of Domain Knowledge in Data Mining, Proc. ACM CIKM '95, Baltimore MD USA, pp. 37-43.
6. Van Heijst G., Schreiber G., CUE: Ontology Based Knowledge Acquisition, Proc. 8th European Knowledge Acquisition Workshop, EKAW 94, vol 867 of Lecture Notes in AI, pp. 178-199, Springer-Verlag, Berlin/Heidelberg (1994).
7. Wielinga B.J., Schreiber A.T., Breuker J.A., KADS: A modelling approach to knowledge Engineering, Knowledge Acquisition, 4(1), 5-53 (1992).
8. Fayyad U.M., Piatetsky-Shapiro G., and Smyth P., The KDD Process for Extracting Useful Knowledge from Volumes of Data, Communications of the ACM, 39(11), (1996)
9. Liebowitz J., Knowledge management and its link to artificial intelligence, Expert Systems with Applications 20, (2001) 1-6
10. Gur Ali, O.F., Wallace, W.A., Bridging the gap between business objectives and parameters of data mining algorithms, Decision Support Systems, 21, (1997) 3-15
11. Daskalaki S., Kopanas I., Goudara M., Avouris N., Data Mining for Decision Support on Customer Insolvency in Telecommunications Business, European Journal of Operations Research, submitted (2001)
12. Ankerst M., Ester M., Kriegel H-P, Towards and Effective Cooperation of the Computer and the user in Classification, ACM SIGKDD Int. Conf. on Knowledge Discovery & Data Mining (KDD'2000), Boston, MA (2000)
13. Williams G. J. and Huang Z, Modelling the KDD Process, A Four Stage Process and Four Element Model, TR DM 96013, CSIRO, Canberra, Australia (1996)

Artificial Neural Network Learning: A Comparative Review

Costas Neocleous[1] and Christos Schizas[2]

[2] Senior Lecturer, Mechanical Engineering Department, Higher Technical Institute, POBox 20423, Nicosia, Cyprus
costas@ucy.ac.cy
[2] Professor, Department of Computer Science, University of Cyprus, 75 Kallipoleos, 1678, POBox 20537, Nicosia, Cyprus
schizas@ucy.ac.cy

Abstract. Various neural learning procedures have been proposed by different researchers in order to adapt suitable controllable parameters of neural network architectures. These can be from simple Hebbian procedures to complicated algorithms applied to individual neurons or assemblies in a neural structure. The paper presents an organized review of various learning techniques, classified according to basic characteristics such as chronology, applicability, functionality, stochasticity etc. Some of the learning procedures that have been used for the training of generic and specific neural structures, and will be reviewed are: Hebbian-like (Grossberg, Sejnowski, Sutton, Bienenstock, Oja & Karhunen, Sanger, Yuile et al., Hasselmo, Kosko, Cheung & Omidvar), Reinforcement learning, Min-max learning, Stochastic learning, Genetics-based learning, Artificial life-based learning. The various learning procedures will be critically compared, and future trends will be highlighted.

1 Introduction

Different models of learning based on mathematics, statistics, logic, neural structures, information theory, evolutionary systems, artificial life, and heuristics have been proposed in recent years. The dedicated scientific journals and books on computational intelligence are abundant with learning rules and procedures, both in the general artificial intelligence (AI) context and in specific subfields like in machine learning and neural networks. Many of these rules can be identified as special cases of more generalized ones, usually being of a minor variation and typically given a different name or simply of different terminology and symbolism. In particular, in neural networks, there appears to be considerable confusion on what is what, what is a new rule and what ultimately constitutes a neural learning rule. Extensive expositions of neural learning rules have been given in [1], [2], [3], [4] and many other relevant papers. The various existing neural learning rules have been surveyed, identified and classified in order to gain a global overview of the subject area, and hence explore the possibilities for novel and more effective rules or for novel implementations of the existing rules by applying them in new network structures or strategies. This exploration aims to: i) attempt a systematic organization and generalization of the various neural network learning rules, ii) propose a rational taxonomy, iii) identify what is a generic rule and what is a special case, iv) present a chronological rule scheme and finally v) present a comparison of the rules. The proposed taxonomy will help in identifying which rules can be used for a proposed neural structure and the relative merits of each. Only those

I.P. Vlahavas and C.D. Spyropoulos (Eds.): SETN 2002, LNAI 2308, pp. 300–313, 2002.

considered as most important, employing parameter adaptation (mainly weight) are presented, and this is done in a concise manner in order to keep the extend of the paper within reasonable size.

An all-encompassing systematic and comparative study of the effectiveness of the various learning rules is not available. Since humans have always tried to improve things, some of these rules are better than others at particular tasks. There is, thus, room for even more rules, which will hopefully produce even better results than the existing paradigms in both aspects of accuracy and speed of execution.

2. Definitions of Learning – Learning in Neural Networks

2.1 Learning in General

The Webster's dictionary defines **learn** as: "To learn is to gain knowledge, or understanding of, or skill in, by study, instruction or experience". In the general AI context, learning may be defined as: "Learning is a dynamical process by which a system responding to an environmental influence, reorganises itself in such a manner that it becomes better in functioning in the environment". In machine learning: "Learning denotes changes in the system that are adaptive in the sense that they enable the system to do the same task or tasks drawn from the same population more effectively the next time" or "Learning involves changes to the content and organization of a system's knowledge, enabling it to improve it's performance on a particular task or set of tasks" [5]. Thus, a computational system learns from experience with respect to a class of tasks and some performance measure, if its performance for some task(s), as evaluated by the performance measure, improves with experience. The three important issues are the Experience, Task, and Performance. Learning in artificial neural systems may be thought of as a special case of machine learning.

2.2 Learning in Artificial Neural Networks

Once an apparently suitable neural network structure has been decided, it needs to be adapted in order to be able to provide the desired results at appropriate times. In most existing neural network paradigms a somewhat restrictive approach to learning is adopted. This is usually done by systematically modifying a set of suitable controllable parameters, the so-called synaptic weights. In this manner, learning is identified as any change in the weight set **W** (generally known as the synaptic weight matrix, or long term memory) that minimizes a suitable criterion [6], [7].

A more general approach is adopted by Haykin, where learning is defined as: "Learning is a process by which the free parameters of a neural network are adapted through a continuing process of stimulation by the environment in which the network is embedded. The type of learning is determined by the manner in which the parameter changes take place" [3].

The free parameters have been given different names such as synaptic weights, synaptic efficacies, controllable parameters and others.

An alternative, more general approach is [8]: "Learning is achieved through any change, in any characteristic of a neural network, so that improved meaningful results are achieved". Thus learning could be achieved, among others, through i) synaptic weight modification, ii) network structure modifications (creating or deleting neurons or synaptic connections), iii) use of suitable attractors or other suitable stable state points, iv) learning through forgetting [9], [10], v) through appropriate choice of activation functions [11], [12] or vi) even learning through modifying controllable parameters in a look-up table defining an activation scaling. Combinations of such rules (e.g. competitive learning systems) to make more diverse and versatile learning systems may also be explored and implemented.

By meaningful results it is meant that a desired objective is met with a satisfactory degree of success that improves prior state. When the objective is quantified by a suitable criterion or cost function, a process of minimization of the error function or maximization of a specified benefit function is usually adopted. In this respect, learning resembles the optimization.

Based on the previous general definitions, one may wonder how are knowledge discovery, recognition, creativity, memory, mapping, classification, and categorization, related to learning and to what extend are these processes considered as learning tasks. What are the basic differences among these tasks, and what is the difference between learning and knowing? How can systems operate in a self-organizing, self-learning, and unsupervised mode? What are the relations with statistical procedures used for data manipulation and feature extraction?

Table 1. Characteristic feature taxonomy

Characteristic feature	Comment
The degree to which a neural learning paradigm resembles learning in biological systems	One has to note that there is no universal agreement among researchers on what constitutes biological learning and how it is implemented. The rules that cannot be autonomous, cannot be considered as belonging to this class, unless one emphasizes a specific local interaction (e. g. the Hebbian locality). Thus, all algorithmically defined rules (PAC, EM, Boosting, ...) cannot be included in this category. Typical rules of the class are the basic Hebbian and its closely related rules, as well as Hebbian-like rules used in spiking neuron networks [13].
Extend of applicability	Learning rules may be classified according to their depth of applicability. That is, on whether the rule applies to diverse environments, or to some special cases.
External guidance during learning	The process of adaptation may be externally guided by a teacher, in which case it is known as supervised training or internally, in which case it is known as unsupervised training. It is debatable whether truly unsupervised learning does exist. Even in natural-biological systems, some guidance either internal or external, by analogy or necessity, exists. Learning through pure intuitional guidance is rather a largely philosophical question. Typical learning rules that may be used in unsupervised manner are those used in self-organized maps, in learning vector quantizers, in principal component analysis (PCA) and in independent component analysis (ICA) procedures.

The type of adaptable parameters	Learning rules may be classified depending on whether the parameters that are adapted are the synaptic weights or any others such as some activation function characteristics (slope, amplitude, offsets, …) [14], [15].
The degree of "rigidity" of the neural structure	Inflexible structures (hardwired systems) In such cases, there is no learning. A random generation of parameters, is hoped to give some meaningful results. Constructive learning (growing networks) In constructive learning, groups of neurons (layers, slabs …) or individual neurons or connections are added in the network during training. A popular constructive algorithm is the cascade correlation [16] and its variants such as upstart, tiling, etc. The Boosting algorithm [17], [18] has recently gained significant attention because by a combination of poorly performing nets one can get a very good classifier. Destructive learning (shrinking networks) In destructive learning usually groups of neurons (layers, slabs …) or individual processing units (neurons) or connections are removed from a network during training. The process is usually called pruning [19], [20].
The degree of evolution as a dynamical system	Classification on whether the learning rule/algorithm is expressed in terms of differential equations where some time-dependent evolution is implemented. Learning with non-dynamical equations does not involve time evolution, delays or recurrencies. Instead, the various parameters are changed in a nearly instantaneous manner.
The degree of stochasticity employed	The neural learning rules may or may not include stochastic elements (eg Simulated Annealing, Boltzman machines …) [21], [22].
On whether learning is algorithmic or non-algorithmic	Rules may be algorithmic (Genetic algorithm-based, artificial life-based, growing an pruning algorithms, …), in the sense that a sequence of procedures is needed to define the rule. Non-algorithmic rules are those that can easily be expressed with a mathematical equation, such that the system may grow autonomously. This is a rather artificial distinction, and from a practical point of view, the end result is what counts most.

3 Characteristic Features of Neural Learning

A taxonomy of neural learning and learning strategies may be done based on different characteristics. Such characteristics can be (among other possible features) the degree of resemblance to biological learning, the degree of extend of applicability, the degree of external guidance/supervision, the type of adaptable parameters, the degree of "rigidity" of the neural structure, the degree of dynamical system evolution, the degree of stochasticity, and finally on whether it is algorithmic or non-algorithmic. Suggested characteristic feature taxonomy may be as described in Table 1.

The most well-known neural learning paradigms, as proposed by different researchers, have been identified and examined with respect to their characteristics as related to the characteristics specified in Table 1. A general description of these rules with specific reference to the above categorization is presented in Table 2 (Appendix).

4 Taxonomy of Neural Learning Rules

Various taxonomies have been used. For example, Haykin [3] uses the following categorization: Error correction, Hebbian, Competitive, Boltzman and Thorndike law of effects. Simpson [23] uses the following: Hebbian, PCA, Differential Hebbian (Basic form, Drive Reinforcement form, Covariance correlation form), Competitive, Min-max, Error correction, Reinforcement, Stochastic, and Hard-wired.

Based on the comments on characteristic features of the learning rules (section 3), a proposed taxonomy of distinct rules could be:

- Hebbian (and many of its special cases as depicted in table 2)
- Reinforcement learning
- Min-max
- Stochastic
- Stochastic search in combination with steepest descent
- Genetics based
- Artificial life based
- Principle of maximum information preservation

In this taxonomy the Error Correction and the Competitive rules are considered as special cases of the generalized Hebbian, while Haykin [3] considers them as distinct rules. Such taxonomy helps in organizing the learning paradigms and in identifying what is a truly new learning rule.

5 Learning as Optimization and Optimization-Type Learning Rules

The majority of learning rules are such that a desired objective is met by a procedure of minimizing a suitable associated criterion (also known as Computational energy, Lyapunov function, or Hamilton function), whenever such exists or may be constructed, in a manner similar to the optimization procedures. Thus, a network global criterion function is desired to be minimized. In many cases the form of these functions resembles the physical energy. Many methods have been proposed for the implementation of the desired minimization, such as the 0th order, 1st order gradient-descent (Newton's, Steepest-descent), damped Newton (Levenberg-Marquardt), quasi-Newton (Broyden-Fletcher-Goldfarb-Shanno, Barnes-Rosen) and conjugate gradient methods [2]. Many of these rules are special cases of the generalized unconstrained optimization procedure, briefly described below:

For a neural network described by equation 1, the optimization procedure interpreted as learning may be defined as finding a W* that minimizes the perturbed computational energy criterion given by equation 2.

$$\dot{y}(t) = \psi(\boldsymbol{x}, \boldsymbol{y}, \mathbf{W}) \tag{1}$$

$$E(\boldsymbol{x}, \boldsymbol{y}, \mathbf{W}) = E_{cost} + E_{perturbation} \tag{2}$$

Where, y is the network output, x the network input, E_{cost} a suitable cost (error, objective, or computational energy) function, and $E_{perturbation}$ a shake-up component used to enable the system to hopefully escape from local minima. **W** here, even though is generally known as the set of synaptic weights, it is considered to be a more general set of adaptable parameters that when adapted may drive a network to better minima as far as the error landscape is concerned.

If E is continuous in the domain of interest, the minima of equation 2 with respect to the adaptable parameter (weights), **W**, are obtained when the gradient of E is zero, or when:

$$\nabla_{\boldsymbol{w}} E = \mathbf{0} \tag{3}$$

Due to the generally non-linear nature of the artificial neural networks, and the need for developing intelligent optimization techniques, an exact solution of equation 3 is not easily obtained an it is not usually sought. Different, non-analytical methods for finding the minima of E have been proposed as neural learning rules. These are mainly implemented as iterative procedures suitable for computer simulations. The general iterative approach is:

Starting from a $\mathbf{W}^{(0)}$ find $E(\mathbf{W}^{(0)})$, then use the iteration,

$$\mathbf{W}[\kappa+1] = \mathbf{W}[\kappa] + \eta_\kappa \boldsymbol{d}_\kappa \tag{4}$$

Where η_κ is the search step and $\boldsymbol{d}_{\kappa_\kappa}$ the search direction. Then find $\mathbf{W}[\kappa+1]$ and compare it with $\mathbf{W}[\kappa]$. If $\mathbf{W}[\kappa+1]$ is less than $\mathbf{W}[\kappa]$, keep the change and repeat until an E minimum is reached. The search direction $\boldsymbol{d}_\kappa$ and the search step η_κ may be randomly picked or guided by an intelligent drive/guess. If this strategy is followed, a stochastic search approach is adopted. Alternatively, $\boldsymbol{d}_\kappa$ may be guided so that a speedier search may be implemented (hopefully). Typically, $\boldsymbol{d}_\kappa$ is proportional to the gradient (1st order methods), as for example in the steepest descent, damped Newton (Levenberg-Marquardt), quasi-Newton (Broyden-Fletcher-Goldfarb-Shanno, Barnes-Rosen), conjugate gradient and variable metric (or quasi-Newton) or it is proportional to the Hessian (2nd order methods).

A popular approach used in artificial neural network learning in order for the network to reach these minima, is based on allowing multi-dimensional dynamical systems to relax, driven by a scaled gradient descent. In such a case, the system is allowed to settle by following its trajectories. It will then, hopefully, reach the minima of the hypersurface defined by E. A general parameter adaptation approach, which is a generalization of equation 4 may be adopted, as shown in equation 5.

$$f(\mathbf{w}, \dot{\mathbf{w}}, \ddot{\mathbf{w}} \ldots) = -\nabla_{\mathbf{w}} E \tag{5}$$

The function f is so-specified so that it drives the system to acceptable minima. It is rarely needed to be of higher than second degree, and in most cases a first degree model is used.

Let a second-degree dynamical system that is forced to seek the desired minima, in which the input of the system is the negative of the gradient of E (gradient descent).

$$\alpha(t)\,\ddot{\mathbf{w}} + \beta(t)\mathbf{T}\dot{\mathbf{w}} = -\nabla_{\mathbf{w}} E \tag{6}$$

Where $\alpha(t)$ and $\beta(t)$ are positive real-valued functions and $\mathbf{T}$ a suitable matrix. Equation 6 may be considered as a generalized second order learning equation based on gradient descent. Specific instances of this equation, as maybe used in optimization-learning are described in Table 3.

Table 3. Specialization of equation 6

$E_{perturbation} = 0$	
If $\alpha(t)$ and $\beta(t) \neq 0$	→ Second degree optimization
If $\alpha(t) \equiv 0$, $\mathbf{T}$ positive definite and $\beta(t) \equiv \beta_o \neq 0$	→ First degree optimization
If $\alpha(t) \equiv 0$, $\mathbf{T} \equiv \mathbf{I}$ and $\beta(t) = \frac{1}{\eta}$	→ Steepest descent method
If $\alpha(t) \equiv 0$, $\mathbf{T} \equiv \nabla^2 E$ and $\beta(t) = 1$	→ Newton's method
If $\alpha(t) \equiv 0$, $\mathbf{T} \equiv \nabla^2 E + \gamma(t)$ and $\beta(t) = 1$	→ Levenberg-Marquardt method
$E_{perturbation} \neq 0$ In this case different stochastic gradient techniques are obtained. The perturbation is generally used as a "shake-up" that will hopefully force the network to escape from local minima. As this is approached, the perturbation in E is gradually reduced to zero so that the system reaches a state near the global minimum and settles there. Thus, at the end of the procedure the network becomes deterministic. A commonly used form for the perturbation is that shown in equation 7 [24], [25], [2] $E_{perturbation} = c(t) \sum_{j=1}^{n} y_j N_j(t) \quad (7)$ Where $c(t)$ is a suitable decaying function used to gradually reduce the effects of noise and $N_j(t)$ is noise applied to each neuron j.	

6 Concluding Remarks

A survey of learning rules has been done. It is evident that an extensive variety of rules is available. The rules most extensively used by researchers and application users are of gradient descent approach. They are closely related to optimization techniques developed by mathematicians, statisticians and researchers working mainly in the field of "operations research". It is apparent that the suitability of any learning rules for implementation to artificial neural network problems is problem-specific. A comparative list of the most important rules has been prepared and presented as Table 2. A systematic examination of the effectiveness of these rules is a matter of extensive research being conducted at different research centers. Conclusive comparative findings on the relative merits of each learning rule are not presently available. Numerous claims are being made, but they need to be independently verified, a task which is extremely difficult, as there is usually little information provided on the specific conditions and assumptions under which the learning was implemented.

The problem of neural system learning is ultimately very important in the sense that evolvable intelligence can emerge when the learning procedure is automatic and unsupervised. The term "unsupervised" is debatable depending on the level of scrutiny applied when evaluating a rule. It is customary to consider some learning as unsupervised when there is no specific and well defined external teacher. In the so-called self-organizing systems, the system organizes apparently unrelated data into sets of more meaningful packets of information. Ultimately though, how can intelligent organisms learn in total isolation? Looking at supervisability in more liberal terms, one could say that learning is not well-specified supervised or unsupervised procedure. It is rather a complicated system of individual processes that jointly help in manifesting an emergent behavior that "learns" from experience. Ultimately, one may even ask whether consciousness is learned.

References

1. Simpson P: Foundations of Neural Networks. Invited Paper. In: Sinencio E, Lau C: (eds.): Artificial Neural Networks: Paradigms, Applications and Hardware Implementations. IEEE Press, NY (1992)
2. Cichocki A, Unbehauen R: Neural Networks for Optimization and Signal Processing. John Wiley and Sons Ltd, London (1993)
3. Haykin S: Neural Networks: A Comprehensive Foundation. Macmillan College Publishing Co, NY (1994)
4. Hassoun M: Fundamentals of Artificial Neural Networks. MIT Press, MA (1995)
5. Simon H: The Sciences of the Artificial. MIT Press, Cambridge, MA (1981)
6. Simpson P: Fuzzy Min-Max Neural Networks. Proc. of the Int. Joint Conf. on Neural Networks. (1991) 1658-1669
7. Kosko B: Neural Networks and Fuzzy Systems. Prentice Hall International, NJ, (1992)
8. Neocleous C: A Neural Network Architecture Composed of Adaptively Defined Dissimilar Single-neurons: Applications in engineering design. PhD Thesis, Brunel University, UK (1997)
9. Hopfield J., Feinstein D, Palmer G: Unlearning has a Stabilizing Effect in Collective Memories. Nature Vol. 304 (1983) 158-159

10. Wimbauer S., Klemmer N., Van Hemmen L: Universality of Unlearning. Neural Networks Vol.7 (1994) (2):261-270
11. Kruschke J, Movellan J: Benefits of Gain. Speeded Learning and Minimal Layers in Back-propagation Networks. IEEE Trans. on Systems, Man and Cybernetics Vol.21 (1991) 273-280
12. Chen C, Chang W: A Feedforward Neural Network with Function Shape Autotuning. Neural Networks Vol.9 (1996) 4:627-641
13. Ruf B: Computing and Learning with Spiking Neurons – Theory and Simulations. PhD Thesis. Technische Universität Graz, Austria (1998)
14. Trentin E: Networks with Trainable Amplitude of Activation Functions. Neural Networks Vol.14 (2001) (4&5):471-493
15. Poirazi P., Neocleous C., Pattichis C, Schizas C: A Biologically Inspired Neural Network Composed of Dissimilar Single Neuron Models. Proc. of the 23rd IEEE Int. Conf. on Engineering in Medicine and Biology, Istanbul (2001)
16. Fahlman S, Lebiere C: Fast Learning Variations on Backpropagation: An Empirical Study. Proc. of the 1988 Connectionist Models Summer School. Morgan Kaufmann, LA, (1990)
17. Schapire R: The Strength of Weak Learnability. Machine Learning, Vol. 5 (1990) 2:197-227
18. Freund Y: Boosting a Weak Learning Algorithm by Majority. Information and Computation, Vol. 121 (1995) 2:256-285
19. Reed R., Marks R. II: Neural Smithing: Supervised Learning in Feedforward Artificial Neural Networks. MIT Press. Cambridge, MA (1999)
20. Leung C., Wong K., Sum P, Chan L: A Pruning Algorithm for the Recursive Least Squares Algorithm. Neural Networks, Vol.14 (2001) 2:147-174
21. Kirkpatrick S., Gelatt C, Vecchi M: Optimization by Simulated Annealing. Science, Vol. 220 (1983) 671-680
22. Ackley D., Hinton G, Sejnowski T: A Learning Algorithm for Boltzman Machines. Cognitive Science, Vol. 9 (1985) 147-169
23. Simpson P: Foundations of Neural Networks. In Simpson P: (ed) Neural Networks Theory, Technology, and Applications. IEEE Technology Update Series, NY (1996)
24. Aluffi-Pentini F., Parisi V, Zirilli F: Global Optimization and Stochastic Differential Equations. J. on Optimization Theory and Applications, Vol. 47 (1985) 1-16
25. Gelfand S, Mitter S: Recursive Stochastic Algorithms for Global Optimization in R^d. SIAM J. on Control and Optimization, Vol. 29 (1991) 999-1018
26. Hebb D: Organization of Behavior. John Wiley & Sons, NY (1949)
27. Grossberg S: Some Nonlinear Networks Capable of Learning a Spatial Pattern of Arbitrary Complexity. Proc. of the National Academy of Sciences, USA, Vol. 59 (1968) 368-372
28. Amari S: Mathematical theory of neural learning. New Generation Computing, Vol. 8 (1991) 281-294
29. Widrow B, Hoff M: Adaptive Switching Circuits. IRE Western Electric Show and Convention Record. Vol. 4 (1960) 96-104
30. Werbos P: Beyond Regression: New Tools for Prediction and Analysis in the Behavioral Sciences. Ph.D. Dissertation, Harvard University (1974)
31. Parker, D: Optimal Algorithms for Adaptive Networks: Second Order Back Propagation, Second Order Direct Propagation, and Second Order Hebbian Learning. Proc. of the IEEE 1st Int. Conf. on Neural Networks, San Diego, CA, Vol. 2 (1987) 593-600
32. LeCun: Une Procedure D'apprentisage Pour Reseau a Seuil Asymetrique. Cognitiva, Vol. 85 (1985) 599-604
33. Rumelhart D., Hinton G, McClelland J: In McClelland J. L., Rumelhart D. E. and the PDP Research Group (eds.) Parallel Distributed Processing: Explorations in the Microstructure of Cognition Vol. 1. Foundations. MIT Press, MA (1986)
34. Kohonen T: Self-organization and Associative Memories. Springer-Verlag, NY (1984)

35. Carpenter G, Grossberg S: Invariant Pattern Recognition and Recall by an Attentive Self-organizing ART Architecture in a Stationary World. Proc. of the IEEE 1st Int. Conf. on Neural Networks, San Diego CA, Vol. 2 (1987) 737-746
36. Bienenstock E., Cooper E, Munro P: Theory for the Development of Neural Selectivity: Orientation Specificity and Binocular Interaction in Visual Cortex. J. of Neuroscience, Vol. 2 (1982) 32-48
37. Oja E: A simplified neuron model as a principal component analyzer. J. Math. Biol. Vol. 15 (1982) 267-273.
38. Oja E, Karhunen J: On Stochastic Approximation of the Eigenvectors and Eigenvalues of the Expectation of a Random Matrix. J. of Mathematical Analysis and Applications, Vol. 104 (1985) 69-84
39. Oja E., Ogawa H, Wangviwattana: Principal Components Analysis by Homogeneous Neural Networks. IEICE Trans. on Information and Systems. (1992) E75-D:366-382
40. Oja E: Principal Components, Minor Components and Linear Neural Networks. Neural Networks, Vol. 5 (1992) 927-935
41. Sanger T: Optimal Unsupervised Learning in a Single Layer Linear Feedforward Neural Network. Neural Networks, Vol. 2 (1989) 459-473
42. Yuille A., Kammen D, Cohen D: Quadrature and the Development of Orientation Selective Cortical Cells by Hebb Rules. Biological Cybernetics, Vol. 61 (1989) 183-194
43. Hasselmo M: Runaway Synaptic Modification in Models of Cortex: Implications for Alzheimer's Disease. Neural Networks, Vol. 7 (1994) 1:13-40.
44. Sejnowski T: Statistical Constraints on Synaptic Plasticity. J. of Math. Biology, Vol. 64 (1977) 385-389
45. Sutton R, Barto A: Toward a Modern Theory of Adaptive Networks: Expectation and Prediction. Psychological Review, Vol. 88 (1981) 135-171
46. Klopf A: Drive Reinforcement Model of a Single Neuron Function: An Alternative to the Hebbian Neuron Model. In Denker J: (ed.) Proc. of the AIP Conf. on Neural Networks for Computing NY (1986)
47. Kosko B: Differential Hebbian Learning. In Denker J: (ed.) Proc. of the AIP Conf. on Neural Networks for Computing NY (1986)
48. Cheung J, Omidvar M: Mathematical Analysis of Learning Behaviour of Neuronal Models. In Anderson D: (ed) Neural Information Processing Systems NY (1988)
49. Kosko B: Feedback Stability and Unsupervised Learning. Proc. of the IEEE Int. Conf. on Neural Networks, IEEE Press, San Diego, Vol. 1 (1988) 141-152
50. Kosko B: Unsupervised Learning in Noise. IEEE Trans. on Neural Networks. Vol. 1 (1990) 1:44-57
51. Widraw B., Gupta N, Maitra S: Punish/reward: Learning with a Critic in Adaptive Threshold Systems. IEEE Trans. on Systems, Man, and Cybernetics, Vol. 3 (1973) 455-465
52. Barto A., Sutton R, Anderson C: Neuron-like Adaptive Elements that can solve Difficult Learning Control Problems. IEEE Trans. on Systems, Man and Cybernetics, Vol. 13 (1983) 834-846
53. Williams R: Reinforcement Learning in Connectionist Networks: A mathematical Analysis. University of California at San Diego. Institute of Cognitive Science Report 8605 (1986)
54. Barto A: Learning by Statistical Cooperation of Self-interested Neuron-like Computing Units. Human Neurobiology, Vol. 4 (1985) 229-256
55. Minsky M: Theory of Neural-analog Reinforcement Systems and its Application to the Brain-model Problem. PhD Thesis. Princeton University NJ (1954)
56. Minsky M, Selfridge O: Learning in Random Nets. Information Theory. 4th London Symposium, London(1961)
57. Simpson P: Fuzzy Min-max Classification with Neural Networks. Heuristics, Vol. 4 (1991) 7:1-9

58. Szu H: Fast Simulated Annealing. In Denker J: (ed.) Proc. of the AIP Conf. on Neural Networks for Computing NY (1986)
59. Peterson C, Anderson J: A Mean Field Learning Algorithm for Neural Networks. Complex Systems, Vol. 1 (1987) 995-1019
60. Kennedy J, Eberhart R: Particle Swarm Optimization. Proc. IEEE Int. Conf. on Neural Networks, Perth, Australia.(1995)
61. Van den Bergh F, Engelbrecht A: Cooperative Learning in Neural Networks using Particle Swarm Optimizers. SAICSIT 2000 (2000)

Appendix

Table 2. Library of neural network learning rules

Notation: $y_s \equiv x_r$ = Output of sending neuron = An input to a receiving neuron, $\bar{y}$ = Mean of y, x_d = Post-synaptic activation (dendritic), w_{sr} = Controllable parameters (synaptic weights), d_o = Desired response of the oth output neuron, p_o = Predicted response of the oth output neuron, e_o = Error in the oth output neuron $\equiv d_o - p_o$, E = Computational energy function (or Error, or Criterion, or Potential, or Lyapunov, or Hamilton function), $\Delta w_{sr} \equiv w_{sr}[\kappa+1] - w_{sr}[\kappa]$ for time counter $\kappa = 1, 2, \ldots$, η = Learning rate, μ = Momentum rate, [L] = Layer of interest, $\|x\|$ = Suitable norm.

MAJOR GROUP RULE	SUB-GROUP RULE (Discrete – time)	COMMENTS
HEBBIAN LEARNING Hebb statement (1949) [26]:"When an axon of cell A is near enough to excite a cell B and repeatedly or persistently takes part in firing it, some growth process or metabolic changes take place in one or both cells such that A's efficiency as one of the cells firing B, is increased." Haykin statement (1994) [2]: A Hebbian synapse uses a time-dependent, highly local, and strongly interactive mechanism to increase synoptic efficiency as a function of the correlation between the pre-synaptic and postsynaptic activities. General mathematical forms: (Hebb, 1949): $\Delta w_{sr} = \varphi(y_s, y_r) = f(y_s, y_r, y_s - \bar{y}_r)$ (Grossberg, 1968): $\Delta w_s = g(y_s, w_{sr}) \cdot h(y_r, d_o)$ Special cases: A more specific form is given by $w_{sr}[\kappa+1] = w_{sr}[\kappa](1-\xi_r) + \eta_r[\kappa]\delta_r[\kappa]y_s[\kappa]$ where, $\delta_r \equiv \delta(w_{sr}, y_s, u_r, y_r, d_o)$ and ξ_r = Forgetting or leakage factor $0 \leq \xi_r < 1$	**Simple Hebbian** $\Delta w_{sr} = \eta_r y_s y_r$	Known as activity product rule, or passive decay long term memory
	Error correction Hebbian Delta rule (Widrow & Hoff, 1960) [29] $\Delta w_{sr} = \eta_r y_s e_o$ Backpropagation and variants [30], [31], [32], [33] For single-layer nets of linear units: $\Delta w_{sr} = \eta_r y_s e_o$ For multi-layer feed forward nets of non-linear units: $\Delta w_{sr} = \eta_r y_s \delta_r$ where a different δ_j is used for each neuron r of layer as specified below: $\delta_r^{[L]} = \frac{\partial s^{[L]}}{\partial u_r^{[L]}} \left(\sum_r \delta_r^{[L+1]} w_{sr}^{[L+1]} \right)$	It is a gradient descent Least mean square error reduction procedure, closely related to statistical optimization procedures. Some other backpropagation variants are: RPROP, Quickprop, Minkowski-r Recirculation, ELEANNE, Delta-bar-delta, Super SAB, …
	Grossberg (Grossberg, 1969) $\Delta w_{sr} = y_s(\beta y_r - \alpha w_{sr})$ (Grossberg, 1970) $\Delta w_{sr} = \alpha y_r(y_r - w_{sr})$ (Grossberg, 1976) $\Delta w_{sr} = \eta_r y_r(y_s - w_{sr})$ $\alpha = \alpha(t)$ is a decreasing function.	Also known as the simple competitive learning rule, or simple competitive - cooperative learning rule. A similar rule is used in self-organization [34] and ART [35].
	Bienenstock et al. (1982) [36] $\Delta w_{sr} = -\alpha w_{sr} + y_s \varphi(y_r)$	This rule induces a temporal competition between the input patterns.

Amari [28] showed that this form can be derived by minimizing a suitably chosen computational energy function by employing a gradient descent procedure: $\frac{dw_{sr}}{dt} = -\eta_r \frac{\partial E}{\partial w_{sr}}$	**Normalized Hebbian (Oja, 1982)** [37] $\Delta w_{sr} = \alpha y_r y_s - \beta y_r^2 w_{sr}$	This is a gradient descent - principal component rule.
	Symmetrical subspace learning rule (Oja & Karhunen, 1985) [38] $\Delta w_{sr} = \alpha y_r y_s - \beta y_r \sum_{h=1}^{p} w_{rh} y_h$	It is a principal component learning rule closely related to the Oja-Ogawa-Wangviwattana rule [39] and the stochastic gradient ascent rule [40].
	Sanger (1989) [41] $\Delta w_{sr} = \eta_r (y_r y_s - y_r \sum_{h=1}^{s} w_{rh} y_h)$	It is a principal component learning rule also called the generalized Hebbian.
	Yuile et al (1989) [42] $\Delta w_{sr} = \eta_r (y_r y_s - \Vert w_{sr} \Vert^2 w_{sr})$	
	Hasselmo (1994) [43] $\Delta w_{sr} = \eta y_s (y_r + \sum_{i=1}^{n} w_{sr} y_s)$	
	Differential Hebbian - Covariance Correlation [44] $\Delta w_{sr} = \eta_r$ **Covariance**$((y_s - \bar{y}_s)(y_r - \bar{y}_r))$	Also known as the activity covariance rule
	Differential Hebbian - Covariance Correlation [45] $\Delta w_{sr} = \eta_r \bar{y}_s (y_r - \bar{y}_r)$	
	Differential Hebbian - Drive Reinforcement [46] $\Delta w_{sr} = \Delta y_r \sum_{h=k}^{K} \alpha(t-h) \Vert w_{sr}(t-h) \Vert \Delta y_s(t-h)$ Where $\alpha(t-h)$ is a decreasing function of time.	The basic form of a differential Hebbian [47] is: $\Delta w_{sr} = \Delta y_r[\kappa] + \Delta y_r[\kappa-1]$ where, $\Delta y[\kappa] = y[\kappa] - y[\kappa-1]$
	Differential Hebbian - Covariance Correlation [48] $\Delta w_{sr} = \eta_r (\Delta y_s) w_{sr} y_r$	
	Differential Hebbian – (Kosko, 1988) [49] $\Delta w_{sr} = - w_{sr} + u_s u_r + \frac{dS_s}{dt}\frac{dS_r}{dt}$	
	Differential competitive (Kosko, 1990) [50] $\Delta w_{sr} = \frac{dS_s}{dt}(y_r - w_{sr})$	

REINFORCEMENT LEARNING [51], [52], 53]	$\Delta w_{sr} = \eta_r(\varepsilon - r_r)e_{sr}$ where, $\varepsilon = \frac{\text{success}}{\text{failure}}$ r_r = reinforcement threshold value, e_{sr} = canonical eligibility of the weight from neuron s to $r = \frac{\partial(\ln g_s)}{\partial w_{sr}}$ and $g_s = \mathbf{Pr}(y_r = d_r \mid w_r, x)$	The rule is related to the error correction learning. The Adaptive Heuristic Critic [52] and the Associative Reward - Penalty [53] are two similar paradigms of this rule. Reinforcement learning was also considered by Minsky [55] [56].
MIN-MAX LEARNING [57]	For the minimum vector: $v_{sr}[\kappa+1] = \mathbf{min}(y_s - v_{sr}[\kappa])$ For the maximum vector: $w_{sr}[\kappa+1] = \mathbf{max}(y_s - w_{sr}[\kappa])$	
STOCHASTIC LEARNING [21], [22], [58]	Stochastic search by random modification of the parameters (weights) until a suitable energy (or criterion) function settles to a desired value.	This search can be purely random, or guided as in the simulated annealing [21], Boltzman machine [22] Cauchy machine [58] and mean field annealing [59]. It is similar to the Quasi-Newton method
STOCHASTIC HEBBIAN	**Hebbian Annealing** [15] A stochastic local Hebbian rule in which the weights are changed depending on their score in a suitable function.	
GENETICS BASED LEARNING	Evolutionary techniques (genetic algorithms) are used to find weights and other parameters, or to prune or grow neural structures	
ARTIFICIAL LIFE BASED LEARNING	The particle swarm optimizer is one such learning procedure [60], [61]	

Piecewise Neural Networks for Function Approximation, Cast in a Form Suitable for Parallel Computation

Ioannis G. Tsoulos, Isaac E. Lagaris, and Aristidis C. Likas

Dept. of Computer Science, University of Ioannina,
Ioannina - GREECE 45110

Abstract. We present a technique for function approximation in a partitioned domain. In each of the partitions a form containing a Neural Network is utilized with parameterized boundary conditions. This parameterization renders feasible the parallelization of the computation. Conditions of continuity across the partitions are studied for the function itself and for a number of its derivatives. A comparison is made with traditional methods and the results are reported.

1 Introduction

1.1 Rationale and Motivation

Piecewise continuous polynomials are well established tools for approximation and interpolation. As examples we refer to the Natural splines, to B-splines and to Hermite splines[1]. In this article we present a partitioning technique, where instead of polynomials we introduce Neural Networks as the basic approximation element, obtaining so a scheme that may be referred to as "Neural Splines". Other non-polynomial splines have been developed in the past, for instance we mention the "Tension Splines" that are based on the exponential function [2]. Neural Networks are well known for their universal approximation capabilities [3],[4] and have been employed for interpolation, approximation and modeling tasks in many cases, ranging from pattern recognition[5], signal processing, control and the solution of ordinary and partial differential equations [6], [7],[8].

Partitioning a large domain into smaller ones, has the obvious advantage of the reduced problem size and the disadvantage of the increased number of problems. However there are more points to consider. It is not clear if partitioning is always worthwhile, since in most cases is being accompanied by computational overhead, matching discontinuities and increased complexity. However a serious problem with extended domains is that since non-linear optimization is often the only method of choice, the resulting objective function possesses a large number of useless local minima, a fact that corresponds to excessive computational load that diminishes the efficiency of any method, hence in that respect partitioning has an edge. Note also that partitioning schemes may profit dramatically from parallel processing if formulated properly. Taking all the above into account, we

I.P. Vlahavas and C.D. Spyropoulos (Eds.): SETN 2002, LNAI 2308, pp. 314–324, 2002.

developed a method that uses partitions and manages to cope with the mentioned difficulties and in addition is cast in a suitable form so as to benefit when executed on parallel multiprocessor machines or on a distributed system.

1.2 General Description of the Method

Let us first consider the classical fitting problem:

Given M points and associated values (x_i, y_i), $i = 1, 2, ..., M$, where the points $x_i \in R^{(N)}$, draw a smooth hypersurface, that is optimal in the least squares sense.

The traditional way of solving the above is to assume a parametric model $\Psi(x, p)$ for the solution, and consequently adjust the parameters p, so as to minimize the least squares "total error" $E_T[p] = \sum_{i=1}^{M} [\Psi(x_i, p) - y_i]^2$.

In this article we assume that the domain D containing the x-points, is an N-dimensional rectangular hyperbox and we proceed by first partitioning it in several non-overlapping rectangular subdomains D_i. In each of these subdomains, the solution is represented by a proper model $\psi_i(x, p^i, q^i)$ that is constructed in such a way so as to meet certain conditions on the subdomain-boundary ∂D_i, imposed by continuity requirements. These boundary conditions depend on the additional parameters denoted by q^i but are independent of p^i.

If we define the least squares "local error", i.e. the error in the subdomain D_i as:

$$E_L[p^i, q^i] = \sum_{x_k \in D_i} [\psi_i(x_k, p^i, q^i) - y_k]^2, \ \forall\, i = 1, 2 \dots \tag{1}$$

then, the total error is given by:

$$E_T[p, q] = \sum_i E_L[p^i, q^i] \tag{2}$$

The parameters p^i are determined by minimizing $E_L[p^i, q^i]$ for a given set of values for q^i. The additional parameters q^i, are then adjusted so that the complete solution written as:

$$\Psi(x, p, q) = \psi_i(x, p^i, q^i), \ \forall\, x \in D_i$$

minimizes the "total error" given by equation 2. The above steps are repeated until a convergence criterion prevails. A detailed algorithmic description is deferred to section 3.

2 Definitions and Terms

2.1 Obreshkov Polynomials and Related Operators

Consider a continuously differentiable function $f(x)$, with $x \in [a,b]$, and a polynomial $P^{k,m}_{a,b}(f,x)$ with the following properties:

$$\frac{d^j}{dx^j} P^{k,m}_{a,b}(f,a) = \frac{d^j}{dx^j} f(x)|_{x=a} \equiv f^{(j)}(a), \forall\, j = 0,1,\dots,k \quad (3)$$

$$\frac{d^j}{dx^j} P^{k,m}_{a,b}(f,b) = \frac{d^j}{dx^j} f(x)|_{x=b} \equiv f^{(j)}(b), \forall\, j = 0,1,\dots,m \quad (4)$$

Obreshkov [9], obtained the following result for the unique polynomial of the minimal degree $k+m+1$.

$$P^{k,m}_{a,b}(f,x) = \sum_{j=0}^{k} f^{(j)}(a) \frac{(x-b)^{m+1}(x-a)^j}{j!(a-b)^{m+1}} \sum_{i=0}^{k-j} \binom{m+i}{i} \frac{(x-a)^i}{(b-a)^i} + \sum_{j=0}^{m} f^{(j)}(b) \frac{(x-a)^{k+1}(x-b)^j}{j!(b-a)^{k+1}} \sum_{i=0}^{m-j} \binom{k+i}{i} \frac{(x-b)^i}{(a-b)^i} \quad (5)$$

We may then define an operator $L^{m,k}_{x\in[a,b]}$ via the following relation:

$$L^{k,m}_{x\in[a,b]} f(x) = P^{k,m}_{a,b}(f,x) \quad (6)$$

We define the quantities:

$$S^{k,m}_{a,b}(f,x) \equiv f(x) - P^{k,m}_{a,b}(f,x) = (1 - L^{k,m}_{x\in[a,b]}) f(x) \quad (7)$$

with the understanding that outside the domain, i.e. for $x \notin [a,b]$, $S^{k,m}_{a,b}(f,x)$ vanishes, and

$$B^{k,m}_{a,b}(f,x) \equiv f(x) - S^{k,m}_{a,b}(f,x) = (1 - (1 - L^{k,m}_{x\in[a,b]})) f(x) = L^{k,m}_{x\in[a,b]} f(x) = P^{k,m}_{a,b}(f,x) \quad (8)$$

$S^{k,m}_{a,b}(f,x)$ has the property that at $x = a$, $(x = b)$ vanishes along with all its derivatives up to k^{th}, (m^{th}) order. We call it an f-spline (since it is based on the function f) and the quantity $B^{k,m}_{a,b}(f,x)$ a boundary match (since it resembles f on the boundary).

2.2 Neural Splines and Model Description

When $f(.)$ is chosen to be a Neural Network, then we may call $S(f,.)$ a Neural Spline. In each of the rectangular subdomains D_i we represent our model as:

$$\psi_i(x, p^i, q^i) = B^{k,m}_{a,b}(f,x) + S^{l,n}_{a,b}(N,x) \quad (9)$$

where $N(x, p^i)$ is a Neural Network with weights denoted by p^i. The parameters q^i represent the values of $f(x)$ and possibly of its derivatives on the boundary ∂D_i. In one dimension the model $\psi_i(x, p^i, q^i)$ so defined, satisfies by construction the following boundary conditions:

$$\frac{d^j}{dx^j}\psi_i(x, p^i, q^i)|_{x=a} = f^{(j)}(a),\ j = 0, ..., \min(k, l) \tag{10}$$

$$\frac{d^j}{dx^j}\psi_i(x, p^i, q^i)|_{x=b} = f^{(j)}(b),\ j = 0, ..., \min(m, n) \tag{11}$$

As an example in the case $k = l = m = n = 0$, the one-dimensional model is written as:

$$\begin{aligned}\psi(x, p, q) = f(a)\frac{x-b}{a-b} + f(b)\frac{x-a}{b-a} + \\ N(x, p) - [N(a, p)\frac{x-b}{a-b} + N(b, p)\frac{x-a}{b-a}]\end{aligned} \tag{12}$$

with q referring collectively to $f(a)$ and $f(b)$, and satisfies $\psi(a, p, q) = f(a)$ and $\psi(b, p, q) = f(b)$, as it can readily be verified. For the case $k = l = m = n = 1$, we have the following one dimensional model:

$$\begin{aligned}\psi(x, p, q) = {} & f^{(0)}(a)\pi_{3,0}(x, a, b) + f^{(1)}(a)\pi_{3,1}(x, a, b) \\ & + f^{(0)}(b)\tau_{3,0}(x, a, b) + f^{(1)}(b)\tau_{3,1}(x, a, b) \\ & + N(x, p) - [N(a, p)\pi_{3,0}(x, a, b) + N^{(1)}(a, p)\pi_{3,1}(x, a, b) \\ & \qquad + N(b, p)\tau_{3,0}(x, a, b) + N^{(1)}(b, p)\tau_{3,1}(x, a, b)]\end{aligned}$$

where the following notation is used:

$$\begin{aligned}\pi_{1,0}(x, a, b) &= \frac{x-b}{a-b} \\ \pi_{3,0}(x, a, b) &= \frac{(x-b)^2}{(a-b)^2}\left(1 + 2\frac{x-a}{b-a}\right) \\ \pi_{3,1}(x, t_{i-1}, t_i) &= (x-a)\frac{(x-b)^2}{(a-b)^2} \\ \tau_{2k+1,j}(x, a, b) &\equiv \pi_{2k+1,j}(x, b, a)\end{aligned} \tag{13}$$

3 Partitioning and Procedures

We proceed by first defining a number of knots t_i, i.e. points that partition the domain of interest D in several non-overlapping subdomains $D_i = [t_i, t_{i+1}]$.

1. Introduce a set of external parameters $f_i^{(0)}, f_i^{(1)}, \cdots, f_i^{(k)}$ (collectively denoted by q^i) that specify values for the solution and for a number of its derivatives at each knot t_i.

2. For $i = 1, 2, \ldots$ use a model $\psi_i(x, p^i, q^i)$ for $x \in D_i$ that satisfies the conditions specified at the two bracketing knots t_i and t_{i+1} and minimize the local least squares "error" $E_i[p^i, q^i]$ with respect to p^i, keeping the external q^i parameters fixed.
3. Adjust the external parameters q^i (i.e. the prescribed values at the knots) in such a way so as to minimize the total "error" $E_T\left[p, q\right] = \sum_i E_L\left[p^i, q^i\right]$ keeping p^i fixed.
4. Repeat from step 2, until some termination criterion is satisfied.

Note that the procedure in step 2, can be implemented in parallel, since the local models are being determined independently, given that the external parameters remain constant, as it will become evident shortly. This is not the case for the procedure in step 3, where a change in the external parameters at the knot t_i affects the representation in both the D_{i-1} and the D_i domains. However this part is not time consuming and hence it is not critical. There are some important points that must be stressed. The initial values for the external parameters are extremely important. Far off values, may decelerate the convergence dramatically. Hence we deviced a preprocessing scheme to ensure that the initial values are close to their actual values. This is achieved by fitting a single neural network in every interval and then use this model to generate the initial values for the external parameters. The network parameters resulting from the preprocessing are subsequently used to initialize the weights p^i of the final model $\psi_i(x, p^i, q^i) = B(f, x) + S(N, x)$. In this article the Neural Network used is the sigmoidal perceptron with one hidden layer, given by:

$$N(x, p) = \sum_{i=1}^{H} p_{3i-2}\sigma(p_{3i-1}x + p_{3i}), \quad \sigma(z) = \frac{1}{1 + e^{-z}} \tag{14}$$

Global optimization is used in each subdomain in the phase of preprocessing. In practice, in order to accelerate the process, we proceed by first applying a local search procedure, and only if this proves to be inadequate (i.e. if it produces a local error above a set threshold) we employ global optimization techniques.

4 Numerical Experiments

Experiments were conducted with several data sets. We present in what follows experiments with the function $f(x) = x\sin(x^2)$ whose plot in the interval $[-4, 4]$ is shown in Figure 1

Several cases were examined by varying the number of partitions and the number of hidden units of the Neural Networks in each partition. Two sets of points were used: a rather sparse point set for the training and a dense point set for testing. Since the local models are mutually independent, there are no propagating errors across the subdomains and so a rather modest optimization stopping criterion may be used, that accelerates the process without substantially sacrificing the model's approximation capability.

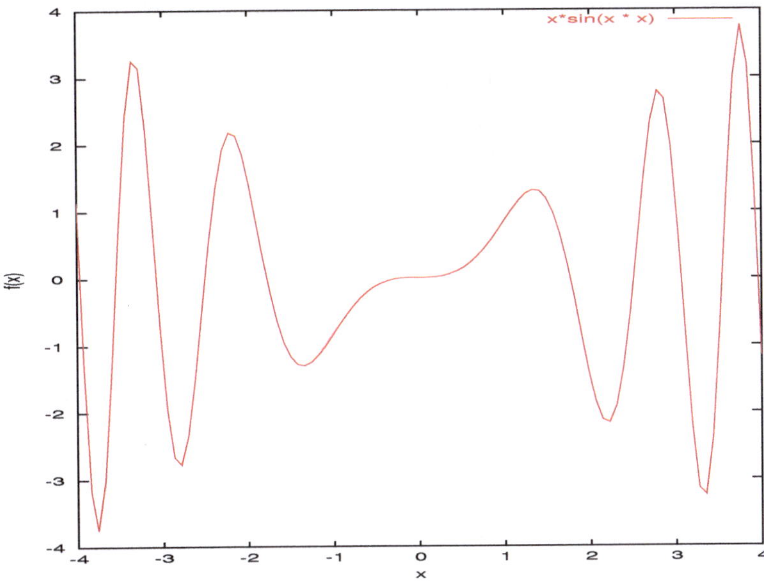

Fig. 1. Plotting of $x \sin x^2$

To test the efficiency we compared solution times for several combinations of the partition number and the number of the hidden nodes of each network keeping their product at comparable values to avoid overblown model complexity. A solution is taken to be one that produces a prescribed value for the max absolute pointwise error for the training set. The solution time is taken to be the cpu time spent by a uniprocessor system. In order to test the gain coming from parallel processing, our implementation that is based on message passing programming, was run on a multiprocessor system and observed how the solution time scaled down.

5 Experiments

5.1 Resources

The following results were obtained by using 25 Pentium III - 450MHZ machines running on Linux with kernel 2.4.0 The Lam v6.5.3 of MPI was employed for the distributed processing.

5.2 Results

In table 1 we list the square approximation error (columns ERR) and the number of knots (columns N) for cubic spline interpolation. 1000 points were used for testing. Diagrammatically tis is represented in figure 2.

Table 1. Approximation error for the cubic spline interpolation

N	ERR	N	ERR
40	168.05	75	7.86
45	90.95	80	6.08
50	52.37	85	4.82
55	32.18	90	3.90
60	21.00	95	3.22
65	14.54	100	2.69
70	10.47		

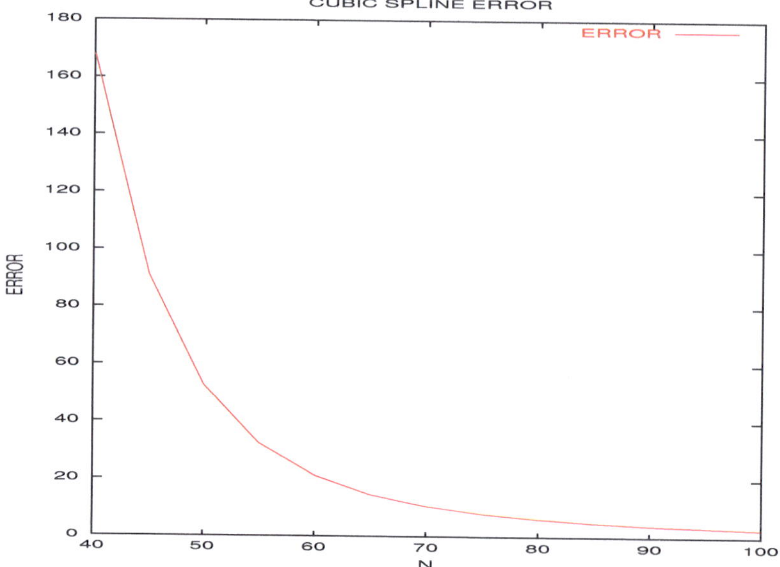

Fig. 2. Approximation error for the cubic spline interpolation

In all of our experiments we used 200 randomly selected points from the interval [-4,4] for training and 1000 points for testing. The reported approximation error refers to the test error. In table 2 we list the square approximation error (column ERR) and the training time (column TIME) for a single neural network. For the train of the neural network we used the single linkage clustering global optimization method due to Kan[10]. The column NODES represents the number of hidden nodes in the neural network.

In table 3 we list the square approximation error (column ERR) and the training time (column TIME) for the suggested method. For the training of the neural networks we used the single linkage clustering global optimization method due to Kan[10] The column INTERVALS represents the number of the intervals,

Table 2. Approximation error and execution time for a single neural network

NODES	ERR	TIME
8	4.52	46.27
10	$1.9 * 10^{-3}$	110.86
12	$2.0 * 10^{-4}$	179.33
14	$1.3 * 10^{-5}$	349.75
16	$2.0 * 10^{-6}$	418.334
18	$1.4 * 10^{-7}$	488.219
24	$9 * 10^{-8}$	598.124
30	$6 * 10^{-8}$	634.896
36	$4.3 * 10^{-8}$	697.150

in which we partitioned the problem. In this experiments we used 4 hidden nodes in each of the neural networks.

Table 3. Approximation error and execution time for the proposed method

INTERVALS	ERR	TIME
2	4.733	56.25
4	0.1497	90.72
8	$2.7 * 10^{-5}$	182.86
10	$1.1 * 10^{-5}$	193.55
15	$2.3 * 10^{-7}$	87.30

In table 4 we list the square approximation error (column ERR) and the training time (column TIME) for the suggested method. For the training of the neural networks we used the single linkage clustering global optimization method due to Kan[10]. The column INTERVALS represents the number of the intervals, in which we partitioned the problem. In this experiments we used 8 hidden nodes in each of the neural networks.

In figure 5.2 we show the absolute difference between $x\sin(x^2)$ and our approximation for 10 intervals and 8 nodes at each interval.

In table 5 we compare the training time for the multiple interval method on one processor (column T_1) in comparison with the training time for the same method run on multiple processors (column T_I, where I is the number of processors). We use column I for the number of intervals and column N for the number of hidden nodes in each of the neural networks. We use column E for the maximum absolute approximation error. In the column DIFF we have the relative difference between the multiple processor case and the single processor case.

Table 4. Approximation error and execution time for the proposed method

INTERVALS	ERR	TIME
2	$1.1 * 10^{-5}$	296.53
4	$3 * 10^{-7}$	126.53
8	$2 * 10^{-7}$	103.076
10	$2 * 10^{-8}$	86.40
15	10^{-8}	276.67

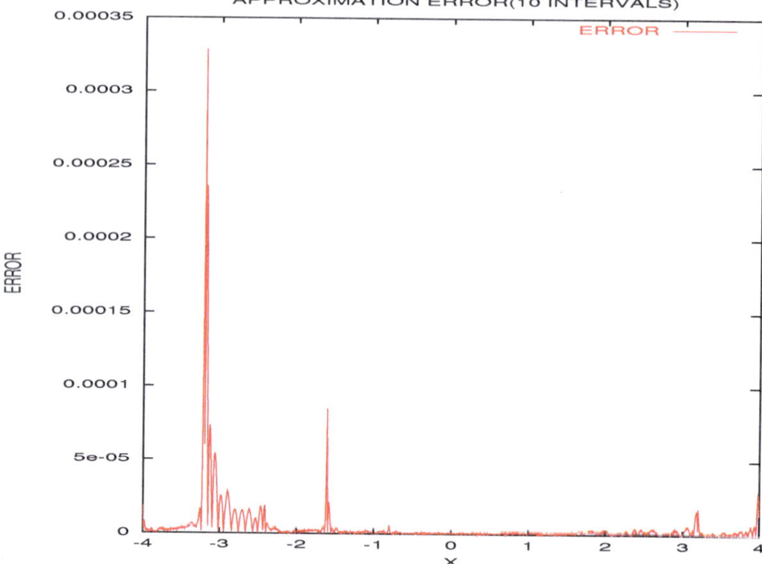

Fig. 3. Approximation error for the proposed method

Table 5. Multiple processors vs one processor

I	N	E	T_1	T_I	$DIFF$
2	8	0.0021	603.19	296.53	-50.84%
4	8	0.00012	476.90	126.53	-73.47%
8	4	0.0038	857.46	182.86	-78.67%
10	2	0.072	620.96	135.71	-78.15%
10	4	0.0054	866.38	193.55	-77.66%
15	1	0.073	1065.74	216.87	-79.65%
15	2	0.015	1187.66	282.51	-76.21%

6 Conclusions

Although our results are only preliminary, we can however draw some conclusions.

- The Neural Splines seem to be quite convenient and offer a flexible basis for functional approximation.
- Parallel processing plays an important role to the efficiency of the method, as can be realised by comparing the times spent on uniprocessor and multiprocessor systems. For large problems this will be the key advantage of our method.
- The scaling behaviour seems to be described by:

$$\frac{T_1}{T_I} = \frac{1 - e^{-\gamma I}}{1 - e^{-\gamma}}, \quad \gamma > 0$$

which for small values of I, scales linearly.(I, denotes the number of processors that is equal to the number of the partitions). The value of γ reflects the overhead of the calculation as well as the non-parallelized parts of it. Note that the optimization with respect to the external parameters can be accelerated by applying even-odd knot parallelization that will further reduce the value of γ. This will be important for problems in higher dimensions, since there the number of the external parameters is expected to grow significantly.

Future research will focus on higher dimensional problems and to the solution of differential equations.

References

1. De Boor C., *A practical guide to Splines*, Springer-Verlag, New York 1978.
2. Kincaid D., and Cheney W., *Numerical Analysis*, Brooks/Cole Publishing Company 1991.
3. Hornik K., Stinchcombe M., and White H., Neural Networks 2(1989) 359
4. Cybenko G., Approximation by superpositions of a sigmoidal function, Mathematics of Control Signals and Systems 2(1989)303-314
5. Bishop C., *Neural Networks for Pattern recognition*, Oxford University Press,1995.
6. Lagaris I. E., Likas A., Fotiadis D. I., *Artificial Neural Networks for solving ordinary and partial differential equations*, IEEE Trans. on Neural Networks, 9(1998)987-1000.
7. Lagaris I. E., Likas A., Fotiadis D. I., *Artificial Neural Network methods in Quantum Mechanics*, Computer Physics Communications, 104(1997)1-14
8. Lagaris I. E., Likas A., Papageorgiou D. G., *Neural Network methods for boundary value problems with irregular boundaries*, IEEE Trans. on Neural Networks, 11(2000)1041-1049
9. Obreshkov N., *On the Mechanical Quadratures*, J. Bulgar. Acad. Sci. and Arts LXV-8,(1942)191-289
10. Stochastic Global Optimization Methods: Clustering Methods. A.H.G Rinnooy Kan, G.T. Timmer, Mathematical Prograaming 39(1987) pp:27-56.

11. F. Theos, Master Thesis, June 2001, Department of Computer Science, University of Ioannina, Greece.
12. Papageorgiou D. G., Demetropoulos I. N. and Lagaris I. E., *The Merlin Control Language for strategic optimization,* Comput. Phys. Commun. 109(1998)250-275
13. Papageorgiou D. G., Demetropoulos I. N. and Lagaris I. E., *MERLIN-3.0 A multidimensional optimization environment,* Comput. Phys. Commun. 109(1998)227-249

Using Hopfield Networks to Solve Assignment Problem and N-Queen Problem: An Application of Guided Trial and Error Technique*

Christos Douligeris[1] and Gang Feng[2]

[1] Department of Informatics, University of Piraeus, Piraeus, 18534, Greece.
[2] Telecommunications and Information Technology Institute, Florida International University, Miami, FL 33174.

Abstract. In the use of Hopfield networks to solve optimization problems, a critical problem is the determination of appropriate values of the parameters in the energy function so that the network can converge to the best valid solution. In this paper, we first investigate the relationship between the parameters in a typical class of energy functions, and consequently propose a "guided trial-and-error" technique to determine the parameter values. The effectiveness of this technique is demonstrated by a large number of computer simulations on the assignment problem and the N-queen problem of different sizes.

1 Introduction

The continuous Hopfield neural network (CHNN) [1] can be used to solve an optimization problem in such a way that the cost function and constraints are first mapped to an energy function (if possible) and then a solution is obtained as the network stabilizes. Ever since Hopfield and Tank applied this network to solve the traveling salesman problem (TSP) [2], it has been employed to solve a variety of combinatorial optimization problems. However, a critical problem arising in the use of the HNN to solve optimization problem is how to choose the best parameters in the energy function so that the network can converge to valid solutions of high quality. In this paper, we will propose a relatively general method to determine the parameters.

In the past decade, the most extensively used method is the trial-and-error technique, and to our point of view, this technique (at most with more constraints) will still be used in the future, especially for those problems that are NP-hard or NP-complete. This is based on the observation that given an energy function for a specific problem, it seems that we can at most determine a range for each parameter that might result in better solutions. Therefore, what we need to do is to find as many constraints for these parameters as possible, and thus considerably reduce the number of trials before good parameters are found. This method for determining parameters, slightly different from the original trial-and-error technique, can be called "guided trail and error" method. Previous related works include Aiyer's eigenvalue analysis [4], Abe's suppressing spurious states [5], and Gee's application of polytope concept [3]. All of these works, however, are solely based

* This was partially supported by the Univ. of Piraeus Research Center.

I.P. Vlahavas and C.D. Spyropoulos (Eds.): SETN 2002, LNAI 2308, pp. 325–336, 2002.

on the analysis of the TSP. Matsuda published a series of papers [6]-[7] to study this problem. His basic idea is to analyze the stability of feasible and infeasible solutions and thus obtain some constraints for the parameters. However, we notice that in his most recent publication [7] even using the "optimal" network that he claimed can distinguish optimal solutions *most sharply* among all the networks to solve the 20×20 assignment problem, the percentage of experiments that the network converges to optimal solutions is only 58%, which leaves much to be desired considering that assignment problems of such small size are rather easy to be solved [8]-[9]. Moreover, the stability analysis in [7] is based on the assumption that any neuron in the network can exactly converge to "0" or "1", which is definitely not the case for a continuous HNN. Therefore there is a need for a methodology that will draw upon this experience and present more practical and efficient results.

The rest of the paper is organized as follows. We first discuss the relation of the parameters for a specific class of Hopfield energy functions in Section 2. In Section 3, the effectiveness of the convergence theorem and parameter selection method is demonstrated through a large number of tests on two combinatorial optimization problems. Finally, Section 4 concludes this paper.

2 The Relation of Parameters for a Class of Energy Functions

In this Section, we first provide a general form for a class of Hopfield energy functions, and then analyze what values should be chosen for the parameters so that the CHNN can converge to valid solutions of high quality. As a result, a "guided trial-and-error" technique is presented to determine the parameter values.

2.1 The General Form of a Class of Energy Functions

There exists a class of optimization problems [2], [7], [16], [17] that can be described as follows:

$$\left.\begin{array}{lll} \text{minimize} & \sum_{x}^{n}\sum_{i}^{n} f_{xi}V_{xi} & \\ \text{subject to} & \sum_{j}^{n} V_{xj} = k & \text{for any } x \\ & \sum_{y}^{n} V_{yi} = k & \text{for any } i \\ & V_{xi} \in \{0,1\} & \text{for any } x, i \end{array}\right\} \quad (1)$$

where $V = (V_{xi}) \in \{0,1\}^{n\times n}$ is a two dimensional variable matrix with each entry being the output of a neuron, $k(\leq n)$ is an integer representing the number of nonzero variables in each row and each column, and generally $k \in \{1,2\}$. Function f_{xi} is a linear combination of the variables in $S = V\backslash\{V_{xi}\}$ and is in the following form:

$$f_{xi}(V) = c_{xi} + \sum_{V_{yj}\in S} c_{yj}^{xi} V_{yj} \quad (2)$$

where c_{xi} and c_{yj}^{xi} are real numbers. Moreover, we assume that for any $x = 1, 2, \cdots, n$, $i = 1, 2, \cdots, n$, f_{xi} is positive at any point in the hypercube. More clearly, for any x and i,

$$f_{xi}(\tilde{V}) \geq 0,$$

where $\tilde{V}$ is a $n \times n$ matrix with $\tilde{V}_{yj} \in [0, 1]$ for any y and j.

When using a CHNN to solve the problem defined by (1), one can construct the following energy function:

$$E = \frac{C}{2}\left[\sum_{x}^{n}\left(\sum_{j}^{n} V_{xj} - k\right)^2 + \sum_{i}^{n}\left(\sum_{y}^{n} V_{yi} - k\right)^2\right] + D\sum_{x}^{n}\sum_{i}^{n} f_{xi}V_{xi} \quad (3)$$

where C and D, the Lagrange multipliers, are positive real numbers. The dynamics of the corresponding CHNN can be obtained in terms of a relation $du_{xi}/dt = -\partial E/\partial V_{xi}$, given by

$$\frac{du_{xi}}{dt} = -C\left(\sum_{j}^{n} V_{xj} + \sum_{y}^{n} V_{yi} - 2k\right) - Df_{xi}, \quad (4)$$

in which u_{xi} denotes the input of neuron xi.

In the rest of this Section, we will investigate ways to determine the values of parameters C and D. To ensure the effectiveness of our approach, we assume that the D term describes the objective function of a specific optimization problem, rather than a constraint. More clearly, there is an additional assumption for f_{xi}: given a valid solution $\tilde{V}$ to (1), assume that for at least some x, i, y and j, $f_{xi}(\tilde{V}) \neq f_{yj}(\tilde{V})$. Throughout this paper the notation $\hat{V}$ is used to denote the output matrix when the CHNN converges to a stable state.

2.2 The Relation between Parameters C and D

Let us first consider what values for C and D could possibly make the network converge to a valid solution. It is clear that a valid solution $\tilde{V}$ to problem (1) must have exactly k "1"s in each row and each column of $\tilde{V}$. When the CHNN converges to a stable state, however, the output of each neuron may not be exactly "1" or "0". Therefore, we cannot expect the network to directly converge to a valid solution; instead, we should try to "extract" a valid solution from the stable state if it is possible. For this reason, we start from the following lemma.

Lemma 1. A necessary condition to guarantee that a valid solution can be extracted from a stable state is that there are at least k nonzero entries in each row and each column in the matrix $\hat{V}$.

It is clear that we can not extract a solution if the number of nonzero entries is less than k in some row or column of $\hat{V}$.

Lemma 2. A necessary condition to guarantee that there are at least k nonzero entries in each row and each column in the matrix $\hat{V}$ can be given by

$$\sum_j^n \hat{V}_{xj} + \sum_y^n \hat{V}_{yi} > 0, \qquad \text{for any } x, i. \tag{5}$$

Theorem 1. A necessary condition for $\sum_j^n \hat{V}_{xj} + \sum_y^n \hat{V}_{yi} > 2\alpha k$, for any x, i, and $\alpha \in [0, 1)$ can be given by

$$Df_{min} < 2(1 - \alpha)kC \tag{6}$$

where $f_{min} = \min\{f_{xi} | x, i = 1, 2, \cdots, n\}$.

Proof: Omitted for saving space. □

Corollary 1. A necessary condition to guarantee that a valid solution can be extracted from the stable state can be given by

$$Df_{min} < 2kC. \tag{7}$$

Proof: In theorem 1, let $\alpha = 0$. From lemma 2 and lemma 1, we get that the corollary holds. □

To better understand the significance of theorem 1, let us assume that at a stable state, there are exactly k nonzero entries in each row and each column of $\hat{V}$, and thus it is clear that the value of α denotes to what degree a nonzero entry approaches "1". On the other hand, given a specific value for C, D must be small enough to ensure that the summation of a row and a column to be greater than $2\alpha k$. Theorem 1 is useful in such cases where the obtained solution becomes satisfactory only if each nonzero entry very closely approaches "1". Nonetheless, one should notice that (6) is neither a necessary nor a sufficient condition to guarantee that a valid solution can be obtained.

Another two necessary conditions stronger than (6) and (7) are given in the following theorem and the subsequent corollary.

Theorem 2. A necessary condition to guarantee that

(a) at a stable state there are in total at least nk (product of n and k) nonzero entries in $\hat{V}$, and
(b) for any x, i, and $\alpha \in [0, 1)$, $\sum_j^n \hat{V}_{xj} + \sum_y^n \hat{V}_{yi} > 2\alpha k$

is the following:

$$D\tilde{f}_{min} < 2(1 - \alpha)kC \tag{8}$$

where $\tilde{f}_{min}$ is the nkth minimum number among all f_{xi}'s.

Proof: Omitted for saving space. □

Corollary 2. A necessary condition to guarantee that a valid solution can be extracted from the stable state can be given by

$$D\tilde{f}_{min} < 2kC. \tag{9}$$

Proof: Omitted for saving space. □

Since $\tilde{f}_{min} \geq f_{min}$ (due to the fact that f_{min} is the minimum number among all f_{xi}'s), the necessary conditions (8) and (9) are stronger than (6) and (7), respectively, in the sense that given specific values for C, k and α, the range of D becomes smaller.

2.3 The Initial Value of D

In a Hopfield energy function, each energy term is usually assigned a parameter. For instance, in (3) the two parameters C and D are used to combine two energy terms. In fact it is obvious that in optimization their relative values are important, and one of them is redundant. Thus, any one of the parameters can be arbitrarily assigned a value as a reference to determine the values of other parameters. For this reason, from now on we assume that parameter C has already been assigned a specific value, and our goal is to find an appropriate value for D. We notice, however, that given a specific value for C, the range of D determined by the strongest necessary condition in the last subsection, i.e. (9), is still very large.

To find a good initial value for D, we need to consider what values of these parameters could possibly result in a good solution since our final goal is to find a solution which is not only valid, but of high quality as well. The difficulty in considering this point lies in that one can hardly find any conditions that can guarantee that better solutions are available. However, researchers in the area have obtained some practical experience [4], [7]. It is well known, for example, that when the network converges to a stable state, the closer the nonzero entry in $\hat{V}$ approaches "1", possibly the better the solution. For this reason, theorem 2 can be used to find a good initial value for D since only if the summation of each row and each column approaches $2k$ is it possible that each nonzero entry approaches "1". Thus the initial value of D can be given as follows:

$$D_{initial} = \frac{2(1-\alpha)k}{\tilde{f}_{min}} C \tag{10}$$

with α being a value close to 1.

For a specific problem, the value of $\tilde{f}_{min}$ can be obtained by estimation. If the expression of f_{xi} does not contain the second term in (2), namely the problem is an assignment problem, then it is possible to find the exact value of $\tilde{f}_{min}$ by greedy search, but it might be very time consuming.

2.4 The Fine-Tuning of D

Once an initial value for D is obtained, by gradually increasing or decreasing its current value, it is not hard to find a good value of D that may result in good valid solutions. To make a fine-tuning of D so that the quality of solutions can be further improved, we find that there is a basic rule that may be helpful.

Theorem 3. Assume that at any stable state of the CHNN defined by (3) and (4), there are exactly k nonzero entries in each row and each column of $\hat{V}$, and each nonzero is approximately equal to the same value, then the ratio of the second energy term in (3) to the first one is approximately in reverse proportion to the value of D.

Proof: Omitted for saving space. □

Theorem 3 indicates that a smaller value for D could possibly increase the proportion of the energy in the second term of (3) to the total energy. Since the second term of (3) is contributed from the objective function in (1), it is possible that a smaller value of D

could lead to a better solution. This is because the CHNN will continuously reduce the energy function until it reaches a stable state. Thus, among the total decreased energy, the more the energy coming from the objective term, most possibly the better the obtained solution. However, the dilemma lies in that if the value of D is too small, the nonzero entries can hardly approach "1". Therefore, one has to make many trials to find a balanced value for D.

2.5 The Value of the Parameter Associated with the Binary Constraint

The CHNN treats any problem it solves as a linear or nonlinear programming problem since the network only tries to find a local minimum of the energy function without caring whether the output of each neuron has reached an integral value. Therefore, if the output of each neuron can not approach a binary value when we try to solve an integer programming problem, another energy term due to the binary constraint should be added to the energy function. For a specific problem that can be formulated as (1), it is well known that we have two ways to describe the binary constraint as an energy term:

$$\sum_{x}^{n}\sum_{i}^{n} V_{xi}\left(1 - V_{xi}\right) \tag{11a}$$

or

$$E_0 = \sum_{x}^{n}\sum_{i}^{n} V_{xi}\left[\sum_{j\neq i}^{n} V_{xj} - (k-1)\right] + \sum_{x}^{n}\sum_{i}^{n} V_{xi}\left[\sum_{y\neq x}^{n} V_{yi} - (k-1)\right]. \tag{11b}$$

The first expression is effective because it becomes zero only when V_{xi} has a binary value. The second expression becomes zero if $V_{xi} = 0$ or in the case where $V_{xi} = 1$ and the bracket part equals to zero. Therefore, it still has the effect to help the output reach a binary value. We prefer the latter expression since the former one includes self-interaction terms which may make our following analysis more complicated. By assuming a positive parameter A is associated with E_0, the energy function (3) is now modified as

$$E = \frac{C}{2}\left[\sum_{x}^{n}\left(\sum_{j}^{n} V_{xj} - k\right)^2 + \sum_{i}^{n}\left(\sum_{y}^{n} V_{yi} - k\right)^2\right] + D\sum_{x}^{n}\sum_{i}^{n} f_{xi}V_{xi} + AE_0. \tag{12}$$

There are three parameters in (12). Although at first glance it seems difficult to analyze the mutual relations between these parameters, we find that (12) can be rewritten to be the same form as (3):

$$E = \frac{C}{2}\left[\sum_{x}^{n}\left(\sum_{j}^{n} V_{xj} - k\right)^2 + \sum_{i}^{n}\left(\sum_{y}^{n} V_{yi} - k\right)^2\right] + D\sum_{x}^{n}\sum_{i}^{n} \hat{f}_{xi}V_{xi} \tag{13}$$

in which

$$\hat{f}_{xi} = f_{xi} + \gamma \left(\sum_{j \neq i}^{n} V_{xj} + \sum_{y \neq x}^{n} V_{yi} - 2k + 2 \right) \tag{14}$$

and $\gamma = A/D$. Now, it is clear that our former analysis on the choice of the values of C and D still applies to this case. Similar to the analysis in the last subsection, in order to let more of the total decreased energy come from the objective term, from (14) we know A/D should be as small as possible. In fact, it has been noted that the binary constraint term will considerably increase the number of local minimums, therefore in most cases A is set to 0. However, we also find that in some cases this term can not be omitted, even if the value of A is very small [10].

2.6 The Guided Trial-and-Error Technique

By summarizing the above analysis, we give a formal statement on the "guided trial-and-error" technique. When using a CHNN to solve a specific problem formulated as (1), and assuming that its energy function is given by (13), the "guided trial-and-error" technique can be described as follows:

1. Initialization.
   (1) Arbitrarily choose a value for C.
   (2) Choose a value for Δt, which satisfies $\Delta t < 1/(\beta_{max} C)$[1]
   (3) Compute the initial value of D by (10) when α is set to a value close to 1, e.g. $\alpha = 0.99$.
   (4) Let $\gamma = 0$.
2. Tuning. Keep tuning the parameters according to the following rules until satisfactory results are found:
   (1) Decrease (increase) Δt if the network converges too fast (slow) to a stable state with unsatisfactory solutions.
   (2) Increase D if the outputs of neurons do not approach binary values; if this has no effect, then increase γ.
   (3) Decrease γ if the outputs of neurons approach binary values, but with solutions of low quality; if γ can not be decreased any more, then try to decrease D.

During the increase of D, inequality (9) should be strictly satisfied. On the other hand, when the values of D and γ are small, the number of iterations should be large enough to ensure that the network can reach a stable state.

3 Experimental Results

In this section, the "guided trial-and-error" technique is applied to solve the assignment problem and the N-queen problem to test its effectiveness. In our following experiments, the sigmoid function is used as the neuron's I/O function:

$$V_{xi} = \frac{1}{2}\left[1 + tanh\left(\frac{u_{xi}}{2u_0}\right)\right]. \tag{15}$$

The maximum slope of this function is $\beta_{max} = 1/(4u_0)$.

[1] Δt is the discretized dt in the dynamic equation, and β_{max} is the maximum slope of the input-output equation of the neuron. For more details regarding this constraint, please see [11].

3.1 The Linear Assignment Problem

The linear assignment problem (AP) needs to assign n jobs to n persons in a one-to-one way such that the total cost is minimized. This problem can be solved by converting it to a minimum cost flow problem [8] or using the Hungarian method [9] in time $O(n^3)$, where n is the problem size. In recent years, instead of using these ordinary linear programming methods, many researchers try to develop parallel algorithms based on, for example, Hopfield-type neural networks [12]-[14] and statistical physics [15] so as to considerably reduce the time complexity. In this paper, we use the original CHNN to solve the assignment problem by formulating it as (1), in which $k = 1$ and f_{xi} equals to a deterministic value, namely (2) becomes $f_{xi} = c_{xi}$.

Now let us show how to choose the parameter values using the "guided trial-and-error technique". First, we let $C = 50$, $\gamma = 0$, and the parameter u_0 in the sigmoid function be 0.01. From the convergence theorem proposed in [11] we know that the time-step Δt should be less than 0.0008 to ensure that the network continuously converges to a stable state. Thus, we let $\Delta t = 0.00075$. To determine an initial value for the parameter D, we assume that each c_{xi} is a randomly generated real number and is uniformly distributed in $(0, 1]$. Thus, from equation (10), the initial value of D is given by $D_{initial} = (n^2 + 1)/n \approx n$ when $\alpha = 0.99$ (we only consider the cases where n is big enough such that $1/n$ is negligible).

We have tested a number of AP instances when the problem size varies from 20 to 200. In our simulations, all of the above parameter values are kept unchanged except that we let $D = n$ when $n \leq 100$, and $D = 100$ when $n > 100$. For a specific problem size n, ten problem instances are randomly generated such that c_{xi}'s are integers uniformly distributed in $[1, 1000]$. For each problem instance, ten simulations are made when the initial values of neurons are changed. Thus, we obtain 100 solutions for problem instances with the size of n. Note that this is same method used in [7].

The initial value of a neuron is given by

$$u_{xi}(t = 0) = -u_0 ln(n - 1) + 0.01 Rand \tag{16}$$

where $Rand$ is a random number in $[-1, 1]$. Using this initialization method, the output of each neuron approximately equals to $1/n$ when $t = 0$, and thus the summation of the entries in a row or a column of the matrix $V(t = 0)$ is approximately 1. The following rule is used to terminate a simulation. For a specific problem instance, the Hungarian method is used to obtain its optimal solution. In every 100 iterations of a specific simulation, the total decrease of energy ΔE in one iteration is computed as follows:

$$\Delta E = \sum_{x,i}^{n} \Delta E_{xi} = \sum_{x,i}^{n} C \Delta V_{xi}^2 - \frac{1}{\Delta t} \Delta u_{xi} V_{xi}. \tag{17}$$

A simulation is terminated if $|\Delta E| < \epsilon$, or if the temporary solution is equal to the optimal solution, whichever condition occurs first. ϵ is set to a value such that when $|\Delta E| < \epsilon$, the network approximately approaches a stable state and the solution can hardly be changed. In our experiments we let $\epsilon = n \times 10^{-8}$.

The statistical results are shown in Table 1. The first row denotes the problem size, the second row is the number of simulations when optimal solutions are obtained, the third row is the average error, and the last row is the average iteration number for a single AP instance. The average error is computed as follows:

$$\frac{1}{100}\sum_{i}^{10}\sum_{j}^{10}\frac{Sol_{ij}-Opt_i}{Opt_i}\times 100\%$$

where Sol_{ij} is the solution obtained in the jth simulation for problem instance i, and Opt_i is the optimal solution of problem instance i. From Table 1, we may find that when the problem size is relatively small, the CHNN can obtain an optimal solution with a very high probability, even though we have not put much effort to tune parameter D. To show the effectiveness of our theoretical analysis, one may make a comparison of our results with those shown in [7]. When using the same problem formulation, the author of [7] can obtain an optimal solution with a probability of only 1% even when the problem size is 20, and the probability was improved to 58% after the energy function was reformulated.

We can further improve the performance of the CHNN by fine-tuning the value of D. As stated in theorem 3, under certain assumptions the ratio of the objective energy term to the constraint energy term is in reverse proportion to the value of D. Therefore, a smaller value of D could possibly improve the quality of the solution. We have done the same experiments as described above when D is set to a fixed value 15. The corresponding results are shown in Table 2. To ensure that the results are comparable, the initial values of the neurons for a specific simulation of Table 2 are set to the same as those for the corresponding simulation of Table 1. From Table 2, one may notice that the probability that an optimal solution can be obtained has been considerably increased. The expense is that the number of iterations also increases.

Table 1. Results of the Assignment Problem when $D = n$ ($n \geq 100$) and $D = 100$ ($n > 100$)

problem size n	20	40	60	80	100	200
optimal solution convergence (%)	100	100	90	85	52	78
average error(%)	0	0	2.59	5.79	17.63	8.91
average iterations	166	255	646	657	932	1523

Table 2. Results of the Assignment Problem when $D = 15$

problem size n	20	40	60	80	100	200
optimal solution convergence (%)	100	100	100	95	99	86
average error(%)	0	0	0	2.60	0.16	4.41
average iterations	193	447	1577	1640	1898	5334

3.2 The N-Queen Problem

The N-queen problem can be stated as follows: given a n by n chessboard, we need to place n queens on the chessboard such that any two queens can not attack each other. The constraints in this problem can be described more precisely as follows: in each row or each column, there is exactly one queen; in each positive or negative diagonal, there is also exactly one queen.

The N-queen problem can also be formulated as (1) when $k = 1$ and f_{xi} are defined as follows:

$$f_{xi} = \sum_{\substack{j \neq 0 \\ 1 \leq x+j \leq n \\ 1 \leq i+j \leq n}} V_{x+j,i+j} + \sum_{\substack{j \neq 0 \\ 1 \leq x-j \leq n \\ 1 \leq i-j \leq n}} V_{x-j,i-j}. \tag{18}$$

However, one should note that the above expression violates the second assumption we impose on f_{xi} in (1), because for a valid solution $\tilde{V}$ to this problem, we always have $f_{xi}\left(\tilde{V}\right) = f_{yj}\left(\tilde{V}\right) = 0$ for any x, i, y and j. In fact, (18) is the expression of a constraint, rather than an objective term in the general sense. For this reason, we can not determine the value of parameter D by means of the theorems in Section 3. Instead, we should choose a value so that the importance of the two constraint-terms (C term and D term) can be balanced.

Although we can only arbitrarily choose an initial value for D, the values of other parameters can be readily determined in accordance with the convergence theorem in [11]. Similarly, we let $\gamma = 0$, $u_0 = 0.01$, $C = 50$, $\Delta t = 0.00075$. After a number of experiments, we find that the network can obtain valid solutions with high probability when D is around 15. Note that for this problem, a valid solution is also an "optimal" solution.

The experimental results when $D = 10$ and $D = 15$ are shown in Tables 3 and 4, respectively. The problem size varies from 30 to 200. For a specific problem size n, we have done 100 simulations, each with different initial values for the neurons. The initialization method is same with the one used in the assignment problem except that the amplitude of the random number is set to 0.005. Also, in every 100 iterations of a specific simulation, the total decrease of the energy is computed according to (17), and the temporary output matrix is processed using the recommended post-processing method described in the previous Section. If $|\Delta E| < 10^{-6}$ or a valid solution is obtained then the simulation is terminated.

From Tables 3 and 4, one may notice that the CHNN can obtain valid solutions with very high probability even when the problem size becomes large. Now let us make a comparison with the results reported by other researchers. In recent years, many works have been done on the use of neural networks (not necessarily the Hopfield networks) to solve the N-queen problem. In [16], the highest probability that a valid solution can be obtained is 73% when $n = 30$, and 90% when $n = 50$, and no results were given when $n > 50$. In [18] and [19], the sizes of the studied problems are restricted to be 10 and 8, respectively. In [20], a dual-mode dynamics neural network is employed to solve this problem and this method is demonstrated to outperform many other methods when $n \leq 40$, but no results are reported for problems of larger size. In [21], the self-feedback controlled chaotic neural network is used to solve this problem of large size, and after the self-feedback factor is finely tuned, the success rate to solve the 200-queen problem is around 98.8%. Thus, our result is comparable with the best result in the literature.

Table 3. Results of the N-queen Problem when $D = 10$

problem size n	30	50	80	100	200
valid solution convergence (%)	98	100	98	99	92
average iterations	131	119	172	204	358

Table 4. Results of the N-queen Problem when $D = 15$

problem size n	30	50	80	100	200
valid solution convergence (%)	95	100	100	100	97
average iterations	170	112	122	133	252

4 Conclusions

In this paper, we have addressed the dynamics of the continuous Hopfield neural networks. In particular, we investigated the mutual relation between the parameters in a typical class of Hopfield energy functions, and thus proposed a "guided trial and error" technique for determining the parameters. The effectiveness of this technique has been demonstrated by a large number of computer simulations when the HNN is used to solve the assignment problem and the N-queen problem. Compared with previous works, the performance of the HNN has been considerably improved.

References

1. J. J. Hopfield, "Neurons with graded response have collective computational properties like those of two-state neurons," *Proc. National Academy of Sciences USA*, vol.81, pp.3088-3092, May 1984.
2. J. J. Hopfield and D. W. Tank, "Neural computation of decisions in optimization problems," *Biological Cybernetics*, vol.52, pp.141-152, 1985.
3. A. H. Gee, "Problem solving with optimization networks," Ph.D. dissertation, Univ. Cambridge, July 1993.
4. S. V. Aiyer, M. Niranjan and F. Fallside, "A theoretical investigation into the performance of the Hopfield model," *IEEE Trans. Neural Networks*, vol.1, no.2, pp.204-215, June 1990.
5. S. Abe, "Global convergence and suppression of spurious states of the Hopfield neural networks," *IEEE Trans. Circuits Syst. I*, vol.40, no.4, pp.246-257, April 1993.
6. S. Matsuda, "The stability of the solution in Hopfield neural network," *Proc. Int. Joint Conf. Neural networks*,pp. 1524-1527, 1993.
7. S. Matsuda, "Optimal" Hopfield network for combinatorial optimization with linear cost function," *IEEE Trans. Neural Networks* , vol.9, no.6, pp.1319-1330, November 1998.

8. E.L. Lawler, *Combinatorial Optimization: Networks and Matroids*, Holt, Rinehart and Winston, 1976.
9. H.W. Kuhn, "The Hungarian method for the assignment problem," *Naval Res. Logist. Quart.*, pp.83-97, 1955.
10. G. Feng and C. Douligeris,"Using Hopfield networks to solve traveling salesman problems based on stable state analysis technique," *Proc. Int. Joint Conf. Neural networks*,Vol.6, pp. 521-526, Jul 24-Jul 27 2000.
11. G. Feng and C. Douligeris,"On the Convergence and Parameter Relation of Discrete-Time Continuous-State Hopfield Networks with Self-Interaction Neurons," *IEICE Trans. Fundamentals*, Vol.E84-A No.12, pp.3162-3173, Dec. 2001.
12. S.P. Eberhardt, T. Duad, DA.Kerns, T.X.Brown and A.P. Thakoor, "Competitive neural architecture for hardware solution to the assignment problem," *Neural networks*,Vol.4, no.4, pp.431-442,1991.
13. J. Wang, "Primal and dual assignment networks," *IEEE Trans. Neural Networks*, vol.8, no.3, pp.784-790, May 1997.
14. W.J. Wolfe, J.M. MacMillan, G. Brady, R. Mathews, J.A. Rothman, M.D. Orosz, C. Anderson and G. Alaghand, "Inhibitory grids and the assignment problem," *IEEE Trans. Neural Networks*, vol.4, no.2, pp.319-331, March 1993.
15. A.L. Yuille and J.J. Kosowsky, "Statistical physics algorithms that converge," *Neural computation*, pp.341-356, 1994.
16. S. Bharitkar and J.M., Mendel,"Hysteretic Hopfield neural network," *IEEE Trans. Neural Networks*, vol.11, no.4, pp. 879-888, Jul 2000.
17. Y. Takefuji and K.C. Lee,"Artificial neural networks for four-coloring map problems and K-colorability problems," *IEEE Trans. Circuits Syst.*, vol.38, no.3, pp.326-333, March 1991.
18. T. Kwok, K. Smith and L. Wang, "Solving combinatorial optimization problem by chaotic neural networks," *Proc. Of the Artificial Neural networks in Eng.*, vol.8, pp.317-322, Nov. 1998.
19. I. N. Silva, A. N. Souza and M. E. Bordon, "A modified Hopfield model for solving the N-queen problem," *IJCNN'2000*, Como, Italy, pp.509-514, 2000.
20. S. Lee and J. Park, "Dual-mode dynamics neural networks for non-attacking N-queen problem," *IEEE Intel. Symp. Intelligent Control*, pp.588-593, August 1993.
21. M. Ohta, "On the self-feedback controlled chaotic neural networks and its application to N-queen problem," *IJCNN'99*, Washington DC, pp.713-716, July 1999.

A Bayesian Regularization Method for the Probabilistic RBF Network

Constantinos Constantinopoulos, Michalis K. Titsias, and Aristidis Likas

Dept. of Computer Science, University of Ioannina,
45110 Ioannina, Greece
{ccostas,mtitsias,arly}@cs.uoi.gr

Abstract. The Probabilistic RBF (PRBF) network constitutes a recently proposed classification network that employs Gaussian mixture models for class conditional density estimation. The particular characteristic of this model is that it allows the sharing of the Gaussian components of the mixture models among all classes, in the same spirit that the hidden units of a classification RBF network feed all output units. Training of the PRBF network is a likelihood maximization procedure based on the Expectation – Maximization (EM) algorithm. In this work, we propose a Bayesian regularization approach for training the PRBF network that takes into account the existence of ovelapping among classes in the region where a Gaussian component has been placed. We also propose a fast and iterative training procedure (based on the EM algorithm) to adjust the component parameters. Experimental results on well-known classification data sets indicate that the proposed method leads to superior generalization performance compared to the original PRBF network with the same number of kernels.

1 Introduction

In pattern recognition it is well-known that a convenient way to construct a classifier is on the basis of inferring the posterior probability of each class. ¿From the statistical point of view this inference can be achieved by first evaluating the class conditional densities $p(x|C_k)$ and the corresponding prior probabilities $P(C_k)$ and then making optimal decisions for new data points by combining these quantities through the Bayes theorem

$$P(C_k|x) = \frac{p(x|C_k)P(C_k)}{\sum_{k'} p(x|C_{k'})P(C_{k'})}, \tag{1}$$

and then selecting the class with maximum $P(C_k|x)$. In the traditional statistical approach each class density $p(x|C_k)$ is estimated using a separate mixture model and considering only the data points of the specific class, therefore the density of each class is estimated independently from the other classes. We will refer to this approach as the *separate mixtures* model.

The probabilistic RBF network [6,7] constitutes an alternative approach for class conditional density estimation. It is an RBF-like neural network [4] adapted

I.P. Vlahavas and C.D. Spyropoulos (Eds.): SETN 2002, LNAI 2308, pp. 337–345, 2002.

to provide output values corresponding to the class conditional densities $p(x|C_k)$. Since the network is RBF [4], the kernels (hidden units) are shared among classes and each class conditional density is evaluated using not only the corresponding class data points (as in the traditional statistical approach [5]), but using all the available data points. In order to train the PRBF network, an Expectation - Maximization (EM) algorithm can be applied [1,2,7]. The treatment of the training procedure as a likelihood maximization problem provides the opportunity to define Bayesian priors on the network parameters. The priors we propose tend to favor solutions that avoid the placement of a kernel in a region with weak overlap among classes. We provide an iterative EM-based procedure for finding the maximum a posteriori probability (MAP) [3] PRBF parameters. The effectiveness of the proposed method is demonstrated using several data sets and the experimental results indicate that the method leads to performance improvement over the classical PRBF training method.

2 The Probabilistic RBF Network

Consider a classification problem with K classes and a training set $X = \{(x^{(n)}, y^{(n)}), n = 1, \ldots, N\}$ where $x^{(n)}$ is a d-dimensional pattern, and $y^{(n)}$ is a label C_k $(k = 1, \ldots, K)$ indicating the class of pattern $x^{(n)}$. The original set X can be easily partitioned into K independent subsets X_k, so that each subset contains only the data of the corresponding class. Let N_k denote the number of patterns of class C_k, ie. $N_k = |X_k|$.

Assume that we have a number of M kernel functions (hidden units), which are probability densities, and we would like to utilize them for estimating the conditional densities of all classes by considering the kernels as a common pool [6,7]. Thus, each class conditional density function $p(x|C_k)$ is modeled as

$$p(x|C_k) = \sum_{j=1}^{M} \pi_{jk} p(x|j), \qquad k = 1, \ldots, K \tag{2}$$

where $p(x|j)$ denotes the kernel function j, while the mixing coefficient π_{jk} represents the prior probability that a pattern has been generated from kernel j, given that it belongs to class C_k. The priors take positive values and satisfy the following constraint:

$$\sum_{j=1}^{M} \pi_{jk} = 1, \qquad k = 1, \ldots, K. \tag{3}$$

It is also useful to introduce the posterior probabilities expressing our posterior belief that kernel j generated a pattern x given its class C_k. This probability is obtained using the Bayes' theorem

$$P(j|x, C_k) = \frac{\pi_{jk} p(x|j)}{\sum_{i=1}^{M} \pi_{ik} p(x|i)}. \tag{4}$$

In the following, we assume that the kernel densities are Gaussians of the general form

$$p(x|j) = \frac{1}{(2\pi)^{d/2}|\Sigma_j|^{1/2}} \exp\left\{-\frac{1}{2}(x-\mu_j)^T \Sigma_j^{-1}(x-\mu_j)\right\} \tag{5}$$

where $\mu_j \in \Re^d$ is a vector representing the center of kernel j, while Σ_j represents the corresponding $d \times d$ covariance matrix. The whole adjustable parameter vector of the model consists of the priors and the kernel parameters (means and covariances) and we denote it by θ.

Training of the PRBF network may efficiently achieved with the EM algorithm [1,2,6,7]. It consists of the application at each iteration t of the following processing steps:

1. E-step: For each training point $(x^{(n)}, y^{(n)}) \in X$ compute the posterior probabilities $P^{(t)}(j|C_k, x^{(n)})$, for $j = 1, \ldots, M$ and $k = 1, \ldots, K$, from (4) using the current parameters $\theta^{(t)}$.
2. M-step: Find the new parameter vector $\theta^{(t+1)}$ using the following equations:

$$\mu_j^{(t+1)} = \frac{\sum_{k=1}^{K} \sum_{x \in X_k} P^{(t)}(j|C_k, x)x}{\sum_{k=1}^{K} \sum_{x \in X_k} P^{(t)}(j|C_k, x)} \tag{6}$$

$$\Sigma_j^{(t+1)} = \frac{\sum_{k=1}^{K} \sum_{x \in X_k} P^{(t)}(j|C_k, x)(x-\mu_j^{(t+1)})(x-\mu_j^{(t+1)})^T}{\sum_{k=1}^{K} \sum_{x \in X_k} P^{(t)}(j|C_k, x)} \tag{7}$$

$$\pi_{jk}^{(t+1)} = \frac{1}{|X_k|} \sum_{x \in X_k} P^{(t)}(j|C_k, x), \; k = 1, \ldots, K \tag{8}$$

It is apparent that the PRBF model is a special case of the RBF network [4] where the outputs correspond to probability density functions and the second layer weights are constrained to represent prior probabilities. Furthermore, it can be shown that the separate mixtures model [5] can be derived as a special case of PRBF.

As discussed in [8] both the PRBF model (trained in a typical manner) and the separate mixtures model, in some cases provide solutions that are not very effective from the classification point of view. More specifically, it has been observed [8] that the PRBF network provides inferior classification solutions when there exist kernels placed on regions with weak overlapping among classes. The motivation behind this work is to exploit Bayesian regularization, by specifying appropriate priors on the PRBF parameters, in order to guide the training process to avoid solutions exhibiting the above undesirable characteristic.

3 Bayesian Regularization

Let $P(C_k)$ denote the prior probability of class C_k. In order to use Bayes rule (1) for unlabeled input data we have to find first appropriate values for both class prior probabilities and parameter vector θ. Thus, the whole adjustable parameter vector is $\Theta = (\theta, P(C_1), \ldots, P(C_k))$. We can utilize Bayes theorem once again to estimate the a posteriori distribution of the parameter vector Θ according to

$$p(\Theta \mid X) = \frac{p(X \mid \Theta)p(\Theta)}{\int p(X \mid \Theta)p(\Theta)\mathrm{d}\Theta} \tag{9}$$

where $p(X \mid \Theta)$ is the density of the observations X given Θ, and $p(\Theta)$ is the prior density on Θ. The configuration $\hat{\Theta}$ that maximizes $p(X \mid \Theta)p(\Theta)$ also maximizes $p(\Theta \mid X)$, and is known as the maximum a posteriori (MAP) estimation of Θ

$$\hat{\Theta} = \arg\max_{\Theta} \; p(X \mid \Theta)p(\Theta) \tag{10}$$

In order to proceed with the MAP estimation, we have to define a proper prior $p(\Theta)$ for PRBF training. At first we introduce the variables μ_{jk} and Σ_{jk}, for $j = 1, \ldots, M$ and $k = 1, \ldots, K$. These represent means and covariance matrices respectively as follows:

$$\mu_{jk} = \frac{\sum_{x \in X_k} P(j|C_k, x)x}{\sum_{x \in X_k} P(j|C_k, x)} \tag{11}$$

$$\Sigma_{jk} = \frac{\sum_{x \in X_k} P(j|C_k, x)(x - \mu_{jk})(x - \mu_{jk})^T}{\sum_{x \in X_k} P(j|C_k, x)}. \tag{12}$$

As shown in [7], μ_{jk} and Σ_{jk} constitute an estimation of the parameters of kernel j, when only data of class C_k are considered. It has been shown [7] that during PRBF training, the parameters of kernel j computed at any EM iteration can be written as

$$\mu_j = \sum_{k=1}^{K} P(C_k|j)\mu_{jk} \tag{13}$$

$$\Sigma_j = \sum_{k=1}^{K} P(C_k \mid j)\Sigma_{jk} \tag{14}$$

where

$$P(C_k \mid j) = \frac{\pi_{jk} P(C_k)}{\sum_{k'=1}^{K} \pi_{jk'} P(C_{k'})} \tag{15}$$

is the probability that pattern x belongs to class C_k, given that it has been generated from kernel j. The above equations indicate that the parameters μ_j, Σ_j of kernel j actually correspond to the mean values of the variables μ_{jk} and Σ_{jk}, for $k = 1, \ldots, K$. For convenience we will refer to a 'component' with parameters μ_{jk} and Σ_{jk} as *subkernel* jk. In other words each subkernel jk defines a Gaussian distribution $p(x \mid jk)$ with mean μ_{jk} and covariance Σ_{jk}. Now we can quantify the overlapping among classes in the region of a kernel using measures of the distance among distributions. The expected value of the distance between the kernel j and its subkernels jk can be used as a measure of class ovelapping in the region of kernel j. Using the *Bhattacharya distance* between $p(x \mid j)$ and $p(x \mid jk)$ we obtain the desirable measure:

$$\delta_j = \sum_{k=1}^{K} P(C_k \mid j) \left\{ -\ln \int [p(x \mid j) p(x \mid jk)]^{1/2} \, \mathrm{d}x \right\} \tag{16}$$

In the case of complete overlapping among classes δ_j equals zero, and the same holds if only one class exists in the region of the kernel j.

Based on this property of δ_j, we define the prior on Θ as

$$p(\Theta) = \prod_{j=1}^{M} \exp\{-\alpha \delta_j\} \tag{17}$$

where α constitutes the regularization *hyperparameter.*

Apparently there is no a priori assumption about class priors, and each factor of the product refers to a kernel of the model. According to the above discussion, solutions where kernels are placed in regions with high overlapping or no overlapping at all are prefered. With this choice of $p(\Theta)$, it is expected that in the case where a subkernel jk exhibits weak overlapping with the remaining subkernels jl, the training algorithm will force π_{jk} to become zero.

3.1 The EM Training Procedure

The posterior log likelihood function of the data set X is

$$L(\Theta) = \sum_{n=1}^{N} \log p(x^{(n)}, y^{(n)} \mid \Theta) + \log p(\Theta) \tag{18}$$

Using that $p(x, C_k \mid \Theta) = p(x \mid C_k, \Theta) P(C_k \mid \Theta)$ and the fact that the data set X consists of K independent subsets X_k, the above equation takes the form

$$\begin{aligned} L(\Theta) = & \sum_{k=1}^{K} |X_k| \log P(C_k \mid \Theta) \\ & + \sum_{k=1}^{K} \sum_{x \in X_k} logp(x \mid C_k, \Theta) + \log p(\Theta) \end{aligned} \tag{19}$$

To simplify the procedure, we maximize the first term of (19) separately, and then use the resulting solution in the maximization of the remaining terms. Maximization of the first term yields

$$P(C_k) = \frac{|X_k|}{|X|}, k = 1, \ldots, K \tag{20}$$

while the maximization of the reamaining terms is equivalent to PRBF training using regularization. Consequently the a posteriori log likelihood function suitable for training of the PRBF network is given by

$$L(\theta) = \sum_{k=1}^{K} \sum_{x \in X_k} logp(x \mid C_k, \theta) + \log p(\theta) \tag{21}$$

and assuming Gaussian mixture models the above equation can be written as

$$L(\theta) = \sum_{k=1}^{K} \sum_{x \in X_k} \log \sum_{j=1}^{M} \pi_{jk} p(x \mid j) - \alpha \sum_{j=1}^{M} \sum_{k=1}^{K} P(C_k \mid j) \beta_{jk} \tag{22}$$

where β_{jk} is the Bhattacharya distance between Gaussian distributions $p(x \mid j)$ and $p(x \mid jk)$

$$\beta_{jk} = \frac{1}{8}(\mu_j - \mu_{jk})^T \left[\frac{\Sigma_j + \Sigma_{jk}}{2} \right]^{-1} (\mu_j - \mu_{jk}) + \frac{1}{2} \ln \frac{\left| \frac{1}{2} \left(\Sigma_j + \Sigma_{jk} \right) \right|}{|\Sigma_j|^{1/2} |\Sigma_{jk}|^{1/2}} \tag{23}$$

In order to maximize $L(\theta)$ we employ the EM algorithm [1,2] and show that PRBF regularization can be performed with a fast, effective and easily implementable scheme.

The Expectation-Maximization (EM) algorithm is a general technique for maximum likelihood estimates in the case where hidden information exists. Given the corresponding incomplete data set X, the complete data set is defined as $X_C = \{(x^{(n)}, y^{(n)}, z^{(n)}),\ n = 1, \ldots, N\}$ where the hidden variable z is a M-dimensional vector of zero-one values, indicating the kernel that generated x. If kernel j is responsible for generating x then $z_j = 1$, otherwise $z_j = 0$. The expected value of z equals the a posteriori probability $P(j \mid x, C_k)$ that kernel j generated x given the class label C_k, defined as

$$P(j \mid x, C_k) = \frac{\pi_{jk} p(x \mid j)}{\sum_{i=1}^{M} \pi_{ik} p(x \mid i)} \tag{24}$$

Following the common procedure, we define the expected complete a posteriori log likelihood as

$$L_C(\theta) = \sum_{k=1}^{K} \sum_{x \in X_k} \sum_{j=1}^{M} P(j \mid x, C_k) \log \pi_{jk} p(x \mid j) - \alpha \sum_{j=1}^{M} \sum_{k=1}^{K} P(C_k \mid j) \beta_{jk} \tag{25}$$

We make the reasonable assumption that $\Sigma_{jk} = \Sigma_j$, and concentrate on the centers of the subkernels. So at iteration t of the algorithm, the quantity to be maximized at the M-step is:

$$Q(\theta; \theta^{(t)}) = \sum_{k=1}^{K} \sum_{x \in X_k} \sum_{j=1}^{M} P^{(t)}(j \mid x, C_k) \log \pi_{jk} p(x \mid j) - \frac{\alpha}{8} \sum_{k=1}^{K} \sum_{j=1}^{M} P(C_k \mid j) (\mu_j - \mu_{jk}^{(t)})^T \left[\Sigma_j^{(t)} \right]^{-1} (\mu_j - \mu_{jk}^{(t)}) \tag{26}$$

Based on several algebraic manipulations, it can be shown that the above maximization can be performed analytically thus leading to the following update equations:

$$\mu_j^{(t+1)} = \frac{\sum_{k=1}^{K} \sum_{x \in X_k} P^{(t)}(j \mid x, C_k)x + \frac{\alpha}{4} \sum_{k=1}^{K} P^{(t)}(C_k \mid j)\mu_{jk}^{(t)}}{\sum_{k=1}^{K} \sum_{x \in X_k} P^{(t)}(j \mid x, C_k) + \frac{\alpha}{4}} \tag{27}$$

$$\Sigma_j^{(t+1)} = \frac{\sum_{k=1}^{K} \sum_{x \in X_k} P^{(t)}(j \mid x, C_k)(x - \mu_j^{(t+1)})(x - \mu_j^{(t+1)})^T}{\sum_{k=1}^{K} \sum_{x \in X_k} P^{(t)}(j \mid x, C_k)} \tag{28}$$

$$\pi_{jk}^{(t+1)} = \frac{\sum_{x \in X_k} P^{(t)}(j \mid x, C_k) + \frac{\alpha}{8} P^{(t)}(C_k \mid j) \left\{ \sum_{l=1}^{K} P^{(t)}(C_l \mid j)\delta_{jl}^{(t)} - \delta_{jk}^{(t)} \right\}}{|X_k| + \frac{\alpha}{8} \sum_{i=1}^{M} P^{(t)}(C_k \mid i) \left\{ \sum_{l=1}^{K} P^{(t)}(C_l \mid i)\delta_{il}^{(t)} - \delta_{ik}^{(t)} \right\}} \tag{29}$$

where

$$\delta_{rs}^{(t)} = (\mu_r^{(t+1)} - \mu_{rs}^{(t)})^T \left[\Sigma_r^{(t+1)} \right]^{-1} (\mu_r^{(t+1)} - \mu_{rs}^{(t)}) \tag{30}$$

It is worthwile to examine the regularization term in (29). Notice that for any kernel j, the regularization terms corresponding to the subkernels jk $(k = 1, \ldots, K)$ sum to zero:

$$\sum_{k=1}^{K} P(C_k \mid j) \left\{ \sum_{l=1}^{K} P(C_l \mid j)\delta_{jl} - \delta_{jk} \right\} = 0 \tag{31}$$

This equation indicates that there is competition among the subkernels. If the distance between the kernel j and one subkernel jk' is less than the average, then the corresponding regularization term is positive, otherwise it is negative. In that way the remote subkernel is penalized, and eventually rejected if the prior $\pi_{jk'}$ becomes zero.

A computational problem that we experience is that sometimes the negative regularization term becomes too high and results in negative priors. To avoid this situation, at each iteration if the minimum prior of any class becomes negative we set it equal to zero, and normalize the remaining priors in order to satisfy (3).

4 Experimental Results and Conclusions

In this section we compare the proposed training method with the typical PRBF training method [6,7]. We considered four well-known data sets from the UCI repository, namely the Phoneme($N = 5404, K = 2$), Satimage($N = 6435, K = 6$), Pima Indians Diabetes($N = 768, K = 2$) and Ionosphere($N = 351, K = 2$) data sets. For each data set, in order to obtain an estimation of the generalization error, we have employed 5-fold cross-validation. In every experiment all training algorithms started from the same initial state. Tables 1-4 provide the obtained results for both methods, for several values of the number of kernel functions M,

Table 1. Generalization error on the Pima Indians Diabetes data set

	Number of kernels				
Algorithm	6	8	10	12	14
PRBF	30.33	30.07	28.26	28.00	27.35
$\alpha = 5N/KM$	31.25	28.25	27.21	26.82	25.78
$\alpha = 10N/KM$	28.91	26.30	**26.56**	27.60	26.82
$\alpha = 15N/KM$	28.00	27.73	27.99	**26.81**	26.43
$\alpha = 20N/KM$	**27.47**	**25.64**	27.86	28.39	**25.38**

Table 2. Generalization error on the Satimage data set

	Number of kernels				
Algorithm	6	9	12	15	18
PRBF	24.12	17.09	17.01	16.08	16.16
$\alpha = 5N/KM$	23.92	17.20	16.92	16.05	15.69
$\alpha = 10N/KM$	24.10	17.08	16.41	15.99	15.71
$\alpha = 15N/KM$	22.74	16.58	**15.80**	15.85	15.68
$\alpha = 20N/KM$	**22.55**	**15.88**	15.99	**15.76**	**15.48**

Table 3. Generalization error on the Phoneme data set

	Number of kernels				
Algorithm	8	10	12	14	16
PRBF	21.12	21.58	21.23	21.57	21.33
$\alpha = 5N/KM$	**20.97**	21.66	21.27	21.64	21.10
$\alpha = 10N/KM$	21.08	21.44	**20.81**	20.70	20.62
$\alpha = 15N/KM$	21.34	21.16	20.99	20.75	**20.38**
$\alpha = 20N/KM$	21.03	**20.81**	20.97	**20.55**	20.57

Table 4. Generalization error on the Ionosphere data set

	Number of kernels				
Algorithm	4	6	8	10	12
PRBF	24.49	17.37	12.83	11.69	9.42
$\alpha = 5N/KM$	19.11	12.26	**10.25**	9.40	9.41
$\alpha = 10N/KM$	**14.52**	**10.26**	10.80	9.11	9.70
$\alpha = 15N/KM$	14.80	12.83	10.82	9.40	9.70
$\alpha = 20N/KM$	14.80	12.83	10.25	**8.83**	**9.11**

and the hyperparameter α. Bold values indicate the best result for each column. The values of α we used were multiples of the quantity $\frac{N}{KM}$.

The results indicate that the proposed regularization technique provides networks with superior performance compared to typical PRBF training. It must also be noted that the method is fast, since in all experiments 100 EM iterations were sufficient for reaching the final solution.

In what concerns future enhancement of the method, our current work focuses on the utilization of alternative distance measures, averaging PRBF networks obtained for different values of the hyperperameter α, and developing an approach for dynamicaly adjusting the number of kernels M. In the last case our aim is to exploit recent results for adjusting the number of kernels in a Gaussian mixture that have been developed in the framework of pdf estimation [9].

References

1. A. P. Dempster, N. M. Laird and D. B. Rubin, "Maximum Likelihood Estimation from Incomplete Data via the EM Algorithm", *Journal of the Royal Statistical Society B*, vol. 39, pp. 1-38, 1977.
2. G. McLachlan, T. Krishnan, *The Em Algorithm and Extensions*, Wiley, 1997.
3. T. Mitchell, *Machine Learning*, McGraw-Hill, 1997.
4. C. M. Bishop, *Neural Networks for Pattern Recognition*, Oxford University Press, 1995.
5. G. McLachlan, D. Peel, *Finite Mixture Models*, Wiley, 2000.
6. M. Titsias, A. Likas, "A Probabilistic RBF network for Classification", *Proc. of International Joint Conference on Neural Networks*, Como, Italy, July 2000.
7. M. Titsias, A. Likas, "Shared Kernel Models for Class Conditional Density Estimation", *IEEE Trans. on Neural Networks*, vol. 12, no. 5, pp. 987-997, Sept. 2001.
8. M. Titsias, A. Likas, "Class Conditional Density Estimation Using Mixtures with Constraint Component Sharing", Tech. Rep. 8-2001, Dept. of Computer Science, Univ. of Ioannina, 2001.
9. N. A. Vlassis and A. Likas, "A Greedy-EM Algorithm for Gaussian Mixture Learning", *Neural Processing Letters*, to appear.

Support Vector Machines with Clustering for Training with Very Large Datasets

Theodoros Evgeniou and Massimiliano Pontil

Technology Management,
INSEAD,
Bd de Constance, Fontainebleau 77300, France
and
Department of Information Engineering,
University of Siena, Siena, Italy, and
Department of Mathematics, City University of Hong Kong, Hong Kong
theodoros.evgeniou@insead.edu, pontil@dii.unisi.it

Abstract. We present a method for training Support Vector Machines (SVM) classifiers with very large datasets. We present a clustering algorithm that can be used to preprocess standard training data and show how SVM can be simply extended to deal with clustered data, that is effectively training with a set of weighted examples. The algorithm computes large clusters for points which are far from the decision boundary and small clusters for points near the boundary. This implies that when SVMs are trained on the preprocessed clustered data set nearly the same decision boundary is found but the computational time decreases significantly. When the input dimensionality of the data is not large, for example of the order of ten, the clustering algorithm can significantly decrease the effective number of training examples, which is a useful feature for training SVM on large data sets. Preliminary experimental results indicate the benefits of our approach.

1 Introduction

The recent development of a new family of learning machines, namely Support Vector Machines (SVM) [2,3,12], whose training can be formulated as optimizing a quadratic programming (QP) problem with box constraints, has lead to a series of fast optimization methods for this type of QP problems [7,6,9]. A lot of work has been done to speed up SVMs through speeding up the corresponding QP problems. A chunking algorithm is proposed by Vapnik [3]. This is an iterative method that at each iteration solves a small subproblem. The chunking algorithm uses the support vectors found in previous batches for use in next batches [3]. Advanced working set algorithms use only a subset of the variables as a working set and optimize the problem with respect to them while freezing the others [6]. The extreme case of the advance working set is to use only two variables in the working set as in Sequential Minimum optimization [7]. In a recent paper, the problem is formulated by using a random rectangular kernel sub-matrix

I.P. Vlahavas and C.D. Spyropoulos (Eds.): SETN 2002, LNAI 2308, pp. 346–354, 2002.

instead of using a full square one [4]. Column generation techniques and Bender's Decomposition can be also applied to this problem [1,10].

Other than methods for speeding up the training of SVM, a lot of work has also been done in the direction of speeding up (scaling up) general data mining methods. Provost and Kolluri [8] give a recent review of various approaches, mostly focusing on learning methods for finding rules and for training decision trees. The paper categorizes the approaches into three groups: designing fast algorithms, partitioning the data, and using relational representations.

In this paper we describe a new approach to training SVM with very large datasets which is different from the three main approaches discussed in [8] and from the standard methods for training SVM using all the training data. The approach is based on the idea of first clustering - in a particular way - the original training data and then training an SVM with a set of new data which represent the found clusters and which are therefore significantly less than the original data. The clustering is done in a way that takes into account the key characteristic of SVM that only training data near the separating boundary (for classification) are important. We therefore present a clustering method that yields only a few clusters away from the separating boundary, and many clusters near the boundary. This way the important information from the training data - namely that of the training data near the separating boundary - is preserved while at the same time the size of the training set is effectively decreased. The approach is similar to that proposed by [5] for the case of radial basis functions. Once clusters have been found, the initial training data are then represented with a set of weighted examples - the centers of the clusters with weights depending on the size of the clusters - which a simple variation of the standard SVM uses for training. The variation of the SVM is such that weighted example data are used during training.

The paper is organized as follows: in section 2 we first define the notation, give a brief overview of SVM, present the setup of the problem, and outline the proposed solution. Section 3 discusses the proposed clustering method. In section 4 we present experiments comparing the proposed method to that of standard SVM training using all the initial training data. Finally section 5 is summary and conclusions.

2 Background and Notation

We are given a training set $S = \{(\mathbf{x}_1, y_1), \ldots, (\mathbf{x}_N, y_N)\}$, where each point $\mathbf{x}_i$ belongs to $\mathbb{R}^n$ and $y_i \in \{-1, 1\}$ is a label that identifies the class of point $\mathbf{x}_i$. Our goal is to determine a function

$$f(\mathbf{x}) = \mathbf{w} \cdot \boldsymbol{\phi}(\mathbf{x}_i) + b, \tag{1}$$

where $\boldsymbol{\phi}(\mathbf{x}) = (\phi_1(\mathbf{x}), \ldots, \phi_m(\mathbf{x}))$ corresponds to a mapping from $\mathbb{R}^n$ into a feature space $\mathbb{R}^m$ - this is the standrad Reproducing Kernel Hilbert Space mapping used for kernel learning machines [3].

Statistical Learning Theory [12] establishes that in order to obtain a function with controllable generalization capability we need to control the VC-dimension of the function through structural risk minimization. SVMs are a practical implementation of this idea. The formulation of SVM leads to the following Quadratic Programming Problem [3]:

Problem **P1**

Minimize $\frac{1}{2}\mathbf{w}\cdot\mathbf{w} + C\sum_{i=1}^{N}\xi_i$

subject to $y_i(\mathbf{w}\cdot\boldsymbol{\phi}(\mathbf{x}_i)+b) \geq 1-\xi_i \; i=1,2,\ldots,N$

$\boldsymbol{\xi} \geq 0.$

The solution $\bar{\mathbf{w}}$ of this problem is given by equation:

$$\bar{\mathbf{w}} = \sum_{i=1}^{N} \bar{\alpha}_i y_i \boldsymbol{\phi}(\mathbf{x}_i), \tag{2}$$

where $\bar{\boldsymbol{\alpha}} = (\bar{\alpha}_1, \ldots, \bar{\alpha}_N)$ is the solution of the *Dual Problem*:

Problem **P2**

Maximize $-\frac{1}{2}\boldsymbol{\alpha}^\top D\boldsymbol{\alpha} + \sum \alpha_i$

subject to $\sum_{i=1}^{N} y_i\alpha_i = 0$

$0 \leq \alpha_i \leq C, \qquad i=1,2,\ldots,N$

where D is a $N \times N$ matrix such that

$$D_{ij} = y_i y_j \boldsymbol{\phi}(\mathbf{x}_i)\cdot\boldsymbol{\phi}(\mathbf{x}_j). \tag{3}$$

Combining Equations (1) and (2), the solution of Problem P1 is given by:

$$\sum_{i=1}^{N} \bar{\alpha}_i y_i \boldsymbol{\phi}(\mathbf{x}_i)\cdot\boldsymbol{\phi}(\mathbf{x}) + \bar{b}.$$

The points for which $\bar{\alpha}_i > 0$ are called Support Vectors (SVs). They are the points that are either misclassified by the computed separating function or are closer than a minimum distance - the margin of the solution - from the separating surface [3]. In many applications they form a small subset of the training points.

For certain choices of the mapping $\boldsymbol{\phi}(\mathbf{x})$ we can express the dot product in the feature space defined by the $\boldsymbol{\phi}$'s as:

$$\boldsymbol{\phi}(\mathbf{x}_i)\cdot\boldsymbol{\phi}(\mathbf{x}_j) = K(\mathbf{x}_i,\mathbf{x}_j) \tag{4}$$

where K is called the kernel of the Reproducing Kernel Hilbert Space defined by the $\boldsymbol{\phi}$'s [3]. Observe that the spatial complexity of Problem **P2** is N^2, independent from the dimensionality of the feature space. This observation allows us to extend the method in feature spaces of infinite dimension [12].

In practice, because of memory and speed requirements, Problem **P2** presents limitations on the size of the training set. To overcome this practical problem, we suggest an approach based on clustering. The idea consists of substituting the original training set with a smaller set of a few weighted points:

$$\{(\mathbf{t}_1, y_1, n_1), \ldots, (\mathbf{t}_g, y_g, n_g)\},$$

so that each point $\mathbf{t}_i$ represents a cluster of n_i points of the input data $\mathbf{x}_i$ of the original training set ($\mathbf{t}_i$ is the "center" of the cluster - although as we will see in the next section it is not necessarily the geometric center), y_i is the class (±1) of the points in cluster i, g is the number of clusters, n_i are also the weights of the new points $(\mathbf{t}_i, y_i)$, and $\sum_{i=1}^{g} n_i = N$. Problem **P1** can then be adjusted to separate the new weighted training data as follows:

Problem **P3**
Minimize $\frac{1}{2}\mathbf{w}\cdot\mathbf{w} + C\sum_{i=1}^{g} n_i\xi_i$
subject to $y_i(\mathbf{w}\cdot\phi(\mathbf{t}_i) + b) \geq 1 - \xi_i \; i = 1, 2, \ldots, g$
$\xi \geq 0.$

where we have modified the second term in the objective function with a weighed sum to take into account the number of points represented by each cluster "center" $\mathbf{t}_i$. The motivation for this is that intuitively the more original points a new point $\mathbf{t}_i$ "represents", the more its importance. Of course other weights can be chosen, but here we choose weights equal to the sizes of the clusters represented by the new points $\mathbf{t}_i$. How the final solution is influenced by this choice of weights is an open question. The Dual Problem then becomes:

Problem **P4**
Maximize $-\frac{1}{2}\boldsymbol{\alpha}^\top D\boldsymbol{\alpha} + \sum_{i=1}^{g}\alpha_i$
subject to $\sum_{i=1}^{g} y_i\alpha_i = 0$
$0 \leq \alpha_i \leq n_i C. \qquad i = 1, 2, \ldots, g$

where now D is a $g \times g$ matrix such that

$$D_{ij} = y_i y_j K(\mathbf{t}_i, \mathbf{t}_j). \tag{5}$$

with y_i corresponding to the class of "center" $\mathbf{t}_i$ - as we will see in the next section each cluster consists of original training points with the same class ±1, which is also the class of the new y_i. Notice that the differences from Problem **P2** are the new matrix D and the new upper bounds $n_i C$ for the variables α_i. Unlike in Problem **2**, matrix D now has size $g \times g$ instead of $N \times N$. So for $g << N$ the new problem is smaller and therefore training is expected to be faster. So the question now is how to cluster the initial training data without "loosing information".

3 The Clustering Algorithm

In this section we introduce the clustering algorithm that we use as a preprocessing step to train SVM on large data sets.

The algorithm computes clusters for each of the two classes separately. We illustrate it in the case of class +1.

First we initialize the set A_1 of clusters of class 1: $A_1 = \{(\mathbf{x}_i, 1) \mid (\mathbf{x}_i, y_i) \in S,\ y_i = 1\}$.

1. Set $\ell = 0$.
2. For each point $(\mathbf{x}_k, n_k) \in A$:
   (a) Compute the nearest point[1] in $A_1 \setminus \{(x_k, n_k)\}$ to $(\mathbf{x}_k, n_k)$. Let $(\mathbf{x}_j, n_j)$ be this point and d their distance, $d = \|x_k - x_j\|$.
   (b) Compute the center of mass of the two previous points, $\mathbf{v} = \frac{n_k \mathbf{x}_k + n_j \mathbf{x}_j}{n_k + n_j}$.
   (c) Compute the distance D between $\mathbf{v}$ and the nearest training point in class -1.
   (d) If $\frac{d}{D} < \gamma$ delete the two previous points from A_1, add $(\mathbf{v}, n_k + n_j)$ to A_1, and set $\ell = \ell + 1$.
3. If $\ell > 0$ goto step 1, otherwise stop.

After the algorithm has stopped, A_1 is the set of clusters of class 1. The same procedure is then repeated to compute the set of clusters of class 2, A_2. Notice that the number of clusters is not fixed a priori and it clearly depends on the parameter γ. Notice also that the clusters are not found "explicitly": at the end of the algorithm we only have the final points $\mathbf{t}_i$ representing the clusters, which are not necessarily the geometric centers of the original training points they represent.

Notice that the algorithm tends to produce large clusters of points which are far away from the boundary between the two classes and small clusters of points near the boundary. Thus, we expect that the original points that are candidates to be support vectors are not strongly affected by the clustering procedure, while the others are heavily reduced. The parameter γ controls the meaning of "near". If the dimensionality of the input space is not too big (say $n \approx 10$), we expect that the overall algorithm (clustering and then training using the centers of the clusters) can considerably improve the training time compared to an SVM using all original training data.

4 Experimental Results

In this section we compare the performance of standard SVM with that of the SVM trained on the weighted examples computed by the clustering algorithm discussed above. We performed three sets of experiments in $\mathbb{R}^2$ with linear and non-linear kernels and one experiment in $\mathbb{R}^8$ with non-linear kernels. The experiments were performed on a DEC alpha 430MHz. The SVM is computed by solving the primal Problem **P1** (**P3** for clustered data). We used a software [11] based on Interior Point Methods [13].

[1] We use the Euclidean distance.

Linear kernel: In the first example we randomly generated two sets of points inside two circles of the same radius r and Bayes region of about $.03\pi r^2$. We then trained a linear SVM with and without the clustering preprocessing step. Table 1 shows the number of clusters and the performance of the algorithm we developed in the previous section on training sets of increasing size. The parameter γ was set to 2.5.

Table 1. Experiment 1 - Size of the clustering set and user time of the clustering algorithm for training sets of increasing size.

N	g	Time
5000	470	8.5 sec
10000	849	39.7 sec
20000	1537	137.4 sec

Table 2 is a comparison between the SVM obtained by training on the full set of 5000 points and the SVM trained on the clusters.

Table 2. Experiment 1 - User time and error rate for the full training set (5000 points) and the cluster set for different values of the regularization parameter. The error rate is obtained on a test set of 5000 points. Total training time for the proposed method is the sum of the time reported in this Table and in Table 1 for 5000 points.

C	Full Set		Cluster Set	
3	23.3 sec	2.8%	.73 sec	2.8%
10	22.2 sec	2.8%	.80 sec	2.7%
100	25.0 sec	2.8%	.89 sec	2.7%

Non-linear kernel: In the second example the training points are randomly generated in a circle of radius r and the boundary between the two classes is given by $x_2 = rsin(\pi \frac{x_1}{r})$. We now work with a polynomial kernel of third degree. Tables 3 and 4 show the results of clustering and prediction.

Table 3. Experiment 2 - Size of the clustering set and user time of the clustering algorithm for training sets of increasing size.

N	g	Time
5000	397	9.4 sec
10000	745	41.8 sec
20000	911	145 sec

Table 4. Experiment 2 - User time and error rate of the SVM trained on the full training set (20000 points) and on the cluster set for different values of the regularization parameter C. The error rate was computed on a test set of 5000 points.

C	Full Set		Cluster Set	
3	286 sec	0.48%	1.54sec	0.44%
10	316 sec	0.32%	1.54sec	0.30%
100	364 sec	0.14%	1.82 sec	0.16%

The setting of the third experiment is as in experiment 2 with the addition that now we assign point $\mathbf{x}$ to the first class if $x_2 > rsin(\pi \frac{x_1}{r}) + \epsilon$, where ϵ is a random number $\in (-\frac{1}{10}r, \frac{1}{10}r)$. We again work with a polynomial kernel of third degree.

Table 5. Experiment 3 - User time and error rate for the full training set of 20000 points and for the cluster set obtained with different values of the regularization parameter. The error rate is computed on a test set of 5000 points.

C	Full Set		Cluster Set	
3	327 sec	3.16%	4.51 sec	3.16%
10	385 sec	3.15%	4.95 sec	3.15%
100	356 sec	3.15%	4.82 sec	3.15%

The results are shown in Table 5 which is like Tables 2 and 4. To better understand the dependence on parameter γ, we also run the clustering algorithm for different values of γ. The results are shown in Tables 6 and 7. Table 7 shows that for this particular example the choice of the parameter γ does not modify significantly the true error rate.

Table 6. Experiment 3 - Size of the clustering set and corresponding percentage of reduction of the effective size of the training data for different values of the parameter γ, obtained from the original training set of 20000 points.

γ	g	Reduc. Rate
2.5	2518	87.4 %
1.5	1818	90.9 %
1.25	1582	92.1 %
1	1326	93.4 %

Table 7. Experiment 3 - Error rate for different values of the parameter γ. In all cases the regularization parameter C was 10

γ	Error Rate
2.5	3.15 %
1.5	3.16 %
1	3.17 %

5 Conclusions

We have presented a method for fast training SVM classifiers using a particular method for clustering that does not "distort" significantly training data around the separating boundary. Experimental results indicate that this is a promising direction for research. A number of questions remains open. From the theoretical point of view, it is an open question how close the solution found from the proposed methods is to the global optimal one that a single SVM using all the training data would have found. Appropriate measures of distance between the solutions need to be defined: for example one can probably use the margin and the number of training errors, or the value of the cost function of the QP, or the set of overall (including all points in the clusters found) support vectors, as such measures. From the practical point of view, an important question is how to adapt the proposed methods to other learning techniques. Finally, future work will consist of using the proposed method with very large real datasets.

References

1. Bennett, K., A. Demiriz and J. Shawe-Taylor: 2000, 'A Column Generation Algorithm for Boosting' In *Proc. of 17. International Conferance on Machine Learning*, p. 57-64, Morgan Kaufman, San Francisco
2. Burges, C. J. C. 1998 'A tutorial on support vector machines for pattern recognition' In *Data Mining and Knowledge Discovery* 2(2):121-167.
3. Cortes, C. and V. Vapnik: 1995, 'Support Vector Networks'. *Machine Learning* **20**, 1–25.
4. Lee, Y. J. and O.L. Mangasarian: 2001 'RSVM: Reduced Support Vector Machines' In *First SIAM International Conference on Data Mining*
5. Musavi, M.T., Ahmed, W., Chan, H., Faris, K.B, Hummels, D.M. 1992. "On the Training of Radial Basis Function Classifiers," *Neural Network* **5**: 595–603.
6. Osuna, E., R. Freund, and F. Girosi: 1997 'Improved Training Algorithm for Support Vector Machines' In Proceeding of IEEE Neural Networks and Signal Processing (NNSP'97)
7. Platt, J.: 1999 'Fast training of support vector machines using sequential minimal optimization' In B. Schölkopf, C. J. C. Burges, and A. J. Smola, editors, Advances in Kernel Methods — Support Vector Learning, pages 185-208, Cambridge, MA, 1999. MIT Press.
8. Provost, F., and V. Kolluri: 1999 'A survey of methods for scaling up inductive algorithms' In *Machine Learning*, 1999, p. 1-42.

9. Rifkin, R.: 2000 'SvmFu a Support Vector Machine Package' In http://five-percent-nation.mit.edu/PersonalPages/rif/SvmFu/index.html
10. Trafalis T. and H. Ince: 2001, 'Benders Decomposition Technique for Support Vector Regression' *Working Paper, School of Industrial Engineering, University of Oklahoma, Norman, OK*
11. Vanderbei, R.J. 1997. "LOQO User's Manual - Version 3.04." *Statistical and Operations Research* Tech. Rep. **SOR-97-07** Princeton University.
12. Vapnik, V. N.: 1998, *Statistical Learning Theory.* New York: Wiley.
13. Wright, M.H. 1992. "Interior Methods for Constrained Optimization" **Tech. Rep.** AT&T Bell Lab.

A Temporal Network of Support Vector Machine Classifiers for the Recognition of Visual Speech

Mihaela Gordan[1], Constantine Kotropoulos[2], and Ioannis Pitas[2]

[1] Faculty of Electronics and Telecommunications
Technical University of Cluj-Napoca
15 C. Daicoviciu, 3400 Cluj-Napoca, Romania
mihag@bel.utcluj.ro

[2] Artificial Intelligence and Information Analysis Laboratory
Department of Informatics, Aristotle University of Thessaloniki
Box 451, GR-54006 Thessaloniki, Greece
{costas, pitas}@zeus.csd.auth.gr

Abstract. Speech recognition based on visual information is an emerging research field. We propose here a new system for the recognition of visual speech based on support vector machines which proved to be powerful classifiers in other visual tasks. We use support vector machines to recognize the mouth shape corresponding to different phones produced. To model the temporal character of the speech we employ the Viterbi decoding in a network of support vector machines. The recognition rate obtained is higher than those reported earlier when the same features were used. The proposed solution offers the advantage of an easy generalization to large vocabulary recognition tasks due to the use of viseme models, as opposed to entire word models.

1 Introduction

Visual speech recognition refers to the task of recognizing the spoken words based only on the visual examination of the speaker's face. This task is also referred as lipreading, since the most important visible part of the face examined for information extraction during speech is the mouth area. Different shapes of the mouth (i.e. different mouth openings, different position of the teeth and tongue) realized during speech cause the production of different sounds. One can establish a correspondence between the mouth shape and the phone produced, even if this correspondence will not be one-to-one, but one-to-many, due to the fact that invisible parts of the vocal tract are also involved in speech production as well. For small size word dictionaries, we can still perform good quality speech recognition using the visual information regarding the mouth shape only.

So far, many methods have been reported in the literature for solving the visual speech recognition problem. The different types of solutions adopted vary widely with respect to: 1) the feature types; 2) the classifier used; and 3) the class definition. For example, Bregler uses time-delayed neural networks (TDNN) for visual classification, and the outer lip contour coordinates as visual features [6].

I.P. Vlahavas and C.D. Spyropoulos (Eds.): SETN 2002, LNAI 2308, pp. 355–365, 2002.

Luettin uses active shape models for representing different mouth shapes, gray level distribution profiles (GLDPs) around the outer and/or inner lip contours as feature vectors, and finally builds whole-word hidden Markov models (HMMs) for visual speech recognition [7]. Movellan employs also HMM for building visual word models, but using as features directly the gray levels of the mouth images, after some simple preprocessing to exploit the vertical symmetry of the mouth [5].

Despite the big variety of existing strategies for visual speech recognition, there is still ongoing research in this area, attempting: 1) to find the most suitable features and classification techniques to discriminate efficiently between the different mouth shapes, but to keep the mouth shapes corresponding to the same phone produced by different individuals in the same class (i.e., to develop speaker independent techniques); 2) to require limited processing of the mouth image so that the implementation of the mouth shape classifier in real time is feasible; 3) to facilitate the easy integration of audio and video speech recognition.

In this paper, we aim to contribute to the first of the above mentioned aspects in visual speech recognition, by examining the suitability of a new type of classifiers for visual speech recognition tasks, the support vector machines (SVMs). We are motivated by the success of SVMs in various pattern recognition applications including visual classification tasks such as biometric person authentication, medical image processing, etc.

The use of SVMs as classifiers for automatic speech recognition is a new idea. Very good results in audio speech recognition using SVMs were recently reported in [1]. No attempts in applying SVMs for visual speech recognition have been reported so far, although a somehow closely related application is described in [11], where SVMs were applied for detecting the degree of opening/smile of mouth images in videosequences. This work uses SVMs for linear regression, not for classification task. Thus, according to the best of the author's knowledge, the use of SVMs as visual speech classifiers is a novel idea. Regarding SVMs applications as visual classifiers, there are some very good results in face detection and face recognition [2,3] and in dynamical object detection in videosequences [13].

One of the reasons for not using SVMs in automatic speech recognition so far is the fact that they are inherently static classifiers, whilst speech is a dynamic process, where the temporal information is essential for recognition. This means one cannot use directly SVMs for speech recognition. A solution to this problem is presented in [1], where a combination of HMM and SVM is proposed. In this paper we adopt a similar strategy for modeling the visual speech dynamics with the difference that we shall use only the Viterbi algorithm to create dynamical visual word models.

Another novel aspect in the visual speech recognition approach proposed here refers to the strategy adopted for building the word models: while most of the applications presented in the literature [1,7,5] build whole word models as basic visual models, our basic visual models are mouth shape models (viseme models), and the visual word model is obtained by the combination of these basic models into a temporal dynamic sequence. This approach offers the advantage of an easy generalization to large vocabulary word recognition tasks without a significant increase in storage requirements by maintaining the dictionary of basic visual models needed for word modeling to a reasonable limit.

The visual speech recognition results obtained are very promising as compared to similar approaches reported in the literature. This shows that SVMs are a promising alternative for visual speech recognition and encourages the continuation of the research in this direction.

The outline of the paper is as follows. Section 2 details the proposed visual speech recognition using SVMs. The modeling of temporal speech dynamics is described in Section 3. Experimental results are presented in Section 4 and conclusions are drawn is Section 5.

2 Description of the Proposed Visual Speech Recognition Approach Using Support Vector Machines

The problem of discriminating between different shapes of the mouth during speech production, the so-called *visemes*, can be viewed as a pattern recognition problem. In this case the feature vector comprises a representation of the mouth image, either low-level at pixel-level, or by extracting several geometric parameters, or by applying some linear transform of the mouth image. The different pattern classes are the different mouth shapes occurred during speech. For example, in the case of producing the sound "o", the mouth will have an open-rounded shape, while for example in the case of sound "f", the mouth will have an almost closed position, not rounded, the upper teeth will be visible and the lower lip will be moved inside.

Obtaining the phonetic description of each word from a possible dictionary is a simple task, and there are currently many publicly available tools to do this. Correlations can be established between the different phones produced during speech and the visemes corresponding to them. However, this correspondence is not one-to-one, since non-visible parts of the vocal tract are also involved in speech production, and even more, it depends on the nationality of the different speakers given the fact that the pronunciation of the same word varies and is not always according to the "standard" one. Furthermore, although there are phoneme-to-viseme correspondence tables available in the literature [4], currently there is not a universally accepted mapping, as in the case of phonemes (cf. [12]). The solution adopted here is to define the viseme classes and the viseme-to-phoneme mapping dependent on the application (i.e., the recognition of the first four digits in English, as spoken by the different individuals in the Tulips1 database [5]). The viseme classes defined and their corresponding phonemes are presented in Table 1.

Once we have defined the mapping between the classes of visemes needed in our application and their corresponding phonemes based on the phonetic description of each word from the dictionary, we can build the *visemic models* of the words as sequences of mouth shapes which could produce the phonetic

Table 1. Viseme-to-phoneme mappings for the first four digits.

Phoneme	Corresponding viseme classes
W	w (small rounded open mouth state)
	ao (larger rounded open mouth state)
	wao (medium rounded open mouth state)
AH	ah (medium ellipsoidal mouth state)
N	n (medium open, not rounded, mouth state; teeth visible)
T	t (medium open, not rounded, mouth state; teeth and tongue visible)
UW	SAME AS W
TH	$\text{th}_{1,2}$ (medium open, not rounded)
R (context C-**C**-V)	w (small rounded open mouth state)
	ao (larger rounded open mouth state)
IY	iy (longitudinal open mouth state)
	ah (medium ellipsoidal mouth state)
F	$\text{f}_{1,2,3}$ (almost closed position; upper teeth visible; lower lip moved inside)
AO	SAME AS W

realizations of the words. Thus, for the small four word dictionary of the first four digits in English from our application, we have the phonetic and the visemic models given in Table 2.

SVMs is a principled technique to train classifiers that stems from statistical learning theory [8,9]. Their root is the optimal hyperplane algorithm. They minimize a bound on the empirical error and the complexity of the classifier at the same time. Accordingly, they are capable of learning in sparse high-dimensional spaces with relatively few training examples. Let $\{\mathbf{x}_i, y_i\}$, $i = 1, 2, \ldots, N$, denote N training examples where $\mathbf{x}_i$ comprises an M-dimensional pattern and y_i is its class label. Without any loss of generality we shall confine ourselves to the two-class pattern recognition problem. That is, $y_i \in \{-1, +1\}$. We agree that $y_i = +1$ is assigned to positive examples, whereas $y_i = -1$ is assigned to counterexamples.

The data to be classified by the SVM might be linearly separable in their original domain or not. If they are separable, then a simple linear SVM can be used for their classification. However, the power of SVMs is demonstrated better in the nonseparable case, when the data cannot be separated by a hyperplane in their original domain. In the latter case, we can project the data into a higher dimensional Hilbert space and attempt to linearly separate them in the higher dimensional space using kernel functions. Let Φ denote a nonlinear map $\Phi : \mathcal{R}^M \rightarrow \mathcal{H}$ where $\mathcal{H}$ is a higher-dimensional Hilbert space. SVMs construct the optimal separating hyperplane in $\mathcal{H}$. Therefore, their decision boundary is of the form:

$$f(\mathbf{x}) = sign\left(\sum_{i=1}^{N} \alpha_i \, y_i \, K(\mathbf{x}, \mathbf{x}_i) + b\right) \tag{1}$$

Table 2. Phonetic and visemic description models of the four spoken words from Tulips1 database.

Word	Phonetic model	Visemic models
"one"	W-AH-N	w-ah-n
		ao-ah-n
		wao-ah-n
"two"	T-UW	t-w
		t-wao
		t-ao
"three"	TH-R-IY	$\text{th}_{1,2}$-w-iy
		$\text{th}_{1,2}$-w-ah
		$\text{th}_{1,2}$-ao-iy
		$\text{th}_{1,2}$-ao-ah
		$\text{th}_{1,2}$-iy
"four"	F-AO-R	$\text{f}_{1,2,3}$-ao
		$\text{f}_{1,2,3}$-w
		$\text{f}_{1,2,3}$-wao
		$\text{f}_{1,2,3}$-ao-ah

where $K(\mathbf{z}_1, \mathbf{z}_2)$ is a kernel function that defines the dot product between $\Phi(\mathbf{z}_1)$ and $\Phi(\mathbf{z}_2)$ in $\mathcal{H}$, and α_i are the nonnegative Lagrange multipliers associated with the quadratic optimization problem that aims to maximize the distance between the two classes measured in $\mathcal{H}$ subject to the constraints

$$\begin{aligned} \mathbf{w}^T \Phi(\mathbf{x}_i) + b \geq 1 \;\; \text{for } y_i = +1 \\ \mathbf{w}^T \Phi(\mathbf{x}_i) + b \leq 1 \;\; \text{for } y_i = -1. \end{aligned} \tag{2}$$

The sign function in the decision boundary (1) simply makes the optimal separating hyperplane an indicator function. In the following we will omit this sign function and use as the output of the SVM classifier the real valued function:

$$f(\mathbf{x}) = \sum_{i=1}^{N} \alpha_i \; y_i \; K(\mathbf{x}, \mathbf{x}_i) + b, \tag{3}$$

as a measure of confidence in the class assignment.

A single SVM can recognize a single mouth shape. To recognize all the mouth shapes we shall need to define and train one SVM classifier for each mouth shape and to arrange the SVMs in a parallel structure. The input mouth image is simultaneously presented to the input of all the SVMs and each of them gives a real output value showing the confidence in assigning the mouth shape in the corresponding class. Figure 1 depicts the topology of SVM network built.

The selection of the type of feature vector to be classified by the SVMs takes into account that by their nature SVMs have the ability of separating the input data into classes even when the correlation among the data and the dimensionality of the feature vector is high, due to the projection of the data into a higher dimensional space performed inside the SVM. This allows us to

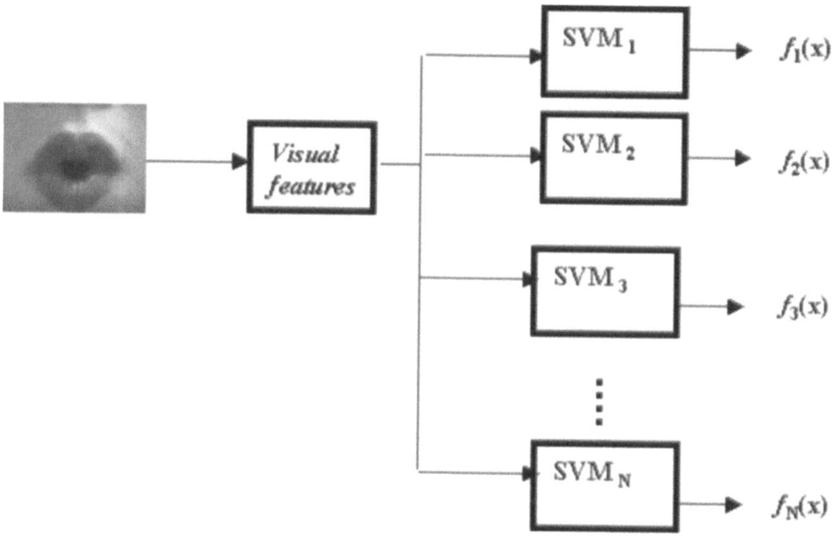

Fig. 1. Topology of SVM network used for visual speech recognition

use very simple features to represent the mouth image, e.g. pixel-level features. As a consequence, we decided to use as feature vector for the mouth image whose shape we want to recognize, the vector comprising the gray levels of the pixels from the mouth image, scanned in row order. The labeling of the mouth images is done manually. To ensure a good training, only the unambiguous positive and negative examples are included in the training set of each SVM. Preprocessing of the mouth images from Tulips1 was needed due to the fact that the mouth has different scale, position in the image and orientation towards the horizontal axis from utterance to utterance, varying with the position of the subject in front of the camera. To compensate for these variations we applied the normalization procedure of mouth images with respect to scale, translation and rotation described in [7].

3 Modeling the Temporal Dynamics of Visual Speech

In every audiovisual speech sequence, a word is described as a sequence of phonemes in the audio domain and visemes in the video domain covering a number of frames. The symbolic phonetic/visemic models show only the sequence of the different symbols in a word realization without specifying the duration of each symbol, as this is strongly person-dependent.

The most natural way of representing the word models in the temporal domain, starting only from the symbolic visemic model and from the total number of T frames in the word pronunciation, is to assume that the duration of each viseme in the word pronunciation can be whatever, but *necessarily not zero.*

Thus, we can create a temporal network of models corresponding to the different possible durations of the visemes in the model, containing as many states as many frames we have in the videosequence, that is, T. The most straightforward way to represent such a network of models is the Viterbi algorithm [14]. One of the possible visemic models and the resulting Viterbi lattice are shown in Figures 2 and 3 for the example of the word "one", where the visemes present in the word pronunciation have been denoted according to Table 1. The paths formed by the solid lines in the Vitterbi lattice from Figure 3 show the possible model realizations. Each node of the Vitterbi lattice in Figure 3 signifies the realization of the corresponding viseme at that particular time instant. Each visemic word model from the set of D visemic description models of the four words in the dictionary, given in Table 2, w_d, $d = 1, 2, \ldots, D$, will have its own Viterbi lattice model. In the current application, $D = 15$.

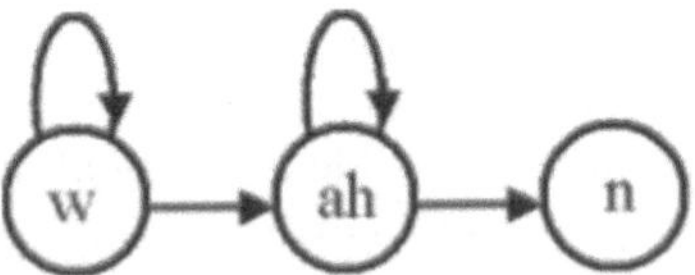

Fig. 2. Temporal sequence for the pronunciation of the word "one"

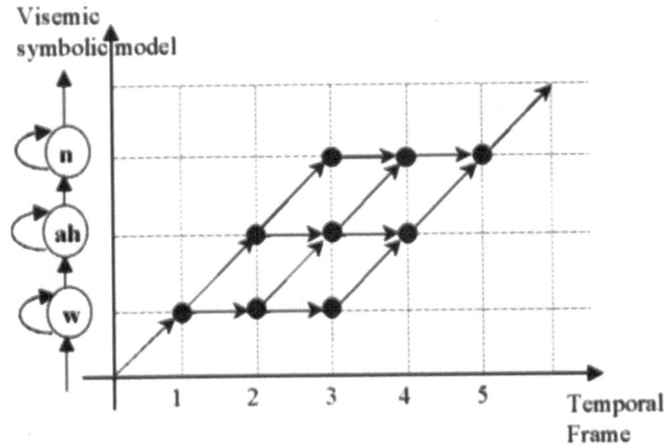

Fig. 3. The temporal Viterbi lattice for the pronunciation of the word "one" in a videosequence of 5 frames

Let us interpret each node in the lattice of Figure 3 as a measure of confidence that the corresponding symbol o_k is emitted at the time instant k. We denote this measure of confidence by $c_{o_k k}$. Each solid line between the nodes corresponding to the symbol o_k at time instant k and o_{k+1} at time instant $k+1$ represents the transition probability from the state that is responsible for the generation of o_k to the state that generates the symbol o_{k+1}. We denote the latter probability by $a_{o_k o_{k+1}}$, where o_k and o_{k+1} may be different or not. To a first approximation, we assume equal transition probabilities $a_{o_k o_{k+1}}$ between whatever two symbol emission states. Thus, they do not contribute to differentiate between the costs of following different paths in the Viterbi lattice.

Having a videosequence of T frames for a word pronounced and such a Viterbi model for each visemic word model w_d, $d = 1, 2, \ldots, D$, we can compute the confidence for the visemic word model w_d to be produced following a path ℓ in the Viterbi lattice as:

$$c_{d,\ell} = \sum_{k=1}^{T} c_{o_k k} \, |d, \ell \; , \tag{4}$$

independent of $a_{o_k o_{k+1}}$, and the confidence score that the visemic word model w_d was produced is the maximum over all possible $c_{d,\ell}$. Among the words that can be produced following all the possible paths in all the D Viterbi lattices, the most plausible word, that is, the one corresponding to the visemic model with the maximum confidence score c_d, $d = 1, 2, \ldots, D$, is finally recognized. In the visual speech recognition approach discussed in this paper, the symbol emission measures of confidence $c_{o_k k}$ are given by the corresponding SVMs, SVM_{o_k}.

4 Experimental Results

To evaluate the recognition performance of the proposed SVM-based visual speech recognizer, we choose to solve the task of recognizing the first four digits in English. As experimental data we used the small audiovisual database Tulips1 [5], frequently used in similar visual speech recognition experiments. The phonetic and visemic description of the four words and the phoneme to viseme mapping for this application are given in Tables 1 and 2. The visual speech recognizer requires the training of 12 different SVMs, one for each distinct mouth shape considered in the Table 1. We used for our experiments SVMs with a polynomial kernel of degree 3. For the training of the SVMs we used the publicly available SVMLight toolkit [10]. The complete visual speech recognizer was implemented in C++ programming language. In the module implementing the Viterbi decoder for all the possible visual word models, the SVM classifiers in the nodes of a Viterbi decoder were implemented using the classification module of the SVMLight toolkit. We performed speaker-independent visual speech recognition tests, using the leave-one-out testing strategy for the 12 subjects in the Tulips1 database. More precisely, the testing strategy was as follows: we trained the system 12 times separately, each time using 11 subjects in the training set and leaving the 12*th* subject out for testing. In this way, we obtained actually 24 test sequences per word, due to the fact that Tulips1 database contains 2 pronunciations per subject for each word (Set1 and Set2). This gives a total of 24×4 words $= 96$ video test sequences.

We examine the overall word recognition rate (WRR) comparing this result with those reported in literature under similar conditions (i.e., using the same features, the same database and the same testing procedure) [7,5] in Table 3.

Table 3. The overall WRR of the proposed system of SVM classifiers as compared to other techniques (without delta features)

Method	Dynamic SVM network (our method)	Stochastic networks [5]	AAM and HMM shape model inner+ outer lip contour [7]	AAM and HMM intensity model outer lip contour [7]
WRR [%]	76	60	75	65.6

We can see that, for similar features used, our system achieves a slightly higher word recognition performance than those reported in the literature. The WRR is lower than the best rate reported without delta features in [7], i.e., 87.5 %, where the shape + intensity information is used with the inner and outer lip contour model. In the latter model, the intensity is sampled in the exact subregion of the mouth image comprising the lips and not including the skin areas. However, the computational complexity of this method is higher to that of our solution, due to the need for re-definition of the region of interest at each frame.

To assess the statistical significance of the rates observed, we model the ensemble {test patterns, recognition algorithm} as a source of binary events, 1 for correct recognition and 0 for an error, with probability p of drawing a 1 and $(1-p)$ of drawing a 0. These events can be described by Bernoulli trials. Let us denote by $\hat{p}$ the estimate of p. The exact ϵ confidence interval of p is the segment between the two roots of the quadratic equation [15]:

$$(p-\hat{p})^2 = \frac{z^2_{(1+\epsilon)/2}}{K}\, p\,(1-p) \tag{5}$$

where z_u is the u-percentile of the standard Gaussian distribution having zero mean and unit variance, and $K = 96$ is the total number of tests conducted. We computed the 95% confidence intervals ($\epsilon = 0.95$) for the WRR of the proposed approach and also for the WRRs reported in literature [7,5], as summarized in Table 4.

5 Conclusions

In this paper we examined the suitability of SVM classifiers in visual speech recognition. Due to the inherent temporal dependency of the speech, we also propose a solution to build a dynamic SVM-based classifier. We tested the proposed method on a small visual speech recognition task, namely, the visual recognition

Table 4. Confidence interval for the WRR of the proposed system of SVM classifiers as compared to other techniques (without delta features)

Method	Dynamic SVM network (our method)	Stochastic networks [5]	AAM and HMM shape model inner+outer lip contour [7]	AAM and HMM intensity model outer lip contour [7]
Confidence interval [%]	[66.6%;83.5%]	[49.9%;69.2%]	[65.5%;82.5%]	[55.6%;74.3%]

of the first four digits in English. The features used are the simplest possible: directly the raw gray level values of the mouth image. Under these circumstances, we obtained good word recognition rates as compared to the similar results from the literature. This shows that SVMs are promising classifiers for visual speech recognition tasks. Another advantage of the viseme-oriented modeling method proposed here is the possibility of easy generalization to large vocabularies. The existing correlation between the phonetic and visemic models can also lead to an easy integration of the visual speech recognizer with its audio counterpart. In our future research, we will try to enhance the performance of the visual speech recognizer by including delta features in the feature vector, by using other type of kernel functions and by including the temporal constraints at symbol level in the temporal word models trough the learning of the state transitions probabilities for the Vitterbi decoding lattice.

Acknowledgement. This work has been supported by the European Union funded Research Training Network on "Multi-modal Human-Computer Interaction" (HPRN-CT-2000-00111).

References

1. Ganapathiraju, A., Hamaker, J., Picone, J.: Hybrid SVM/HMM architectures for speech recognition. Proc. of Speech Transcription Workshop. College Park, Maryland, USA (May 2000).
2. Yongmin, Li, Shaogang, Gong, Liddell, H.: Support vector regression and classification based multi-view face detection and recognition. Proc. 4th IEEE Int. Conf. Automatic Face and Gesture Recognition. Grenoble, France (March 2000) 300–305.
3. Terrillon, T.J., Shirazi, M. N., Sadek, M., Fukamachi, H., Akamatsu, S.: Invariant face detection with support vector machines. Proc. 15th Int. Conf. Pattern Recognition. Barcelona, Spain. **4** (September 2000) 210–217.
4. Chen, T.: Audiovisual speech processing. IEEE Signal Processing Magazine. **18(1)** (January 2001) 9–21.
5. Movellan, J. R.: Visual speech recognition with stochastic networks. In: Tesauro, G., Toruetzky, D., Leen, T. (eds.): Advances in Neural Information Processing Systems. **7**. MIT- Press, Cambridge, MA (1995).
6. Bregler, C., Omohundro, S.: Nonlinear manifold learning for visual speech recognition. Proc. IEEE Int. Conf. Computer Vision (1995) 494–499.

7. Luettin, J., Thacker, N. A.: Speechreading using probabilistic models. Computer Vision and Image Understanding. **65(2)** (February 1997) 163–178.
8. Vapnik, V.N.: Statistical Learning Theory. J. Wiley, N.Y. (1998).
9. Cristianini, N., Shawe-Taylor, J.: An Introduction to Support Vector Machines. Cambridge University Press, Cambridge, U.K. (2000).
10. Joachims, T.: Making large-scal SVM learning practical. In: Schoelkopf, B., Burges, C., Smola, A. (eds.): Advances in Kernel Methods - Support Vector Learning. MIT-Press (1999)
11. Kumar, V. P., Poggio, T.: Learning-based approach to real time tracking and analysis of faces. Proc. 4th IEEE Int. Conf. Automatic Face and Gesture Recognition. Grenoble, France (March 2000) 96–101.
12. Ezzat, T., Poggio, T.: MikeTalk: A talking facial display based on morphing visemes. Proc. Computer Animation Conference. Philadelphia, Pennsylvania (June 1998).
13. Papageorgiou, C., Poggio, T.: A pattern classification approach to dynamical object detection. Proc. IEEE Int. Conf. Computer Vision. **(2)** (1999) 1223–1228.
14. Young, S., Kershaw, D., Odell, J., Ollason, D., Valtchev V., Woodland, P.: The HTK Book. HTK version 2.2. Edition. Entropic, Ltd., Cambridge, UK (1999).
15. Papoulis, A.: Probability, Random Variables, and Stochastic Processes. 3rd Edition. McGraw-Hill (1991)

Fuzzy Stochastic Automata for Reactive Learning and Hybrid Control

Gerasimos G. Rigatos

Industrial Systems Institute
University of Patras
Rion Patras 26500, Greece
grigat@isi.gr

Abstract. Fuzzy Stochastic Automata (FSA) are suitable for the modelling of the reactive (memoryless) learning and for the control of hybrid systems. The concept of FSA is to switch between a fuzzy increase and a fuzzy decrease of the control action according to the sign of the product $e\dot{e}$, where $e = x - x_d$ is the error of the system's output and is its first derivative. The learning in FSA has stochastic features. The applications of FSA concern mainly autonomous systems and intelligent robots.

1 Introduction

Fuzzy Automata have been studied extensively in [1]. Fuzzy Stochastic Automata (FSA) are a tool for the control of hybrid systems and for the modelling of the reactive learning. The FSA have been introduced in [2-5].

Fuzzy Stochastic Automata are the graphs of switching control laws. The concept described by FSA is to maintain or to change the control action according to the sign of the product $e\dot{e}$, where $e = x - x_d$ is the error of the system's output and $\dot{e}$ is its first derivative. The control action can be either an *increase* or a *decrease* of the control signal that is performed through fuzzy inference.

Petri Net analysis is used to describe the interaction of the FSA with dynamic systems. Three theorems have been proved : i) if the FSA are applied to a system with *Strictly Positive Real* (*SPR*) error transfer function, then the resulting closed-loop converges asymptotically to the desirable setpoint, ii) the control signal u converges under FSA to its optimal value u^* almost linearly, iii) for a class of systems (see Theorem 2) the FSA are equivalent to the switching term of sliding mode control .

The learning modelled by FSA has several advantages : i) it needs only the sign of the output error e and the sign of the error's first derivative $\dot{e}$, ii) it memorizes a minimal number of past control actions or past states of the system, iii) the expert knowledge that is contained in its rule base is minimal, iv) it imitates closely the tuning performed by humans. Applications of FSA can be found in autonomous systems and intelligent robots ([1-4]). The paper unifies and extends the results of [2-5] thus presenting the complete theory of fuzzy stochastic automata.

I.P. Vlahavas and C.D. Spyropoulos (Eds.): SETN 2002, LNAI 2308, pp. 366–377, 2002.

2 Fuzzy Switching Control Laws

It will be shown that switching control laws which are based on the sign function of the error and its first derivative, i.e. $\mathrm{sgn}(e_k \dot{e}_k)$, can be modelled as an FSA. Fuzzy Stochastic Automata are the graphs of these switching control laws. An analysis of the fuzzy switching control law that has inspired the concept of FSA is given first.

2.1 A Switching Control Algorithm for Uncertain Systems

Consider the general form of a SISO nonlinear non-autonomous system:

$$x^{(n)}(t) = f(x,t) + b(x,t)u + \tilde{d} \tag{1}$$

with scalar output $x(t)$ and desirable set-point $x_d(t)$. $f(x,t)$ and $b(x,t)$ are known nonlinear functions and $\tilde{d}$ is an unknown additive disturbance. The tracking error is $e(t) = x(t) - x_d(t)$ and the rate of error change is $\dot{e}(t) = \dot{x}(t) - \dot{x}_d(t)$. The error convergence conditions are :

$$\text{If} \quad \mathrm{e(t)}\,\dot{e}(t) < 0 \ \text{ then } \ x(t) \to x_d(t) \quad \text{implies } \ e(t) \to 0 \tag{2}$$

$$\text{If} \quad \mathrm{e(t)}\,\dot{e}(t) > 0 \ \text{ then } \ x(t) \text{ deviates from } x_d(t) \tag{3}$$

These conditions follow from the Lyapunov's stability criterion with $V = \frac{1}{2}e^2 \Rightarrow \dot{\mathrm{V}} = e\dot{e}$. As long as the state vector $[e(t), \dot{e}(t)]^T$ remains on the quarter-plane $e(t)\dot{e}(t) < 0$ then it gradually approaches the origin $[0,0]^T$. Thus the goal is to find a control law u that :

- will be able to keep the error vector $[e(t), \dot{e}(t)]^T$ on the quarter-plane $e(t)\dot{e}(t) < 0$
- will reduce the magnitude of the control signal changes Δu as the origin $[0,0]^T$ is approached.

To this end the following simple control law is proposed:

a) If $\mathrm{sgn}(e_k \dot{e}_k) < 0$, then the control action leads to convergence and should be maintained

b) If $\text{sgn}(e_k \dot{e}_k) > 0$, then the control action leads to divergence and should be altered

c) At each crossing of $e = 0$, i.e. at change of $\text{sgn}(e_k e_{k-1})$, reduce the magnitude of the control action Δu

Two possible control actions Δu are considered : *increase* or *decrease* the control signal u, which are realised through the following $n-1$ fuzzy rules :

IF u_k is U_1 THEN u_{k+1} is U_2 (IF u_k is U_2 THEN u_{k+1} is U_1)
IF u_k is U_2 THEN u_{k+1} is U_3 (IF u_k is U_3 THEN u_{k+1} is U_2)
. .
. .
IF u_k is $\mathrm{U}_{\mathrm{n-1}}$ THEN u_{k+1} is U_{n} (IF u_k is U_{n} THEN u_{k+1} is $\mathrm{U}_{\mathrm{n-1}}$)

$U_1, U_2, \ldots\ldots, U_{n-1}, U_n$ are the fuzzy subsets in which the universe of discourse U of the control u is partitioned. The sets U_i are selected to have the same spread and to satisfy the equality $\sum_{i=1}^{n} \mu_{U_i}(x) = 1$ (strong fuzzy partition). The fuzzifier is selected to be a triangular one. The min t-norm is used for the derivation of the fuzzy relational matrices R_n^i and R_n^d where $U_n = R_n^i \circ U_{n-1}$ (increase operation) and $U_{n-1} = R_n^d \circ U_n$ (decrease operation). The *max-min inference* mechanism is used while the defuzzifier is a center-of-average one.

To reduce Δu when approaching $e = 0$ the last two values of the control signal u are taken into account, namely :

u_{k-1} : the last control signal below (above) $e = 0$
u_k : the last control signal above (below) $e = 0$

Recalling the bisection method, the control signal u^* that will produce zero error should be searched in the range [u_{k-1}, u_k]. The fuzzy subsets $U_1, U_2, \ldots\ldots, U_{n-1}, U_n$ are updated so as to divide the interval between [u_{k-1}, u_k] in n equal segments (see Fig. 1). From (a), (b) and (c) a control law of the following form is obtained:

$$\Delta u_k = -K(\text{sgn}(e_k e_{k-1}))\text{sgn}(e_k \dot{e}_k) \quad (4)$$

K is a function of $\text{sgn}(e_k e_{k-1})$. When $\text{sgn}(e_k e_{k-1})$ changes the width of the membership functions is reduced, and consequently the switching gain K is reduced too. The initial control value u_0 is randomly chosen.

If $f(x,t)$ and $b(x,t)$ are known then the overall control law for the system (1) should be :

$$u = b^{-1}(x,t)[x_d^{(n)} - f(x,t) + \sum_{k=1}^{n} \binom{n}{k} \lambda^k e^{(n-k)}] - K_{fuzz}(\mathrm{sgn}(e_k e_{k-1}))\,\mathrm{sgn}(e_k \dot{e}_k) \quad (5)$$

with $\lambda > 0$ such that $\sum_{k=0}^{n} \binom{n}{k} \lambda^k e^{(n-k)}$ to have stable poles, while $K(\mathrm{sgn}(e_k e_{k-1}))$ denotes that the gain K is a function of $\mathrm{sgn}(e_k e_{k-1})$. In [2-3] it has been proved that the above control law assures convergence.

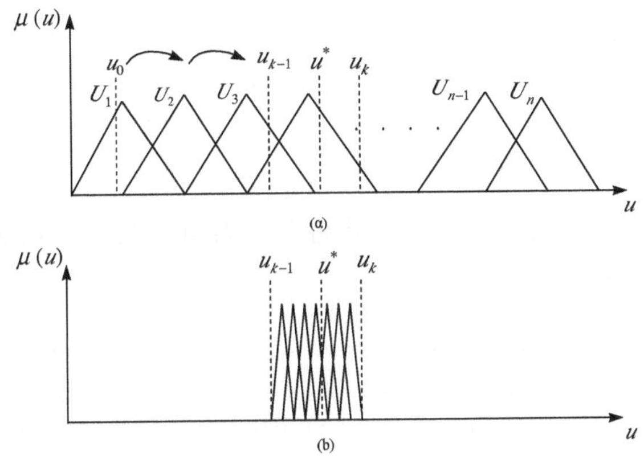

Fig. 1. Adaptation of the membership functions at every change of $\mathrm{sgn}(e_k e_{k-1})$.

2.2 The Rule Base for the Tuning of the Switching Control Δu_k

The switching control Δu_k in (4) can be described by the following IF-THEN rules :

R_1 : IF $e_k > 0$ AND $\dot{e}_k > 0$ AND $\mathrm{sgn}(e_k e_{k-1}) = -1$ THEN change the control action AND reduce $\| \Delta u_k \|$

R_2 : IF $e_k > 0$ AND $\dot{e}_k > 0$ AND $\mathrm{sgn}(e_k e_{k-1}) = 1$ THEN change the control action AND maintain $\| \Delta u_k \|$

R_3 : IF $e_k > 0$ AND $\dot{e}_k < 0$ AND $\mathrm{sgn}(e_k e_{k-1}) = 1$ THEN maintain the control action AND maintain $\| \Delta u_k \|$

R_4 : IF $e_k < 0$ AND $\dot{e}_k > 0$ AND $\mathrm{sgn}(e_k e_{k-1}) = 1$ THEN maintain the control action AND maintain $\| \Delta u_k \|$

R_5 : IF $e_k < 0$ AND $\dot{e}_k < 0$ AND $\mathrm{sgn}(e_k e_{k-1}) = -1$ THEN change the control action AND reduce $\| \Delta u_k \|$

R_6 : IF $e_k < 0$ AND $\dot{e}_k < 0$ AND $\mathrm{sgn}(e_k e_{k-1}) = 1$ THEN change the control action AND maintain $\| \Delta u_k \|$

Each change of $\mathrm{sgn}(e_k e_{k-1})$ clips the fluctuation ranges of the control signal. This causes a reduction of the gain K. However, between two successive changes of $\mathrm{sgn}(e_k e_{k-1})$, K remains the same. The proposed switching control $R_1 - R_6$ is a *discrete-event* control algorithm which is fired at appropriate sampling instances denoted by the index k. Sampling of e_k takes place at intervals greater than the settling time T_s of the plant.

3 Modelling of the Switching Control Law as a Learning Automaton

The proposed switching controller of $R_1 - R_6$ can be interpreted with the use of Discrete Event Dynamic Systems (DEDS) theory and can be modelled with the aid of Petri-Nets [6]. The associated Petri Net diagram contains the following places :

p_1 : $e > 0$ and $\dot{e} > 0$ and last control action = increase and $\mathrm{sgn}(e_k e_{k-1}) = 1$

p_2 : $e > 0$ and $\dot{e} > 0$ and last control action = increase and $\mathrm{sgn}(e_k e_{k-1}) = -1$

p_3 : $e > 0$ and $\dot{e} > 0$ and last control action = decrease and $\mathrm{sgn}(e_k e_{k-1}) = 1$

p_4 : $e > 0$ and $\dot{e} > 0$ and last control action = decrease and $\mathrm{sgn}(e_k e_{k-1}) = -1$

p_5 : $e > 0$ and $\dot{e} < 0$ and last control action = increase and $\mathrm{sgn}(e_k e_{k-1}) = 1$

p_6 : $e > 0$ and $\dot{e} < 0$ and last control action = increase and $\mathrm{sgn}(e_k e_{k-1}) = -1$

p_7 : $e > 0$ and $\dot{e} < 0$ and last control action = decrease and $\mathrm{sgn}(e_k e_{k-1}) = 1$

p_8 : $e > 0$ and $\dot{e} < 0$ and last control action = decrease and $\mathrm{sgn}(e_k e_{k-1}) = -1$

p_9 : $e < 0$ and $\dot{e} > 0$ and last control action = increase and $\mathrm{sgn}(e_k e_{k-1}) = 1$

p_{10} : $e < 0$ and $\dot{e} > 0$ and last control action = increase and $\mathrm{sgn}(e_k e_{k-1}) = -1$

p_{11} : $e < 0$ and $\dot{e} > 0$ and last control action = decrease and $\mathrm{sgn}(e_k e_{k-1}) = 1$

p_{12} : $e<0$ and $\dot{e}>0$ and last control action = decrease and $\text{sgn}(e_k e_{k-1}) = -1$

p_{13} : $e<0$ and $\dot{e}<0$ and last control action = increase and $\text{sgn}(e_k e_{k-1}) = 1$

p_{14} : $e<0$ and $\dot{e}<0$ and last control action = increase and $\text{sgn}(e_k e_{k-1}) = -1$

p_{15} : $e<0$ and $\dot{e}<0$ and last control action = decrease and $\text{sgn}(e_k e_{k-1}) = 1$

p_{16} : $e<0$ and $\dot{e}<0$ and last control action = decrease and $\text{sgn}(e_k e_{k-1}) = -1$

The transitions that link the above places are :

t_1 : increase t_5 : decrease t_9 : increase

t_2 : increase t_6 : increase t_{10} : increase

t_3 : decrease t_7 : decrease t_{11} : increase

t_4 : decrease t_8 : decrease t_{12} : decrease

The states-transitions diagram of Fig. 2 is an automaton. This automaton is named *Fuzzy Stochastic Automaton* (FSA) because its transitions denote fuzzy control actions and because its learning procedure has stochastic properties.

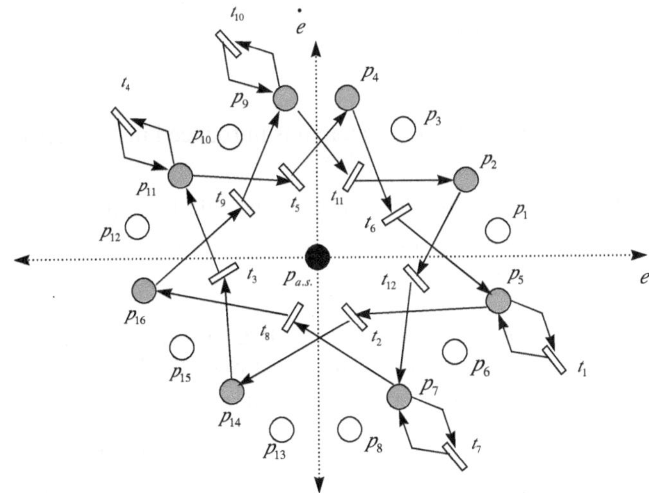

Fig. 2. The fuzzy stochastic automaton that models the rule base $R_1 - R_6$

3.1 Stochastic Properties of the FSA Learning

The learning of the FSA shown in Fig. 2 consists in finding the control value u^* that results in zero steady-state error of (1) starting from a random initial value u_0. This learning is reactive and stochastic . It is reactive because it is based on the memorisation of a minimal number of past system states or past control actions unlike the learning from data. The FSA learning is based on the current error and the error one step in the past. Unlike this, in batch training of neural networks averaging is performed over a large number of error values.

It is stochastic because: i) being at place p and applying the control action $t_i \in \{increase, decrease\}$ will result in a new place p' that is drawn stochastically from the set of the reachable places, ii) the change of the sign of $e_k e_{k-1}$ and the associated reduction of Δu_k is a stochastic event iii) the probability that a control action is repeated switches stochastically from 0 to 1 according to the result of the previous control action.

The probability vector $p(n) = [p(t_i(n)) \in \{0,1\} \mid t(n-1) = t_i]$ of the control actions t_i $i = 1,...N$ is updated within a reinforcement scheme, i.e. "0" for penalty when the system goes to one of the states that lie in the quarterplane $e\dot{e} > 0$, and "1" for reward when the system goes to one of the states that lie in the quarterplane $e\dot{e} < 0$. If at the time instant $n-1$ the control action "increase" results in convergence then at the time instant n the probability vector will be $p(n) = [1,0]$ otherwise it will be set to $p(n) = [0,1]$.

3.2 Convergence of the FSA Control

It remains to find out for which class of systems the control law of $R_1 - R_6$ assures the closed-loop convergence. Three theorems analyse the convergence conditions for the FSA control. The proofs of Theorems 1 and 2 are given in [3] and [2] respectively. The proof of the third theorem is introduced in this paper.

Theorem 1. If the control law, described by the rule base $R_1 - R_6$, is applied to a system with SPR error transfer function then closed-loop asymptotic convergence is assured. For proof see [3].

Here a heuristics proof of Theorem 1 will be given. As it has been shown in Lemma 1 (see [3]) a SPR dynamic error equation sampled at time intervals larger than the settling time T_s is monotonous. Since $e_k = f(u_k)$ is monotonous the problem of finding the optimal control signal u^* that will result in a zero steady-state error is that of finding the root of $e_k = f(u_k)$. Starting from a random initial value u_0 the update of u under FSA keeps on moving to the direction of error decrease with the use of the "increase" , "decrease" operators. At every crossing of $e = 0$, the step of this search is reduced from Δu to $\Delta u / N$ where N is the number of the fuzzy sets U_i thus permitting to approximate the root u^* with infinite accuracy (Fig.3).

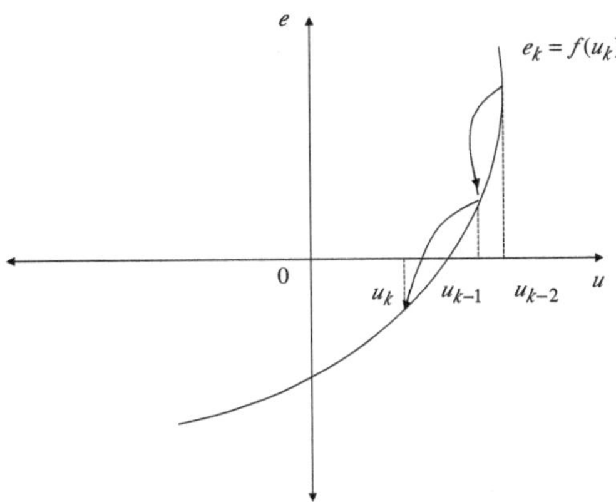

Fig. 3. Fuzzy search of a root in a monotonous error function

Theorem 2. For the class of systems $x^{(n)} = f(x,t) + b(x,t)u + \tilde{d}$ where $f(x,t)$, $b(x,t)$ are known nonlinear functions and $\tilde{d}$ is unknown additive disturbance the FSA are equivalent to the switching term of sliding mode control. For proof see [2].

Theorem 3. The control signal u_k that is generated by an FSA converges almost linearly to the optimal value u^*, i.e. to the value that results in zero steady-state error.

Proof. The proof will be given for symmetric triangular fuzzy sets (strong fuzzy partition, i.e. for two adjacent fuzzy sets $\mu_{R_k}(\rho_k) + \mu_{R_{k+1}}(\rho_k) = 1$) and can be generalized for Gaussian membership functions with symmetric overlapping and finite support.

Let us denote by N the number of the fuzzy sets in which u is partitioned and by i the $i-th$ switch from $e_k e_{k-1} > 0$ to $e_k e_{k-1} < 0$ (or vice versa). Due to the piecewise linear nature of the triangular membership functions, for a random value u_k holds (see Fig. 4.):

$$\mu_{U_k}(u_k) = \frac{-u_k + (k+1)\Delta c}{\Delta c} \tag{6}$$

$$\mu_{U_{k+1}}(\rho_k) = \frac{u_k - k\Delta c}{\Delta c} \tag{7}$$

where u_k is the current value of the control signal, Δc is the distance between the centres of two adjacent membership functions, i.e. $\Delta c = c_{k+1} - c_k$ and k indicates the $k-th$ fuzzy membership function.

From (6) and (7) one gets

$$u_{k+1} = \mu_k c_{k+1} + \mu_{k+1} c_{k+2} \Rightarrow$$

$$u_{k+1} = \frac{-u_k + (k+1)\Delta c}{\Delta c}(k+1)\Delta c + \frac{u_k - k\Delta c}{\Delta c}(k+2)\Delta c \Rightarrow$$

$$u_{k+1} = \frac{-u_k(k+1)\Delta c + (k+1)^2 \Delta c^2}{\Delta c} + \frac{u_k(k+2)\Delta c - k(k+2)\Delta c^2}{\Delta c} \Rightarrow$$

$$u_{k+1} = \frac{u_k \Delta c[(k+2)-(k+1)] + \Delta c^2[(k+1)^2 - k(k+2)]}{\Delta c} \Rightarrow$$

$$u_{k+1} = u_k + \frac{(k^2+2k+1-k^2-2k)}{\Delta c}\Delta c^2 \Rightarrow u_{k+1} - u_k = \Delta c \Rightarrow \Delta u_k = \Delta c$$

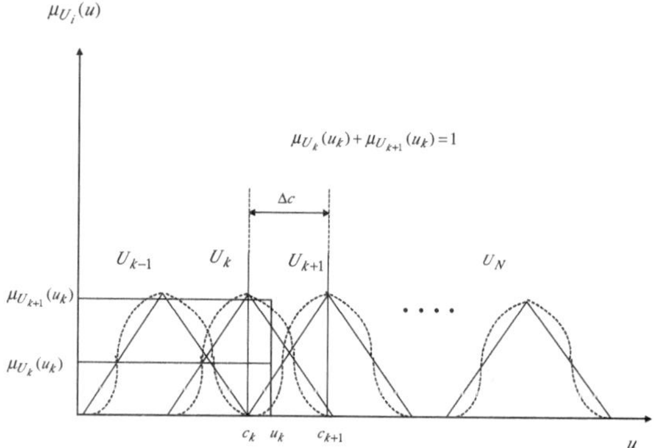

Fig. 4. Strong fuzzy partition in triangular fuzzy sets (solid line) and in Gaussian fuzzy sets (dashed line)

Assume that the permitted variation range of u is $[a,b]$. The step of the FSA learning evolves with respect to the $i-th$ switch from $e_k e_{k-1} > 0$ to $e_k e_{k-1} < 0$ as follows:

$$Step^{(0)} = \Delta u^{(0)} = \frac{b-a}{N-1}, \qquad Step^{(1)} = \Delta u^{(1)} = \frac{\Delta u^{(0)}}{N-1} = \frac{(b-a)}{(N-1)^2},$$

$$Step^{(2)} = \Delta u^{(2)} = \frac{\Delta u^{(1)}}{N-1} = \frac{(b-a)}{(N-1)^3} \quad \ldots\ldots \quad Step^{(i)} = \Delta u^{(i)} = \frac{\Delta u^{(i)}}{N-1} = \frac{(b-a)}{(N-1)^{(i+1)}}$$

i.e. $\Delta u^{(i)} \underset{i\to\infty}{\to} 0$ i.e. $\Delta u^{(i)}$ converges linearly to 0

Taking into account that the optimal value of the control signal $u^* \in \Delta u^{(i)}$ it can be stated that the uncertainty $\Delta u^{(i)}$ on u_k reduces linearly, i.e. the fuzzy search algorithm converges linearly to u_k.

Remark: Convergence for Gaussian membership functions

If the triangular membership functions with finite support are replaced by Gaussian membership functions with infinite support, i.e. $\mu_{U_i}(u_k) \neq 0$ for $u_k \in (-\infty,+\infty)$ then the symmetric properties for the adjacent membership functions now vanish i.e.

$$\forall i \in \{0,1,\dots,\mathrm{N}-1\}: \mu_{U_i}(u_k) + \mu_{U_{i+1}}(u_k) \neq 1$$

and $\exists\, j \neq i, i+1 \quad \mu_{U_j}(u_k) \neq 0$

However the case of an infinite support is viewed more from a mathematical point of view since we can choose the spread of the Gaussians to be such that

$$\exists i \in \{0,1,\dots,\mathrm{N}-1\}: \mu_{U_i}(u_k) + \mu_{U_{i+1}}(u_k) \approx 1$$

and $\forall\, j \neq i, i+1 \quad \mu_{U_j}(u_k) \approx 0$

Under the previous assumption the Gaussian membership functions can be approximated by triangular membership functions. Thus the result of the previous analysis is also valid , i.e. $\Delta u_k \approx \Delta c$.

4 Applications of FSA

Due to space limitations only a one example of the FSA applications is given. The reader is referred to [2-5] for a more detailed analysis.

4.1 Fuzzy Stochastic Automata for Reactive Learning and Hybrid Control

As already mentioned the learning that is performed by FSA is reactive , which means that past states of the FSA-environment interaction and past control actions do not influence the choice of the current control action. Reactive learning is reflexive and is contrasted to deliberative planning. Two examples of reactive learning based on FSA are : i) learning of the robot deburring task for a metal surface of unknown stiffness (see [5]), ii) parallel parking of a non-holonomic vehicle of unknown kinematic model (see [2]).

4.2 Fuzzy Stochastic Automata for Hybrid Control

The FSA can be also used in hybrid control schemes, i.e. control structures that contain both continuous time and discrete event components. In [4] the FSA has been applied to the motion control of an autonomous vehicle moving on a surface with unknown slopes. The dynamic model of the mobile robot is :

$$\ddot{s}(t)+\frac{I'_R(s)}{(m+I_R(s))}\dot{s}^2(t)+\frac{mgz'(s)}{(m+I_R(s))}=\frac{1}{(m+I_R(s))}u(t) \tag{8}$$

The control signal that leads the closed-loop system to convergence is:

$$u(t)=\ddot{s}(t)+\frac{I'_R(s)}{(m+I_R(s))}s^2(t)+K_p e(t)+K_d\dot{e}(t)+u_{RC-SMFLC}(t) \tag{9}$$

This results in $\ddot{e}(t)+K_d\dot{e}(t)+K_p e(t)=\frac{mgz'(s)}{(m+I_R(s))}-u_{FSA}(t)$. Therefore, if $\lim_{t\to\infty}[\frac{mgz'(s)}{(m+I_R(s))}-u_{RC-SMFLC}(t)]=0$ and the gains K_p and K_d are appropriately selected (so as the above dynamic error equation to be SPR), then $\lim_{t\to\infty}e(t)=0$. The RC-SMFLC controller which is modelled by the FSA of Fig. 2 guarantees that the above condition will be satisfied.

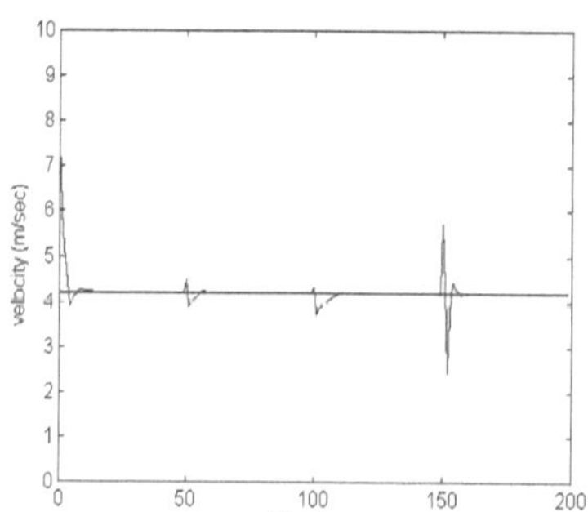

Fig. 5. Velocity fluctuation when the vehicle mounts an uphill slope.

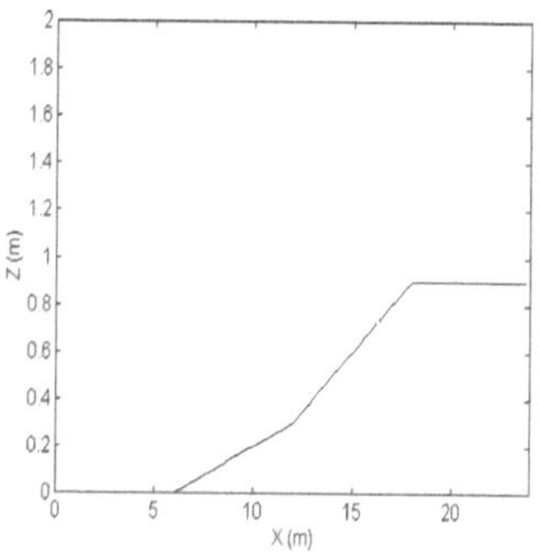

Fig. 6. The corresponding vehicle trajectory on a positive slope.

5 Conclusions

Fuzzy Stochastic Automata (FSA) have been proposed for hybrid control and for the modelling of the reactive (memoryless) learning. FSA can be considered as the graph of switching control laws.

The applications of FSA concern mainly autonomous systems and intelligent robots. Three theorems analyse the convergence of the FSA control. It has been proved that : i) if the FSA is applied to a system with SPR dynamic error equation that is excited by an unknown additive disturbance then closed-loop convergence is assured, ii) under FSA the control signal u converges almost linearly to the optimal value u^*, i.e. to the value that results in zero steady state error, iii) for a class of systems the FSA are equivalent to the switching term of sliding mode control. Fuzzy stochastic automata can be considered as a step towards machine intelligence.

References

1. Kandel A. and Lee A.: Fuzzy and Switching Automata. Taylor and Francis (1979)
2. Rigatos G., Tzafestas S., Evangelidis G.: Reactive parking control of a nonholonomic vehicle via a Fuzzy Learning Automaton. IEE Proceedings : Control Theory and Applications , (2001) 169-179
3. Tzafestas S. and Rigatos G.: Stability analysis of an Adaptive Fuzzy Control System Using Petri-Nets Modeling and Learning Automata Theory. Mathematics and Computers in Simulation , vol. 51. Elsevier, (1999), 351-359
4. G.G. Rigatos , C.S. Tzafestas and S.G. Tzafestas: Mobile Robot Motion Control in Partially Unknown Environments Using a Sliding-Mode Fuzzy-Logic ControllerRobotics and Autonomous Systems, vol. 33, Elsevier, (2000) 1-11
5. Tzafestas S., Rigatos G:. Fuzzy Reinforcement Learning Control for Compliance Tasks of Robotic Manipulators , accepted for publication in : IEEE Trans. on Syst. Man and Cybern – Part B: Cybernetics (2001)
6. Passino K., Burgess K.:, Stability Analysis of Discrete Event Systems , J. Wiley & Sons New York (1998)

Overview of Wave Probe-Based High-Resolution Subsurface Sensing, Imaging, and Vision

George A. Tsihrintzis and Konstantinos G. Girtis

Department of Informatics, University of Piraeus
Piraeus 185 34, Greece
{geoatsi, kgirtis}@unipi.gr

Abstract. We propose a general paradigm for image formation from data collected by wave-based sensory probes of subsurface structures. We discuss methodologies that are directly applicable in several robotic subsurface sensing, imaging, and vision technologies, including buried waste clean-up, excavation planning, de-mining, archaeological investigations, environmental pollution monitoring, water quality assessment, etc. The proposed methodologies are, therefore, crucial in the development of automated robotic vision systems. A large number of references to the relevant literature are included.

1 Introduction

A key challenge for the 21st century will be to maximize the effective use of the planet's diminishing physical resources through the use of information resources. To bring the full benefits of the information revolution to bear the physical world, the staggering advances in computation and communication of the past decades must be matched by similar progress in our ability to extract and manage information about our environment through sensing and imaging technology.

Some of the most difficult and intractable problems in sensing and imaging involve detecting, locating, and identifying objects that are obscured beneath a covering medium (e.g., underground or underwater). Mapping pollution plumes under the ground, for example, is a problem of deconvolution of the effect of a dispersive, diffusive, and absorptive medium from the desired details of the subsurface structure and functionality. Subsurface sensing and imaging problems arise in a wide range of areas of critical interest: geophysical exploration, environmental remediation under the earth or ocean, pollution monitoring, or biological cycle study. Clearly, the benefits from solving these problems are immense.

While subsurface sensing and imaging problems involve many sensing modalities, (acoustic, electromagnetic induction, ground–penetrating radar, ultrasound, or optical), they all seek to infer internal structure from complex and distorted signals and, fortunately, can be formulated in a similar way whether the wave probe is electromagnetic or acoustic and whether the target is a pollution plume or a land mine or a fish population.

I.P. Vlahavas and C.D. Spyropoulos (Eds.): SETN 2002, LNAI 2308, pp. 378–389, 2002.

Precise and accurate subsurface sensing and imaging is inaccessible today because modalities that penetrate deeply beneath the surface do not resolve accurately enough or are not sensitive to relevant functional characteristics. Conventional image processing and computer vision techniques fail because those signals from useful modalities that are received are contaminated by diffracted or scattered radiation. Fourier–based backpropagation or backprojection inverse algorithms cannot be easily extended to complex nonlinear interactions in the subsurface medium. Additionally, effective recognition strategies have not been developed for these cases of partial and obscured information and techniques for manipulating, cataloging, and retrieving the enormous data sets associated with sensing and imaging are still in their infancy.

The grand challenge in subsurface sensing and imaging is to create a unified problem–solving platform with techniques, tools, and infrastructure, applicable to a wide range of next–generation sensing and imaging systems (i.e., a 3D multi–sensor imager). For this goal to be achieved, basic research is required in subsurface sensing and modeling, physics–based signal and image processing and understanding, and image information management.

2 State of the Art in Wave–Based Imaging

A wave is a signal that varies with spatial coordinates and time. Waves play a pervasive role in nature, and get excited and propagate in every type of physical system. Mechanical systems exhibit wave phenomena in the form of seismic, acoustic, and water waves. Electromagnetic waves cover a very broad range of frequencies, from the low frequency biological signals and radio waves to microwaves to optical waves to the very high frequency X–ray and γ–ray waves. Underlying all matter, there are quantum mechanical waves. Waves have dominated twentieth century mathematical physics. From Rayleigh's explanation of why the sky is blue to modern computerized imaging, wave phenomena have constantly fascinated, perplexed and challenged physicists, mathematicians, and engineers.

Despite their broad diversity, however, wave phenomena are understood on the basis of a few unifying mathematical concepts that can be summarized in the form of a limited number of classes of partial differential equations. In broad terms, these equations are models of the effects, such as refraction, diffraction, and scattering, that inhomogeneities in the propagating medium have on an incident wave (see Fig. 1). Determining the effect of given (known) inhomogeneities on a given (known) incident wave is the *direct scattering problem.* Perhaps more challenging, however, are ***I**nverse **S**cattering **P**roblems* (**ISP**), that is problems of determining the structure (and representing it in the form of multidimensional images) of an inhomogeneous object from observations of the manner in which it modifies probing waves. In mathematical terms, ISP consist of reconstructing the partial differential equation that the wave satisfies and/or its domain of definition from the behavior of (many of) its solutions [1,2,3]. Applications from a number of seemingly different scientific disciplines, such as crystal structure determination [4], X–ray tomography [5,6], medical ultrasound tomography [7], acoustic and electromagnetic underground surveying [8,9,10,11,12,13], optical and coherent X–ray microscopy [14], and elastic wave inverse scattering [15] can be addressed within the same unified mathematical theory of ISP.

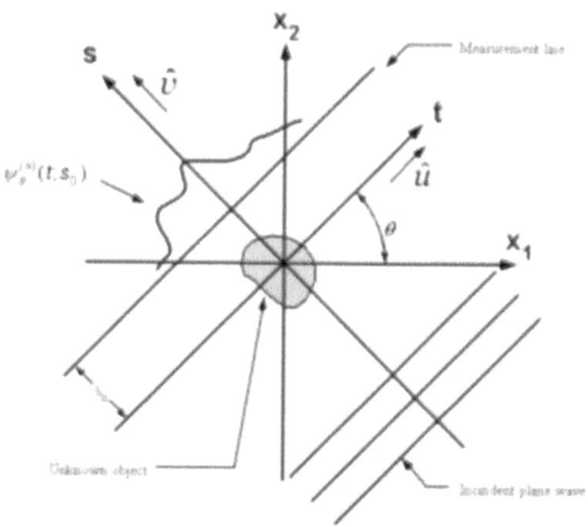

Fig. 1. The classical scan configuration of diffraction tomography

The structure determination objective of ISP usually consists of an attempt to estimate the spatial distribution of the complex–valued index of refraction of the object by inverting the mathematical mapping relating the probing wave, the refraction index, and the measurable total wave. This objective is non trivial to achieve due to the inherent non–uniqueness and non–local (i.e., with memory) non–linearity of the mapping from index of refraction to scattered wave in any single scattering experiment [16]. The non–uniqueness issue can be partially addressed by employing a multiplicity of experiments, where the object is probed from several incident wave directions, and the full scattering data set is then available for the inversion. However, the issue of non–linearity is significantly harder to address. To date, research has only produced mathematical results or computationally intensive iterative algorithms as opposed to practically implementable reconstruction algorithms to exact non–linear ISP.

Over the past twenty years, an alternative approach to ISP has been employed based on certain linearizing approximations [17,18,19], which has led to an expanded discipline within the regime of imaging and tomography, known as ***Diffraction Tomography*** (**DT**). The first application of linearized Inverse Scattering seems to date back in 1912, when von Laue suggested that Friedrich and Knipping try diffracting X–rays by crystals in order to test the hypothesis that X–rays had wavelengths on the order of 10^{-10} m. The experiment was successful and led, within less than a year, to the first structure determination by X–ray methods (sodium chloride by W.L. Bragg) [3]. Since then, X–ray probes are typically used to determine the structure of crystals using reconstruction algorithms based on the Born scattering model and measurement of far field intensity distributions [3]. Indeed, the foundation of modern linearized DT lies in the generalized projection–slice theorem (see Figure 2), which forms the core of X–ray crystal structure determination and the basis of Wolf's pioneering work in 1969 [17].

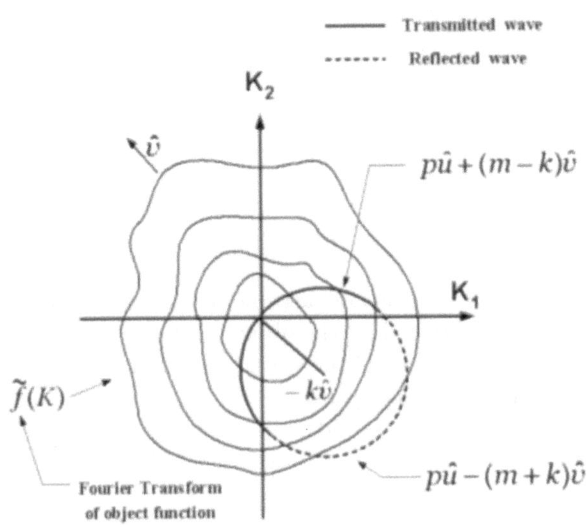

Fig. 2. The generalized projection–slice theorem

In [17], Wolf showed how near field measurements can be employed to generate reconstructions within the Born model. Wolf's formulation was extended in 1974 by Iwata and Nagata [20] to determine the structure of a less restrictive class of scattering objects satisfying the Rytov rather than the Born approximation. In 1979, Mueller et al. [21] employed the same concepts of the Born and Rytov approximations and presented Fourier interpolation–based algorithms for the inverse problem of ultrasound tomography, while in 1982 Devaney [18] derived an elegant, FFT–based inversion algorithm, named the ***F****iltered* ***B****ackpropagation* ***A****lgorithm* (**FBA**) of DT, for the inversion of full view, scattered wave data under the Born or Rytov approximations. When scattering experiments are done at a wavelength λ, the filtered backpropagation algorithm returns an estimate of the unknown index of refraction distribution whose frequency content is the same as of the true distribution over a circular disk in Fourier space of radius $\frac{2\pi}{\lambda}$ and zero elsewhere [22].

The filtered backpropagation algorithm has been recognized as the one providing highest quality in the reconstructed images and modifications to it have been presented by Devaney [23] in 1984 and Deming and Devaney [24] in 1996 to adjust it to the configurations employed in geophysical tomographic surveys. Hansen and Johansen [25] also addressed the underground imaging problem using a ground penetrating radar system. While the Deming and Devaney algorithms [24] compute the pseudoinverse of the linearized wave scattering model of the ground penetrating radar system, the Hansen and Johansen [25] approach utilizes asymptotic expansions of the model valid for deeply buried (practically, two or more wavelengths into the ground) objects, which are FFT–implementable. The reconstruction problem of linearized DT from noisy scattered wave data was addressed by Tsihrintzis and Devaney [26,27] who showed that the optimum (Wiener) estimation filter attains again the form of a filtered backpropagation algorithm. Recently, the same problem was also addressed by Pan who presented a class of DT reconstruction algorithms with noise control [28]. Finally, the mathematical framework to solve the problem of inversion of an angularly limited set of noise–free linearized wave scattering data was addressed by Devaney [22] and was given solution in the form of algebraic reconstruction (iterative) algorithms of the Kaczmark type by Ladas and Devaney [29].

In several practical ISP, it is not possible to measure both the phase and the intensity of the waves scattered off the object of interest. In optical tomography, for example, the high frequency of the electromagnetic waves does not permit direct phase measurement. In acoustic traveltime tomography, on the other hand, attenuation can be immeasurable and, thus, the image formation algorithm needs to rely on phase measurements only. Fortunately, the wave propagation process tends to mix wave phase and intensity information as the wave propagates, in a manner that at a large distance from a scattering object the wave phase distribution has intensity information encoded in it and, vice versa, the wave phase distribution can be retrieved from measurements of the wave intensity. This fact has been recognized by Kawata et al. [30] and Devaney et al. [31,32,14] in the development of image formation algorithms and by Tsihrintzis and Devaney [33] in the context of object detection, location estimation, and classification.

Most of the above developments assume that the object under probing is embedded in a *homogeneous* background medium, i.e., a medium whose properties are constant with respect to position in space. However, generalizations to other types of background media that arise in practical applications are possible. The Deming and Devaney [24] and the Hansen and Johansen [24] work, for example, addresses ISP in which the background medium consists of two semi–infinite media separated by a planar interface. More generally, Devaney and Zhang [34] addressed ISP in which the background medium consisted of an arbitrary number of non–parallel layers, while object detection, location estimation, and classification ISP were addressed by Tsihrintzis, Johansen, and Devaney [35]. The general formal theory of obtaining linearized approximate models for wave scattering off objects embedded in non–uniform background media has been presented by Beylkin and Oristaglio [36], while the general formal procedure for image formation from such linearized wave scattering data was described by Devaney and Oristaglio [37].

Linearized DT has reached today the stage of being implemented in prototype commercial tomographic scanners for ultrasonic [38,39], underground [10,12,13], and optical [14] imaging systems. Particularly successful have been geophysical DT algorithms when applied to a range of underground imaging problems such as oil field prospecting and reservoir monitoring, locating underground tunnels between North and South Korea [10], searching for dinosaur bones in the New Mexico desert [12], mapping buried waste sites [11], and locating archaeological artifacts [13]. The success of the linearized DT algorithms depends critically, however, on the two assumptions of linearity and availability of multiple experiments and, in many cases, the linearity assumption fails, while different constraints (economic, safety, operating, geometric, or physical) limit the number of scattering experiments that can be performed and/or provide low signal–to–noise ratio data. Even though algebraic reconstruction techniques reduce the effect of availability of only a small number of scattering experiments, the effects of non–linearity are much harder to combat and remain an issue of current research. Two different research avenues can be identified accordingly. The first avenue addresses alternative, simpler ISP, that, often, provide sufficient information about the object structure. The second avenue addresses the complex–valued refraction index reconstruction problem, but utilizes more accurate, non–linear approximate scattering models.

Along the lines of the first research avenue, more modest ISP were addressed by Tsihrintzis and Devaney, originally within the framework of linearized [40,33,39,42] and later exact [41,39,43,35] scattering theory, and found significant in practical applications [12,39]. The goal of these more modest ISP was to estimate the location of a known scattering object having unknown central location from noisy scattered wave data. It was found that for monochromatic plane–wave probing the optimum (in the maximum likelihood sense) location estimate could be obtained via a filtered backpropagation algorithm, in which partial images formed by filtering and backpropagating scattered wave data for different probing directions were coherently summed. The algorithm yields an image of the log likelihood function of the object's location and can be used for target detection and classification, as well as for target location estimation. The detection/estimation/classification procedure is optimum (in the maximum likelihood sense) for any given number of scattering experiments and returns good estimates even from a single experiment as long as the wavelength of the probing radiation is comparable with the typical dimensions of the target [40]. On the other hand, the second research avenue addresses the practically important tomographic imaging situation where the object consists of a number of distinct scatterers. As pointed out by Slaney, Kak, and Larsen [44], even though each scatterer individually may be weak enough for validity of the linear approximate models, multiple scattering interactions among several scatterers degrade the performance of linearized DT reconstruction algorithms. The situation can be partially ameliorated if the reconstruction algorithms are based on higher–order (non–linear) scattering models and, indeed, formal series solutions to the inverse scattering problem have been presented in the literature. In [45] more specifically, perturbative expansions of the scattering object's Fourier transform were utilized to develop DT reconstruction algorithms of arbitrary order, which contained linear reconstruction algorithms as special cases and effectively attained the form of non–linear data filtering followed by a linear operation. On the other hand, recent attempts ([46,47] and references therein) to invert a second-order scattering model have resulted in algorithms of the form of iterative numerical solutions of systems of quadratic equations and revealed significantly higher fidelity than their linear counterparts. More recently, non–linear tomographic reconstruction algorithms were developed by Tsihrintzis and Devaney for imaging from scattered wave data modeled up to an arbitrarily large number of terms in the Born [48] or Rytov [49] series. The algorithms attained the form of a Volterra series of non–linear operators, with the usual filtered backpropagation algorithm of DT as the leading linear term. Tsihrintzis and Devaney also followed the same approach for imaging from travel time data and Volterra series of non–linear inversion operators were developed, in which the filtered backprojection algorithm of conventional X–ray tomography appears as the leading linear term [50].

The early and the later developments of algorithms to solve ISP outlined above have led to a vast amount of published literature and, combined with the availability of inexpensive computational power, have opened the door to potential new imaging modalities and systems. Thus, the term *Diffraction* Tomography should, perhaps, be replaced by the more general term *Inverse Scattering* Tomography to reflect both the use of non–linear approximate models in the image formation process and the consideration of other ISP besides the traditional complex–valued refraction index reconstruction problem. It seems, however, that the published literature on ISP is fragmented and scattered around in several journals and its progress is monitored only by a specialized community. An article such as the present is, therefore, justified as an attempt to familiarize broader audiences (the environmental engineers is this case) with only a general education in engineering or science with the rapidly growing field of computerized tomographic imaging.

3 Computer Simulation

In this section, we implement and study nonlinear tomographic imaging algorithms, originally developed in [48,49]. For simplicity, the object of interest consists of a circular core and three concentric circular coatings and constitutes a realistic model for cylindrical objects such as optical fibers, large molecules, or buried pipes. In this simulation, the probing wave number was equal to $k = 2\pi$, corresponding to a wavelength $\lambda = \frac{1}{3}$ and the measurement distance was set to $s_0 = 0$. This is a fairly big object, sixty wavelengths in diameter, for which the Born series [48] converges slowly. The sampling rate was set to 0.04, which corresponds to approximately eight samples per wavelength and thus equals about four times the Nyquist rate. Thus the sample density is high enough to provide good numerical approximations to the continuous space signals and algorithms considered in here.

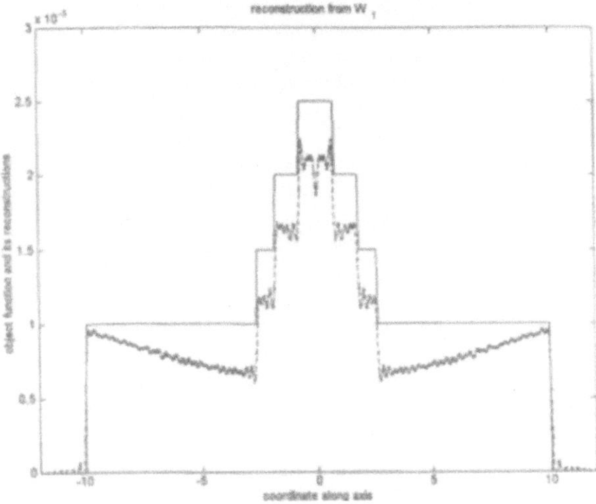

Fig. 3. Reconstruction from the first–order Rytov approximation.

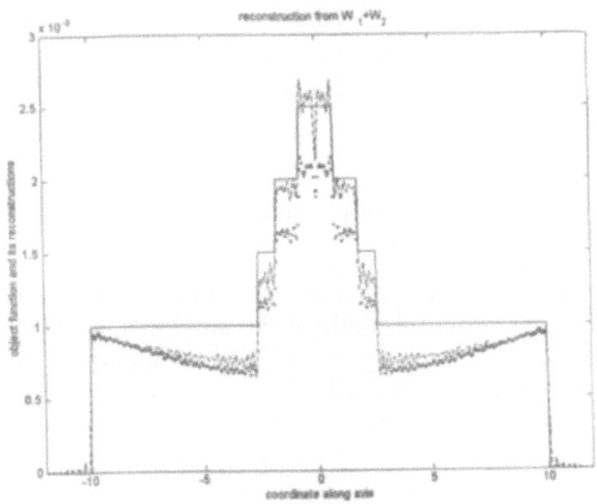

Fig. 4. Reconstruction from the second–order Rytov approximation.

In figures (3–5) original object function (solid line) and reconstruction returned from the FBA (dotted line) and the second–order algorithm based on Rytov series (dashed line) in the computer simulation. These figures show the object function reconstruction returned by the FBA and a second–order nonlinear algorithm based on the Rytov series applied to data synthesized from first– (Figure 3), second– (Figure 4), and third–order (Figure 5), Rytov approximations. Clearly, the second–order nonlinear algorithm returns the same reconstruction as the FBA in the case of data consisting of only the Rytov term,

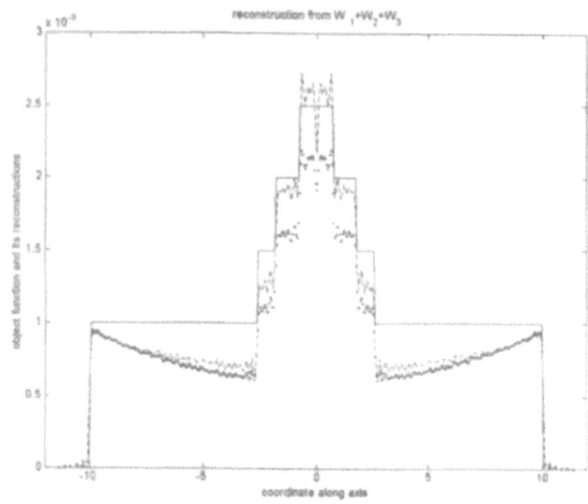

Fig. 5. Reconstruction from the third–order Rytov approximation.

as theoretically expected. In the other cases, however, the FBA underperforms the second–order algorithm by a significant margin, especially in the area close to the core of the object.

4 Conclusions and Future Research

Inverse scattering tomography already spans a century of research and development. It has emerged from the study of the physics of crystals at the beginning of the 20th century and, with the growth of the computer industry, has evolved in the direction of computerized data processing for a large and diverse area of applications. The fields of impedance and diffuse–photon density wave tomography are very active areas of research and technology development. The problem of extraction of information and features of objects hidden under the interface between two media is only beginning to be addressed. The technological potential of this activity is tremendous and spans areas such as demining, buried waste clean–up, pollution monitoring, excavation planning, archaeological investigations, medical imaging and diagnosis, genetic defect screening, and large molecule imaging. The challenges for the development of imaging modalities in these and related application areas include understanding of the interaction of waves and matter, efficient wave data modeling for arbitrary strentgh scattering [51], signal processing and information extraction methodologies, efficient numerical analysis techniques, hardware design for algorithm implementation, and visualization methodologies for the presentation of the reconstructed multidimensional images. Therefore, besides the required research activity, a new educational paradigm is also needed to train professionals of the imaging science, that exposes students in all of these areas of study. It is hoped that the present article will contribute towards this goal, too.

References

[1] R G Newton, "Scattering Theory of Waves and Particles," Springer Verlag, Berlin, 1982
[2] K Chadan, D Colton, L Paivarinta, and W Rundell, "An Introduction to Inverse Scattering and Inverse Spectral Problems," SIAM Publications, Philadelphia, 1997
[3] H Lipson and W Cochran, "The Determination of Crystal Structures," Cornell University Press, Ithaca, 1966
[4] G T Herman, "Image Reconstruction from Projections: The Fundamentals of Computerized Tomography," Academic Press, New York, 1980
[5] A C Kak and M Slaney, "Principles of Computerized Tomographic Imaging," IEEE Press, New York, 1988
[6] J F Greenleaf and R C Bahn, "Computerized Tomography with Ultrasound," Proc. IEEE, vol. 71, p. 330, 1983
[7] D Colton and R Kress, "Inverse Acoustic and Electromagnetic Scattering," Springer Verlag, Berlin, 1998
[8] A Witten and E Long, "Shallow Applications of Geophysical Diffraction Tomography," IEEE Trans. Geosc. Rem. Sens., vol. GE-24, p. 654, 1986
[9] A Witten, J Tuggle, and R C Waag "A Practical Approach to Ultrasonic Imaging Using Diffraction Tomography," J. Acous. Soc. Amer., vol. 83, p. 1645, 1988
[10] A Witten and W C King, "Acoustical Imaging of Subsurface Features," J. Envir. Eng., vol. 116, p. 166, 1990
[11] A Witten, "Sounding out Buried Waste," Civil Engineering, vol. 60, p. 62, 1990
[12] A Witten, D Gillette, W C King, and J Sypniewski, "Geophysical Diffraction Tomography at a Dinosaur Site," Geophysics, vol. 57, p. 187, 1992
[13] T E Levy and A Witten, "Denizens of the Desert," Archaeology Magazine, p. 36, 1996
[14] M H Maleki, A J Devaney, and A Schatzberg, "Tomographic Reconstruction from Optical Scattered Intensities," J. Opt. Soc. Am. A, vol. 9, p. 1356, 1992
[15] A J Devaney, "Elastic Wave Inverse Scattering," in: S K Datta, J D Achenbach and Y S Rajapakse (eds.), "Elastic Waves and Ultrasonic Nondestructive Evaluation," Elsevier Science Publishers, New York, 1990
[16] A J Devaney, "Non-uniqueness in Inverse Scattering Problems," J. Math. Phys., vol. 19, p. 1526, 1978
[17] E Wolf, "Three-Dimensional Structure Determination of Semi-transparent Objects from Holographic Data," Opt. Comm., vol. 1, p. 153, 1969
[18] A J Devaney, "A Filtered Backpropagation Algorithm for Diffraction Tomography," Ultr. Imag., vol. 4, p. 336, 1982
[19] A J Devaney, "Reconstructive Tomography with Diffracting Wavefields," Inv. Problems, vol. 2, p. 161, 1986
[20] K Iwata and R Nagata, "Calculation of Refractive Index Distribution from Interferograms Using the Born and Rytov's Approximation," Japan. J. Appl. Phys., vo.l. 14, p. 379, 1974
[21] R K Mueller, M Kaveh, and G Wade, "Reconstructive Tomography and Applications to Ultrasonics," Proc. IEEE, vol. 67, p. 567, 1979

[22] A J Devaney, "The Limited-View Problem in Diffraction Tomography," Inv. Problems, vol. 5, p. 501, 1989
[23] A J Devaney, "Geophysical Diffraction Tomography," IEEE Trans. Geosc. Rem. Sens., vol. GE-22, p. 3, 1984
[24] R W Deming and A J Devaney, "Diffraction Tomography for Multi-Monostatic Ground Penetrating Radar Imaging," Inv. Problems, vol. 13, p. 29, 1997
[25] T B Hansen and P M Johansen, "Inversion Scheme for Ground Penetrating Radar that Takes into Account the Air-Soil Interface," IEEE Trans. Geosc. Rem. Sens., Jan. 2000
[26] G A Tsihrintzis and A J Devaney, "Stochastic Diffraction Tomography: Theory and Computer Simulation," Sign. Proc., vol. 39, p. 49, 1993
[27] G A Tsihrintzis and A J Devaney, "Stochastic Geophysical Diffraction Tomography," Int. J. Imag. Syst. Techn., vol. 5, p. 239, 1994
[28] X Pan, "Unified Reconstruction Theory for Diffraction Tomography with Consideration of Noise Control," J. Opt. Soc. Am. A, vol. 15, p. 2312, 1998
[29] K T Ladas and A J Devaney, "Iterative Methods in Geophysical Diffraction Tomography," Inv. Problems, vol. 8, p. 119, 1992
[30] S Kawata, Y Touki, and S Minami, "Optical Microscopic Tomography," in: A J Devaney and R H T Bates (eds.), Inverse Optics II, SPIE 558, 1985
[31] A J Devaney, "Structure Determination from Intensity Measurements in Scattering Experiments," Phys. Rev. Letts., vol. 62, p. 2385, 1989
[32] A J Devaney, "Diffraction Tomographic Reconstruction from Intensity Data," IEEE Trans. Im. Proc., vol. IP-1, p. 221, 1992
[33] G A Tsihrintzis and A J Devaney, "Estimation of Object Location from Diffraction Tomographic Intensity Data," IEEE Trans. Sign. Proc., vol. SP-39, p. 2136, 1991
[34] A J Devaney and X Zhang, "Geophysical Diffraction Tomography in a Layered Background," Wave Motion, vol. 14, p. 243, 1991
[35] G A Tsihrintzis, P M Johansen, and A J Devaney, "Buried Object Detection and Location Estimation from Electromagnetic Field Measurements," IEEE Trans. Ant. Prop., vol. AP-47, p. 1742, 1999
[36] G Beylkin and M L Oristaglio, "Distorted-Wave Born and Distored-Wave Rytov Approximation," Opt. Comm., vol. 53, p. 213, 1985
[37] A J Devaney and M L Oristaglio, "Inversion Procedure for Inverse Scattering within the Distorted Wave Born Approximation," Phys. Rev. Letts., vol. 51, p. 237, 1981
[38] N Sponheim, L-J Gelius, I Johansen, and J J Stamnes, "Quantitative Results in Ultrasonic Tomography of Large Objects Using Line Sources and Curved Detector Arrays," IEEE Trans. Ultr. Ferr. Freq. Contr., vol. UFFC-38, p. 370, 1991
[39] G A Tsihrintzis and A J Devaney, "Application of a Maximum Likelihood Estimator in an Experimental Study of Ultrasonic Diffraction Tomography," IEEE Trans. Med. Imag., vol. MI-12, p. 545, 1993
[40] G A Tsihrintzis and A J Devaney, "Maximum Likelihood Estimation of Object Location in Diffraction Tomography," IEEE Trans. Sign. Proc., vol. SP-39, p. 672, 1991
[41] G A Tsihrintzis and A J Devaney, "Maximum Likelihood Estimation of Object Location in Diffraction Tomography, Part II: Strongly Scattering Objects," IEEE Trans. Sign. Proc., vol. SP-39, p. 1466, 1991
[42] G A Tsihrintzis and A J Devaney, "Maximum Likelihood Techniques in Ultrasonic Diffraction Tomography," in: C T Leondes (ed.), "Medical Imaging Techniques and Applications, Vol. 6," p. 43-126, Gordon and Breach Publ. Newark, 1998

[43] G A Tsihrintzis, A J Devaney, and E Heyman, "Estimation of Object Location from Wideband Scattering Data," IEEE Trans. Im. Proc., vol. IP-8, p. 996, 1999

[44] M Slaney and A C Kak and L E Larsen, "Limitations of Imaging with First-Order Diffraction Tomography," IEEE Trans. Microw. Th. Techn., vol. MTT-32, p. 360, 1984

[45] A J Devaney and E Wolf, "A New Perturbation Expansion for Inverse Scattering from Three-Dimensional Finite-Range Potentials," Phys. Letts., vol. 89A, p. 269, 1982

[46] R Pierri and A Brancaccio, "Imaging of a Rotationally Symmetric Dielectric Cylinder by a Quadratic Approach," J. Opt. Soc. Am. A, vol. 14, p. 2777, 1997

[47] A Brancaccio and R Pierri, Information Content of Born Scattered Fields: Results in the Circular Cylindrical Case," J. Opt. Soc. Am. A, vol. 15, p. 1909, 1998

[48] G A Tsihrintzis and A J Devaney, "Higher-Order (Nonlinear) Diffraction Tomography: Reconstruction Algorithms and Computer Simulation," IEEE Trans. Im. Proc., vol. IP-9, p. 1560, 2000

[49] G A Tsihrintzis and A J Devaney, "Higher-Order (Nonlinear) Diffraction Tomography: Inversion of the Rytov Series, " IEEE Trans. Inf. Th., Special Issue on Information-Theoretic Imaging, vol. IT-46, p. 1748, 2000

[50] G A Tsihrintzis and A J Devaney, "A Volterra Series Approach to Nonlinear Traveltime Tomography," IEEE Trans. Geosc. Rem. Sens., Special Issue on Computational Wave Issues in Remote Sensing, Imaging and Target Identification, Propagation, and Inverse Scattering, vol. GRS-38, p. 1733, 2000

[51] G.A. Tsihrintzis, Polynomial Approximators to Plane Wave Scattering and Applications in Nonlinear Diffraction Tomographic Imaging, CISS'2001, Johns Hopkins University, Baltimore, MD, March 21-23, 2001.

3D Volume Reconstruction by Serially Acquired 2D Slices Using a Distance Transform-Based Global Cost Function

Stelios Krinidis, Christophoros Nikou, and Ioannis Pitas

Aristotle University of Thessaloniki
Department of Informatics
Box 451, 54006 Thessaloniki, Greece

Abstract. An accurate, computationally efficient and fully-automated algorithm for the alignment of 2D serially acquired sections forming a 3D volume is presented. The method accounts for the main shortcomings of 3D image alignment: corrupted data (cuts and tears), dissimilarities or discontinuities between slices, missing slices. The approach relies on the optimization of a global energy function, based on the object shape, measuring the similarity between a slice and its neighborhood in the 3D volume. Slice similarity is computed using the distance transform measure in both directions. No particular direction is privileged in the method avoiding global offsets, biases in the estimation and error propagation. The method was evaluated on real images (medical, biological and other CT scanned 3D data) and the experimental results demonstrated the method's accuracy as reconstruction errors are less than 1 degree in rotation and less than 1 pixel in translation.

1 Introduction

Three-dimensional reconstruction of medical images (tissue sections, CT and autoradiographic slices) is now an integral part of biomedical research. Reconstruction of such data sets into 3D volumes, via the registrations of 2D sections, has gained an increasing interest. The registration of multiple slices is of utmost importance for the correct 3D visualization and morphometric analysis (e.g. surface and volume representation) of the structures of interest. Several alignment algorithms have been proposed in that framework. A review of general medical image registration methods is presented in [1], [2], [3].

The principal 3D alignment (reconstruction from 2D images) methods may be classified in the following categories: fiducial marker-based methods [4], feature-based methods using contours, crest lines or characteristic points extracted from the images [5], [6], and gray level-based registration techniques using the intensities of the whole image [7], [8], [9], [10]. Most of the above mentioned techniques do not simultaneously consider the two major difficulties involved in medical and CT scanned data registration.

I.P. Vlahavas and C.D. Spyropoulos (Eds.): SETN 2002, LNAI 2308, pp. 390–400, 2002.

At first, consecutive slices may differ significantly due to distortions, discontinuities in anatomical structures, cuts and tears. These effects are more pronounced when distant slices are involved in the registration. From this point of view, a registration method must be robust to missing data or outliers [7], [10].

Besides, registering the slices sequentially (the second with respect to the first, the third with respect to the second, etc.) leads to different types of misregistration. If an error occurs in the registration of a slice with respect to the preceding slice, this error will propagate through the whole volume. Also, if the number of slices to be registered is large, a global offset of the volume may be observed, due to error accumulation [8].

In this paper, a solution to the above mentioned shortcomings is presented. A global energy function having as variables the rigid transformation parameters (2D translation and rotation) of a given slice with respect to a local symmetric neighborhood is proposed. Global energy functions are a powerful tool in computer vision applications but they have not yet been considered for the registration of serially acquired slices.

Our approach was inspired by the technique presented in [11], which consists in minimizing a global energy function with the Iterative Closest Point algorithm [12], to register multiple, partially overlapping views of a 3D structure. The global energy function implemented in our approach is associated with a pixel similarity metric based on the Euclidean distance transform [13].

The remainder of the paper is organized as follows. The global energy function formulation and the associated registration algorithm is presented in section 2, experimental results are presented in section 3 and conclusions are drawn in section 4.

2 A Global Energy Function Formulation

Before presenting the alignment method, the notations used in our formulation are introduced. A set of 2D serially acquired slices is represented by:

$$V = \{I_i | i = 1 \dots N\} \tag{1}$$

where I_i is a slice (a 2D image) and N denotes the total number of slices. A pixel of a 2D slice is represented by: $p = (x, y)^T$, so that $I_i(p)$ corresponds to the gray level (intensity) of pixel p of slice i. N_x and N_y designate the number of pixels of each slice in the horizontal and vertical direction respectively.

Standard two-dimensional rigid alignment consists of estimating the rigid transformation parameters (translation t_x, t_y and rotation by angle θ) that have to be applied to the image to be aligned (floating image) in order to match a reference image.

In the approach proposed here, the alignment of the 2D sections, within the 3D volume, is considered globally by minimizing an energy function $E(\cdot)$, which expresses the similarity between the 2D sections:

$$E(\Theta) = \sum_{i=1}^{N} \sum_{j=1}^{N} \sum_{p=1}^{N_x \times N_y} f(I_i(T_{\Theta_i}(p)), I_j(T_{\Theta_j}(p))) \tag{2}$$

where $f(\cdot)$ is a similarity metric, I_k denotes slice k and T_{Θ_k} designates a rigid transformation with parameters $\Theta_k = \{t_x^k, t_y^k, \theta^k\}$.

Equation (2) indicates that for a given set of rigid transformation parameters T_{Θ_i}, applied to the slice to be aligned I_i, the similarity between the *transformed slice* $I_i(T_{\Theta_i}(p))$ and *all of the other already transformed slices* $I_j(T_{\Theta_j}(p))$ in the volume is accumulated in the energy function.

Assuming that function $f(\cdot)$ is symmetric:

$$f(I_i(T_{\Theta_i}(p)), I_j(T_{\Theta_j}(p))) = f(I_j(T_{\Theta_j}(p)), I_i(T_{\Theta_i}(p))) \tag{3}$$

which is the case for the pixel similarity functions considered here, yields the following global minimization problem:

$$\hat{\Theta} = arg \min_{\Theta} E(\Theta) = arg \min_{\Theta} \sum_{i=1}^{N} \sum_{\substack{j=1 \\ j<i}}^{N} \sum_{p=1}^{N_x \times N_y} f(I_i(T_{\Theta_i}(p)), I_j(T_{\Theta_j}(p))) \tag{4}$$

Without additional constrains, the optimization problem (4) has clearly an infinite number of solutions (if the set of rigid transformations $\{T_{\hat{\Theta}_1}, T_{\hat{\Theta}_2}, \ldots T_{\hat{\Theta}_N}\}$ is a solution, the same holds true for $\{T_{\hat{\Theta}_1} \circ T_\Delta, T_{\hat{\Theta}_2} \circ T_\Delta, \ldots T_{\hat{\Theta}_N} \circ T_\Delta\}$, where T_Δ is an arbitrary 2D rigid transformation). To remove this ambiguity, the transformation $T_{\hat{\Theta}_l}$ applied to an arbitrary chosen slice k is constrained to the identity transformation (we have chosen $k = 1$ in our implementation). As a result, there are $3(N-1)$ parameters to estimate.

It is common sense that distant slices present very little similarity due to anatomy and it would be more appropriate to measure the energy function only for slices presenting at least some similarities. Therefore, the support region of function $f(\cdot)$ has been limited to a neighborhood of radius R centered at each slice and set:

$$f(I_i(T_{\Theta_i}(p)), I_j(T_{\Theta_j}(p))) = 0, \quad \forall \ |i-j| > R \tag{5}$$

Thus, the following alignment algorithm is associated with the energy function (4):

- **do** until convergence.
  - declare all slices unvisited.
  - **do** until all slices are declared visited.
    - randomly chose an unvisited slice $I_i \in V$.

  * update the rigid transformation parameters T_{Θ_i} bringing into alignment slice I_i with the other slices in the neighborhood of i, by minimization of the following local energy function:

$$E_i(\Theta_i) \stackrel{\text{def}}{=} \sum_{i=1}^{N} \sum_{\substack{j=1 \\ |i-j|\leq R}}^{N} \sum_{p=1}^{N_x \times N_y} f(I_i(T_{\Theta_i}(p)), I_j(T_{\Theta_j}(p))) \tag{6}$$

  * declare slice I_i visited.
- **end do**

– **end do**

The minimization of the local energy function (4) is conducted by a deterministic optimization algorithm, known as Iterated Conditional Modes (ICM) [14]. ICM is a discrete Gauss Seidel-like optimization technique, accepting only configurations decreasing the objective function. Let us notice that the parameter $\hat{\Theta}_i$ corresponding to the minimum value of the local energy function $E_i(\Theta_i)$ (Equ. 6) also corresponds to a local minimum value of the global energy function $E(\Theta)$ with respect to Θ_i, keeping all other parameters $\Theta_j, j \neq i$ fixed. It is thus easy to see that the described algorithm converges towards a local minimum of the initial energy function (2). This local minimum corresponds to a satisfactory registration, since the initial alignment of the 2D sections is generally close to the desired solution (if this is not the case, a good initialization may be obtained by a standard coarse alignment technique such as principal axes registration). It is thus not necessary to resort here to greedy global optimization procedures, such as simulated annealing or genetic algorithms.

Further improvement of the solution is obtained by a gradient decent technique. To speed the algorithm up a multigrid data processing is also implemented.

The pixel similarity metric associated with the above described global energy function is based on a distance transform ([13], [15]) (also known as chamfer matching technique [16]) and it is computed from the 3D object contours [17]. A distance transformation is an operation that converts a binary picture, consisting of feature and non-feature elements (contours), to a picture where each pixel has a value that approximates its distance to the nearest contour point.

Thus, using the distance transform $D(p)$ of the reference slice the method aligns the floating slice by minimizing the distance between the contours of the images. For further details of the chamfer matching method the reader may refer to [16].

Considering the slices per triplets, which is very common for standard reconstruction problems (i.e. setting R=1 in eq. 5), the estimation of the alignment parameters Θ involves the non-linear similarity metric:

$$f(T_{\Theta_i}(p)) = D_{i-1}(T_{\Theta_{i-1}}(p)) + D_{i+1}(T_{\Theta_{i+1}}(p)), \qquad I_i(T_{\Theta_i}(p)) \neq 0 \tag{7}$$

where $I_i(T_{\Theta_i}(p)) \neq 0$ means that only the contour points of I_i are involved.

A large number of interpolations are involved in the alignment process. The accuracy of estimation of the rotation and translation parameters is directly related to the accuracy of the underlying interpolation model. Simple approaches such as the nearest neighbor interpolation are commonly used because they are fast and simple to implement, though they produce images with noticeable artifacts. Besides, as the translation and rotation parameters should compensate for accuracy by having subvoxel values, this type of interpolation would not be appropriate. More satisfactory results can be obtained by small-kernel cubic convolution techniques, bilinear, or convolution-based interpolation. According to sampling theory, optimal results are obtained using sinus cardinal interpolation, but at the expense of a high computational cost. As a compromise, a bilinear interpolation technique has been used in the optimization steps. At the end of the algorithm, the alignment parameters are refined using a sinus cardial interpolation that preserves the quality of the image to be aligned. This technique has proven to be fast and efficient.

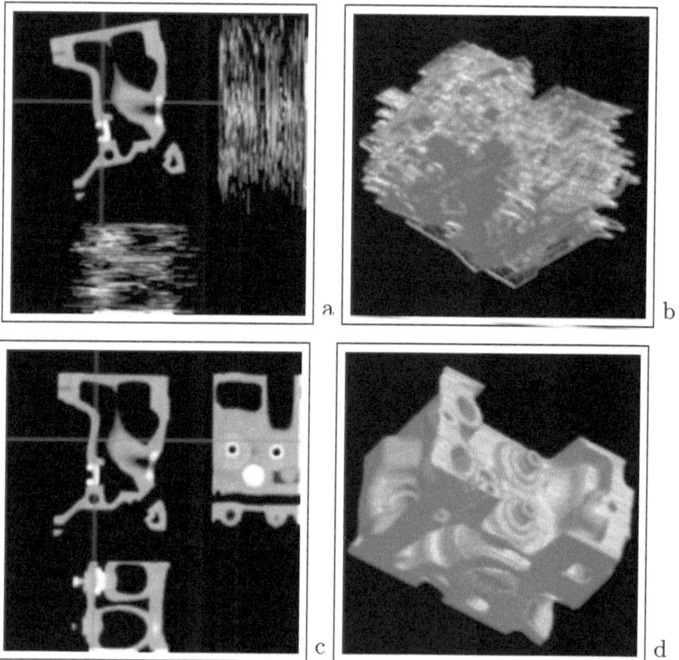

Fig. 1. Reconstruction of a 3D scanned mechanical part volume of 109 slices. **(a)** Multiplanar view of the volume before registration. **(b)** Three-dimensional view of the volume before registration. **(c)** Multiplanar view of the volume after registration. **(d)** Three-dimensional view of the volume after registration.

Table 1. A set of 109 slices of a 3D CT scanned mechanical part volume were artificially transformed using different rigid transformation parameters. Each slice was randomly transformed using translations varying from -10 to +10 pixels and rotations varying from -20 to +20 degrees. Statistics on the alignment errors for the rigid transformation parameters are presented. Translation errors are expressed in pixels and rotation error in degrees.

	Δt_x	Δt_y	$\Delta\theta$
median	0.33	0.31	0.06
maximum	1.07	0.93	0.25
mean ± s. dev	0.35 ± 0.25	0.38 ± 0.25	0.07 ± 0.06

3 Experimental Results

To evaluate our method, we applied the algorithm to the reconstruction of an artificially misaligned 3D CT scanned mechanical part (figure 1). The slices of the original 256 × 256 × 109 CT volume were transformed using translations varying from -10 to +10 pixels and rotations varying from -20 to +20 degrees.

Table 2. A set of 100 slices of a 3D CT scanned mechanical part volume were artificially transformed using different rigid transformation parameters. Each slice was translated by 0.2 pixels in both directions and rotated by 0.4 degrees with respect to its preceding slice. Different statistics on the errors for the rigid transformation parameters are presented. Translation errors are expressed in pixels and rotation error in degrees.

	Δt_x	Δt_y	$\Delta\theta$
median	0.19	0.23	0.05
maximum	0.99	0.87	0.32
mean ± s. dev	0.29 ± 0.26	0.31 ± 0.26	0.07 ± 0.07

The transformations for each slice were random following a uniform distribution in order not to privilege any slice (figures 1(a) and 1(b)). Table 1 presents statistics on the alignment errors. The algorithm revealed robust in aligning this type of image providing small registration errors. Figures 1(c) and 1(d) present the reconstructed volume.

Moreover, we have uniformly transformed 100 slices of the same 3D volume (mechanical part of an engine) by applying to each slice I_i a translation of $t_x^i = t_x^{i-1} + 0.2$ pixels and $t_y^i = t_y^{i-1} + 0.2$ pixels and a rotation of $\theta^i = \theta^{i-1} + 0.4$ degrees. As the volume has 100 slices, the last slice is translated by 20 pixels in both directions and rotated by 40 degrees with respect to its initial position. Table 2 presents the registration errors of the method. It is illustrated that our approach has subvoxel mean, median and maximum errors.

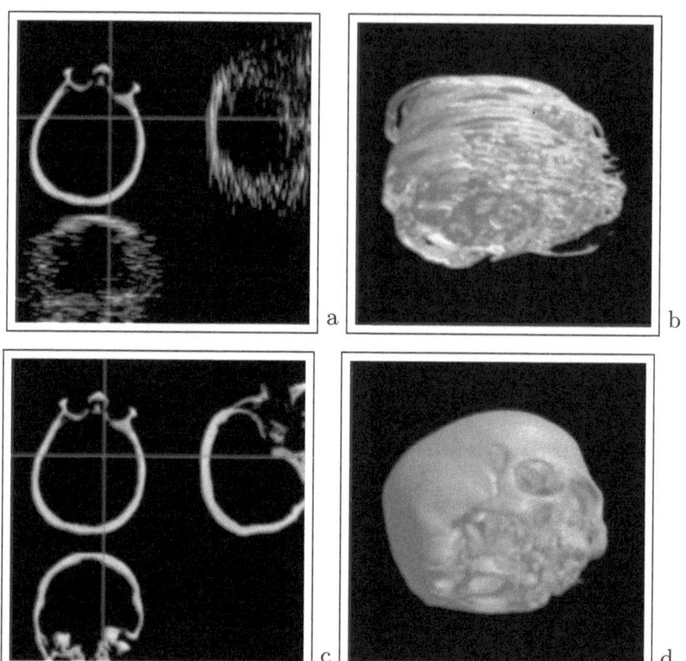

Fig. 2. Reconstruction of a 3D human skull volume of 140 slices. **(a)** Multiplanar view of the volume before registration. **(b)** Three-dimensional view of the volume before registration. **(c)** Multiplanar view of the volume after registration. **(d)** Three-dimensional view of the volume after registration.

Table 3. A set of 140 slices of a 3D CT human skull volume were artificially transformed using different rigid transformation parameters. Each slice was randomly transformed using translations varying from -10 to +10 pixels and rotations varying from -20 to +20 degrees. Different statistics on the errors for the rigid transformation parameters are presented. Translation errors are expressed in pixels and rotation error in degrees.

	Δt_x	Δt_y	$\Delta\theta$
median	2.10	0.33	0.07
maximum	1.45	2.02	2.42
mean $\pm$ s. dev	0.37 $\pm$ 0.28	0.38 $\pm$ 0.30	0.19 $\pm$ 0.35

The same evaluation procedure was performed on a 3D human skull volume with 140 slices (figure 2). The algorithm aligned the artificially (randomly and uniformly) misaligned slices of the volume and the errors are drawn in Tables 3 and 4. Human skull presents discontinuities, and consecutive slices may differ significantly due to anatomy but the global energy function is robust to these shortcomings. As it can be seen, median and mean translation and rotation errors are less than 1 pixel and 1 degree respectively. Also maximum errors are

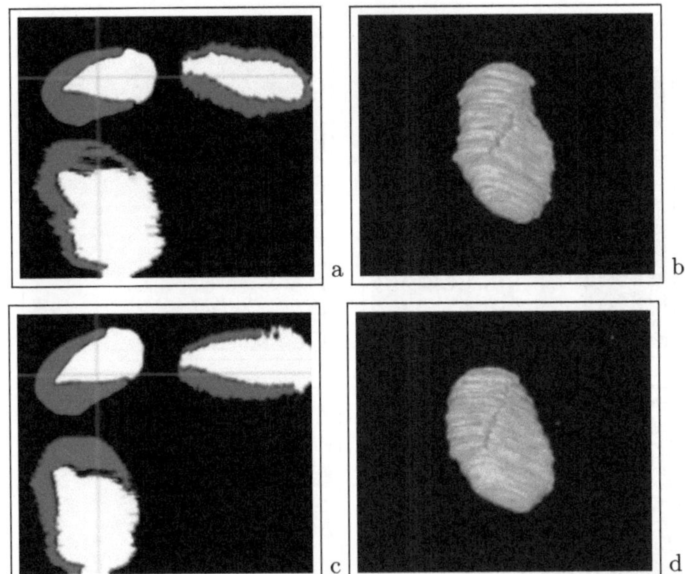

Fig. 3. Reconstruction of a 3D tooth volume of 265 slices. **(a)** Multiplanar view of the volume after alignment by an expert dentist. **(b)** Three-dimensional view of the volume after alignment by an expert dentist. **(c)** Multiplanar view of the volume after registration. **(d)** Three-dimensional view of the volume after registration.

Table 4. A set of 140 slices of a 3D CT human skull volume were artificially transformed using different rigid transformation parameters. Each slice was translated by 0.15 pixels in both directions and rotated by 0.3 degrees with respect to its preceding slice. Different statistics on the errors for the rigid transformation parameters are presented. Translation errors are expressed in pixels and rotation error in degrees.

Alignment error statistics

	Δt_x	Δt_y	$\Delta\theta$
median	0.23	0.21	0.26
maximum	1.95	1.94	1.64
mean ± s. dev	0.33 ± 0.32	0.34 ± 0.33	0.25 ± 0.25

slightly superior to 1 pixel and 1 degree respectively showing the robustness of the technique.

Furthermore, the algorithm was applied to the reconstruction of volumes (tooth germs, biological tissues) with unknown ground truth. The method's performance was compared with the manual alignment accomplished by an expert physician. Figure 3 shows the reconstruction of a tooth germ by an expert dentist (fig. 3(a) and 3(b)) and by our method (fig. 3(c) and 3(d)). It is illustrated that human intervention fails to correctly align the slices, whilst our method is efficient and can achieve alignment with high accuracy.

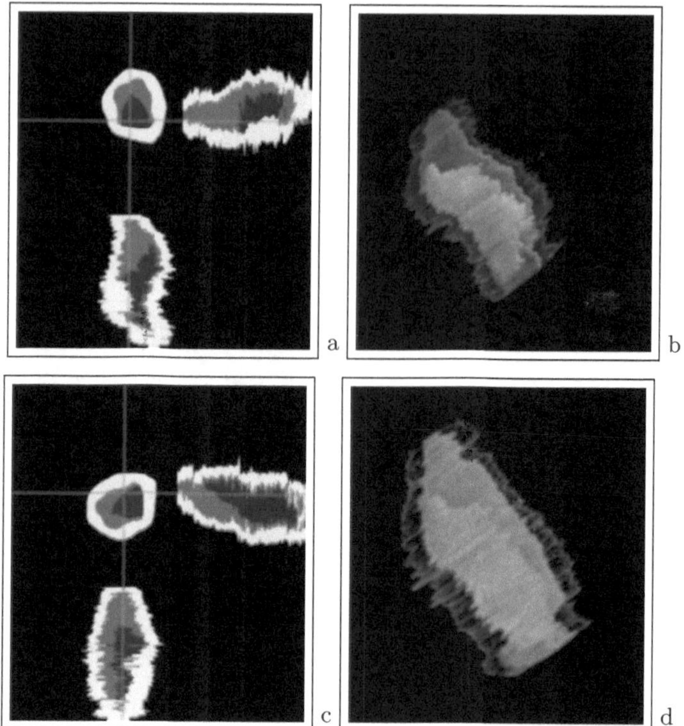

Fig. 4. Reconstruction of a 3D tooth volume of 194 slices. **(a)** Multiplanar view of the volume after alignment by an expert dentist. **(b)** Three-dimensional view of the volume after alignment by an expert dentist. **(c)** Multiplanar view of the volume after registration. **(d)** Three-dimensional view of the volume after registration.

The same stands for the example presented in figure 4 where another tooth reconstruction is presented.

Also, Figure 5 depicts a 3D tissue containing a large number of vessels. Figures 5(a) and 5(b) show the volume aligned by an expert biologist and Figures 5(c) and 5(d) the tissue after alignment by our method.

This volume presents cuts and discontinuities and the tissues had been stretched during the cut procedure. Despite these drawbacks, according to the expert biologist, the algorithm aligned correctly the slices.

Finally, let us notice that the algorithm has a computational complexity $O(N_x N_y N)$ and requires approximately 10 min. to reconstruct a $256 \times 256 \times 140$ volume on a Pentium III (800 MHz) workstation.

4 Conclusion

The alignment method described in this paper is akin to the global energy function formulation proposed in [11] to register multiple views of a 3D surface in

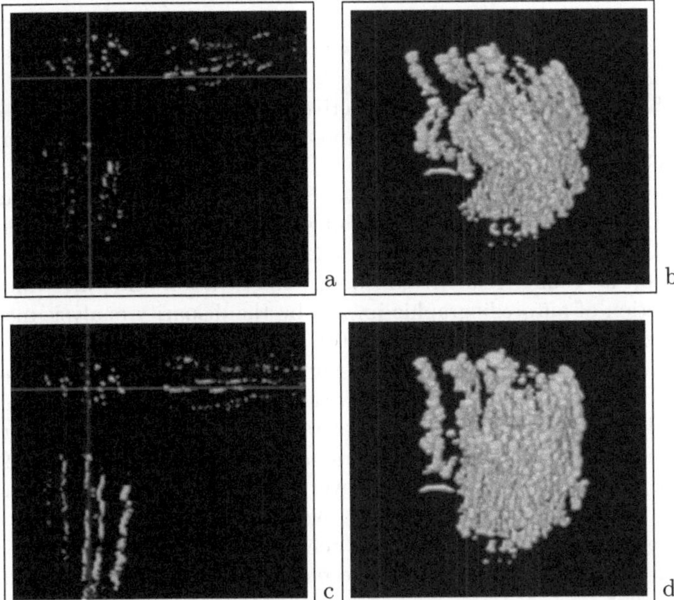

Fig. 5. Reconstruction of a 3D tissue volume of 237 slices. **(a)** Multiplanar view of the volume after alignment by an expert biologist. **(b)** Three-dimensional view of the volume after alignment by an expert biologist. **(c)** Multiplanar view of the volume after registration. **(d)** Three-dimensional view of the volume after registration.

computer vision applications. The main contribution of the approach is to consider the alignment problem globally on the 3D volume, by minimizing a global objective function expressing the similarity between neighboring slices. The approach does not privilege any particular direction in the registration process. By these means, the major problems set by the registration of serially acquired slices are addressed. With the global (isotropic) formulation of the registration problem (rather than a standard step by step, sequential formulation), no global offset nor error propagations are observed in the final alignment. The approach seems promising and its association to more sophisticated but time consuming pixel similarity metrics (mutual information [18], robust estimation-based measures [19]) may improve its accuracy and is a perspective of this work.

References

1. L. Gottesfeld-Brown. A survey of image registration techniques. *ACM Computing Surveys*, 24(4):325–376, 1992.
2. J. B. A. Maintz and M. A. Viergever. A survey of medical image registration techniques. *Medical Image Analysis*, 2(1):1–36, 1998.
3. P. Van den Elsen, E. J. D. Paul, and M. A. Viergever. Medical image matching - a review with classification. *IEEE engineering in Medicine and Biology*, 12(1):26–39, 1993.

4. A. F. Goldszal, O. J. Tretiak, P. J. Hand, S. Bhasin, and D. L. Mac Eachron. Three-dimensional reconstruction of activated columns from 2-[^{14}c] deoxy-d-glucose data. *NeuroImage*, 2:9–20, 1995.
5. L. Hibbard and R. Hawkins. Objective image alignment for three-dimensional reconstruction of digital autoradiographs. *Journal of Neuroscience Methods*, 26:55–75, 1988.
6. A. Rangarajan, H. Chui, E. Mjolsness, S. Pappu, L. Davachi, P. Goldman-Rakic, and J. Duncan. A robust point-matching algorithm for autoradiograph alignment. *Medical Image Analysis*, 1(4):379–398, 1997.
7. W. Zhao, T. Young, and M. Ginsberg. Registration and three-dimensional reconstruction of autorediographic images by the disparity analysis method. *IEEE Transactions on Medical Imaging*, 12(4):782–791, 1993.
8. A. Andreasen, A. M. Drewes, J.E. Assentoft, and N. E. Larsen. Computer-assisted alignment of standard serial sections without use of artificial landmarks. a practical approach to the utilization of incomplete information of 3d reconstruction of the hippocampal region. *Journal of Neuroscience Methods*, 45:199–207, 1992.
9. B. Kim, J. Boes, K. Frey, and C. Meyer. Mutual information for automated unwarping of rat brain autorediographs. *NeuroImage*, 5:31–40, 1997.
10. S. Ourselin, A. Roche, G. Subsol, X. Pennec, and C. Sattonnet. Automatic alignment of histological sections for 3d reconstruction and analysis. Sophia Anipolis, France, 1998.
11. R. Ben-Jemaa and F. Schmitt. A solution for the registration of multiple 3d points sets using unit quaternions. In *Notes in Computer science. Proceedings of the* 5th *European Conference on Computer Vision (ECCV'98)*, volume 2, pages 34–50, Freiburg, Germany, June 1998.
12. M. J. Besl and N. McKay. A method for the registration of 3d shapes. *IEEE transactions of Pattern Analysis and Machine Intelligence*, 14(2):239–256, 1992.
13. G. Borgefors. Distance transformations in arbitrary dimensions. *Computer Vision, Graphics, and Image Processing*, 27:321–345, 1984.
14. J. Besag. On the statistical analysis of dirty pictures. *Journal of the Royal Statistical Society*, 48(3):259–302, 1986.
15. Per-Erik Danielsson. Euclidean distance transform. *Computer Graphics and Image Processing*, 14:227–28, 1980.
16. G. Borgefors. Hierarchical chamfer matching: A parametric edge matching algorithm. *IEEE transactions of Pattern Analysis and Machine Intelligence*, 10:849–965, November 1988.
17. J. Canny. A computational approach to edge detection. *IEEE Transactions on Pattern Analysis and Machine Intelligence*, pages 679–698, 1986.
18. W. Wells III, P. Viola, H. Atsumi, S. Nakajima, and R. Kikinis. Multimodal volume registration by maximization of mutual information. *Medical Image Analysis*, 1(1):33–51, 1996.
19. C. Nikou, J. P. Armspach, F. Heitz, I. J. Namer, and D. Grucker. Mr/mr and mr/spect registration of brain images by fast stochastic optimization of robust voxel similarity measures. *NeuroImage*, 8(1):30–43, 1998.

Definition and Extraction of Visual Landmarks for Indoor Robot Navigation

Dimitrios I. Kosmopoulos and Konstantinos V. Chandrinos

National Centre for Scientific Research "Demokritos"
Institute of Informatics and Telecommunications, 15310 Ag. Paraskevi, Greece
{dkosmo, kostel}@iit.demokritos.gr

Abstract. This paper presents a new method for defining and extracting visual landmarks for indoor navigation using a single camera. The approach considers that navigating from point A to point B amounts to navigating to intermediate positions, which are signified by recognition of local landmarks. To avoid the pose problem we seek scene representations that rely on clustered corners of physical objects on corridor walls. These representations are scale and translation independent and allow for the construction of a metric that can match pre-detected landmarks of a learning phase with landmarks extracted from images captured at run-time. The validity of our approach has been verified experimentally.

1 Introduction

The use of visual information has been studied excessively in recent years as the most promising approach to intelligent mobile platform navigation. Two distinct strands of approach have been those utilizing a metric map and those using a topological map to control navigation. A metric map is usually pre-loaded to the robot and includes extended detail of the environment through some geometric modeling [4]. The redundant for the purpose of robot navigation and hard to compile information required for a complete metric map has led researchers into examining construction of topological maps, i.e. maps that model aspects of the environment critical to the task at hand usually as a graph of intermediate navigational tasks [5]. Visual landmarks have been explored as a possible solution to the problem, more so as they lend themselves nicely to the prevailing anthropocentric metaphor applied to robot navigation. On the face of it, visual landmarks have to face the 'pose' problem, namely the fact that the same visual landmark may look different when viewed under different perspectives. To resolve ambiguity a number of solutions have been proposed, ranging from information fusion from other sensors [6] to Kalman filters on odometer input [7].

As regards the pure visual methods various approaches have been used. According to the *environment engineering* approach (e.g. [17]) predetermined patterns are installed in the workspace ensuring robust recognition. This approach is out of the scope of our research, which seeks to identify "natural" scenes. The *template matching* and the *appearance-based* methods such as PCA (e.g. [12], [16]) entail big computational expense and suffer from pose constraints. The holistic image representations, which employ omnidirectional cameras such as in [14] seem more

I.P. Vlahavas and C.D. Spyropoulos (Eds.): SETN 2002, LNAI 2308, pp. 401–412, 2002.

promising. The selective feature extraction methods such as edges in constrained orientation (e.g. [15]) or point set invariants (e.g. cross-ratio [8], SIFT [11]) overcome the pose constraints but are still computationally expensive.

Our work aims to define and extract pose-independent visual landmarks for topological navigation by feature extraction. It considers that navigating from point A to point B amounts to intermediate navigations to points A_1, A_2, ... A_n and arrival to these intermediate positions is signified by recognition of local landmarks. To avoid the pose problem we seek scene representations that rely on clustered corners of physical objects on corridor walls. These representations are scale and translation independent and allow for the construction of a metric that can match pre-detected landmarks of a learning phase with landmarks extracted from images captured at run-time. The visual system described has been designed and tested during the national project "Hygeiorobot" and was meant to provide assistance in the navigation of an autonomous mobile platform in health related applications. In this paper, we describe only issues concerning acquisition and representation of the visual information and more particularly the method for visual landmark discovery and matching. Section 2 presents an overview of the method for the landmark extraction and representation while section 3 presents the comparison metric used for landmark identification. Experimental results are described in section 4, while section 5 concludes the paper.

2 Method Overview

The method employed in this work is destined to be used for vision-based topological navigation. The typical tasks to be executed in that framework are

- the construction of a topological map of the environment,
- the definition of the current position as of this map by comparing real-time input with previously stored images
- the assistance to autonomous navigation after translation of path plan to sub-goals through successful recognition of visual cues between start point and destination

Landmark recognition runs across all these tasks. In our approach we have sought to define landmarks that are robustly recognized, pose-independent and can be calculated efficiently.

We have decided to employ object corners in the image due to the fact that in most cases they constitute quite robust features for sequential tracking [9]; the pose-independency is achieved by clustering the identified corners, so that higher-level entities with pose independent attributes are formulated (see section 3); we have used a similarity metric to compare the sets of clusters extracted from the current image with the ones resulting from an offline training procedure; we use this metric along with a predefined threshold in order to decide in a "binary manner" whether the robot has approached a node of the map, which is signified by an expected landmark[1]. The whole process can be implemented within acceptable processing cycles (as described in section 4) and an overview is given in figure 1.

---

[1] The term "expected landmark" is justified by the assumption that path planning is already available, which along with data such as odometry can define which landmarks are likely to be seen next.

We now describe the image processing procedure. Initially the image is fed to the *Edge Detector.* The output is a set of edge points, from which the corners are going to be extracted in the next processing stage. The identified edges are also used for detecting the far end of the workspace and the vanishing point. The edge points are Hough - transformed (*Hough Transformer* in figure 1) and the resulting lines are given as input to the *Vanishing Point Calculator.* The resulting lines allow us to perform workspace segregation. The segregation data and the identified corners are input to the *Corner Selector* that decides which of the corners are actually reliable to track. The output of this module is received from *Point Clusterer*, which forms clusters of the corners according to their proximity in the image. The vectors of those clusters are calculated and stored in order to be used during the operation phase. While in operation the system performs a metric calculation (*Metric Calculator* in figure 1) to decide the similarity metric between the currently grabbed image and the stored one in the *Landmark Database.* The database contains landmarks that were defined following the same extraction procedure for the reference robot poses, which are defined as nodes in the topological map. In the following sections the aforementioned modules will be described in detail.

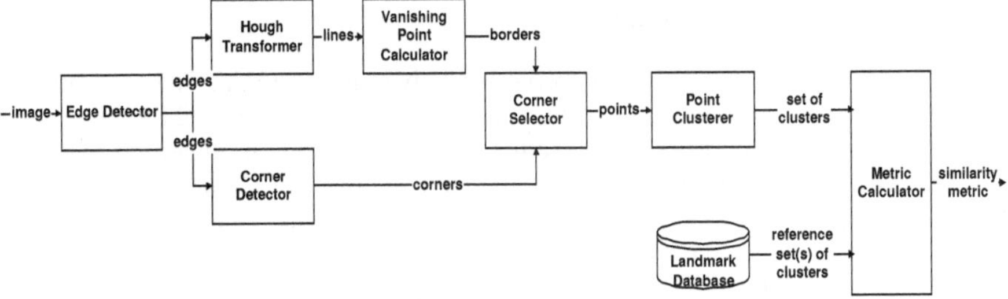

Fig. 1. Overview of the processing modules of the machine vision subsystem of Hygeiorobot

2.1 Edge Detector

The edge detector that we have selected to use is the SUSAN edge detector [1] due to its speed, robustness and accuracy compared to other popular algorithms such as Canny or Sobel. Furthermore, as we want to end up with corners in the images we evaluated SUSAN as a corner detector. A comparative study with the Kanade-Lucas-Tomasi (KLT [9]) corner detector can be found in [10]. The SUSAN edge detector is a non-linear algorithm. A circular mask (having a center pixel called the nucleus) moves on the image. The brightness of each pixel within the mask is compared with the nucleus; then an area of the mask is extracted, which has the same or similar brightness as the nucleus. This means that the brightness difference between each pixel belonging in that area and the nucleus is within some threshold. This area is called the "Univalue Segment Assimilating Nucleus"–USAN. From the size, centroid and second moments of the USAN two-dimensional features such as edges can be detected. Furthermore from the results of the SUSAN edge detector it is very simple to extract the corners as it will be presented in section 2.2. For the detection of edges we select a threshold for identification of edges equal to $g = 3n_{max}/4$, where n_{max} is the number of pixels belonging to the circular (and thus isotropic) mask. Whenever the application of the mask returns a value higher than g, the nucleus is regarded to be an edge point. The threshold defining the difference in the intensity in order to have an edge is set to 25, which gives acceptable results for typical corridor images.

2.2 Corner Detector

We showed earlier how we detect edges using the SUSAN algorithm. From those edges we are able to detect the corners, because the set of corners is a subset of the set of edge points. The method is quite simple and first we set the threshold g equal to $n_{max}/2$. From the resulting candidate corners we eliminate the thin lines that give a response similar to that of a corner by checking the center of gravity of the USAN. It has to be far from the center of the mask otherwise it has to be rejected [1]. In addition to that, for a corner to be detected, all of the pixels within the mask, lying in a straight line pointing outwards from the nucleus in the direction of the center of gravity of the USAN must be part of the USAN.

2.3 Vanishing Point Calculator

A typical image when navigating in corridors is given in figure 2a. The estimation of the vanishing point is achieved through the following procedure. From the edges detected in the step described in section 3, through the application of Hough transform we are able to extract the lines that have an angle of about 45 degrees (GC, HD in figure 2a). These lines are almost always detectable under normal lighting conditions. We assume that the end points C, D of the previously identified lines define the horizontal line CD (many times it is detectable) and that from those points also the vertical line segments CA and DB are initiated (detected in the image). The horizontal linear segment that is detected above the vanishing point and has a similar length with the segment CD is the AB.

The accuracy of the method depends on the quality of the edge detection. This accuracy can be improved by tracking the vanishing point over a sequence of images and by defining areas within which the lines are expected to appear [3].

2.4 Corner Selector

Our goal is to detect the points that lie within the "wall regions" of the image. Our choice is spurred from the fact that wall features tend to be permanent. On the contrary, features detected on the floor may not always be present. Additionally, features detected on the floor may be a result of reflections and thus unreliable. Features detected on the ceiling must also be excluded due to the presence of lights, which may be on or off and thus altering the image characteristics around them. Finally the "far end" in the image must be excluded due to low resolution. Therefore, using the vanishing point and the lines detected as described in the previous section we have to perform the so-called workspace segregation.

A typical corridor image looks like the one in figure 2a. From the module *Vanishing Point Calculator* we have detected the lines depicted in figure 2a and the vanishing point. The point selection is performed as following:

Initially we exclude all the points whose x-coordinate lies between the x coordinates covered by the "far end" frame ABCD. This is simply done by comparing with the minimum and maximum x-coordinates of the points A, B, C, D. Then from the remaining points we detect the ones that lie on the left of the line EACG and on the right of the line FDBH. The conditions that have to be fulfilled for a point P, in the first case are:

$$(\mathbf{PG} \times \mathbf{GC})_z > 0 \text{ and } (\mathbf{PA} \times \mathbf{AE})_z > 0. \quad \textbf{(1)}$$

Similarly for the second case the conditions are:

$$(\mathbf{PH} \times \mathbf{HD})_z < 0 \text{ and } (\mathbf{PB} \times \mathbf{BF})_z < 0 \quad \textbf{(2)}$$

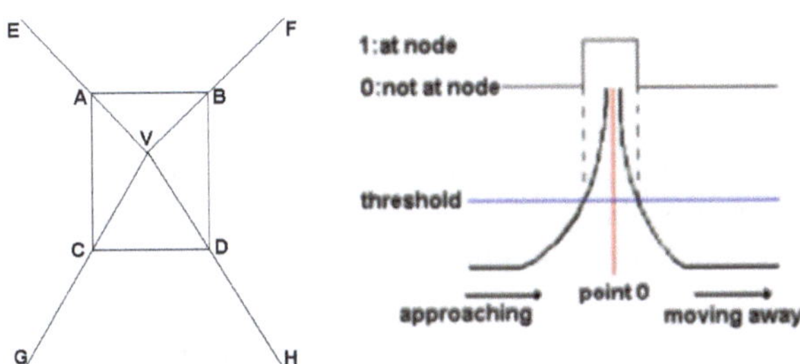

Fig. 2. (a) The workspace in images taken during robot navigation in corridors (b) The ideal metric response during approaching and moving away from a reference point 0 (landmark). When a threshold is exceeded the robot is assumed to have reached the corresponding node in the topological map.

2.5 Point Clustering

We employ point-clustering techniques in order to use a high-level representation for the detection of landmarks. The input constitutes of filtered points and the output is clusters of points that are described by attribute vectors. The fields of those vectors should not be affected by changes in the scale and the position, which are expected due to the robot movement.

The points are clustered according to their positions in the image. The results of such a process for arbitrarily located points can not be verified using universally acceptable criteria and only the human operator can decide for the success of the method.

The method that we have used for clustering utilizes a metaphor, by considering the filtered corner points in the image as particles of uniform mass m, which can exert attraction forces to each other. For a pair of such particles m_1, m_2 the force exerted in each of them is of the following form:

$$F = \hat{r} \cdot K \cdot \frac{m_1 \cdot m_2}{r^2} = \hat{r} \frac{K}{r^2} \quad \textbf{(3)}$$

if we define that $m_1 = m_2 = 1$, where $\hat{r}$ is the vector that connects m_1 with m_2. The result is that the particles will start moving towards each other until their collision. From that moment on, the two particles will behave as a single one with double mass. This procedure is simulated iteratively and finishes when no particle is able to move because no significant force will be exerted. Then we say that the system is in balance and the clustering is complete. Under this balance state we use the compound particles that resulted from the collision of single ones to form clusters.

At this point, we should mention that the size of the constant K affects the returned clusters. A big value of K would result in big forces, thus creating a small number of bigger clusters. On the other hand, if the value of K is small the forces will be weak resulting in a large number of smaller clusters. The value of K is decided experimentally to suit the needs of the specific application.

3 Comparing Images Using Clusters of Corners

As previously mentioned, the comparison between images is performed using the clusters of the corners. The attributes used for each cluster are stored as vectors. Thus each processed image is characterized by N such vectors, where N is the number of clusters, which resulted from the previous procedure. These vectors are of the type (x_A, x_B, x_C), where:

x_A = The number of points belonging to the cluster.

x_B = The Mahalanobis distance of the center of gravity of the cluster from the vanishing point in the image.

x_C = The angle of the center of gravity of the cluster from the vanishing point.

The fields of this vector are scale- and translation – invariant. This is a mandatory requirement considering that the images are taken from a camera mounted on a moving robot.

The employment of the vanishing point in combination with the x_B, x_C results in increased reliability. It would be quite possible to have two totally different images but with quite similar clusters. The introduced methods avoid a false positive in such cases by considering the Mahalanobis distance and the angle from the vanishing point. Thus the probability of false positive is dramatically reduced and only in case of really similar images (and not just similar representations via corners) a high metric value would be returned. Given that for two images close in succession it is possible to find corners at a close distance but in different image coordinates, the clustering of those points is affected and thus it is not possible to compare directly the clusters using e.g. Euclidean distances. For instance, a cluster in image A may have split into two in image B or it is quite possible that there is overlaying of clusters.

For this reason we have chosen to compare two images using a metric, which reaches a maximum when the vectors of the two images coincide and it gives a high result when the vectors are “close” to each other. By employing such a metric the robot will be able to perceive that it approaches a landmark, because the application of the metric in a set of consecutive images will give an increasing value much above the noise level (with regard to the reference image). Similarly the robot will be able to perceive that it is moving away from the target landmark when the metric gives clearly decreasing values for a set of consecutive images. When the metric with regard to the current image gives a very high result it is clear that the robot is very close to the landmark. This is depicted in figure 2b. As already mentioned in section 2, in our current approach we are only interested to know if the robot is at the region of the node defined in the topological map or not. This can be decided by setting an appropriate threshold. Calculating the distance from the node is not within the scope of this method.

To provide grounds for metric comparison between stored image representations via clusters and actual run-time images, we first analyse run-time images and reduce them to a point-cluster representation employing the same method as used in the learning phase.

The metric is calculated as follows: For each cluster of the current image we calculate a similarity metric with each cluster of the reference image. This metric is inversely proportional to the square root of the sum of squares of the differences in the fields of the corresponding vectors.

$$F_{ij} = k \cdot \frac{1}{(x_{Ai} - x_{Aj})^2 + (x_{Bi} - x_{Bj})^2 + (x_{Ci} - x_{Cj})^2} \quad \textbf{(4)}$$

The sum of those metrics gives the total similarity metric between the two images:

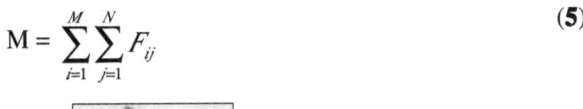

$$\mathrm{M} = \sum_{i=1}^{M} \sum_{j=1}^{N} F_{ij} \quad \textbf{(5)}$$

Fig. 3. The Hygeiorobot mobile robotic platform

4 Experimental Results

In order to evaluate the method we used the mobile robotic platform of the NTUA lab constructed by Robosoft (Figure 3), with a CCD SONY EVI-371D with auto focus and automatic gain control capabilities mounted on it. The whole system was running on a 500Mhz PC under Windows 2000. The source code used for edge and corner detection is a modified version of the code freely distributed at [2]. The rest of the system has been programmed using C++.

We performed experiments to test (a) the ability of the method to decide when the robot approaches a reference position according to the situation described in figure 2b, (b) the influence of displacement.

4.1 Target Approaching

More than ten image sequences from various corridors were acquired (each one comprising 8 to 15 images) in order to test the consistency of the method. Each of the images was compared (played the role of the reference image) using the similarity metric with all the images of the sequence, which were taken from neighboring poses with a constant distance between them. We expected to get increased similarity values from images taken from the closest poses to the reference one.
A typical image sequence is illustrated in figure 4. The results of the procedure for this sequence are presented analytically in the following.

The results of the clustering tests are presented in figure 5. We have rejected all clusters containing less than three points. The presented results appear to be very satisfactory and are in most cases very close to what a human would consider as appropriate clustering, taking the point proximity as criterion.

In figure 6 we present the results of matching each one of the images illustrated in figure 5 with all the others based on the clustering of the corners as presented in figure 5. We have programmed the software to give a maximum value to the metric in case of high returned values (e.g. in cases of division by numbers close to zero). During the experiments the value was selected empirically to be $V_{\max} = 3$. It is clear from figure 6 that in almost all cases the metric seems to give results, which are quite close to the ideal case that was described in figure 2b. The space intervals between the images are approximately 100cm. Of course the efficiency of the method can be dramatically improved if the space intervals between two consecutive images decrease and in that case the metric response becomes even closer to the ideal case. The time t_g needed for grabbing a new image and the time t_p needed to process it place an upper limit to the robot velocity V_R as follows:

$$V_R \leq \frac{d}{t_g + t_p} \tag{6}$$

where d is the required space distance between the consecutive images (we have assumed linear translational robot movement when approaching the target). Therefore, in order to increase the efficiency of the method the robot speed should be reduced every time the metric values, which are higher than the noise levels were detected. This comes well with the intuitive expectation that a mobile platform should slow down and examine its sensors on a need-to-know basis. According to the results of figure 6 a threshold that indicates the robot is approaching a reference pose (node) would be T=0.5.

In the conducted experiments the following timing has been measured with the help of the profiler of the Microsoft Integrated Environment: t_g=40ms, which is defined by the frame grabber cycle and remains almost constant and t_p=420ms, where the 340ms are consumed for the edge/corner detection and the rest is consumed in clustering, Hough transformation and image matching (using a set of ten stored landmarks). The above numbers for t_p are typical values and may vary according to the image size and the number of the detected corners. In our experiments images of 768×576 were grabbed and the detected corners were around 100. The performance can be significantly improved by grabbing smaller images, but the reliability of the method would be reduced as well.

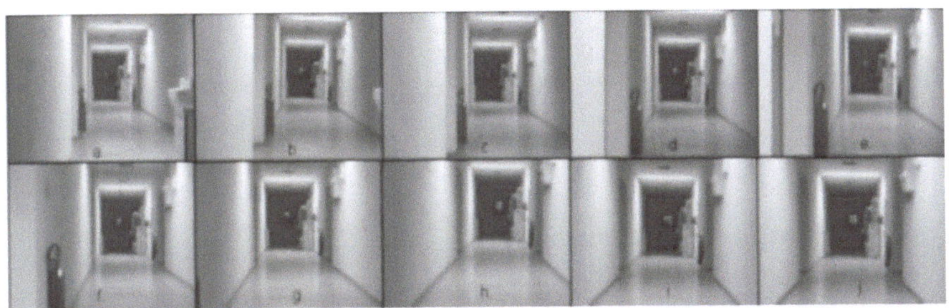

Fig. 4. The sequence of images used for the evaluation of the landmark identification method

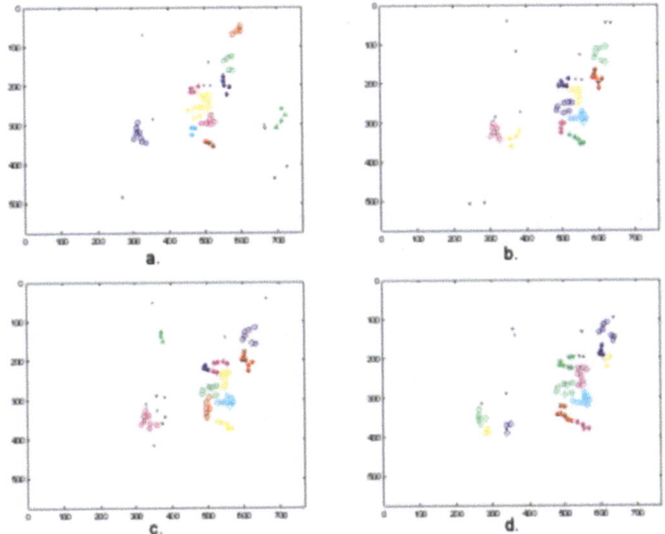

Fig. 5 a-d. The results of the clustering procedure. The points with the same color and shape belong to the same cluster. There is a one to one correspondence with the images of figure 4. The grey "x"s are unclustered points.

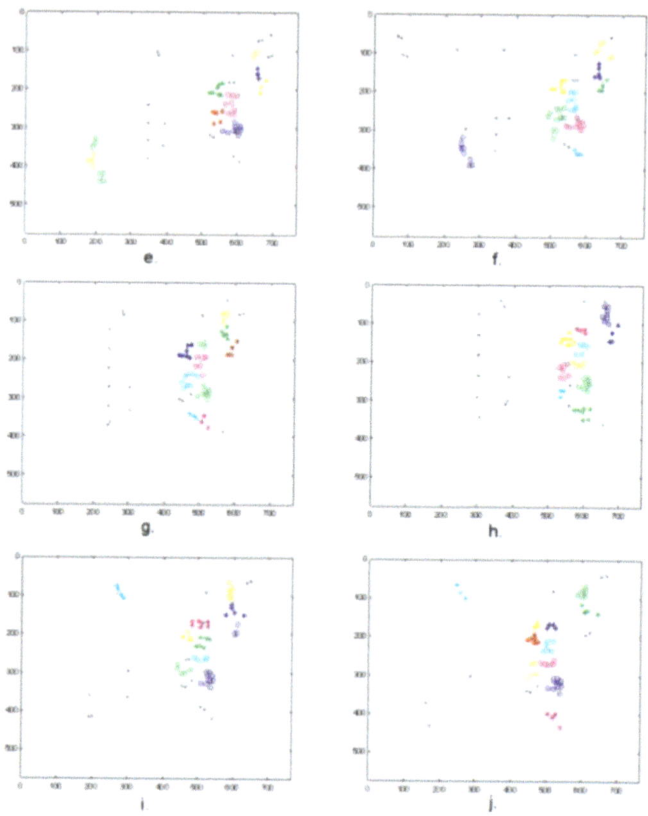

Fig. 5. e-j (continued)

4.2 Influence of Displacement and Constraints

This paper describes work on the construction of a reliable visual system used for the guidance of a robotic platform in corridors. It would be unwise not to take into account the physical constraints posed by the problem itself and the ambiguity resolution provided by other sub-systems and/or the overall system design. For example, we never have to solve the 'kidnapped robot' problem, nor do we need to compare real-time detected landmarks in corridor A with those that are known at learning time to appear in corridor B. Also, in a case like ours, landmark redundancy such as that of storing the same landmark twice, according to the direction the robot moves in a certain corridor can be very helpful.

In view of the above, we need to clarify that by the term "pose independence" we mean that the method can reliably recognize a landmark although the viewpoint has been translationaly and rotationaly displaced with regard to a reference point. As demonstrated in the previous experiment the system is able to recognize the landmark with a certainty that is proportional to the value of the metric. Therefore there is no general pose independence due to the fact that the displacement affects the clustering procedure. However, there *is* pose independence within small areas (in the experiment +/- 100cm) and rotation which is expected to show up in our scenarios.

In general, the constraints of the method have mainly to do with the working environment, i.e. the corridors of a building. Changes regarding the objects put on the walls with respect to the ones already taught offline can seriously affect the stability of the method. Furthermore, it is assumed that the illumination variances do not alter the brightness and the contrast of the image by more than ±10% so that the image corners can be stably identified 10. Last, the method relies on the ability of the edge detector to extract the lines from which the vanishing point is calculated. These constrains have to be considered when seeking optimal landmarks.

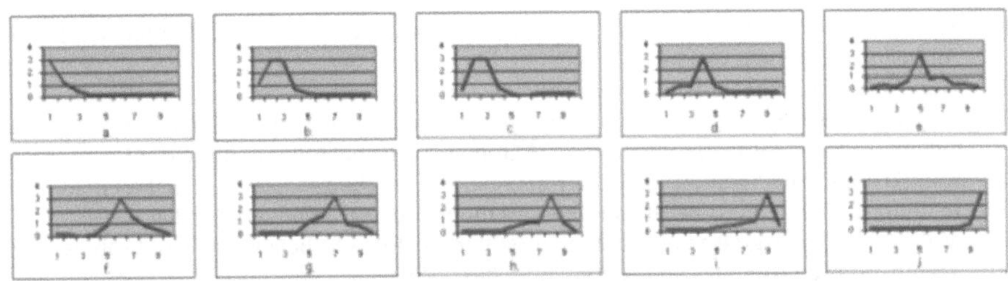

Fig. 6. The results of the metric-based matching for each of the ten images of figure 4 with all the others in the same figure. The x-axis represents the image with which the current image is matched and the y-axis represents the metric result.

5 Conclusions

We have introduced a new method for defining and extracting landmarks for indoor topological navigation using a single camera and its basic capabilities and constraints have been discussed. The method by-passes the pose and correspondence problems and gave promising results in a corridor environment. Considerable experimentation indicates that it could be possible to relax constraints and complexity induced by relying on complex invariants by employing a qualitative metric. However the dependency on the vanishing point limits the application of the method to indoor corridor environments.

Our approach has been designed to guide the robot based plainly on visual (and eventually odometric) data. Occasionally –depending on the environment-the visual input is not sufficient and then the method has to be extended to work in cooperation with other types of sensors such as ultrasonic or laser range sensors (e.g. vanishing point specification). In most mobile platforms such sensors are already used for local navigation and obstacle avoidance and thus their employment to solve the global problem would not introduce a hardware overhead.

In the next steps we plan to improve the clustering method, in order to take into consideration the clusters in the reference image before attempting clustering in run time. This is expected to increase the similarity metric between similar images and if designed appropriately we will be able to avoid false positives.

Acknowledgements. The authors would like to thank Dr. C. D. Spyropoulos, Research Director at the Institute of Informatics & Telecommunications, NCSR "Demokritos", for his critical reading of an earlier version of the manuscript.

This research work is supported by the General Secretariat for Research and Technology (Greek Ministry of Development and the European Community, under Grant PENED-99-ED623)

References

1. S.M. Smith and J.M. Brady. SUSAN - a new approach to low level image processing. Int. Journal of Computer Vision, 23(1):45--78, May 1997.
2. http://www.fmrib.ox.ac.uk/~steve/susan/
3. P. Trahanias, S. Velissaris, S. Orphanoudakis, "Visual recognition of workspace landmarks for topological navigation", Autonomous Robots, 7, 143-158, 1999.
4. Kampman, P. and Schmidt, G. Indoor navigation of mobile robots by use of learned maps, In "Information processing in Autonomous mobile robots", Springer-Verlag, 1991.
5. Mataric, M. J. Integration of representation into goal-driven behaviour-based robots. IEEE Transactions on Robotics and Automation, 8(3), 1992
6. Kortencamp, D. and Weynmouth, T. Topological mapping for mobile robots using a combination of sonar and video sensing. In Proceedings of the AAAI, 1994
7. Kurz, A. Constructing maps for mobile robot navigation based on ultrasonic range data. IEEE Transactions on System, Man and Cybernetics, 26(2):233-242, 1996.
8. Chandrinos, K.V. , Tsonis ,V. and Trahanias, P. Automated Landmark Extraction and Retrieval, SIRS, Edinburgh, 1998
9. Carlo Tomasi and Takeo Kanade. Detection and Tracking of Point Features. Carnegie Mellon University Technical Report CMU-CS-91-132, April 1991
10. D. I. Kosmopoulos, K.V. Chandrinos, Technical Report DEMO2000/14, Athens, November 2000
11. S. Se, D. Lowe, J. Little, "Vision – based mobile robot localization and mapping using scale-invariant features", International Conference on Robotics and Automation, Seoul, Korea, pp. 2051-2058, 2001
12. V.C. Verdiere, J. L. Crowley, "Local appearance space for recognition of navigation landmarks", Robotics and Autonomous Systems, 31, pp 61-69, 2000.
13. N. Vlassis, Y. Motomura, I. Hara, H.Asoh, T. Matsui, "Edge-based features from omnidirectional images for robot localization", International Conference on Robotics and Automation, Seoul, Korea, pp. 1579-1584, 2001.
14. P. Lamon, I. Nourbakhsh, B. Jensen, R. Siegwart, "Deriving and matching image fingerprint sequences for mobile robot localization", International Conference on Robotics and Automation, Seoul, Korea, pp. 1609-1614, 2001.
15. L. Tang, S. Yuta, "Vision based navigation for mobile robots in indoor environment by teaching and playing-back scheme", International Conference on Robotics and Automation, Seoul, Korea, pp. 3072-3077, 2001.
16. R. F. Vassallo, H. J. Schneebeli, J. Santos-Victor, "Visual servoing and appearance for navigation", Robotics and Autonomous Systems, 31, pp. 87-97, 2000.
17. M. Mata, J. M. Armingol, A. Escalera, M.A. Salichs, "A visual landmark recognition system for topological navigation of mobile robots", International Conference on Robotics and Automation, Seoul, Korea, pp. 1124-1129, 2001.

Factors Affecting the Accuracy of an Active Vision Head

Antonios Gasteratos [1] and Giulio Sandini [2]

[1] Laboratory of Electronics
Section of Electronics and Information Systems Technology
Department of Electrical and Computer Engineering
Democritus University of Thrace
GR-671 00 Xanthi, Hellas
agaster@ee.duth.gr

[2] Laboratory for Integrated Advanced Robotics
Department of Communication, Computer and System Sciences
University of Genoa
Viale Causa 13, I-16145 Genoa, Italy
sandini@dist.unige.it
http://www.lira.dist.unige.it

Abstract. In any measuring system the categorization of the error generation factors leads to simplification of complex error problems and to higher suppression of the error. In this paper we categorize, quantify and analyze the errors that affect a binocular active vision head. Simulations have been made and experimental results on a high resolution pan-tilt-vergence mechanism are also proposed. As a conclusion it can be said that the system performs optimal when it is initialized so that the two cameras are perfectly aligned and perpendicular to the baseline. Small variations in the vergence angle or small horizontal deviations of the principal point alters the measurement dramatically. On the other hand, variations in pan and tilt and vertical deviations of the principal point, affect the measurement insignificantly.

1 Introduction

Stereo is used widely in artificial vision to extract 3D information such as depth, surface normal and the exact position of a point [1-3]. The most widely applied method is disparity, i.e. the difference of the projection of the same point on the left and the right image. Using this information, the focal length of the cameras and the baseline, the 3D coordinates of any point can be determined. Let us consider the simple case of Figure 1: the 3D coordinates of the point P are given by:

$$[x, y, z]^T = \frac{d}{2(x_l' - x_r')}[x_l' + x_r', y_l' + y_r', f]^T \tag{1}$$

where: d is the baseline, f is the focal length of the two cameras (it is supposed that both cameras have the same f) and $x_l - x_r$ is the stereo disparity.

I.P. Vlahavas and C.D. Spyropoulos (Eds.): SETN 2002, LNAI 2308, pp. 413–422, 2002.

However, several problems arise when attempting to realize the above formula. The first is the *correspondence problem* [4]. It is obvious that in order to be able to apply eq. (1), one should know which are the x_l', and x_r' that correspond to the same point P in space. An analysis of the errors due to false correspondence has been carried out in [5]. The second problem is that of *camera calibration.* As is obvious in Figure 1 the distortion introduced by the lenses has not been taken into consideration and, moreover, the focal lengths of the two cameras were considered as equal. The lens distorted images are usually rectified using a of the camera calibration method (e.g. [6, 7]). An equally important issue is the *stereo setup alignment.* Eq. (1) demands that the two cameras are aligned exactly and also that they are perpendicular to the baseline. The camera calibration/alignment issue is studied in [8, 9], where a taxonomy and quantification of the errors due to misalignment of the stereo pair and due to misalignment of the sensor on the camera has been done.

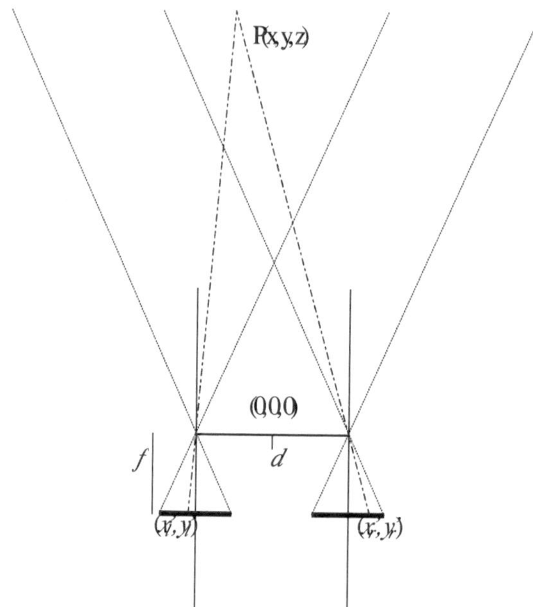

Fig. 1. Simple stereo geometry for 3D estimation

In [10] a method based on the measure of the vergence angle, was presented. In this method the cameras are not calibrated, because they are moved in a closed loop, so that the point under measure is put on the principal points of the two cameras. In this paper we attempt a complete analysis of the errors that may affect the method in [10]. These can basically be discriminated into visual errors, misalignment errors and mechanical errors. We also provide a theoretical analysis, supported by simulations for the above errors. Experiments have been carried out. These show that for the given setup the most critical errors are the visual and the misalignment ones, as the mechanical ones tend to be zeroed. The critical parameters for a high accuracy measurement are: the principal point identification; the initial alignment of the pair of cameras on the head and an image processing method eliminating the errors due to false correspondence.

2 The Stereo Head

Our stereo head is shown in Figure 2. It has been designed and implemented to be an accurate vision-based measuring device. For the control of the pan, tilt and vergence, four harmonic drive actuators are used. These actuators have been chosen according to their mechanical characteristics, which, due to their harmonic drive gearing, provide high reduction ratios in a single stage, zero backlash and high precision. Teeth belts have been used for the movement transmission. This gives better results in term of accuracy than usual gearing transmission.

Fig. 2. The head. The head has been utilized as an accurate measuring device for the purpose of ROVISION project [11, 12]. More specifically, it has been mounted on a walking/climbing and the measurements obtained by it have been used for self-localization of the robot.

3 Error Generation Factors

As has been stated above, the method in [10] utilizes a recursive method, so that a junction under measure is put on the principal points of both the images. The junctions are tracked by intersecting two different lines. The measurement is taken as:

$$l = d/(2\sin\nu) \tag{2}$$

where ν is the vergence angle.

Because of the fact that the baseline d of the head is comparatively small (190mm), the measured distance is very sensitive to small variations of the vergence angle. The measurement is obviously more sensitive in long distances, where $\nu\rightarrow 0$ and, consequently, $\sin\nu\rightarrow 0$. The 3D position of a point given the pan (p), tilt (t) and vergence angles is given by:

$$[x,y,z]^T = \mathbf{T}(p,t,\nu,d)\cdot[l,0,0]^T \tag{3}$$

with $\mathbf{T}$ being the 4x4 matrix of the kinematics of the head.

The factors that affect the accuracy of this measurement can be summarized as:

- Visual errors
- Alignments errors
- Mechanical errors

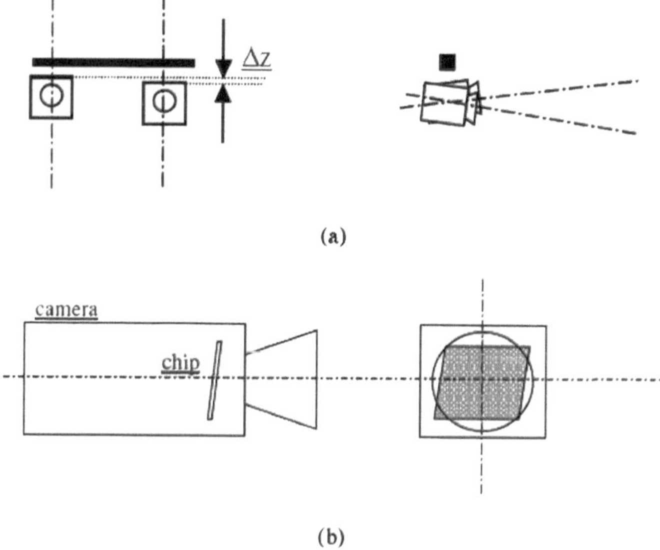

Fig. 3. (a) Misalignments of two cameras on a stereo head and (b) misalignment of the chip on a single camera

If the junction is not on the principal point of each camera, then we call that error visual error. This error is almost eliminated by the closed loop procedure to approach the junction. We say almost, because we have two degrees of freedom (dof) to move each camera separately in the horizontal direction but none on the vertical one. Therefore it is easy to compensate horizontal disparities using the vergence dof, but we are not able to compensate vertical ones. It may be expected that since the cameras are mounted on the same horizontal plane, with respect to the head, no vertical disparities should exist. However, in a real system no matter how well are mounted the cameras on the head or the sensor on camera, there are always displacements as these shown in Figures 3a and 3b. Moreover, due to the fact that the lenses are not identical they introduce different distortions around different principal points. In other words the different lenses may decline the optical axis from the perpendicular to the baseline position, though the bodies of the two cameras might be perfectly parallel.

It is only in the case where the junction under measure appears on the principal point when we know that the two optical axes form a proper triangle, from which we can obtain the measurement. However, this is a necessary but not sufficient condition to form the proper triangle. In order that the measurement according to eq. (2) is correct the triangle must be isosceles and the vergence angle precisely known. This brings us to the second point of the error classification, i.e. the head calibration method (cameras alignment). The head calibration method should ensure the following two conditions: (i) Initially the two cameras are perfectly aligned on the horizontal plane of the head; (ii) they are perpendicular to the baseline ($\nu = 0$). If these conditions are fulfilled, then equally we can derive the previously described statement.

4 Experiments

In this section we describe several experiments carried out to measure the accuracy of the overall system. Cameras with nominative focal length 6mm lenses were used. For the measurement a perfect metallic cube of dimension 100mm was used. Several experiments were carried out in order to measure the sensitivity and the tolerance of the system to several kinds of errors, as described below. The experiments were carried out with human supervision, to avoid problems of choosing a wrong pixel due to image processing. However, an unsupervised experiment is also included at the end of this section to test the overall efficiency of the system. Analytical presentation of the experimental results can be found in [13].

a. Visual Errors

Let us consider first the visual errors due to horizontal displacement of the principal point. This case is graphical illustrated in Figure 4a. In this figure we have considered a displacement on the left camera. Taking into consideration the pin-hole model we can directly reduce the displacement in pixel into an angle as:

$$\varepsilon = \arctan(p_d CL / p_t f) \quad \textbf{(4)}$$

where ε is the reduced angle of the displacement, p_d is the displacement in pixels, p_t the total pixel number in one line and CL the chip length.

In Figure 4b the resulting error is shown. Due to the fact that $(p_d CL)/ p_t$ and f are negligible compared to the distance l' of the point to the left camera and the measured distance l, we can say that Figure 4b is a very good approximation. It is easily derived from that figure that:

$$l' = d \cos \nu / \sin(2\nu + \varepsilon) \quad \textbf{(5)}$$

which for ε=0 it is reduced to eq. (2).

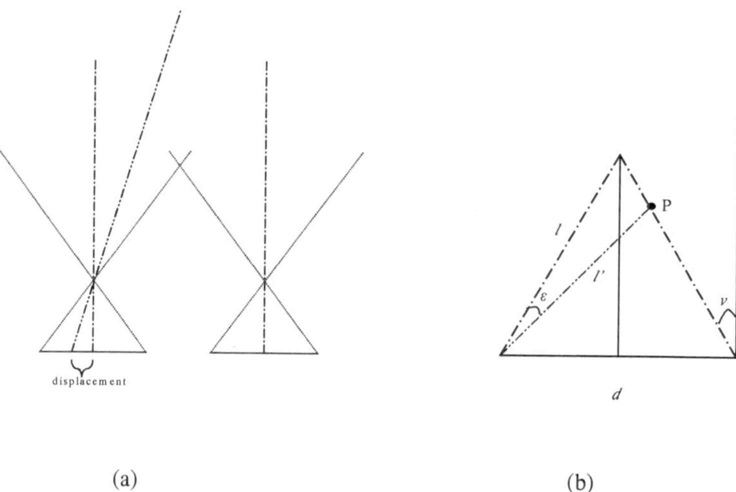

Fig. 4. (a) Horizontal displacement of the principal point and (b) the resulting error due to this displacement

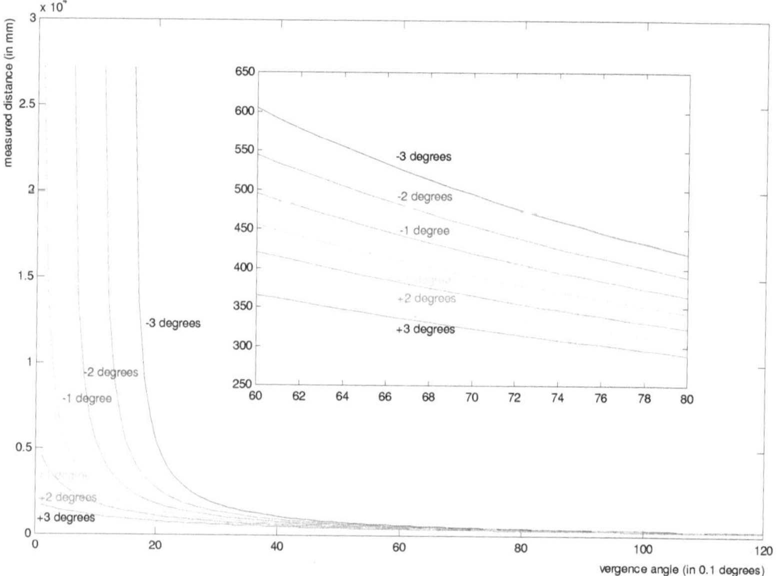

Fig. 5. The distance l' as a function of the vergence angle, for several displacement angles ε

A graphical illustration of the distance error, for several displacements, is provided in Figure 5. As shown a displacement of 1 degree, which corresponds to a displacement of about 16 pixels, may result in an error of several meters in the distance measurement, according to eq. (4). From eq. (3) it is obvious that this affects directly to the determination of the 3D coordinates of the point.

We evaluated this simulation by real measurements. The cube was positioned at a distance such that its center of mass was approximately 800mm from the center of the head. We inserted intentionally a displacement of –20, -10, 10 and 20 pixels at the principal point of the left camera. When the displacement is 0 the distance l was optimal and near to the correct one l'. However, for displacement different to 0 l was varying accordingly.

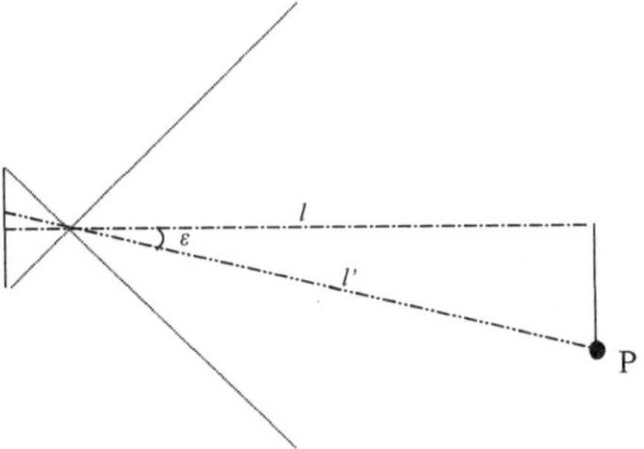

Fig. 6. Vertical displacement of the principal point and the resulting error.

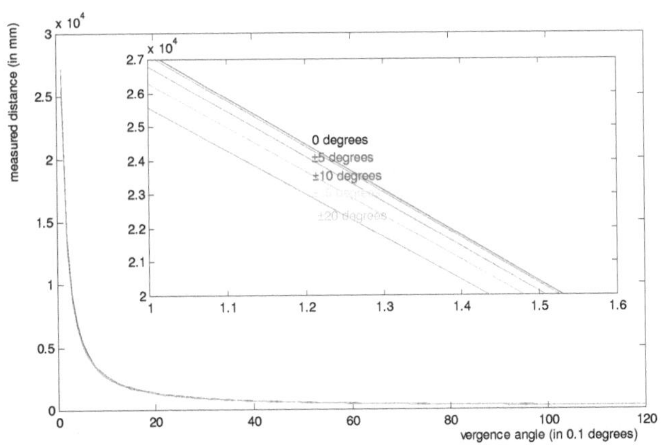

Fig. 7. The distance l' as a function of distance l and the displacement angle ε

Let us now consider a vertical displacement of the principal points. Because of the nature of the measurement method in [10], a triangular cannot be formed and, therefore, no measurement can be taken, unless the vertical displacement has taken place simultaneously in both cameras. In Figure 6 we present the profile of one of the two cameras with a vertical displacement corresponding to angle ε and for the other camera we consider exactly the same case. As one can see in this figure the actual distance l' is related with the measured distance l, as: $l' = l / \cos\varepsilon$. Intuitively it is apparent that the distance l' should not vary much with respect to l. This is also shown in Figure 7, where the curves for ε equal to 0, ±5, ±10, ±15 and ±20 degrees, respectively, are almost overlapping. In the top-right corner snapshot it is shown that for vergence angles from 0.1 to 0.16 degrees (about 54m to 34m distance) the error is not grater than 1.5m for displacement of ±20, which in our setup corresponds to about 380 pixels. Therefore, we can deduce that vertical displacements do not affect the accuracy of the system as much as the horizontal ones. The same effect was evaluating by our experimental setup.

b. Alignment Errors

Taking into consideration eqs. (2) and (3) we can easily derive that from the three head angles the most dominant in affecting the accuracy of the measurements is the vergence. The other two affect the absolute 3D coordinates of a point, but do not distort the shape of the measured object. Let us consider the case of Figure 8, where one of the two cameras declines from the perpendicular position. In that case, when the two cameras are verging the case is identical to the one presented in Figure 4b and studied with eq. (5) and Figure 5. Indeed, in our experiments we observed same effect as in the case of the horizontal displacement of the principal point, as was expected.

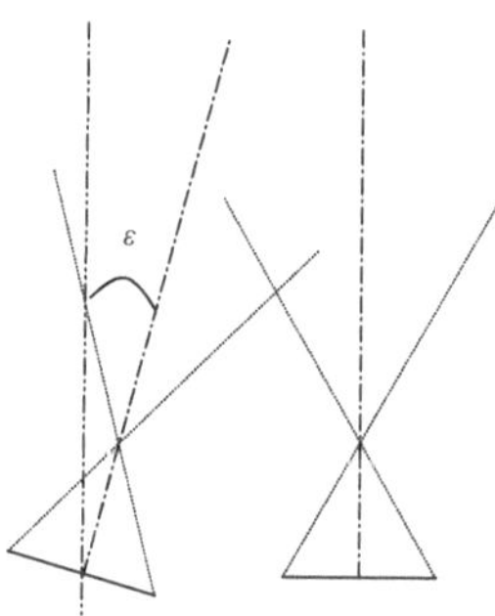

Fig. 8. Declination of the left camera from the perpendicular position.

c. Mechanical Errors

These are the errors due to transmission of the belts of the head. In our experiments the motor of each separate joint was moved by a constant angle, the encoders were read and the angle difference on the encoder was calculated. Images were taken before and after the movement. Any movement of any joint is directly measurable on the rectified image, with the value of the angle being:

$$\phi = \arctan(disp / f) \tag{6}$$

where *disp* is the disparity (horizontal or vertical, depending on the case) from one view to the other.

In order to extract eq. (6) we considered that the two lines, formed by the sensor and the observed point in the two consequent views, are parallel. This assumption can be made due to the fact that the sensor size and the focal length are insignificant compared to the distance of the observed point (about 4m). We measured the mechanical errors according to eq. (6) in our setup and we find them almost zero. Due to the fact that we did not apply a method to estimate the disparity with sub-pixel accuracy, it can be concluded that the error is mainly due to image quantization rather than the motors.

d. Overall System Efficiency

In order to test the accuracy of the whole system (the head employing image processing) we performed an unsupervised junction tracking. The cube was placed in several positions. The relative distances from one cube corner to the other were estimated as in the previous experiments. The tolerance that was set in order to take a measurement was ±1 pixel. The experiments resulted a maximum error of about 1.5cm at a distance of 1.1m. The main error factor in this case was false correspondence, as was observed during the experiment. The other crucial factor is the lighting conditions, due to which the tracked point may be several pixels away from the exact junction.

5 Conclusions

The main factors that affects the measurement with such an active vision stereo head are small variations in the vergence angle or small horizontal deviations of the principal point. On the other hand variations in pan and tilt and vertical deviations of the principal point do not significantly affect the measurement. When the image processing is used, i.e. unsupervised junction determination, other factors such as false correspondence or lighting conditions are also important. From the experiments carried out it can be deduced that the overall system can be very accurate in the absence of false correspondences, which may lead to large errors.

Acknowledgments. The work presented in this paper has been supported by the Esprit project ROBVISION (EP-28867).

References

1. Horn, B. K. P.: Robot Vision, MIT Press, Cambridge MA (1986)
2. Haggren H., Mattila, S.: 3-D Indoor Modeling from Videography, in Proc. SPIE, Vol. 3174, San Diego (1997) 14-20
3. Lim, H. S., Binford, T. O.: Curved Surface Reconstruction using Stereo Correspondence, in DARPA88, Cambridge, MA (1988) 809-819

4. Barnard, S. T., Thompson, W. B.: Disparity Analysis of Images. IEEE Trans. PAMI **2** (1980), 333-340
5. Mohan, R., Medioni, G., Nevatia, R.: Stereo Error Detection, Correction and Evaluation. IEEE Trans. PAMI **11** (1989) 13-120
6. Tsai, R. Y.: A Versatile Camera Calibration Technique for High-Accuracy 3D Machine Vision Metrology Using off-the Shelf TV Cameras and Lenses. IEEE J. Robotics and Automation **5** (1987)
7. Heikkila, J., Silven, O.: A Four-step Camera Calibration Procedure with Implicit Image Correction, in CVPR '97, San Juan, Puerto Rico (1997) 1106-1112
8. Zhao, W., Nandhakumar, N: Relative Influence of Camera Alignment Errors on 3D Stereoscopic Measurements, in ACCV95, Singapore (1995)
9. Zhao W., Nandhakumar, N: Effects of Camera Alignment Errors on Stereoscopic Depth Estimates. PR **29** (1996) 2115-2126
10. Gasteratos, A., Martinotti, R., Metta, G., Sandini, G.: Precise 3D Measurements with a High Resolution Stereo Head, in IWISPA 2000, Pula, Croatia (2000) 171-176
11. Vincze, M., Ayromloy, M., Beltran, C., Gasteratos, A., Hoffgaard, S., Madsen, O., Ponweiser W., Zillich, M.: A System to Navigate a Robot into a Ship Structure in Lecture Notes in Computer Science, Schiele, B., Sagerer, G., (Eds.), Vol. 2095, Springer-Verlag Berlin-Heidelberg (2001) 268-283
12. Gasteratos, A., Beltran, C., Metta, G., Sandini, G.: PRONTO: A System for Mobile Robot Navigation via CAD-Model Guidance, to appear in Microprocessors and Microsystems.
13. Gasteratos, A, Sandini, G.: On the Accuracy of the Eurohead. TR-2/00, LIRA-Lab, DIST, University of Genova, Genova, (2000)

Query Translation for Mediators over Ontology-Based Information Sources

Yannis Tzitzikas[1], Nicolas Spyratos[2*], and Panos Constantopoulos[1]

[1] Department of Computer Science, University of Crete, Greece, and
Institute of Computer Science, ICS-FORTH
{tzitzik, panos}@csi.forth.gr

[2] Laboratoire de Recherche en Informatique, Université de Paris-Sud, France
spyratos@lri.fr

Abstract. We propose a model for providing integrated and unified access to multiple information sources. Each source comprises: (a) an *ontology* i.e. a set of terms structured by a subsumption relation, and (b) a *database* that stores descriptions of objects using terms of the ontology. We assume that different sources may use different ontologies, i.e., different terminologies with terms that correspond to different natural languages or to different levels of granularity. Information integration is obtained through a mediator comprising two parts: (a) an *ontology*, and (b) a set of *articulations* to the sources, where an articulation to a source is a set of relationships between terms of the mediator and terms of that source. Information requests (queries) are addressed to the mediator whose task is to analyze each query into sub-queries, send them to the appropriate sources, then combine the results to answer the original query. We study the querying and answering process in this model and we focus on query translation between the mediator and the sources.

1 Introduction

The need for integrated and unified access to multiple information sources has stimulated the research on *mediators* (initially proposed in [1]). Roughly a mediator is a "secondary" information source aiming at providing a uniform interface to a number of underlying sources (which may be primary or secondary). Users submit queries expressed over the ontology of the mediator. Upon receiving a user query, the mediator has to query the underlying sources. This involves selecting the sources to be queried and formulating the query to be sent to each source. These tasks are accomplished, based on what the mediator "knows" about the underlying sources. Finally, the mediator has to appropriately combine the returned results and deliver the final answer to the user.

In this paper we consider information *sources* over a domain consisting of a denumerable set of objects. For example in the environment of the Web, the

---

* Work partially conducted while this author was visiting at the National Technical University of Athens, supported by the PENED/GGET project.

I.P. Vlahavas and C.D. Spyropoulos (Eds.): SETN 2002, LNAI 2308, pp. 423–436, 2002.

domain is the set of all Web pages, specifically, the set of all pointers to Web pages. Each source has an *ontology*, that is, a set of names, or *terms*, that are familiar to the users of the source, structured by a *subsumption* relation. In addition each source maintains a database storing objects that are of interest to its users. Specifically, each object in the database of a source is associated (indexed) with a description (conjunction of terms) over the ontology of that source. A user who looks for objects of interest can browse the ontology of a source until he reaches the desired objects, or he can query the source by submitting a boolean expression of terms. The source will then return the appropriate set of objects. Specifically, the general purpose catalogs of the Web, such as Yahoo! or Open Directory[1], the domain specific catalogs/gateways (e.g. for medicine, physics, tourism), as well as the personal bookmarks of the Web browsers can be considered as examples of such sources.

However, although several sources may carry information about the same domain, they usually employ different ontologies with terms that correspond to different natural languages, or to different levels of granularity, and so on. For example Figure 1 sketches graphically the ontologies of two sources S_1 and S_2 which provide access to electronic products. Now suppose that we want to provide unified access to the databases of these sources through an ontology such as the one shown in Figure 1.(c). A mediator is a system that can bridge these heterogeneities and provide a unified access to a set of such sources. Specifically, a mediator has an *ontology* with terminology and structuring that reflects the needs of its potential users, but does not maintain a database of objects. Instead, the mediator has a number of *articulations* to other sources. An articulation to a source is a set of relationships between the terms of the mediator and the terms of the source. These relationships are defined by the designer of the mediator. The mediator uses the articulations in order to translate queries over its own ontology to queries over the ontologies of the articulated sources. Figure 2 shows the general architecture of a mediator.

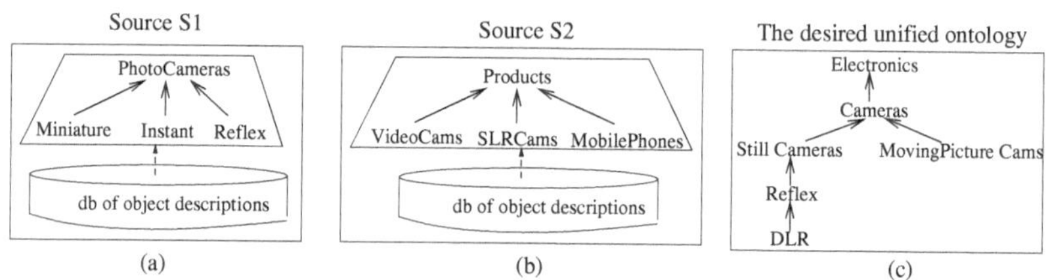

Fig. 1. Two sources providing access to electronic products and the desired unified ontology

In this paper we describe this mediator-based architecture and we present algorithms for source selection and query translation. The objective that governs these tasks is to minimize the "semantic difference" between the received query and the query finally answered by the mediator. Our approach can complement

[1] http://dmoz.org

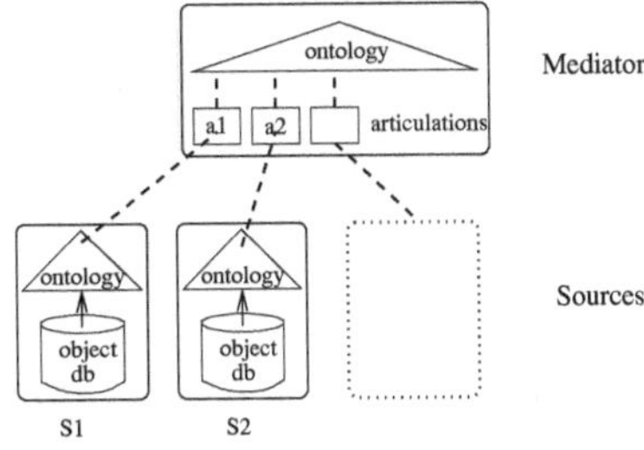

Fig. 2. The mediator architecture

mediators over relational databases so that to support approximate translations of values that are partially ordered. Another essential feature that distinguish our work is that our mediators can operate differently for those users (or information needs) that focus on recall and those that focus on precision. Our model can be used for defining user views over existing Web catalogs.

The paper is organized as follows: Section 2 describes the information sources, and Section 3 the mediators. Section 4 defines the query translation problem, and Section 5 presents the algorithms for translating queries. Finally, Section 6 discusses related work and concludes the paper.

2 The Information Sources

Let *Obj* denote the set of all objects of a domain (e.g. the set of all pointers to Web pages). Each source has an *ontology*, i.e. a pair $(T, \preceq)$ where T is a *terminology*, i.e. a set of names, or *terms*, and $\preceq$ is a *subsumption* relation over T, i.e. a reflexive and transitive relation over T. If a and b are terms of T, we say that a is *covered* or *subsumed* by b if $a \preceq b$; we also say that b *covers* or *subsumes* a, e.g. `Databases` $\preceq$ `Informatics`, `Canaries` $\preceq$ `Birds`. We write $a \sim b$ if both $a \preceq b$ and $b \preceq a$ hold, e.g., `Computer Science` $\sim$ `Informatics`. Note that $\sim$ is an equivalence relation over T and that $\preceq$ is a partial order over the equivalence classes of T.

In addition each source has a stored *interpretation* I of its terminology, i.e. a function $I : T \rightarrow 2^{Obj}$ that associates each term of T with a set of objects[2]. Figure 3 shows an example of a source.

Concerning queries, each source responds to queries over its own terminology:

Definition 1. Let T be a terminology. A *query* over T is any string derived by the following grammar, where t is a term of T: $q ::= t \mid q{\wedge}q' \mid q{\vee}q' \mid q{\wedge}\neg q' \mid (q)$. We will denote by Q_T the set of all queries over the terminology T.

Any interpretation I of T can be extended to an interpretation $\hat{I}$ of Q_T, as follows: $\hat{I}(q \wedge q') = \hat{I}(q) \cap \hat{I}(q')$, $\hat{I}(q \vee q') = \hat{I}(q) \cup \hat{I}(q')$, $\hat{I}(q \wedge \neg q') = \hat{I}(q) \setminus \hat{I}(q')$, $\hat{I}(t) = I(t)$. For simplicity, hereafter we shall use the symbol I to denote both

[2] We use the symbol 2^{Obj} to denote the power set of *Obj*.

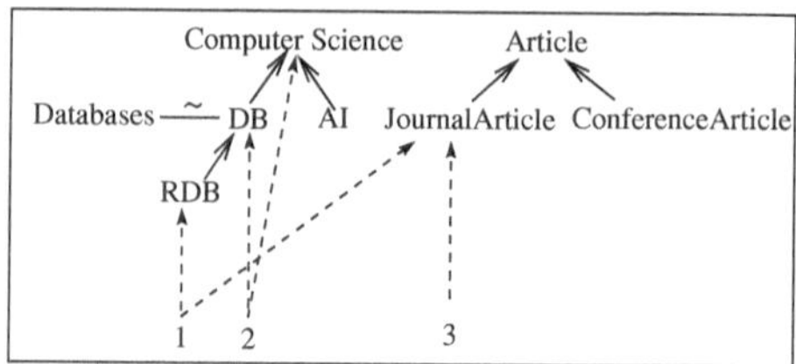

Fig. 3. Graphical representation of a source. Here the stored objects are denoted by the natural numbers 1,2 and 3, dashed oriented lines are used to connect each term t with the elements of $I(t)$, solid arrows indicate subsumption, and solid non-oriented lines equivalence.

the interpretation and its extension over queries. Given two interpretations I, I' of T, we call I less or equal than I', and we write $I \sqsubseteq I'$, if $I(t) \subseteq I'(t)$ for each term $t \in T$. Note that $\sqsubseteq$ is a partial order on interpretations.

Now, the interpretation that a source uses for answering queries must respect in some sense the structure of its ontology (i.e. the relation $\preceq$). For example, assume that a source has stored two sets of objects under the terms `Databases` and `AI`, and no objects under the term `Computer Science` - although the latter term subsumes the former two. However, such a stored interpretation is acceptable since we can "satisfy" $\preceq$ by defining the interpretation of `Computer Science` to be the union of the sets of objects associated with `Databases` and `AI`. In order to define this formally we introduce the notion of *model.*

Definition 2. An interpretation I of T is a *model* of $(T, \preceq)$ if for each t, t' in T, if $t \preceq t'$ then $I(t) \subseteq I(t')$.

Clearly, we can always extend an interpretation I to a model of $(T, \preceq)$, and we assume that each source answers queries from a model of its stored interpretation. However in order to respond to a query, a source must select one among several possible models, and as such we assume the minimal model which is greater than I, denoted by $\bar{I}$ (and it can be easily proved that there is always a unique minimal model). We shall refer to this model as the *answer model.* Thus if a source $[(T, \preceq), I]$ receives a query $q \in Q_T$ it returns the set of objects $\bar{I}(q)$.

For answering queries there are two distinct approaches. In the first approach the source computes and stores the answer model $\bar{I}$. However, whenever the ontology or the interpretation I changes, $\bar{I}$ must be appropriately updated. This requires an efficient method for handling updates since recomputing the whole $\bar{I}$ from scratch would be inefficient. In the second approach, only the interpretation I is stored, and whenever a query q is received the source computes and returns $\bar{I}(q)$. This evaluation is based on the (easily proved) proposition that for any $t \in T$: $\bar{I}(t) = \bigcup\{I(s) \mid s \preceq t\}$. However, evaluating $\bar{I}(t)$ in this manner requires computing the transitive closure of $\preceq$. More about the implementation and the inference mechanisms of a source can be found [2].

3 The Mediator

Suppose that we want to build a mediator M over a set of sources S_1,...,S_k. Even if all sources carry information about the same domain, they usually employ different ontologies, i.e. different terminologies with terms that correspond to different natural languages, or to different levels of granularity, and so on. A mediator M is a system that can bridge these heterogeneities and provide a unified access to a set of such sources. Specifically a mediator M has an ontology $(T, \preceq)$ with terminology and structuring that reflects the needs of its potential users. For achieving integration we enrich the mediator with a set of relationships that relate its terms with the terms of the sources. These relationships, or *articulations*, are defined by the designer of the mediator. Formally:

Definition 3. A mediator M over k sources $S_1=[(T_1, \preceq_1), I_1]$,..., $S_k=[(T_k, \preceq_k), I_k]$ consists of:
1) an ontology $(T, \preceq)$, and
2) a set of *articulations* a_i, one for each source S_i. Each a_i is a subsumption relation over $T \cup T_i$

For example, consider the sources S_1 and S_2 shown in Figure 4 and suppose that we want to provide access to these sources through a mediator M with ontology as shown this figure. For achieving integration we enrich the mediator with two articulations a_1 and a_2:

$$\begin{aligned} a_1 = \{&\texttt{PhotoCameras} \preceq \texttt{Cameras},\ \texttt{StillCameras} \preceq \texttt{PhotoCameras},\\ &\texttt{Miniature} \preceq \texttt{StillCameras},\ \texttt{Instant} \preceq \texttt{StillCameras},\\ &\texttt{Reflex}_1 \preceq \texttt{Reflex},\ \texttt{Reflex} \preceq \texttt{Reflex}_1\}\\ a_2 = \{&\texttt{Products} \preceq \texttt{Electronics},\ \texttt{SLRCams} \preceq \texttt{Reflex},\\ &\texttt{VideoCams} \preceq \texttt{MovingPictureCams},\ \texttt{MovingPictureCams} \preceq \texttt{VideoCams}\} \end{aligned}$$

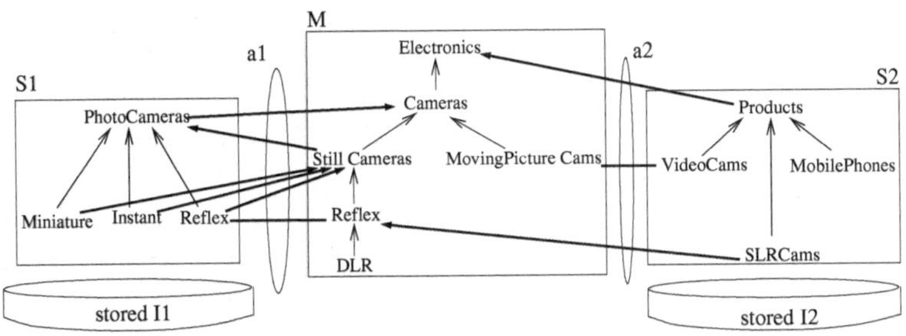

Fig. 4. A mediator over two catalogs of electronic products

3.1 The Answer Model of the Mediator

In this section we define the interpretation that M uses for answering queries. Given an articulation a_i, we will use R_i to denote those terms of T_i that appear in a_i (clearly $R_i \subseteq T_i$). Now, let $G = (T_G, \preceq_G)$ denote the ontology defined as follows:

$$T_G = T \cup R_1 \cup ... \cup R_k \quad \text{and} \quad \preceq_G = \preceq \cup\, a_1 \cup ... \cup a_k$$

Roughly, the terminology T_G is made up from the mediator terminology T augmented by the sets R_i of source terms that the mediator knows (through the articulations a_i), while the subsumption $\preceq_G$ is the mediator subsumption $\preceq$ augmented by the articulations a_i to the sources. Note that if two terms in two sources have the same name e.g. DB, then by default they are considered different ($\mathtt{DB}_i \not\sim \mathtt{DB}_j$). This is reasonable as the same term can have different interpretations (meanings) in different sources. Thus for every $i \neq j$ we assume $T_i \cap T_j = \emptyset$; and for every i we assume $T \cap T_i = \emptyset$. In this way we overcome the problems of homonyms. Two terms are considered equivalent, e.g. $\mathtt{DB}_i \sim_G \mathtt{DB}_j$, only if they belong to the same equivalence class of G, e.g. if there is a term $t \in T$ such that $t \sim_G \mathtt{DB}_i$ and $t \sim_G \mathtt{DB}_j$.

The interpretation that the mediator uses in answering queries is defined with respect to the ontology $G = (T_G, \preceq_G)$ just defined. We call *mediator interpretation* the function $I_G : T_G \to 2^{Obj}$ defined as follows:

$$I_G(t) = \begin{cases} \emptyset & \text{if } t \in T \\ \bar{I}_i(t) & \text{if } t \in R_i \end{cases}$$

Recall that $\bar{I}_i$ denotes the answer model of the source S_i. This means that the interpretation of a term t is empty if t belongs to the terminology of the mediator, otherwise it is the set of objects that will be returned if we query the source that owns the term t. We can now extend I_G to a model of G and by $\bar{I}_G$ we will denote the minimal model which is larger than I_G (which again is unique). Upon reception of a query q, the mediator returns $\bar{I}_G(q)$, i.e., $\bar{I}_G$ is the *answer model* of M. Figure 5.(a) shows an example of a mediator with two articulations, while the table of Figure 5.(b) shows the (current) answer models $\bar{I}_1$ and $\bar{I}_2$ of the sources S_1 and S_2, and the induced answer model $\bar{I}_G$ of the mediator M.

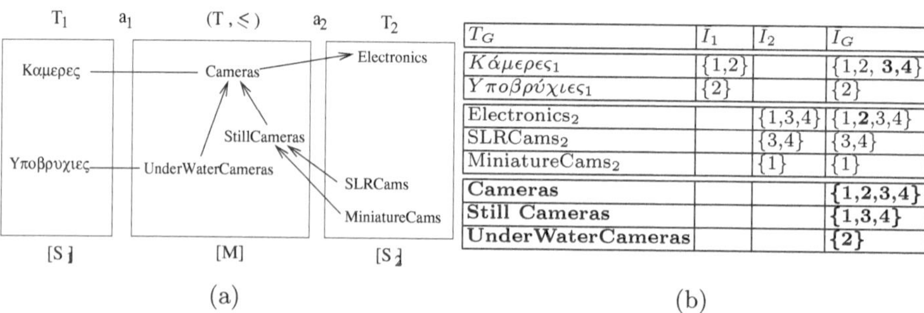

T_G	$\bar{I}_1$	$\bar{I}_2$	$\bar{I}_G$
$Κάμερες_1$	{1,2}		{1,2, **3,4**}
$Υποβρύχιες_1$	{2}		{2}
Electronics$_2$		{1,3,4}	{1,**2**,3,4}
SLRCams$_2$		{3,4}	{3,4}
MiniatureCams$_2$		{1}	{1}
Cameras			**{1,2,3,4}**
Still Cameras			**{1,3,4}**
UnderWaterCameras			**{2}**

(b)

Fig. 5. A mediator with two articulations to sources S_1 and S_2

3.2 Answering Queries at the Mediator

Answering queries at the mediator is done based on the answer model $\bar{I}_G$, and we can easily see that: $\bar{I}_G(t) = \bigcup\{I(s) \mid s \preceq_G t\}$. For example, suppose that the mediator shown in Figure 4 receives the query $q = \texttt{Cameras}$. The answer to this query is defined as follows:

$$\begin{aligned}
\bar{I}_G(\texttt{Cameras}) &= I_G(\texttt{Cameras}) \cup I_G(\texttt{StillCameras}) \cup I_G(\texttt{MovingPictureCams}) \cup \\
&\quad I_G(\texttt{Reflex}) \cup I_G(\texttt{DLR}) \cup I_G(\texttt{PhotoCameras}_1) \cup I_G(\texttt{Miniature}_1) \cup \\
&\quad I_G(\texttt{Instant}_1) \cup I_G(\texttt{Reflex}_1) \cup I_G(\texttt{VideoCams}_2) \cup I_G(\texttt{SLRCams}_2) \\
&= \emptyset \cup \emptyset \cup \emptyset \cup \emptyset \cup \emptyset \cup \\
&\quad \bar{I}_1(\texttt{PhotoCameras}_1) \cup \bar{I}_1(\texttt{Miniature}_1) \cup \bar{I}_1(\texttt{Instant}_1) \cup \bar{I}_1(\texttt{Reflex}_1) \cup \\
&\quad \bar{I}_2(\texttt{VideoCams}_2) \cup \bar{I}_2(\texttt{SLRCams}_2)
\end{aligned}$$

However query answering cannot be performed as in the individual sources, because the interpretation I_G is not stored at the mediator. For evaluating a query the mediator has to query the underlying sources and then to combine the returned answers. Suppose first that the query is just a term t of T. In order to evaluate $\bar{I}_G(t)$, the mediator has to retrieve from each source S_i the set of objects $\bigcup\{\ \bar{I}_i(s) \mid s \in R_i \text{ and } \ s \preceq_G t\}$. If we define

$$q_i(t) = \bigvee\{s \in R_i | s \preceq_G t\}$$

then for evaluating $\bar{I}_G(t)$ the mediator sends the query $q_i(t)$ to each source S_i and then it takes the union of the returned answers. That is:

$$\bar{I}_G(t) = \bigcup_{i=1..k} \bar{I}_i(q_i(t)) \tag{1}$$

In our example, we have:

$$\begin{aligned}
q_1(\texttt{Cameras}) &= \texttt{PhotoCameras}_1 \vee \texttt{Miniature}_1 \vee \texttt{Instant}_1 \vee \texttt{Reflex}_1 \\
q_2(\texttt{Cameras}) &= \texttt{VideoCams}_2 \vee \texttt{SLRCams}_2
\end{aligned}$$

Now, if the query q is not just a term of T then the mediator can evaluate the set $\bar{I}_G(q)$ by combining, through set operations, the interpretations of the terms that appear in q. This time, however, the evaluation presents certain problems as we will show next.

Consider, for simplicity, the case where M has decided to query only one particular source S_i. Since M will query only one source, it does not have to combine results from multiple sources. Instead, M just sends (at most) one query to S_i and then delivers the answer returned by S_i to the user. For simplicity hereafter we shall write S instead of S_i, and R instead of R_i. If M receives a query q over T, M actually sends a query q_R over R to the source S. The following question arises:

What is the relationship between the original query q and the query q_R with respect to the ontology G ?

Let us introduce a definition prior to answering this question. If q, q' are queries over G, we write $G \models q \preceq q'$, or $q \preceq_G q'$, if $I(q) \subseteq I(q')$ in every model I of G. Moreover, we write simply $q \preceq q'$ instead of $G \models q \preceq q'$, when G is understood. Two queries q, q' are called *equivalent*, denoted $q \sim q'$, if $q \preceq q'$ and $q' \preceq q$. Returning to our question, note that it may will be that $q \preceq q_R$, or $q_R \preceq q$, or both (i.e. $q_R \sim q$), or none of the three. If $q \preceq q_R$, we will call q_R *including*, if $q_R \preceq q$, we will call q_R *included*, and if $q \sim q_R$, we will call q_R *perfect*.

In the case where q is a single term $t \in T$, then the query q_R is actually the query $q_i(t) = \bigvee\{s \in R | s \preceq_G t\}$, and clearly $q_R \prec q$. For example consider the mediator shown in Figure 4 and assume only the source S_1. If $q = \texttt{Cameras}$ then $q_R = \texttt{PhotoCameras}_1 \vee \texttt{Miniature}_1 \vee \texttt{Instant}_1 \vee \texttt{Reflex}_1$. Clearly here we have $q_R \preceq q$, thus q_R is an included translation.

Let us now consider the query $q = \texttt{Cameras} \wedge \neg\texttt{DLR}$. Assume that we derive the query q_R by replacing each term t appearing in q by the query $q_1(t)$. This means that $q_R = q_1(\texttt{Cameras}) \wedge \neg q_1(\texttt{DLR}) =$ $(\texttt{PhotoCameras}_1 \vee \texttt{Miniature}_1 \vee \texttt{Instant}_1 \vee \texttt{Reflex}_1) \wedge \neg\ \epsilon$, where ϵ denotes the empty query and clearly $\bar{I}(\epsilon) = \emptyset$ in every source. Thus, the query finally answered is the query $\texttt{PhotoCameras}_1 \vee \texttt{Miniature}_1 \vee \texttt{Instant}_1 \vee \texttt{Reflex}_1$ and notice that this is not an included query, meaning that the answer returned by M may contain objects about DLR although the user does not want them. However, note that there is actually an included query, i.e the query $q'_R = (\texttt{PhotoCameras}_1 \vee \texttt{Miniature}_1 \vee \texttt{Instant}_1 \vee \texttt{Reflex}_1) \wedge \neg\texttt{Reflex}_1$, for which it holds: $q'_R \preceq q$, and which the mediator did not evaluate. This example shows that if we derive q_R by replacing each term appearing in q by the query $q_1(t)$, then we do not always get an included query. This problem is the subject of the subsequent section.

4 The Query Translation Problem

In this section we study the problem of *query translation*: how, for a given query q, the mediator can choose the "best" translation of q that can be answered by the underlying sources.

Roughly, among the many possible translations the mediator should select those with the "minimum" change of "semantics". Ideally, we want to find a query q_R "equivalent" to q, that is, a perfect translation. If a perfect translation is not possible, then the mediator should be able to compute the "biggest included" and the "smallest including" query, if any of these queries exist. The former is appropriate for those users (or information needs) that focus on *precision*, while the latter for those that focus on *recall*. For example consider the mediator shown in Figure 4 and assume that a user submits the query StillCameras. If the user is interested in precision, that is, if he does not want to retrieve objects which are not StillCameras, then he may prefer an answer to the query $\texttt{Miniature}_1 \vee \texttt{Instant}_1 \vee \texttt{Reflex}_1$. On the other hand, if the user is interested in recall, that is, if he does not want to miss objects which are StillCameras, then he may prefer the answer to the query $\texttt{PhotoCameras}_1$. Also note that a user interested in precision may ask an answer to the smallest including query, if the biggest included query yielded no results (e.g. if $q = \texttt{DLR}$), or if the query yielded less objects than those wanted.

Let us now define formally the criteria for identifying the preferred translations. Assume that M receives a query q (over T) and suppose that M has decided to query only one particular source S_i. For brevity we shall hereafter write S instead of S_i and R instead of R_i. Among the possibly many including translations of q we prefer the "*smallest*", i.e. the queries in the set $up(q, R)$ defined as follows:

$$up(q, R) = glb\{q_R \in Q_R \mid q \preceq q_R\}$$

Among the possibly many included translations of q we prefer the "*biggest*", i.e. the queries in the set $down(q, R)$ defined as follows:

$$down(q, R) = lub\{q_R \in Q_R \mid q_R \preceq q\}$$

If there is a query q_R such that $q_R \in up(q, R)$ and $q_R \in down(q, R)$, then $q \sim q_R$, thus q_R is a *perfect* translation.

Concerning including translations, we can easily see that the set $\{q_R \in Q_R | q \preceq q_R\}$ may be empty, (e.g. if $q = \texttt{Electronics}$ in Figure 4). If not empty then it is infinite and $glb\{q_R \in Q_R | q \preceq q_R\}$ exists, specifically, it is the set of queries equivalent to the query:

$$\bigwedge\{q_R \in Q_R | q \preceq q_R\}$$

Analogously, the set $\{q_R \in Q_R | q_R \preceq q\}$ may be empty (e.g. if $q = \texttt{DLR}$), but if not empty then $lub\{q_R \in Q_R | q_R \preceq q\}$ exists, specifically, it is the set of queries equivalent to the query:

$$\bigvee\{q_R \in Q_R | q_R \preceq q\}$$

In conclusion, given a query q over T we would like the mediator to be able to compute a query in $down(q, R)$, and a query in $up(q, R)$, if these exist.

Now assume that M receives a query q, and decides to query a *set* of sources S_1,...,S_k. This set can be the set of all sources, or it may be the set of those sources which are online currently, or it may be the set of sources that have been selected on the basis of some criterion or cost fuction. Recall that the mediator will return an answer which will be the combination of the answers of the queries sent to the underlying sources. Thus the answer of the mediator will be an answer to a query over R where $R = R_1 \cup ... \cup R_k$. This again raises the question about the relation between q and q_R, and, as in the single source case, we would like a q_R such that $q_R \sim q$, or $q_R \in down(q, R)$, or $q_R \in up(q, R)$. Thus in order to find the biggest included or the smallest including (or the perfect) translation of q, the mediator needs the same translation mechanism as in the single source case. The only difference is that here $R = R_1 \cup ... \cup R_k$.

5 Translating and Evaluating Queries

In this section we describe the algorithms for computing the *up* and *down* of a query. Hereafter we will use $up(q,R)$ to denote any query contained in the set $up(q,R)$, and $down(q,R)$ to denote any query contained in the set $down(q,R)$. Let us first consider the case where q is a single term $t \in T$. In this case one can easily see that

$$up(t,R) \sim \bigwedge\{r \in R | t \preceq r\} \quad \text{and} \quad down(t,R) \sim \bigvee\{r \in R | r \preceq t\}$$

The queries $up(t,R)$ and $down(t,R)$ can be derived by algorithms which traverse G and "collect" the appropriate terms of R. However if $\{r \in R | t \preceq r\} = \emptyset$ then the algorithm that derives $up(t,R)$ will return *Nil*. Analogously, if $\{r \in R | r \preceq t\} = \emptyset$ then the algorithm that derives $down(t,R)$ will return *Nill* too.

Let us now generalize to the general case where q is a query in Q_T. The following propositions allow us to derive the *up* and *down* of a query q, by synthesizing the *up* and *down* of the terms that appear in q. For brevity we shall write $up(q)$ (and $down(q)$) instead of $up(q,R)$ (and $down(q,R)$).

1. $up(q \wedge q') = up(q) \wedge up(q')$
2. $up(q \vee q') = up(q) \vee up(q')$
3. $up(q \wedge \neg q') = up(q) \wedge \neg down(q')$
4. $down(q \wedge q') = down(q) \wedge down(q')$
5. $down(q \vee q') = down(q) \vee down(q')$
6. $down(q \wedge \neg q') = down(q) \wedge \neg up(q')$

Thus in order to produce $down(q)$ or $up(q)$ the mediator parses the query q and composes the *up* or *down* of the terms that appear in q according to the above propositions. Due to limitations of space the proofs of these propositions are not included in this paper. Figure 6 gives some examples of translations where the elements of R are denoted by white circles.

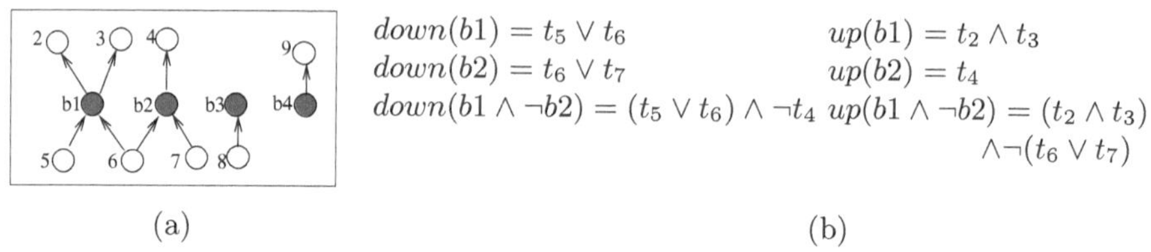

Fig. 6. Examples of translations

However, notice that we cannot derive the desired translated query if the *up* or *down* of one subterm of q is empty (*Nil*). Nevertheless, there are cases where we can overcome this problem, and for doing so we introduce the special symbols $\top$ and $\bot$. If for a term t, we have $up(t) = \emptyset$, then we set $up(t) = \top$, and if $down(t) = \emptyset$, then we set $down(t) = \bot$. However the query q_R that we want to construct should not contain any of these special symbols. We can reduce all or some of these symbols according to the following rules:

(a) Delete the substrings "$\wedge\top$" or "$\top\wedge$". Example: $up(b_1 \wedge b_3) = (t_2 \wedge t_3) \wedge \top = t_2 \wedge t_3$

(b) Delete the substrings "$\vee\bot$" or "$\bot\vee$" . Example: $down(b_1 \vee b_4) = (t_5 \vee t_6) \vee \bot = t_5 \vee t_6$

(c) Delete the substrings "$\wedge\neg\bot$" . Example: $up(b_2 \wedge \neg b_4) = t_4 \wedge \neg\bot = t_4$

So, the process for translating a query q consists of the following steps:

(1) Parse q and synthesize the *up* and *down* of the terms that appear in q using propositions 1 to 6, seen earlier. Let q_t be the resulting query.
(2) Delete the symbols $\top$ and $\bot$ that can be reduced using rules (a), (b) and (c) seen earlier. Let $q_{t'}$ be the resulting query.
(3) If $q_{t'}$ does not contain any of the symbols $\top$ and $\bot$ then $q_R = q_{t'}$, else $q_R = Nil$.

Below we give some examples of translations assuming the ontology of Figure 6.

$down(b3) = t_8$	$up(b3) = \top = Nil$
$down(b4) = \bot = Nil$	$up(b4) = t_9$
$down(b1 \wedge b3) = (t_5 \vee t_6) \wedge t_8$	$up(b1 \wedge b3) = (t_2 \wedge t_3) \wedge \top = t_2 \wedge t_3$
$down(b1 \wedge b4) = (t_5 \vee t_6) \wedge \bot = Nil$	$up(b1 \wedge b4) = (t_2 \wedge t_3) \wedge t_9$
$down(b1 \vee b4) = (t_5 \vee t_6) \vee \bot = t_5 \vee t_6$	$up(b1 \vee b4) = (t_2 \wedge t_3) \vee t_9$
$down(b3 \vee b4) = t_8 \vee \bot = t_8$	$up(b3 \vee b4) = \top \vee t_9 = Nil$
$down(b2 \wedge \neg b4) = (t_6 \vee t_7) \wedge \neg t_9$	$up(b2 \wedge \neg b4) = t_4 \wedge \neg\bot = t_4$
$down(b3 \wedge \neg b4) = t_8 \wedge \neg t_9$	$up(b3 \wedge \neg b4) = \top \wedge \neg\bot = Nil$

Let us now summarize how the mediator operates. Whenever the mediator receives a query q, at first it computes the translation $up(q)$ or $down(q)$ (according to the user's desire), then it evaluates each term that appears in the translated query (as described in section 3.2), and finally, it combines through set operations the obtained results in order to compute the final answer.

6 Related Work – Concluding Remarks

We proposed a model for building mediators over sources which index their objects using terms from ontologies. The ontologies that we consider although simple, they fit to the content-based organizational structure of Web catalogs and portals, keyword hierarchies and personal bookmarks. Besides most of the ontologies that are used for indexing and retrieving objects are term hierarchies ([3], [4], [5]). Concerning the functionality offered by our mediators, the objective that governs the selection of the sources to be queried (and the formulation of the queries to be sent to each source) is to minimize the "semantic difference" between the received query and the query finally answered by the mediator. We defined the desired translations and we described the algorithms for computing these translations.

The concept of mediator is not new. After the introduction of the mediator concept by Wiederhold [1], many different approaches have been proposed and developed in order to build mediators over relational databases (e.g. see

[6,7,8,9]), SGML documents (e.g. see [10]), information retrieval systems (e.g. see [11,12,13,14,15]) and Web-based sources (e.g. see [16,17]). The techniques for building relational mediators are appropriate for rendering the structural (schema) heterogeneities of the sources transparent to the users (e.g. see the systems TSIMMIS [18], [7], HERMES [19], Information Manifold [6]). Our work can complement these techniques so that to support approximate translations of values that are partially ordered. The difference with the approach presented in [20] is that in this approach the reasoning services for supporting translations have exponential complexity (it employs very expressive description logics), as opposed to the complexity of our mediators which is clearly polynomial. This is very important because usually the ontologies (e.g. those employed by Web catalogs) contain very large numbers of terms, e.g. the catalog of Open Directory contains 300.000 terms. Our work differs from other approaches that support approximate translations. The difference with [17] is that we also support negation in queries, while the difference with the system presented in [21], [22], is that the described system merges the ontologies of all underlying sources. We propose articulation instead of merging, because merging the ontologies of all underlying sources would introduce storage and performance overheads. In addition, full integration is a laborious task which in many cases does not pay-off because the integrated ontology becomes obsolete when the involved ontologies change.

An alternative approach for query translation which offers more operation modes is given in [23], while the optimization of query evaluation, i.e. the minimization of the number of queries that the mediator has to send to the sources in order to evaluate a user query, is described in [24].

One can easily see that our approach allows the users of the Web to define views over the existing Web catalogs: by defining a mediator the user can use his own terminology in order to access and query several Web catalogs, specifically those parts of the catalogs that is of interest to him. We plan to use our approach for building mediators over sources such as Google[3]. Google allows (1) browsing through the hierarchical catalog of Open Directory, and (2) searching through natural language queries. Using Google, one can first select a category, e.g. `Sciences/CS/DataStructures`, from the ontology of Open Directory and then submit a natural language query, e.g. "`Tree`". The search engine will compute the degree of relevance with respect to the natural language query, "`Tree`", only of those documents that fall in the category `Sciences/CS/DataStructures` in the catalog of Open Directory. A mediator over such sources will allow the user to use the ontology of the mediator in order to browse those parts of the catalogs that is of interest to him. Moreover he will be able to query the databases of these sources by natural language queries. However, this implies that the mediator will send two kinds of queries to the sources: queries evaluated over the catalog and queries which are evaluated over the contents of the pages. In this case, since each source will return an ordered set of objects, we also need a method (e.g. [14]) for fusing these orderings in order to derive the ordering to be delivered to the user.

[3] www.google.com

Acknowledgements. Many thanks to Anastasia Analyti for proof reading the paper, and to Agiolina Dellaporta.

References

1. G. Wiederhold. "Mediators in the Architecture of Future Information Systems". *IEEE Computer*, 25:38–49, 1992.
2. Yannis Tzitzikas, Nicolas Spyratos, and Panos Constantopoulos. "Deriving Valid Expressions from Ontology Definitions". In *11th European-Japanese Conference on Information Modelling and Knowledge Bases*, Maribor, Slovenia, May 2001.
3. Nicola Guarino. "Formal Ontology and Information Systems". In *Proceedings of FOIS'98*, Trento, Italy, June 1998. Amsterdam, IOS Press.
4. Deborah L. McGuinness. "Ontological Issues for Knowledge-Enhanced Search". In *Proceedings of FOIS'98*, Trento, Italy, June 1998. Amsterdam, IOS Press.
5. Alexander Pretschner. "Ontology Based Personalized Search". Master's thesis, Department of Electrical Engineering and Computer Science - University of Kansas, 1999.
6. Alon Y. Levy, Divesh Srivastava, and Thomas Kirk. "Data Model and Query Evaluation in Global Information Systems". *Journal of Intelligent Information Systems*, 5(2), 1995.
7. Hector García-Molina, Yannis Papakonstantinou, Dallan Quass, Anand Rajaraman, Yehoshua Sagiv, Jeffrey Ullman, Vasilis Vassalos, and Jennifer Widom. "The TSIMMIS Approach to Mediation: Data Models and Languages". In *Proceedings of IPSJ*, Tokyo, Japan, October 1994.
8. Hector García-Molina, Jeffrey D. Ullman, and Jennifer Widom. *"Database System Implementation"*, chapter 11. Prentice Hall, 2000.
9. R. Yerneni, Chen Li, H. García-Molina, and J.Ullman. "Computing capabilities of mediators". In *Proceedings of ACM SIGMOD'99*, Philadelphia, 1999.
10. Sophie Cluet, Claude Delobel, Jérôme Siméon, and Katarzyna Smaga. "Your mediators need data conversion!". In *Proceedings of the ACM SIGMOD International Conference on Management of Data*, 1998.
11. E. Vorhees, N. Gupta, and B. Johnson-Laird. "The Collection Fusion Problem". In *Proceedings of the Third Text Retrieval Conference (TREC-3)*, Gaithersburg, MD, 1995.
12. L. Gravano and H. García-Molina. "Generalizing GlOSS To Vector-Space Databases and Broker Hierarchies". In *Proc 21st VLDB Conf.*, Zurich, Switzerland, 1996.
13. Norbert Fuhr. "A Decision-Theoretic Approach to Database Selection in Networkded IR". *ACM Transactions on Information Systems*, 17(3), July 1999.
14. Yannis Tzitzikas. "Democratic Data Fusion for Information Retrieval Mediators". In *ACS/IEEE International Conference on Computer Systems and Applications*, Beirut, Lebanon, June 2001.
15. Henric Nottelmann and Norbert Fuhr. "MIND: An Architecture for Multimedia Information Retrieval in Federated Digital Libraries". In *DELOS Workshop on Interoperability in Digital Libraries*, Darmstadt, Germany, September 2001.
16. José Luis Ambite, Naveen Ashish, Greg Barish, Craig A. Knoblock, Steven Minton, Pragnesh J. Modi, Ion Muslea, Andrew Philpot, and Sheila Tejada. Ariadne: a system for constructing mediators for Internet sources. In *Proceedings of the ACM SIGMOD International Conference on Management of Data*, pages 561–563, 1998.

17. Chen-Chuan K. Chang and Héctor García-Molina. "Mind Your Vocabulary: Query Mapping Across Heterogeneous Information Sources". In *Proc. of the ACM SIGMOD*, pages 335–346, 1999.
18. Sudarshan Chawathe, Hector Garcia-Molina, Joachim Hammer, Kelly Ireland, Yannis Papakonstantinou, Jeffrey Ullman, and Jennifer Widom. "The TSIMMIS project: Integration of Heterogeneous Information Sources". In *Proceedings of IPSJ*, Tokyo, Japan, October 1994.
19. V. S. Subrahmanian, S. Adah, A. Brink, R. Emery, A. Rajput, R. Ross, T. Rogers, and C. Ward. "HERMES: A Heterogeneous Reasoning and Mediator System", 1996. (www.cs.umd.edu/projects/hermes/ overview/paper).
20. D. Calvanese, G. de Giacomo, M. Lenzerini, D. Nardi, and R. Rosati. "Description Logic Framework for Information Integration". In *Proceedings of the 6th Int. Conf. on the Principles of Knowledge Representation and Reasoning (KR-98)*, 1998.
21. E. Mena, V. Kashyap, A. Sheth, and A. Illarramendi. "OBSERVER: An Approach for Query Processing in Global Information Systems based on Interoperation across Preexisting Ontologies.". In *Proceedings of the First IFCIS International Conference on Cooperative Information Systems (CoopIS'96)*, Brussels, Belgium, June 1996. IEEE Computer Society Press.
22. Vipul Kashyap and Amit Sheth. "Semantic Heterogeneity in Global Information Systems: the Role of Metadata, Context and Ontologies ". In *Cooperative Information Systems: Trends and Directions*. Academic Press, 1998.
23. Yannis Tzitzikas, Nicolas Spyratos, and Panos Constantopoulos. "Mediators over Ontology-based Information Sources". In *Second International Conference on Web Information Systems Engineering, WISE 2001*, Kyoto, Japan, December 2001.
24. Yannis Tzitzikas, Nicolas Spyratos, and Panos Constantopoulos. "Mediators over Ontology-based Information Sources", December 2001. (submitted for publication in journal).

Intelligent Querying of Web Documents Using a Deductive XML Repository

Nick Bassiliades[1] and Ioannis P. Vlahavas

Dept. of Informatics
Aristotle University of Thessaloniki
54006 Thessaloniki, Greece
{nbassili,vlahavas}@csd.auth.gr

Abstract. In this paper, we present a deductive object-oriented database system, called X-DEVICE, which is used as a repository for XML documents. X-DEVICE employs a powerful rule-based query language for intelligently querying stored Web documents and data and publishing the results. XML documents are stored into the OODB by automatically mapping the DTD to an object schema. XML elements are treated either as objects or attributes based on their complexity, without loosing the relative order of elements in the original document. The rule-based language features second-order logic syntax, generalized path and ordering expressions, which greatly facilitate the querying of recursive, tree-structured XML data and the construction of XML trees as query results. All the extended features of the rule language are translated through the use of object metadata into a set of first-order deductive rules that are efficiently executed against the object database using the system's basic inference engine.

1 Introduction

Currently information is captured and exchanged over Internet through HTML pages, without any conceptual structure. XML is the currently proposed standard for structured or even semi-structured information exchange over the Internet. However, the maintenance of the information captured from XML documents is essential for building long-lasting applications of industrial strength. The enormous research and development of DBMSs should be re-used for managing XML data with the minimum of effort. There already exist several proposals on methodologies for storing, retrieving and managing XML data stored in relational and object databases.

Another important aspect of managing XML is effective and efficient querying and publishing these data on the Web. There have been several query language proposals ([11], [2], [9]) for XML data. Furthermore, recently the XML Query Working Group [22] of the WWW consortium issued a working draft proposing XQuery, an amalgamation of the ideas present in most of the proposed XML query languages of the literature. Most of them have functional nature and use path-based syntax. Some of them, including XQuery, have also borrowed an SQL-like declarative syntax, which

[1] Supported by a post-doctoral scholarship from the Greek Foundation of State Scholarships (F.S.S. - I.K.Y.).

I.P. Vlahavas and C.D. Spyropoulos (Eds.): SETN 2002, LNAI 2308, pp. 437–448, 2002.

is popular among users. Some of the problems relating to most of the above approaches is the lack of a comprehensible data model, a simple query algebra and query optimization techniques. There are proposals for a data model and a query algebra for XQuery, however it is not yet clear how these will lead to efficient data storage and query optimization.

In this paper, we present a deductive object-oriented database system, called X-DEVICE, which is used as a repository for XML documents. X-DEVICE employs a powerful rule-based query language for intelligently querying stored Web documents and data and publishing the results. X-DEVICE is an extension of the active object-oriented knowledge base system DEVICE ([4]). DEVICE integrates deductive and production rules into an active OODB with event-driven rules [13], on top of Prolog. This is achieved by translating the condition of each declarative rule into a set of complex events that is used as a discrimination network to incrementally match the condition against the database.

In X-DEVICE, XML documents are stored into the OODB by automatically mapping the DTD to an object schema. XML elements are treated either as objects or attributes based on their complexity, without loosing the relative order of elements in the original document. The rule-based language features second-order logic syntax, generalized path and ordering expressions, which greatly facilitate the querying of recursive, tree-structured XML data and the construction of XML trees as query results. All the extended features of the rule language are translated through the use of object metadata into a set of first-order deductive rules that are efficiently executed against the object database using the system's basic inference engine. The formal translation procedures can be found in [21]. In this paper we mainly focus on the use of the X-DEVICE query language on intelligently querying XML documents.

The advantages of using a logic-based query language for XML data come from the well-understood mathematical properties and the declarative character of such languages, which both allow the use of advanced optimization techniques, such as magic-sets. Furthermore, X-DEVICE compared to the XQuery functional query language has a more high-level, declarative syntax that allows users to express everything that XQuery can express, in a more compact and comprehensible way, with the powerful addition of general path expressions, which is due to fixpoint recursion and second-order variables.

The outline of this paper is as follows: in section 2 we overview some of the related work done in the area of storing and querying XML data in databases. Section 3 describes the mapping of XML data onto the object data model of X-DEVICE. Section 4 presents the X-DEVICE deductive rule language for querying XML data through several examples. Finally, Section 5 concludes this paper and discusses future work.

2 Related Work

There exist two major approaches to manage and query XML documents. The first approach uses special purpose query engines and repositories for semi-structured data (e.g. [18], [19]). These database systems are built from scratch for the specific purpose of storing and querying XML documents. This approach, however, has two potential disadvantages. Firstly, native XML database systems do not harness the sophisticated storage and query capability already provided by existing database systems. Secondly, native XML database systems do not allow users to query seamlessly across XML documents and other (structured) data stored in database systems. The second approach captures and manages XML data within the data models of either relational ([20], [12]) or object databases ([23], [10]). Our system, X-DEVICE, stores XML data into the object database ADAM [14], because XML documents have by nature a hierarchical structure that better fits the object model. Also references between or within documents play an important role and are a perfect match for the notion of object in the object model.

When XML data are mapped onto relations there are some limitations: First, the relational model does not support set-valued attributes, therefore when an element has a multiply-occurring sub-element, the sub-element is made into a separate relation and the relationship between the element and the sub-element is represented by a foreign key. The querying and reconstruction of the XML document requires the use of "expensive" SQL joins between the element and sub-element relations. On the other hand, object databases support list attributes; therefore, references to sub-elements can be stored with the parent element and retrieved in a non-expensive way. Furthermore, relations are sets with no ordering among their rows or columns. However, in XML documents ordering of elements is important, especially when they contain textual information (e.g. books, articles, Web page contents).

Object database approaches usually treat element types as classes and elements as objects. Attributes of elements are treated as text attributes, while the relationships between elements and their children are treated as object referencing attributes. There are some variations of the above schema between the various approaches. For example, in [1] and [23] all the elements are treated as objects, even if their content is just PCDATA, i.e. mere strings. However, such a mapping requires a lot of classes and objects, which wastes space and degrades performance, because queries have to traverse more objects than actually needed. In X-DEVICE this problem is avoided by mapping PCDATA elements to text attributes.

Another major issue that must be addressed by any mapping scheme is the handling of the flexible and irregular schema of XML documents that includes alternation elements. Some mapping schemes, such as [20], avoid handling alternation by using some simplification rules, which transform alternation to sequence of optional elements: `(X|Y)->(X?,Y?)`. However, some of these transformation do not preserve equivalence between the original and the simplified document. In the previous simplification rule, for example, the element declaration on the left-hand side accepts either an `X` or a `Y` element, while the right-hand side element declaration allows also a sequence of both elements or the absence of both.

Alternation is handled by union types in [1], which required extensions to the core object database O_2. This approach is efficient, however it is not compatible with the ODMG standard and cannot easily be applied in other object database system. In X-DEVICE instead of implementing a union type, we have emulated it using a special type of system-generated class that its behavior does not allow more than one of its attributes to have a value. Furthermore, the parent-element class hosts aliases for this system generated class, so that path resolution is facilitated.

Logic has been used before for querying semi-structured documents in F-Logic/FLORID [16] and its successor XPathLog/LoPix [17]. The semantics of these languages are defined by bottom-up evaluation, similarly to X-DEVICE, however negation has not been implemented. Both languages can express multiple views on

XML data; XPathLog, in addition, can export the view in the form of an XML document, much like X-DEVICE. However, none of the languages offers incremental maintenance of materialized views when XML base data get updated, as X-DEVICE does.

Both F-Logic and XPathLog are based on a graph data model, which can be considered as a schema-less object-oriented (or rather frame-based) data model. However, alternation of elements is not supported. Furthermore, F-Logic does not preserve the order of XML elements. Both languages support path expressions and variables; XPathLog is based on the XPath language syntax [22]. The main advantage of both languages is that, similar to X-DEVICE, they can have variables in the place of element and/or attribute names, allowing the user to query without an exact knowledge of the underlying schema. However, none of the languages supports generalized path expressions that X-DEVICE does, which compromises their usefulness as semi-structured query languages.

3 The Object Model of XML Data

The X-DEVICE system translates DTD definitions into an object database schema that includes classes and attributes, while XML data are translated into objects. Generated classes and objects are stored within the underlying object-oriented database ADAM ([14]). The mapping of a DTD element to the object data model depends on the following:

- If an element has PCDATA content (without any attributes), it is represented as a string attribute of the class of its parent element node. The name of the attribute is the same as the name of the element.
- If an element has either a) children elements, or b) attributes, then it is represented as a class that is an instance of the `xml_seq` meta-class. The attributes of the class include both the attributes of the element and the children elements. The types of the attributes of the class are determined as follows:
  - Simple character children elements and element attributes correspond to object attributes of string type. Attributes are distinguished from children elements through the `att_lst` meta-attribute.
  - Children elements that are represented as objects correspond to object reference attributes.

The order of children elements is handled outside the standard OODB model by providing a meta-attribute (`elem_ord`) for the class of the element that specifies the correct ordering of the children elements. This meta-attribute is used when (either whole or a part of) the original XML document is reconstructed and returned to the user. The query language also uses it, as it will be shown later.

Alternation is also handled outside the standard OODB model by creating a new class for each alternation of elements, which is an instance of the `xml_alt` meta-class and it is given a system-generated unique name. The attributes of this class are determined by the elements that participate in the alternation. The structure of an alternation class may seem similar to a normal element class, however the behavior of alternation objects is different, because they must have a value for exactly one of the attributes specified in the class.

The mapping of the multiple occurrence operators, such as "star" (*), etc, are handled through multi-valued and optional/mandatory attributes of the object data model. The order of children element occurrences is important for XML documents, therefore the multi-valued attributes are implemented as lists and not as sets.

Due to space limitations, examples of OODB schemata that are generated using our mapping scheme cannot be presented here, but can be found in [21].

4 The Deductive XML Query Language

X-DEVICE queries are transformed into the basic DEVICE rule language and are executed using the system's basic inference engine. The query results are returned to the user in the form of an XML document. The deductive rule language of X-DEVICE supports constructs and operators for traversing and querying tree-structured XML data, which are implemented using second-order logic syntax (i.e. variables can range over class and attribute names) that have also been used to integrate heterogeneous schemata [5]. These XML-aware constructs are translated into a combination of a) a set of first-order logic deductive rules, and/or b) a set of production rules that their conditions query the meta-classes of the OODB, they instantiate the second-order variables, and they dynamically generate first-order deductive rules.

Throughout this section, we will demonstrate the use of X-DEVICE for querying Web documents in XML format using examples taken from the “TEXT” XML Query Use Case proposed by the XML Query Working Group ([22]). This use case is based on company profiles and a set of news documents which contain data for mergers, acquisitions, etc. Given a company, the use case illustrates several different queries for searching text in news documents and different ways of providing query results by matching the information from the company profile and the content of the news items. The X-DEVICE object schema for this case can be found in [21].

In this section, we give a brief overview of the X-DEVICE deductive rule language. More details about DEVICE and X-DEVICE can be found in [4] and [6]. The general algorithms for the translation of the various XML-aware constructs to first-order logic can be found in [21]. Here, due to space limitations, we will present only few translation cases, so that the reader can have an idea of the process.

4.1 First-Order Deductive Query Language

In X-DEVICE, deductive rules are composed of condition and conclusion, whereas the condition defines a pattern of objects to be matched over the database and the conclusion is a derived class template that defines the objects that should be in the database when the condition is true. The following rule defines that an object with attribute `partner` with value `P` exists in class `partner_of_xyz` if there is an object with OID `C` in class `company` with an attribute `name='XYZ Ltd'` and an attribute `partners` which points to an object of class `partners` which in turn has an attribute `partner` with value `P`.

```
if C@company(name='XYZ Ltd',partner.partners ∋ P)
then partner_of_xyz(partner:P)
```

Class `partner_of_xyz` is a derived class, i.e. a class whose instances are derived from deductive rules. Only one derived class template is allowed at the THEN-part (head) of a deductive rule. However, there can exist many rules with the same derived class at the head. The final set of derived objects is a union of the objects derived by the two rules. For example, the transitive closure of the set of direct and indirect partners of company 'XYZ Ltd' is completed with the following (recursive) rule:

```
if P@partner_of_xyz(partner:P1) and
   C@company(name=P1,partner.partners ∋ P2)
then partner_of_xyz(partner:P2)
```

The syntax of such a rule language is first-order. Variables can appear in front of class names (e.g. `P`, `C`), denoting OIDs of instances of the class, and inside the brackets (e.g. `P1`, `P2`), denoting attribute values (i.e. object references and simple values, such as integers, strings, etc). Variables are instantiated through the ':' operator when the corresponding attribute is single-valued, and the '∋' operator when the corresponding attribute is multi-valued. Since multi-valued attributes are implemented through lists (ordered sequences) the '∋' operator guarantees that the instantiation of variables is done in the predetermined order stored inside the list. Conditions also can contain comparisons between attribute values, constants and variables. Negation is also allowed if rules are safe, i.e. variables that appear in the conclusion must also appear at least once inside a non-negated condition.

The path expressions are composed using dots between the "steps", which are attributes of the interconnected objects, which represent XML document elements. The innermost attribute should be an attribute of "departing" class, i.e. `partners` is an attribute of class `company`. Moving to the left, attributes belong to classes that represent their predecessor attributes. Notice the right-to-left order of attributes, contrary to the common C-like dot notation, that stress out the functional data model origins of the underlying ADAM OODB [14]. Under this interpretation the chained "dotted" attributes can be seen as function compositions.

A query is executed by submitting the set of stratified rules (or logic program) to the system, which translates them into active rules and activates the basic events to detect changes at base data. Data are forwarded to the rule processor through a discrimination network (much alike in a production system fashion). Rules are executed with fixpoint semantics (semi-naive evaluation), i.e. rule processing terminates when no more new derivations can be made. Derived objects are materialized and are either maintained after the query is over or discarded on user's demand. X-DEVICE also supports production rules, which have at the THEN-part one or more actions expressed in the procedural language of the underlying OODB.

The main advantage of the X-DEVICE system is its extensibility that allows the easy integration of new rule types as well as transparent extensions and improvements of the rule matching and execution phases. The current system implementation includes deductive rules for maintaining derived and aggregate attributes. Among the optimizations of the rule condition matching is the use of a RETE-like discrimination network, extended with re-ordering of condition elements, for reducing time complexity and virtual-hybrid memories, for reducing space complexity [3]. Furthermore, set-oriented rule execution can be used for minimizing the number of inference cycles (and time) for large data sets [4].

4.2 Generalized Path Expressions

X-DEVICE supports several types of path expressions into rule conditions. The previous example demonstrated the simplest case, where all the steps of the path are known. Another case in path expressions is when the number of steps in the path is determined, but the exact step name is not. In this case, a variable is used instead of an attribute name. This is demonstrated by the following example, which searches for companies that contain in any of their immediate (PCDATA) children elements a specified string.

```
if C@company(A $ 'XYZ')
then a_xyz_comp(company:list(C))
```

The ($) operator searches its right-hand-side argument (string 'XYZ') inside its left-hand-side argument (a string attribute A). The list(C) construct in the rule conclusion denotes that the attribute company of the derived class a_xyz_comp is an attribute whose value is calculated by the aggregate function list. This function collects all the instantiations of the variable C (since many companies can contain the string 'XYZ' in any of their string attributes) and stores them under a strict order into the multi-valued attribute company. More details about the implementation of aggregate functions in X-DEVICE can be found in [4].

Variable A is in the place of an attribute name, therefore it is a second-order variable, since it ranges over a set of attributes, and attributes are sets of things (attribute values). Deductive rules that contain second-order variables are always translated into a set of rules whose second-order variable has been instantiated with a constant. This is achieved by generating production rules, which query the meta-classes of the OODB, instantiate the second-order variables, and generate deductive rules with constants instead of second-order variables [5]. The above rule is translated as follows:

```
if company@xml_seq(elem_order ∋ A)
then new_rule('if C@company(A $ 'XYZ')
               then a_xyz_comp(company:list(C))')
     => deductive_rule
```

Notice that variable A is now a first-order variable in the condition of the production rule, while the deductive rule generated by the action of the production rule has A instantiated. The above rule will actually produce as many deductive rules, as many attribute names there are in class company. The result consists of the union of the results of all the deductive rules. Notice that optimized execution of multiple such deductive rules is guaranteed by the compact discrimination network that is produced by the underlying DEVICE system.

The most interesting case of path expressions is when some part of the path is unknown, regarding both the number and the names of intermediate steps. This is handled in X-DEVICE by using the "star" (*) operator in place of an attribute name. Such path expressions are called "generalized". The previous example can be re-written using the "star" (*) operator as:

```
if C@company(* $ 'XYZ')
then a_xyz_comp(company:list(C))
```

However, the semantics of the above query are significantly different, since now the search for the `'XYZ'` string is not done only at the immediate children elements of `company`, but on any element of the XML sub-tree that starts from the `company` element.

4.3 Ordering Expressions

X-DEVICE supports expressions that query an XML tree based on the ordering of elements. The following query, taken from the "TEXT" XML Query Use Cases in [22], demonstrates X-DEVICE's absolute numeric ordering expressions.

TEXT Case - Q5. *For each news item that is relevant to the "Gorilla Corp", create an "item summary" element. The content of the item summary is the content of the title, date, and first paragraph of the news item, separated by periods. A news item is relevant if the name of the company is mentioned anywhere within the content of the news item.* This query is expressed in X-DEVICE as:

```
if N@news_item(*.content $ 'Gorilla Corp',
               par.content ∍1 PAR, title:T, date:D)
then item_summary(title:T,date:D,par:PAR)
```

The $\ni_1$ operator (a shortcut notation for the $\ni_{=1}$ operator) is an absolute numeric ordering expression that returns the first element of the corresponding list-attribute. More such ordering expressions in X-DEVICE exist for every possible position inside a multi-valued attribute [6]. The ordering expression part of the above rule is translated as follows:

```
if N@news_item(*.content $ 'Gorilla Corp',
               par.content ∍ XX1, title:T, date:D)
then tmp_elem1(tmp_var1:T,tmp_var2:D,tmp_obj:list(XX1))

if XX3@tmp_elem1(tmp_var1:T,tmp_var2:D,tmp_obj:XX1) and
   prolog{select_sub_list('='(1),XX1,XX2)}
then tmp_elem2(tmp_var1:T,tmp_var2:D,tmp_obj:XX2)

if XX1@tmp_elem2(tmp_var1:T,tmp_var2:D,tmp_obj ∍ PAR)
then item_summary(title:T,date:D,par:PAR)
```

The first rule collects all the paragraphs that satisfy the condition, the second rule isolates a sub-list of all the paragraphs that satisfy the ordering expression (through the use of a Prolog goal), and the third rule actually iterates over all qualifying results. Using Prolog goals in the rule condition, the system can be extended with several new features. However these features are outside of the deductive rule language and, therefore, cannot be optimized.

4.4 Exporting Results

So far, only the querying of existing XML documents through deductive rules has been discussed. However, it is important that the results of a query can be exported as an XML document. This can be performed in X-DEVICE by using some directives around the conclusion of a rule that defines the top-level element of the result document. When the rule processing procedure terminates, X-DEVICE employs an algorithm that begins with the top-level element designated with one of these directives and navigates recursively all the referenced classes constructing a result in the form of an XML tree-like document [6].

The following example demonstrates how XML documents (and DTDs) are constructed in X-DEVICE for exporting them as results.

TEXT Case - Q6. *Find news items where two company names and some form of the word "acquire" appear in the title or in the same sentence in one of the paragraphs. A company name is defined as the content of a <name>, <partner>, or <competitor> element within a <company> element.* This query is expressed in X-DEVICE as the following logic program:

```
R1: if C@company(name:N)
    then company_names(name:N)
R2: if C@company(partner.partners ∋ N)
    then company_names(name:N)
R3: if C@company(competitor.competitors ∋ N)
    then company_names(name:N)
R4: if C1@company_names(name:N1) and
       C2@company_names(name:N2\=N1) and
       N@news_item(title:T) and
       prolog{cont_in_same_sentence(T,N1,N2,'acquire')}
    then result(news_item:list(N))
R5: if C1@company_names(name:N1) and
       C2@company_names(name:N2\=N1) and
       N@news_item(par.content ∋ P) and
       prolog{cont_in_same_sentence(P,N1,N2,'acquire')}
    then xml_result(result(news_item:list(N)))
```

Rules `R1` to `R3`, in the above program, iterate over all company elements, their partners and competitors and store their names in the auxiliary class `company_names`. Notice that the same company name is not stored twice because the semantics of derived classes require that not two objects with exactly the same attribute values should exist [4]. Rules `R4` an `R5` take the Cartesian product of all identified company names and try to establish an acquisition relationship between them either in the title or in any of the paragraphs of a news item. This is achieved through the use of `cont_in_same_sentence/4`, a user-defined Prolog predicate.

The keyword `xml_result` is a directive that indicates to the query processor that the encapsulated derived class (`result`) is the answer to the query. This is especially important when the query consists of multiple rules, as the above example. Notice that although both `R4` and `R5` rules refer to the derived class `result`, only one of them contains the `xml_result` directive. However, this is not a strict language rule; it does not matter if several rules contain the `xml_result` or any other result directive ([6]), as long as the following constraints are satisfied:

- Only one type of result directive is allowed in the same query.
- Only one derived class is allowed at the result.

In order to build an XML tree as a query result, the objects that correspond to the elements must be constructed incrementally in a bottom-up fashion, i.e. first the simple elements that are towards the leaves of the tree are generated and then they are combined into more complex elements towards the root of the tree. Another way to generate an XML tree as a result is to include in the result parts of the (or even the whole) original XML document, as it is the case in the current example. The above query produces a tree-structured XML document, with the following DTD:

```
<!DOCTYPE result [
   <!ELEMENT result (news_item*)>
   <!ELEMENT new_item ...]>
```

Notice how the `list` aggregate function is used to construct XML elements with multiple children. The definition for the `news_item` element is exactly the one found at the original XML document of the “TEXT” XML Query Use Case in [22].

The following is an example of “building” an XML result from scratch.

TEXT Case - Q2. *Find news items where the “Foo Corp” company and one or more of its partners are mentioned in the same paragraph and/or title. List each news item by its title and date.* This query is expressed in X-DEVICE as follows:

```
if C@company(name='Foo Corp',partner.partners ∋ P) and
   N@news_item(title:T $ 'Foo Corp' & $ P,date:D)
then news_item1(title:T,date:D)

if C@company(name='Foo Corp',partner.partners ∋ P) and
   N@news_item(*.par.content $ 'Foo Corp' & $ P,
               title:T, date:D)
then xml_result(news_item1(title:T,date:D))
```

The ‘`&`’ operator denotes conjunction of attribute-testing conditions. For example, in the first rule the `title` attribute should contain both the string ‘`Foo Corp`’ and a string `P` that represents a partner of the above company. Also notice that an attribute can be simultaneously tested and unified with a variable (`title:T`).

The DTD for the above query is:

```
<!DOCTYPE news_item1 [
   <!ELEMENT news_item1 (title, date)>
   <!ELEMENT title (#PCDATA)>
   <!ELEMENT date (#PCDATA)>   ]>
```

The structure of the `title` and `date` elements is automatically determined by the type of the `T` and `D` variables, respectively. Notice that the result generates a class/element `news_item1`, because the class/element `news_item` already exists.

5 Conclusions and Future Work

In this paper, we have considered how XML-formatted Web documents can be intelligently queried and managed using the deductive object-oriented database system X-DEVICE. This has been achieved by storing the XML documents into an OODB through automatic mapping of the schema of the XML document (DTD) to an object schema and storing XML elements as database objects. Our approach maps elements either as objects or attributes based on the complexity of the elements of the DTD, without loosing the relative order of elements in the original document.

Furthermore, X-DEVICE features a deductive rule query language for expressing queries over the stored XML data. The deductive rule language has certain constructs (such as second-order variables, generalized path expressions and ordering expressions) for traversing tree-structured data that were implemented by translating them into first-order deductive rules. The translation scheme is mainly based on the querying of meta-data (meta-classes) about database objects. Comparing X-DEVICE with other XML query languages (e.g. XQuery) seems that the high-level, declarative syntax of X-DEVICE allows users to express everything that XQuery can express, in a more compact and comprehensible way, with the powerful addition of generalized path expressions, fixpoint recursion and second-order variables.

Users can also express complex XML document views using X-DEVICE, a fact that can greatly facilitate customizing information for e-commerce and/or e-learning [7]. Furthermore, the X-DEVICE system offers an inference engine that supports multiple knowledge representation formalisms (deductive, production, active rules, as well as structured objects), which can play an important role as an infrastructure for the impending Semantic Web. Production rules can also be used for updating an XML document inside the OODB, a feature not yet touched upon the XQuery initiative. However, the study of using production rules for updating XML documents is outside the scope of this paper and is a topic of future research.

Among our plans for further developing X-DEVICE is the definition of an XML-compliant syntax for the rule/query language based on the upcoming RuleML initiative [8]. Furthermore, we plan to extend the current mapping scheme to documents that comply with XML Schema.

References

[1] Abiteboul S., Cluet S., Christophides V., Milo T., Moerkotte G., Siméon J., Querying Documents in Object Databases, Int. J. on Digital Libraries, 1(1): 5-19 (1997)

[2] Abiteboul S., Quass D., McHugh J., Widom J., and Wiener J.L., The Lorel Query Language for Semistructured Data, *Int. Journal on Digital Libraries*, 1(1), pp. 68-88, 1997.

[3] Bassiliades N. and Vlahavas I., "Processing Production Rules in DEVICE, an Active Knowledge Base System", *Data & Knowledge Engineering*, 24(2), pp. 117-155, 1997.

[4] Bassiliades N., Vlahavas I., and Elmagarmid A.K., E-DEVICE: An extensible active knowledge base system with multiple rule type support, *IEEE TKDE*, 12(5), 824-844, 2000.

[5] Bassiliades N., Vlahavas I., Elmagarmid A.K., and Houstis E.N., "InterBaseKB: Integrating a Knowledge Base System with a Multidatabase System for Data Warehousing," *IEEE TKDE*, (to appear) 2002.

[6] Bassiliades N., Vlahavas I., Sampson D., Using Logic for Querying XML Data, to appear in *Web-powered Databases*, Taniar D., Rahayu W. (eds.), Idea Group Publishing, 2002.
[7] Bassiliades N., Kokkoras F., Vlahavas I., Sampson D., An Intelligent Educational Metadata Repository, to appear in *Intelligent Systems, Techniques and Applications*, Leondes C.T. (ed.), CRC Press, 2002.
[8] Boley H., Tabet S. and Wagner G., Design Rationale of RuleML: A Markup Language for Semantic Web Rules, Int. Semantic Web Working Symposium, 2001, pp. 381-402.
[9] Chamberlin D., Robie J., and Florescu D., Quilt: an XML Query Language for Heterogeneous Data Sources, *Int. Workshop WebDB*, pp. 53-62, 2000.
[10] Chung T.-S., Park S., Han S.-Y., and Kim H.-J., Extracting Object-Oriented Database Schemas from XML DTDs Using Inheritance, *Proc. 2nd Int. Conf. EC-Web 2001*, Munich, Germany, 2001, LNCS 2115, pp. 49-59.
[11] Deutsch A., Fernandez M., Florescu D., Levy A., and Suciu D., A Query Language for XML, *WWW8 / Computer Networks*, 31(11-16), pp. 1155-1169, 1999.
[12] Deutsch A., Fernandez M.F., Suciu D., Storing Semistructured Data with STORED, *ACM SIGMOD Conf.*, pp. 431-442, 1999.
[13] Diaz O., Jaime A., EXACT: An Extensible Approach to Active Object-Oriented Databases, *VLDB Journal*, 6(4), pp. 282-295, 1997.
[14] Gray P.M.D., Kulkarni K.G., and Paton N.W., *Object-Oriented Databases, A Semantic Data Model Approach*, Prentice Hall, London, 1992.
[15] Lakshmanan L.V.S., Sadri F., Subramanian I. N., A Declarative Language for Querying and Restructuring the WEB. RIDE-NDS 1996: 12-21
[16] Ludäscher B., Himmeröder R., Lausen G., May W., Christian Schlepphorst, Managing Semistructured Data with FLORID: A Deductive Object-Oriented Perspective, *Information Systems*, Vol. 23, No 8, 1998, 589-613.
[17] May W.: XPathLog: A Declarative, Native XML Data Manipulation Language. IDEAS 2001: 123-128
[18] McHugh J., Abiteboul S., Goldman R., Quass D., Widom J., Lore: A Database Management System for Semistructured Data, *ACM SIGMOD Record*, 26(3), pp. 54-66, 1997.
[19] Naughton J., et al, The Niagara Internet Query System, *IEEE Data Eng. Bulletin*, 24(2), June 2001, 27-33.
[20] Shanmugasundaram J., Tufte K., Zhang C., He G., DeWitt D.J., and Naughton J.F., "Relational Databases for Querying XML Documents: Limitations and Opportunities," *Int Conf. VLDB*, pp. 302-314, 1999.
[21] X-DEVICE, http://www.csd.auth.gr/~lpis/systems/x-device.html
[22] XML Query Working Group, http://www.w3.org/XML/Query
[23] Yeh C.-L., A Logic Programming Approach to Supporting the Entries of XML Documents in an Object Database, *Int. Workshop PADL*, pp. 278-292, 2000.

Roles in Collaborative Activity

Ioannis Partsakoulakis and George Vouros

Department of Information and Communication Systems
School of Sciences University of the Aegean 83200, Karlovassi, Samos
{jpar,georgev}@aegean.gr

Abstract. Cooperative activity involves collaboration and communication. Through the stages of collaboration, agents may play different roles either for performing domain tasks, or for forming decisions concerning the collaborative activity itself. Collaboration and communication can be enhanced if dependencies between agents' intentions are captured. Role-specification is expected to be a vital factor towards this goal. This is evidenced by roles' importance in many implemented systems. Agents' coordination, plan monitoring and re-planning in these systems rely on contextual information and agents' roles. However, there is not an implemented generic agent architecture that realizes the importance of roles for flexible cooperative activity. This paper shows how the ICAGENT development framework has been evolved to support cooperative activity through representing and reasoning about multi-role recipes.

1 Introduction

In the last few years, due to the increased degree of complexity in domains where the role of intelligent systems is foreseen and the need to employ systems in complex, dynamic and unpredictable environments, there is a great interest in building multi-agent systems where (homogeneous or heterogeneous) agents are collaborating and communicating towards achieving a shared objective. Examples of multi-agent systems with advanced cooperative abilities can be met in real-time, non-deterministic and dynamic environments such as in the RoboCup-Rescue [3] and RoboSoccer [9,10] domains, as well as in multi-robot space explorations, battlefield simulations [15,14] and information integration [13]. In these cases, due to agents' actions interferences and dependencies, agents must be able to coordinate their actions and communicate effectively in all stages of the cooperative activity.

Generic models for collaborative activity such as the SharedPlans model, the Joint Intentions and Joint Responsibility models [1,4,6,7] provide the principles that underpin social activity and reasoning, and describe the necessary constructs for defining cooperative and individual behaviour of agents in social contexts. Intentions play a major role in these models and drive agents to (a) commit to bring about a particular state of affairs, (b) organize and perform appropriate actions within the overall context of action in a coherent and consistent manner and (c) contact means-end reasoning for working the low-level details of their actions.

I.P. Vlahavas and C.D. Spyropoulos (Eds.): SETN 2002, LNAI 2308, pp. 449–460, 2002.

Implemented systems [12,6,15,5], aim to make explicit the cooperation model upon which agents' behaviour is based. The objective is to provide flexibility towards solving problems related to [6] "how individual agents should behave when carrying out their local activities in the overall context of action", "how the joint action may come unstuck", "how problems with the joint action can be repaired", "how individuals should act towards their fellow team members when problems arise" and "how agents should re-organize their local activity in response to problems with the joint action". Major issues of concern are the following: (a) Coordinating agents' activity towards coherent group action, (b) reducing the amount of communication messages exchanged between agents, and (c) communicating the necessary amount of information at the appropriate time point, so that effective coordination to be achieved.

To address these concerns, implemented systems, driven by the high-level cooperation models that they implement, employ constructs and methods such as the intentional context, common recipes [6], fixed organizations with discrete roles interchanged among agents [11], and dynamic assignment of agents to pre-specified roles in conjunction with plan monitoring and repair [15]. The aim is to provide the means for systems to track the mental state of individual agents participating in the cooperative activity in a coherent and integrated way. Although the importance for the employment of roles and contextual information is well evidenced in implemented systems, there is not an implemented generic agent architecture that provides the full range of facilities for collaboration and communication provided by common recipes and roles.

The objective of this paper is to report on the evolution of the ICAGENT agent development framework, that employs the SharedPlans model, to support cooperative activity through representing and reasoning about multi-role recipes.

The paper is structured as follows: Section 2 motivates our work by presenting previous approaches related to the employment of roles in cooperative activity. Section 3 briefly presents the ICAGENT agent development framework and describes its evolution towards representing and exploiting multi-role recipes for cooperative activity. Finally, section 4 concludes the paper with remarks and future work.

2 Motivation and Previous Work

Collaborative activity comprises the phases of recognition, in which an agent identifies the potential for collaboration, team formation, in which the agent solicits assistance, plan formation, in which the newly formed team attempts to construct an agreed shared plan, and finally execution, in which members of the team try to achieve the objectives they have committed [16].

It is during team formation that a set of agents shares an intention to achieve an action. Each action is realized by one or more alternative recipes. Recipes comprise conditions for being selected, applicability conditions and, as far as complex actions are concerned - actions that need further planning and refinement - the recipe specifies a sequence of sub-actions that the agent must perform for completing the plan. A *role* is a specification of a subset of actions that an individual or a team undertakes in the context of a recipe.

For instance, teaching a course, which with no doubt is a complex action, requires careful planning. This means that agents shall form intentions towards their common goal and choose a recipe that achieves courses' objectives in the required context. The context comprises the curriculum in which the course is being taught, the time available for the course, restrictions on the way it shall be examined, the specific programme in which it is being taught. The selected recipe may involve two roles: One for the lecturer and one for the teaching assistant. Each agent has its own responsibilities during cooperative activity: Each one must perform its local activities in the overall context of action, must inform the other in case he/she is not able to perform its role in the context of the joint activity, shall try to provide the necessary resources for the joint task to be performed successfully, and shall try to re-organize the overall activity in case there is any problem with the joint action.

Distinct, well-defined and clear roles, which are motivated in the context of the overall activity, provide agents with information about activities' interdependencies, activities' coordination and communication requirements. For instance, in case the lecturer in our teaching scenario fails to achieve its weakly task, then it must inform the teaching assistant about this failure, since the weakly task of the latter depends on the task of the former. This is evidenced by interdependencies[1] between actions in roles. The assistant, exhibiting helpful behaviour must either perform the task, or in case this is not possible, the team must re-plan its overall activity for the next weeks. However, the teaching assistant must not perform its individual activity, as it would do in case the lecturer had performed its task successfully.

It must be noticed that in case a recipe involves two or more roles, it does not mean that it is necessarily a multi-agent recipe: In case there is not a teaching assistant with the necessary abilities, and if the lecturer's commitments allow, he/she may also be assigned the role of the teaching assistant. In this case the recipe would be performed, as it would be a single-agent recipe.

On the other hand, in case more agents could be employed in the respective roles, for instance, experts in specific areas could give lectures, or assistants - each with a given specialty - provide teaching assistance, then each role may have been filled with a team of agents. In this case, sub teams must cooperate and contact means-end analysis towards performing a single role. This leads to a dynamic organization, in the sense that cooperating agents, or sub-teams of agents, are assigned roles depending on needs and availability, resulting in a hierarchy of roles that is formed in parallel to the joint plan.

According to the above, it is conjectured that roles' specifications in the context of recipes must provide great flexibility for the agents to build teams and cooperate towards achieving their common objectives. Specifically, roles must

[1] Such an interdepedency can be a common parameter, or a temporal relation between actions.

a. Specify the actions that an individual or a team must undertake in the context of a recipe,
b. Facilitate agents to decide whether a recipe shall be utilised as a single or as a multi-agent recipe,
c. Allow agents to decide on the best way for filling roles and performing actions in an arbitrary level of detail. This may result in building dynamic organizations in the sense specified above,
d. Facilitate agents to coordinate their activities during planning and execution, by capturing actions interdependencies,
e. Provide support for effective agents communication, reducing the amount of communication messages and communicating the necessary information. This can be achieved by inferring roles interdependencies from role specifications.

As it is already pointed in section 1, the need for roles and contextual information is well evidenced in implemented systems. However, there is not an implemented agent architecture that provides the full range of facilities for collaboration and communication provided by commonly agreed recipes and roles. The only known system that allows agent developers to specify roles in conjunction with plans is STEAM [15]. The developer has to specify three key aspects of a team of collaborating agents: A team organization hierarchy, a team reactive plan hierarchy and assignments of agents to execute plans. The latter is done by assigning the roles in the organization hierarchy to plans, and then assigning agents to roles by exploiting only agents' capabilities. Agents do not exploit contextual information for this assignment. This is justified by the use of reactive plans: Agents do not deliberate whether they should be committed to an action by reconciling their intentions and desires. Consequently, whether an operator is a team operator or an individual operator is dynamically determined only by agents' capabilities. Developers specify domain-dependent coordination constraints for agents assigned to roles, while domain independent ones are inferred from roles specifications. Role specifications are used mainly for plan performance monitoring and re-planning.

In [5] recipes are specified to be either single or multi-agent. The number of agents in multi-agent recipes is fixed. In this case, variables in recipes represent certain agents. In GRATE* [6], the organizer of the cooperative activity agrees on a common recipe with other team members, and decides which part of the recipe can undertake and which part is going to delegate to other agents. Each agent adopts one or more recipe actions. In GRATE* there are no roles defined in conjunction with recipes. Roles are dynamically identified and assigned to agents by the organizer who exploits the temporal relations between actions. Furthermore, agents are not able to plan in an arbitrary level of detail (planning reaches only the second level). This prohibits agents from planning and building dynamic organization hierarchies at an arbitrary level of detail.

This paper evolves the ICAgent framework for developing cooperative agents, by providing an enhanced version of recipes that contain role specifications. Roles dynamically define organizational relationships among agents.

Our aim is to provide agents with the necessary flexibility for solving complex problems in dynamic and unpredictable environments in cooperation with other agents, through the definition of multi-role recipes. Agents, depending on context and their mental state may deliberate about role assignment, or be reactively assigned to roles. Therefore, the role, and consequently the task assignment, is done in a flexible way.

3 The Multi-agent Tileworld Domain

The Multi-Agent Tileworld (MAT) [2] is an abstract, dynamic, simulated environment, with embedded agents, developed to support controlled experimentation with agents in dynamic environments.

As it is shown in figure 1, MAT is a chessboard like environment with empty squares, obstacles, holes and agents. Each agent is a unit square with the ability to move in all directions, except diagonally, by one square per move. Holes and obstacles are also unit squares that appear and disappear randomly. Obstacles and tiles have varying weights. Each agent is able to carry tiles whose weight is less than a maximum weight. The expected time for a tile to disappear (TTL) is known and the goal is to fill as many holes as possible in the minimum time.

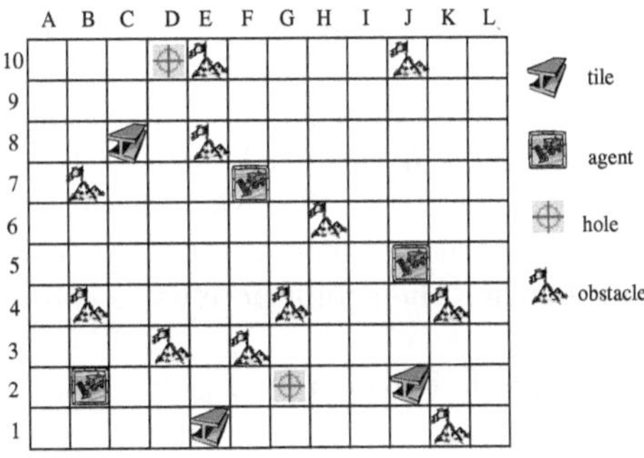

Fig. 1. The MA-Tileworld domain

To show the importance of roles in the cooperative activity, let us consider the following scenario: Assume that agent in 7F desires to fill the hole in 10D. The agent is not able to load tile 8C by himself and the other tiles are too far: The cost associated with these tiles is two high compared to the cost associated with 8C. In this case the agent should check the potential for collaboration. Agent in 7F should ask for the help of other known agents in the MAT in order to load the desired tile. Assume that agent in 2B is able to load 8C. Having agreed on the principle for joint action, the two agents (7F and 2B) must find a common recipe towards the desired state. To collaborate effectively, it is not enough for the agents to commit to a common recipe. Agents must also commit to specific roles in the context of the common recipe. For instance, the action of loading the tile 8C shall be done by the agent with the corresponding capability, while the action of putting the tile to the corresponding hole shall be done by the originator agent 7F. However, both agents have to move to square 8C. In case any of the agents fails to perform its role successfully, the other must exhibit helpful behaviour, making the best for the completion of their shared activity.

Having agreed on a common recipe and being committed to specific roles in the context of this recipe, agents have already decided that the recipe shall be utilised as a multi-agent recipe.

Proceeding deliberatively, agents decide on the best way for filling roles: Each agent reconciles roles' conditions and restrictions imposed by their common recipe, with constraints holding in its individual context of action and with further desires and commitments it may hold. In case more than one agents fill a recipe role (for instance many agents may help loading the tile), this drives the system to contact further planning, making the roles of these agents discrete. This results in building dynamic organizations in the sense specified above. Agents may also proceed reactively. In this case they do not reconcile the intentions to perform some roles with other intentions and desires they may hold, but they just check the capabilities each role requires.

Having committed to specific roles, agents coordinate their activities by means of actions interdependencies. For instance, agents shall meet in a specific square in the MAT. In case agent 2B arrives first at the meeting point, gets the tile and waits for the agent 7F to arrive there. On the contrary, if agent 7F arrives first, it waits for the other to get there and pick the tile. The context of roles' performance is also crucial for agents' cooperation: In case agents' roles are in the context of a recipe for filling a hole, agent 2B shall wait for the agent 7F to fill the hole, until it knows that their shared activity has been performed successfully. However, in case agents have committed to roles in the context of a recipe for loading a tile, then their joint activity is completed when the agent 7F has the tile been loaded.

In case any of the agents fails to perform its role successfully, it must communicate to the other its failure, as well as any information needed for the other to proceed. For instance, the failure of any agent to perform its role may lead the other to seek for alternative partner(s) or alternative recipes. Furthermore, roles help agents interpret each others' actions: the agent in 7F can interpret the motion of the agent in 2B towards their meeting point.

4 ICAGENT Framework and Multi-role Recipe Specification

As already pointed, this paper evolves the ICAGENT generic framework towards the representation and exploitation of multi-role recipes for agents' coordination and communication. ICAGENT allows for the development of agents that reason about their plans and balance between deliberation and reaction. Key issues towards this aim are the following:

- Equip agents with advanced plan management tasks, so that agents are able to balance between reaction and deliberation.
- Provide a clear distinction between deliberation and reaction in terms of agents' reasoning tasks and management of agents' mental state. Agents may contact "careful" planning (deliberation) by reconciling desires and intentions.
- Provide an explicit and an as detailed as possible representation of agents' mental state. Agents utilize a comprehensive set of mental attitudes based on the SharedPlans model for cooperation.

Key points for the evolution of ICAGENT towards our aim are the following:

- Specification of the multi-role recipe structure
- Extension of agents' reasoning tasks and plan management abilities for deliberating and reacting in a collaborative setting by exploiting multi-role recipes.
- Exploitation of roles' interdependencies for effective agents' coordination and communication.

As figure 2 shows, the ICAGENT overall architecture comprises two units: the Deliberation Control Unit (DCU) and the Plan Elaboration and Realization Control Unit (PERCU). These units, as well as the perception module consult and update agent's knowledge base.

Based on this architecture, an agent monitors its environment via the perception module and updates its beliefs about the environment. The term environment denotes the external, physical or simulated, environment as well as the mental attitudes of other agents acting in the environment. Although the perception module can be quite sophisticated, involving planning and multi-modal perception, this paper assumes that the agent, somehow, is aware of everything occurring in its environment.

The agent recognizes situations and forms desires to perform actions. While the agent may have many and possibly conflicting desires, depending on the situation at a specific time point, it must decide which action to pursue and whether it shall elaborate its plan towards that action reactively or deliberatively. Depending on whether the agent reacts or deliberates, it commits to the corresponding action, or it reconciles its desires with its intentions, reasoning about the relative strength of conflicting actions, about the strength of its commitments and its desires, and about the overall context of action.

As already noted, each action is realized by one or more alternative recipes. During plan formation, the agent selects relevant recipes, tests for their applicability and adds them in the overall plan. In this way, the agent constructs a hierarchical plan. This plan, augmented with constraints that must hold during plan formation and execution (e.g. preconditions of recipes) is referred as the context of action. Elaborating a plan, the agent reaches basic-level actions (i.e., actions that may be performed directly in the environment) and decides whether these actions shall be performed at the current time point, interleaving

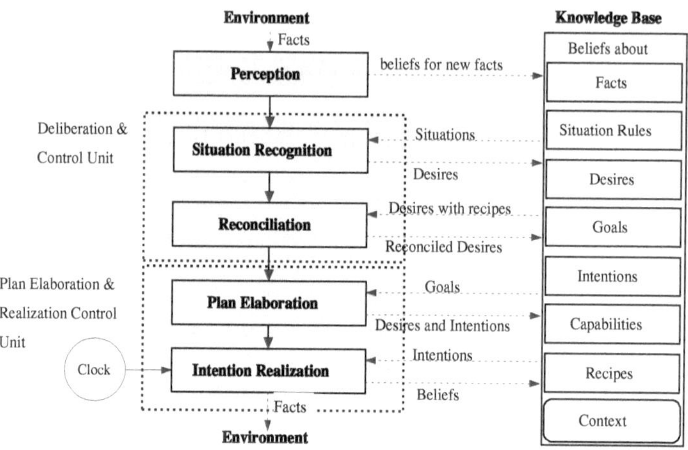

Fig. 2. The ICAGENT Architecture

planning with execution, or whether their execution shall be postponed until it has completed the corresponding part of the plan.

The structure and content of the resources depicted in figure 2, as well as the function of the individual modules are described in detail in [8].

4.1 The Recipe Structure

A recipe has the structure: `rec(action,recId,mntlCond,mode,type(recType, interleave),capConstr,cConstr,actionList,effects)` where:

- `action`, describes the action that the recipe realizes and has the form: `actionName(time,actionArgument`$_1$`,actionArgument`$_2$`,...)` where `time` is the time point that the action will be performed. Action arguments are either constants or variables. Variables are instantiated by checking the `mntlCond` constituent of the recipe, or during recipe selection.
- `recId` is an id for the recipe.
- `mntlCond` is a list of logical propositions. Each proposition specifies conditions for a certain role and combines mental attitudes using and, or and not logical connectives. The general form of the mental condition is: `[roleid`$_1$`: logicalProp`$_1$`,roleid`$_2$`:logicalProp`$_2$`,...]`, where `roleid`$_i$ is a list of role names.
- `mode` has the form: `[roleid`$_1$`:mode`$_1$`,roleid`$_2$`:mode`$_2$`,...]` where `mode`$_i$ has the form: `mode(BMntlCond,Behaviour)`. `BMntlCond` is a logical proposition and `Behaviour` is a variable that is instantiated to a, possibly empty, list of check directives that involve features that must be checked during reconciliation. It is this feature that enables each agent to balance between reactive and deliberative behaviour.

- `recType` is used to distinguish among domain recipes and communication protocols.
- `interleave` is a true/false variable. If true, then the agent interleaves planning with execution. Otherwise, the agent constructs the full plan for the corresponding action (either reactively or deliberatively) and executes the resulting plan afterwards. This argument is specified either by the agent developer or it is instantiated by checking the mental conditions of the recipe.
- `capConstr` stands for capability constraints and is a list that represents constraints that should hold during performance/reconciliation of roles. The list has the following form: $\texttt{[roleid}_1\texttt{:capConstr}_1\texttt{,roleid}_2\texttt{:capConstr}_2\texttt{,...]}$. $\texttt{capConstr}_i$ comprises a logical proposition that combines agent mental attitudes using and, or and not logical connectives.
- `cConstr` stands for contextual constraints. This is a list that represents constraints that should be maintained when the agent plans deliberatively towards actions under some specified role. The list has the following form: $\texttt{[roleid}_1\texttt{:conConstr}_1\texttt{,roleid}_2\texttt{:conConstr}_2\texttt{,...]}$. $\texttt{conConstr}_i$ is a logical proposition that combines agent mental attitudes using and, or and not logical connectives. Capability and contextual constraints constitute the preconditions of some recipe role and determine the applicability of that role and consequently the applicability of the recipe.
- `actionList` is a list that specifies the sequence of sub-actions that each role must perform. If this list is empty, then the action is a basic level one. The form of the action list is as follows: $\texttt{[roleid}_1\texttt{:action}_1\texttt{,roleid}_2\texttt{:action}_2\texttt{,...]}$. Agents that have committed to a role must perform the appropriate actions.
- `effects` is a list of facts that each agent that performs a role in the context of the recipe shall believe, when the plan towards `action` has been performed successfully.

4.2 Recipe's Example and Exploitation

Below is the definition of a recipe for the MAT, which is used in order one agent to get the tile that is closer to it. This recipe comprises two roles, `carrier` and `loader`.

The first role specifies that someone must get the tile, while the second role specifies that someone must load the tile to the first one. Mental conditions specify that `carrier` must recognize the closest tile that is not reserved by some other agent, while `loader` must check and confirm the existence of that tile. As far as the capabilities that agents should have are concerned, `loader` must be able to lift the desired tile and `carrier` must be able to carry it. Concerning context constraints, both roles should check if there is plenty of time in order to get to the tile's position. This is done by calculating the time needed to go to the position that the tile is located, comparing this with the lifetime of the tile. Concerning actions that must be performed, `carrier` must reserve the tile, both must go to the position of the tile, and finally, `loader` must load the tile to `carrier`.

```
rec( get_tile(_T),
    get_tile,
    [[carrier]: bel(agent_name(Agent1)) and
                bel(tile(TileId,Position,TTL,Type)) and
                not( bel(tile(TileId2,Position2,_,_)) and
                    TileId \== TileId2 and
                    closer_than(Position2,Position) ) and
                not bel(reserved(_SomeAgent,TileId)),
    [loader]: bel(agent_name(Agent2)) and
            bel(tile(TileId,Position,TTL,Type)) ],
    [[carrier,loader]: behaviour(reconc(...,ReconcDirect),failure(...)) ],
    type(domain([Agent1,Agent2]),true),
    [[carrier]: null, [loader]: bel(cap(Agent2,lift,tile_type(Type))) ],
    [[carrier]: bel(tile(TileId,Position,TTL,Type)) and
                calc_path(Position,_Path,PathCost1) and TTL > PathCost1,
    [loader]: bel(tile(TileId,Position,TTL,Type)) and
            calc_path(Position,_Path,PathCost2) and TTL > PathCost2 ],
    [[carrier]:         reserve(t(now,_),tile,TileId),
    [carrier,loader]: move_to(t(now,_),Position),
    [loader]:           load_tile(t(now,_),Agent1)],
    [[carrier,loader]: [not tile(TileId,Position,TTL,Type),
                         location(Agent1,Position),location(Agent2,Position)]]).
```

Fig. 3. The get_tile multi-role recipe.

This recipe explicitly specifies the actions that an individual or a team must undertake for performing action "get_tile". This is done by specifying the sequence of actions that must be performed, and the roles that should perform these actions. Consequently, a recipe captures interdependencies between roles by means of actions' temporal relations, as well as by arguments that these actions share.

Agents decide whether they shall utilize the recipe as a single or as a multi-agent recipe. An agent can commit to one or more roles according to its mental state, capabilities and the overall context of action. In case more than one agents commit to both roles, then the recipe is considered to be a multi-agent recipe.

Assume that agent in 7F adopts the recipe shown in figure 3 in order to get tile 8C. Agent identifies that it is not able to undertake the role `loader` of that recipe and decides to broadcast a request to the other agents in the MAT chessboard. Let us assume that agents 2B and 5J are willing to adopt the role `loader` in order to help agent 7F. If done deliberatively, these agents reconcile their desire to adopt `loader` role with other desires and commitments that may hold. If done reactively, these agents, based on their capabilities, commit to role `loader`. In case both agents commit to role `loader`, then the agent that maximizes team performance is chosen, while the other one retracts its intention to perform this role. In case both agents fill this role, then for each action that this role shall perform, they shall find a recipe and plan further towards their shared objective. In this way the recipe allows agents to decide on the best way for filling roles and performing actions in an arbitrary level of detail, building dynamic agent organizations.

The major stages, steps, and flow of control for agents involved in collaborative activity are shown in figure 4: agents form desires, form teams of collaborators, select recipes and allocate roles, and finally execute their roles. When an agent achieves, or fails to achieve the role to which it has committed, then it must inform the agents that share the same context with it. This may drive the team to reallocate roles or to select another recipe. This may further lead

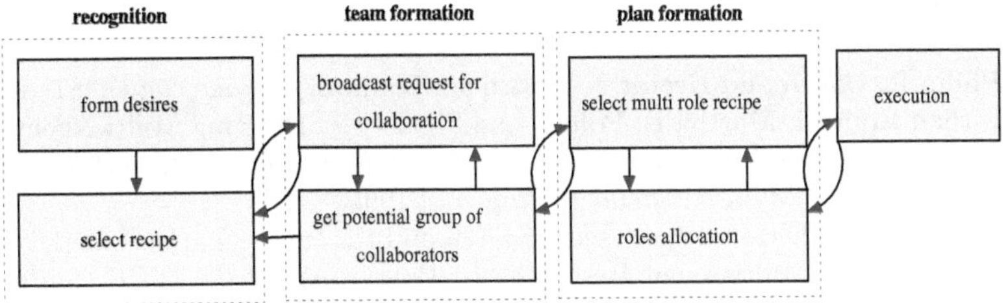

Fig. 4. The process of collaboration.

to the selection of another potential group of collaborators or even abandon the collaboration process. The organization of the group of collaborators through roles specifications provide the communication paths during cooperation. This is achieved via roles' interdependencies that can be inferred from the specification of multi-role recipes. These dependencies reduce the communication overhead, since agents communicate only with those collaborators on which their tasks depend (or depend by) and communicate only the necessary information for achieving their tasks. Therefore, roles provide an additional constraint that can be exploited by agents to decide on the messages and amount of information exchanged. Furthermore, roles specifications provide agents with necessary information to interpret other agents' actions in the context of their joined activity. This can also lead to the reduction of the communication overhead during collaboration. However, the ways that multi-role recipes affect communication is an issue of further work.

5 Concluding Remarks

ICAGENT is an agent architecture implemented for real-time dynamic and unpredictable environments. This paper evolves ICAGENT by introducing multi-role recipes. Recipes constitute the know-how of agents and comprise one or more roles. Roles allow agents to decide on the actions that an individual or a team must undertake in the context of a recipe, facilitate agents to decide whether a recipe shall be utilised as a single or as a multi-agent recipe, and allow agents to decide on the best way for performing actions, planning in an arbitrary level of detail. Furthermore, being committed to common multi-agent recipes, agents coordinate their activities during planning and execution by capturing actions interdependencies, and communicate effectively by reducing communication overhead.

Further work concerns further evolution of the cooperation model introduced by multi-role recipes in both, the theoretical and the applications level. Moreover, we conjecture that using roles' recipes for modelling communication protocols, it is possible to catch the constraints and the dependencies among the interlocutors. This may enhance communication modelling and facilitate message interpretation.

References

[1] Philip R. Cohen and Hector J. Levesque. Teamwork. *Nous*, 25(4):487–512, 1991.

[2] Eithan Ephrati, Martha E. Pollac, and Sigalit Ur. Deriving Multi-Agent Coordination through Filtering Strategies. In *Proceeding of the fourteenth International Joint Conference on Artificial Intelligence*, 1995.

[3] H. Kitano et al. Robocup-Rescue: Search and Rescue for Large Scale Disasters as a Domain for Multi-Agent Research. In *Proceedings of the IEEE Conference on Man, Systems, and Cybernetics (SMC-99)*. 1999.

[4] Barbara J. Grosz and Sarit Kraus. Collaborative plans for complex group action. *Artificial Intelligence*, 86(2):269–357, October 1996.

[5] Merav Hadad and Sarit Kraus. SharedPlans in Electronic Commerce. In M. Klusch, editor, *Intelligent Information Agents*, chapter 9, pages 204–231. Springer, 1999.

[6] Nicholas Jennings. Controlling cooperative problem solving in industrial multi-agent systems using joint intentions. *Artificial Intelligence*, 75, 1995.

[7] D. Kinny, M. Ljungberg, A. Rao, E. Sonenberg, G. Tidhard, and E. Werner. Planned Team Activity. In C. Castelfranchi and E. Werner, editors, *Artificial Social Systems*, LNAI 830. 1992.

[8] Vangelis Kourakos Mavromichalis and George A. Vouros. Balancing between Reactivity and Deliberation in the ICAGENT Framework. In Markus Hannebauer et. al., editor, *Balancing Reactivity and Social Deliberation in Multi-Agent Systems*, LNAI 2103, pages 53–75. 2001.

[9] Itsuki Noda. Soccer server: A simulation of robocup. In *Proceedings of AI symposium '95 Japanese Society for Artificial Intelligence*, pages 29–34, 1995.

[10] Itsuki Noda, Hitoshi Matsubara, Kazuo Hiraki, and Ian Frank. Soccer server: A tool for research on multiagent systems. *Applied Artificial Intelligence*, 12:233–250, 1998.

[11] Luís Paulo Reis, Nuno Lau, and Eugénio Costa Oliveira. Situation Based Strategic Positioning for Coordinating a Team of Homogeneous Agents. In Markus Hannebauer et. al., editor, *Balancing Reactivity and Social Deliberation in Multi-Agent Systems*, LNAI 2103, pages 175–197. 2001.

[12] Charles Rich, Candace Sidner, and Neal Lesh. COLLAGEN: Applying Collaborative Discourse Theory to Human-Computer Interaction. *AI Magazine, Special Issue on Intelligent User Interfaces*, 2002. (to appear).

[13] K. Sycara, M.Paolucci, M van Velsen, and J. Giampapa. The RETSINA MAS Infrastructure. Technical Report CMU-RI-TR-01-05, CMU Technical Report, 2001.

[14] M. Tambe, K. Schwamb, and P. S. Rosenbloom. Constraints and design choices in building intelligent pilots for simulated aircraft pilots for simulated aircraft: Extended Abstract. In *AAAI Spring Symposium on Lessons Learned from Implemented Software Architectures for Physical Agents*, 1995.

[15] Milind Tambe. Towards flexible teamwork. *Journal of Artificial Intelligence Research*, 7:83–124, 1997.

[16] Michael Wooldridge and Nicholas R. Jennings. The Cooperative Problem Solving Process. *Journal of Logic and Computation*, 9(4):563–592, 1999.

Formal Modelling of Reactive Agents as an Aggregation of Simple Behaviours

Petros Kefalas

Dept. of Computer Science, CITY Liberal Studies,
Affiliated Institution of the University of Sheffield
13 Tsimiski Street, Thessaloniki 546 24, Greece
kefalas@city.academic.gr

Abstract. Agents, as highly dynamic systems, are concerned with three essential factors: (i) a set of appropriate environmental stimuli, (ii) a set of internal states, and (iii) a set of rules that relates the previous two and determines what the agent state will change to if a particular stimulus arrives while the agent is in a particular state. Although agent-oriented software engineering aims to manage the inherent complexity of software systems, there is still no evidence to suggest that any proposed methodology leads towards correct systems. In the last few decades, there has been a strong debate on whether formal methods can achieve this goal. In this paper, we show how a formal method, namely X-machines, can deal successfully with agent modelling. The X-machine possesses all those characteristics that can lead towards the development of correct systems. X-machines are capable of modelling both the changes that appear in an agent's internal state as well as the structure of its internal data. In addition, communicating X-machines can model agents that are viewed as an aggregation of different behaviours. The approach is practical and disciplined in the sense that the designer can separately model the individual behaviours of an agent and then describe the way in which these communicate. The effectiveness of the approach is demonstrated through an example of a situated, behaviour-based agent.

1 Introduction

An agent is an encapsulated computer system that is situated in some environment and that is capable of flexible, autonomous action in that environment in order to meet its design objectives [1]. Agents, as highly dynamic systems, are concerned with three essential factors: (i) a set of appropriate environmental stimuli or inputs, (ii) a set of internal states of the agent, and (iii) a set of rules that relate the two above and determines what the agent state will change to if a particular stimulus arrives while the agent is in a particular state.

Although *agent-oriented software engineering* aims to manage the inherent complexity of software systems [2], there is still no evidence to suggest that any methodology proposed so far leads towards correct systems. In the last few decades, there has been a strong debate on whether *formal methods* can achieve this goal. Academics and practitioners adopted extreme positions either for or against formal

I.P. Vlahavas and C.D. Spyropoulos (Eds.): SETN 2002, LNAI 2308, pp. 461–472, 2002.

methods [3]. It is, however, apparent that the truth lies somewhere in between and that there is a need for use of formal methods in software engineering in general [4], while there are several specific cases proving the applicability of formal methods in agent development. One of them was to formalize *PRS* (Procedural Reasoning System), a variant of the *BDI* architecture [5] through the use of *Z*, in order to understand the architecture in a better way, to be able to move to the implementation through refinement of the specification and to be able to develop proof theories for the architecture [6]. In an attempt to capture the dynamics of an agent system, an agent can be viewed as a situated automaton that generates a mapping from inputs to outputs, mediated by its internal state [7]. Alternatively, the *DESIRE* framework focuses on the specification of the dynamics of the reasoning and acting behaviour of multi-agent systems [8]. Finally, in a less formal approach, extensions to *UML* were proposed (*AUML*) in order to accommodate the distinctive requirements of agents [9].

Although all the above have contributed to formal modelling of intelligent agents, they were not able to solve the complexity problem of a single or a multi-agent system. In this paper, we describe a formal method for modelling agents through its behaviours. We decompose modelling into simpler independent steps that facilitates and simplifies the development process. In section 2, the motivation of our work is given and the background theory is introduced. Section 3 defines the proposed formal method and section 4 demonstrates its capability to express complex systems through an example. The practical advantages and the evaluation of the method are discussed in Section 5. Finally, section 5 concludes this paper by presenting further work.

2 Motivation

One of the challenges that emerge in *intelligent agent engineering* is to develop agent models and agent implementations that are correct. The criteria for correctness, as stated in [10], are: (i) the initial agent model should match with the requirements, (ii) the agent model should satisfy any necessary properties in order to meet its design objectives, and (iii) the implementation should pass all tests constructed using a complete functional test generation method.

All the above criteria are closely related to three stages of agent system development, i.e. *modelling*, *verification* and *testing*. Proving correctness is facilitated when modelling of an agent is done in a formal way. So far, however, little attention has been paid in formal methods that could aid all crucial stages of correct system development. The main reason for this drawback of formal methods is that they focus on one part of the system modelling only. For example, system specification has centered on the use of models of data types, either functional or relational models such as *Z* [11] or *VDM* [12]. Although these have led to some considerable advances in software design, they lack the ability to express the dynamics of the system. Other formal methods, such as *Finite State Machines* [13] or *Petri Nets* [14] have little or no reference at all to the internal data and how this data is affected by each operation in the state transition diagram. Finally, *Statecharts* [15] capture the requirements of dynamic behaviour and modelling of data but are rather informal with respect to clarity and semantics.

2.1 Modelling of Change and Data

Among all the above mentioned formal methods, Finite State Machines (*FSM*) manage to capture the essential feature of an agent system, which is the change of its internal state. FSM is a rather straightforward way for modelling reactive agents that receive inputs from the environment and act upon these inputs according to their current state. For example, consider a robotic agent that collects objects from some environment and carry them to its base. The agent can be modelled with the following tuple: (i) a set of states in which the agent can be, (ii) a set of inputs which correspond to its stimuli, (iii) a set of transitions that change its current state according to a stimulus and (iv) a set of outputs that define its actions (Fig.1).

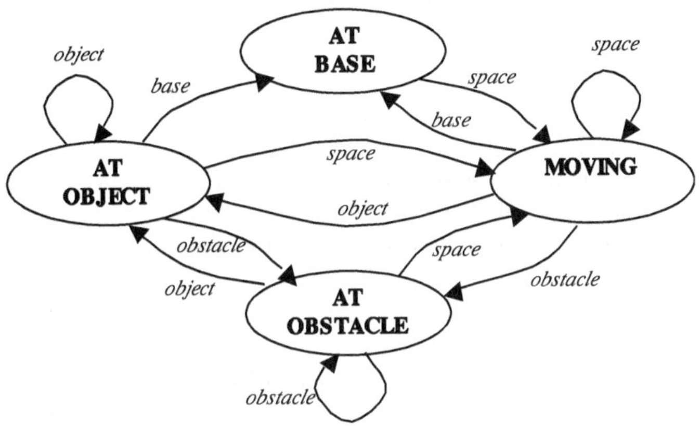

Fig. 1. An example of a reactive agent modelled as Finite State Machine.

The FSM, however, lacks the ability to model any non-trivial data structures. In more complex tasks, one can imagine that the actions of the agents will also be determined by the values stored in its memory. For example, the previously described robotic agent may know its position, remember the position of the objects that meets on the way or the position of obstacles, thus building a map of the environment in order to eventually carry out the task in a more efficient way. Using FSM or their variants [7,16] is rather complicated, since the number of states increases in combinatorial fashion to the possible values of the memory structure.

2.2 Modelling as an Aggregation of Simpler Models That Communicate

Agents can be modelled as stand-alone FSMs as shown above, but with the risk of resulting to an extremely complex model. However, an agent can be also viewed as an aggregation of simpler components, which model various different behaviours of the agent. This fits with the three principles of complex agent systems: (i) decomposition, (ii) abstraction, and (iii) organization [17]. Another approach for reactive agents is described in the *subsumption architecture* [18], in which behaviours can communicate with each other in order to result in a situated agent with the desired overall robust performance. Similarly, in the *Cassiopeia* method [19], the agents are defined by following three steps: (i) identifying the elementary behaviours that are implied by the overall task, (ii) identifying the relationship between elementary behaviours, and (iii) identifying the organizational behaviours of the system.

Based on the latter, we believe that such a methodology can be practical in developing agent models only if it can be able to cope with modelling of the behaviours separately from the description of the behaviour interaction. This approach has several advantages for the developer who: (i) does not need to model a new agent from scratch, (ii) can re-use existing behaviours in other agent models, and (iii) can view agent modelling as two separate distinct activities.

With respect to the above, certain approaches for building an agent require a brand new conceptualisation and development of the system as a whole. This approach has a major drawback, i.e. one cannot re-use existing behaviour models that have been already verified and tested for their correctness. Often, in agent systems, components from other agents are required. A desirable approach would be to conceptualise an agent as an aggregation of independent smaller models of behaviours, which need to communicate with each other. Thus, one does not need to worry about the individual components, in which *verification* and *testing* techniques are applied, but only with appropriately linking those components. This would lead to a disciplined development methodology, which implies two distinct and largely independent development activities, i.e. building simple models and then employing communication between them.

3 A Formal Method for Agent Modelling

Bearing in mind the above, a formal method in order to be useful to modelling of intelligent agents should be able:

- to model both the data and the changes of an agent,
- to model separately the behaviours of an agent and the ways the behaviours interact with each other,
- to be intuitive, practical and effective towards implementation of an agent, and
- to facilitate development of correct agents.

All the above are prominent characteristics of the X-machine. A X-machine is a general computational machine [20,21] that resembles a FSM but with two significant differences: (i) there is memory attached to the machine, and (ii) the transitions are not labeled with simple inputs but with functions that operate on inputs and memory values. X-machines employ a diagrammatic approach of modelling the control by extending the expressive power of the FSM. Data is held in memory, which is attached to the X-machine. Transitions between states are performed through the application of functions, which are written in a formal notation and model the processing of the data. Functions receive input symbols and memory values, and produce output while modifying the memory values (Fig.2). The machine, depending on the current state of control and the current values of the memory, consumes an input symbol from the input stream and determines the next state, the new memory state and the output symbol, which will be part of the output stream. The formal definition of a deterministic stream X-machine [22] is an 8-tuple $XM = (\Sigma, \Gamma, Q, M, \Phi, F, q_0, m_0)$, where:

- Σ, Γ is the input and output finite alphabet respectively,
- Q is the finite set of states,
- M is the (possibly) infinite set called memory,
- Φ is the type of the machine XM, a finite set of partial functions φ that map an input and a memory state to an output and a new memory state, $\varphi: \Sigma \times M \rightarrow \Gamma \times M$
- F is the next state partial function that given a state and a function from the type Φ, denotes the next state. F is often described as a transition state diagram, $F: Q \times \Phi \rightarrow Q$
- q_0 and m_0 are the initial state and memory respectively.

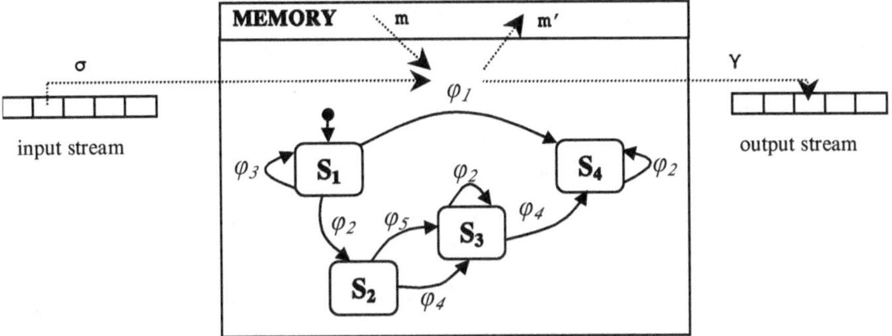

Fig. 2. An abstract example of a X-machine; φ_i: functions operating on inputs and memory, S_i: states. The general formal of functions is: $\varphi(\sigma,m) = (\gamma,m')$ if condition

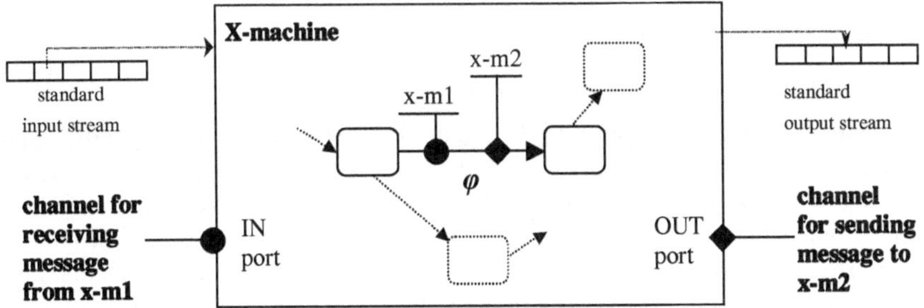

Fig. 3. An abstract example of a Communicating X-machine component.

Several theoretical approaches for communicating X-machines have been proposed [23,24,25,26]. All of them lead to the development of large-scale systems as a set of X-Machines that communicate with each other. In this section we will describe the approach that focuses on the practical development of communicating systems but also subsumes all others [26].

The functions of a X-machine, if so annotated, read input from a communicating stream instead of the standard input stream. Also, the functions may write to a communicating input stream of another X-machine. The normal output of the functions is not affected. The annotation used is the solid circle (*IN port*) and the solid box (*OUT port*) to indicate that input is read from another component and output is directed to another component respectively. For example, function φ in Fig.3 accepts its input from the model *x-m1* and writes its output to model *x-m2*. Multiple communications channels for a single X-machine component may exist.

4 Modelling Reactive Agents as X-Machines

Consider a reactive agent that is working in some environment and collects objects, which are then carried to its base. Initially, the agent knows no object and searches in random to find some of them. When an object is found, the agent carries it to its base, but while going back records the objects met on the way in its memory. When the object is dropped at the base, the agent sets an object from its list of objects as the current goal and looks for it, thus performing a directed search. At all times the agent is able to avoid obstacles found on its way. The agent is modelled by the X-machine shown in Fig.4., which shows the next state partial function.

First of all, the input set of the X-machine consists of the percept and the x and y coordinate it is perceived:

$$\Sigma = (\{space, base\} \cup OBSTACLE \cup OBJECT) \times COORD \times COORD,$$

where *[OBSTACLE, OBJECT]* are basic types and *COORD* is of type *integer*, that is $COORD \subseteq Z$. A basic type is the kind of abstraction made in a specification language in the attempt to define "anything", without getting into details concerning their implementation. The set of outputs is defined as a set of messages:

$$\Gamma = \{\text{"moving freely"}, \text{"moving to base"}, \text{"dropping food"}, \ldots\}.$$

The states in which the agents can be are:

$$Q = \{At\ Base, Searching, At\ Obstacle, Going\ Back, Directed\ to\ Object\}.$$

The state "*Searching*" applies to an agent that does not have a specific goal and searches in random for an object. The state "*Going Back*" applies when the agent is carrying an object and it is on its way back to its nest. The state "*Directed to Object*" applies when the agent has a goal, i.e. remembers where an object is found during previous explorations of the terrain. The memory consists of three elements, i.e. what the agent carries, the current position of the agent, and the sequence of positions where objects are found during its exploration:

$$M = (OBJECT \cup \{none\}) \times (COORD \times COORD) \times seq\ (COORD \times COORD)$$

where *none* indicates that no object is carried. The initial memory and the initial states are respectively $m_0 = (none, (0,0), nil)$ and $q_0 = \text{"At Base"}$. It is assumed that the base is at position $(0,0)$. The type Φ is a set of functions of the form:

$$function\_name(input, memory) \rightarrow (output, memory'), \text{ if } condition.$$

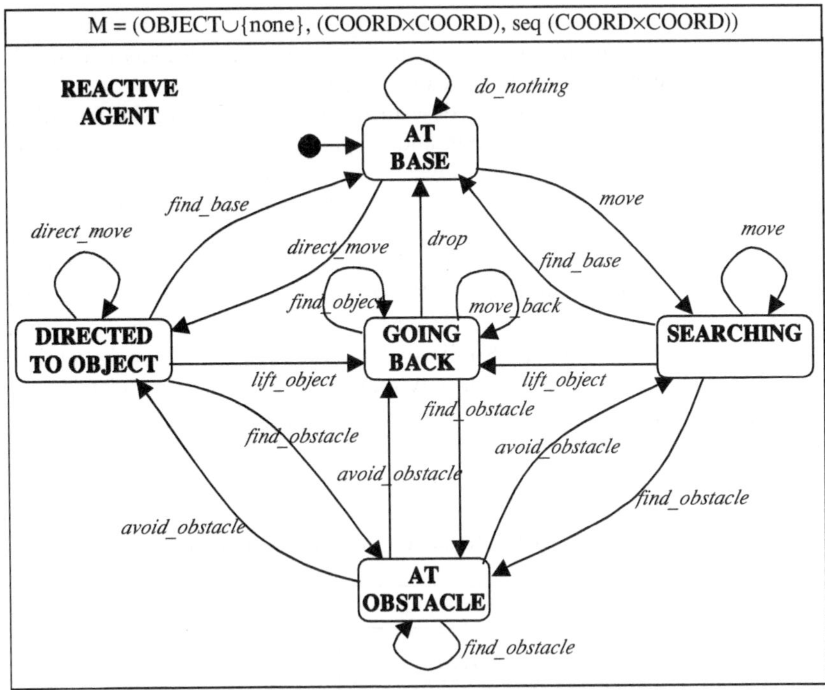

Fig. 4. An example of a reactive agent modelled as X-machine.

For example, the following are some of the functions of the agent model:

$move(\ (space,xs,ys),\ (none,(x,y),nil)\ ) \rightarrow (\text{"moving freely"},(none,(xs,ys),nil)),$
$\quad if\ next(x,y,xs,ys)$

$direct\_move\ (\ (space,xs,ys),(none,(x,y),\langle(px,py)::rest\rangle)\ ) \rightarrow$
$\quad (\text{"moving to object"},(none,(nx,ny),\langle(px,py)::rest\rangle)),$
$\quad if\ next(x,y,xs,ys) \wedge closer\_to\_object(px,py,xs,ys)$

$lift\_object(\ (obj,x,y),(none,(x,y),objectlist)\ ) \rightarrow$
$\quad (\text{"lifting object"},(obj,(x,y),\langle(x,y)::objectlist\rangle)),$
$\quad if\ obj \in OBJECT$

$find\_object(\ (obj,x,y),(item,(x,y),objectlist)\ ) \rightarrow$
$\quad (\text{"record object position"},(item,(x,y),\langle(x,y)::objectlist\rangle)),$
$\quad if\ item \neq none \wedge obj \in OBJECT \wedge (x,y) \notin objectlist$

where the functions *next*, *closer_to_object* are considered as external functions:

$next: COORD \times COORD \times COORD \times COORD \rightarrow BOOLEAN$
$closer\_to\_object: COORD \times COORD \rightarrow BOOLEAN$

External functions are functions that are already defined elsewhere or they are possibly X-machines themselves. The X-machine theory allows for hierarchical refinement of models, and therefore a X-machine can be considered as a function that can be used in modelling of other X-machines [10].

An agent, however, can be conceptualized as a set of simple behaviours. The methodology for building such an agent model should is based around three steps: (a) identification of the behaviours, (b) modeling of individual behaviours, and (c) aggregation of behaviours in order to construct the whole agent model. Towards this approach, communicating X-machines can be used.

The behaviours of the previously described are: (a) searching for an object, (b) moving directly to an object, (c) lifting and dropping objects, (d) avoiding obstacles, (e) traveling back to the base, (f) building a map of the environment.

Each behaviour can be modelled as simple X-machines, as long as the states, the input set (percepts in which this behaviour will react) and the memory is determined. For example, "*moving directly to an object*" is an X-machine (Fig.5), called *MD*, with three states *Q={"Waiting for Goal", "Starting Search", "Moving Directly"}*, an input set *Σ={space, base}*, a memory *M=(agent_position, object_position)*, an initial state q_0*="Waiting for Goal"*, etc. Similarly, "*building map of the environment*" is an X-machine (Fig.5), called *BEM*, with only one state *Q={"Building Map"}*, an input set *Σ=OBJECT×COORD×COORD*, a memory *M=(seq COORD×COORD)*, which holds the objects positions, etc. The rest of the behaviours can be modelled accordingly. Each machine has different memory, inputs (percepts), and functions. Symbols used for inputs a memory need not be the same, i.e. models can be independently built without any reference to other models at this stage.

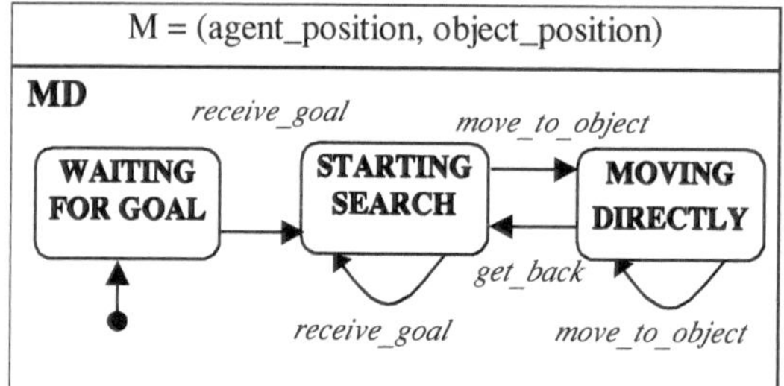

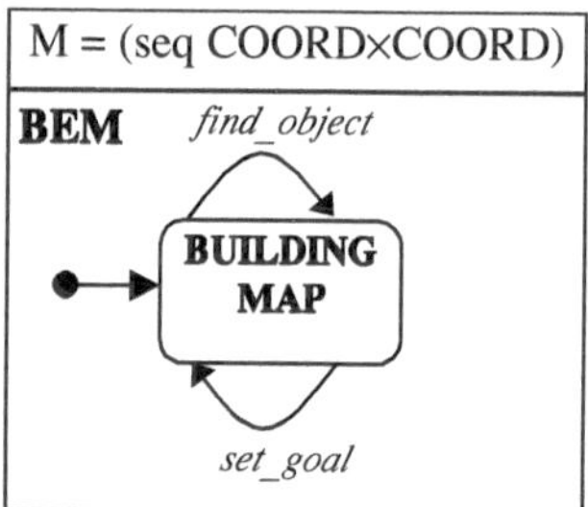

Fig. 5. The behaviours of an agent "moving directly to an object" and "building map of the environment" modelled separately as X-machine components.

The next task is to set up the communication between the components. For example, the behaviour of building the map of the environment should set a goal to the behaviour of moving directly to an object. This is done by utilising the notation of communicating X-machines, as shown in Fig.6. When an object is found, *find_object* is applied and the memory of *BEM* is updated. The *set_goal* function sends a message of type *COORD×COORD* to *MD*, which is perceived as input from *receive_goal.* The memory (*object_position*) is updated. Model *MD* continues to receive inputs and apply its functions. In the meantime, if other objects are found, their position is communicated form *BEM* to *MD* through the communication channel between the two X-machines.

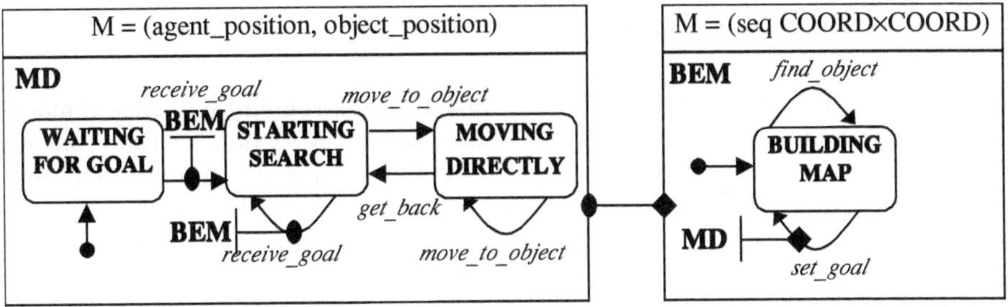

Fig. 6. Communicating agent behaviours modelled as X-machines.

In the same manner, the rest of the behaviours can participate in the complete agent model, which is built of simple but communicating X-machines components (Fig.7). Each machine "works" separately and concurrently in an asynchronous manner. Each machine may read inputs from a communication channel instead of its standard input tape. Also, each machine may send a message through a communication channel that acts as input to functions of another component.

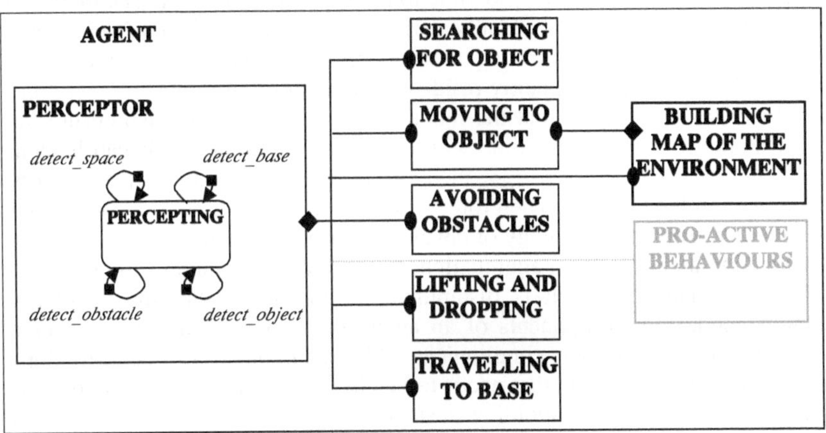

Fig. 7. The complete agent model modelled as an aggregation of different behaviours.

Modelling of an agent can be incremental by providing components, which will advance further the level of intelligent behaviour. More complex behaviours can be modelled, as for example, the X-machine that builds an environment map for free positions and positions of obstacles. Information held in the memory of this machine could be used to efficiently move around the environment, or even to model a pro-active behaviour for the agent (Fig.7). In principle, one can use X-machines to model even more complex behaviours, like planning. Although the modelling complexity is high, the theory behind X-machines allows modelling through hierarchical development, refinement and use of communicating X-machines for building large-scale systems [10].

5 Discussion and Evaluation

The approach described in this paper aims towards the development of formal models of situated agents and meets the requirements set up in section 2. There are two fundamental concepts associated with any dynamic or reactive system, such as an agent, that is situated in and reacting with some environment [10]. Firstly, it is the environment itself, which could be precisely or ill-specified or even completely unknown, but nevertheless it involves identifying the important aspects of the environment and the way in which they may change in accordance with the activities of the agent. And also, it is the agent, which will be responding to environmental changes by changing its basic parameters and possibly affecting the environment as well. Thus, there are two ways in which the agent reacts, i.e. it undergoes internal changes and it produces outputs that affect the environment. These concepts are captured by X-machines as demonstrated by the example presented. The X-machine method is rather intuitive, while formal descriptions of data types and functions can be expressed in any known mathematical notation.

An important issue in the use of X-machines as a modelling formal method is that they can lead towards the development of correct agents. Having constructed a model of an agent as a X-machine, it is possible to apply existing *model checking* techniques to verify its properties. A specifically defined logic, namely *XmCTL*, can verify the model expressed as X-machine against the requirements, since it can prove that certain properties, which implicitly reside on the memory of X-machine are true [27]. In addition, having ensured that the model is valid, we need to also ensure that the implementation is correct, this time with respect to the model. This can be achieved through a *complete testing strategy*, such as the one presented in [10], which finds all faults in the implementation. Therefore, X-machines can be used as a core method for an integrated formal methodology of developing correct systems.

By viewing an agent as an aggregation of behaviours, communicating X-machines can be used. This approach is disciplined, in the sense that the developer can separately model the components of an agent and then describe the way in which these components-behaviours communicate. Also, components can be re-used in other systems, since the only thing that needs to be changed is the communication part. For example, the behaviour for avoiding obstacles is a component of any robotic agent. The major advantage is that the methodology also lends itself to modular model checking and testing strategies in which X-machines are individually tested as components while communication is tested separately with existing methodologies, mentioned above.

Communicating X-machines may be used to model multi-agent systems. Modelling of multi-agent systems imposes the consideration of the means of communication between agents, in order to coordinate tasks, cooperate etc. Also, modelling of artificial environments in which agents act imposes the need of interaction between agents and the environment. These requirements are met by the communicating X-machines and shown to be effective in modelling of biology-inspired agents, such as a colony of ants or bees for collective foraging [28,29].

Finally, through the use of *XMDL* [30], the X-machine formal method aims to overcome one of the main criticisms for formal methods, i.e. practicality. *XMDL* (X-Machine Description Language) is a declarative mark-up language, which permits the designer to write ASCII code in order to describe a X-machine model, rather than using any other ad-hoc mathematical notation. A number of tools have been developed, like test-case generators, model checkers, automatic translators to executable languages, such as *Prolog* or *Java*, animators etc., with *XMDL* as a common modelling language.

6 Conclusions and Further Work

We have presented a formal way to model behaviour-based agents, through the use of X-machines. X-machines provide the ability to model individual behaviours of an agent and then describe the way in which these behaviours can communicate with each other. The main advantage of using the particular formal method is that it can model both the internal changes of an agent state as well as the information stored in an agent. Such features are particularly interesting in agent systems, since they act on a dynamic environment and perceive the changes of the environment as inputs that alter their internal states as well as their knowledge or beliefs. In addition, the formal method can lead towards the disciplined development of correct agents using formal verification and complete testing strategies.

Current and future work involves the applicability of the approach to simple robotic agents, through the automatic translation of X-machine models to a higher level programming language. Having based their design on X-machines we are trying to guarantee that on one hand they possess the desired properties through model checking, and on the other hand that they behave correctly under all circumstances through complete testing.

References

1. Jennings, N.R.: On agent-based software engineering. Artificial Intelligence 117 (2000) 277-296
2. Wooldridge, M., & Ciancarini, P.: Agent-oriented software engineering: The state of the art. To appear in the Handbook of Software Engineering and Knowledge Engineering, World Scientific Publishing Co. (2001)
3. Young, W. D.: Formal Methods versus Software Engineering: Is There a Conflict? In Proceedings of the Fourth Testing, Analysis, and Verification Symposium (1991) 188-899
4. Clarke, E., Wing, J. M.: Formal Methods: State of the Art and Future Directions, ACM Computing Surveys 28 (4) (1996) 26-643
5. Rao, A.S., & Georgeff, M.: BDI Agents: from theory to practice. In Proceedings of the First International Conference on Multi-Agent Systems (ICMAS-95) (1995) 312-319
6. Inverno, d' M., Kinny, D., Luck, M., & Wooldridge, M.: A formal specification of dMARS. In: M.P.Singh, A.Rao, and M.J.Wooldridge (Eds.): Intelligent Agents IV – LNAI, Vol.1365. Springer-Verlag (1998) 155-176
7. Rosenschein, S. R., & Kaebling, L. P.: A situated view of representation and control. Artificial Intelligence 73 (1-2) (1995) 149-173
8. Brazier, F., Dunin-Keplicz, B., Jennings, N., & Treur, J.: Formal specification of multi-agent systems: a real-world case. Proceedings of International Conference on Multi-Agent Systems (ICMAS'95), MIT Press (1995) 25-32

9. Odell, J., Parunak, H. V. D., & Bauer, B.: Extending UML for agents. In Proceedings of the Agent-Oriented Information Systems Workshop at the 17th National conference on Artificial Intelligence (2000)
10. Holcombe, M., & Ipate, F.: Correct systems: Building a business process Solution. Springer Verlag (1998)
11. Spivey, M.: The Z notation: A reference manual. Prentice-Hall (1989)
12. Jones, C. B.: Systematic software development using VDM. 2nd edn. Prentice-Hall (1990)
13. Wulf, W. A., Shaw, M., Hilfinger, P.N., & Flon, L.: Fundamental structures of computer science. Addison-Wesley (1981)
14. Reisig, W.: Petri nets - an introduction. EATCS Monographs on Theoretical Computer Science 4. Springer-Verlag (1985)
15. Harel, D.: Statecharts: A visual approach to complex systems. Science of Computer Programming 8 (3) (1987)
16. Brooks, R. A.: A robust layered control system for a mobile robot. IEEE Journal of Robotics Automation 2 (7) (1986) 14-23
17. Jennings, N.R.: An agent-based approach for building complex software systems. Communications of the ACM 44 (4) (2001) 35-41
18. Brooks, R. A.: Intelligence without reason. In: J.Mylopoulos, & R.Reiter (Eds.): Proceedings of the 12th International Joint Conference on Artificial Intelligence, Morgan Kaufmann (1991) 569-595
19. Collinot, A., Drogul, A. & Benhamou, P.: Agent oriented design of a soccer robot team. In proceedings of the 2nd International Conference on Multi-Agent Systems (1996) 41-47
20. Eilenberg, S.: Automata, Machines and Languages. Vol. A. Academic Press (1974)
21. Holcombe, M.: X-machines as a basis for dynamic system specification. Software Engineering Journal 3 (2) (1988) 69-76
22. Ipate, F., & Holcombe, M.: Specification and testing using generalised machines: a presentation and a case study. Software Testing, Verification and Reliability 8 (1998) 61-81
23. Balanescu, T., Cowling, A.J., Gheorgescu, H., Gheorghe, M., Holcombe, M., & Vertan, C.: Communicating stream X-machines systems are no more than X-machines. Journal of Universal Computer Science 5 (9) (1999) 494-507
24. Cowling, A.J., Gheorgescu, H., & Vertan, C.: A structured way to use channels for communication in X-machines systems. Formal Aspects of Computing 12 (2000) 485-500
25. Barnard, J.: COMX: a design methodology using communicating X-machines. Journal of Information and Software Technology 40 (1998) 271-280
26. Kefalas, P., Eleftherakis, G., & Kehris, E.: Modular modelling of large-scale systems using communicating X-machines. In: Y.Manolopoulos & S.Evripidou (Eds.): Proceedings of the 8th Panhellenic Conference in Informatics, Greek Computer Society (2001) 20-29
27. Eleftherakis, G., & Kefalas P.: Towards model checking of finite state machines extended with memory through refinement. In: G.Antoniou, N.Mastorakis, & O.Panfilov (Eds.): Advances in Signal Processing and Computer Technologies, World Scientific and Engineering Society Press (2001) 321-326
28. Georghe, M., Holcombe, M., & Kefalas, P.: Computational models for collective foraging, BioSystems 61 (2001) 133-141
29. Kefalas P., Holcombe M., Eleftherakis G., Gheorghe M.: A formal method for the development of agent-based systems. In: V.Plekhanova & S.Wermter (Eds.): Intelligent Agent Software Engineering, Idea Group Publishing Hershey, PA, USA (2002) (to be published)
30. Kapeti, E., & Kefalas, P.: A design language and tool for X-machines specification. In: D.I.Fotiadis, S.D.Nikolopoulos (Eds.): Advances in Informatics. World Scientific Publishing Company (2000) 134-145

On the Application of Artificial Intelligence Techniques to the Quality Improvement of Industrial Processes

Pavlos Georgilakis[1] and Nikos Hatziargyriou[2]

[1] Schneider Electric AE, Elvim Plant, P.O. Box 59, 32011, Inofyta, Viotia, Greece
pavlos_georgilakis@mail.schneider.fr

[2] National Technical University of Athens, 9 Heroon Politexneiou str., 15780, Athens, Greece
nh@mail.ntua.gr

Abstract. In this paper, the combined use of decision trees and artificial neural networks is examined in the area of quality improvement of industrial processes. The main goal is to achieve a better understanding of different settings of process parameters and to be able to predict more accurately the effect of different parameters on the final product quality. This paper also presents results from the application of the combined decision tree - neural network method to the transformer manufacturing industry. In the environment considered, quality improvement is achieved by increasing the classification success rate of transformer iron losses. The results from the application of the proposed method on a transformer industry demonstrate the feasibility and practicality of this approach for the quality improvement of industrial processes.

1 Introduction

In this paper, the combined use of decision trees and artificial neural networks is examined in the area of quality improvement of industrial processes. The main goal is to achieve a better understanding of different settings of process parameters and to be able to predict more accurately the effect of different parameters on the final process (or product) quality.

A hybrid Decision Tree – Neural Network classifier is proposed in this paper. This approach combines the attractive features of two artificial intelligence techniques, namely the transparency and model interpretability of Decision Trees (DTs) and the information accuracy of multi layer perceptrons (MLPs). In the proposed method, first, DTs identify the critical parameters affecting the quality of the industrial process (or product) and express in a clear hierarchical fashion their influence on process (or product) quality. Second, the obtained trees are reformulated in terms of an equivalent four-layer feed-forward neural network (NN) [1] to which they provide structural information, i.e., number of neurons and topology.

This paper also presents results from the application of the combined decision tree - neural network method (hybrid method) to the transformer manufacturing industry. In

I.P. Vlahavas and C.D. Spyropoulos (Eds.): SETN 2002, LNAI 2308, pp. 473–484, 2002.

the environment considered, quality improvement is achieved by increasing the classification success rate (CSR) of transformer iron losses.

This paper is organized as follows: a short description of DTs and MLPs is given in Sections 2 and 3, respectively. In Section 4, the proposed hybrid DT - NN classifier is presented. In Section 5, this methodology is applied to transformer quality improvement. Conclusions are finally presented in Section 6.

2 Overview of DT Methodology

The Decision Tree methodology [2] is a non-parametric learning technique able to produce classifiers about a given problem in order to reduce information for new, unobserved cases. The DT is a tree structured upside down, built on the basis of a Learning Set (LS). The LS comprises a number of preclassified states defined by a list of candidate attributes. The construction of a DT starts at the root node with the whole LS of preclassified measurement sets (MS). These MS are analyzed in order to select the test T which splits them "optimally" into a number of most "purified" subsets. The test T is defined as:

$$T : A_i \leq t, \qquad (1)$$

where A_i is the value of attribute i of a particular MS, and t is the optimal threshold value. Selection of the optimal test is based on maximizing the additional information gained through that test. A measure of the information provided by a test of form (1) is based on the entropy of the examined subset and is obtained from the normalized correlation measure between the test and the goal partition in the subset of the LS, as defined in [2]. The α-risk of the hypothesis test determines the amount of evidence required at each node in order to split it. Thc confidence level is defined as $1-\alpha$.

In order to detect if a node is terminal, i.e. "sufficiently" class pure, the classification entropy of the node with a minimum preset value H_{min} is compared. If it is lower than H_{min}, then the node is sufficiently class-pure and it is not further split. Such nodes are labeled LEAVES. Otherwise, a suitable test is sought to divide the node, by applying the optimal splitting rule. In the case that no test can be found with a statistically significant information gain, the node is declared a DEADEND and it is not split.

3 Multilayer Perceptrons

Multi layer perceptrons are feedforward neural networks consisting of one input layer, one or more hidden layers and one output layer (Fig. 5). Each layer is made out of neurons and each neuron is connected to the neurons in the adjacent layer with different weights.

The neurons in the input layer are passive; each simply broadcasts a single data value over weighted connections to the hidden neurons. The hidden and output neurons process their inputs in two steps. Each neuron multiplies every input by its weight, adds the product together with neuron's threshold value (bias) to a running total, and then passes the sum through a transfer (activation) function to produce its result. This transfer function is usually a steadily increasing S-shaped curve, commonly called a sigmoid function. The backpropagation (BP) algorithm [3] is the most frequently used training procedure for MLPs.

4 A Hybrid DT-NN Classifier

A MLP with two hidden layers used for classification performs the following functions. The first hidden layer is the partitioning layer that divides the entire feature space into several regions. The second hidden layer is the ANDing layer that performs ANDing of partitioned regions to yield convex decision regions for each class. The output layer is the ORing layer that combines the results of the previous layer to produce disjoint regions of arbitrary shape.

On the other hand, a binary DT induces a hierarchical partitioning over the decision space. Starting with the root node, each internal (test) node partitions its associated decision region into two half spaces. It is obvious that all the conditions along any particular path from the root to the terminal node of the DT must be satisfied in order to reach the particular terminal node. Thus, each path of a DT implements an AND operation on a set of half spaces. If two or more terminal nodes result in the same class, then the corresponding paths are in an OR relationship.

From the previous mentioned reasons, it is obvious that a DT and a four-layer perceptron are equivalent in terms of input-output mapping. In addition, a DT can be reformulated as a neural network by following the rules proposed in [1]. According to this technique the neural network, called entropy network (EN), has the following four-layer architecture.

a. **The Input Layer (IL)** consists of one neuron per attribute selected and tested by the DT.
b. **The Partitioning or Test Layer (TL)** consists of one neuron per DT test node.
c. **The ANDing Layer (AL)** consists of one neuron per DT terminal node.
d. **The ORing Lyer (OL)** consists of one neuron per DT class.

The connections between the neurons of the above four layers implement the hierarchy of the DT. In particular, each neuron of the TL is connected to the neuron of the IL corresponding to the tested attribute. In addition, each neuron of the AL is linked to the neurons of TL corresponding to the test nodes located on the path from the top node towards the terminal node. Finally, each neuron of the OL is connected to the neurons of AL corresponding to the DT terminal nodes. In comparison to the standard MLPs that are fully connected, the entropy network has fewer connections, or equivalently fewer number of parameters, reducing the time needed for training.

The entropy network can be used only for classification. However, some modifications to the structure of the EN are required in order to use it for prediction purposes [4]. In this case the OL layer would be replaced by a single output neuron, fully connected to all neurons of the AL and the resulted network should be trained again. This methodology is called hybrid DT - NN (HDTNN) approach. Since the entropy network is used only for classification, the comparison between the EN and the HDTNN can be done only on their classification performance. For that reason, after HDTNN convergence, the network is used to predict the test states and after that to classify them accordingly, providing the so-called hybrid DT - NN classifier (HDTNNC).

5 Industrial Applications

In this section, results from the application of DTs, ENs and the HDTNNC are used in order to improve transformer quality through better classification of both individual core and transformer specific iron losses.

In the specific industrial environment, accurate classification of iron losses is an important task, since the latter constitute one of the main parameters of transformer quality. In addition, accurate estimation of transformer iron losses protects the manufacturer of paying loss penalties. In order to avoid this risk, the transformer is designed at a lower magnetic induction, resulting in increase of the transformer cost, since more magnetic material is required. In case of wound core type transformers, classification of iron losses of individual cores is also desired. Satisfactory classification of iron losses however can be achieved only if various parameters, involved in the process, both qualitative and quantitative, are taken into consideration. Instead, in the current practice, only the loss curve is used, i.e. only the influence of the rated magnetic induction on iron losses, for each specific type of magnetic material, is considered. This is dictated by the fact that there is no analytical relationship expressing the effect of the other parameters on transformer iron losses.

5.1 Wound Core Distribution Transformer

In order to construct a three-phase wound core distribution transformer, two small individual cores (width of core window equal to F1) and two large individual cores (width of core window equal to F2) should be assembled (Fig. 1). In general, the width F2 is twice F1.

The theoretical iron losses, say W1 (in Watt), of the small individual core are given by:

$$W1 = WPK_1 * CTW_1 , \tag{2}$$

where WPK_1 are the theoretical individual core specific iron losses at the rated magnetic induction (Fig. 2) and CTW_1 is the theoretical weight of the small core as defined in [5].

The theoretical iron losses, say W2 (in Watt), of the large individual core are:

$$W2 = WPK_1 * CTW_2 , \tag{3}$$

where CTW_2 is the theoretical weight of the large core.

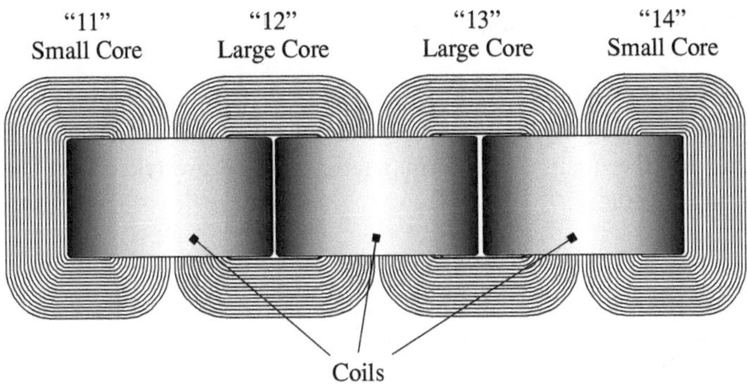

Fig. 1. Assembled active part of wound core distribution transformer.

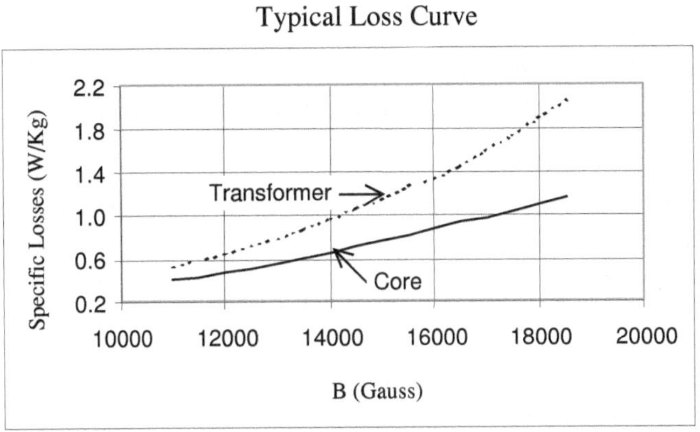

Fig. 2. Typical loss curve.

Consequently, the theoretical total iron losses, say $W1_{tot}$ (in Watt), of the four individual cores are:

$$W1_{tot} = 2*(W1+W2) . \tag{4}$$

The theoretical iron losses of the three-phase transformer, TFLosses, are:

$$TFLosses = WPK_3 * CTW , \tag{5}$$

where WPK_3 are the theoretical transformer specific iron losses at the rated magnetic induction, also obtained from Fig. 2 and CTW is the theoretical total weight of transformer.

5.2 Application on Individual Core

The objective is the improvement of the quality of individual cores. In particular, the impact of the annealing cycle, the divergence of the actual core weight from the theoretical value and the quality of core magnetic material are taken into consideration as input attributes (Table 1).

Table 1. Attributes for the classification of specific losses of individual cores.

Symbol	Description
ATTR1	Annealing final temperature
ATTR2	Temperature rising time
ATTR3	Furnace opening temperature
ATTR4	Duration of constant temperature
ATTR5	Position of core in the furnace
ATTR6	Protective atmosphere
ATTR7	Actual over theoretical core weight ratio
ATTR8	Specific losses of core magnetic material

768 samples were collected for the creation of the learning and test sets. The 3/4 (576) of them were used as learning set and the rest (192) as test set (TS).

The criterion considered for the classification of specific iron losses of individual core as non-acceptable (NA) is the actual specific iron losses being greater than 15% of the theoretical specific iron losses. Otherwise, individual core is acceptable (A).

In Fig. 3 a characteristic DT is illustrated, developed with the 8-attribute list and 0.999 confidence level. The notation used for the DT nodes is explained in Fig. 4.

The Acceptability Index of a node is defined as the ratio of the acceptable MS in the subset E_n of node n to the total number of MS in E_n. If the Acceptability Index of a terminal node is greater than 0.5, then the MS "falling" to this node are characterized as acceptable, otherwise as non-acceptable.

It should be noticed that the DT consists of 3 test and 4 terminal nodes, and has automatically selected only 3 attributes among the 8 candidate ones. These attributes in decreasing order of significance are ATTR8, ATTR2 and ATTR7. The DTs' classification success rate is 94%.

Based on the Decision Tree of Fig. 3 and the methodology described in section 4 the EN of Fig. 5 can be derived. The EN is composed of 3 input, 3 test, 4 ANDing and 2 ORing (output) neurons. The output discrete information is a two-class classification, i.e., acceptable (A) and non-acceptable (NA) transformers with respect to the DT acceptability criterion considered. The correspondence used between the DT nodes and EN neurons is described in Table 2.

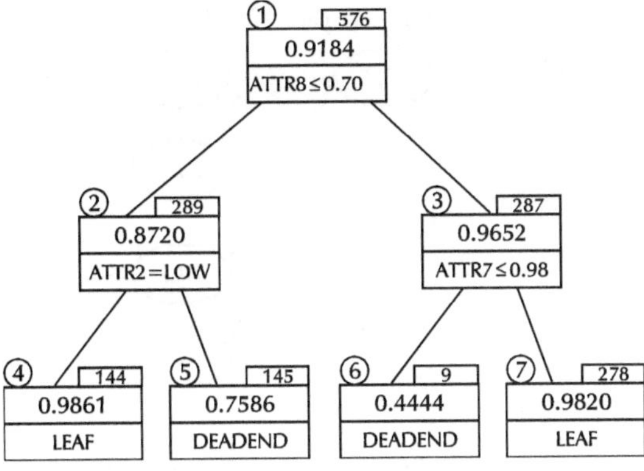

Fig. 3. DT developed using the 8-attribute set.

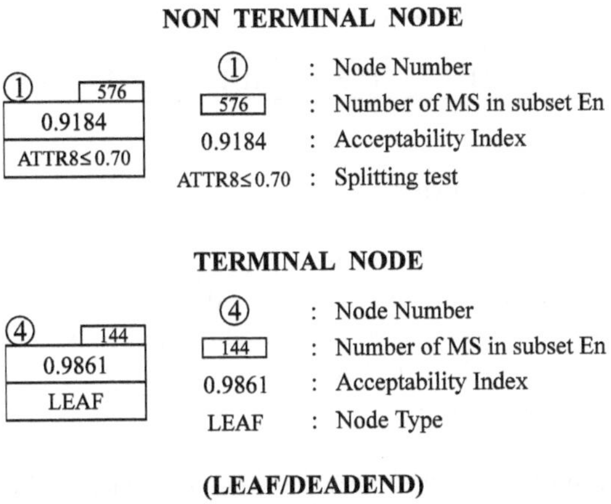

NON TERMINAL NODE

① 576 / 0.9184 / ATTR8≤0.70

① : Node Number
576 : Number of MS in subset En
0.9184 : Acceptability Index
ATTR8≤0.70 : Splitting test

TERMINAL NODE

④ 144 / 0.9861 / LEAF

④ : Node Number
144 : Number of MS in subset En
0.9861 : Acceptability Index
LEAF : Node Type

(LEAF/DEADEND)

Fig. 4. Notation of the DTs' nodes.

If a very high value of the sigmoidal slope of the transfer function is selected, e.g. λ=20, the EN replicates as closely as possible the discrete classification of the DT. The EN is trained using the NNET package [6]. At convergence the CSR on the TS is 94.2%. Using smaller values for λ, it is possible to improve the CSR. For example, for λ=10, and after further adaptation of the weights the CSR of the EN is increased from 94.2% to 94.6%.

Furthermore, the output layer of the EN is replaced by a single neuron representing transformer specific iron losses and the HDTNN approach, described in section 4, is applied using a value of λ=0.5. After training with NNET and convergence, the NN is used to predict the transformer specific iron losses of the TS and classify them accordingly to the criterion used for DT building. The HDTNNC significantly improves the CSR to 95.7%. This important result is obtained due to the enhancement of the EN information.

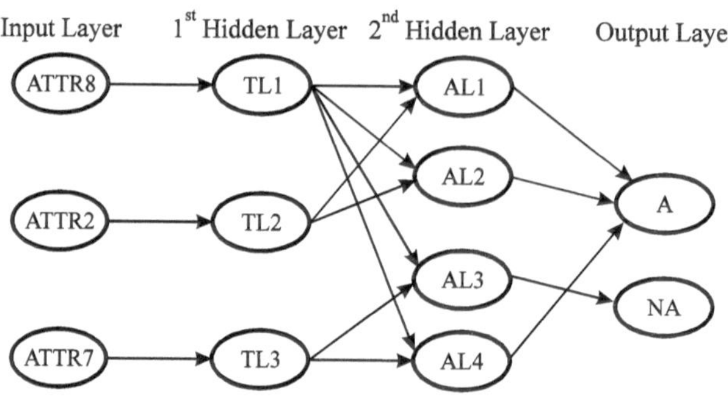

Fig. 5. Entropy network for the DT of Fig. 3.

Table 2. Correspondence between DT nodes (Fig. 3) and EN neurons (Fig. 5).

DT	1	2	3	4	5	6	7
EN	TL1	TL2	TL3	AL1	AL2	AL3	AL4

5.3 Application on Transformer

The objective is the improvement of the quality of transformer, by accurately classifying specific iron losses. However, in this case different attributes have been selected, since at the transformer level the specific iron losses of individual cores are taken for granted and geometrical characteristics are of primary importance. The attributes considered are shown in Table 3.

Table 3. Attributes for the classification of transformer specific iron losses.

Symbol	Attribute Name
ATTR1	Ratio of actual over theoretical total iron losses of the four individual cores
ATTR2	Ratio of actual over theoretical total weight of the four individual cores
ATTR3	Magnetic material average specific losses of the four individual cores (Watt/Kg at 15000 Gauss)
ATTR4	Rated magnetic induction
ATTR5	Thickness of core leg
ATTR6	Width of core leg
ATTR7	Height of core window
ATTR8	Width of core window
ATTR9	Transformer volts per turn

For the creation of the LS and TS 2595 actual industrial measurements were used, 2/3 (1730) of the MS were used as the LS, and the rest as the test set.

The criterion considered for the classification of specific iron losses of transformer as non-acceptable (NA) is the actual specific iron losses being greater than 9% of the theoretical specific iron losses. Otherwise, transformer is acceptable (A).

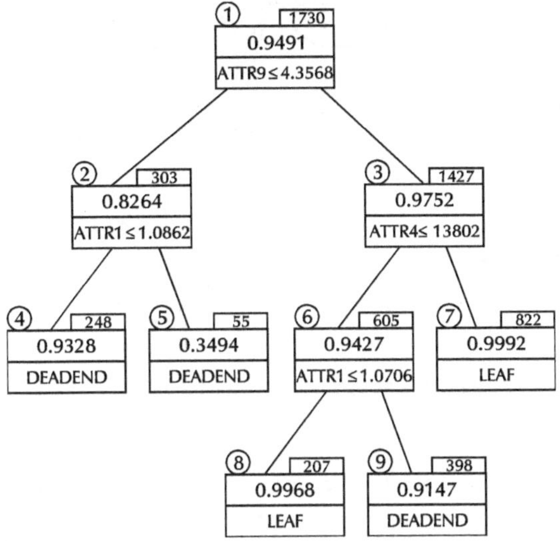

Fig. 6. DT developed using the 9-attribute set.

In Fig. 6 a characteristic DT is illustrated, developed with the 9-attribute list and 0.999 confidence level.

The DT of Fig. 6 consists of 4 test and 5 terminal nodes, and has automatically selected only 3 attributes among the 9 candidate ones. These attributes in decreasing order of significance are ATTR9, ATTR1 and ATTR4. The DTs' classification success rate on the TS is 96%.

Based on the Decision Tree of Fig. 6 the EN of Fig. 7 can be derived. The EN is composed of 3 input, 4 test, 5 ANDing and 2 ORing (output) neurons. The correspondence used between the DT nodes and EN neurons is described in Table 4.

If a value of λ=20 is selected, and training the EN again, the CSR on the TS amounts to 96.3%. Using a value of λ=10, and after further adaptation of the weights the CSR of the EN is increased from 96.3% to 96.7%.

Furthermore, the output layer of the EN is replaced by a single neuron representing transformer specific iron losses and the HDTNN approach is applied using a value of λ=0.5. After training with NNET and convergence, the NN is used to predict the transformer specific iron losses of the TS and classify them accordingly to the criterion used for DT building. The HDTNNC significantly improves the CSR to 97.8%.

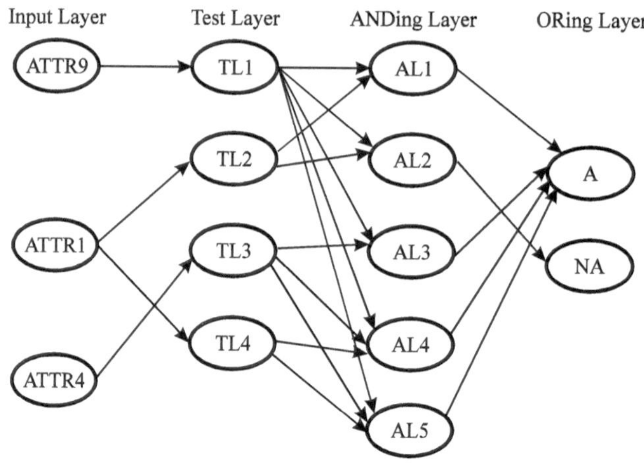

Fig. 7. Entropy network for the DT of Fig. 6.

Table 4. Correspondence between DT nodes (Fig. 6) and EN neurons (Fig. 7).

DT	1	2	3	4	5	6	7	8	9
EN	TL1	TL2	TL3	AL1	AL2	TL4	AL3	AL4	AL5

Table 5. Comparing methods for classification of transformer iron losses.

Method	Structure	*CSR* (%)
DT	-	96.0%
EN	6-6-7-2	96.7%
HDTNNC	6-6-7-1	97.8%
MLP (9 attributes)	9-5-2	98.6%
MLP (3 DT attributes)	3-7-2	96.8%

Moreover, two fully connected MLPs were constructed for the same classification problem. The first MLP comprises 9 input neurons corresponding to the candidate attributes of Table 3, while the second comprises the 3 attributes selected by the decision tree of Fig. 6. Both MLPs have only one single hidden layer and two output neurons corresponding to the acceptable and non-acceptable transformers. The first MLP comprises 5 hidden neurons, i.e. a 9-5-2 structure, and presents a classification success rate of 98.6%. The second MLP has a 3-7-2 structure and a 96.8% CSR.

Table 5 summarizes the results of classification of transformer iron losses. The EN, which is derived by translating the decision tree structure and the second MLP with the 3 attributes identified by the tree, provide very similar classification results. The HDTNNC is more accurate than the EN and the second MLP. The first MLP with the 9 attributes provides the best classification results. Concerning training computational performance, decision trees are by far the fastest method, while among the different neural network approaches the slowest method corresponds to the fully connected MLP.

5.4 Discussion of Results

The 3 attributes appearing in the node splitting tests of the DT of Fig. 3 in decreasing order of significance are ATTR8, ATTR2 and ATTR7. Parameter ATTR8 reflects the quality of the material, as it is equal to the specific losses (Watt/Kg at 15000 Gauss) of core magnetic material. Parameter ATTR2 represents the temperature rising time of the annealing cycle, while parameter ATTR7 expresses the actual over theoretical core weight ratio. The selection of these attributes is reasonable and expected, since they are all related to the quality of individual core. It is notable that the only variable, relevant to the annealing cycle that appears in the node splitting tests of the DT is ATTR2. This is due to the fact that ATTR2, ATTR4 and also the duration of the slow and fast cooling stages are strongly correlated, since the duration of the annealing cycle is considered to be constant. On the other hand ATTR5, which declares the position of core in the furnace, is not important.

Based on the DTs methodology, practical rules, useful for the industrial process, are derived.

In case of individual core, it is concluded from Fig. 3 that it is desirable to construct cores leading to nodes 4 and 7, if it is technically and economically feasible. These nodes have Acceptability Indices greater than 98%. The measurement sets following the rule ATTR8>0.7 and ATTR7≤0.98 are led to node 6, and characterised as non-acceptable. In order to avoid this, the Production Department must increase ATTR7. This is equivalent to increasing the real weight of core by adding more magnetic material, so that the actual over theoretical core weight ratio (ATTR7) is greater than 0.98.

In case of transformer, it is concluded from the DT of Fig. 6 that the measurement sets following the rule ATTR9≤4.3568 and ATTR1>1.0862 are led to node 5, and characterized as non-acceptable. In order to avoid this, ATTR1 should be reduced. The method is to reduce the actual total iron losses of individual cores, by removing from the transformer cores set one or more cores with high iron losses, and add cores with lower ones. The measurement sets following the rule ATTR9>4.3568 and ATTR4>13802 are led to node 7, and characterized as acceptable. This is equivalent to increasing the volts per turn (ATTR9), and also increasing the rated magnetic induction (ATTR4). Design engineers determine both these parameters. In fact, the rated magnetic induction offers enough flexibility, therefore it is desirable to design transformers leading to this node, if it is technically and economically feasible.

Regarding the iron loss classification problem, for the individual core as well as for the transformer, it is concluded that the EN provides very similar classification results with the DT. The HDTNNC is more accurate than the EN. The fully connected MLP provides the best classification results. Concerning training computational performance, decision trees are by far the fastest method, while among the different neural network approaches the slowest method corresponds to the fully connected MLP.

Using the hybrid method, instead of the standard MLP, the tedious task of network structure optimization is avoided. Moreover, training time is significantly reduced (more than a factor 10). Furthermore, the HDTNNC approach can be used to increase the classification success rate, as shown in subsections 5.2 and 5.3, resulting in transformer quality improvement.

6 Conclusions

In this paper, a hybrid decision tree - neural network classifier is proposed for the quality improvement of industrial processes. The method is applied for the increase of the classification success rate of the specific iron losses of both individual core and transformer. The basic steps in the application of the method, like the selection of candidate attributes, the generation of the learning and test sets and the derivation of the appropriate DTs and ENs are presented. Using the HDTNNC the CSR is increased from 94% to 95.7% for the individual core problem, and from 96% to 97.8% for the transformer problem. This significant result is obtained because the HDTNNC combines the advantages of DTs and MLPs while bypasses their weaknesses. Consequently, in the industrial environment considered, the HDTNNC is very suitable for classification of specific iron losses for both individual core and transformer.

References

1. Sethi, I.K.: Entropy Nets: From Decision Trees to Neural Networks. Proceedings of the IEEE, 78(10), October 1990, pp. 1605-1613
2. Wehenkel, L., Pavella, M.: Decision trees and transient stability of electric power systems. Automatica, 27 (1), 1991, 115-134
3. Rumelhart, D.E., Hinton, G.E., Williams, R.J.: Learning internal representation by error propagation. In Rumelhart, D.E., McClelland, J.L., (eds.): Parallel Distributed Processing: Explorations in the Microstructure of Cognition, Vol. 1: Foundations, Cambridge, MA: M.I.T. Press, 1986
4. Wehenkel, L.: Automatic Learning Techniques in Power Systems. Kluwer Academic (1998)
5. Hatziargyriou, N.D., Georgilakis, P.S., Spiliopoulos, D.S., Bakopoulos, J.A.: Quality improvement of individual cores of distribution transformers using decision trees. Int. Journal of Engineering Intelligent Systems, 6 (3), September 1998, 29-34
6. AI Ware "NNET 210 User's Manual", AI Ware Incorporated, Cleveland, OH, 1989

Using Non-uniform Crossover in Genetic Algorithm Methods to Speed up the Generation of Test Patterns for Sequential Circuits

Michael Dimopoulos and Panagiotis Linardis[1]

Department of Informatics
Aristotle University of Thessaloniki
GR-54006 Thessaloniki - GREECE
[1] linardis@csd.auth.gr

Abstract. Due to the high complexity of the problem of generating test patterns for digital circuits Genetic Algorithms (GA) have been investigated as an alternative to deterministic algorithms for test generation. In this paper a Genetic Algorithm "GATPG" is presented for generating sequences of test vectors for sequential circuits. The aim is to produce compact test sequences that attain high fault coverage. Because of the constraints imposed on a GA by the peculiar characteristics of sequential circuits it is proposed here a non-uniform selection probability for crossover combined with individuals (test sequences) of variable length and a two-phase fitness function. For the evaluation of candidate test sequences is used a 3-valued fault simulator, allowing the test patterns to be applied on faulty circuits that start from an arbitrary (unknown) state. Experimental results with respect to the ISCAS'89 benchmarks are presented to show the viability of the proposed approach.

1 Introduction

Digital circuits must be tested to assure that they function properly. Testing is needed: (a) during production, so that no faulty circuits leave the factory, and (b) during the periodic service of the appliances in which they reside. The testing process itself is very time consuming, in particular when it comes to test the large scale digital circuits (VLSI) which are part of the computer hardware and of other digital devices.

Testing in digital Integrated Circuits is done by applying a vector of input values (bits), called *test pattern*, and observing the response (vector of bits) at the outputs of the circuit. The good or faulty state of the circuit is then determined by comparing its response with the expected (good) circuit output. In the so called *exhaustive testing* the time to test a combinational circuit with n inputs is proportional to 2^n, because there are 2^n input vectors, and for a sequential circuit it takes much more time because of the inherent memory of the circuit. However, in exhaustive testing not all input vectors produce useful information about the state of the circuit, the information from many of them is redundant.

The purpose of Automatic Test Pattern Generation (ATPG) is to use a methodology that will lead to a subset of input vectors, called *test set*, which is as small as possible and which is sufficient to detect (reveal) the presence of faults in the

I.P. Vlahavas and C.D. Spyropoulos (Eds.): SETN 2002, LNAI 2308, pp. 485–493, 2002.

circuit. In sequential circuits the order by which the test vectors are applied to the circuit is also important, so here it is necessary to determine a sequence of test vectors, called *test sequence*.

The ATPG problem for combinational circuits is itself a highly complex problem, typically it is NP-complete [1]. For sequential circuits, which is the subject of this paper, it is even more complex.

One class of ATPG methods for sequential circuits is Deterministic [1, 2, 3]. These methods use branch and bound techniques with the aid of heuristics to prune the search space. Due to the vast search space these methods are often unable to handle large sequential circuits [1, 4].

The other class is the Simulation-based methods [1], which in essence are *trial-and-error* methods. Randomly generated input vectors are evaluated by *fault simulation*, according to a "cost" function. The best *trial* vector is selected and added to the test sequence.

Test generation techniques based on Genetic Algorithms (GA) [4, 5, 6, 7, 8, 9, 10] belong to the "simulation" class of methods. In a GA method [11, 12], a population of, initially, randomly generated input sequences is evaluated by simulation and guided by genetic operators until it evolves into a highly fit solution. Compared to Deterministic methods GA methods are simpler because there is no need for them to perform the operations of *justification* and *backtracking* [1], since processing happens only in the forward direction.

Considerable work has been done for improving GA based ATPG algorithms. GATEST [5] tries to maximize the number of detected faults by using a fitness function that gives emphasis to the fault effects propagated to flip-flops. CRIS [6] and GATTO [7] take into account circuit activity. IGATE [13, 14] uses distinguishing sequences for propagating faults from flip-flops to the outputs and for state justification uses the sequences *set*, *clear* and *pseudoregister justification*.

One requirement for a GA to be efficient is that it must be able to inherit to the next generation the good "genes" of the present generation (through crossover-fitness). However, in a sequential circuit it is very difficult, if not impossible, to identify the "genes" of the circuit. The behavior of a large (even small) sequential circuit is so complicated that the effect of the change of one bit in a sequence of input vectors may take many generations to be seen. Further, because of the *ordering* requirement for input vectors (test sequence), the disruption of an input sequence at a random point may have catastrophic effects on the "genes" contained in the tail of the sequence. The tails of the crossed sequences may become completely useless.

In this paper we propose a GA simulation-based method, called GATPG, which tries to improve the effectiveness of the GA by considering the above remarks. GATPG puts emphasis on producing shorter, more compact, test sequences by introducing a non-uniform crossover operator and by varying the length of the individuals.

The paper is organized as follows: In section 2 is presented the testing problem for sequential circuits. In section 3 the structure of the GATPG algorithm is analyzed. In section 4 experimental results are given, supporting the potential of the proposed method.

2 Problem Formulation

Let a digital integrated circuit with n inputs and m outputs. Testing is done by applying a set of values V_I (test pattern) to the inputs I_i (i=1,..,n) and then comparing the responses V_{TO} at the outputs O_i (i=1,..,m) with the corresponding responses V_{GO} of a, known, good circuit. The purpose of ATPG, as was mentioned, is to find a subset of input vectors which is as small as possible and which is sufficient to detect the presence of faults in the circuit.

The internal structure of the good circuit (logic gates and their connections) is known from factory data so to find the corresponding responses V_{GO} is sufficient to simulate the circuit. In general, the operation of a synchronous sequential circuit may be represented by a Finite State Machine M=(I,O,S,s,o), where I is the set of input vectors, O is the output set, S is the set of states, s is the next state function and o is the output function.

Furthermore, the behavior of a faulty digital circuit, irrespectively of the physical cause of the fault, may be predicted by using, mainly, the so-called *stuck-at* fault model. Because of the binary nature of these circuits, a malfunction in a gate will cause this gate to be either *stuck-at-1* i.e its output to be "1" though it should be "0" under the present input conditions or vice versa (*stuck-at-0*). In general, the presence of a stuck-at fault *f* in the given circuit transforms the machine M into a machine $M_f=(I,O_f,S_f,s_f,o_f)$. The effect of this fault on the outputs may be computed by simulating M_f for V_I .

Under the *stuck-at* fault model the variety of possible faulty circuits is finite, it is a function of the number of gates and the number of multiple connections inside the circuit [1]. Because of the finite, though quite large, number of possible faulty circuits their responses to a given V_I may be computed in advance.

Let a sequential circuit M and a list $F=\{f_1,f_2,\ldots,f_n)$ of stuck-at faults for M. The test generation problem for sequential circuits consists of finding a sequence of input vectors V, called *Test Sequence*, that detects the n faults in F i.e. when V is applied to each M_f it will produce different responses from those of M. This problem is quite involved because not one vector but a sequence of input vectors must be evaluated, through simulation, before their effect is shown at the outputs, as was mentioned in section 1. The evaluation (by fault simulation) of a given input sequence, having a length of v vectors, requires *v(n+1)* vector simulations (n faulty circuits + 1 good) and it is one of the most time consuming phases of an ATPG algorithm.

The simulation of a sequential circuit M requires that M start from a given initial state. For a faulty circuit no assumption can be made about its initial state. For that purpose, as is usually the case, a three-valued simulator [2] is used here, a logic simulator that includes the unknown state "X", and each simulation starts here by assuming that the initial states of M and M_f are unknown. The presence of unknown states requires from the algorithm to find and insert at the beginning of the input sequence an *initializing subsequence*, further extending the input sequence, that will drive the circuits M and M_f into valid ("0" or "1") states.

In this work the test sequences V are generated with the help of genetic algorithms, modified to take into account the remarks made in Section 1.

3 The GATPG Algorithm

The proposed GA algorithm for test generation, GATPG, is shown in Fig.1. Starting with an initial population of randomly produced sequences of candidate test vectors (*Create_random_population*) each sequence (individual) is evaluated (*Evaluate_fsim*) by performing fault simulation to find the faults which are: (a) *detected* and (b) *activated* (propagated to flip-flops), and to find also the state and output differences between M and M_f. These results are used to determine the fitness value of each sequence (section 3.4). The crossover operation (*cross_over*) applied here follows a non-uniform probability of cut-point selection (section 3.2).

```
Create_random_population
For each individual
        Evaluate_fsimulation(individual)
Sort_population                                  /* with descending fit. value */
ngen=0                                           /* generation num. */
do {
    for (j=0, i=0; i<ncross; j +=2, i++)         /* *** crossover *** */
            {cross_over(Individual[j], Individual[j+1], child1, child2)
             Evaluate_fsimulation (child1)
             Evaluate_fsimulation (child2)
             }
    for (i=0; i<nmut; i +=2)                     /* *** mutation *** */
            {mutation(Individual[0], child1)
             mutation(Individual[1], child2)
             Evaluate_fsimulation (child1)
             Evaluate_fsimulation (child2)
             }
    Sort_population
    If ( (ngen % 3) == 0 )
            {Expand_sequence(EXPAND_STEP)
             Evaluate_fsim(Individual[0])                 /* check best */
             }
    ngen++ } while (ngen<MAX_GENERATIONS)
```

Fig. 1. The GATPG algorithm

For the reasons mentioned in section 2 about the initial state, the simulator for evaluating the individuals is a PROOFS-based [2] three-valued fault simulator developed by the authors.

The experimental results for GATPG were taken using the following parameter values:

POPULATION SIZE =32
MAX_GENERATIONS = 300
CROSSOVER RATE = 0.60
MUTATION RATE = 0.20
EXPAND STEP = 1

3.1 Individuals

An individual may be considered either as a sequence of binary-valued input vectors of length L_v or as a 2-dimensional bit string having (bit) length $L_s = n^* L_v$ where n is the number of circuit inputs.

As was mentioned in section 1, in the case of sequential circuits it is rather impossible to identify separate "genes" within individuals. The whole (2-dimensional) bit string appears as one large "gene". Also, the effect of changing one bit in an individual may remain obscure until many (unpredictable how many) vectors further down the "tail" of the sequence have been evaluated.

The apparent "single gene" property of these circuits weakens very much the effect of the crossover operator. Here, because of the sequential nature of the circuits, if the k-th vectors of two individuals are crossed (fig. 2) then all vectors after the k-th (i.e. vectors k+1 to L_v) may loose their old properties. Applying multiple crossover operators is not the answer to this problem. Finally, to this problem we must add the high cost of fault simulating the circuit.

The approach taken here was to vary the length of the individuals. Starting with a small initial sequence length L_v of 5 vectors, L_v is slowly increased from generation to generation, by appending at the end a randomly generated vector, according to the progress made so far. This approach has the advantage of lower simulation cost (section 2).

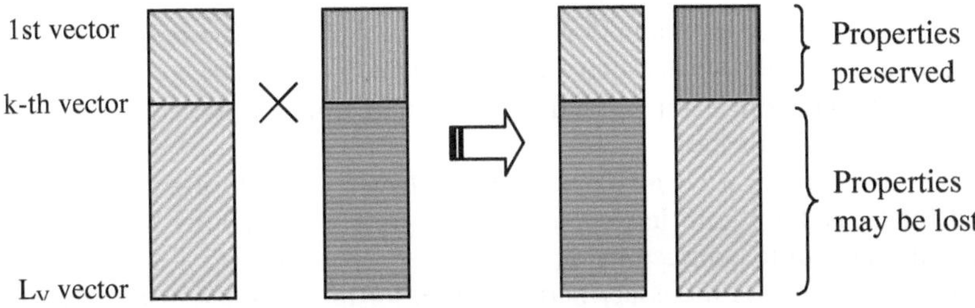

Fig. 2. Crossover of test sequences

3.2 Non-uniform Crossover Selection

Following the remarks made in sections 1 and 3.1 about the effect of crossover on the tails of the generated test sequences, a crossover operator was introduced here having a non-uniform probability density. The vector on which crossover is applied is selected using a random number generator having a square probability distribution (linear density). As shown in Fig. 3, under this distribution halve of the selected vectors lie in the upper 70% of the test sequence and 80% of the selections are made at the upper 90% (near the tail). This non-uniform selection increases the chances to optimize the tail of the sequence while it reduces the risk of destroying "good" sequences by cutting them near their beginnings. Once a vector is selected the bit within the vector is selected with a uniform probability.

This technique, by optimizing the tails of the individuals (test sequences) as these individuals get longer from generation to generation, helps to produce also very compact (short) test sequences.

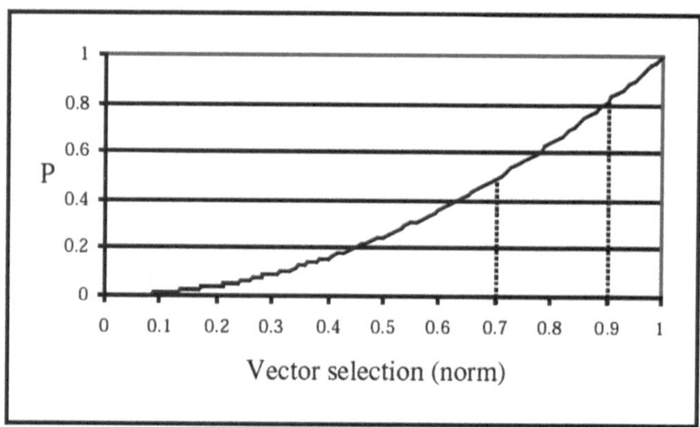

Fig. 3. Square probability distribution (normalized) for crossover selection

3.3 Mutation

Mutation is performed with a uniform selection probability. The best 2 individuals in the population are mutated and two different mutation operations are used:

- Single-bit mutation: a bit is randomly selected from the best 2-dimensional bit string and complemented.
- Multi-bit-mutation: a vector is randomly selected from the best vector sequence and for every bit within it a choice is made with a probability of 1/2 whether to keep its value or to complement it.

A high mutation rate is necessary here because, for the reasons explained earlier, the crossover operation is not so productive for this type of problem. A high mutation rate is proposed for other problems, also, when crossover ceases to be productive [15].

3.4 Fitness Function

The results from the simulation are used to rank the individuals according to certain evaluation rules, which form the so-called *fitness function.* In the present fitness function emphasis is given in the maximization of detected faults while favoring smaller test sequences.

A two-phase function is used. Because in practice there are "easy" and "difficult" to test faults [5] the GA starts with function f_1 and after a number of generations switches to a form f_2 . Further, in order to escape from stagnation an aging factor is incorporated so that offsprings having the same fitness value with their parents are given higher precedence in the next generation.

The fitness function used here is:

fitness = if (ngen < 0.25*MAX_GENERATIONS) f_1 else f_2

where:

$f_1 = 20 \,.\, R_1 + R_2 \,.\, R_3$

$f_2 = 20 \,.\, R_1 + R_3 + R_2 \,.\, R_4 \,.\, R_5$

and

$R_1 = f_{detected}$

R_2 = (sequ_length – eff_length) / sequ_length

$R_3 = f_{activated} / (f_{remaining}+1)$

R_4 = (faults propagated to FFs) / (num_FF . f_{active} . seq_length)

R_5 = (faults propagated to outputs) / (num_ouputs . f_{active} . sequ_length)

4 Experimental Results

The GATPG algorithm was implemented in C and its efficiency was measured by using a subset of the ISCAS'89 benchmark circuits [16]. The main characteristics of these benchmark circuits are given in Table 1, where *i*, *o*, *ff* and gates denote the number of inputs, outputs, flip-flops and gates of each circuit. Column *Total detected faults* presents the total number of faults that can be detected in the circuit and against which the results are judged.

In Table 2 are compared the results regarding two versions of GATPG: with uniform and with square probability of cut-point selection. Columns *Det.*, *Vec.* and *Gen.* represent the number of detected faults, of test sequence lengths and of the generations required to produce these sequences.

As it is seen from Table 2 the square selection probability is better than uniform selection probability because, in order of importance, on the average: (a) it detects more faults, (b) in relatively small sequences, and (c) in fewer generations (shorter time). It is reminded that the sequences under *square probability* may be longer but they are more useful because they detect more faults.

Table 1. Sample of ISCAS'89 benchmark circuits

circuit	I /o / ff / gates	Total Detected Faults
s298	3 / 6 / 14 / 119	265
s344	9 / 11 / 15 / 160	329
s349	9 / 11 / 15 / 161	335
s382	3 / 6 / 21 / 158	364
s386	7 / 7 / 6 / 159	314
s400	3 / 6 / 21 / 164	384
s444	3 / 6 / 21 / 181	424

Table 2. Results for GATPG with uniform and with square selection probability

	uniform probability			*square probability*		
Circuit	**Det.**	**Vec.**	**Gen.**	**Det.**	**Vec.**	**Gen.**
s298	264	79	242	265	89	282
s344	327	56	266	329	61	225
s349	332	51	295	335	59	287
s382	316	88	284	332	91	272
s386	254	39	284	286	52	233
s400	329	86	293	347	79	227
s444	360	91	258	383	76	272
Sum	2182	490	1922	2277	507	1798

In Table 3 are compared the results of GATPG (square) with results from [3, 5, 14]. Columns *f.c* and *Vec.* represent the *fault coverage* (detected faults to total detectable faults) and the test sequence lengths.

Methods [5, 14] belong to the same category with our method. There is no comparison with the methods presented in [4, 7] because they assume that the circuit starts from a given initial state instead of the more general case of an unknown (arbitrary) one, as in our case. We must note that HITEC is a state-of-the art deterministic test pattern generator that achieves high fault coverage but requires long CPU time to achieve satisfactory results.

As it is seen from Table 3 the fault coverage for the first three circuits is the same with those of the others (for IGATE are given the available results). For the remaining circuits although our fault coverage (GATPG) is lower, i.e. average fault cov. 0.947 compared to 0.972 [5] and 0.997 [14], the average size of our test sequences is 2.6 times smaller than [5] and many times smaller than that of HITEC and IGATE.

Table 3. Comparison of GATPG (square) with results from literature

	GATPG		*ref[5]*		*IGATE[14]*		*HITEC [3]*	
Circuit	**f.c.**	**Vec.**	**f.c.**	**Vec.**	**f.c.**	**Vec.**	**f.c.**	**Vec.**
s298	1.000	89	1.000	161	1.000	232	1.000	306
s344	1.000	61	1.000	95	1.000	120	0.994	142
s349	1.000	59	1.000	95			1.000	137
s382	0.911	91	0.953	281	0.994	2047	0.997	4931
s386	0.911	52	0.939	154			1.000	311
s400	0.904	79	0.951	280	0.994	2162	0.997	4309
s444	0.902	76	0.958	275	1.000	1970	0.976	2240
Averages:								
f.c.	0.947		0.972		0.997		0.995	
Vec.		72		191		1306		1768

5 Conclusion

A GA-based test generation algorithm is presented which has some unique features. Apart from the fitness function used here, crossover is enhanced with a non-uniform crossover-selection probability and individuals of varying length. This "directed" cut-point selection in crossover combined with the varying length of the individuals performs better than the classical one with uniform probability cut-point selection, as is evident from experimental results presented here.

Although the preliminary results that were presented are quite competitive with those of others the GATPG algorithm may be further improved by adding more circuit specific knowledge in the fitness function and elaborating on GA-operators.

References

1. M. Abramovici, M. Breuer, A. Friedman: Digital Systems Testing and Testable Design. IEEE Press (1990).
2. T. M. Niermann, W. T. Cheng, and J. H. Patel: PROOFS: A fast, memory-efficient sequential circuit fault simulator. IEEE Trans. Computer-Aided Design (1992) 198-207.
3. T. M. Niermann and J. H. Patel: HITEC: A test generation package for sequential circuits. Proceedings of the European Conference on Design Automation (1991) 214-218.
4. F. Corno, P. Prineto, M. Rebaudengo, M. Sonza Reorda, R. Mosca: Advanced Techniques for GA-based sequential ATPGs. European Design & Test Conf. (1996).
5. E. M. Rudnick, J. H. Patel, G. S. Greenstein, and T. M. Niermann: Sequential circuit test generation in a genetic algorithm framework. Proc. Design Automation Conf. (1994) 698-704.
6. D. G. Saab, Y. G. Saab, J. A. Abraham: CRIS: A Test cultivation program for sequential VLSI circuits. ICCAD (1992) 216-219.
7. F. Corno, P. Prinetto, M. Rebaudengo, M. Sonza Reorda: GATTO: A Genetic Algorithm for Automatic Test Pattern Generation for Large Synchronous Sequential Circuits. IEEE Trans. on CAD, Vol. 15, No 8 (1996) 991-1000.
8. M. Hsiao, E. Rudnick, J. Patel: Sequential Circuit Test Generation Using Dynamic State Traversal. European Design & Test Conf. (1997) 22-28.
9. E. Rudnick, J. Patel: Combining deterministic and genetic approaches for sequential circuit test generation. DAC. (1995) 183-188.
10. M.H.Hsiao, E.M.Rudnick, J.H.Patel: Alternating strategies for sequential circuit atpg. European Design &Test Conf. (1996) 368-374.
11. D. E. Goldberg: Genetic Algorithms in Search, Optimization, and Machine Learning, Reading. MA: Addisson-Wesley (1989).
12. Zbigniew Michalewicz: Genetic Algorithms+ Data Structures=Evolution Programs. Springer (1996).
13. M. Hsiao, E. Rudnick, J. Patel: Application of Genetically Engineered Finite-State Machine Sequences to Sequential Circuit ATPG. IEEE Trans. CAD (March 1998) 239-254.
14. Pinaki Mazumder, Elizabeth M. Rudnick: Genetic Algorithms for VLSI Design, Layout & Test Automation. Prentice Hall (1999).
15. J. E. Beasly, P. C. Chu: A genetic algorithm for the set covering problem. European Journal of Operational Resaearch 94 (1996) 392-404.
16. F. Brglez, D. Bryan and K. Kozminski: Combinational profiles of sequential benchmark circuits. Int. Symposium on Circuits and Systems (1989) 1929-1934.

Hybrid Computational Intelligence Schemes in Complex Domains: An Extended Review

Athanasios Tsakonas and George Dounias

University of the Aegean,
Business School, Dept. of Business Administration,
8 Michalon St., 82100 Chios, Greece,
TEL. +30-271-35165, FAX:+30-271-93464,
tsakonas@stt.aegean.gr, g.dounias@aegean.gr
http://decision.ba.aegean.gr

Abstract. The increased popularity of hybrid intelligent systems in recent times lies to the extensive success of these systems in many real-world complex problems. The main reason for this success seems to be the synergy derived by the computational intelligent components, such as machine learning, fuzzy logic, neural networks and genetic algorithms. Each of these methodologies provides hybrid systems with complementary reasoning and searching methods that allow the use of domain knowledge and empirical data to solve complex problems. In this paper, we briefly present most of those computational intelligent combinations focusing in the development of intelligent systems for the handling of problems in real-world applications. We emphasize the appropriateness of hybrid computational intelligence techniques for dealing with specific problems, we try to point particularly suitable areas of application for different combinations of intelligent techniques and we briefly state advantages and disadvantages of the "hybrid" idea, seen as the next theoretical step in the evolving impact and success of artificial intelligence tools and techniques.

1 Computational Intelligent Components

Hybrid computational intelligence is defined as any effective combination of intelligent techniques that performs superior or in a competitive way to simple standard intelligent techniques. A very thorough analysis of what is meant by computational intelligence and what the trends of modern AI are, can be found in [1] and [2]. Lately more and more researchers recognize and define as main components of computational intelligence, four areas of research that dominate the area of AI, namely, (1) fuzzy sets and soft computing, (2) neural networks, (3) genetic algorithms and evolutionary computing and (4) machine learning and data mining. A collection of research work on computational intelligence and learning techniques in the sense presented above can also be found in [3]. Advantages and disadvantages of each individual approach, as well as reasons that make hybrid schemes attractive in modern AI research, are given in brief at the end of this paper, together with a description of the main clusters of application areas that hybrid appears particularly capable to be applied. Below we attempt a reference to the basic concepts of the most popular

I.P. Vlahavas and C.D. Spyropoulos (Eds.): SETN 2002, LNAI 2308, pp. 494–511, 2002.

intelligent components of hybrid intelligent architectures, and then a review of more than 100 related research papers found in recent literature, is made.
Fuzzy logic [4] is a language, which uses syntax and local semantics where we can imprint any qualitative knowledge about the problem to be solved. The main attribute of fuzzy logic is the robustness of its interpolative reasoning mechanism. Neural networks were introduced by [5] and [6]. They are computational structures that can be trained to learn by examples. Using a supervised learning algorithm, such as the back-propagation [7], and a training set that samples the relation between input and output, we can perform fine local optimization. Genetic algorithms [8] give us a method to perform randomized global search in a solution space. Usually a population of candidate solutions, encoded internally as chromosomes, is evaluated by a fitness function in terms of its accuracy. The best chromosomes are combined and reproduced in subsequent generations. Genetic programming, proposed by [9] is an extension to the original concept of genetic algorithms. The population in genetic programming is composed by variable length tree-like candidate solutions. Each of these individual candidates, called program, may have functional nodes, enabling the solution to perform arbitrarily large actions. Machine Learning [10], [11], [12], [13], was conceived four decades ago for the development of computational methods that could implement various forms of learning, in particular mechanisms capable of inducing knowledge from examples or data [14, p.3]. Knowledge induction seems particularly desirable in problems that lack algorithmic solutions, are ill-defined, or only informally stated. Most research in machine learning has been devoted to developing effective methods for building learning systems that will acquire high-level concepts and/or problem solving strategies through examples in a way analogical to human learning. Most of the complex domain problems are ill-defined, difficult to model and they have large solution spaces. Any relevant information about these problems is the prior domain knowledge, usually incomplete, and input-output instances of the system's behavior, which is also incomplete. Therefore, in many cases, hybrid combinations are capable of describing an approximate reasoning for these domains. These hybrid systems are proved superior to each of their underlying computational intelligent components, thus providing us with better problem solving tools.

Table 1. Publications related to hybrid schemes in this paper, summarized by subject and date published

	<= '91	'92-'93	'94-'95	'96-'97	'98-'99	'00-'01	Total
Neural Networks and Fuzzy Logic (NN+FL)	5	6	3	7	-	10	*31*
Fuzzy Logic and Evolutionary Algorithms (FL+EA)	5	7	9	19	1	4	*45*
Neural Nets and Evolutionary Algorithms (NN+EA)	2	3	2	1	2	2	*12*
Machine Learning and Evol. Algorithms (ML+EA)	1	1	-	-	2	4	*8*
Other Hybrid Schemes (HS)	1	-	1	3	1	6	*12*
Total	*14*	*17*	*15*	*30*	*6*	*26*	

Table 1 summarizes those publications related to hybrid systems, that are presented in this paper, based on a classification by subject and date published, while *Table 2* is a digest of the hybrid application papers shown in this work classified by subject and task.

Table 2. Publications related to hybrid applications presented in this work, summarized by subject and task

	NN+FL	FL+EA	NN+EA	ML+EA	Other HS	Total
Fuzzy control	4	6	-	-	-	*10*
Function approximation	2	1	1	1	-	*5*
Forecasting	6	-	2	-	-	*8*
Knowledge discovery	1	-	-	-	-	*1*
Decision making	2	1	-	-	-	*3*
Scheduling	-	1	-	-	1	*2*
Feature selection	-	-	-	2	1	*3*
System design	-	1	-	-	-	*1*
Data classification	1	1	-	1	-	*3*
Image processing	2	-	-	-	-	*2*
Financial, medical, industrial appl.	5	2	1	2	-	*10*
Other / benchmarking	-	1	1	-	-	*2*
Total	*22*	*14*	*5*	*6*	*2*	

As observed from the above tables, combinations of machine learning and evolutionary algorithms are relatively few as compared e.g., with the fuzzy-neural systems. The main reason may be that these two domains (i.e. machine learning and evolutionary algorithms) were evolved separately, and only recently the number of this kind publications increases. Regarding the combination of neural networks and evolutionary algorithms, although there exists a sufficient number of (most theoretical) publications, the number of real-world applications remains relatively small as compared to the fuzzy-neural systems. This may be a result of the particular success of the fuzzy-neural approach in real-world complex domains, a fact that leads researchers to substitute neural-evolutionary approaches with the fuzzy-neural ones, although those two competitive hybrid schemes address mostly common domains. Similar observations exist for the comparison between fuzzy-evolutionary systems and fuzzy-neural ones. Fuzzy-evolutionary systems are commonly used -but not always- in the same complex domains as with the fuzzy-neural systems. However, the uniqueness in some of the fuzzy-evolutionary systems, which is the incorporation of fuzzy logic into an evolutionary algorithm (and not for example, the fuzzy rule-base construction using an evolutionary approach, which can also be done by fuzzy-neural systems) lets these hybrid schemes to work effectively in a larger scale of application domains. The literature presented above, is by no means exhaustive, though it can be considered as representative. The collection of these papers was mainly done from IEEE publications, edited books, research monographs, as well as from web databases such as the ScienceDirect and the Citeseer. No specific strategy was used for performing keyword-search, as a "hybrid" system is not always defined under this term in literature. The paper is organized as follows:

Next section describes different major categories of hybrid systems and attempts to classify and analyze them, while section 3 presents some brief conclusions drawn from the comparison of the performance of all the alternative hybrid approaches into various domains of application.

2 Hybrid Systems and Combinations

Below we approach the concept of hybrid computational intelligence by presenting evidence found in literature, concerning effective combinations of two, either competitive or, complementary intelligent approaches to specific domains of application. Later in this text we also refer to more complex hybrid schemes that usually combine more than two techniques at the same time, in a more complicated manner.

2.1 Neural Networks and Fuzzy Logic

Neural networks and fuzzy logic is maybe proved to be the most successful combination of intelligent techniques in modern literature around AI, also called as neuro-fuzzy systems and techniques[1]. Neuro-fuzzy systems have shown a high rate of success when applied in complex domains of application, either when fuzzy set theory is the heart of such a system, or when the neural mechanism is the dominant component in the architecture. The main principle of this combination, as seen by a neural network expert, can be roughly described as the adoption of fuzzy functions in (mostly consisted of 3-layers) neural networks' nodes. On the other hand, a fuzzy systems' expert may realize a neural-like training (such as back-propagation) for the membership functions of a fuzzy system. However, combinations and approaches in these hybrid systems can be less obvious and descriptive, concerning different NN or FS structures, such as self-organizing maps or radial basis functions.

Neural networks controlled by fuzzy logic. Some basic theoretical aspects, detailed description of the characteristics of the methodological components, as well as the early adoptions of neural networks controlled by fuzzy logic, can be found in a series of publications [15], [16], [17], [18], [19], [20], [21] and [22]. In [23], is addressed the concept of a fuzzy neural network to implement syllogistic fuzzy reasoning. In syllogistic fuzzy reasoning, the consequence of a rule in one reasoning stage is passed to the next stage as a fact. The approach is shown to be essential to effectively build up large-scale systems, with high-level intelligence, when applied in two benchmark problems from the fuzzy control and nonlinear function approximation domains. In [24], the problem of adaptive regularization in image restoration is addressed, by adopting a neural network learning approach. Instead of explicitly specifying the local regularization parameter values, the authors regard them as network weights, which are then modified through the supply of appropriate training examples. In addition, they consider the separate regularization of edges and textures due to different noise masking capabilities and they propose a new edge-texture characterization measure,

[1] See for example the Neuro–Fuzzy International Conference NF-2002, La Habana, Cuba, January 2002, http://www.icsc-naiso.org/conferences/nf2002/.

which is incorporated in a fuzzified form to the neural network. In [25], is proposed the fuzzy neural network for tuning the proportional-integral-derivative controller for plants with under-damped step responses. Several simulation examples demonstrate the effectiveness and robustness of the obtained fuzzy neural network. In [26], is proposed a supervisory control system using a recurrent fuzzy neural network to control the mover of a permanent magnet linear synchronous motor servo drive for the tracking of periodic reference inputs. The system combines a supervisory control subsystem and an intelligent control subsystem. The overall approach is shown to be effective to track various periodic reference inputs with robust control performance.

Fuzzy logic controllers tuned by neural networks. The early adoptions of fuzzy logic controllers tuned by neural networks can be found again in [27], [28], [29], [30], [31], and [32]. Since then, the term neuro-fuzzy has covered both previous areas.

Neuro-fuzzy systems. In [33], a distributed approach to genetic-neuro-fuzzy learning is presented, for a class of low-cost form of personal computers, built at the University of Messina. The performance of the serial version is significantly enhanced with the parallelization scheme described in the paper. In [34], the authors propose a neuro-fuzzy function approximator combining the reasoning method with stochastic reinforcement learning. The model is proved in the examples superior to back-propagation in simple non-linear approximation tasks. In [35], the authors show which elements have to be extracted from a chaotic time series in order to define the architecture of a forecasting neuro-fuzzy system. They test the model on Mac Key - Glass time series, concluding that the system is promising. In [36], the author presents a fuzzy-neural approach to the prediction of nonlinear time-series. The underlying mechanism governing the time series is expressed in the form of If-Then rules and is discovered by a modified self-organizing counter-propagation network. Tests over three different time-series demonstrate the efficiency and the effectiveness of this approach, over other network approaches. In [37], is presented a neuro-fuzzy system combining neural computation and heuristics fuzzy rule generation. The system is proved very efficient and effective in various complex domains in other publications [38]. In [39], the authors propose a combination of chaos analysis, neuro-fuzzy systems and evolutionary training for stock exchange daily trading. The system is demonstrated to be efficient in various test cases and superior to buy and hold strategies. In [40], the modeling of the German stock index DAX is attempted with a neuro-fuzzy approach.

2.2 Neural Networks and Evolutionary Algorithms

Fundamental implementations of neural networks generated and tuned by genetic algorithms can be found in a series of publications [41], [42], [43], [44], [45], [46]. The idea behind the implementation of such a hybrid system is the adoption of an evolutionary algorithm for the determination of neural network's weights or the neural network's architecture, or both. In the first case, neural networks are tuned by evolutionary algorithm, rather than generated by, which is the case in the second approach. The third approach may contain both generation and tuning. A special case of tree-like neural networks may also be served by genetic programming training.

Neural networks generated by genetic algorithms. In [47], the authors use a hybrid scheme combining neural networks and genetic training to forecast the three-month spot rate of exchange for four currencies. The forecasts are compared to the predictions made by the forward and futures rates and are evaluated based on their degree of accuracy and their ability to correctly forecast the direction of the change in the exchange rate movement. In [48], is proposed a more comprehensive evolution of network design, enabling all aspects of the network to evolve and all varieties of networks to be discovered. In their chromosome, they represented various neural network properties, intended to permit all possible connectivity. The system has been tested effectively in various benchmarking problems, such as the XOR and the parity problem, and a potential has been shown in this model.

Neural networks tuned by genetic algorithms. The work presented in [49], has proposed the neural networks weight selection by encoding these parameters in real-valued chromosomes. The authors of [49] applied this methodology in both feed-forward neural networks and to a new, at that time, topology, the weighted probabilistic neural networks. In [50], the authors compare the genetic algorithm training with the back-propagation for neural networks for five chaotic time series, showing that the genetic algorithms training is superior to back-propagation in terms of effectiveness, ease-of-use and efficiency.

Neural networks and genetic programming. In [51], the authors present the development of a hybrid system of neural networks and genetic programming trees for problem domains where a complete input space can be decomposed into several different sub-regions, and these are well represented in the form of oblique decision tree. The overall architecture of this system is called federated agents and consists of a facilitator, local agents, and boundary agents. Neural networks are used as local agents, each of which is expert at different sub-regions. Genetic programming trees serve as boundary agents.

2.3 Fuzzy Logic and Evolutionary Algorithms

Genetic algorithms and fuzzy logic have been used in the past collaboratively for various control engineering applications and complex optimization problems. Both, fuzzy logic driven genetic approaches and genetic driven fuzzy logic based schemes have been proved effective in modern AI literature, as described in the following paragraphs. The fuzzy logic driven genetic approaches primarily concern the use of fuzzy logic, either for genetic parameters' tuning, or for fuzzy encoding of the chromosomes. The genetic driven fuzzy logic based schemes usually are consisted by fuzzy rule-based systems, using a genetic approach for the determination of the rule base. On the other hand, the prime theoretical aspects of implementing complex structures such as the fuzzy systems into genetic programming trees, is developed in a series of publications [52], [53], [54], [55] and [56], where the main concept, the grammar-driven or strongly-typed genetic programming is proved capable of describing arbitrarily large structure hierarchies. As it is shown in the following paragraphs, the fuzzy-genetic-programming approach, goes beyond a simple cooperation between two intelligent domains, while such a system may be seen as a single component that includes the attributes of both sub-components, such as fuzzy inference and genetic-based self-training.

Genetic algorithms controlled by fuzzy logic. Applications of genetic algorithms controlled by fuzzy logic can be found in a series of publications [57], [58], [59], [60], [61], [62], [63] and [64]. In [65], the authors use fuzzy coding for genetic optimization. This approach enables to establish a relevant level of information granularity and to provide with some search guidance. In [66], fuzzy logic controllers are used for the adaptation of genetic algorithms parameters. In [67], is proposed a bi-directional scheme, where fuzzy logic controllers are used for the tuning of a genetic algorithm and another genetic algorithm is used simultaneously for the tuning of these fuzzy logic controllers. The empirical study of this model has shown that it adapts the parameter settings according to the particularities of the search space allowing significant performance to a variety of problems.

Fuzzy logic controllers tuned by genetic algorithms. Some fundamentals of theory and description of individual components, as well as the early implementations of fuzzy logic controllers tuned by genetic algorithms can be found in a series of publications [57], [68], [69], [70], [71], [72], [61], [22], [73], [74] and [75].

Fuzzy logic controllers' learning by genetic algorithms. In [76], two different approaches to apply genetic algorithms to fuzzy logic controllers are described. The first approach uses the knowledge base as the individual of the genetic system, while the second uses the knowledge base as the population of the genetic system. Both systems are applied to complex control problem and their efficiency is demonstrated. In [77], hybrid fuzzy-genetic approaches are explored to intelligent systems design. The paper contains demonstrations of techniques on robotics control and biomedical diagnosis applications. The work in [78], proposes the training of fuzzy rule systems using messy genetic algorithms. The method is applied to a control problem in robotics. The control behavior proves robust enough, in order to compensate differences of sensory perception between simulation and reality. In [79], the authors describe a fuzzy rule learning system, developed for working with noise-affected systems. The system is proved capable of obtaining a reasonable small set of rules as compared with other algorithms. The paper described in [80], presents an evolutionary process based on genetic algorithms and evolution strategies for learning the fuzzy logic controller knowledge base from examples. Tests demonstrate the effectiveness of the proposed model and the results are compared with other methods. In [81], is proposed an algorithm for generating the rule-base of fuzzy systems via symbiotic evolution. In symbiotic evolution each chromosome in the population represents only one fuzzy rule and not the whole rule base. The authors have applied successfully this methodology for the design of an active control suspension system.

Fuzzy logic controllers' optimization by genetic algorithms. The work presented in [82], presents a genetic algorithm optimization method for fuzzy control and decision systems. The method extends traditional fuzzy systems by a learning ability without changing the fuzzy rule framework. The author uses the entropy of the fuzzy rule set in the fitness function together with a genetic optimization with different concurrent fuzzy systems in the population. A test case for charging high-power NiCd batteries, demonstrate the effectiveness of the proposed method. In [83], the cart-centering problem is addressed using a new controller concept called analytical influence controller, which is based on a general control surface structure. This concept is suited for optimization by a genetic algorithm. Tests show that with proper tuning, the results can have high accuracy. In [84], is proposed a self-tuning fuzzy controller with virus-evolutionary genetic algorithm. This algorithm realizes a horizontal propagation and a vertical inheritance of genetic information in a population. The effectiveness of the proposed method is shown through the simulations of the cart-centering problem. In [85], is proposed a hybrid method combining an evolutionary computation technique for input membership function parameters and a stochastic gradient descent, for rule conclusion parameters, for constrained optimization of fuzzy inference systems. The optimization process is shown to be able to find the optimal size of fuzzy inference systems for a given problem.

Fuzzy-Evolutionary systems. Early work in this domain can be found in [86], [87], and [88]. In [89], is proposed the evolutionary fuzzy modeling for various aerospace applications. Various test are conducted to analyze the stability and performance robustness of the methodology, demonstrating the feasibility of the model in non-linear control of the space station. In [90], it is addressed the problem of multi-objective job-shop scheduling using fuzzy processing time and fuzzy due-date. They formulate the multi-objective fuzzy job-shop scheduling as three-objective ones which not only maximize the minimum agreement index but they also maximize the average agreement index and minimize the maximum fuzzy completion time. With two examples, they demonstrate the feasibility and effectiveness of the proposed method by comparing with the simulated annealing method.

Fuzzy logic controllers generated by genetic programming. In [91] and [92], the authors present an evolutionary approach for the design of fuzzy logic controllers. They apply the genetic programming paradigm to evolve fuzzy rule-bases, internally represented as type-constrained syntactic trees. The obtained results from an application to the cart-centering problem, show that a good parameterization of the algorithm and an appropriate evaluation function can lead to near-optimal solutions. In [93], a model for the construction of fuzzy rule-based systems incorporating the fuzzy mechanism into the genetic programming functional nodes is proposed. The model has been tested effectively in the medical domain, showing the potential of its future use.

2.4 Machine Learning and Fuzzy Logic

Fuzzy logic is used for the modeling of ambiguity contained in decision attributes, before these attributes are subjected to further process using machine learning for classification and diagnosis tasks. The process followed for the definition of boundaries of the examined attributes, are defined by methods often called "fuzzy or soft thresholds". On the other hand, machine learning can assist the formation of fuzzy membership functions by defining successfully the fuzzy boundaries among neighboring linguistic areas. In [94], a comparison between three different learning methods for fuzzy decision trees is presented. An early hybrid approach consisting of fuzzy rule based systems and inductive machine learning was presented in [95] where the cut-off points of different linguistic areas of the fuzzy membership functions used, where obtained by rules induced from experimental data, with the aid of entropy based inductive learning algorithms [96], [97]. In [98], fuzzy machine learning is introduced, through the application of a fuzzy machine learning technique in the knowledge acquisition process. Fuzzy logic support for the application of automated knowledge acquisition is presented by [99] with the construction of Fuzzy-ID3, an inductive decision tree generator. A very interesting study on heuristic algorithms for generating fuzzy decision trees is also presented by [100]. Fuzzy sets and machine learning are also working together in [101], where a fuzzy inference system learning by reinforcement methods is presented. Finally, another similar attempt for combining fuzzy set theory and inductive machine learning is given in [102].

2.5 Machine Learning and Evolutionary Algorithms

Machine learning often works as feature selection or feature extraction methodology applied in large collections of data, prior to the application of evolutionary approaches for generalization from data. In this way, machine learning works as a mechanism for reducing complexity, a task which is necessary for time consuming approaches such as evolutionary computation. Genetic-based machine learning approaches are also described in literature, see [103]. The goal of this study is the automatic development of a rule set for an industrial production process. The problem is solved successfully, by applying a largely modified Learning Classifier System (a class of genetic based Machine Learning methods), called Fuzzy Efficiency-based Classifier System. On the other hand, machine learning and genetic programming form another very effective hybrid scheme for handling various applications in literature. In [9], was primarily introduced a genetic based approach for decision tree generation in a way that a result equivalent to that of pure machine learning [96] was obtained. In [104], a regularization approach to inductive genetic programming tuned for learning polynomials is presented. The presented experimental results within that work show that the suggested regularization approach outperforms traditional genetic programming on benchmark data mining and practical time-series prediction tasks. Credit scoring problems can also be handled with the combined use of inductive machine learning and genetic programming [105]. Inductive machine learning is used in first step as feature selector technique and then the reduced feature set serves as input of reduced complexity to a genetic programming approach for generalization purposes. The attempt to perform feature selection with the aid of inductive learning has proved effective in past literature [106], [107].

Decision trees generated by genetic programming. In [108], is proposed a study of inductive genetic programming with decision trees. The paper presents the development of fitness functions for improving the search guidance, where it is demonstrated that with careful design of the fitness function the global search space becomes smoother, thus facilitating the search. The overall method is shown to guarantee maintenance of decision trees with low syntactic complexity and high predictive accuracy. As stated above, in [9] was primarily introduced a genetic based approach for decision tree generation in a way that a result equivalent to that of pure machine learning [96] was obtained.

2.6 Other Hybrid Intelligent Schemes

Before closing this brief review to effective hybrid schemes of well-known intelligent techniques, it should be added that a number of other techniques are also combined in real world applications. This paper will not attempt any extensive reference to those methods as part of hybrid architectures, but it should be noted that rough sets, Petri nets and wavelets are very often found useful and intelligent enough to be included in hybrid methodologies. Specially wavelets that are particularly capable of de-noising signal data, have been used in collaboration to neural networks for separation between order and disorder in stock index [109], as well as with fuzzy sets for function learning [110], and for real time tool condition monitoring [111]. The following paragraphs show a classification among hybrid systems not belonging clearly to one of the presented hybrid classes.

Hybrid Neural Network Systems. In [112], a hybrid neural network scheme for face recognition is proposed. The model combines local image sampling, a self-organizing map neural network and a convolutional neural network. The system provides a measure of confidence in its output and classification error approaches zero when rejecting as few as 10% of examples from a database of 400 images of 40 individuals which contains quite a high degree of variability in expression, pose and facial details. In [113], the authors use three alternative methods to empirically select predictors for neural networks in bankruptcy prediction. Among these methods -linear discriminant analysis, logit analysis and genetic algorithms- the best prediction results are achieved from the neural network when the prediction variables are selected using genetic algorithms. In [114], is proposed a structured model with multiple stages combining case-based forecasting, neural networks and discriminant analysis for bankruptcy prediction. This integrated approach produced higher prediction accuracy than the individual components. In [115], is proposed an integrated thresholding design of the optimal or near-optimal wavelet transformation by genetic algorithms to represent a significant signal most suitable for neural networks. The approach is applied to Korean won / US-dollar exchange rate forecasting. The results show that the proposed system has better performance than three other wavelet thresholding algorithms (cross-validation, best basis selection and best level tree). In [116] and [117], the authors propose a multistage hybrid system combining wavelet thresholding, neural networks and neuro-fuzzy systems for stock exchange daily trading. The system is proved to be superior to individual components performance and to buy and hold strategies. In [118] knowledge discovery is attempted by an inductive neural network scheme.

Hybrid genetic algorithms. Early findings and studies on hybrid genetic algorithms can be found in [119] and [120]. In [121], a hybrid genetic algorithm model is suggested for scheduling storage tanks. The proposed approach integrates genetic algorithms and heuristic rule-based techniques, decomposing the complex mixed-integer optimization problem into integer and real number sub-problems. The model is applied to three scenarios of a water treatment facility to a port and is found to be robust and to give a significantly better schedule as compared to heuristic or random search. In [122] is proposed a hybrid genetic scheme using genetic and micro-genetic algorithms (genetic algorithms with small population and short evolution), which has enhanced search capabilities. The suggested model, over a significant number of tests, has shown better performance in terms of solution accuracy, feasibility percentage of the attained solutions, and robustness. In [123], is proposed a parallel hybrid method that combines cellular genetic algorithms and the random walk strategy for solving the "satisfiability" problem. This method uses a cellular genetic algorithm to perform a global search and specializes this search in local search by adopting the random walk strategy. The aim of this work is to deal with large-sized problems and it is realized on a parallel machine with satisfactory results. In [124], is addressed the uncertainty of the estimated fitness of the solution in genetic algorithms. This uncertainty is either due to environmental changes (process noise), or due to noisy evaluations (observation noise). The Kalman formulation provides a well-developed formal mechanism for treating uncertainty within the genetic algorithms framework. In the paper, is developed a Kalman-extended genetic algorithm to determine when to generate a new individual, when to re-evaluate an existing individual and which one to re-evaluate. The overall approach shows efficient discovery of better-adapted solutions in examples with several levels of process and observation noise.

Hybrid genetic programming. In [125], the genetic programming is used to enhance the simulated annealing search by replacing the simulating annealing key parameter search (called the *simulated annealing schedule*), usually searched manually, by a genetic programming search. Two new algorithms are presented that are proved to be superior to existing simulated annealing algorithms. In [126], the authors apply a two-stage procedure for the identification of crack profiles using genetic programming and fuzzy inference. The genetic programming is used for feature extraction and a fuzzy inference system detects presence, position and size of a defect using the extracted features. The effectiveness of the proposed method is demonstrated through simulation studies.

3 Conclusions

For many years, in most applications of intelligent methodologies, the trend has been to use the most proper approach for each field of study. Usually, a successful application of the selected intelligent technique corresponds to the comparison of the performance of some competitive intelligence techniques in contrast to the proposed one. Superiority of the latter over the other techniques proves the correctness of the selection. After a large collection of such real-world applications of intelligent techniques within the past decade, scientists of today should attempt to draw general conclusions on the advantages and disadvantages of each category of intelligent methods (i.e. machine learning, neural nets, soft computing, genetic algorithms, etc.).
In this sense, machine learning seems more capable of handling large databases consisting of incomplete and/or nominal data by taking advantage of mathematical logic, induction and elements of information theory. Neural networks can perform ideally in domains of purely numerical nature, as well as in making effective predictions in time series data. Genetic algorithms could competitively perform

optimization tasks in a very large search space, identifying sub-optimal solutions of high quality, becoming thus the methods of choice for domains suffering from combinatorial explosion phenomena such as operations research, manufacturing etc. Soft computing and fuzzy rule-based systems have been proved ideal for handling approximate concepts, human characterizations and domains having unclear boundaries. Moreover, it has been observed that the highly increasing computing power and technology, could make possible the use of more complex intelligent architectures, taking advantage of more than one intelligent techniques, not in a competitive, but rather in a collaborative sense. This last fact corresponds to what is called a hybrid computational intelligence methodology throughout this paper.

Application areas for computational intelligence can be seen as almost any complex domain with the need for diagnosis, decision-making, supervision, modeling and analysis. Most of computational intelligence techniques seem to focus on (1) control engineering, data analysis and function approximation, (2) monitoring and diagnosis of complex dynamic systems, chaotic domains and time-series data, with a special emphasis on economic/financial problems and electromechanical devices and systems, (3) numerous medical diagnosis problems and, (4) managerial decisions and strategic decision-making. The need for the design of a generalized hybrid architecture combining both, theoretical intelligent components and suitable areas of application is currently under construction by the authors. More details are to be provided and discussed during the presentation of this work, together with evidence that authors have gained during their work on more than 15 different domains of real-world applications in the last decade.

References

1. Chen Z. Computational Intelligence for Decision Support. CRC Press, 2000
2. Nilsson N. Artificial Intelligence: A New Synthesis. Morgan Kaufmann, 1998
3. Zimmermann H-J., Tselentis G., Van Someren M., Dounias G. (Eds.). Advances in Computational Intelligence and Learning: Methods and Applications. Kluwer Ac. Publ., 2001
4. Zadeh L.A., Fuzzy Sets, Information Control 8, 338-353, 1965
5. Rosenblatt F., Two theorems of statistical separability in the perceptron, Mechanization of Thought Processes, London HM Stat.Office, 421-456
6. Widrow B. and Hoff M.E., Adaptive switching circuits, IRE WesternElectric Show and Convention Record - Part 4, pp 96-104, 1960
7. Werbos P., Beyond regression: new tools for predictions and analysis in the behavioral science, PhD Thesis, Harvard University, 1974
8. Holland J.H., Adaptation in Natural and Artificial Systems, Cambridge, MA:MIT Press, 1975
9. Koza J. R. 1992. Genetic Programming – On the Programming of Computers by Means of Natural Selection. The MIT Press.
10. Michalski R.S., Carbonell J.G., and Mitchell T.M.: Machine Learning: An Artificial Intelligence Approach, Morgan Kaufmann, 1983
11. Michalski R.S., Carbonell J.G., and Mitchell T.M.: Machine Learning: An Artificial Intelligence Approach, Vol. 2, Morgan Kaufmann, 1986
12. Kodratoff Y. and Michalski R.S.: Machine Learning: An Artificial Intelligence Approach, Vol. 3, Morgan Kaufmann, 1990

13. Mitchell T.M. Machine Learning. McGraw-Hill, New York, 1997
14. Kubat M., Bratco I. and Michalski R.S.: A Review of Machine Learning Methods, in Michalski R.S., Bratco I. and Kubat M. (eds), Machine Learning And Data Mining – Methods and Applications, Wiley, pp. 3-69, 1997
15. Rumelhart D E, McClelland J. L. and Hinton G. E., Parallel Distributed Processing vols l, 2, Cambridge, MA:MIT Press, 1986
16. Jacobs R.A. Increased rates of convergence through learning rate adaptation, Neural Networks Vol.1, 295-307, 1988
17. Wasserman P. D., Neural Computing: Theory and Practice, N.Y:Van Nostrand Reinhold, 1989
18. Arabshahi P., Choi J. J., Marks R. J. and Caudell T. P., Fuzzy control of backpropagation Proc. l st IEEE lnt. Conf.on Fuzzy Systems, Fuzz-IEEE'92 , 967-972, 1992
19. Wong F.S., Wang P.Z., Goh T.H., Quek B.K., Fuzzy neural systems for stock selection, Fianancial Analysts Journal 48:1, 61-64 , 1992
20. Kuo R. I., Chen Y. T., Cohen P. H. and Kumara S., Fast convergence of error back propagation algorithm through fuzzy modeling, Intelligent Engineering Systems through Artificial Neural Networks, 239-244, 1993
21. Bonissone P. P., Badami V., Chiang K., Khedkar P., Marcelle K. and Schutten M., Industrial applications of fuzzy logic at General Electric Proc. IEEE 83, 450-465, 1995
22. Bonissone P. P., Khedkar P. and Chen Y., Genetic algorithms for automated tuning of fuzzy controllers: a transportation application Proc. 5th IEEE lnt. Conf. Fuzz-IEEE'96, 674-680, 1996
23. Duan J.-C., Chung F.-L., Cascaded Fuzzy Neural Network Model Based on Syllogistic Fuzzy Reasoning, in IEEE Trans. on Fuzzy Systems., Vol 9, No 2, April 2001, 293-306
24. Wong H.-S., Guan L., A Neural Learning Approach for Adaptive Image Restoration Using a Fuzzy Model-Based Network Architecture, in IEEE Trans. on Neur.Net., Vol 12, No 3, May 2001, 516-531
25. Shen J.-C., Fuzzy Neural Networks for Tuning PID Controller for Plans with Unterdamped Responses, in IEEE Trans. on Fuzzy Systems., Vol 9, No 2, April 2001, 333-342
26. Lin F.-J., Wai R.-J., Hong C.-M., Hybrid Supervisory Control Using Recurrent Fuzzy Neural Network for Tracking Periodic Inputs, in IEEE Trans. on Neural Net., Vol 12, No 1, Jan-2001, 68-90.
27. Lee S. C. and Lee E. T., Fuzzy sets and neural networks J. Cybernet. 4, 83-103, 1974
28. Takagi H., Fusion technology of fuzzy theory and neural networks-survey and future directions, Proc. lnt. Conf. on Fuzzy Logic and Neural Networks, Izuka'90, pp 13-26, 1990
29. Jang J. S. R., ANFIS: adaptive-network-based-fuzzy-inference-system IEEE Trans. Syst. Man Cybernet. SMC-23,665-85, 1993
30. Kawamura A., Watanabe N., Okada H. and Asakawa K. A., prototype of neuro-fuzzy cooperation systems Proc. 1st IEEE Int. Conf. on Fuzzy Systems, Fuzz-lEEE'92 , 75-82, 1992
31. Bersini H., Nordvik J. P. and Bonarini A. , A simple direct adaptive fuzzy controller derived from its neural equivalent, Proc. IEEE lnt. Corf. IEEE-ICNN'93, 345-350, 1993
32. Bersini H., Nordvik J. P. and Bonarini A., Comparing RBF and fuzzy inference systems on theoretical and practical basis, Proc. Int. Conf. on Artificial Neural Networks, 169-174, 1995
33. Russo M, Distributed Fuzzy Learning Using the MULTISOFT Machine, in IEEE Trans. on Neur.Net., Vol 12, No 3, May 2001, 475-484
34. Zikidis K.C., Vasilakos A.V., ASAFES2:a novel, neuro-fuzzy architecture for fuzzy computing based on functional reasoning, Fuzzy Sets and Systems 83, 1996, 63-84
35. Studer L., Masulli F., Building a neuro-fuzzy system to efficiently forecast chaotic time-series, Nuclear Instruments and Methods in Physics Research A 389, 1997, 264-267
36. Nie J., Nonlinear time-series forecasting: A fuzzy-neural approach, Neurocomputing 16, 63-76, 1997

37. Nauck D., Kruse R., Designing Neuro-Fuzzy Systems Through Backpropagations, in Witold Pedrydz (Ed.), Fuzzy Modeling – Paradigms and Practice, pp 203-231, Kluwer Academic Publishers, 1996
38. Nauck Detlef and Kruse Rudolf , NEFCLASS – a Neuro-Fuzzy approach for the classification of data, In K.M.George,Janice H.Carrol, Ed Deaton, Dave Oppenheim and Jim Hightower (Eds.), Applied Computing, 1995, ACM Symposium on Applied Computing, Nashville, Feb. 26-28, pages 461-465. ACM Press, New York, February 1995.
39. Tsakonas A., Dounias G., Decision making on noisy time-series data under a neuro-genetic fuzzy rule-based system approach, in Proc. of 7th UK Workshop on Fuzzy Systems, 80-89,2000
40. Zimmermann H. G., Neuneier R., Siekmann S., Dichtl H., Modeling the German Stock Index DAX with Neuro-Fuzzy, EUFIT'96, Aachen, Germany, Sept. 2-5, pp. 2187-2190, 1996
41. Maniezzo V., Genetic evolution of the topology and weight distribution of neural networks, IEEE Trans. Neural Networks NN 5 39-53, 1994
42. Patel M. J. and Maniezzo V., NN's and GA's: evolving co-operative behavior in adaptive learning agents, Proc. 1st IEEE Conf. on Evolutionary Computation, ICEC'94, pp 290-295 , 1994
43. Montana D. J. and Davis L., Training feedforward neural networks using genetic algorithms, Proc. l I th lnt. Joint Conf. on Artificial Intelligence, IJCAI, 762-767, 1989
44. Kitano H., Empirical studies on the speed of convergence of neural networks training using genetic algorithms. Proc. 8th Natl Conf. on Artificial Intelligence, AAAI'90, 789-796, 1990
45. McInerney M. and Dhawan A. P., Use of genetic algorithms with backpropagation in training of feedforward neural networks, Proc. IEEE lnt. Conf. on Neural Networks, IEEE-ICNN'93 , 203-208, 1993
46. Schaffer J. D., Whitley D. and Eshelman L. J., Combinations of genetic algorithms and neural networks: a survey of the state of the art, Proc. Int. Workshop on Combinations of Genetic Algorithms and Neural Networks, COGANN'92, pp 1-37, 1992
47. Shazly M.R.E., Shazly H.E.E., Forecasting currency prices using a genetically evolved neural network architecture, International Review of Financial Analysis, 8:1, 1999, 67-82
48. Edwards D., Taylor N., Brown K., Comprehensive Evolution of Neural Networks, in Proc. of the 2001 UK Workshop of Computational Intelligence, University of Edinbourgh, 2001, 75-80
49. Montana D.J., Neural Network Weight Selection Using Genetic Algorithms, 1992
50. Sexton R.S., Gupta J.N.D., Comparative evaluation of genetic algorithm and backpropagation for training neural networks, Information Sciences 129, 2000, 45-49
51. Yeun Y.-S., Lee K.-H., Yang Y.-S., Function approximation by coupling neural networks and genetic programming trees with oblique decision trees, Artif. Intell. in Eng. 13, 223-239, 1999
52. D.J.Montana, "Strongly Typed Genetic Programming", Evolutionary Computation Vol 3:2, 1995
53. F.Gruau, "On Using Syntactic Constraints with Genetic Programming"", in P.J.Angeline, K.E.Jinnear,Jr., "Advances in Genetic Programming", MIT,1996
54. T.D.Haynes, D.A.Schoenefeld,R.L.Wainwright, "Type Inheritance in Strongly Typed Genetic Programming", in P.J.Angeline, K.E.Jinnear,Jr., "Advances in Genetic Programming", MIT,1996
55. C.Z.Janikow, "A Methodology for Processing Problem Constraints in Genetic Programming", in Computers Math.Applic. Vol.32:8,pp 97-113, 1996
56. C.Ryan, J.J.Collins, M. O'Neil, "Grammatical Evolution: Evolving Programs for an Arbitrary Language", in W.Banzhaf, R.Poli, M.Schoenauer, T.C.Fogarty (Eds.), "Genetic Programming", Lecture Notes in Computer Science, Springer, 1998

57. Cordon O., Herrera H. and Lozano M., A classified review on the combination fuzzy logic-genetic algorithms bibliography, Technical Report 95129, Department of Computer Science and AI, Universidad de Granada, 1995, url: http://decsai.ugr.es/difuso/tr.html
58. Herrera F., Lozano M. and Verdegay J. L., Tackling fuzzy genetic algorithms, in G. Winter, J. Periaux, M. Galan and P. Cuestapages (eds.), Genetic Algorithms in Engineering and Computer Science , New York: Wiley, 167-189, 1995
59. Lee M. A. and Tagaki H., Integrating design stages of fuzzy systems using genetic algorithms, Proc. 2nd IEEE lnt. Conf, on FuzzySystems, Fuzz-IEEE'93, 1993
60. Herrera F. and Lozano M., Adaptive genetic algorithms based on fuzzy techniques, Proc. lnt. Conf. on Information Processing and Management of Uncertainty, IPMU'96 ,775-780, 1996
61. Lee M. A. and Tagaki H., Dynamic control of genetic algorithm using fuzzy logic techniques, Proc. 5th lnt. Conf. on Genetic Algorithms, lCGA'93, 76-83 , 1993
62. Lee M. A., Automatic design and adaptation of fuzzy systems and genetic algorithms using soft computing techniques, PhD Thesis, University of California, Davis, 1994
63. Grefenstette J., Optimization of control parameters for genetic algorithms, IEEE Trans. Syst. Man Cybernet. SMC-16, 122-128, 1986
64. De Jong K. A., An analysis of the behavior of a class of genetic adaptive systems, PhD Thesis, University of Michigan, 1975
65. Witold Pedrycz and Marek Reformat, Genetic Optimization with Fuzzy Coding, in Herrera F. and Verdegay J.L. (Eds), Genetic Algorithms and Soft Computing, Physica-Verlag, 1996, 51-67
66. Francisco Herrera and Manuel Lozano, Adaptation of Genetic Algorithm Parameters Based on Fuzzy Logic Controllers, in Herrera F. and Verdegay J.L. (Eds), Genetic Algorithms and Soft Computing, Physica-Verlag, 1996, 95-125
67. Herrera F., Lozano M., Adaptive Genetic Operators Based on Co-evolution with Fuzzy Behaviors, in IEEE Trans. on Evol.Comp., Vol 5, No 2, April 2001, 149-165
68. Karr C. L., Design of an adaptive fuzzy logic controller using genetic algorithms, Proc. 4th Int. Conf. on Genetic Algorithms, ICGA'91, 450-456, 1991
69. Karr C. L., Genetic algorithms for fuzzy controllers. Al Expert 6, 27-33, 1991
70. Karr C. L., Fuzzy control of pH using genetic algorithms, IEEE Trans. Fuzzy Syst. FS, 146-153, 1993
71. Herrera F., Lozano M. and Verdegay J. L., Tuning fuzzy logic control by genetic algorithms, Int. J. Approx. Reasoning 12, 299-315, 1995
72. Kinzel, J., Klawoon F. and Kruse R., Modifications of genetic algorithms for designing and optimizing fuzzy controllers, Proc. 1st IEEE Conf. on Evol. Computation, ICEC'94, 28-33, 1994
73. Takagi T. and Sugeno M., Fuzzy identification of systems and its applications to modeling and control, IEEE Trans.Syst. Man Cybernet. SMC-15, 116-132, 1985
74. Surmann H., Kanstein A. and Goser K., Self organizing and genetic algorithms for an automatic design of fuzzy control and decision systems, Proc. EUFIT'93, Aachen, 1993, pp 97-104, 1993
75. Zheng L., A practical guide to tune proportional and integral (PI) like fuzzy controllers, Proc. 1st IEEE Int.Conf. on Fuzzy Systems, Fuzz-IEEE'92, 633-640, 1992
76. Magdalena L. and Velasco J.R.,Fuzzy Rule-Based Controllers that Learn by Evolving their Knowledge Base, in Herrera F. and Verdegay J.L. (Eds), Genetic Algorithms and Soft Computing, Physica-Verlag 1996, 172-201
77. Lee M.A. and Takagi H., Hybrid Genetic-Fuzzy Systems for Intelligent Systems Design, in Herrera F. and Verdegay J.L. (Eds), Genetic Algorithms and Soft Computing, Physica-Verlag, 1996, 226-250
78. Hoffman F. and Pfister G., Learning of a Fuzzy Control Rule Base Using Messy Genetic Algorithms, in Herrera F. and Verdegay J.L. (Eds), Genetic Algorithms and Soft Computing, Physica-Verlag, 1996, 279-305

79. Gonzalez A. and Perez R., A Learning System of Fuzzy Control Rules Based on Genetic Algorithms, in Herrera F. and Verdegay J.L. (Eds), Genetic Algorithms and Soft Computing, Physica-Verlag, 1996, 202-225
80. Cordon O. and Herrera F., A Hybrid Genetic Algorithm-Evolution Strategy Process for Learning Fuzzy Logic Controller Knowledge Bases, in Herrera F. and Verdegay J.L. (Eds), Genetic Algorithms and Soft Computing, Physica-Verlag, 1996, 251-278
81. Jamei M., Mahfouf M., Linkens D.A., Rule-Base Generation via Symbiotic Evolution for a Mamdani-Type Fuzzy Control System, in Proc. of the 2001 UK Workshop of Computational Intelligence, University of Edinbourgh, 2001, 15-20
82. Surmann H., Genetic Optimization of Fuzzy Rule-Based Systems, in Herrera F. and Verdegay J.L. (Eds), Genetic Algorithms and Soft Computing, Physica-Verlag, 1996, 389-402
83. Schroder M., Klawonn F., Kruse R., Sequential Optimization of Multidimensional Controllers Using Genetic Algorithms and Fuzzy Situations, in Herrera F. and Verdegay J.L. (Eds), Genetic Algorithms and Soft Computing, Physica-Verlag, 1996, 419-444
84. Shimojima K., Kubota N., Fukuda T., Virus-Evolutionary Genetic Algorithm for Fuzzy Controller Optimization, in Herrera F. and Verdegay J.L. (Eds), Genetic Algorithms and Soft Computing, Physica-Verlag, 1996, 369-388
85. Glorennec P.Y., Constrained Optimization of FIS Using an Evolutionary Method, in Herrera F. and Verdegay J.L. (Eds), Genetic Algorithms and Soft Computing, Physica-Verlag, 349-368.
86. Linkens D.A., Okola H., Real time acquisition of fuzzy rules using genetic algorithms, Artificial Intelligence in Real-Time Control, 1992, 17, 335-339
87. Lee M.A., Saloman R., Hybrid evolutionary algorithms for fuzzy system design, Proc. 6th Int. Fuzzy Systems Assoc. World Congress, IFSA 95, Vol 1, 269-272, 1995
88. Pedrycz W., Genetic algorithms for learning in fuzzy relational structures, Fuzzy Sets and Systems, 69, 37-52 , 1995
89. Satyadas A. and KrishnaKumar K., EFM-based Controllers for Space Station Attitude Control: Application and Analysis, in Herrera F. and Verdegay J.L. (Eds), Genetic Algorithms and Soft Computing, Physica-Verlag, 1996, 152-171
90. Sakawa M., Kubota R., Fuzzy programming for multiobjective job shop scheduling with fuzzy processing time and fuzzy duedate through genetic algorithms, European Journal of Operational Research 120, 2000, 393-407
91. Alba E., Cotta C., Troya J.M., Evolutionary Design of Fuzzy Logic Controllers Using Strongly-Typed GP, 1996
92. Alba E., Aldana J.F., Troya J.M., Genetic Algorithms as Heuristics for Optimizing ANN Design, 1996
93. Tsakonas A., Dounias G., Axer H., von Keyserlingk D.G., Data Classification using Fuzzy Rule-Based Systems represented as Genetic Programming Type-Constrained Trees, in Proc. of the 2001 UK Workshop of Computational Intelligence, University of Edinbourgh, 2001, 162-168
94. Wang X.-Z., Yeung D.S., A Comparative Study on Heuristic Algorithms for Generating Fuzzy Decision Trees, in IEEE Trans. on SMC, Part B, Vol 31, No 2, Apr 01, 215-226 , 2001
95. Dounias G. D. and Tsourveloudis N.C., Power Plant Fault Diagnosis Using a Fuzzy Knowledge-Based System, Engineering Intelligent Systems, CRL Publ., Vol. 3, No. 2, pp. 109-120, 1995
96. Quinlan J.R., Induction of Decision Trees. Machine Learning 1, 81-106, 1986
97. Quinlan J.R., C4.5: Programs for Machine Learning. San Mateo: Morgan Kaufmann,1993
98. J.L. Castro, J.J. Castro-Schez, J.M. Zurita , Use of a fuzzy machine learning technique in the knowledge acquisition process, Fuzzy Sets and Systems, Vol. 123, No. 3, pp 307-320, 2001

99. Weber R., Fuzzy-ID3: A Class of Methods for Automatic Knowledge Acquisition, Proc. of the 2nd Int. Conference on Fuzzy Logic & Neural Networks, Iizuka, Japan, July 17-22, 1992, pp. 265-268.
100. Wang X-Z., Yeung D. S., and Tsang E.C.C.: A Comparative Study on Heuristic Algorithms for Generating Fuzzy Decision Trees, IEEE Trans. on Systems Man & Cybernetics, PART B: Cybernetics, Vol. 31, No. 2, Apr. 2001, pp. 215-226.
101. Jouffe L.: Fuzzy Inference System Learning by Reinforcement Methods, IEEE Trans. on Systems Man & Cybernetics, PART C: Applications & Reviews, Vol. 28, No. 3, Aug. 1998, pp. 338-355.
102. Nomikos, G. Dounias, G. Tselentis, K. Vemmos (2000): "Conventional vs. Fuzzy Modeling of Diagnostic Attributes for Classifying Acute Stroke Cases", in ESIT-2000, European Symposium on Intelligent Techniques, Aachen, Germany, 14-15 September 2000, pp. 192-200.
103. Sette S., Boullart L., An implementation of genetic algorithms for rule based machine learning, Engineering Applications of Artificial Intelligence, 13, 2000, 381-390
104. Nikolaev N.Y. and Iba H., Regularization Approach to Inductive Genetic Programming, IEEE Trans. on Evolutionary Computation, Vol. 5, No. 4, Aug. 2001, pp. 359-375.
105. Dounias G., Tsakonas A., Hatas D., Michalopoulos M., Introducing Hybrid Computational Intelligence in Credit Management, submitted to the Int. Journal of "Managerial and Decision Economics", Special Issue on Credit Management, Sept. 2001.
106. Weiss S.M., Indurkhya N. Predictive Data Mining: A Practical Guide. M. Kaufmann, 1998
107. Dounias G., Tselentis G., Moustakis V.S.:Feature selection in washing machines using inductive learning. Journal of Integrated Computer Aided Engineering, Vol. 8, No. 4, pp. 325-336., 2001
108. Nikolaev N.I., Slavov V., Inductive Genetic Programming with Decision Trees, Intelligent Data Analysis 2, 1998, 31-44
109. Echauz J.and Vachtsevanos G.: Separating Order from Disorder in a Stock Index Using Wavelet Neural Networks, EUFIT'97, Aachen, Germany, Sept. 8-11, pp. 434-437., 1997
110. Ho D.W.C, Zhang P-A, and Xu J.: Fuzzy Wavelet Networks for Function Learning, IEEE Trans on Fuzzy Systems, Vol. 9, No.1, Feb. 2001, pp. 200-211.
111. Li Xiaoli, Tso Shiu Kit: Real-Time Tool Condition Monitoring Using Wavelet Transforms and Fuzzy Techniques, IEEE Trans. on Systems Man & Cybernetics, Part C, Applications and Reviews, Vol. 30, No.3, Aug. 2000, pp. 352-357.
112. Lawrence S., Giles C.L., Tsoi A.C., Back A.D., Face Recognition: A Hybrid Neural Network Approach, Technical Report, UMIACS-TR-96-16 and CS-TR-3608, Institute for Advanced Computer Studies, University of Maryland, College Park, MD 20742, 1996
113. Back B., Laitinen T., Sere K., Neural Networks and Genetic Algorithms for Bankruptcy Predictions, Expert Systems with Applications 11, 1996, 407-413
114. Jo H., Han I., Integration of Case-Based Forecasting, Neural Network, and Discriminant Analysis for Bankruptcy Prediction, Expert Systems with Applications, Vol 11, No 4, 1996, 415-422
115. Shin T., Han I., Optimal signal multi-resolution by genetic algorithms to support artificial neural networks for exchange-rate forecasting, Expert Systems with Applications 18, 257-269
116. Tsakonas A., Dounias G. and Tselentis G., "Using Fuzzy Rules in Multilayer Perceptron Neural Networks for Multiresolution Processed Signals: A Real World Application in Stock Exchange Market",in Proc. of Symposium on Comput. Intelligence and Learning, CoIL 2000, 154-170.
117. A.Tsakonas, G.Dounias and A.Merikas, The Role of Genetic Algorithms and Wavelets in Computational Intelligence-based Decision Support for Stock Exchange Daily Trading,in Proc. of VII Congress of SIGEF, 195-208, 2000
118. Fu L.: Knowledge Discovery by Inductive Neural Networks, IEEE Trans. on Knowledge and Data Engineering, Vol. 11, No. 6, Nov/Dec 1999, pp. 992-998

119. Renders J. M. and Bersini H., Hybridizing genetic algorithms with hilt climbing methods for global optimization: two possible ways, Proc. 1 st IEEE Conf. on Evol. Comput.,,ICEC'94, 312-317, 1994
120. Renders J. M. and Flasse S. P., Hybrid methods using genetic algorithms for global optimization, IEEE Trans. Syst. Man Cybernet. SMC-26 243-258, 1976
121. Dahal K.P., Burt G.M., McDonald J.R., Moyes A., A Case Study of Scheduling Storage Tanks Using a Hybrid Genetic Algorithm, in IEEE Trans. on Evol.Comp., Vol 5, No 3, June 2001, 283-294
122. Kazarlis S.A., Papadakis S.E., Theocharis J.B., Petridis V., Microgenetic Algorithms as Generalized Hill-Climbing Operators for GA Optimization, in IEEE Trans. on Evol.Comp., Vol 5, No 3, 204-217, 2001
123. Folino G., Pizzuti C., Spezzano G., Parallel Hybrid Method for SAT That Couples Genetic Algorithms and Local Search, in IEEE Trans. on Evol.Comp., Vol 5, No 4, August 2001, 323-334
124. Stroud P.D., Kalman-Extended Genetic Algorithm for Search in Nonstationary Environments with Noisy Fitness Evaluations, in IEEE Trans. on Evol. Comp., Vol 5, No 1, Feb 01, 66-77, 2001
125. Bolte A., Thonemann U.W., Optimizing simulated annealing schedules with genetic programming, European Journal of Operational Reasearch 92, 1996, 402-416
126. Kojima F., Kubota N., Hashimoto S., Identification of crack profiles using genetic programming and fuzzy inference, Journal of Materials Processing Technology 108, 2001, 263-267
127. Pena-Renes C.A., Sipper M., Evolutionary computation in medicine: an overview, Artificial Intelligence in Medicine, 19, 2000, 1-23
128. Wong B.K., Selvi Y., Neural Network applications in finance: A review and analysis of literature (1990-1996), Information and Management 34,1998, 129-139.

Author Index